"Unravelling the story of MAiD in Canada is a daunting undertaking. It requires untangling misinformation, distilling complex data, and examining issues from a multitude of perspectives. It also demands reckoning with what drives suffering Canadians to no longer want to live. With editors Coelho, Gaind, and Lemmens and their carefully selected coauthors, this task couldn't be in more capable hands."

– Harvey Chochinov, co-founder of the Canadian Virtual Hospice, co-editor of the *Handbook of Psychiatry in Palliative Medicine*, and author of *Dignity in Care: The Human Side of Medicine*

"Thorough analysis of data and a review of individual cases approved for 'assisted dying' with a critical and reflective eye are crucial. This book's balanced approach sheds light on aspects often overlooked or avoided by campaigners. The authors clarify the profound challenges faced by those who are socially disadvantaged in societies that are increasingly ableist. Disabled individuals, and those whose autonomy is deeply constrained by poverty or illness, face the risk of being further devalued. The societal mechanisms and approaches revealed in *Unravelling MAiD in Canada* are thought-provoking – every caring physician, legal expert, and policymaker should read it carefully."

– Ilora Finlay, Baroness of Llandaff, Cardiff University School of Medicine

"*Unravelling MAiD in Canada* is an interesting and insightful examination of one of the most profound issues in Canadian healthcare and law. At a time when the UK debate surrounding assisted suicide is heating up, the broadening of MAiD criteria in Canada and the disproportionate influence this has had on a number of disabled people in choosing an assisted death is something that I find particularly concerning. UN rapporteurs recently suggested that the UK 'devalues Disabled people's lives.' I fear that if assisted suicide is introduced in the UK, there is the potential that we will be led down the same dark path as Canada."

– Tanni, Baroness Grey-Thompson, DBE, member of the House of Lords and paralympic champion

"This book is exceptional. Coelho, Gaind, and Lemmens have edited a deeply informative collection that unpacks the history of medical assistance in dying in Canada and reveals its disproportionately harmful impact on persons with disabilities. The chapters helpfully bring together law, politics, medicine, and disability studies as they discuss and interrogate Canada's rapid policy developments – developments that increasingly favour death in lieu of social supports, therapy, and palliative care."
– Laverne Jacobs, University of Windsor and co-author of *Law and Disability in Canada: Cases and Materials*

"Canada's dysfunctional policy-making process around its MAiD law has made it an international case study in how not to debate and implement an assisted dying law. But how and why did it happen? Historians will surely rely on this collection of well-researched, evidence-based, and scholarly contributions that trenchantly yet carefully explain the disturbing truths behind this Canadian tragedy."
– Scott Kim, National Institutes of Health and Council of Canadian Academies Expert Panel on Medical Assistance in Dying

"This extraordinary book provides desperately needed, penetrating insight into many serious failings and dangers in Canada's accelerated liberalization of doctor-assisted suicide. Its revealing analysis is enriched by evidence and principle, by front-line realities wedded to insightful policy analysis. It should be required reading for anyone making policy or undertaking medical practice in the area of MAiD."
– David Lepofsky, University of Western Ontario and University of Ottawa

"This important collection traces the rapid expansion of Canada's MAiD system over recent years and the far-reaching implications in contexts ranging from medical ethics to impacts on Indigenous peoples and persons with disabilities. The book offers perspectives on the current system and on likely future developments around

matters like advance requests, mature minors, and mental illness. Distinctively comprehensive in its coverage, it is an essential read for anyone interested in Canada's MAiD system, whether in Canada or elsewhere."
– Dwight Newman, University of Saskatchewan and author of *Revisiting the Duty to Consult Aboriginal Peoples*

"This collection of essays educates the reader about the ethics, law, and acceptability of assisted dying as it touches on vulnerable groups. It will interest anyone concerned about the gradual extension of MAiD, especially to those groups whose architecture of choice continues to be effectively restricted. It broadens and deepens the terms of conversation about assisted dying. In setting polemics to one side, it is an indispensable reference tool for anyone who takes an interest in one of the defining issues of the early twenty-first century."
– Gerard Quinn, former UN special rapporteur on the rights of persons with disabilities

"A reasoned, data-based, and multidisciplinary caution about the implications of providing state-funded assisted suicide to people with disabilities who are not dying, to those experiencing mental illness, to those who no longer have the capacity to consent to MAiD, and to 'mature' minors. Compassion for human suffering and commitment to ethical practice shine out from every page."
– Elizabeth Sheehy, author of *Defending Battered Women on Trial: Lessons from the Transcripts*

"The subject of MAiD is more than a political or academic debate, more than a question of bodily autonomy and dignity – it is an existential threat to disabled people. *Unravelling MAiD in Canada* is a necessary book that analyzes this issue through race, gender, disability, and class. As MAiD expands to more countries, it becomes even more critical to document the history of these policies and their implications for the future."
– Alice Wong, author of *Year of the Tiger: An Activist's Life*

UNRAVELLING MAID IN CANADA

Unravelling MAiD in Canada

Euthanasia and Assisted Suicide as Medical Care

Edited by Ramona Coelho,
K. Sonu Gaind, and Trudo Lemmens

McGill-Queen's University Press
Montreal & Kingston • London • Chicago

© McGill-Queen's University Press 2025

ISBN 978-0-2280-2369-2 (paper)
ISBN 978-0-2280-2452-1 (ePDF)
ISBN 978-0-2280-2453-8 (ePUB)

Legal deposit second quarter 2025
Bibliothèque nationale du Québec

Printed in Canada on acid-free paper that is 100% ancient forest free (100% post-consumer recycled), processed chlorine free

This book has been published with the help of a grant from the Federation for the Humanities and Social Sciences, through the Awards to Scholarly Publications Program, using funds provided by the Social Sciences and Humanities Research Council of Canada.

We acknowledge the support of the Canada Council for the Arts.
Nous remercions le Conseil des arts du Canada de son soutien.

McGill-Queen's University Press in Montreal is on land which long served as a site of meeting and exchange amongst Indigenous Peoples, including the Haudenosaunee and Anishinabeg nations. In Kingston it is situated on the territory of the Haudenosaunee and Anishinaabek. We acknowledge and thank the diverse Indigenous Peoples whose footsteps have marked these territories on which peoples of the world now gather.

Library and Archives Canada Cataloguing in Publication

Title: Unravelling MAiD in Canada : euthanasia and assisted suicide as medical care / edited by Ramona Coelho, K. Sonu Gaind, and Trudo Lemmens.
Names: Coelho, Ramona. | Gaind, K. Sonu. | Lemmens, Trudo.
Description: Includes bibliographical references and index.
Identifiers: Canadiana (print) 20240507266 | Canadiana (ebook) 20240508114 | ISBN 9780228023692 (paper) | ISBN 9780228024521 (PDF) | ISBN 9780228024538 (ePUB)
Subjects: LCSH: Assisted suicide—Law and legislation—Canada. | LCSH: Assisted suicide—Social aspects—Canada. | LCSH: Assisted suicide—Moral and ethical aspects—Canada. | LCSH: Euthanasia—Law and legislation—Canada. | LCSH: Euthanasia—Social aspects—Canada. | LCSH: Euthanasia—Moral and ethical aspects—Canada. | LCSH: Medical care—Canada.
Classification: LCC KE3663.E94 U57 2025 | LCC KF3827.E87 U57 2025 kfmod | DDC 344.7104/197—dc23

This book was typeset by Sayre Street Books in 10.5/13 Sabon.
Copyediting by Lesley Trites.

Contents

Preface   vii
Ramona Coelho, K. Sonu Gaind, and Trudo Lemmens

Introduction   3
Ramona Coelho, K. Sonu Gaind, and Trudo Lemmens

1 MAiD in Canada: A Tale of Rapidly Expanding Euthanasia   12
Ramona Coelho and Trudo Lemmens

2 Fall of Duty: The Breach of Trust and Moral Failure of Canada's Entrusted Experts   59
K. Sonu Gaind

3 Assisting Dying: A Policy Framework Developed without Adequate Ethical Consideration   100
Alexander I.F. Simpson and Roland M. Jones

4 How Canada's MAiD Law Has Made Death a "First-Line Therapy" for Suffering   111
Trudo Lemmens, Mary J. Shariff, and Leonie Herx

5 Conscience and MAiD   151
Ramona Coelho

6 MAiD and Palliative Care   166
Leonie Herx

7 Disability and MAiD   188
Ramona Coelho

Contents

8 Creating a Killable Class and Manufacturing Selective Suicidality: Thoughts of a Past and Future Ironing Board 204
Gabrielle Peters

9 Indigenous Peoples and MAiD 277
Hon. Graydon Nicholas

10 Ableism in Canada: Why Track 2 MAiD Violates the *Canadian Charter of Rights and Freedoms* 294
Isabel Grant

11 Mental Illness, Health Care, and Assisted Death: Part I – Examining Parameters for Expanding or Restricting MAiD under Canada's *Charter* 330
Mary J. Shariff, Derek B.M. Ross, and Trudo Lemmens

12 Mental Illness, Health Care, and Assisted Death: Part II – Examining Parameters for Expanding or Restricting MAiD under Canada's Federal System 381
Mary J. Shariff, Derek B.M. Ross, and Trudo Lemmens

13 Evaluating the Existing Scientific Evidence for Physician-Assisted Death for Mental Illness 417
Mark Sinyor and Ayal Schaffer

14 MAiD by Advance Request: Vulnerability, Stigma, and the Myth of Free and Informed Advance Consent 451
Catherine Ferrier

15 Mature Minors and MAiD 473
Ramona Coelho

Conclusion | Insights on Canada's MAiD Expansion: Is This About Autonomy or Privilege? 487
K. Sonu Gaind, Ramona Coelho, and Trudo Lemmens

Contributors 499

Index 505

Preface

Ramona Coelho, K. Sonu Gaind, and Trudo Lemmens

This book grew out of our involvement in parliamentary, public, and academic debates following the 2015 Supreme Court of Canada *Carter v. Canada (AG)* decision and the subsequent legislative and policy initiatives. As editors we have in common that we have been critical of various components of Canada's medical assistance in dying (MAiD) regime and participate in those debates. The policy and parliamentary debates were also the context in which we started working with several of the authors included in this volume. If you had asked us ten years ago where we would devote the bulk of our professional time in the next decade, we doubt that MAiD, the awkward acronym introduced in Canada for euthanasia and assisted suicide, would have been our first thought. Some of us had worked on end-of-life care issues before and continued to teach and publish on related issues, but none of us predicted the extent to which this topic would come to dominate so much of Canada's health law and policy debates and as a result our lives. In fact the intensity of the debate, partly the result of the continuing changes that are described in several chapters of this volume, means that our involvement far exceeded our professional work. We are particularly grateful to our spouses, families, and friends for having put up with how this debate has thereby also intruded upon their lives.

As editors we come to this project from different professional backgrounds that are reflected in the interdisciplinary variety of the chapters we selected to be part of this book, including general medicine, psychiatry, palliative care, law, health policy, and ethics. Some chapters discuss intricacies of constitutional law and medico-legal concepts such as the standard of care. Others reflect disability scholarship and lived experience. There are further short reflections on the ethical arguments invoked in the debate around the legalization of MAiD and on the need to respect conscientious objections for health care professionals. Still other chapters provide a critical review of Canadian policy-making in relation to MAiD and evidence-based analyses of the expansion of MAiD for mental illness and its impact on suicide prevention.

The topic of this book touches on one of our most profound and universal human experiences: the end of life. Personal and professional experiences influence our approach to the challenging issues this book discusses. The following narratives explain how our experiences have shaped our work on this topic.

RAMONA COELHO

Fifteen years ago I was living in Montreal, working as a family physician and also a mother of young children while my husband was a busy surgical resident. My time was mostly spoken for. My interest and concern have always been for the disenfranchised, so in my chosen work as a family physician half of my practice was composed of home care. I cared for those with end-stage organ failure, dementia, severe physical disabilities, and mental health struggles including addiction. As a young physician I was deeply and negatively affected by observing my patients experience serious barriers to accessing specialized care and witnessing discrimination against them as well as their social isolation.

I became depressed, which was likely exacerbated by other factors such as postpartum changes. Every day for some years I had to struggle against a growing ambivalence about being able to restore my patients' health, and I was admittedly ambivalent about the meaning of life itself. The fact that suffering is a common experience for all humanity frightened me deeply. Fear of illness, disability, and growing old haunted me.

However, through those same relationships with patients I experienced an extraordinary gift – a gift my patients gave me with the privilege of knowing their inner lives and thoughts. My patients were so kind, good, and thoughtful despite what I perceived to be significant suffering. In time, I realized some of my own biases were influencing how I perceived my patients' lives and colouring my impressions of their suffering. My patients often had great joys, and I did have a lot to offer even in just being there for them. A lot of solutions relied on peer support, allied health care workers, and answers outside the strict realm of traditional medicine. I also realized I could use my creative energy and skills to advocate for resources and find care solutions that truly offered large benefits for my patients. I gained lived experience through working with my patients. I began to understand that coping, recovery, and healing were possible in circumstances that had previously terrified me.

When the Select Committee on Dying with Dignity was introduced in Quebec, I testified. I shared experiences of healing and recovery in contrast to the overworked, overburdened health care system that could make MAiD the easiest option. I was concerned that MAiD would further the inhumanity that so many experience in health care and that offering MAiD as an option would negatively impact the work of healing and my patients' lives.

Fast forward to 2020. MAiD was legalized in 2016 and although I was still concerned, I was more preoccupied with conscience protection. I felt that I couldn't continue to practise medicine with marginalized communities, which I continued to do in London, Ontario, without conscience protection. (Conscience protection in health care involves policies or laws that give health care providers the right to opt out of participating in medical procedures or practices that, based on their moral, ethical, or professional understandings, they consider not to be in the patient's best interests.)

When patients lacked access to so many things in a way that exacerbated suffering and delayed the work of healing, I needed to be fully in their court to help them live. I needed to be able to exercise my conscience freely to serve my patients. When Bill C-7 was introduced, I was appalled to learn that my patients who were not dying but were blocked from care by many hurdles, often created by our government, would be offered death by the same government. My apprehension became despair as I realized there was a lack of stringent safeguards. Patients requesting MAiD didn't need to be able to access treatment beforehand to qualify, and patients could die within ninety days of their first MAiD assessment. This didn't match any medical evidence I was aware of, and my work experience had taught me that the work of recovery from serious illnesses, accidents, and trauma takes much more time, especially when compounded by a lack of services. I dutifully reached out to my local politicians and soon found myself invited to speak in Parliament. I was inundated with requests to speak in different venues and write on this issue until it became my main focus. I had become an activist. I see this work as an extension of my original passion, protecting disenfranchised patients who need and deserve care to live.

K. SONU GAIND

When I entered the field of medicine years ago I had no idea that I would eventually become so heavily involved in the area of medically assisted death, or as Canada now calls it, medical assistance in dying (MAiD). Following my psychiatry residency at the University of Toronto, I did a fellowship in psycho-oncology and cross-cultural psychiatry and subsequently started working as a psycho-oncology consultant at Princess Margaret Hospital. In 2014 I shifted to Humber River Hospital to take on the role of chief of psychiatry there and was elected president of the Canadian Psychiatric Association (CPA), a role I stepped in to in late 2015. This was when my involvement with MAiD began, and it has intensified ever since.

As I outline in some detail in my chapter, "Fall of Duty: The Breach of Trust and Moral Failure of Canada's Entrusted Experts," my time as CPA president began after the *Carter* ruling in 2015 and prior to Bill C-14's enactment in 2016. This time period was critical in informing our initial MAiD laws. In this context we engaged psychiatrists and stakeholders across the country in consultations on MAiD, with a view to inform evolving policies with as robust evidence as possible. I also chaired the time-limited CPA Task Force on MAiD and Mental Illness as we surveyed members and developed guidance on emerging policies. Independent of the CPA, I was selected to sit on the Council of Canadian Academies Expert Panel on MAiD for Mental Disorders as a Sole Underlying Medical Condition and was retained by the then attorney general of Canada as an expert in the *Truchon* and *Lamb* cases. In addition to such broad policy involvement, I was the physician chair of our hospital MAiD team at Humber River.

Through these experiences and ongoing consultations and teaching nationally and internationally on MAiD, I have followed the development and nuances of Canada's MAiD laws and expansions. I am not a conscientious objector to MAiD in general (had I been, I would never have chaired my former hospital's MAiD team). I have seen its appropriate use in appropriate circumstances.

I have also had an inside view of much of the politics and hidden dynamics fuelling Canada's MAiD expansions. What I have seen consistently over several years has led me to become increasingly concerned not just by the inherent risks that ongoing MAiD expansion poses to vulnerable fellow Canadians, but by what can only be described as ideologically driven activism fuelling Canada's MAiD expansion to the wilful disregard of evidence-based cautions. Despite being a past president of the CPA, I have seen my own former national professional association as one such example of an expert body that has failed to contribute expected evidence and due diligence to this complex topic. Unfortunately this has allowed policies to develop that put the most vulnerable and marginalized among us at risk, exposing them to avoidable deaths as they seek escape from social and life suffering. Responding to this and attempting to bring relevant evidence to policy discussions and decisions has motivated my ongoing work in the area.

In addition to these professional experiences, many of us who have expressed caution about Canada's rapid euthanasia expansion have had unexpected personal experiences related to this issue, facing ad hominem attacks and significant blowback from some quarters. This is particularly ironic given that most psychiatrists overwhelmingly share the concerns being raised and do not agree with the minority ideological positions being pushed by the leadership of a few associations – yet those who have been vocal in expressing concerns and caution have paid a price.

For my own part, I have faced intimidation, bullying, and attempts at academic stifling, from expansion advocate university peers seeking to have my presentations cancelled or to silence my use of evidence related to marginalization and suicidality, to organization leaders attempting public shaming and using racialized tropes (I am a brown male of East Indian descent). As discussed in chapter 2, "Fall of Duty," activist senators went as far as using their national platform to denounce my critiquing the lack of evidence informing CAMAP's suicidality training, suggesting I had destroyed the future of medical education in Canada.

While unpleasant, and without dwelling on such unfortunate distractions, these experiences can also be motivation to push for positive change and attempt to model academic integrity and respectful discourse. The issue of MAiD and euthanasia, as with any complex issue, should engender academic debate and most of all should be informed by evidence rather than be hostage to ideology.

An echo chamber may have so far shaped much of Canada's MAiD expansion policies, but there has been an increasing groundswell of dedicated and compassionate peers, confreres, disability advocates, and others fighting to ensure that our most marginalized fellow Canadians are not simply swept under the rug, or swept aside, in a wave of expanding policies of privilege. Parts of this volume may be difficult to read; however, if through this book you not only learn something you didn't know but learn to appreciate a perspective you may not have previously considered, then the hoped for goal of contributing to needed academic discourse will have been met – and it is for this reason that I am thrilled to be joining my colleagues Dr Coelho and Prof. Lemmens as a co-editor of this important volume.

TRUDO LEMMENS

As a professor of health law, policy, and bioethics, I have taught and published on issues related to euthanasia, assisted suicide, and end-of-life care since the mid-1990s. It had not been the dominant focus of my more recent scholarship and teaching. But being of Dutch-speaking Belgian origin, I had been closely following what had been happening in Belgium and the Netherlands after the legalization of euthanasia and physician-assisted suicide in those countries in 2002. In earlier work in the mid-1990s, I had expressed concern about how legalization of euthanasia and assisted suicide could fundamentally alter societal perception of disability and aging; how it could also impact self-perception; and how demands for legalization reflected an illusory desire to enable medicine to offer full control over death and dying. My later publications focused more on legal developments in Canada and the United States, and I had become curious about how legalization unfolded in Belgium and the Netherlands.

But when observing the significant expansion of the euthanasia practice outside the end-of-life context in those countries, particularly after 2010, I had become increasingly concerned about how legalization appeared to be changing health care practices and norms around death and dying, impacting elderly and disabled persons. I was writing a chapter documenting some of these issues when the Supreme Court's *Carter* decision came out. When a Provincial-Territorial Expert Advisory Group subsequently made sweeping recommendations for open-ended legalization of euthanasia and assisted suicide, I was alarmed about how the report ignored the lessons we had to learn from the Belgian and Dutch developments.

I testified about my concerns before the Joint Parliamentary Committee, which largely took over the same recommendations for an open-ended regime, disturbingly, with few safeguards that would prevent premature deaths. I prioritized several publications and editorials on the Belgian and Dutch experience, and also translated some Belgian and Dutch editorials to help inform the Canadian policy debate.

What really struck me when I presented my concerns before parliamentary committees and at various scholarly events was the strong resistance from supporters of broad legalization, including several parliamentary members. They appeared to embrace the narrative that there were no problems whatsoever in countries that had legalized euthanasia or assisted suicide. Documented instances of problems were routinely presented as "anecdotal." Some also explicitly tried to frame objections against broad legalization of euthanasia as inherently conservative or based on religious beliefs, as if the protection of the right to life is not a core human rights obligation. This type of framing has remained characteristic of the Canadian debate.

Because of my concerns about the broad legalization of MAiD, I supported the first Canadian law that contained as a key safeguard the restriction to an already broad end-of-life context. Prior to the development of that law some colleagues and I co-organized an event at the University of Toronto where we brought together various experts and stakeholders, including government officials, to share some of the concerns about expansive euthanasia. I was also an expert witness for the federal attorney general in two court cases in which plaintiffs challenged the restriction of access to MAiD to people whose death is "reasonably foreseeable," as documented in chapter 1. In these court cases, my testimony focused on the implications of abandoning the "reasonably foreseeable death" criterion, based on my study and observations of foreign jurisdictions, particularly Belgium and the Netherlands.

Following the adoption of the first law, I was a member of the Advance Request for Medical Assistance in Dying Subcommittee of the Council of Canadian Academies Expert Panel on MAiD. The subcommittee's report highlights how the Dutch experience of euthanasia for persons with advanced dementia should be a clear warning sign about the in my view insurmountable ethical problems with the practice of ending the life of persons who no longer fully understand and appreciate what is happening to them, on the basis of a prior request.

My scholarly and policy work has shifted significantly in the last couple of years. I used to focus on what we can learn from Belgium and the Netherlands about the pitfalls and dangers of more open-ended assisted dying regimes. I now primarily document and analyze what is happening in Canada and how other countries must learn from Canada's MAiD regime to see what they should avoid. Interestingly, even Belgian and Dutch colleagues supportive of legalization now often comment on how Belgium and the Netherlands can learn from Canada to strengthen their own regimes to counter the problems we face.

Working on this topic has been an emotional rollercoaster. Like many others, I have been confronted with death and dying around me while working on this topic, often directly witnessing issues we discuss in this book, including with people who received MAiD. Many, particularly disabled people and family members of people who received MAiD, have reached out to me in the context of this debate with deeply human, often tragic, and sometimes uplifting experiences. It has frequently been deeply frustrating not to be able to do more for people in their struggle to be heard and helped. The resistance of some of the most ardent supporters of Canada's MAiD regime, including people in government, academia, and the health professions, to engage in reasoned discussion and to recognize concerns has often been hard to digest, and the indifference of others has been disappointing. But at the same time, it has been an incredibly enriching privilege to encounter so many engaged and thoughtful *compagnons de route*, deeply dedicated health professionals, academic scholars of various disciplines, disabled persons, and strong advocates for disability justice and human rights. Many of them are part of this book as authors or are represented by the insights they offered.

ACKNOWLEDGMENTS

The editors, as full co-editors ranked alphabetically in this volume, are deeply indebted to all contributing authors, who supported this book project from the start and were patient when the project encountered delays. Without their continued support, this book would not have seen the light. We are further grateful to Rowan

Meredith and Manreet Brar for their diligent work on the references and formatting and to Jennifer Nason for painstaking work on the index. Two anonymous peer reviewers provided very helpful comments on the various chapters and on the organization of the volume. The Scholl Chair in Health Law and Policy provided financial support for the editing and formatting work.

We dedicate this book to:

Ramona: To my amazing husband, Philippe Violette, and my wonderful children, Isabelle, Madeleine, Kevin, Eric, and Joseph: I thank them for their patience, for filling in the gaps at home while I worked, and for the beauty, joy, and humour they brought to this journey, making it all the more bearable. To my father and mother, whose example of caring for newcomers and marginalized persons has been a guiding light throughout my life – I am grateful for the opportunity to care for my dad, who would have been proud to know I edited a book! To my sisters, Kareena, who read and edited my chapters countless times with love and patience, and Marisa, who provides psychiatric care to my patients who have suffered so much – I adore and thank my dear family. To my fabulous patients: many of them taught me what it means to suffer while living with hope and gratitude in adversity. To those who have passed: it was a privilege. For those who continue to be my patients, I am further privileged.

Sonu: To my life love Lystra, and my life purposes Dante and Sabine, all and each of whom provided much wisdom and thankfully shared the joys, and sadly also felt the slings and arrows, of this journey. To Nemo Maru, whose four paws and endless hugs provide enduring comfort. To Flora and Ram, for modelling strength of spirit and raising such a wonderful daughter. And of course to my father Virindar for opening the eyes of a child to the injustices of the *Komagata Maru*, and to Narinder, for her caring companionship of my father. And last but first, to my late mother, Harinder, for showing an imperfect world that there is no defence against grace and dignity, and for ingraining in me the prime directive to always strive to Bend the Arc with integrity.

Trudo: To my wife and love Pascale Chapdelaine, and my sons Rafaël and Albéric. They endured many conversations on this challenging topic, always with excellent feedback and thoughtful reflections. They offered a safe retreat from work and patiently accepted many intrusions on our family life. To my parents Cecile Vanassche and Jos Lemmens, who passed away in the years that I worked on this topic, for the values they instilled in us and their exemplary dedication to public service. After my mother's death, I was moved by hearing more details about how in her volunteer work she was among a small group of pioneers of palliative care in Brugge, my city of birth. To my brother Willem, who shared his insights working on these issues in Belgium, for the many conversations and the support of this work. To my dear friend, the late Louis Charland, whose wise counsel we miss in this debate. And to the many disabled persons who shared their concerns, experiences, and insights, and made me understand so much better what is at stake.

UNRAVELLING MAiD IN CANADA

Introduction

Ramona Coelho, K. Sonu Gaind, and Trudo Lemmens

In 2016 Canada joined what was then still only a handful of jurisdictions with euthanasia or assisted suicide laws. Canada's Parliament carved out an exemption to the Criminal Code prohibitions of homicide and aiding and abetting suicide and partially legalized the practice under the term *medical assistance in dying* (MAiD). Since then the country has accumulated the highest number of euthanasia deaths in the world, with one of its provinces, Quebec, now the jurisdiction with the highest number of deaths induced by health care providers as a percentage of overall deaths.

Canada's MAiD regime also stands out internationally for reasons other than its sheer number of deaths. First, most other assisted dying laws were created following lengthy societal and legislative debates and in some cases, such as in New Zealand, following a referendum of the population. Canada partially legalized MAiD in response to the 2015 Supreme Court decision of *Carter v. Canada (AG)*, which declared an absolute prohibition of physician-assisted suicide and euthanasia to be a violation of Canadians' constitutional right to life, liberty, and security of the person. And a recent expansion of the MAiD law again happened in response to a judicial decision, this time of a lower trial court in Quebec.

Second, Canada opted for a legislative euthanasia regime inspired by Belgium and the Netherlands. Most countries that have legalized some form of assisted dying focus primarily on assisted suicide, with some allowing euthanasia only for persons incapable of taking medication themselves. Third, even though Canada originally included as a safeguard that MAiD was only to be provided for those broadly at the end of their lives, which was already more flexible than most assisted suicide regimes – these tend to have a strict survival prognosis of less than six months or less than one year as key criteria – the law was expanded remarkably quickly to provide access to MAiD for disabled persons not approaching their death, and it is also scheduled to offer MAiD to persons with mental illness as of 2027. With those expansions, introduced in 2021, Canada will offer even broader access to euthanasia than Belgium and the Netherlands because of some unique features of the Canadian law documented in this volume that are already impacting the practice of MAiD in Canada.

Various controversies discussed throughout this book show that intersecting factors of poverty, disability, mental health, and barriers of access to care may increasingly put marginalized Canadians at risk of premature death through MAiD. The fact that poverty and lack of adequate care may drive at least some of the demands for euthanasia and assisted suicide is one of the most striking and for many deeply disturbing components of Canada's regime.

Readers will find in this volume critical reflections about these components of Canada's MAiD law and practice. They will learn about Canada's rapid expansion, from an already relatively broad end-of-life focused regime to one that offers death as an intervention to address the suffering of disabled persons who may otherwise have years or decades of life left and that will soon also include persons with mental illnesses and addictions.

Since the expansion of our MAiD law, the debate over the desirability and consequences of offering death as a solution to various forms of illness and disability-related suffering has increased significantly in Canada. Various chapters focus on the concerns this expansion raises. Some chapters also look at the future and discuss ways in which Canada's MAiD law may further expand to include, for example, mature minors and MAiD on the basis of advance requests for persons with dementia.

Canada's developments have understandably drawn attention from around the world. Euthanasia and assisted suicide remain illegal in most countries. Since 2016, however, a growing number of jurisdictions have legalized some form of these practices, particularly focusing on the end-of-life context. In some of these countries, there are ongoing discussions about potential expansion of the law, as has happened in Canada. Other countries are faced with debates about whether legalization is desirable, and if so, in what format: Should it be restricted to the prescription of lethal medicines, or should physicians be allowed to end patients' lives? Should a terminal illness diagnosis be an essential access criterion? The editors and many of the authors of this book are frequently invited to share their insights about Canadian developments before disability, Indigenous, academic, and parliamentary audiences around the world. Many want to understand how Canada has had such striking developments, how Canada has already bypassed the most liberal euthanasia regimes in the world with its MAiD practice, and how it has pushed through legislation against the explicit and strong opposition of disability advocacy and Indigenous organizations. International readers will find in this book reflections on why Canada's MAiD regime expanded so rapidly, and on the concerns this has raised. We hope this book will thereby contribute to further reflections on the path other countries should take or avoid.

The framework of medical care and indeed our social fabric has undergone a profound change in Canada with the introduction and implementation of MAiD in Canada. Drawing upon the insights provided by our authors, experts with legal, medical, and lived experience, this book clarifies legal intricacies, ethical dilemmas faced by health care practitioners, and the impact on palliative, supportive, and psychiatric care. It documents in detail how the Canadian MAiD regime is affecting marginalized populations, including those who are discriminated against based on Indigeneity, ageism, disability, and mental illness.

The book is organized into four main sections. The initial section, spanning chapters 1 to 3, delves into the evolution of MAiD in Canada and the ethical arguments underlying the country's legal framework. The second section, encompassing chapters 4 to 10, explores the integration of MAiD into Canadian medical practice and the broader context and societal implications. It examines the impact of MAiD on patient care and on specific populations, scrutinizing elements of ableism, colonialism, economic injustice, and ageism. The third section (chapters 11–13) concentrates on the planned expansion of MAiD to include mental illness as a sole criterion. Finally, chapters 14 and 15 in the fourth section discuss federal recommendations for future expansions, including the consideration of advance directives and extending eligibility to minors.

In chapter 1, which provides a broad overview, Ramona Coelho, a physician, and Trudo Lemmens, a law and bioethics professor, cover the evolving landscape of MAiD in Canada, a journey marked by legislative changes, ethical debates, and shifting public perceptions. This chapter examines the backdrop of MAiD legalization in several landmark cases, the subsequent legal battles, and the foundations that paved the way for further legislative changes. Shifting societal attitudes towards increasing support for MAiD are contrasted with the concerns of the disability community, legal experts, medical professionals, and Indigenous leaders, leaving the reader to grapple with the implications of the evolving landscape associated with the rapid increase in MAiD rates across Canada.

In chapter 2, K. Sonu Gaind, an academic and hospital psychiatrist as well as the former president of the Canadian Psychiatric Association and previous head of his former hospital's MAiD team, discusses the concerning lack of expertise and ethical responsibility demonstrated by some of Canada's expert bodies in shaping policies related to MAiD. Gaind's chapter provides a detailed, critical inside perspective on the flawed processes that resulted in the planned expansion of MAiD for mental illness and addictions. A significant focus of the chapter is how ideologically driven leaders of a few key psychiatric associations came to endorse this expansion and contributed to shaping governmental policy. The chapter also illustrates more broadly how an ideological commitment to expansive MAiD influenced various policy initiatives and how basic rules of transparent evidence-based policy-making established on broad consultation with experts were ignored. Gaind also critiques the removal of the "reasonably foreseeable natural death" safeguard.

Alexander I.F. Simpson and Roland M. Jones, psychiatrists at the Centre for Addiction and Mental Health and professors at the University of Toronto, discuss in chapter 3 the historical roots and ethical foundations of assisted dying legislation. They critically analyze what advocates for legalization of assisted dying put forward as the key concepts that seem to underpin the Canadian MAiD regime: respect for autonomy, eligibility based on compassion for suffering, and the designation of ending life as a medical procedure provided by the state. They question the coherence of invoking these concepts for the broad legalized regime of assisted dying that Canada has developed outside the end-of-life context. They argue that should the state wish to provide assisted suicide for competent individuals, a different process of assessment and delivery of assisted death is required.

In chapter 4, Mary J. Shariff and Trudo Lemmens, both law professors, along with Leonie Herx, a palliative care physician, discuss the amendments to Canada's MAiD law through Bill C-7, particularly highlighting concerns about the impact on medical practice, the standard of care, and the role of physicians. The chapter emphasizes the unique nature of Canada's MAiD law, in how it ignores, or even undermines, the crucial role of the concept of the standard of care. The authors argue that Canada's MAiD law, particularly since it has expanded beyond a strict end-of-life context, distorts the role of informed consent in health care decision-making. Informed consent, they argue, has under Canada's MAiD law been elevated as a norm that replaces the operation of the standard of care. While informed consent is obviously a key requirement for medical care, the authors point out that, in the context of evidence-informed medical practice, this does not imply that patients have a right to insist on receiving health care interventions that are not professionally indicated. The authors discuss how Canada's MAiD law and also MAiD policy and guidance documents contradict this fundamental idea, particularly in how they recommend MAiD be put on the table and made available even when patients may have years or decades of life left and other medical options are indicated. This, they argue, constitutes an internationally unprecedented assault on the normal operation of medicine as a professional practice.

Ramona Coelho discusses the exercise of conscience in medicine and the problematic implications of the effective referral policy in Ontario and the subsequent model practice guidelines developed by Health Canada. Chapter 5 provides an argument against the policy of the College of Physicians and Surgeons of Ontario that compels physicians to make effective referrals for MAiD, emphasizing the importance of conscience protection. Coelho contends that forced participation compromises physicians' ethical decision-making, potentially leading to worsened health care access and a less diverse and inclusive health care system.

Leonie Herx, a palliative care specialist, explores in chapter 6 the history of palliative care and its principles, alongside the challenges it faces in light of MAiD. Palliative care, originating from Dame Cicely Saunders's work, emphasizes holistic care to alleviate suffering for patients and families facing life-threatening illnesses. The article underscores the ethical distinction between palliative care, which focuses on affirming life, and MAiD, which involves intentionally ending life. It addresses the impact of MAiD implementation on palliative care resources and the lack of access to quality palliative care for most Canadians.

Ramona Coelho's chapter 7 explores the way medical care is provided to those with disabilities. Her chapter argues that due to entrenched inequalities and inadequate resources for people with disabilities, MAiD may disproportionately result in the deaths of those who could benefit from better care. She explores the role of discrimination, ableism, and unequal societal structures in influencing MAiD choices, emphasizing the need for comprehensive care rather than premature assisted suicide.

Chapter 8 is written by Gabrielle Peters, a disabled writer, researcher, consultant, and policy analyst with lived experience of disability and poverty. Voices like hers, in our view, have often been ignored in the Canadian debate. Peters is given significant space with a chapter that situates MAiD in the historical context of the ableist nature of other societal practices, laws, and policies. Arguing against individualistic liberal autonomy, she puts forward that it is essential to consider the role and nature of the state and the forces that restrict, pressure, influence, and coerce "choice." Following a sketch of the history of disability and poverty in Canada, she asserts that through MAiD, the state has expanded its power, now involving itself directly in disabled people's deaths while continuing to fail to support disabled people's lives. To provide privileged people with the illusion of control over death and disability, Peters bluntly states, the state has put those who already face injustice at far greater risk by making them "a killable class." Peters's chapter illustrates why the knowledge of disabled people should feature prominently in all discussions about the legalization of MAiD.

In chapter 9, the Honourable Graydon Nicholas, an Indigenous attorney, judge, and politician who served as the appointed thirtieth lieutenant governor of New Brunswick and was the first Indigenous person to hold this office, covers the concerns within Indigenous communities in Canada about MAiD. Indigenous leaders have argued that their communities have not been adequately consulted in regard to MAiD, which violates their right to self-governance in health care. High suicide rates in Indigenous communities make leaders worry that MAiD will usher in a new cause of intergenerational trauma as the government helps their members to die instead of to live. The text explores historical injustices such as colonialism, coerced sterilization, residential schools, and missing persons, contributing to the social inequalities and mental health issues faced by Indigenous peoples today.

In chapter 10, Isabel Grant, a law professor, discusses the ableist implications of Canada's expansion outside the end-of-life context in a detailed legal analysis. She argues that it is impossible to separate suffering as a result of an irremediable disability and suffering caused by the impacts of systemic ableism. The expanded MAiD law, Grant argues, violates disabled persons' right of equality and right to life, liberty, and security of the person, because it is premised on a view that portrays disability as potentially worse than death and thus denies people with disabilities the protection of the criminal law that is provided to other Canadians. Grant takes the reader through an analysis of the *Charter* compliance of the law, as a Canadian court should do.

Law professors Mary J. Shariff and Trudo Lemmens, and lawyer and constitutional law expert Derek B.M. Ross, then focus in chapter 11 on the question of whether MAiD for those with mental illness as a sole underlying condition is constitutionally required. This has been a recurrent argument among those who push for further expansion of Canada's law; that is, that this expansion is necessary to respect a constitutional right to MAiD. The authors argue, with a detailed analysis of the various MAiD-related constitutional cases, that there is no binding precedent that obliges Parliament to legalize MAiD for mental illness, and that there are, on the contrary, compelling legal arguments to prohibit MAiD outside the end-of-life context.

Chapter 12 by the same authors examines the power provinces have in Canada's federal structure to regulate and potentially restrict MAiD practice. The authors start with a discussion of how the province of Quebec already decided it would not include mental illness in its provincial MAiD law. That raises the question of whether a province could be more restrictive than what is dictated by the federal law in determining what MAiD practice it allows. The chapter explores the interaction between federal and provincial law in areas of overlapping jurisdictions, such as health. It analyzes recent Supreme Court case law that deals with comparable federalism questions. They conclude that based on the overlapping jurisdiction in relation to MAiD, provinces should feel comfortable taking further legislative and regulatory action.

Mark Sinyor and Ayal Schaffer, both academic psychiatrists, cover in their chapter the scientific evidence in relation to MAiD for mental illness. In chapter 13, they challenge the notion that the decision to permit MAiD is purely ethical and not empirical and argue that scientific evidence is crucial in medical decision-making. The chapter scrutinizes the various arguments that are made in the debate. It contrasts what evidence-informed policy would normally require in relation to each argument with the reality of how Canada's MAiD law and policy was shaped. They discuss, for example, the evidence related to irremediability in mental illness and how policy-makers failed to take seriously the evidence that reveals that irremediability cannot be predicted in individual patients. They also put forward that the official endorsement of death as a response to suffering runs counter to the evidence-based messaging of the suicide prevention community. Overall, the authors argue for a more scientific and evidence-based approach in shaping policies related to MAiD, especially regarding mental illness.

In chapter 14, Catherine Ferrier, a physician with capacity assessment and elder care expertise, addresses the contentious issue of MAiD by advance request, particularly for individuals who lose decision-making capacity, such as those facing dementia. Despite claims by MAiD advocates that their goal is to uphold autonomous decision-making about one's death, concerns arise about the vulnerability, stigma, and lack of informed advance consent for those unable to consent at the time of the procedure. The author discusses what we can learn from the Netherlands, where significant controversies have erupted over the practice of euthanizing patients with dementia based on a written prior request.

Ramona Coelho next discusses the controversial topic of MAiD for mature minors in Canada. Chapter 15 reviews the recommendations of the Special Joint Committee on MAiD, which suggested expanding MAiD to mature minors despite concerns about safeguards and potential abuses. She examines the legal perspective and the impact of MAiD on parental roles, questioning whether it could compromise guardianship and lead to government overreach. Additionally, the discussion delves into the scientific understanding of brain maturation in adolescents, highlighting the potential capacity limitations that make informed decisions about choosing death problematic for mature minors.

Our last chapter provides insights on Canada's MAiD expansion based on what was documented throughout the book. The editors reflect on what appears to have been driving the rapid developments in Canadian MAiD law and practice and what that means for the future. They remind the reader of how rapidly the official attitude shifted in the last couple of years, and how the ideological commitment of some promoters of assisted dying appears to have been instrumental in this. They ask what this reveals: Is our society promoting autonomy or privilege?

We hope these chapters will help readers critically examine the evolving landscape of MAiD in Canada: the role of law and legal concepts, the potential legal challenges that lie ahead, and the ethical considerations that accompany this paradigm shift in care with significant impacts on medical care, on persons who are elderly, ill, and disabled, on family members, on health professionals, and on our society at large. Through this exploration, we hope to encourage a broader dialogue about what measures must be taken to tackle these challenges.

POSTSCRIPT: After this book manuscript had been initially submitted and reviewed, a new Special Joint Parliamentary Committee recommended an indefinite delay to the implementation of MAiD for mental illness. In February 2024 the federal government then passed another bill to pause the introduction of MAiD for sole reasons of mental illness, which was, as discussed in chapter 1, scheduled to begin in March 2024. The special law delayed this expansion to at least March 2027. As much as possible, relevant chapters have been adjusted accordingly to acknowledge this recent information. This is one of the first times since the Canadian Parliament first legalized some form of MAiD that a parliamentary committee explicitly recognized potential problems with the further expansion of MAiD. Our hope is that this book will contribute to careful reflection about where we go from here.

1

MAiD in Canada: A Tale of Rapidly Expanding Euthanasia

Ramona Coelho and Trudo Lemmens

The Supreme Court declared in its 2015 *Carter v. Canada (AG)* decision that an absolute prohibition on assisted suicide and euthanasia was a violation of the constitutional right to life, liberty, and security of the person.[1] One year later, Canada moved to allowing medical assistance in dying (MAiD) for persons approaching their natural death, and in 2021 it expanded this to MAiD outside the end-of-life context.[2] The 2021 legislation removed the safeguards constructed around the concept of a "reasonably foreseeable natural death" for those with a serious and irremediable medical illness, disease, or disability that involves an irreversible decline of capability and "intolerable suffering." And while the 2021 Bill C-7 originally excluded MAiD for sole reasons of mental illness, that exclusion was lifted in the final bill and replaced by a sunset provision that ultimately will make MAiD also available for mental illness.[3]

The legalization and subsequent expansion outside the end-of-life context has been pushed through as compassionate care, coupled with the right of persons to decide for themselves when and how they want to die. Yet United Nations experts, national disability and many social justice organizations, and Indigenous leaders along with hundreds of physicians and several law professors have expressed concern that Bill C-7 leaves Canadians at risk of wrongful and premature death when they would have recovered with care and resources.[4] Developments since then, in terms of rapidly increasing numbers of death by MAiD and fact-checked media reports and declarations and findings by some official agencies, appear to confirm that these concerns are warranted.

This chapter sketches the road to the legalization of MAiD, looking at how earlier policy initiatives, court challenges, and legislative initiatives paved the way for the 2015 *Carter* decision and the legal responses to it. We describe some of the political dynamics during this process and clarify how we ended up with the current terminology. The chapter further describes how MAiD eligibility has concretely expanded in Canada, how numbers have increased, and how controversial practices emerged. Some of the problematic components of the practice are discussed in more detail in subsequent chapters.

DEFINITIONS: WHAT IS MEDICAL ASSISTANCE IN DYING (MAiD)?

Medical assistance in dying (MAiD) was introduced as a legal term in Canadian law following the *Carter* decision. In its Criminal Code definition, the term encompasses both euthanasia (active and intentional ending of life by a health care practitioner) and assisted suicide (prescription of lethal medication to be self-administered).[5] It is an exemption to the normal application of the Criminal Code provisions related to culpable homicide (s. 222.4), aiding or abetting suicide (s. 241), or the provision of a noxious substance (s. 245), which allows physicians or nurse practitioners to do what is otherwise a serious criminal offence.[6] In Canada, MAiD has overwhelmingly consisted of euthanasia: in 2022, out of more than thirteen thousand reported cases, only seven cases consisted of self-administered MAiD.[7]

The term *MAiD* is now widely used in the Canadian context and is increasingly used in debates in other countries by those who advocate legalizing the practice or broadening existing assisted suicide regimes. It remains controversial because it obfuscates what is involved and seems particularly inappropriate since the law expanded outside the end-of-life context. Even in Canada it was introduced only recently. In the *Carter* decision, the Canadian Supreme Court used the term "physician-assisted dying." A 2011 report commissioned by the Royal Society of Canada and finalized at the start of the *Carter* trial still used the term "assisted death" as an "umbrella term" that encompasses the "full spectrum of conduct ... that contributes to the death of an individual," including euthanasia, assisted suicide, and withholding or withdrawing life-sustaining treatment.[8]

Practical and strategic considerations are at the origin of the term. There was a need to use a broader term than *physician-assisted dying*, since Canadian law also allows nurse practitioners to perform the procedure. The term MAiD closely resembles the term *medical aid in dying*, which was introduced in a 2015 provincial Quebec law, but there it only refers to euthanasia, that is, the administration of a lethal substance by physicians. Strategically, the term MAiD was preferred to obscure similarities with well-known historical instances of physicians' involvement in euthanasia and to avoid stirring up concerns that Canada could be facing problems similar to those arising in the few jurisdictions that legalized euthanasia, particularly Belgium and the Netherlands. The use of the term MAiD arguably also helped circumvent discussions about potential tension with suicide prevention.

Before the Joint Parliamentary Committee that ended up recommending the term MAiD for all future legislation, a senior counsel of the Department of Justice pointed out that some – she likely meant legalization supporters – were worried that "euthanasia" and "assisted suicide" were "loaded and stigmatizing terms."[9] *Medical assistance in dying* seemed from that perspective perfect. Who could be against "medical assistance in dying"? Although most Canadians now likely understand, at least in general, what MAiD stands for, we were struck by how people were often convinced that Canada was permitting something very different from what had been legalized in Belgium and the Netherlands.[10] In fact, some supporters of broad legalization continue to object very strongly when the internationally accepted terms euthanasia and assisted suicide are used in public discussions, as if this disparages MAiD.

Public officials contributed to this confusion. Véronique Hivon, Quebec's minister of social services and youth protection who was in charge of the province's MAiD file, claimed for example that there was a clear difference between "assisted suicide" and "euthanasia" on the one hand, and "aide médicale à mourir" on the other hand. "In contrast with euthanasia," she stated in an interview, "medical aid in dying is very well defined and takes place in a medical context,"[11] thereby ignoring the experience with legalized euthanasia in Belgium and the Netherlands, regimes that significantly informed the Quebec law.

Although the term is now part of the Canadian legal landscape, and we therefore use it in this book, we do so reluctantly. Indeed, particularly since the expansion of the law outside the end-of-life context, the term is incoherent and misleading. In the end-of-life context, it was already confusing, since it seemingly suggested that it encompassed the long-standing support of the dying process through palliative care and created confusion with various medical practices aimed at "assisting" in the dying context. For that very reason, palliative care specialists in particular have been very critical of the term, as discussed further in this volume, since they have always been "assisting" in dying. Balfour Mount, a founder of Canadian palliative care medicine, stated in an interview: "The very name of that intervention, 'medical aid in dying,' is misleading ... Medical aid in dying is what I have been doing for fifty years. This bill is not talking about medical aid in dying."[12]

At least the original bill was arguably still aimed at facilitating a process that was independently already leading to death. But since it now involved a process of ending the life of persons with decades of life left, we and others suggested that the term *medically administered death* would be more apt to describe this practice.[13] We also see no reason to avoid terms clearly established by their use in the literature and in other jurisdictions: "euthanasia" and "assisted suicide."

It should be understood that MAiD is not the withholding or stopping of inappropriate, unwanted, or ineffective medical treatment or the provision of palliative care.[14]

THE PATH TOWARDS THE FIRST MAiD LAW

The fight for MAiD by proponents of its legalization and expansion spans decades. One key component of Canada's MAiD history is the pivotal role of some landmark legal cases and how these cases interacted with policy initiatives. It is therefore important to briefly expand on some of these cases and initiatives.

The first case to explicitly deal with the question of legalization of assisted suicide was launched in British Columbia by Sue Rodriguez, who suffered from amyotrophic lateral sclerosis (ALS). She argued that the Criminal Code prohibition on "giving assistance to commit suicide" (the language used in the case) violated her *Charter* right of life, liberty, and security of the person (s. 7), her right not to be submitted to cruel and unusual punishment (s. 12), and her right to equality (s. 15). The case went up to the Supreme Court, where the court rejected her claim with a small majority (five to four). All but one of the justices analyzed the case under the right to liberty and security of the person. They all found that the Criminal Code prohibition did impinge on her right to security and liberty, but the majority found the absolute prohibition justified because of the state interest in protecting "the sanctity of life," here thus recognized as a core constitutional value.

Justice Sopinka, speaking for the majority, held that "the prohibition against assisted suicide serves a similar purpose [to the prohibition of capital punishment]. In upholding the respect for life, it may discourage those who consider that life is unbearable at a particular moment, or who perceive themselves to be a burden upon others, from committing suicide. To permit a physician to lawfully participate in taking life would send a signal that there are circumstances in which the state approves of suicide."[15] This prohibition, he further ruled, "is grounded in the state interest in protecting life and reflects the policy of the state that human life should not be depreciated by allowing life to be taken."[16]

It is noteworthy that Justice McLachlin, the only justice who was still on the bench two decades later when the court ruled in the *Carter* case, considered that the prohibition was disproportionately restricting Rodriguez's right to liberty and security of the person.

In the same year as the *Rodriguez* case, Robert Latimer killed his twelve-year-old disabled daughter Tracy by placing her in his truck and pumping gas from the exhaust pipe back into the truck via a hose. He claimed he was compelled to do so out of compassion, to end her physical pain and suffering. Tracy had cerebral palsy. She was scheduled to undergo hip surgery to reduce her physical discomfort and pain, which Latimer opposed as, in his word, "mutilation." Her mother testified about Tracy as a happy girl. Latimer was convicted of second-degree murder after a lengthy legal saga that included a Supreme Court order of a new trial.[17] In a second trial, the trial judge failed to apply the mandatory minimum sentence of ten years, instead declaring a "constitutional exemption" and sentencing him to one year in jail and one year under house arrest on his farm.[18] This decision was overturned by the Saskatchewan Court of Appeal and the mandatory sentence was eventually imposed.[19]

The fact that many people sympathized with Robert Latimer and that one judge even invoked a constitutional exemption to soften his conviction deeply troubled many in the disability community. In their view, Latimer and those sympathizing with him disregarded the equal value of Tracy Latimer's life. They were also troubled by calls to soften the penalty for so-called "mercy killings."

In the wake of the *Rodriguez* and *Latimer* cases, a special Senate committee on euthanasia and assisted suicide studied the question of whether the practice should be legalized.[20] It recommended against legalization. Although the *Latimer* case is not mentioned in the report, the committee controversially recommended that a "separate offence of compassionate homicide" with a less severe penalty *could* be established.[21]

The report, the defeat in the *Rodriguez* case, and the controversy surrounding the killing of Tracy Latimer may have contributed to a relative silence around the topic of assisted suicide and euthanasia in Canada for some time, even though private member bills were brought forward in support of some form of legalization.

The debate intensified again around 2010. That year, federal Parliament again rejected a private member's bill to legalize assisted suicide by a wide margin of 228–59.[22] But other initiatives were already underway that had a serious impact on the Canadian end-of-life policy scene. In December 2009 the Quebec legislature mandated a *Commission spéciale sur la question de mourir dans la dignité* (Special Committee on the Question of Dying with Dignity) with the mandate to study the potential legalization of physician involvement in ending life. This parliamentary initiative followed in the footsteps of a public statement by the Quebec College of Physicians and Surgeons that euthanasia could in exceptional circumstances be justified.[23] For two years the special committee consulted with relevant experts and with the general public on the topic of end-of-life care, including the potential legalization of some form of assisted dying.[24] Its 2012 report contained detailed recommendations for the legalization of "medical aid in dying" for adults with a serious and incurable disease and an advanced decline of capabilities with no prospect of improvement that causes permanent physical or psychological intolerable suffering that cannot be alleviated in circumstances they find tolerable. It also recommended that an oversight body be established to review "medical aid in dying" procedures. The recommendations situated this newly proposed practice in the context of overall end-of-life care, with the report emphasizing the need for the government to promote palliative care, including palliative home care. The organization Vivre dans la dignité, opposed to the legalization, analyzed the submissions to the parliamentary committee and found that 60 per cent of the submissions opposed "any opening of euthanasia" and that only 34 per cent of those who submitted or presented to the committee were "either somewhat or strongly in favour" of it.[25]

Nevertheless, in 2014 the National Assembly of Quebec adopted a law on "mourir dans la dignité," legalizing "medical aid in dying" as a key component of broader end-of-life care.[26] The integration of the practice into a set of medical measures to promote "dying with dignity" permitted Quebec to frame it as being about health care and thus under provincial jurisdiction. It created, however, the remarkable situation that a provincial health care act was contradicting an explicit prohibition in the Criminal Code, which is squarely within federal jurisdiction.[27]

MAiD was presented to the Quebec population as a measure of last resort that would rarely be needed. Minister Véronique Hivon framed MAiD as an "exceptional measure for exceptional cases,"[28] in line with the Special Parliamentary Committee's view that legalization was needed to address the unique needs of "un petit nombre de personnes" (a small number of people),[29] while minister of health Gaétan Barrette admitted after the first year of practice that he had expected less than one hundred requests per year.[30] Quebec's more than three thousand MAiD deaths in 2022 reveal how policy-makers clearly underestimated how the practice would explode in less than a decade.

Meanwhile, at the federal level, a lawsuit launched in 2012 by a group of plaintiffs in British Columbia against Canada's Criminal Code prohibition on assisted suicide and euthanasia was slowly making its way through the courts. The coalition involved as individual plaintiffs: Gloria Taylor, a woman who like Sue Rodriguez lived with amyotrophic lateral sclerosis and wanted to have the option to have a physician end her life; two family members of Kathleen Carter, a woman with degenerative spinal stenosis, who had accompanied Carter at risk of criminal prosecution to Switzerland where she died with assisted suicide; and Dr William Shoichet, a physician who wanted to participate in physician-assisted dying if it were legal. Justice Lynne Smith of the British Columbia Supreme Court, who presided over the case, used her judicial discretion to also accept the British Columbia Civil Liberties Association as a public interest co-plaintiff, notwithstanding a challenge by the defendants (the federal and provincial attorneys general). Justice Smith, a former board member of the British Columbia Civil Liberties Association, pointed out that "the BCCLA is a large, well-established organization" and that it "has been extensively involved in advocacy and education regarding end-of-life choices, including assisted suicide and voluntary euthanasia."[31] She also approvingly noted that Joseph Arvey, counsel for the individual plaintiffs, indicated that the plaintiffs would have been unable to launch such a lawsuit on their own or to continue it should Gloria Taylor die during the proceedings.

The plaintiffs argued that the various Criminal Code provisions related to aiding someone with suicide and to homicide violated their right to life, liberty, and security of the person and the right to equality to the extent that these provisions collectively prohibit physician-assisted dying.

In June 2012 Justice Smith sided with the applicant and ruled the Criminal Code prohibition restricted both the right to life, liberty, and security of the person and the equality right of the applicants, and that this restriction was grossly disproportionate. To justify overturning the *Rodriguez* precedent, Justice Smith invoked two issues: (1) the Supreme Court had developed a new proportionality test after *Rodriguez*; and (2) new social circumstances and new international developments justified a re-examination. In support of the latter, Justice Smith cited broader public support for legalization in Canada and accumulated evidence about the practice from jurisdictions that had legalized euthanasia and assisted suicide.

Justice Smith's ruling has been discussed elsewhere in more detail.[32] Some have lauded the judgment as an example of solid, comprehensive judicial engagement with complex evidence.[33] Others have been critical of the judgment, particularly of some of its evidentiary findings.[34] For example, Justice Smith remarkably stated that there was a "preponderance of evidence of ethicists," that is, her framing of what she found the most convincing statements from the expert witnesses who she identified as "ethicists" – with one of them clearly not being an ethicist – that there is no distinction between actively ending the life of a patient and withdrawing life support. She also all too easily brushed aside concerns about practices in Belgium and the Netherlands by suggesting that they are the result of a different medico-legal culture.[35]

A detailed discussion of the case itself exceeds the scope of this overview chapter. But it is worth emphasizing here how some components reflect the carefully planned nature of this judicial challenge, the apparent coordination with other policy initiatives seemingly aimed at feeding into the judicial process, and broader institutional support. With respect to the level of preparedness, it is striking how many expert witnesses for the plaintiff were heard in court, in contrast with the defendant federal and provincial attorneys general: thirty-nine for the plaintiff, with only eighteen for the defendant attorneys general.[36] The defendants were given little time to respond. Justice Smith emphasized the urgency of the case, since it involved a person who was waiting to be able to access physician-assisted dying. The trial proceeded as a summary and expedited trial, based on affidavit evidence. When the defendants later challenged this decision and asked for permission to produce more evidence, their request failed on appeal because of procedural issues.

A remarkably well-timed initiative by the Royal Society of Canada further fed into the judicial process. Around 2010, the Royal Society set up the Expert Panel on End-of-Life Decision-Making, seemingly because it felt that "assisted dying is a critically important public policy issue, where opinion, practice and the law seem out of alignment" and that "the time has come for a national debate on end-of-life decision making."[37] The Royal Society's mandate is to serve Canada and Canadians "by mobilizing [leading intellectuals, scholars, researchers, and artists] *in open discussion and debate*, to advance knowledge, encourage integrated interdisciplinary understandings and address [critical] issues."[38] An effort to balance various perspectives on what was then and still remains a challenging and controversial issue would have seemed proper. Yet, with utilitarian philosopher Udo Schüklenk as chair, the panel consisted of members who all but one had explicitly supported legalization of assisted dying in public declarations and publications, with none on record expressing concerns. This seems a departure from what historically was the respected practice for advisory panels on important ethical debates to ensure some balance of perspectives. Not surprisingly, the panel concluded that there were no substantial problems in the countries that legalized euthanasia and assisted suicide, and it came out with strong recommendations for broad legalization in Canada.

The panel's report was not ready yet when the plaintiffs in *Carter* went to court, but it was introduced as evidence during the proceedings through cross-examination of one of the defendants' witnesses. The attorney general's lawyers pointed out the report's one-sided arguments, and the fact that three of its members were now expert witnesses for the plaintiffs, while another member was assisting the plaintiffs' legal team with the cross-examination of witnesses. One of the attorney general's witnesses, Dr Harvey Chochinov, himself a fellow of the Royal College, suggested that the report was written with "a pre-ordained conclusion." He noted the speed by which it had been put together, and the fact that there was no expert in palliative care on the panel.[39] The lawyers indicated they wanted to cross-examine the expert panel members if their report were to be considered as evidence. Still, the report was "provisionally" admitted by Justice Smith and was referenced in her judgment.

The timing of the Royal Society initiative and the fast integration of it in a court case where all but two of the members of the panel contributed as expert witnesses or as direct advisors to the plaintiffs hardly seems coincidental. It suggests that this initiative was intended to produce "evidence" that could be used in court. One wonders whether the Royal Society, or at least the person(s) in charge of this file, was informed of this goal and wittingly participated, and if so, whether this was in line with the Royal Society's mandate, particularly in light of the selection of the panel members.

Some other aspects of Justice Smith's ruling are worth mentioning, since they appear to contrast with later developments of Canada's MAiD law and practice, as is also discussed further in this volume. Justice Smith did not express support for a specific form of legalization. That was, of course, not a question she had to address. Her inquiry focused on whether an absolute prohibition was a justifiable, proportionate restriction of the plaintiffs' *Charter* rights. Her ruling dealt with the situation of the plaintiffs, in particular Gloria Taylor, who was also asking for a constitutional exemption to be able to obtain a physician's assistance in dying. As is discussed in subsequent chapters, Justice Smith referred to end-of-life situations and gave examples of jurisdictions such as Oregon to illustrate how legalization could work. She also acknowledged that there might very well have been some problems with the euthanasia practices in Belgium and the Netherlands, and that official self-reported data may not be fully reliable. In other words: she did not clearly embrace a broad style of legalization of euthanasia as in Belgium or the Netherlands, nor did she declare that the evidence of those jurisdictions clearly indicated that this form of legalized assisted dying was preferable and should be introduced in Canada.

In the end, Justice Smith concluded that "the risks inherent in permitting physician-assisted death can be identified and very substantially minimized through a carefully designed system imposing stringent limits that are scrupulously monitored and enforced."[40] She gave the government one year to design new legislation and granted a constitutional exemption to Gloria Taylor so that she could obtain a physician's aid in dying.

After the British Columbia Court of Appeal reversed Justice Smith's judgment, declaring that Rodriguez remained a good precedent, the Supreme Court accepted to hear the case.[41] In February 2015, it ruled, in an unusually unanimous judgment of "The Court," that the absolute prohibition on "physician-assisted dying" was an unjustifiable infringement of the right to life, liberty, and security of the person.[42] It gave Parliament one year to create a "carefully crafted" exemption to the Criminal Code prohibition and provided broad parameters that the law ought to reflect. The judgment and its legal implications are discussed in detail elsewhere in this volume.[43] But it bears repeating here that the judgment confirmed the legitimate role of the Criminal Code in protecting the right to life through provisions prohibiting among other things assisted suicide and homicide. What it asked the legislature to do is to allow physicians to be involved in "physician-assisted dying" in exceptional circumstances. It declared the provisions of the Criminal Code void "insofar as they prohibit physician-assisted death for a competent adult person who (1) clearly consents to the termination of life; and (2) has a grievous and irremediable medical condition (including an illness, disease, or disability) that causes enduring suffering that is intolerable to the individual in the circumstances of his or her condition. 'Irremediable,' it should be added, does not require the patient to undertake treatments that are not acceptable to the individual."[44]

As is emphasized further in this volume, the Supreme Court explicitly stated that its declaration was "intended to respond to the factual circumstances of the case," and that it made "no pronouncement on other situations where physician-assisted dying may be sought."[45] Finally, the court also explicitly invited Parliament to enact a new law before the invalidity of the relevant provisions would kick in, one year after the judgment. It approvingly cited Justice Smith's judgment, which had mentioned that the government could enact "a stringently limited, carefully monitored system of exceptions."[46]

One other point is also worth mentioning here, since it relates to several chapters in this volume related to mental health.[47] In discussing why the "right to life" was infringed by an absolute prohibition, the court appeared to accept the claim that allowing assisted death would prevent premature suicides of people who would end their life sooner because of the fear that they would later be unable to do so. Neither they nor the trial court offered any concrete empirical evidence for this. Also relevant is that the Supreme Court had exceptionally allowed the hearing of new evidence in support of the attorney general's claim that there were troubling developments in Belgium that the court should take into consideration that highlighted the dangers of legalization. However, after hearing the evidence, it rejected the relevance of this evidence, indicating that the court was not dealing with euthanasia for minors, for minor conditions, or for mental illness.[48]

POST-*CARTER* INITIATIVES

The Supreme Court suspended the declaration of invalidity for one year to allow Parliament to design an appropriate regulatory regime. Five months into this year, in July 2015, the conservative Harper government set up the Expert Panel on Options for a Legislative Response to *Carter v. Canada*, mandated to consult broadly and to come up with options for legalization of assisted dying.[49] It consisted of Benoit Pelletier, Dr Harvey Chochinov, and Catherine Frazee, the latter two having been expert witnesses for the attorney general in the *Carter* case. The panel consulted with various stakeholders, including within the broader population, and travelled to Belgium, the Netherlands, Switzerland, and the US to learn about their experiences. But before the panel finalized its work, federal elections brought a new Liberal government under Justin Trudeau into power. The new government reduced the panel's mandate to reporting on consultations and key findings. The panel submitted its report to minister of justice Jody Wilson-Raybould in December 2015.[50] Noteworthy is that the report spent several pages discussing how several organizations recommended introducing a system of prior authorization by judicial or administrative tribunals, an option that was not given much attention in other reports. It also discussed Oregon's system of assisted suicide in some detail.

Two other reports did make recommendations for legalization, one of them feeling remarkably comfortable to do so even without a mandate from the federal government or Parliament. First, an advisory committee had been set up, seemingly at the initiative of the Ontario government, but officially by eleven provinces and territories, with Quebec notably absent and British Columbia only participating as an "observer." The Provincial-Territorial Expert Advisory Group on Physician-Assisted Dying, set up in August 2015, simply noted that the federal expert panel was not mandated to make recommendations, and "with this in mind, our report includes recommendations that ask provinces and territories to advocate for certain changes to federal legislation."[51] The advisory group did its own consultations with stakeholders, and in a record time of three months, put this in a report with sweeping recommendations for broad legalization of assisted dying. Jennifer Gibson and Maureen Taylor co-chaired the advisory group. Gibson, a bioethics professor and director of the Joint Centre for Bioethics, had not focused on assisted dying in her prior research or policy work and did not appear to have taken any public position on this topic. Taylor, on the other hand, was a vocal advocate for legalization of assisted dying, inspired by her former partner, Dr Donald Low, who in 2013 had recorded a passionate plea for legalization of assisted suicide while he was dying from brain cancer. His testimony, widely distributed after his death, had captivated Ontarians perhaps even more because he had been the professional, reassuring public face of the public health response during the 2003 Toronto SARS crisis.[52]

Other members of the advisory group included law professor Jocelyn Downie, who had been an advisor for the plaintiffs in *Carter* and a member of the Royal Society expert panel; bioethics professor Arthur Schafer; emeritus professor of pediatrics and bioethics Dr Nuala Kenny; and human rights lawyer and commissioner Ruth Goba. Downie and Schafer had already been outspoken supporters of broad legalization of euthanasia and assisted suicide, whereas Kenny, a Catholic nun, had expressed serious reservations about it.

The report reads as a consensus document, but Kenny fundamentally disagreed with some of the recommendations and key points. In conversations we had with her, she indicated that she tried but was unable to have her disagreements clearly reflected as a minority statement in the report. She pointed to an introductory section in the report where, after her insistence, reference was made to "a diversity of perspectives ... which we sought to reconcile through our deliberations in light of the background briefings and stakeholder input. In some cases, this involved re-considering and sometimes putting aside deeply held personal views and common ground in the interest of Canadian patients and the public."[53] This can hardly be seen as a clear and transparent recognition of a lack of consensus.

Kenny's experience, the speed with which the consultations were conducted, the explicit recommendations for broad legalization just before a federal Joint Parliamentary Committee was to issue its recommendations, and the remarkable fact that the recommendations targeted policy outside of provincial mandates suggests this initiative was likely a strategic political move to influence the new federal legislation.

Comparably broad recommendations, and this time with an explicit federal mandate to explore legislative options, were also made in a 2016 report by the Special Joint Committee on Physician-Assisted Dying of the House of Commons and the Senate.[54] Over two weeks, this committee held eleven sets of hearings with experts and stakeholders and published its report the same month. Perhaps not surprisingly considering this time frame, the report appeared to borrow heavily from the Provincial-Territorial Expert Advisory Group report, including its recommendations. Both the majority report of the Special Joint Committee and the Provincial-Territorial Expert Advisory Group recommended not to impose an end-of-life safeguard, to consider expanding MAiD toward mature minors in the coming years, to include MAiD for sole reasons of mental illness, and to permit advance requests for MAiD.

Four Conservative committee members wrote a firm dissenting report, arguing that insufficient safeguards were recommended in the majority report and that the recommendations went beyond, and even against, *Carter*.[55] They pointed out that Quebec had more carefully connected its law to improved palliative care, and they opposed the recommendation for an "effective referral" obligation for conscientious objectors. Two New Democrat members of the committee, while agreeing with the majority's recommendations, emphasized that broader health care issues, including access to palliative and mental health care, had to be addressed.[56] They also called for careful consultation with Indigenous people, which did not happen.

The sweeping recommendations of the majority caused concern, particularly within the disability community and among several of the experts who had testified before the committee, whose concerns and warnings about developments in other euthanasia regimes were largely ignored. With Dr Harvey Schipper, one of us (TL) organized on 20 February 2016 an invitation-only "Open Discussion on Legalizing Physician-Assisted Dying" event at the University of Toronto, where academic experts and stakeholders from various professional organizations and ministries explored some of these concerns.[57] Several representatives of the federal and Ontario ministries of justice and health participated in the meeting. Some of the presentations focused specifically on what was happening in Belgium and the Netherlands in terms of the expansion of the practice, including in the context of mental health. We were later told that the meeting consolidated the views of at least some government officials and strengthened or provided additional arguments as to why a more restricted MAiD law than the one recommended by the Joint Parliamentary Committee would be advisable and also reconcilable with the *Carter* decision.

The ministers who were at the time responsible for the MAiD file, minister of justice Jody Wilson-Raybould and minister of health

Jane Philpott, resisted the strong pressure, seemingly from within the Liberal party, in favour of widely accessible legalized MAiD; instead, they designed a law that focused on an albeit rather broad end-of-life regime. Considering the concerns expressed by Indigenous people and the social justice concerns associated with open-ended MAiD, it is likely not coincidental that Wilson-Raybould was the first Indigenous minister of justice, and that Philpott has a strong social justice–focused medical practice background.

THE FIRST MAiD LAW: BILL C-14

Bill C-14, adopted in June 2016, attempted to balance access to assisted death for adult patients approaching their natural death who wanted to have control over the timing and manner of their death with protecting others from wrongful death.[58] Importantly, the explicitly stated goals of the legislation included avoiding negative perceptions of the quality of life of persons who are elderly, ill, or disabled; affirming the inherent and equal value of every person's life; and promoting suicide prevention as a public health goal. The first two goals reflected the disability-related concerns of offering death as a solution to suffering, which is discussed in various chapters in this volume.[59]

The law created an exemption to the continuing Criminal Code prohibitions on culpable homicide and aiding a person to die by suicide. The exemption means that if specific access criteria are respected, the prohibitions do not apply. The access criteria largely repeated the parameters in the *Carter* decision, but a definition of "grievous and irremediable medical condition" was added to the bill. Under the new law, capable adult Canadians eligible for health care services who have a grievous or irremediable medical condition and who make a voluntary request for assisted dying can ask a physician or nurse practitioner to end their life or to prescribe lethal medication. A grievous medical condition was defined in the law as (1) a serious and incurable illness, disease, or disability; (2) with an irreversible decline of capability; (3) that causes enduring, intolerable physical or psychological suffering that cannot be alleviated in circumstances that the person finds acceptable; (4) and with the person's natural death being "reasonably foreseeable" (RFND). As we discuss further, as part of the 2021 expansion of the MAiD law, this fourth criterion would be moved out of the definition and integrated as a selection criterion to determine what procedural criteria apply.

The law introduced specific procedural requirements and safeguards, which reflected the notion that MAiD was clearly an exceptional procedure and not standard medical practice. The key procedural requirements were: the patient had to submit a written request, signed in the presence of two co-signing independent witnesses; a second independent physician had to provide a written assessment in which they agree that the patient meets the criteria; and ten days had to elapse between the signing of the request and the provision of MAiD – a period that could be shortened if loss of capacity was imminent. The patient also had to explicitly reconfirm their desire to die by MAiD just prior to the procedure. As we will mention further, several of these procedural safeguards also disappeared with the 2021 revision.

The most contested aspect, which ran counter to the recommendations of the Joint Parliamentary Committee not to specifically define any terms from the *Carter* "parameters," was precisely the RFND criterion, which meant that a person had to approach their natural death. It was not explicitly stated in the *Carter* decision, but as some of the other chapters point out in more detail, that does not mean, in our view, that it was unreasonable or clearly unconstitutional to add this overall as a key safeguard.[60]

However, "reasonably foreseeable natural death" was not defined in the law, and since it is a vague term, the term was quickly interpreted very broadly, particularly also by those who had been strongly pushing for an open-ended MAiD law.[61] An unusual "clarification" in an Ontario Superior Court decision, which stated that a seventy-seven-year-old patient (patient AB) with osteoarthritis would qualify for MAiD under the "reasonably foreseeable natural death" provision, also contributed to this broad interpretation. Superior Court Justice Paul Perell told the courtroom that a patient's death does not have to be imminent, and their condition does not have to be terminal.[62]

Instead of providing access to MAiD for mental illness, on the basis of advance requests, and for mature minors as the Joint Parliamentary Committee had recommended, the law instructed the government to study these three aspects of assisted dying in the coming years. The law further mandated a review of the developing MAiD practice after five years, the same period given for the study of the three controversial areas. Shortly after the bill was adopted, the Council of Canadian Academies was mandated to study the three topics and report on the evidence, but it was explicitly instructed not to make any specific recommendations. The council brought together a broad group of experts for each of the three topics, including two of the editors of this volume. It published three voluminous reports in 2018.[63]

Meanwhile, some of the same players who supported the plaintiffs in *Carter* also coordinated new court challenges against what they framed as "discriminatory" and unconstitutional "restrictions" of the right to MAiD.

The first case was that of Julia Lamb, a young woman who had a degenerative neuromuscular disorder and wanted to have MAiD. The case was adjourned in September 2019 when an expert for the attorney general, Dr Madeline Li, clarified that if Julia Lamb would refuse regular treatment, she could make herself sick enough that her death would become reasonably foreseeable, and she would thereby qualify for MAiD under the Bill C-14 regime.[64]

While the *Lamb* case was dropped by the plaintiffs – it would have been very difficult in the circumstances to obtain a declaration that Lamb's rights were violated – a challenge before the Quebec Superior Court did result in a judgment in favour of the plaintiffs. Jean Truchon, who lived with cerebral palsy and quadriplegia, and Nicole Gladu, who had post-polio syndrome, argued that both the Quebec "end of life" and the federal "reasonably foreseeable natural death" criteria violated their right to equality and their right to life, liberty, and security of the person. Justice Christine Baudouin ruled that these two *Charter* rights were breached by limiting MAiD according to these two safeguards in Quebec and federal law.[65]

A more detailed discussion of the *Truchon* case and its implications can be found further in this volume.[66] But some points about the *Truchon* case are worth emphasizing here, since they add to concerns about how strong political commitments appear to have driven MAiD expansion in Canada rather than cautious, evidence-informed, and reasoned policy-making. In and of itself, the attorney general's failure to appeal the decision was unusual, particularly for a law that was adopted so recently and with such a strong majority. But what gave it even more the appearance of a purely political decision was the fact that it was Prime Minister Justin Trudeau and not the attorney general, whose core mandate is to defend the laws of Parliament, who announced there would be no appeal – and this in the midst of a federal election during a televised debate in Quebec, the province where expanding MAiD appeared to have broad support.[67] A letter signed by seventy-two organizations, primarily disability advocacy organizations, had strongly urged the attorney general to file a "disability-rights based appeal" of the decision.[68] It appears electoral interests carried more weight than the demands of disability advocates or the duty to defend the laws of Parliament.

But there is more. While the government, particularly then minister of justice David Lametti, argued that the case was not appealed because its reasoning was so solid, there were strong constitutional and evidence-related reasons to appeal the judgment.[69] First, neither the Supreme Court nor any court of appeal had ever ruled that prohibiting or restricting access to assisted dying would be discriminatory. There was no higher court precedent for relying on the discrimination provision. On the contrary, as pointed out further in this volume, there are strong reasons to argue that offering assisted death to disabled persons deprives them of their equal right to protection against premature death, since only they, and no one else, are offered state-facilitated death as an allegedly proper response to their suffering.[70] Justice Baudouin's analysis focusing on the individual plaintiffs, rather than on broader contextual disability concerns, was facilitated by her controversial rejection of explicitly stated goals of the law, in particular the need to avoid negative perceptions of the quality of life of persons who are elderly, ill, or disabled and suicide prevention as a public health goal.[71] She argued that these explicitly stated goals were mere "vehicles used to affirm social values or stakes" ("vecteurs d'affirmation de valeurs ou d'enjeux sociaux"[72]), and that the only relevant goal of the law was preventing vulnerable persons from ending their life in a moment of weakness.

Secondly, the plaintiffs in the *Truchon* case claimed that the safeguards of both the federal and provincial laws violated their *Charter* rights. But as the development in the *Lamb* case already illustrated, many MAiD practitioners interpreted the RFND criterion very broadly. In fact, as Thomas McMorrow and colleagues put forward, the plaintiffs in *Truchon* would likely have obtained access to MAiD outside Quebec under the RFND criterion.[73] In Quebec at the time, the federal law's criterion was interpreted in line with what appears to be a more narrow "end-of-life" ("fin de vie") criterion in Quebec law. In other words, there was arguably no need to declare the federal provision unconstitutional since plaintiffs would already have access to MAiD if the Quebec law's provision was declared unconstitutional.

Moreover, Justice Baudouin's treatment of the evidence also raised concerns. First, in an interim judgment related to the production of evidence, she had already expressed some skepticism about the government's need to produce substantial evidence about what happens when assisted dying goes beyond an end-of-life context, seemingly opining that the evidence in the *Carter* trial decision had provided most of the relevant evidence related to the legalization of assisted dying and its goal.[74] But the constitutional question before the court was clearly entirely different than in *Carter*. Indeed, as is argued also further in this volume, the question in *Truchon* was whether a restriction to end-of-life in the existing new regulatory scheme could be considered to provide a proportionate balance between access to MAiD and protecting against premature death.[75] A fresh constitutional analysis was required to answer that. Evidence about what had happened in Belgium and the Netherlands, two regimes offering euthanasia outside the end-of-life context, and particularly evidence that needed to be updated with developments since 2012 was so much more important. Yet Justice Baudouin significantly limited the production of evidence.[76]

Second, Justice Baudouin's treatment of some expert witnesses raised concern about unreasonable treatment of the evidence. For example, she chastised two expert witnesses for the government for not having had any prior involvement or experience with MAiD practice in Canada. Yet, one of them, Dr Sonu Gaind, was at the time the lead of his hospital's MAiD team, while the other, Dr Scott Kim from the United States's National Institutes of Health, is a top expert on capacity for decision-making who conducted some of the first analyses on capacity and mental health euthanasia in the Netherlands, and who is lead or co-author on widely cited publications on euthanasia and assisted suicide. Both experts had been members of the Council of Canadian Academies Expert Panel on MAiD for Sole Reasons of Mental Illness. They testified, not about *existing* MAiD practice, since of course the question was not about MAiD for persons at the end of life, but about the challenges that would arise if Canada's law was expanded, particularly as it would apply in the mental health context. Yet Justice Baudouin completely rejected the relevance of Dr Kim's testimony, instead relying on the testimony of two persons involved in MAiD in Canada: Dr James Downar, a palliative care expert with no particular scholarly expertise in capacity for decision-making in the mental health context, and Dr Justine Dembo, a psychiatrist. Both were associated with the lobby group Dying with Dignity. All this makes it even more remarkable that the government failed to appeal the decision and introduced legislation in response to one judge's ruling.

After multiple extensions given by the Quebec court, on 17 March 2021, Bill C-7 received royal assent, allowing administered death now also for those not remotely approaching their natural death.[77]

Remarkably, Bill C-7 not only focused on adjusting the law to this lower court decision, but it also discarded many of the safeguards that had been initially put in place to protect Canadians from having a wrongful death. Gone was, for example, the mandatory ten-day reflection period, which was originally introduced as an important safeguard to ensure that persons were given an opportunity to change their mind in the challenging end-of-life context. But most importantly, Bill C-7 allowed health care providers to end the life of those living with a chronic illness or disability who may have otherwise had years or decades of life left. It also introduced a sunset provision, stipulating that MAiD for sole reasons of mental illness would be introduced in a two-year period. How Bill C-7 was pushed through deserves more discussion, since it illustrates the remarkable drive and prioritization of a government and some parliamentary members, particularly also senators, committed to expanding MAiD as a seemingly inherently beneficial practice to which people who are not dying urgently needed access.

THE PASSING OF BILL C-7

Since March 2020, Canadians had been living with the stresses of COVID-19. We experienced lockdowns, financial difficulties, fear, and loneliness. The media justifiably kept its focus on COVID-19, and the news was dominated daily by medical evidence, speculation, public health sanctions, and information about vaccination development and procurement, all trying to guide our next steps as a nation. This perhaps led to many not following the details of the passing of Bill C-7 amid the pandemic, but it also made it more remarkable that the government prioritized this expansion of MAiD. In fact, a report by Deborah Stienstra and a University of Guelph Live Work Well research group on the impact of the early COVID-19 period on disabled persons had pointed out that many disabled persons experienced the practice of MAiD as an additional threat to them.[78]

Yet justice minister David Lametti, who as a Liberal backbencher had voted against the earlier legislation, considering it too restrictive, introduced Bill C-7 in February 2020. Support and opposition to Bill C-7 by members of Parliament tended to depend on party affiliation.

Minister Lametti strenuously argued that suffering was being prolonged by denying some Canadians immediate access to MAiD.[79]

However, all national disability advocacy and many social justice and Indigenous organizations raised concerns about the lack of resources to live well, the discrimination they already faced, and the direct risks these inequalities pose to their communities. They argued that being offered death as a solution for life's suffering would add to these challenges, not solve them. Liberal minister of employment, workforce development, and disability inclusion Carla Qualtrough seemed to acknowledge some of the concerns and admitted to the Standing Committee on Justice and Human Rights that "it is easier to access MAiD than to get a wheelchair in some parts of the country."[80] She nonetheless voted in favour of Bill C-7.

Bill C-7 first passed in the House of Commons on 10 December 2020, with votes recorded as 213–106 in favour.[81] In the end, the vast majority of Conservatives voted against the bill and only one notable Liberal, MP Marcus Powlowski, vocally broke from the Liberal party whip. MP Powlowski, a doctor and lawyer by training, stated in an interview why he could not support his party's bill: "My biggest concern ... is that we end up using MAiD for people who don't really want to die."[82] His concerns were prescient.

All other parties, including the NDP, Green, and the Bloc Québécois parties, voted unanimously in favour of MAiD expansion in the bill. Notably, former Liberal justice minister Jody Wilson-Raybould, sitting now as an independent, who had taken a more cautionary approach with the introduction of the RFND criterion in the 2016 MAiD legislation, voted against the expanded bill.[83]

As the bill went to the Senate, justice minister David Lametti urged that it be passed before the December 2020 holiday break, using the court deadlines imposed by the Quebec court to exert pressure to rush the bill's consideration.[84] Remarkably, since this was a Quebec Superior Court decision, it was not binding in any other province or in higher courts in Quebec. Even if the deadline had passed, nothing would have happened outside Quebec and even in Quebec; the decision would arguably only have had persuasive authority.

Many within the Senate pushed back. Independent Senator Kim Pate questioned whether they could amend the bill to ensure Canadians can access palliative care, disability support services, home care, housing, and income support before being eligible for MAiD. Her colleague, independent Senator Julie Miville-Dechêne, similarly remarked, "If it's easier to get MAiD than palliative care, what kind of society are we living in?"[85]

The bill that had passed in the House of Commons specifically precluded accessing MAiD solely on the basis of suffering from a mental illness. There had therefore been little debate in the House about this issue. In the Senate, Senator Pierre Dalphond and Senator Claude Carignan raised the issue that excluding MAiD for those with mental illness was discriminatory and argued that the bill should be further expanded to avoid it quickly coming back to the Senate after a mental health court challenge.[86] They received strong support from Senator Stan Kutcher, a former psychiatrist.[87]

The Senate held more extensive hearings on Bill C-7 than the House had. Included among the witnesses were legal experts, medical practitioners, Indigenous representatives, mental health advocates, faith group representatives, and caregivers. The minister of justice, minister of health, and the minister of employment, workforce development, and disability inclusion also appeared.[88] However, despite concerns raised by many witnesses, the federal ministers advised against extensive amendments, saying incorporating other services would threaten the ability to pass the legislation quickly.

Still, the initial Senate committee report of December 2020, which was informed by the hearings, appeared balanced and showed that many witnesses and experts had raised concerns about this bill. Ultimately justice minister David Lametti was unable to make the December court deadline and repeatedly asked for extensions. In total four extensions were requested from the court.[89] In one of the judicial extensions, a Superior Court justice ruled that awaiting a new law, patients could obtain judicial permission for accessing MAiD under the *Truchon* criteria.[90] Nicole Gladu never accessed MAiD even after the law was expanded. She died naturally at home two and a half years after the *Truchon* decision.[91]

After their winter holiday break, the Senate resumed and signalled to the public through various interviews that there was political will among them to expand MAiD to those whose sole underlying condition was mental illness. There was also mention of the constitutionality of the bill and the need to increase Indigenous consultation. In February 2021, more witnesses and experts were called to address these questions in particular.[92] No Indigenous witness supported the expansion of MAiD in C-7.

Despite extensive opposition from a range of experts, the Senate passed the bill on 17 February 2021 with five amendments that expanded it further. Most notably, the Senate approved an amendment introduced by Senator Kutcher, which introduced a sunset clause, according to which persons with mental illness as their sole diagnosis would become eligible for MAiD eighteen months after the adoption of the law. Another amendment added MAiD on the basis of advance requests to the bill. To address concerns about the lack of information on how MAiD is impacting disadvantaged communities, yet another amendment introduced a legal duty to collect data on race.[93] Amendments that were introduced to avoid coercion to choose death and another to protect health care workers from being forced to participate in MAiD were not passed, despite being backed by the disability community and by Indigenous and physician voices.[94] Importantly, Senator McPhedran argued that track 2 MAiD was discriminatory against people living with disabilities and therefore drafted an amendment to strike it from the bill. This amendment was disallowed and so no vote took place on the matter.[95]

Once the Senate-amended bill returned back to the House, the government removed part of the additional advanced directive Senate amendment, added a duty to also collect Indigenous demographic data, and changed the sunset cause to twenty-four months instead of eighteen months for mental illness as a sole basis for eligibility.[96] Alarmed by mental illness as the sole criterion being added without the House having ever studied this, several MPs held a press conference, which hosted Indigenous leaders along with psychiatrists and geriatricians.[97] Other MPs also held a press conference about one week later saying they were ready to debate for hours and study this transformed, and at least on some essential components basically new, bill.[98] But three days later, on 11 March 2021, the Liberal government forced a closure motion, making it mandatory to vote on the amendments the same day.[99]

There were two votes following the introduction of the closure motion. Firstly, there was a vote on an amendment introduced by MP Michael Barrett to exclude mental illness with its sunset clause from the bill altogether. Secondly, there was a vote on including the Senate motion bundle as revised by the Liberals. MP Luc Theriault, while encouraging all to vote for the inclusion of MAiD for mental illness, stated: "The Bloc Québécois is far from convinced that MAiD should be broadened to include individuals whose sole medical condition causing suffering is mental illness. Why? Because suicidal ideation is often a manifestation, a symptom of mental illness, and suicidal ideation is reversible. If the expert panel and the special committee arrive at the conclusion that mental health should be excluded, it will be excluded. I do not see why they insist on remaining within the parliamentary framework of a debate which is getting us nowhere."[100]

Almost all Conservative, NDP, and Green Party MPs voted against the Senate bundle amendment and voted for the amendment to exclude mental illness. The Liberal MPs, except for five, and those of the Bloc Québécois voted almost uniformly in favour of including the sunset provision for MAiD for mental illness.[101] On 17 March 2021, Bill C-7 passed quickly in the Senate and received royal assent.[102]

BILL C-7'S TWO-TRACK SYSTEM

Bill C-7 introduced a two-track system for MAiD. The RFND concept, removed from the definition of "grievous medical condition," remained part of the federal MAiD law: it now defined "track 1 requests." Bill C-7 made access to MAiD for RFND easier: the ten-day reflection period was abolished; the number of witnesses who must co-sign the request was reduced to one; and a limited form of advance requests was even introduced, defined as a "waiver of consent," for situations where people may lose consciousness between the approval and the procedure. In principle, applicants whose death is reasonably foreseeable can now even obtain MAiD the same day, obviously only if all requirements, including a second "positive" assessment, are met.

Persons who are not approaching their reasonably foreseeable natural death are submitted to a track 2 route. The most important requirement is a ninety-day assessment period. This period should start from the moment of the first MAiD assessment, but a recent controversy highlighted that some physicians may interpret this ninety-day requirement more flexibly, as including discussions prior to the formal MAiD assessment of the patient.[103]

The assessment period is intended to allow for a more thorough assessment of the underlying reasons for requesting MAiD and to enable an exploration of other options. This is also connected to additional "consent" requirements: where appropriate, health care providers have to inform the patient of relevant counselling services, mental health and disability supports, community services, and palliative care options. Physicians further have to agree that the applicant has "seriously considered" other options. Remarkably, some, such as the end-of-life working group of the Canadian Bar Association, expressed their disagreement with even those rather minimal additional safeguards.[104] The requirements are indeed minimal: there is no obligation that other options are exhausted or even that they are being made available. Considering the lengthy wait times for many crucial health care and disability support services, the ninety-day assessment period seems insufficient.[105]

For track 2 cases, there is also a requirement that one of the assessors must have expertise in the patient condition that underlies the MAiD request, or alternatively, if none has such expertise, that a third health care provider with expertise must be consulted. But there is no detail about how extensive this consultation needs to be, and the consulted professional is not further involved in the decision-making. Remarkably, the person with "expertise" (so either one of the assessors or the consulted expert) does not have to be a specialist. Here again, we see the focus in Canadian law on access to MAiD rather than to adequate medical care: legal terminology was carefully drafted to avoid the unavailability of a medical specialist with professionally recognized expertise in the patient's condition potentially hindering or delaying access to MAiD. What "expertise" really means is further not specified.

The most striking aspect of the law is that even persons who are not remotely approaching their death ultimately decide if they want to avail themselves of available treatments – physicians do not have to agree that there are no other options left,[106] and physicians do not have an obligation to make sure treatment options or social supports are concretely made available.[107] For some Canadian MAiD providers, wait times for required specialized care can very well render an illness irremediable and would thus qualify a person for MAiD.[108]

SHIFTING PERCEPTIONS AND DISCOURSE SURROUNDING MAiD

The earlier discussion of the parliamentary debate over Bill C-7 documents how remarkably fast and in an arguably haphazard way Canada's MAiD law was expanded in response to court cases. These court cases were consciously used or interpreted by advocates, including MPs and senators who strongly supported the expansion of MAiD, as creating or affirming a constitutional right to assisted dying. As is discussed elsewhere and further in this volume, this rhetorical use of a constitutional claim is problematic.[109] But it appears to have shaped Canada's MAiD law and policy to a significant extent and likely explains the steep increases and rapid expansion to some degree.[110] Even professional organizations that were originally opposed, neutral, or only cautiously supportive of some form of assisted dying embraced this rights-based rhetoric and gradually stopped engaging with the policy and evidentiary arguments about what expanding the practice would mean.[111]

For example, throughout the early years of the debate, the Canadian Medical Association's Committee on Ethics was consistent in affirming its stance against euthanasia and assisted suicide. This was clearly stated in its Canadian Medical Association policy in 2007 and upheld in 2013. However, when the Canadian Medical Association (CMA) intervened in the Supreme Court of Canada *Carter* case, it emphasized that it would change its ethical policy based on the conclusions of the justices. The CMA therefore conceded and changed its policy to approve physician-assisted suicide and euthanasia, subject only to legal constraints.[112] More recently, it even abstained from criticizing the expansion of MAiD outside the end-of-life context.

Other professional organizations have also embraced the rhetoric of a constitutional right. For example, in recent hearings about the implementation of MAiD for mental illness before the Special Joint Parliamentary Committee, a representative of Canada's regulatory colleges stated that any delay in implementing MAiD for mental illness would deprive Canadians suffering from mental illness of their constitutional rights.[113] And when in the same hearings the head of the Canadian Psychiatric Association was questioned about Canada's readiness for implementing MAiD for mental illness, she admitted she could not answer this affirmatively, but that there was no other option since it was a constitutional right.[114]

Public perceptions have clearly also shifted. The federal Bill C-14 had assured Canadians that MAiD practice would balance offering assisted suicide and euthanasia for competent patients suffering in an end-of-life context with safeguards that would protect everyone else from premature and wrongful death. However, in less than five years we have seen the government and some Canadians abandon this approach. Polls now show a majority of Canadians support MAiD.

In October 2020, an Angus Reid polling of 1,500 Canadians showed that respondents supported MAiD, with 77 per cent saying access to MAiD was important. A February 2021 Ipsos survey of 3,500 Canadians found that 69 per cent of respondents favoured expanding MAiD to those not dying.[115]

The emphasis has seemingly moved from protecting disabled Canadians from wrongful death and allowing exceptional access to claiming it is discrimination to limit who can end their life with MAiD. An atomistic concept of autonomy has been considered paramount, and any discussion about the safety of the broader community seems increasingly frowned upon.

There is scientific and statistical evidence that people who ask for death at the end of their lives often change their minds with good care, many within two weeks of their first request.[116] Statistically, the 2019 Health Canada report on MAiD also demonstrated that 3.1 per cent of the people who had requested a MAiD assessment changed their minds and did not go on to have MAiD, suggesting that their suffering was not in fact intolerable.[117] Yet Bill C-7 now allows someone whose death is reasonably foreseeable to die the same day they make a first request if two assessors agree the criteria are met. As justice minister David Lametti summed up, "I've had friends who have lost family and had access to MAiD who said to me that we've got to get rid of the 10 days ... we should let people and their families get on with it."[118]

Even calling MAiD by its parts (euthanasia and assisted suicide) has been met with indignation. The Liberal government itself made many attempts to separate MAiD from any connection to assisted suicide or euthanasia. Health minister Patty Hajdu went so far as to say that "referring to this bill as 'euthanasia' legislation, which I have heard in the House of Commons, is incredibly demeaning to the dignity of people who are attempting to access this service and incredibly demeaning to the professionalism of the incredible physicians and other MAiD assessors whom I had the privilege of meeting while I did the consultation."[119] In contrast, another MP pointed out, in our view appropriately so, that if we as a society are so uncomfortable hearing about sick people dying by lethal injection, perhaps we should ask ourselves why we feel uncomfortable instead of demanding that the images and clear language be put aside.[120]

Concerning MAiD for those with a sole diagnosis of mental illness, the majority of psychiatrists and most psychiatry organizations disagree with the government, as there is no convincing scientific evidence that it is possible to predict whose mental illness is irremediable.[121] But disturbingly, the Canadian Psychiatry Association reversed its position on this matter in 2020, not based on emerging scientific evidence but rather on a questionable legal argument that excluding those living with mental illness from assisted death is discriminatory.[122]

In short, MAiD is no longer an exceptional medical service for those with end-of-life suffering. It has now been framed as a right to have one's life ended by health care professionals and with funding by the government for many Canadians with disabilities.

Do Canadians have any hesitations about the further expansion of MAiD? The above quoted Angus Reid poll found that 69 per cent of respondents were concerned that mental health struggles such as depression would influence the choice to die if MAiD were expanded, and the majority, 68 per cent, believed the United Nations's concerns towards expanding MAiD for people with disabilities, while lacking in providing alternatives to live, should be given government attention.[123] And in 2022, a Postmedia-Leger poll of 1,501 online panelists found that fewer than half (45 per cent) supported MAiD for those living with serious mental illness.[124] Finally, a 2024 public survey conducted by researchers at the National Institutes of Health suggested that while a large majority of Canadians are generally supportive of MAiD, many appear to disagree with key components of the law.[125] When confronted with specific scenarios that are currently legal under Canadian law, including MAiD for patients who lack access to standard care and MAiD for persons who receive effective treatment, an equally large majority of respondents disagreed that MAiD should be available in those circumstances. Remarkably, the survey also revealed that only 19 per cent of respondents knew that terminal illness is not required, and only 20 per cent knew that treatment refusal does not exclude a person from obtaining MAiD instead.

MAiD PRACTICE SINCE 2016

Politicians had promised Canadians that the expansion of MAiD was well considered, and that it would move forward cautiously. However, the opposite has been the case. Illustrating the lack of caution, the parliamentary review of Canada's new MAiD practice, which was supposed to be undertaken before any further expansion, was conducted only after the expansion introduced by Bill C-7.[126] Moreover, the politicians who supported expansion quoted and drew most of their conclusions from the 2019 Health Canada report on MAiD. The evidence from this report was acquired from MAiD providers self-reporting after MAiD deaths and by that very factor, it is unlikely that it would uncover abuses.[127] For example, the report claimed that patients dying by MAiD had high rates of access to palliative care. In contrast, a study by Camille Munro and colleagues published in November 2020 demonstrated that palliative care access prior to having MAiD is much lower than was purported in the Health Canada report on MAiD. The Munro et al. study was conducted in a location with better access to palliative care than most places in Canada.[128]

Also, Canadian evidence up to 2019 offered no insights into what would happen when MAiD was offered outside of the end-of-life context and could not reassure us regarding what would happen when Bill C-7 allowed access for those not dying.

An independent review article in the *Canadian Journal of Bioethics* by Dr Jaro Kotalik concludes that oversight of MAiD has been grossly inadequate.[129] Furthermore, problematic MAiD practices have been documented by different oversight bodies, including the chief coroner of Ontario, the Commission on End-of-Life Care in Quebec (the only provincial body in Canada explicitly set up to verify post-factum all provincial MAiD declarations), and the correctional investigator of Canada.[130]

In August 2023, the Commission on End-of-Life Care in Quebec issued a memorandum warning MAiD assessors to follow the law. The chair of the commission, Dr Michel Bureau, said in an interview: "We're now no longer dealing with an exceptional treatment, but a treatment that is very frequent." He noted a slight increase in the number of cases that violate legislation.[131] And shortly thereafter, the chief coroner of Ontario set up a Medical Assistance in Dying Death Review Committee (MDRC) in response to increasing health, social, and intersectional complexities arising from current and pending legislative changes. The purpose of the MDRC is to provide independent expert review of MAiD deaths to assist in evaluating potential public safety.[132] The MDRC does not review all MAiD applications, as these applications are reviewed internally by the coroner's office staff, but reviews a selection of cases to discuss potential challenges and formulate recommendations and guidance. The authors of this chapter are both members of this review panel. The establishment of this panel appears to indicate that there is at least a recognition of potential concerns.

Many fact-checked media accounts of problematic applications of MAiD illustrate growing concerns about some components of the practice, particularly how social and economic factors may be driving MAiD requests.[133]

A striking component of Canada's MAiD policy-making has also been that federal governmental agencies and decision-makers have nearly exclusively relied upon those who pushed most aggressively for the broad legalization of MAiD. This already occurred, as we mentioned, prior to the *Carter* decision, at the level of the Royal Society. It continued immediately after the decision came out, when some of the same experts were allowed to shape the implementation and further direction of MAiD policy and practice in Canada. Their strong commitment to expand MAiD as if it were a constitutional right is reflected in the recommendations and standards they put forward, which focus primarily on ensuring broad access, not protection against premature death. For example, in the context of mental health, some of the staunch supporters of the legalization of MAiD for sole reasons of mental illness were tasked with evaluating, as members of an expert panel, how Canada ought to prepare for the future implementation of MAiD. The federal Expert Panel on MAiD and Mental Illness, headed by Dr Mona Gupta, failed to recommend additional legal safeguards.[134] The panel was marred by controversy. Two members resigned from the panel, expressing in editorials their concern about the panel's apparent unwillingness to consider recommendations for additional safeguards in the panel's report and the committee's lack of disability accommodation and respect for the views of persons with lived experience.[135] One of the members who resigned explicitly associated an unwillingness to consider stronger safeguards with the chair's strong prior commitment to expansion. And yet, the government failed to question the findings and gave some of those involved further opportunities to implement MAiD policies.

For example, Health Canada mandated some of the same committed experts to design the *Model Practice Standard for Medical Assistance in Dying*, aimed at clarifying the legal requirements and safeguards and at providing a model for practice standards by provincial regulatory colleges.[136] One of the proposed professional rules is worth mentioning here, because it is remarkable that a federal health agency would endorse, at least indirectly – after all, it published the *Model Practice Standard* on its website – such recommendations. The *Model Practice Standard* states, in its discussion of conscientious objection, that a health care practitioner who objects to providing MAiD, even only in a specific situation and because of "specific circumstances," becomes a "conscientious objector."[137] This comes with an effective referral obligation in certain provinces, including Ontario, which means that the health care provider has to actively refer the patient to a health care provider willing to provide

MAiD in that situation. This reveals again the remarkable focus on ensuring the broadest possible access to MAiD.[138]

Finally, the federal government also entrusted advocates for broad MAiD access with the education of MAiD assessors and providers. It gave $3.3 million to the Canadian Association of MAiD Assessors and Providers (CAMAP), a newly established organization that is dominated by some of the most prolific MAiD providers and has only a limited number of members. While it is not unusual to mandate a professional group of practitioners to organize professional education, some of CAMAP's educational sessions and materials have raised serious concerns about an overly zealous promotion of access to MAiD.[139]

The most remarkable illustration of this is how the CAMAP guide on the interpretation of the RFND criterion explains how MAiD assessors can transform a request for MAiD under track 2 into a track 1 request. This then allows applicants to circumvent the ninety-day assessment period and the other additional procedural requirements of track 2, which were presented as key safeguards when Bill C-7 was introduced. The guide remarkably states: "A person may meet the 'reasonably foreseeable' criterion if they have demonstrated a clear and serious intent to take steps to make their natural death happen soon or to cause their death to be predictable. Examples might include stated declarations to refuse antibiotic treatment of current or future serious infection, to stop use of oxygen therapy, to refuse turning if they have quadriplegia, or to voluntarily cease eating and drinking."[140]

CAMAP's focus on ensuring access, not protection, is also apparent in other policies. Its policy "Bringing up Medical Assistance In Dying (MAID) as a clinical care option," which is now similarly adopted in the *Model Practice Standard* published by Health Canada, recommends raising MAiD with all potentially eligible individuals if the health care provider believes it may align with the patient's values and preferences.[141] In contrast, in some other jurisdictions where assisted suicide is legalized, such as New Zealand and Victoria, Australia, initiating discussions about these options is prohibited.[142] Such a prohibition reflects the idea that the inherent power dynamics between physicians and patients, as well as a patient's expectation that health care providers will only propose options that prioritize their well-being, can result in undue pressure on patients to consider and choose MAiD.

CONCLUSION

In Canada, one Supreme Court case initiated the process of legalization of some form of assisted dying as an exemption to the Criminal Code prohibitions on homicide and aiding and abetting suicide. While Canada's first law still focused on the end-of-life context and reflected some sense of constraint and an attempt to balance access to MAiD with protection against premature death and other important societal values, strident advocacy, further lower court cases, strong political commitment on the part of the federal government, and a remarkable reliance by governmental agencies and legislators on a core group of experts strongly committed to an expansive practice for further guidance, policy-making, and standard setting have led to a rapid expansion of MAiD. Although legislated as being largely the responsibility of the medical community, MAiD does not operate on the same premise on which medicine traditionally operates. The practice of medicine largely turns around careful weighing of risks and potential harms against benefits of treatment in individual patients, informed by evidence from research and clinical expertise.[143] Yet when it comes to MAiD, clearly a new practice with significant implications for the everyday practice of medicine, it has largely been court cases, zealous advocacy, and political will that have pushed the practice forward. As some have emphasized, there has been no serious evidence-informed assessment of how to balance the risks and potential benefits of this new and radical procedure.[144] A chapter later in this volume explicitly discusses how the normal operation of the standard of care has been suspended as a result of Canada's unique approach to MAiD, which fails to require that all other reasonable treatment options have been exhausted.[145]

While early political commentary had predicted a very restricted pattern of use with projections of few MAiD completions, there had already been more than 21,000 MAiD deaths under the Bill C-14 regime in the period from June 2016 to the end of 2020. The rate of deaths has continued to increase yearly.[146] In 2022 alone, there were 13,241 MAiD deaths in Canada, bringing the total number since legalization in 2016 to 44,958 deaths.[147] Two provinces, Quebec and British Columbia, already bypass the percentage of euthanasia deaths in Belgium and the Netherlands, until recently the most liberal euthanasia regimes in the world, which legalized the practice more than a decade before Canada. In Quebec, more than 7 per cent of deaths are now the result of a health care provider's lethal injection.[148]

Within six years of the introduction of MAiD, Canada has surpassed all other countries for its number of euthanasia and assisted suicide deaths reported in 2022. As Daryl Pullman observed, the huge contrast with the number of people who died by assisted suicide in a jurisdiction such as California, which legalized assisted suicide for persons with terminal illness around the same time that Canada introduced its first law, is particularly striking.[149]

The expansion will further augment the numbers and increasingly so for people not remotely approaching their death. In the first nine months of Bill C-7, 219 Canadians who were not at the end of life died from MAiD. In 2022, that number increased to 463. This does not account for MAiD assessors who transformed a request for MAiD under track 2 into a track 1 request, which likely means many more died than the total of close to seven hundred who died by MAiD while they were not remotely close to their natural death. And as we discussed, the interpretation of the RFND criterion has been so expansive that we can presume a very significant number of Canadians with years of life left have died with a lethal injection.

Several cases of MAiD for psychosocial suffering in persons with disabilities (poverty or lack of access to care) are being reported,[150] while an increasing number of MAiD expansionists are openly arguing that MAiD driven by poverty and inequality is supporting choice or is even a form of harm reduction.[151]

Bill C-14 introduced MAiD as a medical act to cause death for those with intolerable suffering and whose death was reasonably foreseeable. Our current regime under Bill C-7 allows for MAiD for intolerable suffering (psychological or physical) for those with a disability and soon is expected to include those with psychiatric diseases as well. The Special Joint Committee on MAiD, composed of senators and House of Commons members, completed a final report in February 2023. It recommended expansion of MAiD for mature minors with RFND, saying parents could be consulted when appropriate but the decision rests with the child. It also recommended advance directives for MAiD, along with other recommendations on the regulation of psychiatric MAiD, the state of palliative care in Canada, and the protection of disabled persons, to which the current government has responded.[152] As we note in this chapter, some of these practices, for example MAiD on the basis of advance requests, has already been introduced via a broad interpretation of the legal provisions related to a "waiver of informed consent."

Given the documented problems with the existing practice and the lack of research to validate these changes in law as safe, if Parliament would indeed decide to move forward with further expansion, Canada would again be choosing to abandon caution and continuing to proceed recklessly.

POSTSCRIPT

As mentioned in our introduction, the chapters in this book were completed in 2023. In the wake of significant opposition from within the broader mental health community and expressions of concerns by provincial health ministries, a joint committee of the House of Commons and the Senate was set up in October 2023 to verify whether Canada's health care system was ready to start providing MAiD for sole reasons of mental illness. The committee recommended in its January 2024 report that the introduction of MAiD for sole reasons of mental illness should continue to be postponed indefinitely. The government subsequently submitted new legislation to postpone implementation until March 2027, which was approved with an overwhelming majority. This is the first time since the introduction of MAiD in Canada that governmental officials and Parliament has decided to show restraint and to postpone further expansion. During the public and parliamentary debates around the further suspension of MAiD for sole reasons of mental illness, we have urged, as others, that this further suspension be used as an occasion to carefully reflect on how our existing practice of MAiD is already problematic and how it needs to be adjusted.[153] We hope that this first halting of further expansion is a sign that our federal and provincial governments and parliaments, and professional regulators, are starting to realize they must go back to the drawing table.

NOTES

Authors are in alphabetical order. TL is responsible for the legal analysis.

1 *Carter v. Canada (Attorney General)*, 2015 SCC 5, [2015] 1 SCR 331.
2 Bill C-14, *An Act to Amend the Criminal Code and to Make Related Amendments to Other Acts (medical assistance in dying)*, 42nd Parliament, 1st Session (2016), SC 2016, c. 3 (Can.), https://www.parl.ca/DocumentViewer/en/42-1/bill/C-14/royal-assent.

3 Bill C-7, An Act to Amend the Criminal Code (medical assistance in dying), 43rd Parliament, 2nd Session (2021), SC 2021, c. 2 (Can.), https://parl.ca/DocumentViewer/en/43-2/bill/C-7/royal-assent.
4 Gerard Quinn, Claudia Mahler, and Olivier De Schutter to Canada, "Mandates of the Special Rapporteur on the Rights of Persons with Disabilities; the Independent Expert on the Enjoyment of All Human Rights by Older Persons; and the Special Rapporteur on Extreme Poverty and Human Rights," 3 February 2021, ref OL CAN 2/2021, https://spcommreports.ohchr.org/TMResultsBase/DownLoadPublicCommunicationFile?gId=26002; Vulnerable Persons Standard to Members of Parliament, February 2021, http://www.vps-npv.ca/stopc7; CPSO Consultation to Senators, Elected Federal and Provincial Leaders, and Regulators, "Indigenous Peoples Should Not Be Compelled to Provide or Facilitate Medical Assistance in Dying," February 2021, https://policyconsult.cpso.on.ca/wp-content/uploads/2021/05/Indigenous-Peoples-Should-Not-Be-Compelled-to-Provide-or-Facilitate-MAID_Redacted.pdf; Ramona Coelho et al., "Bill C-7, From MAiD to MAD: Medical Assistance in Dying Becomes Medically Administered Death," Physicians Together with Vulnerable Canadians to Parliament, 2020, last modified 2022, https://maid2mad.ca/#-DeclarationEnglish; Archilbald Kaiser et al., "MAID Bill Is an Affront to Equality," *Toronto Star*, 11 March 2021, https://www.thestar.com/opinion/contributors/2021/03/11/maid-bill-is-an-affront-to-equality.html.
5 *Criminal Code of Canada*, RSC 1985, c. C-46, s. 241.1.
6 *Criminal Code of Canada*, RSC 1985, c. C-46.
7 Health Canada, *Fourth Annual Report on Medical Assistance in Dying in Canada 2022*, October 2023, 20, https://www.canada.ca/en/health-canada/services/publications/health-system-services/annual-report-medical-assistance-dying-2022.html#a3.1.
8 Udo Schuklenk et al., *The Royal Society of Canada Expert Panel: End-of-Life Decision Making* (Ottawa: The Royal Society of Canada, 2011), 8, https://rsc-src.ca/sites/default/files/RSCEndofLifeReport2011_EN_Formatted_FINAL.pdf.
9 See Hon. Kelvin Kenneth Ogilvie and Robert Oliphant, *Medical Assistance in Dying: A Patient-Centred Approach – Report of the Special Joint Committee on Physician-Assisted Dying* (Ottawa: Parliament of Canada, 2016), 10, https://www.parl.ca/Content/Committee/421/PDAM/Reports/RP8120006/pdamrp01/pdamrp01-e.pdf, citing Joanne Klineberg, *Meeting of the Special Joint Committee on Physician-Assisted Dying – Evidence*, 42nd Parliament, 1st Session (18 January 2016), 1405.
10 See, however, a recent study by William J.W. Choi and others, which reveals that while Canadians generally have a favourable view of MAiD, a

majority appears to ignore how broadly accessible the practice really is and disagrees with several key components of Canada's MAiD law when confronted with concrete scenarios. William J.W. Choi et al., "When Medical Assistance in Dying Is Not a Last Resort Option: Survey of the Canadian Public," *BMJ Open* 14 (2024): e087736, https://doi.org/10.1136/bmjopen-2024-087736.

11 "À la différence de l›euthanasie, l›aide médicale à mourir est très balisée et se déroule dans un contexte médical," Nathalie Collard, "10+1 questions avec Véronique Hivon," *La Presse*, 20 January 2013, https://www.lapresse.ca/actualites/politique/politique-quebecoise/201301/19/01-4612915-101-questions-avec-veronique-hivon.php.

12 Devon Phillips, "Balfour Mount," Palliative Care McGill, 2021, https://www.mcgill.ca/palliativecare/portraits-o/balfour-mount.

13 Coelho et al., "Bill C-7, From MAiD to MAD."

14 Canadian Medical Association, "CMA Policy: Medical Assistance in Dying," 2017, https://policybase.cma.ca/flipbook?pdfUrl=%2Fmedia%2FPolicyPDF%2FPD17-03.pdf.

15 *Rodriguez v. British Columbia* (Attorney General), [1993] 3 SCR 519, 609.

16 Ibid., 595.

17 Dick Sobsey, "The Latimer Case: The Reflections of People with Disabilities – Media," *Council of Canadians with Disabilities*, August 1995, http://www.ccdonline.ca/en/humanrights/endoflife/latimer/reflections/media; *R. v. Latimer*, 124 Sask. R. 180, [1994] SJ No. 480 (QL) (Sask., Can.); *R. v. Latimer*, 1995 CanLII 3993 (SKCA), 126 DLR 4th 203 (Sask., Can.); *R. v. Latimer*, 1997 CanLII 405 (SCC), [1997] 1 SCR 217 (Can.).

18 *R. v. Latimer*, 1997 CanLII 11316 (SKKB), [1997] SJ No. 701 (QL) (Sask., Can.).

19 *R. v. Latimer*, 1998 CanLII 12388 (SKCA), [1998] SJ No. 731 (QL) (Sask., Can.); upheld in *R. v. Latimer*, 2001 SCC 1 (CanLII), [2001] 1 SCR 3 (Can.).

20 Special Senate Committee on Euthanasia and Assisted Suicide, *Of Life and Death – Final Report*, Senate of Canada, January 1995, https://sencanada.ca/en/content/sen/committee/351/euth/rep/lad-e.

21 Ibid.

22 *Bill C-384, An Act to Amend the Criminal Code (Right to Die with Dignity)*, 40th Parliament, 2nd Session (2009), RS, c. C-46 (Can.).

23 Collège des médecins du Québec, "Le médecin, les soins appropriés et le débat sur l'euthanasie – Document de réflexion," 16 October 2009, 9.

24 Commission Spéciale, *Rapport: Mourir dans la dignité* (Quebec: Assemblée nationale, 2012), https://numerique.banq.qc.ca/patrimoine/details/52327/2103522.

25 "The Quebec Select Committee on Dying with Dignity Full Report Is Now Available in English," *Vivre Dans La Dignité* (blog), 14 August 2012, accessed 8 December 2022, https://vivredignite.org/the-quebec-select-committee-on-dying-with-dignity-full-report-is-now-available-in-english-2/.

26 *Act Respecting End-of-Life Care*, CQLR c. S-32.001 (Can.).

27 Owen Dyer, "Quebec Passes Right-to-Die Law," *Canadian Medical Association Journal* 186, no. 10 (2014): E368, https://doi.org/10.1503/cmaj.109-4830.

28 Nathalie Collard, "10+1 questions."

29 Commission Spéciale, *Rapport: Mourir dans la dignité*, 60.

30 David Gentille, "Aide médicale à mourir: Barrette étonné par le nombre de cas," Radio Canada, 27 October 2016, https://ici.radio-canada.ca/nouvelle/811258/aide-medicale-mourir-barrette-surpris-nombre-cas; Caroline Plante, "More Seeking Medical Aid to Die Than Expected: Barrette," *Montreal Gazette*, 27 October 2016, https://montrealgazette.com/news/quebec/more-seeking-medical-aid-to-die-than-expected-barrette.

31 *Carter v. Canada (Attorney General)*, 2012 BCSC 886, [2012] BCJ No. 1196 (QL), para. 86.

32 See Trudo Lemmens, Heeso Kim, and Elizabeth Kurz, "Why Canada's Medical Assistance in Dying Legislation Should Be C(h)arter Compliant and What It May Help to Avoid," *McGill Journal of Law and Health* 11, no. 1 (2018): S61–148, S72–84.

33 See, for example, Jody Lazare, "Judging the Social Sciences in Carter v Canada (AG)," *McGill Journal of Law and Health* 10, no. 1 (2016), S35–68.

34 See Benny Chan and Margaret Somerville, "Converting the 'Right to Life' to the 'Right to Physician-Assisted Suicide and Euthanasia': An Analysis of *Carter v Canada (Attorney General)*, Supreme Court of Canada," *Medical Law Review* 24, no. 2 (2016): 143–75; Lemmens, Kim, and Kurz, "Canada's Medical Assistance in Dying Legislation," S72–83; John Keown, *Euthanasia, Ethics, and Public Policy*, 2nd ed. (Cambridge: Cambridge University Press, 2018), 397–431, in particular 414–21.

35 See the discussion in Lemmens, Kim, and Kurz, "Canada's Medical Assistance in Dying Legislation," S72–83.

36 See ibid., S70.

37 Udo Schuklenk et al., *End-of-Life Decision Making*.

38 "Our Mandate," Royal Society of Canada, https://rsc-src.ca/en/about/our-mission (emphasis added).

39 *Carter*, 2012 BCSC 886, para. 128.

40 Ibid., para. 883.

41 *Carter v. Canada (Attorney General)*, 2013 BCCA 435, [2013] BCJ No. 2227 (QL).
42 *Carter*, 2015 SCC 5.
43 See chapters 10 (Grant) and 11 (Shariff, Ross, and Lemmens).
44 *Carter*, 2015 SCC 5, para. 127.
45 Ibid., para. 127.
46 Ibid., para. 29.
47 See in particular chapters 2 (Gaind), 3 (Simpson and Jones), 11 (Shariff, Ross, and Lemmens), and 13 (Sinyor and Schaffer). For a discussion of the evidence in relation to suicide and MAiD, see in particular chapter 13.
48 For the relevance of the reference to mental illness, see chapter 11 (Shariff, Ross, and Lemmens). For the relevance of the reference to minors, see chapter 15 (Coelho).
49 Department of Justice, "Government of Canada Establishes External Panel on Options for a Legislative Response to Carter v. Canada," Government of Canada, 17 July 2015, https://www.canada.ca/en/news/archive/2015/07/government-canada-establishes-external-panel-options-legislative-response-carter-v-canada-.html.
50 External Panel on Options for a Legislative Response to *Carter v. Canada*, "Consultations on Physician-Assisted Dying – Summary of Results and Key Findings," Government of Canada, last modified 3 February 2023, https://www.justice.gc.ca/eng/rp-pr/other-autre/pad-amm/toc-tdm.html.
51 Provincial-Territorial Expert Advisory Group on Physician-Assisted Dying, *Final Report*, 30 November 2015, 2, https://novascotia.ca/dhw/publications/Provincial-Territorial-Expert-Advisory-Group-on-Physician-Assisted-Dying.pdf.
52 "SARS Doctor Donald Low's Posthumous Plea for Assisted Suicide," CBC News, 24 September 2013, https://www.cbc.ca/news/canada/toronto/sars-doctor-donald-low-s-posthumous-plea-for-assisted-sucide-1.1866332.
53 Provincial-Territorial Expert Advisory Group on Physician-Assisted Dying, *Final Report*, 14.
54 Hon. Kelvin Kenneth Ogilvie and Robert Oliphant, *Medical Assistance in Dying: A Patient-Centred Approach*.
55 Ibid., 51–6.
56 Ibid., 57–61.
57 "Open Discussion on Legalizing Physician Assisted Dying," invitation-only meeting, Munk Centre of Global Affairs and Public Policy, University of Toronto, 20 February 2023.
58 Bill C-14, *An Act to Amend the Criminal Code and to Make Related Amendments to Other Acts (Medical Assistance in Dying)*.

59 See chapters 7 (Coelho), 8 (Peters), and 10 (Grant).
60 See chapters 10 (Grant) and 11 (Shariff, Ross, and Lemmens).
61 See, for example, Jocelyn Downie and Jennifer A. Chandler, *Interpreting Canada's Medical Assistance in Dying Legislation*, IRPP Report, Institute for Research on Public Policy, March 2018, https://irpp.org/wp-content/uploads/2018/03/Interpreting-Canadas-Medical-Assistance-in-Dying-Legislation-MAID.pdf.
62 *A.B. v. Canada (Attorney General)*, 2017 ONSC 3759.
63 Expert Panel on Medical Assistance in Dying, *Medical Assistance in Dying* (Ottawa: Council of Canadian Academies, 2018), https://cca reports.ca/reports/medical-assistance-in-dying/.
64 Jocelyn Downie, "A Watershed Month for Medical Assistance in Dying," *Policy Options*, 20 September 2019, https://policyoptions.irpp.org/magazines/september-2019/a-watershed-month-for-medical-assistance-in-dying/.
65 *Truchon v. Canada (Attorney General)*, 2019 QCCS 3792.
66 See chapter 11 (Shariff, Ross, and Lemmens).
67 John Sikkema, "Opinion: Federal Leaders Still Don't Seem to Understand the Attorney General's Role," *National Post*, 10 October 2019, https://nationalpost.com/news/politics/election-2019/opinion-federal-leaders-still-dont-seem-to-understand-the-attorney-generals-role; Caroline Touzin, Mélanie Marquis, and Tommy Chouinard, "Décision de Québec sur l'AMM: 'Je suis tellement heureuse,'" *La Presse*, 4 October 2019, https://www.lapresse.ca/actualites/sante/2019-10-04/decision-de-quebec-sur-l-amm-je-suis-tellement-heureuse.
68 Council of Canadians with Disabilities et al. to Hon. David Lametti, "Advocates Call for Disability-Rights Based Appeal of the Quebec Superior Court's Decision in Truchon & Gladu," Inclusion Canada, 4 October 2019, https://inclusioncanada.ca/2019/10/04/advocates-call-for-disability-rights-based-appeal-of-the-quebec-superior-courts-decision-in-truchon-gladu/.
69 See Trudo Lemmens and Laverne Jacobs, "The Latest Medical Assistance in Dying Decision Needs to Be Appealed: Here's Why," *Conversation*, 9 October 2019, https://theconversation.com/the-latest-medical-assistance-in-dying-decision-needs-to-be-appealed-heres-why-124955 (perma.cc/MX6V-NECR).
70 See chapters 4 (Lemmens, Shariff, and Herx), 10 (Grant), and 11 (Shariff, Lemmens, and Ross).
71 See the discussion in Lemmens and Jacobs, "Latest Medical Assistance in Dying Decision."
72 *Truchon*, 2019 QCCS 3792, para. 555.

73 Thomas McMorrow et al., "Interpreting Eligibility under the Medical Assistance in Dying Law: The Experiences of Physicians and Nurse Practitioners," *McGill Journal of Law and Health* 14, no. 1 (2020): 51–108, 57.
74 See *Truchon v. Canada* (Attorney General), 2018 QCCS 317.
75 See chapter 11 (Shariff, Ross, and Lemmens).
76 Trudo Lemmens, "Charter Scrutiny of Canada's Medical Assistance in Dying Law and the Shifting Landscape of Belgian and Dutch Euthanasia Practice," *Supreme Court Law Review* (2nd Series) 85 (2018): 459–544.
77 Bill C-7, *An Act to Amend the Criminal Code (medical assistance in dying)*.
78 Deborah Stienstra et al., *Disability Inclusion Analysis of Lessons Learned and Best Practices of the Government of Canada's Response to the covid-19 Pandemic*, University of Guelph Live Work Well Research Centre and DAWN Canada, March 2021, https://liveworkwell.ca/sites/default/files/pageuploads/DisabilityInclusionAnalysisCOVID-19_Final_031621_protected.pdf.
79 Kathleen Harris, "Lametti Urges MPs to Pass Assisted Death Bill as Disability Groups Demand a Halt," CBC News, 8 December 2020, https://www.cbc.ca/news/politics/lametti-maid-assisted-dying-bill-disabilities-1.5831436.
80 "Testimony of Hon. Carla Qualtrough," in *Meeting of the Standing Committee on Justice and Human Rights – Evidence*, 43rd Parliament, 2nd Session (3 November 2020), https://www.ourcommons.ca/DocumentViewer/en/43-2/JUST/meeting-4/evidence#Int-10988133.
81 Parliament of Canada, "Vote No. 39," 43rd Parliament, 2nd Session (10 December 2020), https://www.ourcommons.ca/members/en/votes/43/2/39.
82 Kathleen Harris, "Liberal MP and Doctor Says He'll Vote Against Assisted Death Bill," CBC News, 9 December 2020, https://www.cbc.ca/news/politics/liberal-mp-marcus-powlowski-maid-c7-assisted-dying-lametti-1.5833493.
83 Parliament of Canada, "Vote No. 39."
84 Rachel Emmanuel, "MAiD Protections More Important than Court Deadline, Says Sen. Batters," *iPolitics*, 10 December 2020, https://ipolitics.ca/2020/12/10/maid-protections-more-important-than-court-deadline-says-sen-batters/.
85 "Speech of Senator Julie Miville-Dechêne," in *Debates of the Senate*, 43rd Parliament, 2nd Session (15 December 2020), 19:50, https://sencanada.ca/en/content/sen/chamber/432/debates/021db_2020-12-15-e?language=e.

86 Peter Mazereeuw, "Senators Preparing 'Sunset Clause' Amendment to Scrap Mental Health Exclusion from Assisted Dying Law," *Hill Times*, 8 February 2021, https://www.hilltimes.com/2021/02/08/senators-preparing-sunset-clause-amendment-to-scrap-mental-health-exclusion-from-assisted-dying-law/282466.

87 Trudo Lemmens, "How Parliament and Our Federal Government Are Playing MAID Politics with the Lives of People with Mental Illness," *University of Toronto Faculty of Law* (blog), 23 February 2021, https://www.law.utoronto.ca/blog/faculty/how-parliament-and-our-federal-government-are-playing-maid-politics-lives-people-mental.

88 Standing Senate Committee on Legal and Constitutional Affairs, "Senate Legal Committee Releases Pre-Study Report on Bill C-7," news release, Senate of Canada, 10 December 2020, https://sencanada.ca/en/newsroom/lcjc-senate-legal-committee-releases-pre-study-report-on-bill-c-7/.

89 Joan Bryden, "Federal Government Seek Fourth Extension to Update Assisted-Dying Law," *Globe and Mail*, 19 February 2021, https://www.theglobeandmail.com/politics/article-federal-government-seek-fourth-extension-to-update-assisted-dying-law/.

90 *Truchon v. Canada (Attorney General)*, 2021 QCCS 590.

91 The Canadian Press, "Nicole Gladu, Quebec Advocate of Medical Aid in Dying, Dies of Natural Causes," CTV News, 1 April 2022, https://montreal.ctvnews.ca/nicole-gladu-quebec-advocate-of-medical-aid-in-dying-dies-of-natural-causes-1.5844322.

92 Standing Committee on Legal and Constitutional Affairs, *Fourth Report*, Senate of Canada, 8 February 2021, https://sencanada.ca/en/committees/report/90681/43-2.

93 Senate of Canada, "Vote Details – Bill C-7," 43rd Parliament, 2nd Session (17 February 2021), https://sencanada.ca/en/in-the-chamber/votes/details/554941.

94 "Speech of Senator Donald Plett," in *Debates of the Senate*, 43rd Parliament, 2nd Session (11 February 2021), https://sencanada.ca/en/Content/Sen/Chamber/432/Debates/027db_2021-02-11-e#49.

95 Hon. Marilou McPhedran, "Bill to Amend – Third Reading – Debate," Senate of Canada, 43rd Parliament, 2nd Session (11 February 2021), https://sencanada.ca/en/senators/mcphedran-marilou/interventions/553872/26.

96 Kady O'Malley K., "Libs to Stop Debate of Senate Rewrite of Proposed Changes to MAiD Laws," *iPolitics*, 11 March 2021, https://www.ipolitics.ca/news/ipolitics-am-libs-to-stop-debate-of-senate-rewrite-of-proposed-changes-to-maid-laws.

97 Michael Cooper and Tamara Jansen, "Conservative MPs on Medical-Assistance-in-Dying Bill," CPAC, 26 February 2021, https://www.cpac.ca/en/programs/headline-politics/episodes/66336975/.

98 Garnett Genuis and Rob Moore, "Conservative MPs on Medical-Assistance-in-Dying Bill," CPAC, 8 March 2021, https://www.cpac.ca/en/programs/headline-politics/episodes/66342113/.

99 Joan Bryden, "Federal Government Approves Senate Amendment to Allow Mentally Ill to Access Assisted Dying – But Not for Two Years," *National Post*, 23 February 2021, https://nationalpost.com/news/politics/government-agrees-mentally-ill-should-have-access-to-maid-in-two-years.

100 "Remarks of MP Luc Theriault," in *House of Commons Debates*, 43rd Parliament, 2nd Session (11 March 2021), https://www.ourcommons.ca/DocumentViewer/en/43-2/house/sitting-71/hansard#Int-11182937.

101 House of Commons, "Vote No. 71 – Bill C-7," 43rd Parliament, 2nd Session (11 March 2021), https://www.ourcommons.ca/Members/en/votes/43/2/71.

102 Senate of Canada, "Vote Details – Bill C-7," 43rd Parliament, 2nd Session (17 March 2021), https://sencanada.ca/en/in-the-chamber/votes/details/555864.

103 For a documentary with Dr Joshua Tepper's approval of twenty-three-year-old Kiano Vafeian's MAiD request, apparently for vision loss associated with diabetes, see, for example, "Is It Too Easy to Die in Canada?," video, CBC *Fifth Estate*, 19 January 2023, https://www.youtube.com/watch?v=plinQAHZRvk.

104 See Kimberly Jakeman to Iqra Khalid (Chair, Committee on Justice and Human Rights), "Bill C-7, Criminal Code Amendments (medical assistance in dying)," Canadian Bar Association, https://www.cba.org/CMSPages/GetFile.aspx?guid=4165f9e8-f212-4dff-bae5-b8b849626c9f.

105 Trudo Lemmens and Leah Krakowitz-Broker, "Why the Federal Government Should Rethink Its New Medical Assistance in Dying Law," CBC News, 10 November 2020, https://www.cbc.ca/news/opinion/opinion-medical-assistance-in-dying-maid-legislation-1.5790710.

106 Scott Kim, "In Canada, MAID Has Become a Matter of Ideology," *Globe and Mail*, 25 February 2023, https://www.theglobeandmail.com/opinion/article-in-canada-maid-has-become-a-matter-of-ideology/.

107 Trudo Lemmens, "When Death Becomes Therapy: Canada's Troubling Normalization of Health Care Provider Ending of Life," *American Journal of Bioethics* 23, no. 11 (2023): 79–84.

108 Avis Favaro, "The Death Debate: Why Some Welcome Canada's Move to Assisted Death for Mental Illness and Others Fear It," CTV News, 16 December 2022, https://www.ctvnews.ca/w5/the-death-debate-why-some-welcome-canada-s-move-to-assisted-dying-for-mental-illness-and-others-fear-it-1.6109646; "Testimony of Dr. Ellen Wiebe," in *Meeting of the Special Joint Committee on Medical Assistance in Dying – Evidence*, 44th Parliament, 1st Session (26 May 2022), 1440.

109 See chapter 11 (Shariff, Ross, and Lemmens) and Trudo Lemmens, "When Death Becomes Therapy," 79–84.

110 See Lemmens, "When Death Becomes Therapy," 79–84.

111 See, for example, chapter 2 (Gaind).

112 Sean Murphy, "Canadian Medical Association and Euthanasia and Assisted Suicide in Canada: Critical Review of CMA Approach to Changes in Policy and Law," The Protection of Conscience Project, September 2018, https://www.consciencelaws.org/background/procedures/assist029-01.aspx.

113 "Meeting of the Special Joint Committee on Medical Assistance in Dying," video, Parl VU, 21 November 2023, https://parlvu.parl.gc.ca/Harmony/en/PowerBrowser/PowerBrowserV2/20231121/-1/40405?Embedded=true&globalstreamId=20&viewMode=3.

114 "Meeting of the Special Joint Committee on Medical Assistance in Dying," video, Parl VU, 7 November 2023, https://parlvu.parl.gc.ca/Harmony/en/PowerBrowser/PowerBrowserV2?fk=12411264.

115 Sharon Kirkey, "Fewer than Half of Canadians Support Assisted Death for Mental Disorders: Poll," *National Post*, 20 July 2022, https://nationalpost.com/news/canada/fewer-than-half-of-canadians-support-assisted-death-for-mental-disorders-poll/wcm/e82777c7-c818-4a6d-a41d-0318d9749efb/amp/.

116 H. M. Chochinov et al., "Desire for Death in the Terminally Ill," *American Journal of Psychiatry* 152, no. 8 (August 1995): 1185–91.

117 "Medical Assistance in Dying, 2019 and 2020," Statistics Canada, 10 January 2022, https://www150.statcan.gc.ca/n1/daily-quotidien/220110/dq220110d-eng.htm.

118 "Remarks of Hon. David Lametti (Justice Minister)," in *Meeting of the Standing Committee on Justice and Human Rights – Evidence*, 43rd Parliament, 2nd Session (3 November 2020), https://www.ourcommons.ca/DocumentViewer/en/43-2/JUST/meeting-4/evidence.

119 "Remarks of Hon. Patty Hajdu (Health Minister)," in *Meeting of the Standing Committee on Justice and Human Rights – Evidence*, 43rd Parliament, 2nd Session (3 November 2020), https://www.ourcommons.ca/DocumentViewer/en/43-2/JUST/meeting-4/evidence.

120 Garnett Genuis, "Speaking on Same-Day Death Bill C-7," Facebook Live video, 8 December 2020, https://www.facebook.com/MPGenuis/videos/2914508042165753/.

121 Expert Advisory Group on Medical Assistance in Dying, *Canada at a Crossroads: Recommendations on Medical Assistance in Dying and Persons with Mental Disorder – An Evidence-based Critique of the Halifax Group IRPP Report* (Toronto: Expert Advisory Group, 2020), https://static1.squarespace.com/static/5e3dcbaafb-4d851392a9298f/t/5e4843a7dd83d25c7dc9140c/1581794218609/EAG+-+Canada+at+Crossroads+-+FINALdoi.pdf.

122 Canadian Psychiatric Association, "Position Statement: Medical Assistance in Dying: An Update," October 2021, https://www.cpa-apc.org/wp-content/uploads/2021-CPA-Position-Statement-MAID-Update-EN-web-Final.pdf.

123 Janet E. Silver, "Canadians Concerned with Medically-Assisted Dying Bill: Poll," *iPolitics*, 10 November 2020, https://ipolitics.ca/2020/11/10/canadians-concerned-with-medically-assisted-dying-bill-poll/.

124 Kirkey, "Fewer than Half of Canadians."

125 Choi et al., "When Medical Assistance in Dying Is Not a Last Resort Option."

126 Senate of Canada, *Report of the Committee – Standing Committee on Legal and Constitutional Affairs*, 10 December 2020, https://sencanada.ca/en/committees/report/89384/43-2.

127 Health Canada, *First Annual Report on Medical Assistance in Dying in Canada*, 2019, July 2020, https://www.canada.ca/en/health-canada/services/medical-assistance-dying-annual-report-2019.html.

128 Camille Munro et al., "Involvement of Palliative Care in Patients Requesting Medical Assistance in Dying," *Canadian Family Physician* 66, no. 11 (November 2020): 833–42, https://www.cfp.ca/content/66/11/833?rss=1.

129 Jaro Kotalik, "Medical Assistance in Dying: Challenges of Monitoring the Canadian Program," *Canadian Journal of Bioethics* 3, no. 3 (2020): 202–9, https://doi.org/10.7202/1073799ar.

130 Dirk Huyer, "Minister of The Solicitor General: Office of the Chief Coroner Memorandum," 9 October 2018, accessed 8 December 2022, https://www.mcscs.jus.gov.on.ca/english/Deathinvestigations/OfficeChiefCoroner/Publicationsandreports/MedicalAssistanceDyingUpdate.html (link defunct); Commission sur les soins de fin de vie, *Rapport annuel d'activitiés*, 2018–19, https://drive.google.com/file/d/1V1T4g_t1wxPR13xONOWBr3K_Ibjfxl2u/view; Office of the Correctional Investigator, *Office of the Correctional Investigator Annual Report*

2019–2020, 26 June 2020, https://oci-bec.gc.ca/sites/default/files/2023-06/annrpt20192020-eng.pdf.

131 Canadian Press, "Quebecers No Longer Seeing Doctor-Assisted Deaths as Exceptional, Says Oversight Body," CTV News, 15 August 2023, https://montreal.ctvnews.ca/quebecers-no-longer-seeing-doctor-assisted-deaths-as-exceptional-says-oversight-body-1.6519503.

132 Chief Coroner of Ontario, MAID *Death Review Committee Application*, accessed 20 September 2023, https://forms.mgcs.gov.on.ca/dataset/6ac44375-42f7-4d35-8120-aa49a3c4ef27/resource/5e6025de-2902-4305-b513-ab375a2c385a/download/on00366e.pdf (link defunct).

133 For some examples, see Ferrukh Faruqui, "'Nothing about This Felt OK': The Troubling Debate over a 'Good' Death for All," *National Post*, 1 April 2022, https://nationalpost.com/news/canada/the-troubling-debate-over-a-good-death-for-anyone-who-chooses; Penny Daflos, "B.C. Woman behind 'Dystopian' Commercial Found 'Death Care' Easier than Health Care," CTV News, 2 December 2022, https://bc.ctvnews.ca/b-c-woman-behind-dystopian-commercial-found-death-care-easier-than-health-care-1.6177877; Alexander Raikin, "No Other Options: Newly Revealed Documents Depict a Canadian Euthanasia Regime that Efficiently Ushers the Vulnerable to a 'Beautiful' Death," *The New Atlantis* 71 (Winter 2023): 3–24, https://www.thenewatlantis.com/publications/no-other-options; Avis Favaro, "Woman with Chemical Sensitivities Chose Medically-Assisted Death after Failed Bid to Get Better Housing," CTV News, 13 April 2023, https://www.ctvnews.ca/mobile/health/woman-with-chemical-sensitivities-chose-medically-assisted-death-after-failed-bid-to-get-better-housing-1.5860579?cache=yes?clipId=89925; "A Complicated Death," video, CBC *Fifth Estate*, 17 January 2023, https://www.cbc.ca/news/fifthestate/a-complicated-death-1.6717266; Yuan Yi Zhu, "Why Is Canada Euthanizing the Poor?," *Spectator*, 30 April 2022, https://www.spectator.co.uk/article/why-is-canada-euthanising-the-poor-; and "Do You Want to Die Today: Inside Canada's Euthanasia Program," video, *Al Jazeera*, Fault Lines, 17 November 2023, https://www.aljazeera.com/program/fault-lines/2023/11/17/do-you-want-to-die-today-inside-canadas-euthanasia-program.

134 Health Canada, *Final Report of the Expert Panel on maid and Mental Illness*, 13 May 2022, https://www.canada.ca/en/health-canada/corporate/about-health-canada/public-engagement/external-advisory-bodies/expert-panel-maid-mental-illness/final-report-expert-panel-maid-mental-illness.html.

135 Jeffrey Kirby, "MAID Expert Panel Recommendations Are Inadequate, Contends Panel Member Who Resigned," *Hill Times*, 16 June 2022,

https://www.hilltimes.com/story/2022/06/16/maid-expert-panel-recommendations-are-inadequate-contends-panel-member-who-resigned/270807/; Ellen Cohen, "Why I Resigned from the Federal Expert Panel on Medical Assistance in Dying," *Globe and Mail*, 14 October 2022, https://www.theglobeandmail.com/opinion/article-expert-panel-maid-mental-illness/.

136 Health Canada, *Model Practice Standard for Medical Assistance in Dying (MAID)*, March 2023, https://www.canada.ca/en/health-canada/services/publications/health-system-services/model-practice-standard-medical-assistance-dying.html.

137 See ibid., at "5.0: Responsibilities of [Physicians or Nurse Practitiones] Unable or Unwilling to Participate in MAID," in particular reference 8.

138 See the discussion in Lemmens, "When Death Becomes Therapy."

139 See Raikin, "No Other Options."

140 Canadian Association of MAID Assessors and Providers, "The Interpretation and Role of 'Reasonably Foreseeable' in MAID Practice," February 2022, 1, https://camapcanada.ca/wp-content/uploads/2022/03/The-Interpretation-and-Role-of-22Reasonably-Foreseeable22-in-MAID-Practice-Feb-2022.pdf.

141 Canadian Association of MAID Assessors and Providers, "Bringing Up Medical Assistance in Dying (MAID) as a Clinical Care Option," accessed 4 October 2023, https://camapcanada.ca/wp-content/uploads/2022/02/Bringing-up-MAID.pdf; Health Canada, *Model Practice Standard*.

142 "End of Life Choice Act 2019: Section 10," Parliamentary Counsel Office, New Zealand Legislation, 2019, https://www.legislation.govt.nz/act/public/2019/0067/latest/LMS195465.html; "About Voluntary Assisted Dying," Department of Health Victoria (Australia), accessed 6 December 2022, https://www.health.vic.gov.au/patient-care/general-information-about-voluntary-assisted-dying#can-someone-be-pressured-into-asking-for-voluntary-assisted-dying.

143 Association of Faculties of Medicine of Canada, "Chapter 5: Assessing Evidence and Information," in *AFMC Primer on Population Health*, 2021, https://phprimer.afmc.ca/en/part-ii/chapter-5/.

144 Harvey Schipper, "Delaying Medically Assisted Death for Mental Illness Will Give Us Time to Find an Acceptable Place for MAID," *Toronto Star*, 13 March 2024, https://www.thestar.com/opinion/contributors/delaying-medically-assisted-death-for-mental-illness-will-give-us-time-to-find-an-acceptable/article_3d1e6c72-dfc8-11ee-998c-c7c6c82c4f1c.html.

145 See chapter 4 (Lemmens, Shariff, and Herx).

146 Health Canada, *Fourth Annual Report*.

147 Ibid., 20.
148 Lemmens, "When Death Becomes Therapy."
149 Daryl Pullman, "Slowing the Slide Down the Slippery Slope of Medical Assistance in Dying: Mutual Learnings for Canada and the US," *American Journal of Bioethics* 23, no. 11 (2023): 64–72.
150 Daflos, "B.C. Woman behind 'Dystopian' Commercial"; Favaro, "Woman with Chemical Sensitivities"; Fifth Estate, "A Complicated Death"; Zhu, "Why Is Canada Euthanizing the Poor?"; Raikin, "No Other Options."
151 For an example of over-reliance on choice, see Udo Schuklenk, "Argumenta Ad Passiones: Canada Debates Access Thresholds to MAiD," *Bioethics* 36, no. 6 (July 2022): 611–12, https://pubmed.ncbi.nlm.nih.gov/35708595/. For the argument that offering MAID in situations of absence of timely care or support is a form of harm reduction, see Kayla Wiebe and Amy Mullin, "Choosing Death in Unjust Conditions: Hope, Autonomy and Harm Reduction," *Journal of Medical Ethics*, April 2023, https://pubmed.ncbi.nlm.nih.gov/37100589/.
152 Hon. Marc Garneau and Hon. Yonah Martin, *Medical Assistance in Dying in Canada: Choices for Canadians, Report of the Special Joint Committee on Medical Assistance in Dying*, Parliament of Canada, 15 February 2023, https://www.parl.ca/DocumentViewer/en/44-1/AMAD/report-2; Parliament of Canada, *Government Response to the Second Report of the Special Joint Committee on Medical Assistance in Dying*, 15 June 2023, https://www.parl.ca/DocumentViewer/en/44-1/AMAD/report-2/response-8512-441-200.
153 Ramona Coelho, "Barriers to Care Persist but Access to MAiD Keeps Expanding: Ramona Coelho for Inside Policy," MacDonald Laurier Institute, 21 February 2024, https://macdonaldlaurier.ca/maid-keeps-expanding-ramona-coelho-for-inside-policy/; Trudo Lemmens, "Opinion: It's Too Late for the Supreme Court: Ottawa Needs to Step Up and Fix MAID," *Globe and Mail*, 9 February 2024, https://www.theglobeandmail.com/opinion/article-its-too-late-for-the-supreme-court-ottawa-needs-to-step-up-and-fix/.

2

Fall of Duty: The Breach of Trust and Moral Failure of Canada's Entrusted Experts

K. Sonu Gaind

Developing sound national policy on complex issues requires both transparent and well-informed public consultation and input from those considered experts in the field. Society provides experts with a platform for their views to be heard; in return, experts have a moral obligation to provide guidance based on their areas of expertise and not to simply use their platforms to espouse personal or ideological opinions while neglecting evidence. In the charged and complex area of medical assistance in dying (MAiD) and mental illness, other than brief dalliances with responsibility and sporadic exceptions, Canada's expert bodies have unfortunately contributed surprisingly little expertise to consultations on legislation enacted in 2021 that significantly expanded eligibility for MAiD. Instead, many leaders acknowledged as experts through their positions have acted as ideological advocates, focusing on particular agendas while neglecting to provide any significant input or evidence in the complex area of mental illness and death, as might be expected given their expertise.

This chapter provides a summary of these events from my perspective as an insider to the MAiD policy evolution during Canada's first several years of MAiD. Despite not being a conscientious objector (I was the physician chair of my previous hospital's MAiD team), I have become increasingly concerned about the flawed processes that have shaped our national MAiD expansion policies, the zealotry of ideologically driven agendas masquerading as expert advice, and the most vulnerable and marginalized Canadians those expansionist policies place at risk.

For those who understandably assume, or trust, that national policy is set following thoughtful and unbiased due diligence, this chapter may be difficult to read. For me, as a past president of the Canadian Psychiatric Association (CPA), the national medical association historically entrusted to provide evidence-based expert input on these challenging issues and whose involvement I outline in some detail below, this chapter has been difficult to write.

EARLY DAYS – LEADING UP TO BILL C-14

When Canada embarked on working through the complexities of introducing MAiD in response to the 2015 *Carter v. Canada (AG)* Supreme Court ruling, there was no clarity on how MAiD policies would apply to mental illnesses. While the *Carter* ruling did acknowledge that psychological suffering was to be considered, the court did not review any issues related to mental illness, nor did the ruling set any precedent for mental illnesses per se.[1] Thus, while the ruling acknowledged the validity of psychological suffering, it did not review or provide any guidance on how to address the issue of MAiD and mental illness. The February 2015 ruling provided a one-year deadline for the implementation of MAiD policies, but for many months there was no consultation on how issues related to mental illness should be addressed, and there remained a dearth of policy development in the area.

When I began my term as CPA president in October 2015, consulting with members and providing input in this important area became a key priority. The CPA did not have to wait long to contribute. Within weeks, in November 2015 I had opportunities to present on MAiD and mental illness as CPA president before two expert panels, the federal External Panel on Legislative Options to *Carter v. Canada* and the Provincial-Territorial Expert Advisory Group on Physician-Assisted Dying, and I again testified in January 2016 before the Special Joint Committee on Physician-Assisted Dying in Ottawa.[2] By this time, the Supreme Court had granted a three-month extension, until May 2016, for the implementation of MAiD legislation.

While the CPA had not gone through the process of developing a formal position on MAiD and mental illness in the short time since beginning to contribute to the consultations in November 2015, there was significant expertise that we, as the national psychiatric association, could contribute regarding issues relevant to mental illness and discussions of MAiD. These broad principles, based on evidence and not ideology, formed the basis of CPA input at the time, and we concurrently kept CPA members fully apprised of the consultations we were engaged in and the submissions we were making. We also established a time-limited task force on MAiD at the CPA that I chaired. Over the next two years the task force regularly presented at CPA conferences, consulted with members, and developed a guidance document for Canadian psychiatrists to assist with navigating the newly implemented MAiD legislation.

Despite the complexities involved, and despite the range of views on MAiD in general and MAiD and mental illness in particular, this early time period showed what could be accomplished by a professional association if it undertook transparent and meaningful consultation and provided thoughtful and expert guidance. Public policy-makers at the highest level responded accordingly. Both the federal Ministry of Health and Ministry of Justice sought advice from the CPA before drafting MAiD legislation, and as CPA president I had the chance to meet both federal minister of health Jane Philpott and the attorney general/ minister of justice Jody Wilson-Raybould to ensure evidence-based input regarding issues relevant to mental illness were considered as Canada's initial MAiD laws were being formed.

Perhaps most tellingly, when media reports began circulating that draft Bill C-14 legislation was expected to allow for MAiD for mental illness, the CPA provided the only evidence-based expert input we could.[3] Since MAiD was ostensibly meant only for irremediable conditions, as CPA president I wrote to Minister Philpott and Minister Wilson-Raybould that "there is no established standard of care in Canada, or as far as CPA is aware of in the world, for defining the threshold when psychiatric conditions should be considered irremediable."[4] Within days, media reports changed to indicate that MAiD for mental illness would not be included in Bill C-14 legislation, and that instead further study would be mandated prior to determining how to address the issue of MAiD and mental illness, which is precisely how draft Bill C-14 was reframed when it was subsequently released in April 2016.[5]

Prior to a final reading of Bill C-14, the government continued to seek input from the CPA at hearings of the Standing Senate Committee on Legal and Constitutional Affairs on Physician-Assisted Death, and I testified virtually before that committee via video link from Hong Kong (which, pre-COVID, actually retained some novelty!) as president of the association in May 2016 prior to my presidential term ending in fall 2016.[6] In all these consultations, the focus was to provide evidence-informed input regarding clinical issues relevant to discussions of mental illness and MAiD. This included providing evidence related to how mental illness symptoms could impact suffering and thoughts of suicidality, the influence of cognitive processes in mental illness beyond the narrow consideration of only legal capacity, issues of autonomy, stigma, and discrimination, the psychosocial contexts and high levels of social suffering often experienced by those with mental illness, risk factors associated with suicide, evidence-based considerations regarding the concept of predicting irremediability in mental illnesses, concerns about the impact of poor access to mental health care on those suffering and the marginalized, and the need for the presence of evidence-based standards to inform policy.

AFTER BILL C-14, LEADING UP TO *TRUCHON*

Following the introduction of Bill C-14 and Canada's initial MAiD legislation, which included the safeguard that natural death needed to be "reasonably foreseeable," the federal government also tasked the Council of Canadian Academies (CCA) with studying three issues regarding MAiD, specifically MAiD for sole mental illness conditions, MAiD for mature minors, and advance directives for MAiD. The CCA Expert Panel on MAiD and Mental Illness (on which I sat as an individual, not related to my CPA role) reviewed worldwide evidence and released its report in December 2018.[7] The panel found no evidence of standards for determining irremediability of mental illnesses, nor any evidence that predictions of irremediability could be accurately or scientifically made. Similarly, the panel found no evidence that suicidality due to mental illness could be differentiated from motivations driving requests for MAiD for mental illness. Tellingly, after deliberating for nearly a year and a half, the panel continued to have five fundamental areas of disagreement that are highlighted in the report.[8] The report also indicated that "some Working Group members believe that, even with safeguards in place, some of the previously identified risks of over-inclusion would still not be mitigated" if MAiD were provided for sole mental illness conditions – in other words, that such "safeguards" would not actually work as safeguards.

Concurrent with the work of the CCA expert panel, the time-limited CPA task force continued to consult with psychiatrists and stakeholders and to present at national conferences and engage with the CPA membership. Following the delivery of a guidance document on

MAiD to the CPA board, the task force was sunset in 2018. At that time, the CPA committed to engage membership and consult experts to further develop its position on MAiD and mental illness.

Unfortunately, after 2018 the CPA did not consult or engage any further on the topic of MAiD for the next two years, despite the crucial developments regarding national MAiD policies with significant implications for those with mental illness that occurred during that time (by 2019, I had rotated off the CPA Board).

2019 *TRUCHON* RULING AND IMPLICATIONS FOR MAiD AND MENTAL ILLNESS (AND SUBSEQUENT RENDERING OF "MAiD" A MISNOMER)

On 11 September 2019, Quebec Superior Court justice Christine Baudouin declared the federal "reasonably foreseeable natural death" (RFND) safeguard unconstitutional in her ruling in the *Truchon v. Canada (AG)* case.[9] By this time minister of justice and attorney general Jody Wilson-Raybould had been removed as justice minister and replaced by the Honourable David Lametti as the new minister of justice and attorney general. The two ministers who had introduced Bill C-14 containing the RFND safeguard in 2016, former justice minister Jody Wilson-Raybould and former health minister Jane Philpott, were both subsequently expelled from caucus by Prime Minister Justin Trudeau in the SNC-Lavalin affair.[10] (In disclosure, I had been retained by the former attorney general and minister of justice Wilson-Raybould to act as an expert in the Quebec *Truchon* case, which was heard in January and February 2019, and the British Columbia *Lamb* case, which never went to trial.)

Rather than test the provincial lower court ruling that was non-binding on courts outside Quebec (which some legal scholars were advising warranted appeal to a higher court),[11] the Trudeau government decided to neither appeal the Quebec provincial court ruling nor to issue a referral to the Supreme Court and chose to change national policy instead. This set the stage for the removal of the initial RFND safeguard nationally and the expansion of MAiD to the non-dying disabled and had significant implications for those with mental illness.

The pending removal of the RFND safeguard also rendered the term that Canada initially coined in 2016, *medical assistance in dying* or MAiD, a misnomer. Medical assistance *in* dying implies a process that facilitates or assists the death of someone who is dying.

Justice Baudouin's opinion that assisted death needed to be provided even when death was not foreseeable rendered the term MAiD misleading – soon death would be provided to people who were not otherwise dying. For the balance of this chapter, to avoid misleadingly implying that Canada's expanded laws are only assisting facilitating deaths of those who are already dying, the term MAiD will be preferentially avoided. Given these deaths are being provided by the state to those who are not dying but wish to die (i.e., have suicidal thoughts) and given that in Canada the vast majority of medically assisted deaths are administered through lethal injection by medical teams (i.e., euthanasia) rather than self-administered, a more accurate term for assisted deaths under Canada's expanded MAiD regime is *state-provided euthanasia* (SPE) or *state-assisted suicide* (SAS). While SPE or SAS are now more appropriate terms for Canada's expanded assisted death policies, to avoid confusion for the balance of this chapter the terms *assisted suicide* or *euthanasia* will preferentially be used, other than when referencing specific literature, legislation, nomenclature, or time periods that warrant using the inaccurate term MAiD.

In 2016 Bill C-14 had not specifically excluded assisted suicide for sole conditions of mental illness. However, since the vast majority of cases of mental illness do not lead to naturally foreseeable death, with the initial RFND safeguard in place mental illnesses would typically not fulfill the requirements for MAiD in the C-14 framework. The *Truchon* ruling and pending removal of the RFND safeguard flagged that the situation was about to change, and that more focused consideration had to be given regarding how to appropriately address mental illness in the post-*Truchon* euthanasia framework.

In February 2020 a subset of the CCA expert panel on euthanasia and mental illness calling itself the Halifax Group published a report advocating for the provision of assisted suicide for mental illness.[12] Amongst other things, the Halifax Group also advocated against the inclusion of a "non-ambivalence" safeguard prior to assisting with the suicide of those with mental illness (ambivalence has been long recognized in mental illness literature as being a marker for suicidality).[13] In response, a group of colleagues, including others who sat on various CCA expert panels and those with lived experience, and I conducted an evidence-based review and critique of the Halifax Group report under the auspices of the Expert Advisory Group (EAG) on MAiD.[14]

The EAG found that there continued to be no evidence that it was possible to predict irremediability in cases of mental illness, consistent with the Centre for Addiction and Mental Health's conclusion that "there is simply not enough evidence available in the mental health field at this time for clinicians to ascertain whether a particular individual has an irremediable mental illness,"[15] and the EAG advised that legislation should accordingly and explicitly acknowledge that fact. Specifically, the EAG issued a core recommendation that "MAID policy and legislation should explicitly acknowledge that determinations of irremediability and irreversible decline cannot be made for mental illnesses at this time, and therefore applications for MAID for the sole underlying medical condition of a mental disorder cannot fulfill MAID eligibility requirements." The EAG also issued two ancillary recommendations, that a "non-ambivalence criterion should be required for MAID in situations when death is not reasonably foreseeable," and that a "'lack of reasonable alternative' criterion should be required prior to being eligible for MAID in situations when death is not reasonably foreseeable" (this last recommendation was in consideration of Canada being the only country in the world that did not require "due care" having been provided, or a "lack of reasonable alternatives" or "treatment futility" or similar safeguard, prior to providing euthanasia – meaning that in Canada, people can receive euthanasia even if routine treatment options have not been tried or been able to be accessed).

EARLY FAILURES OF OMISSION

Despite being aware of the pending implications of the *Truchon* ruling, and despite the fact that Canadian psychiatrists had not been consulted by the CPA on the issue of MAiD since 2018, the CPA conducted no consultation or engagement with their membership after the *Truchon* ruling; indeed, they did not communicate to members whatsoever about the issue, not even communicating any updates about the *Truchon* decision and its pending relevance to potential MAiD for mental illness policies. Instead, with no membership consultation, the new CPA board released a position statement on psychiatric euthanasia in March 2020 (the statement is dated 10 February 2020, since that is apparently when the board approved it, and CPA members became aware of it with its public release on 12 March 2020).[16]

The CPA statement generated significant concern in many quarters, both because of the process followed and because of its content. The CPA had failed to engage membership for nearly two years, despite a prior commitment by CPA to engage in future member and stakeholder consultations following the sunsetting of the previous task force in 2018. The statement was developed by a small non-representative internal CPA committee with no particular expertise in MAiD (the Professional Standards and Practice [PSP] Committee) and without the benefit or input of external experts or even internal consultations with other CPA committees like the CPA Research Committee.

The March 2020 CPA position statement mostly identified generic principles that provided no guidance on any of the complex issues related to mental illnesses and assisted suicide. Strikingly for a national psychiatric association providing input on consultations on mental illness and death seeking, there were no references to any evidence or scientific literature related to mental illness, mental health, psychosocial suffering, vulnerability, marginalization, or suicidality (there actually were no references to any medical or psychiatric literature or evidence whatsoever). The statement failed to mention the importance of suicide prevention or known mental illness–related suicide risks and did not once use the words "suicide" or "suicidal," despite talking about mental illnesses and wishes for death. Instead of presenting evidence, the authors of the statement took an ideological stance proclaiming that "patients with a psychiatric illness should not be discriminated against … and should have available the same options regarding MAiD as available to all patients," yet it remained silent on how or whether irremediability (a fundamental requirement for MAiD assessments) could be assessed in mental illnesses.

After nearly two years without any member input or expert consultation, the CPA statement emerged at a crucial time, post-*Truchon*, when new MAiD policies were being formed. Beyond the lack of member, expert, and stakeholder engagement, the evidence-free content of the statement led to public opinion editorials expressing concern about potential negative impacts of the CPA position on MAiD policies and to pieces in the CPA's own peer-reviewed journal calling for the statement to be revisited.[17] However, the CPA refused to reconsider the statement.

With the CPA framing it as an issue of "discrimination," with no cautions about evidence-based issues specific to mental illness such as illness-fuelled death wishes or the high associated prevalence of psychosocial suffering faced by those with mental illness, many cautioned that policy-makers would see this statement as the CPA advocating for blanket expansion of euthanasia for sole mental illness conditions. There were concerns that the CPA's position could misleadingly lead to public and policy-maker perception that most psychiatrists favoured expansion of MAiD for mental illness, despite the CPA receiving no input from membership on the issue in the preceding two years, and that it furthermore could result in the national association becoming complicit in shaping public policy devoid of evidence or standards for irremediability assessments while exposing the most marginalized with mental illness to policies allowing arbitrary assessments based on personal views of individual assessors, leading to premature and avoidable deaths.

By the summer of 2022 these fears were proven correct.

2020–21 "SUNSET CLAUSE" AND THE PENDING REMOVAL OF SAFEGUARD AGAINST EUTHANASIA FOR SOLE MENTAL ILLNESS

When in March 2020 the federal government introduced Bill C-7, the bill removing the RFND safeguard to accommodate the *Truchon* decision that the government had chosen not to appeal, the initial draft excluded assisted suicide for sole mental illness conditions.[18] At the time then justice minister David Lametti acknowledged that "there is a greater risk of providing medical assistance in dying to people whose condition could improve" and that "in the case of some mental illnesses, the desire to die is itself a symptom of the illness, which makes it particularly difficult to determine whether the individual's request is truly voluntary."[19]

Although the federal government continued providing assurances over the following year that it would maintain the safeguard preventing euthanasia for sole mental illness, tea leaves dropped along the way began indicating that other forces were at play and that these assurances were likely to be rendered meaningless in short order. The Trudeau government initiated hearings on MAiD expansion by the Senate in late 2020. When questioned in these hearings about the exclusion of assisted suicide for sole mental illness, Minister Lametti began to presage that this exclusion was only temporary.[20] The Senate eventually recommended eliminating the safeguard preventing psychiatric euthanasia following a "sunset clause" period.

Following a year of assurances that psychiatric euthanasia would not be provided for in Bill C-7, on 23 February 2021 Minister Lametti introduced an amendment to Bill C-7 to add a sunset clause to ensure psychiatric euthanasia would be provided by March 2023. On 11 March 2021, there was a single evening of debate in the House of Commons on the new amendment and the issue of psychiatric euthanasia. This debate was foreshortened by the Trudeau government's invocation of a closure motion. In the end, the sunset clause was adopted after a vote of members of Parliament in the House of Commons that same evening, with the vote being largely along party lines.

Beyond the clear politicization of a process that should have been informed by medical evidence, the political process itself raised concerns. In response to several members of Parliament expressing dismay over the minimal amount of deliberation given to the issue of psychiatric euthanasia prior to the government seeking to commit to providing it, one government parliamentary secretary, member of Parliament Kevin Lamoureux, claimed the debate included "nothing that is new to members," that "we've literally seen hundreds, if not possibly even thousands of hours of debate and discussion," and that "the issue of MAID has been on the floor of the house for years now." Another parliamentary secretary, MP Arif Virani (who in 2023 became the currently sitting minister of justice), claimed that "scrutiny has been provided with respect to this bill. One hundred thirty-nine MPs have spoken, [forty-five] hours of debate have occurred."[21] The claimed "hundreds to thousands of hours of debate" and 139 MPs with forty-five hours of debate did not address the issue of psychiatric euthanasia, which had not been in the initial draft legislation until the sunset clause amendment was introduced by the government at the last minute only two weeks before the vote on 11 March 2021. Psychiatric euthanasia and the sunset clause had not been part of Bill C-7 during the entire preceding House deliberations, and a few hours of debate on the evening of 11 March was the extent of the discussion the elected House had on the topic prior to committing to expand MAID for sole mental illness conditions through the sunset clause.

Interestingly it seemed some MPs who voted may not themselves have been clear on what they were voting on. For up to a week after the vote, a number of Liberal MPs (including a sitting cabinet minister at the time) indicated in boilerplate communication to constituents who raised concerns that they had "voted for a motion that specifies that persons whose sole underlying medical condition is a mental illness are not eligible for medical assistance in dying" and that the motion excluded MAID for mental illness, despite the amendment they voted for having done the opposite.

With the vote on the sunset clause successfully pushed through the House of Commons after a single evening of debate, Bill C-7 predetermined that psychiatric euthanasia would be implemented in March 2023. The only remaining question was how to implement this, which was a task handed over to a new federal panel on mental illness.

HOW DID WE GET TO THE "SUNSET CLAUSE"? COMPOUNDING FAILURES OF COMMISSION AND THE BROKEN ROAD TO EUTHANASIA EXPANSION – A KAFKAESQUE SPIRAL

To understand how the sunset clause was adopted in a political process after a few hours of debate in the House of Commons, it is important to understand the impact of input provided by the CPA. After the sudden release of the CPA position on MAiD and mental illness in March 2020, the leadership of the CPA refused to meaningfully engage members in their calls to revisit the controversial CPA position statement and its flawed development process, instead misleadingly claiming it had engaged members all along by citing different work done by the previous time-limited task force prior to 2018.

The CPA did form a new working group on MAiD to conduct a survey of members in 2020. This working group was co-chaired by the chair of the CPA Public Policy Committee and the chair of the CPA Professional Standards and Practice Committee, Alison Freeland, who was also the second co-author of the controversial position statement and is the current CPA board chair (the first author of the statement, Gary Chaimowitz, was the CPA president, 2022–23). The CPA survey prepared by the working group did not ask whether members agreed with the position statement (indeed, even at the time this chapter was written, over three years after its release of the position statement, the CPA has remarkably never once asked membership whether they agree with CPA's position statement on MAiD and mental illness). The survey provided no background context of the *Truchon* decision (it made no mention of *Truchon*), nor of the implications of the imminent pending removal of the RFND safeguard on potential mental illness MAiD applications, nor of other relevant issues such as Canada being the only jurisdiction allowing MAiD even if standard treatment options have not been tried or accessible. Of the ten questions on the survey dealing with MAiD, half were framed as asking whether respondents agreed with particular potential "safeguards" for MAiD for mental illness, leaving respondents the option of either disagreeing with the importance of safeguards or answering that they supported a safeguard in the narrow context of the question even if they disagreed with MAiD for sole mental illness conditions. There was concern that the results of such leading questions could be misinterpreted as a demonstration of support for MAiD for mental illness, even from members who disagreed with MAiD for sole mental illness. Other than the targeted checkbox responses, the survey allowed for a total of one thousand characters (not words) of additional narrative input. The president of the Ontario ACT and FACT Association critiqued the survey as being an example of Noam Chomsky's manufactured consent.[22]

The working group did conduct two virtual town halls for CPA members, one in English and one in French. These were structured and highly managed virtual events with facilitated discussion guided by the working group co-chairs, with the discussion and questions strictly limited to focus only on a subset of the same questions asked in the working group survey (and once again, absent from the guided discussion was any question or discussion of whether members agreed with the CPA position).

During this time, the CPA continued maintaining to members that its official position was that it had no position on MAiD for mental illness.[23] While claiming it had "not taken a position," in concurrent consultations with policy-makers the CPA repeatedly described the exclusion of MAiD for sole mental illness as "discriminatory," "inaccurate and stigmatizing," "vague, arbitrary and overbroad," and "unconstitutional," all while failing, or perhaps more accurately refusing, to issue any evidence-based cautions about the known suicide risks to vulnerable and marginalized populations suffering from mental illness that members were concerned about.[24] Others have written of how the claimed "false neutrality" of some medical associations regarding assisted suicide expansion is neither appropriate nor truly "neutral."[25] The CPA was similarly criticized for falsely professing so-called neutrality, including by Indigenous healers, elders, and leaders across Canada citing "alarm that, while claiming it is not taking a position, the Canadian Psychiatric Association clearly supports MAID for mental illness"[26] and the Canadian Association for Suicide Prevention calling out that "the CPA is clearly taking a position on the morality of MAID, despite stating otherwise."[27]

CPA membership attempted to initiate discussion of MAiD at the 2020 CPA AGM. Despite formal requests being submitted by several members well before the agenda and notice of the AGM had been sent to members, CPA leadership refused to allow submitted member proposals on MAiD from appearing or being discussed at the 2020 AGM. Instead the CPA relied on obscure federal regulations to justify denying discussion of the submitted proposals. The regulations used by then CPA chair Pamela Forsythe to deny these items from appearing on the agenda are not directly in CPA bylaws or operating policy; they appear in "regulation 66" related to the Canada Not-for-Profit Corporations Act (CNFPA).[28] Regulation 66 had likely never been read by most, or any, CPA members. While the CPA cited these regulations in refusing to allow discussion of MAiD on the AGM agenda, nothing in these regulations prohibited the CPA from allowing these proposals or discussion of MAiD at the 2020 AGM, rather they provided a way for CPA to deny allowing this discussion if leadership wished. And in the new COVID world of virtual meetings, the CPA conducted another highly managed Zoom meeting with no opportunity for members to discuss these proposals, nor were members able to add any items to the agenda during the AGM meeting itself.

NON-EXPERT/EVIDENCE-FREE CONTRIBUTIONS BY MEDICAL BODIES CHARGED WITH PROVIDING EXPERT EVIDENCE

Having successfully blocked members from raising proposals to revisit the 2020 position statement, the CPA's input to the 2020–21 Senate consultations continued to be informed by the controversial statement. Rather than providing evidence-based input, the CPA continued to claim it would be discriminatory not to provide MAiD for mental illness while failing to issue any evidence-based cautions.[29] As members had anticipated and cautioned would be the case over a year before, the public and policy-makers naturally took it that the CPA unequivocally supported expanding MAiD for sole mental illness conditions.[30]

When specifically asked for medical expert input at Senate consultations in November 2020, the CPA explicitly abdicated its role in providing expert clinical input. When asked whether the CPA agreed with other experts that more research was needed into mental disorders prior to providing MAiD for mental illness, then CPA president Grainne Neilson replied: "I guess that is a legislative decision."[31]

Similarly side-stepping evidence-based recommendations, the Quebec psychiatrist association that supported psychiatric euthanasia openly articulated that its support for psychiatric euthanasia was not based on science. When responding to concerns raised in Senate hearings about the lack of evidence regarding the impact of psychiatric euthanasia, the Association des médecins psychiatres du Québec (AMPQ) president Karine Igartua declined to offer evidence-based guidance and instead maintained that "this is not a data-driven question, this is an ethical question."[32] This was consistent with a prior AMPQ report that acknowledged that irremediability of patients receiving MAiD for mental illness could not accurately be predicted and suggested that rather than following standards or evidence, in guessing whether a mental illness was irremediable and fulfilled criteria for purposes of psychiatric euthanasia, assessors would instead "have to answer this ethical question each and every time they evaluate a request."[33] Suicidology researchers and experts raised alarms about the lack of evidence inherent in these consultations, describing such input as "nonsensical gibberish."[34]

Concurrently, despite the longstanding known association between various mental illnesses and increased risk of suicide, in the entire year leading to the final version of Bill C-7 and adoption of the sunset clause, the CPA never once mentioned the importance of suicide prevention in any of its written or oral submissions, never once referenced suicide, suicidality, or mental illness–related suicide risk, and indeed never used any variation of any word related to suicide in its submissions on public consultations on mental illness and death-seeking. The CPA also never mentioned nor commented on known data relevant to psychiatric euthanasia and mental illness that others were raising alarms about, such as the 2:1 female-to-male gender imbalance of those receiving psychiatric euthanasia in the few European countries allowing it or the high prevalence of loneliness and unresolved social suffering of those receiving psychiatric euthanasia. Most would consider this a clear failure to provide the evidence-based expertise expected of a national medical body.

This inexplicable omission bears repeating – during consultations on death and mental illness, Canada's national psychiatric association failed to issue a single caution about suicidal individuals receiving psychiatric euthanasia, despite well-established data (and repeatedly expressed member concerns) regarding risks of exposing the most marginalized suffering from life distress to premature death in those situations. If a respirologist association failed to once mention smoking as a risk factor for lung disease in public policy consultations on lung health, one imagines that association would at least be criticized for being willfully blind, if not negligent. If that respirologist association actively refused to mention smoking as a risk factor even in the face of criticism and concern raised by its own members, most would likely question the integrity and validity of that association's input.

"LIES, DAMNED LIES, AND STATISTICS"

Unknown to CPA members at the time, CPA chair Pamela Forsythe wrote an unusual follow-up letter to the Senate committee in February 2021.[35] The purpose of the letter was to provide selective partial results to a single question of the CPA working group's survey. This was prior to CPA members themselves being informed of any results from their own survey. In presenting partial results to a single question, the CPA chair suggested that "there appears to have been a shift in psychiatrists' perspectives on access to MAiD solely for mental illness," citing that "41 [per cent] of member survey respondents" in the 2020 survey agreed or strongly agreed with MAiD for mental illness, while 39 per cent disagreed or strongly disagreed, with 20 per cent uncertain, compared to 54 per cent who supported the exclusion of MAiD for mental illness in an earlier 2016/2017 survey, with 27 per cent not supporting it and 20 per cent unsure.

Interestingly, when the survey results were later made available to members, it became clear just how selective the above reporting and interpretation had been. While the CPA chair reported "41 [per cent] of member survey respondents" agreed with MAiD for mental illness, versus 39 per cent who did not, to support the CPA's contention that there had been "a shift in psychiatrists' perspective," she failed to mention that in the same question in the survey only 35 per cent of non-members agreed with MAiD for mental illness, versus 47 per cent who did not. Given that nearly 40 per cent of respondents were non-members, this is a significant omission. In addition to neglecting to mention that a much larger percentage of non-members did not agree with MAiD for sole mental illness, the views of these respondents were also omitted in the "41 per cent agreeing" versus "39 per cent disagreeing" comment by the chair, which implied that a plurality agreed with MAiD for mental illness by referencing only the member results. When factoring in all respondents (i.e., combined member plus non-member results), the results actually suggest a plurality of respondents continued to disagree with MAiD for sole mental illness (with 41 per cent disagreeing to 38 per cent agreeing), information that was not provided by the chair in her selective presentation of results.

Additionally, in reporting results of questions rated on a Likert scale of 1 to 5, result ratings across the full scale are often transparently provided. Unlike the Ontario Medical Association (OMA) survey mentioned below, which transparently provided the full results of ratings along the Likert scale used, the CPA provided only summed responses collapsing the "agree" and "strongly agree," and the "disagree" and "strongly disagree" categories. While presenting such summed responses does have value, it obscures differences in strengths of response, which can sometimes be revealing. For example, in the OMA survey discussed below, most psychiatrists were concerned about and opposed to expanding MAiD for mental illness, and when strengths of response were factored in the opposition was even stronger.

After releasing its survey results, the CPA was asked to provide the disaggregated results to these Likert scale questions so such strength of view comparisons could be transparently understood. CPA leadership refused to provide those results even to members who participated in the survey.

POLITICAL PROCESS OF EUTHANASIA EXPANSION

As a past president of the Canadian Psychiatric Association (CPA), I feel qualified to say that the entrusted and expected due diligence of our medical expert bodies to provide unbiased medical evidence-based input to critical public health consultations on Canada's MAiD expansion for sole mental illness was not followed.

In terms of due diligence in the legal and political process, despite many legal scholars raising concerns about the basis of the *Truchon* decision that overturned the initial reasonably foreseeable death safeguard and believing that an appeal was warranted, the Trudeau government decided to not challenge the lower court ruling in a higher court.[36] The failure of the government to test the ruling made by a single Quebec judge on a matter of such national import left the country's policy on MAiD expansion to be driven by an untested lower court decision, despite that ruling not being binding on other courts outside Quebec. Expansionists supporting psychiatric euthanasia repeatedly cited "court-tested evidence" to support their expansion advocacy, yet not a single case referenced in *Carter* or

Truchon involved mental illness. Despite this, many expansion activists who lauded the government's decision not to appeal *Truchon* went as far as claiming that the courts had already settled the question of MAiD for mental illness.[37] For example, prominent legal scholar and MAiD expansion promoter Professor Jocelyn Downie testified in public hearings that "the Minister of Justice has repeatedly said the government needs more time – I assume with respect to the question of how to implement MAID MD-SUMC [i.e., MAID for a mental disorder as the sole underlying medical condition] rather than whether, as the whether question has already been answered by the courts in *Carter* and *Truchon*."[38]

Many other experts, myself included, cautioned strongly about the inability to predict irremediability in mental illnesses, the lack of evidence of being able to distinguish suicidality from psychiatric MAiD requests, and the evidence showing how psychiatric euthanasia placed those most marginalized and suffering from life distress at risk of premature death.[39] Demonstrating the lack of evidence guiding policy, even the expansionist AMPQ that rejected the need for data in 2020 Senate hearings explicitly acknowledged that mental illnesses could not scientifically be predicted to be irremediable in any evidence-based way. While advocating for psychiatric euthanasia, the AMPQ acknowledged that "it is possible that a person who has recourse to MAiD – regardless of his condition – could have regained the desire to live at some point in the future."[40] The fundamental legislative safeguard and public premise in Canada has been that MAiD is provided for irremediable medical conditions. The open acknowledgement that mental illness irremediability cannot be scientifically predicted despite this being the ostensible pretense for MAiD and the suggestion, as mentioned earlier in this chapter, that this should instead be an "ethical" decision based on the subjective values of assessors made under the guise of an expert medical assessment reveals the ideological basis of such positions.

In the end, in the absence of any evidence-based or expert concerns being raised by key psychiatric associations at the time, the Senate committee was able to forward a recommendation that MAiD for sole mental illness conditions should be provided after a temporary sunset clause period. The sunset clause was proposed by a psychiatrist senator, Senator Stan Kutcher, who quoted CPA and AMPQ consultations to support the introduction of MAiD for mental illness.[41] As detailed above, in March 2021, after one evening of debate in the House of Commons, the government amended Bill

C-7 and pushed through the sunset clause to ensure that psychiatric euthanasia would be provided by March 2023.

The failure of expert bodies to provide scientific input or evidence-based cautions regarding mental illness–related suicidality risks undermined the integrity of much of the medical input to the 2020–21 Senate consultations. To introduce a sleeping pill, or any other medication in Canada, requires a transparent and deliberative process.[42] The push to allow psychiatric euthanasia was based on less scientific evidence than that required to introduce a sleeping pill in Canada. With no cases involving mental illness tested in the *Carter* or *Truchon* rulings, the rulings driving Canada's MAiD policies, many legal scholars have argued that there also was no legal mandate requiring the introduction of psychiatric euthanasia.[43]

When the Senate recommended, and the government subsequently adopted, the sunset clause to preordain psychiatric euthanasia by 2023, this decision was built on a house of cards.

ONGOING CONCERNS FOLLOWING BILL C-7'S PASSAGE

Given the lack of nuance and lack of relevant context provided in recent psychiatrist surveys (for example, no context provided in the 2020 CPA survey regarding the implications of the *Truchon* decision for MAiD applications based on sole mental illness conditions), the Ontario Medical Association (OMA) Section on Psychiatry conducted a survey of Ontario psychiatrists in the summer of 2021 after the passage of the sunset clause. (In disclosure, I sit on the OMA Section on Psychiatry executive. The survey was developed and approved by the entire executive.) Recognizing the range of views on the issue, the section attempted to use wording that was as neutral as possible and to also provide relevant background context, including links to arguments both supporting and cautioning about psychiatric euthanasia.

Among other findings, the OMA survey found that most Ontario psychiatrists are not conscientious objectors to MAiD in general, with 86 per cent of respondents agreeing that MAiD should be an option in some situations.[44] However, by a two-to-one margin, respondents did not believe MAiD should be provided for sole mental illness conditions, with 56 per cent opposed and 26 per cent supporting psychiatric euthanasia and 15 per cent unsure (on strength of views End of Range [EOR] responses [i.e., comparing those with the strongest views, those who "strongly oppose" versus those who "strongly support"], the degree of opposition was even stronger, with a three-to-one margin of 36 per cent strongly opposing to 12 per cent strongly supporting). When asked about whether they agreed with "the position that patients with a psychiatric illness should have available the same options regarding MAiD as available to all patients, without issues of irremediability in mental illness having been examined" (which was essentially the position the CPA had taken), 63 per cent disagreed while 23 per cent agreed (with strength of views responses being stronger, a four-to-one-margin with 41 per cent strongly opposed to 9 per cent strongly supporting). By a three-to-one margin, respondents did not support the sunset clause, with 68 per cent believing there should be further review to determine whether MAiD for sole mental illness conditions should be implemented prior to committing to allowing it, and only 23 per cent believing further review was not needed (on strength of views, nearly five to one wanted further review, with 48 per cent strongly believing further review was necessary versus 10 per cent strongly believing it was not).

These survey results from Ontario, which comprises the largest group of psychiatrists in the country, were forwarded to the CPA in response to CPA requested input and consultations. CPA leadership, which still had never asked membership whether they agreed with the March 2020 CPA position, nor asked membership whether they agreed with the sunset clause of Bill C-7, did not act on the results. To the contrary, the CPA president subsequently denied having access to the results shortly before the November 2021 CPA AGM (despite the results having been sent on two different occasions to the CPA working group chairs and to the president directly), and during the 2021 AGM the CPA chair actively prevented another CPA member from mentioning the OMA survey results, citing them as being "irrelevant" to the discussion at hand.

CROSSING THE (FIRST) RUBICON: BEYOND ANY PRETENSE OF CONTRIBUTING EVIDENCE

Shortly before the November 2021 CPA AGM took place, CPA leadership released a revised position statement on MAiD and mental illness. The revised 2021 position failed to address any of the concerns raised in the preceding year and a half and continued to advocate an ideological position while failing to address the issue of predicting irremediability of mental illnesses; still failed to mention mental illness–related suicide risk, suicidality, or suicide prevention; and still failed to issue a single caution about marginalized populations with mental illness being safeguarded against receiving death by MAID for life suffering.

Advocacy groups across Canada were dismayed by these ongoing failings:

- Indigenous leaders expressed "shock that [the CPA] November 2021 Position Statement Update still does not address the phenomenon of suicide contagion and the importance of suicide prevention, or the risks of suicide to marginalized populations," and decried that CPA's position "will adversely impact Indigenous populations in Canada as your organizations actual policy documents and Position Statements provide recommendations that continue policies of privilege."[45]
- The Council of Canadians with Disabilities stated that CPA's position "does not address the negative social determinants of health (trauma, poverty, lack of housing, disability-related supports and other social supports) and how they impact on people with disabilities, including mental health disabilities, seeking MAID" and "does not address suicidality and suicide prevention" and considered this "a serious and dangerous flaw," and criticized CPA's position as having "serious gaps because it has not attended adequately to the influence of ableism on decisions to seek MAID by people with disabilities."[46]
- The Ontario Association for ACT & FACT (OAAF) described CPA leadership's updated position statement as representing "a serious and appalling abrogation of moral and clinical leadership" and characterized CPA leadership's support for Bill C-7 as "suicide facilitation."[47]
- Dignity Denied cited "profound concern, indeed alarm even, by the approach articulated on *Medical Aid in Dying by the Canadian Psychiatric Association (CPA)* in its Position Statement," and raised concerns about "a complete omission of intersectionality and in particular how racism and poverty intersect and impact the 'choices' one may have and the treatment someone receives and has access to in Canada."[48]
- Legal experts wrote to the CPA describing the updated position as "even more problematic" than the earlier 2020 statement. They expressed concern that the CPA position "appears to

embrace a position that undermines the professional-ethical-care commitment of the psychiatric community to Canadians," felt that "the CPA is endorsing a fundamental abandonment of professional practice standards," and suggested that the "CPA statement as it currently stands does exactly the opposite of what the CPA suggests in its mission statement."[49]

These diverse voices echoed concerns raised by CPA members over the preceding year and a half, yet the CPA leadership still did not address these concerns.

On 24 November 2021, the day before the CPA AGM, the then CPA president Grainne Neilson (who was a co-author of the initial 2020 and the revised 2021 CPA position statements) presented on MAiD at McMaster University Department of Psychiatry and Behavioural Neurosciences Grand Rounds.[50] While discussing what Canadian psychiatrists thought about MAiD, she stated "now I know there was a survey done of Ontario psychiatrists a few months ago that was conducted by the OMA and I'm sorry but I don't have access to those results," and went on to present the results of the previous 2020 CPA survey that the president of the Ontario Association for ACT & FACT had described as "manufactured consent."

More surprising than citing lack of access to the Ontario psychiatrist survey results, despite them having been previously sent to the CPA and CPA president directly, was the seeming characterization denying the existence of any concerns regarding the practice of psychiatric euthanasia in the few European countries allowing it. After discussing challenges assessing capacity in MAiD assessments, potential concerns about "differentiating suicidal ideation that needs psychiatric intervention from that which would make a person eligible for MAID," and potential concerns about the impact of mental disorders on decision-making, President Neilson commented that "it is interesting though to note that [in] jurisdictions where MAID is available for mental illness, they don't report difficulties in making these clinical judgements, so that may be our experience going forward." The suggestion by the CPA president that we might expect Canada's experience to be non-problematic since "they don't report difficulties in making these clinical judgements" in other jurisdictions was hard to reconcile with the fact that evidence-based concerns regarding challenges in other jurisdictions had been raised repeatedly, including by members communicating this evidence directly to the CPA.

Regardless of whether one agrees or disagrees, one would expect at the least an acknowledgement of the concerns about practices in other jurisdictions documented in peer-reviewed literature, rather than denial that such concerns existed as Canada was moving to expand MAiD policies.

NOVEMBER 2021 CPA AGM – KAFKA'S SPIRAL DEEPENS

Having been denied the chance to discuss MAiD at the 2020 CPA AGM, in advance of the 2021 AGM several CPA members made sure to forward proposals on MAiD that CPA leadership could not refuse to hear based on regulation 66.

The key proposal was structured to ensure any further CPA policy guidance on MAiD would be evidence-based and to ensure suitable safeguards were in place to prevent vulnerable or marginalized patients from getting MAiD due to psychosocial stressors or lack of access to care. The relevant member proposal raised at the 25 November 2021 AGM was as follows:

> Given that MAID is based on the premise of having an irremediable medical condition, that any CPA policy on MAID explicitly include guidance on:
>
> i *the need for evidence and standards* regarding whether or not mental illnesses can reliably and prospectively be determined to be irremediable medical conditions, prior to any potential consideration of MAID being provided for sole psychiatric conditions;
>
> ii the need for *appropriate treatments* having been tried, *and supports and services* being in place, *to ensure that* MAID *is not requested as a means to escape social exclusion, nor as a response to psychosocial stressors or a dearth of appropriate clinical and community supports.*

Remarkably to many, CPA leadership, including incoming CPA president Doug Urness, spoke against this proposal. At another time during the MAiD discussions, the incoming CPA chair Alison Freeland (who co-authored both the 2020 and revised 2021 CPA position statements) cut off a speaker (Kathy Margittai, a CPA member and at the time president of the Ontario district branch of the

American Psychiatric Association) to advise Dr Margittai that her attempt to provide information on the OMA Ontario psychiatrist survey was irrelevant, and that she would not allow that information to be presented.

Following the opposition of CPA leadership (which includes over fifteen voting board members), the vote on the above proposal was deadlocked, forty-one for and forty-one against, and the motion failed to pass. Problems with the restrictive method of voting during the virtual meeting also emerged, with at least one CPA member (who was president of a provincial psychiatry organization at the time) who wanted to vote "yes" advising the CPA prior to the vote that the CPA's virtual meeting was preventing him from casting a vote, with no follow-up or resolution, hence that member's vote was never counted.

Canada has over four thousand psychiatrists, with less than two thousand being CPA members at the time. After nearly two years of controversy and attempts to bring more nuanced and evidence-guided policy to the CPA's position on MAiD, CPA leadership spoke openly against the need for evidence, standards, and safeguards that most physicians would take for granted as necessary and that most in the public would trust their medical experts to value and advocate for. Based on less than 1 per cent of Canadian psychiatrists voting against this member proposal at the 2021 CPA AGM, Canada's national psychiatric association formally rejected "the need for evidence and standards" and rejected the need for safeguards to ensure "appropriate treatments having been tried" to avoid the unnecessary deaths of those marginalized by a life of suffering.

Several months after the November 2021 AGM, and over a year after the sunset clause to allow psychiatric euthanasia was passed with no objections from the CPA, on 17 March 2022, the CPA working group on MAiD released a "discussion paper" that contained more fulsome discussion of various issues.[51] While presenting a range of views, this after-the-fact discussion paper was just that, a compilation of views – it did not set or change organizational policy. By this time, the CPA had already formally rejected the member proposal that its MAiD policies should be guided by evidence and standards and rejected that its policies should ensure safeguards against the marginalized and vulnerable receiving MAiD due to lack of access to treatments or a dearth of social supports. The timing of the release of the discussion paper was also curious, since the paper indicated it had been approved by the CPA board on 8 June 2021. It is unclear why a full nine months passed before the discussion paper was publicly released, eliminating opportunity for the range of member views to be considered as relevant policy consultations were afoot (similarly, results to the aforementioned CPA member survey were released nearly half a year after the survey, on 18 March 2021, the day after Bill C-7 received royal assent ... naturally precluding any meaningful analysis of member survey results from informing Bill C-7 deliberations).

CROSSING THE (SECOND) RUBICON: BEYOND ANY PRETENSE OF STANDARDS

With the passage of the sunset clause in Bill C-7, the Liberal government appointed a select federal panel on MAiD and mental illness, chaired by a known psychiatric euthanasia expansion advocate (which the panel's ethicist, who eventually resigned, cited as a primary "process-related challenge" with the panel's "governance and work").[52] The panel also included two members of the CPA working group on MAiD, both who had also publicly advocated for psychiatric euthanasia.

Of note, the panel was not tasked with reviewing whether psychiatric euthanasia should be provided, since that was considered a *fait accompli* following the passage of the sunset clause. The panel's mandate was to develop protocols and safeguards for implementing MAiD for mental illness. The panel report tabled in May 2022 provided little specific guidance in this regard.[53] Instead of providing standards, the panel concluded "it is not possible to provide fixed rules for how many treatment attempts, how many kinds of treatments, and over what period of time" treatment should have been tried prior to providing death for mental illness and called for assessors to make case-by-case determinations. This was similar to the earlier proposal in the AMPQ report that determinations of eligibility criteria should be individual "ethical" decisions by assessors in each case (of note, the same federal panel chair, Mona Gupta, also co-authored both the expansionist 2021 AMPQ report and the 2020 Halifax Group report). This again raised concern among those calling for evidence-based policy that such lack of standards would open the door to arbitrary assessments based on individual assessor's personal ideologies rather than scientific evidence or standards.

As previously discussed, the earlier AMPQ report calling for psychiatric euthanasia acknowledged that people who could still improve would have access to MAiD. The new federal panel went further and explicitly acknowledged that *suicidal* people could receive MAiD, stating that "society is making an ethical choice to enable certain people to receive MAID on a case-by-case basis regardless of whether MAID and suicide are considered to be distinct or not." Despite acknowledging that there may be no distinction between suicide and psychiatric MAiD, and despite Canada being the only country in the world allowing MAiD without requiring past access or attempts at treatment, the panel concluded that psychiatric euthanasia could be provided "without adding new legislative safeguards."

Two members of the initial twelve-person panel resigned, including the panel's health care ethicist mentioned above, who wrote that he could not sign off on the report "in good conscience." These resigning members cited flaws in the process and recommendations, including concerns about "the chair being a nationally recognized, strong advocate" for the expansion of MAiD for mental illness, the "lack of reporting transparency regarding dissenting opinions or views," and an unwillingness of panel members "to put forward any serious safeguards that would require the law to change."[54]

In light of the ongoing concerns about the process and evidence-free content shaping Canada's euthanasia expansion, one might have expected the government to slow down and reconsider its expansionist policies. Concerns about those who are not dying but who are disabled and marginalized seeking and getting euthanasia to end a life of suffering had already started appearing in the media, with podcasts of Canadians saying, "I die when I run out of money"[55] and international headlines asking, "Why is Canada euthanizing the poor?"[56] Yet the federal government remained intent on maintaining Canada's expansionist course.

In May 2022, in the face of concerns raised about "the vulnerable falling through the cracks and serious abuses under the MAID regime," Prime Minister Justin Trudeau defended the country's MAiD expansion in the House of Commons.[57] Of concern to many involved in suicide prevention, the normalization of death as a treatment for life suffering had occurred at an alarming pace.[58] Minister of justice David Lametti, responsible for implementing Canada's MAiD expansion, suggested it was humane to help ambivalent people suffering from mental illness to decide to die, saying that MAiD "provides a more humane way for [people with mental illness] to make a decision" about dying when "for physical reasons and possibly mental reasons, [they] can't make that choice themselves to do it themselves."⁵⁹ And shockingly to many, MAiD providers themselves acknowledged to each other, even if not to the public, the range of unmet social needs that fuelled many expanded euthanasia requests.⁶⁰ And through all of this, senior policy-makers aiming to push through further MAiD expansion remained silent about the unvoiced systemic cost savings that providing MAiD to non-dying Canadians could accrue, compared to the costs of prolonged care and community living, and the obvious potential or perceived conflicts of interest arising from such budgetary implications.

At some point through this process, after years of concerns being repeatedly raised but not impacting processes or decisions of key players at the highest levels, one must be reminded of the adage that every system is perfectly designed to get the results it gets (and distasteful as it may be to say, perhaps of another adage: follow the money).

A FIRST DELAY

Canada's 2021 MAiD expansion through Bill C-7, along with passage of the sunset clause requiring the March 2023 introduction of MAiD for sole mental illness conditions, took place while many were preoccupied with adjusting to life during an emerging global pandemic. Most Canadians continued to picture MAiD as something provided to dying individuals to help relieve their end-of-life suffering. Through 2021 and 2022, with growing public awareness, concerns about the planned March 2023 expansion to mental illness increasingly emerged.

A reconstituted Expert Advisory Group (EAG) on MAiD, comprised of well over a dozen experts including those with lived experience and Indigenous leaders, banded together again in 2022 and submitted a brief to the Special Joint Committee on MAiD succinctly highlighting several evidence-based concerns.⁶¹ There was also increasing public discussion of the flawed processes that have led to Canada's MAiD expansion.⁶²

Following two years of attempting to get our current national association, the CPA, to advocate for evidence-based policies, many of us realized that the current national association may be incapable of advocating for the standards, evidence, and safeguards that would be expected of a national medical body. In that realization came awareness of the need to carve a different path forward. This process highlighted the importance of a national expert voice providing evidence-informed medical input with transparency and responsiveness to diverse views. While a daunting challenge, several colleagues across the country began working on establishing a modernized society, the Society of Canadian Psychiatry (SocPsych), to engage members and inform national policy discussions on mental health in ways respecting our entrusted role as medical experts.

While it will formally launch in 2025, the initial act of SocPsych founders was to issue a call to action on 10 November 2022, calling on mental health and policy leaders across the country to support a pause to Canada's planned March 2023 expansion to psychiatric euthanasia, pending proper evidence-based review and recommendations.[63] The SocPsych call was formally endorsed by the Canadian Association for Suicide Prevention (CASP), the Ontario Psychiatric Association, the Ontario District Branch of the American Psychiatric Association, and the Western District Branch of the American Psychiatric Association and was signed by over two hundred individual psychiatrists across the country. CASP additionally issued its own statement on psychiatric MAiD expansion.[64] On 1 December 2022, the Association of Chairs of Psychiatry in Canada, the chairs representing the seventeen academic departments of psychiatry across the country, joined in calling for a delay and issued a statement that more time is needed to develop standards of care before considering MAiD for mental illness.[65]

In response to mounting public pressure, on 15 December 2022, the federal government announced it would delay the planned March 2023 MAiD for mental illness implementation, though it maintained it was still committed to expansion,[66] and in January 2023 it announced that its planned implementation of MAiD for mental illness would be delayed for one year until March 2024. Federal panel chair Mona Gupta (whose committee failed to provide any specific guidelines for determining incurability) and other expansion activists dismissed widespread concerns about the absence of any standards and objected to the delay.[67] Instead, the panel chair continued providing non-specific reassurances that we would have been prepared in three months to assist with suicides for mental illness, wrongly claiming that allowing MAiD for mental illness had "already been litigated" (again, *Carter* and *Truchon* did not involve mental illness) and suggesting that the push for pause reflected ideology rather than the obvious absence of any common sense evidence-based standards. The CPA continued to be publicly supportive of MAiD for mental illness expansion, with CPA president Gary Chaimowitz suggesting that in the CPA's view, existing safeguards sufficiently "protect all vulnerable Canadians" and continuing to claim it "would be discriminatory" to have safeguards specific to psychiatric euthanasia.[68] Prominent expansion activist politicians continued providing evidence-free reassurances that psychiatrists already knew how to, somehow, separate suicidality from psychiatric euthanasia requests, with Senator Stan Kutcher telling a room full of psychiatrists at the Atlantic Provinces Psychiatric Association conference that "my goodness colleagues this is a core competency at the Royal College standards. If a psychiatrist can't assess suicidal intent, you're telling me that you don't have a core competency?"[69]

YET ANOTHER DELAY

Necessary and challenging discussions have been increasingly taking place in media and television,[70] with a range of diverse editorials and columns expressing concerns about Canada's MAiD expansion.[71] Some expansion activists who opposed the one-year delay characterized the pressure leading to pause as a "massive campaign" that has "been effective at creating a sense of public concern and expert concern about this," rather than viewing this increased public awareness and discourse as reflecting legitimate concerns on this complex topic.[72] However, many continued to raise cautions about the still arbitrary date of March 2024 set by the government for the introduction of MAiD for sole mental illness conditions, given that evidence continued to demonstrate the lack of ability to predict irremediability of mental illnesses, the inability to distinguish suicidality from psychiatric MAiD requests, and the continued risk posed in particular to marginalized Canadians.[73] The Society of Canadian Psychiatry issued a brief outlining key evidence and cautions to parliamentarians on 15 October 2023, in advance of a vote on the private member's Bill C-314 that would have paused the planned March 2024 expansion of MAiD for mental illness.[74] Public and media awareness of concerns regarding expansion continued to build, with several major newspaper editorials cautioning against further expansion.[75] While the government continued to oppose Bill C-314, and that vote narrowly failed, it showed increased concern amongst parliamentarians across multiple party lines, and following the vote the government agreed to establish a new Special Joint Parliamentary Committee to review the "state of readiness" for the planned March 2024 implementation of MAiD for mental illness.

During these debates some psychiatrists still advocated for expanding MAiD to sole mental illness;[76] however, more and increasing numbers of psychiatrists continued raising alarm bells about the dangers of the planned expansion.[77] Along with several others, I testified to the Special Joint Committee about the continued lack of evidence and lack of readiness.[78] The CPA continued to frame it as discrimination to not provide MAiD for sole mental illness, even as CPA chair Alison Freeland reluctantly acknowledged that the CPA could not assure that "all the readiness was there."[79] The hearings contained some remarkable moments of expansion activists dismissing concerns about evidence, professing that evidence existed where it did not or suggesting that providing MAiD for mental illness was like any other "innovative" new treatment in psychiatry. Expert panel chair and co-author of the Health Canada *Model Practice Standard* Mona Gupta dismissed concerns about the gender gap in European data showing twice as many woman as men getting MAiD for mental illness, explicitly stating that this gender gap "doesn't concern" her since nobody really "knows what it means."[80] Chair of the Canadian Association of MAiD Assessors and Providers (CAMAP) group that developed the MAiD curriculum, Gordon Gubitz, professed to be able to distinguish suicidality from motivations for psychiatric MAiD requests, testifying "Is the patient suicidal or do they actually have a reason to wish to die, which is not the same thing?"[81] CPA chair Alison Freeland suggested providing assisted suicide for mental illness was like any other "new practice(s)" like ketamine, psilocybin treatment, or transcranial magnetic stimulation, and that psychiatric euthanasia reflected "active, new practices and innovative aspects of psychiatric treatment and care," which initially have a "limited number of people who have expertise in them."[82] While increasing numbers of experts publicly raised evidence-based cautions about risks to vulnerable and marginalized patients posed by MAiD expansion, the CPA continued to provide reassurances without evidence, with past president Gary Chaimowitz claiming that even with widespread lack of access to care, psychiatric MAiD would not be "an avenue" for those seeking suicide.[83]

In early 2024, the Special Joint Committee released its report and recommendations. In the end the committee concluded that Canada was not ready to expand MAiD to mental illness and recommended an indefinite pause be put on this potential expansion.[84] In reaching its conclusions the committee cited precisely the cautions many of us had been raising alarm bells about, specifically the inability to predict irremediability in mental illness, the inability to distinguish suicidality due to mental illness from other motivations leading to psychiatric euthanasia requests, and the risks the planned expansions would have brought to marginalized populations in particular. A subset of senators, who between them met with Dying With Dignity Canada nearly a dozen times between October 2023 and January 2024, issued a dissenting opinion in the report.[85] Though citing their medical expertise to justify their objections, they failed to address any of the preceding three issues that led to the majority committee's conclusions. Of note, these dissenting senators used their national platform to denounce me, writing that my testimony pointing out the lack of evidence informing CAMAP's training module on suicidality and mental illness "may have misled" the parliamentary committee, and that my testimony "will have a profound and negative consequence for how medical education is developed, accredited, and delivered in Canada."

In response to the Special Joint Committee report, the government indicated it would delay implementation of MAiD for mental illness by another three years, until March 2027.

At this time, evidence continues to build regarding risks that Canada's existing MAiD laws, even without further expansion to mental illness, pose to vulnerable and marginalized Canadians. At a recent CAMAP conference, the Ontario chief coroner indicated that "individuals whose deaths were track 2 were much more likely to live in neighbourhoods with higher levels of residential instability, higher material deprivation, and greater dependency than those in track 1."[86] Given that the potential further expansion to mental illness would be in 2027, after the next election, and given that concerns about social suffering and lack of access to care taking the lives of some Canadians through MAiD is already garnering increased international scrutiny, it is unclear whether the government's plans to expand MAiD to mental illness will actually take place in 2027 or whether there will be a third "delay."[87] One thing is clear: it is highly unusual, and unprecedented, for a government to twice be at the brink of implementing very public major policy changes and to twice reverse course at the last minute. This reflects the clear process flaws followed in planning those policies, and hopefully future policy-makers do not make the same mistakes.

CONCLUSION AND MOVING FORWARD

For many, the Rubicon has been crossed. As Maya Angelou said, "When people show you who they are, believe them."

Many key policy-makers and medical bodies have repeatedly shown that their advocacy for psychiatric euthanasia is based on ideology under the guise of medical expertise and have actively dismissed or disregarded evidence in policy formation. In doing so, as discussed in other chapters in this book, the ideological policies that MAiD expansionists have pushed in Canada have placed the non-dying disabled and those with mental illness who are most marginalized and facing social suffering, including those enduring sexism, racism, ageism, and ableism, at risk of premature deaths. These entirely avoidable deaths would be based on arbitrary assessments of individual assessors, with no standards and no evidence, reinforcing the hopelessness of patients during periods of resolvable despair by wrongly making unsupportable claims predicting "irremediability" of mental illness. In essence, the assessor would become an accomplice to the very illness their patient was suffering from.

As a past president of the CPA, it particularly pains me that our country has gotten to this point abetted by the conspicuous absence of evidence-based input from our entrusted expert psychiatric bodies. If a psychiatry resident were to neglect asking about suicidality on their Royal College fellowship certification exams, they would likely fail their exam. If an emergency room psychiatrist were to neglect asking about suicidality in a depressed patient in crisis who then took their own life, they might well face medico-legal consequences. The CPA's failure to caution about or mention mental illness–related suicide risk, known evidence about psychiatric euthanasia, or the need for suicide prevention while advocating that those with a psychiatric illness should have "the same options regarding MAID as available to all patients" during the crucial 2020–21 consultations on death and mental illness that led to Bill C-7's sunset clause is inexplicable and shamefully casts an indelible stain on my former association.

The sunset clause preordaining that psychiatric euthanasia would be provided by 2023 (now extended to 2027) was based on these and other flawed consultations and the politicized process that followed. If in the future family members are unhappy, believing a loved one was provided wrongful death by MAiD for a mental illness that an assessor "ethically" assessed as irremediable despite medical evidence to date informing the medical community that such predictions cannot responsibly or accurately be made and the lack of evidence that assessors can distinguish suicidality from psychiatric MAiD requests, what responsibility is borne by those groups who were entrusted with a public obligation to provide medical expert input but failed to once mention key evidence-based cautions at the crucial time when Canada's MAiD expansion policies were being formed?

On the positive side, while public awareness and coverage of Canada's euthanasia expansion policies was initially overshadowed by the ongoing global COVID-19 pandemic and briefly by two federal elections (2019 and 2021, each resulting in similar Liberal minority governments), recent increased coverage is finally leading to greater public awareness of the processes behind, and implications of, Canada's rapid expansionist policies and the risks inherent in having only the most zealous expansion advocates driving policy change.

The fall, and failing, of duty of our existing expert groups has been disturbing, illuminating, and motivating. At this time, I am unable to provide further updates on CPA activities as I am no longer a member. However, I and increasing numbers of colleagues are realizing that to ensure evidence and expected professional due diligence is brought to bear on this complex topic, we cannot rely on the echo chamber that has developed around a minority currently contributing ideological views under the guise of expert leadership. Within Canada, the initially obscured risks and lack of evidence fuelling expansion activism are increasingly being recognized. As international attention is brought to bear, other jurisdictions are rightly seeing how Canada, rather than being a bright beacon for progressive change, is actually enacting regressive policies of privilege that sacrifice our most marginalized on the altar of increased privileged autonomy for a few. Many in other jurisdictions contemplating expansion of assisted suicide laws are rightly viewing Canada's example as a cautionary tale, which offers some solace that others may learn from Canada's example. Perhaps the increased public awareness and continued pressure demanding evidence-informed policies and meaningful safeguards will bear further fruit and trigger reconsideration of the new arbitrary 2027 date set for further MAiD expansion in Canada.[88]

The situation may be not yet irremediable.

NOTES

1 *Carter v. Canada* (Attorney General), 2015 SCC 5, [2015] 1 SCR 331.
2 Sonu Gaind, "Preliminary Remarks on Physician-Assisted Death: Presented to the External Panel on Options for a Legislative Response to *Carter v. Canada*," Canadian Psychiatric Association, 2015, https://www.cpa-apc.org/wp-content/uploads/External-Panel-Submission-Nov-2015-FIN-Web1.pdf; Provincial-Territorial Expert Advisory Group on Physician-Assisted Dying, *Final Report*, November 2015, 30, https://novascotia.ca/dhw/publications/Provincial-Territorial-Expert-Advisory-

Group-on-Physician-Assisted-Dying.pdf; *Meeting of the Special Joint Committee on Physician-Assisted Dying – Evidence*, 42nd Parliament, 1st Session (27 January 2016), https://www.parl.ca/DocumentViewer/en/42-1/PDAM/meeting-6/evidence.

3   Joan Bryden, "Assisted-Dying Law Coming Soon with Strict Limits, Sources Say," *Globe and Mail*, 8 April 2016, https://www.theglobeandmail.com/news/politics/assisted-dying-law-will-come-with-strict-limits-sources-say/article29564467/.

4   K. Sonu Gaind, CPA President to Minister Jody Wilson-Raybould and Minister Jane Philpott, 11 April 2016 (in the author's possession).

5   Laura Stone, "Liberals Set to Introduce Assisted-Dying Law with Strict Limits, Source Says," *Globe and Mail*, 12 April 2016, https://www.theglobeandmail.com/news/politics/liberals-set-to-introduce-assisted-dying-law-with-limited-scope-source-says/article29614672/.

6   *Proceedings of the Standing Senate Committee on Legal and Constitutional Affairs*, 42nd Parliament, 1st Session (10–17 May 2016), https://sencanada.ca/en/Content/SEN/Committee/421/lcjc/09cv-e.

7   Expert Panel Working Group on Advance Requests for MAID, *The State of Knowledge on Medical Assistance in Dying Where a Mental Disorder Is the Sole Underlying Medical Condition* (Ottawa: Council of Canadian Academies, 2018), chap. 4, https://rapports-cac.ca/wp-content/uploads/2018/12/The-State-of-Knowledge-on-Medical-Assistance-in-Dying-Where-a-Mental-Disorder-is-the-Sole-Underlying-Medical-Condition.pdf.

8   1 **Weighing of outcomes** – balancing the risk between providing MAiD to someone with a mental illness who would have improved and regained the desire to live versus not providing MAiD to someone who would not have improved.

    2 **How and when to die vs whether to die** – whether there is a difference between providing MAiD to someone dying from an illness (an issue of changing the timing and manner of death) versus providing MAiD to someone whose death is not foreseeable (an issue of whether someone dies).

    3 **Distinguishing between suicide and MAiD MD-SUMC** – whether in cases of MAiD for mental illness there can be valid and reliable methods to distinguish between those making an autonomous, well-considered decision for MAiD versus those with suicidality fuelled by mental illness symptoms.

    4 **Potential implications of MAiD MD-SUMC** – whether or not allowing MAiD for mental illness would adversely impact suicide prevention initiatives.

5 Differences between MAiD and other highly consequential decisions – whether or not there is a difference between allowing a dying person to die by non-intervention versus actively ending someone's life.
9 *Truchon v. Canada (Attorney General)*, 2019 QCCS 3792.
10 Mark Gollom, "What You Need to Know about the SNC-Lavalin Affair," CBC News, 13 February 2019, https://www.cbc.ca/news/politics/trudeau-wilson-raybould-attorney-general-snc-lavalin-1.5014271.
11 Trudo Lemmens and Laverne Jacobs, "The Latest Medical Assistance in Dying Decision Needs to Be Appealed: Here's Why," *Conversation*, 9 October 2019, https://theconversation.com/the-latest-medical-assistance-in-dying-decision-needs-to-be-appealed-heres-why-124955 (perma.cc/MX6V-NECR).
12 The Halifax Group, *MAiD Legislation at a Crossroads: Persons with Mental Disorders as Their Sole Underlying Medical Condition* (Montreal: Institute for Research on Public Policy, 2020), https://irpp.org/wp-content/uploads/2020/01/MAiD-Legislation-at-a-Crossroads-Persons-with-Mental-Disorders-as-Their-Sole-Underlying-Medical-Condition.pdf.
13 Expert Panel Working Group on Advance Requests for MAID, *State of Knowledge*.
14 Expert Advisory Group on Medical Assistance in Dying, *Canada at a Crossroads: Recommendations on Medical Assistance in Dying and Persons with a Mental Disorder: An Evidence-Based Critique of the Halifax Group IRPP Report*, 2020, https://www.eagmaid.org/report (perma.cc/XXX3-SFLT).
15 Centre for Addiction and Mental Health, *Policy Advice on Medical Assistance in Dying and Mental Illness*, October 2017, https://www.camh.ca/-/media/files/pdfs---public-policy-submissions/camh-position-on-mi-MAiD-oct2017-pdf.pdf.
16 Canadian Psychiatric Association, "Position Statement: Medical Assistance in Dying," 10 February 2020, https://static1.squarespace.com/static/5ec97e1c4215f5026a674116/t/61956f5ef64d6f77c32ea957/1637183326947/2020-CPA-Position-Statement-MAiD-EN-web-Final.pdf.
17 Mark Sinyor and Ayal Schaffer, "The Lack of Adequate Scientific Evidence Regarding Physician-Assisted Death for People with Psychiatric Disorders Is a Danger to Patients," *Canadian Journal of Psychiatry* 65, no. 9 (2020): 607–9, https://pubmed.ncbi.nlm.nih.gov/32452224/; Karandeep Sonu Gaind, "What Does 'Irremediability' in Mental Illness Mean?," *Canadian Journal of Psychiatry* 65, no. 9 (2020): 604–6, https://pubmed.ncbi.nlm.nih.gov/32441132/.
18 *Bill C-7, An Act to Amend the Criminal Code (medical assistance in dying)*, 43rd Parliament, 2nd Session (2021), cl. 1(2.1), SC 2021, c. 2 (Can.).

19 "Government Orders," in *House of Commons Debates*, 43rd Parliament, 1st Session (26 February 2020), https://www.ourcommons.ca/DocumentViewer/en/43-1/house/sitting-24/hansard.

20 Joan Bryden and Stephanie Levitz, "Exclusion of Mental Health as Grounds for Assisted Death Is Likely Temporary: Lametti," *Winnipeg Free Press*, 23 November 2020, https://www.winnipegfreepress.com/arts-and-life/life/health/exclusion-of-mental-health-as-grounds-for-assisted-death-is-likely-temporary-lametti-573168591.html.

21 *House of Commons Debates*, 43rd Parliament, 2nd Session (11 March 2021), https://www.ourcommons.ca/documentviewer/en/43-2/house/sitting-71/hansard.

22 Sonu Gaind, "I Continue to Wish I Didn't Have to Write This," Canadian Healthcare Network, 23 October 2020, https://www.canadianhealthcarenetwork.ca/i-continue-to-wish-i-didnt-have-to-write-this; Sonu Gaind, "Lessons from the MAiD Debate: Medical Associations Should Give Evidence Based Input Reflecting Diverse Member Views," Canadian Healthcare Network, 18 March 2021, https://www.canadianhealthcarenetwork.ca/lessons-from-the-maid-debate-medical-associations-should-give-evidence-based-input-reflect-diverse-member-views.

23 "Medical Assistance in Dying (MAiD)," Canadian Psychiatric Association, https://www.cpa-apc.org/medical-assistance-in-dying-maid/.

24 Canadian Psychiatric Association, "Brief to the Standing Committee on Justice and Human Rights Bill C-7," 12 November 2020, https://www.cpa-apc.org/wp-content/uploads/Brief-JUST-12-Nov-2020-FIN.pdf; Canadian Psychiatric Association, "Brief to the Senate of Canada Standing Committee on Legal and Constitutional Affairs Bill C-7," 23 November 2020, https://www.cpa-apc.org/wp-content/uploads/Brief-LCJC-23-Nov-2020-FIN.pdf; Canadian Psychiatric Association to Hon. Mobina S.B. Jaffer, Chair, Standing Committee on Legal and Constitutional Affairs, "CPA's Activities with Respect to MAiD," 5 February 2021, https://sencanada.ca/Content/Sen/Committee/432/LCJC/briefs/CanadianPsychiatricAssociation_e.pdf; *Meeting of the Standing Senate Committee on Legal and Constitutional Affairs – Evidence*, 43rd Parliament, 2nd Session (23 November 2020), https://sencanada.ca/en/Content/Sen/Committee/432/LCJC/02ev-55071-e.

25 Aaron Kheriaty, "First, Take No Stand," *New Atlantis* 59 (Summer 2019): 22–35, https://www.thenewatlantis.com/publications/first-take-no-stand; Daniel P. Sulmasy et al., "Physician-Assisted Suicide: Why Neutrality by Organized Medicine Is Neither Neutral Nor Appropriate," *Journal of General Internal Medicine* 33, no. 8 (August 2018): 1394–9, https://pubmed.ncbi.nlm.nih.gov/29722005/.

26 Honourable Graydon Nicholas et al. to Canadian Psychiatric Association, "CPA Support for MAiD for Mental Illness," November 2021, https://static1.squarespace.com/static/5ec97e1c4215f5026a674116/t/619f0a1806 5082544058cc6e/1637812760998/Indigenous+leaders+open+letter+-+FIN+-+CPA+and+MAiD.pdf.

27 Canadian Association for Suicide Prevention to Canadian Psychiatric Association, "CPA's Discussion Paper on Medical Assistance in Dying ('MAiD')," 20 November 2021, https://static1.squarespace.com/static/5ec97e1c4215f5026a674116/t/619bc64ac482815740760931/1637598795070/Letter+to+CPA+re+Discussion+Paper+on+MAiD+per cent282021+11+20 per cent29.pdf.

28 *Canada Not-for-Profit Corporations Regulations*, SOR/2011-223.

29 K.S. Gaind, "Professional Medical Associations Failing to Provide Evidence in MAID Debate," *Hamilton Spectator*, 9 March 2021, https://www.thespec.com/opinion/contributors/2021/03/09/professional-medical-associations-failing-to-provide-evidence-in-maid-debate.html.

30 Joan Bryden, "Senators Amend MAID Bill to Put 18-Month Time Limit on Mental Illness Exclusion," Canadian Press, 9 February 2021, https://www.ctvnews.ca/politics/senators-amend-maid-bill-to-put-18-month-time-limit-on-mental-illness-exclusion-1.5302151.

31 *Meeting of the Standing Senate Committee*, 23 November 2020.

32 *Meeting of the Standing Senate Committee on Legal and Constitutional Affairs – Evidence*, 43rd Parliament, 2nd Session (3 February 2021), https://sencanada.ca/en/Content/Sen/Committee/432/LCJC/12EV-55130-E.

33 Association des médecins psychiatres du Québec, *Access to Medical Assistance in Dying for People with Mental Disorders – Discussion Paper*, November 2020, 28, https://ampq.org/wp-content/uploads/2020/12/mpqdocreflexionammenfinal.pdf.

34 Mark Sinyor, "Lack of Evidence-Based Medicine in Debate Around New MAID Law Should Concern Canadians," CBC News, 4 March 2021, https://www.cbc.ca/news/opinion/opinion-medical-assistance-in-dying-maid-1.5934977.

35 CPA to Jaffer, "CPA's Activities."

36 Lemmens and Jacobs, "Latest Medical Assistance in Dying Decision."

37 Terry Davidson, "Law Professor Deems Medically Assisted Dying Amendments Welcome, Needed," Law360 Canada, 15 October 2020, https://www.law360.ca/ca/articles/1752897/law-professor-deems-medically-assisted-dying-amendments-welcome-needed.

38 *Meeting of the Standing Senate Committee on Legal and Constitutional Affairs*, 43rd Parliament, 2nd Session (24 November 2020), Jocelyn

Downie, https://sencanada.ca/en/Content/Sen/Committee/432/LCJC/03EV-55073-E.

39 K. Sonu Gaind, "Senate Brief on Medical Assistance in Dying (MAiD)," 27 November 2020, https://sencanada.ca/Content/Sen/Committee/432/LCJC/briefs/Dr.K.SonuGaind_e.pdf.

40 AMPQ, *Access to Medical Assistance in Dying*, 28.

41 Stan Kutcher, "Bill to Amend Criminal Code – Third Reading – Debate," Senate of Canada, 9 February 2021, https://sencanada.ca/en/senators/kutcher-stan/interventions/553870/11.

42 "How Drugs are Reviewed in Canada," Health Canada, 12 February 2015, https://www.canada.ca/en/health-canada/services/drugs-health-products/drug-products/fact-sheets/drugs-reviewed-canada.html.

43 Trudo Lemmens, "Parliament is Not Forced by the Courts to Legalize MAID for Mental Illness: Law Professors' Letter to Cabinet," *University of Toronto Faculty of Law* (blog), 2 February 2023, https://www.law.utoronto.ca/blog/faculty/letter-federal-cabinet-about-governments-legal-claims-related-maid-mental-illness.

44 "MAID Survey of OMA Section on Psychiatry Members: Quantitative Results, October 2021," presented at October 2021 Section AGM, https://www.dropbox.com/scl/fi/mqn9ckstbb83ubk43uumf/OMA-2021-Psychiatrist-MAID-Survey.pdf?rlkey=7kcbphpmtbabecb9y3fshlkhi&dl=0.

45 Nicholas et al. to CPA, "CPA Support."

46 Council of Canadians with Disabilities, "An Open Letter from the Council of Canadians with Disabilities (CCD) Concerning the Canadian Psychiatric Association Position Statement on Medical Aid in Dying (MAiD)," 20 November 2021, https://static1.squarespace.com/static/5ec97e1c4215f5026a674116/t/619c28abd62a466fbdc44aaf/1637623980005/2021+Nov+20++CCD+to+CPA+on+MAID+FINAL.pdf.

47 Ontario Association for ACT & FACT to Canadian Psychiatric Association, "CPA Position Statement," 17 November 2021, https://static1.squarespace.com/static/5ec97e1c4215f5026a674116/t/619bc816dbce0d062990693c/1637599254612/OAAF+-+CPA+MAID+letter.pdf.

48 Spring Hawes and Gabrielle Peters, "An Open Letter from Dignity Denied Concerning the Canadian Psychiatric Association Position Statement on Medical Aid in Dying (MAiD)," 21 November 2021, https://static1.squarespace.com/static/5ec97e1c4215f5026a674116/t/619bc9570560e3351off3ed7/1637599575028/Response+to+CPA+MAID+Position+statement.pdf.

49 Trudo Lemmens and Mary Shariff to Canadian Psychiatric Association, "Updated Position Statement re Medical Assistance in Dying November 2021," 20 November 2021, https://static1.squarespace.com/static/5ec97e1c4215f5026a6741116/t/619bcb34a03aa808b8cac137/1637600053179/CPA+Letter+Lemmens+Shariff+Nov+21.pdf.

50 G. Neilson, "MAiD and Mental Illness: Past, Present, and Future" (Presentation, McMaster DPBN Grand Rounds, 24 November 2021).

51 Canadian Psychiatric Association, "Medical Assistance in Dying (MAiD) for Persons Whose Sole Underlying Medical Condition is a Mental Disorder: Challenges and Considerations – Discussion Paper," 8 June 2021, https://www.cpa-apc.org/wp-content/uploads/2021-CPA-Discussion-Paper-MAID-Challenges-and-Considerations-EN-web-Final.pdf.

52 Jeff Kirby, "MAiD Expert Panel Recommendations Are Inadequate, Contends Panel Member Who Resigned," *Hill Times*, 16 June 2022, https://www.hilltimes.com/story/2022/06/16/maid-expert-panel-recommendations-are-inadequate-contends-panel-member-who-resigned/270807/.

53 Health Canada, *Final Report of the Expert Panel on maid and Mental Illness*, May 2022, https://www.canada.ca/content/dam/hc-sc/documents/corporate/about-health-canada/public-engagement/external-advisory-bodies/expert-panel-maid-mental-illness/final-report-expert-panel-maid-mental-illness/final-report-expert-panel-maid-mental-illness.pdf.

54 Kirby, "MAiD Expert Panel Recommendations"; Ellen Cohen, "Why I Resigned from the Federal Expert Panel on Medical Assistance in Dying," *Globe and Mail*, 14 October 2022, https://www.theglobeandmail.com/opinion/article-expert-panel-maid-mental-illness/.

55 Cherise Seucharan, "I Die When I Run Out of Money," *Canadaland*, 24 October 2021, https://www.canadaland.com/madeline-medical-assistance-in-dying-priced-out-of-life/.

56 Yuan Yi Zhu, "Why Is Canada Euthanising the Poor?," *Spectator*, 30 April 2022, https://www.spectator.co.uk/article/why-is-canada-euthanising-the-poor-.

57 "Trudeau Defends MAID Legislation after Conservative MP Points to 'Serious Abuses,'" video, Global News, 11 May 2022, https://globalnews.ca/video/8827777/trudeau-defends-maid-legislation-after-conservative-mp-points-to-serious-abuses/.

58 Ramona Coelho et al., "Normalizing Death as 'Treatment' in Canada: Whose Suicides Do We Prevent, and Whose Do We Abet?," *World Medical Journal* 68, no. 3 (November 2022): 27–35, https://www.wma.net/wp-content/uploads/2023/02/WMJ_2022_03_final-1.jan23.pdf.

59 Althia Raj, "Is Canada Expanding Medical Assistance in Dying Too Quickly?," *Toronto Star*, 18 November 2022, https://www.thestar.com/podcasts/its-political/2022/11/18/is-canada-expanding-medical-assistance-in-dying-too-quickly.html.
60 Alexander Raikin, "No Other Options: Newly Revealed Documents Depict a Canadian Euthanasia Regime that Efficiently Ushers the Vulnerable to a 'Beautiful' Death," *New Atlantis* 71 (Winter 2023): 3–24, https://www.thenewatlantis.com/publications/no-other-options.
61 Expert Advisory Group on Medical Assistance in Dying, *Expert Advisory Group (eag) Brief to Parliamentary Committee*, 30 May 2022, https://www.eagmaid.org/brief.
62 K. Sonu Gaind et al., "Canada's Medically Administered Death (MAD) Expansion for Mental Illness: Targeting the Most Vulnerable," *World Medical Journal* 68, no. 4 (December 2022): 72–82, https://www.wma.net/wp-content/uploads/2023/02/WMJ_2022_04_final.jan23.pdf.
63 Society of Canadian Psychiatry, "2022 Call to Action," 10 November 2022, https://www.socpsych.org/calltoaction.
64 Canadian Association for Suicide Prevention, "Statement – CASP Issues Statement about MAiD for Mental Illness," 14 December 2022, https://suicideprevention.ca/media/casp-issues-statement-about-maid-for-mental-illness/.
65 Erin Anderssen, "Medical Experts Call on Government to Delay Expansion of MAID for Mental Illness," *Globe and Mail*, 1 December 2022, https://www.theglobeandmail.com/canada/article-maid-delay-mental-illness-medical-experts/.
66 Erin Anderssen, "Ottawa Seeking to Delay Expansion of MAID for Mental Disorders," *Globe and Mail*, 15 December 2022, https://www.theglobeandmail.com/canada/article-maid-expansion-delay-mental-disorders/.
67 David Fraser, "Experts Say Delay of Assisted-Dying Expansion Not Necessary, as Some Cheer Decision," *Toronto Star*, 16 December 2022, https://www.thestar.com/politics/experts-say-delay-of-assisted-dying-expansion-not-necessary-as-some-cheer-decision/article_65f34445-0811-5413-be54-ab01ea041292.html.
68 Ibid.
69 Panel on MAiD in cases of psychiatric disorder, Atlantic Provinces Psychiatric Association, Cardigan, PEI, 3 June 2023.
70 "Should Canada Allow Assisted Death for the Mentally Ill?," video, *TVO Today*, 7 December 2022, https://www.tvo.org/video/should-canada-allow-assisted-death-for-the-mentally-ill.
71 Karandeep Sonu Gaind, "Canada Delays Expanding Medical Assistance in Dying to Include Mental Illness, But It's Still a Policy Built on

Quicksand," *Conversation*, 15 December 2022, https://theconversation.com/canada-delays-expanding-medical-assistance-in-dying-to-include-mental-illness-but-its-still-a-policy-built-on-quicksand-196264.

72 Irelyne Lavery, "Feds Looking to Delay Expansion of Assisted Dying: 'Need to Get This Right,'" Global News, 15 December 2022, https://globalnews.ca/news/9352016/medically-assisted-death-maid-expansion-lametti-announcement/; Althia Raj, "Canada is Now No. 1 in World in Terms of MAiD. We Should Think Twice Before Expanding It," *Toronto Star*, 21 November 2022, https://www.thestar.com/politics/political-opinion/canada-is-now-no-1-in-world-in-terms-of-maid-we-should-think-twice/article_d97f737e-568a-5e79-8485-f5e204b6f6aa.html; Erin Anderssen, "Doctors, Disability Advocates Condemn Parliamentary Committee's Recommendation to Expand MAID law," *Globe and Mail*, 6 March 2023, https://www.theglobeandmail.com/canada/article-maid-report-parliamentary-committee/; John Paul Tusker, "Liberal Government Promoting a 'Culture of Death' with Medical Assistance in Dying Law, Conservative MP Says," CBC, 6 March 2023, https://www.cbc.ca/news/politics/culture-of-death-medical-assistance-in-dying-mental-illness-1.6769504.

73 Marie E. Nicolini et al., "Irremediability in Psychiatric Euthanasia: Examining the Objective Standard," *Psychological Medicine* 53, no. 12 (October 2022): 5729–47, https://www.cambridge.org/core/journals/psychological-medicine/article/irremediability-in-psychiatric-euthanasia-examining-the-objective-standard/39CF3F03E81053EA152C63F332478CB4; Ramona Coelho et al., "The Realities of Medical Assistance in Dying in Canada," *Palliative & Supportive Care* 21, no. 5 (July 2023): 871–8, https://www.cambridge.org/core/journals/palliative-and-supportive-care/article/realities-of-medical-assistance-in-dying-in-canada/3105E6A45E04DFA8602D54DF91A2F568.

74 "How We Will Change the Canadian Landscape," Society of Canadian Psychiatry, 2023, https://www.socpsych.org/oct2023bn.

75 K. Sonu Gaind, "MPs Should Be Voting on MAID with Their Eyes Wide Open," *Hamilton Spectator*, 15 October 2023, https://www.thespec.com/opinion/contributors/mps-should-be-voting-on-maid-with-their-eyes-wide-open/article_60da3a2a-57cd-57e1-8378-231d7b215761.html; Editorial Board, "It's Time to Take a Step Back on Assisted Death," *Globe and Mail*, 4 November 2023, https://www.theglobeandmail.com/opinion/editorials/article-its-time-to-take-a-step-back-on-assisted-death/.

76 Alexandra McPherson et al., "Canadian Psychiatrists Respond: MAID and Mental Disorders," *Impact Ethics*, 15 November 2023, https://

impactethics.ca/2023/11/15/canadian-psychiatrists-respond-maid-and-mental-disorders/.

77 K. Sonu Gaind et al., "More Canadian Psychiatrists Respond: No MAID for Mental Illness," *Impact Ethics*, 28 November 2023, https://impact-ethics.ca/2023/11/28/more-canadian-psychiatrists-respond-no-maid-for-mental-illness/.

78 House of Commons, *Special Joint Committee on Medical Assistance in Dying*, 44th Parliament, 1st Session (28 November 2023), https://www.parl.ca/DocumentViewer/en/44-1/AMAD/meeting-40/evidence.

79 *Meeting of the Special Joint Committee on Medical Assistance in Dying – Evidence*, 44th Parliament, 1st Session (7 November 2023), https://www.parl.ca/documentviewer/en/44-1/AMAD/meeting-38/evidence.

80 Ibid.

81 *Meeting of the Special Joint Committee on Medical Assistance in Dying – Evidence*, 44th Parliament, 1st Session (21 November 2023), https://www.parl.ca/documentviewer/en/44-1/AMAD/meeting-39/evidence.

82 *Meeting of the Special Joint Committee*, 7 November 2023.

83 Camille Bains, "Critics Caution against Plan to Expand Medical Assistance in Dying to Those with Mental Illness," CTV News, 17 December 2023, https://www.ctvnews.ca/health/critics-caution-against-plan-to-expand-medical-assistance-in-dying-to-those-with-mental-illness-1.6690978.

84 Parliament of Canada, MAID *and Mental Disorders: The Road Ahead - Report of the Special Joint Committee on Medical Assistance in Dying*, 44th Parliament, 1st Session (29 January 2024), https://www.parl.ca/Content/Committee/441/AMAD/Reports/RP12815505/amadrp03/amadrp03-e.pdf.

85 "Registration – In-house Organization," "Dying with Dignity Canada," Office of the Commissioner of Lobbying of Canada, https://lobbycanada.gc.ca/app/secure/ocl/lrs/do/vwRg?cno=366489&regId=930240#regStart.

86 Dirk Huyer, "Lessons Learned from the Coroner," presented at CAMAP's Changing Landscape Conference, 3 May 2024 (in the author's possession).

87 Gemma Ware and K. Sonu Gaind, "Assisted Dying: Canada Grapples with Plans to Extend Euthanasia to People Suffering Solely from Mental Illness," *Conversation*, 16 May 2024, https://theconversation.com/assisted-dying-canada-grapples-with-plans-to-extend-euthanasia-to-people-suffering-solely-from-mental-illness-230129.

88 Sonu Gaind, "Unpeeling the False Justifications behind MAID Expansion," *National Observer*, 3 January 2023, https://www.nationalobserver.com/2023/01/03/opinion/unpeeling-false-justifications-behind-maid-expansion; K. Sonu Gaind et al., "More Canadian Psychiatrists Respond."

3

Assisting Dying: A Policy Framework Developed without Adequate Ethical Consideration

Alexander I.F. Simpson and Roland M. Jones

Medical assistance in dying (MAiD) is now available in many countries, extending initially from the Benelux countries and Switzerland to other parts of Europe, Canada, some US states, and Australasia. In general it began as assistance with dying for people who were terminally ill, but in some jurisdictions it has been extended to include persons with non-terminal disorders, including mental health disorders, as the sole underlying medical condition to qualify for assistance.[1]

In almost all jurisdictions, assisted dying means medical assistance in dying, although Switzerland has long had a model of assisted suicide that does not involve medical practitioners other than for assessing that the person has the capacity to make the decision. Assisted death includes euthanasia (where the doctor injects the patient with medication to cause death) and assisted suicide (where the doctor prescribes a medication that the patient self-administers). In Canada MAiD is overwhelmingly euthanasia, with only seven out of 10,064 MAiD deaths in 2021 being by self-administration.[2]

From the outset it is important to note that doctors have long known they possess treatments that can kill patients. In 399 BC, Socrates was convicted by an Athenian court of impiety and corrupting the young.[3] He was sentenced to death, which would be achieved by him being poisoned with hemlock. With young friends gathered around him, his jailer brought him the poison. Socrates asked the jailer if he could perform the traditional libation, the pouring of a small amount of the drink on the ground as a gift to the gods before its consumption. The jailer said no, because the amount of poison had been precisely measured to be sufficient to kill a man and no more. Socrates was required to drink it all. He drank it in a single swallow. As he died, he instructed one of his followers to make a sacrifice, saying, "Crito, we ought to offer a cock to Asclepius," a substitute for the lack of a libation.

Hemlock was commonly used by Greek physicians in lower doses as a medicinal agent, and clearly the calculation of the correct dose to kill the philosopher had required the knowledge of a physician. Indeed, it was to Asclepius, the God of medicine and healing, that Socrates instructed one of his followers to give a sacrifice after his death. In Socrates's final words, the state's use of poison to execute him was seen as part of the technology of medicine. Indeed, the word used for the hemlock in Plato's account of Socrates's death is "Pharmakon," which means both medicine and poison.

Contemporaneously, Hippocrates was concerned with defining the ethical boundaries of medicine. Although the precise date of the oath attributed to him is uncertain (Hippocrates died in 370 BC), the oath includes the statement: "I will use treatment to help the sick according to my ability and judgment, but never with a view to injury and wrongdoing. Neither will I administer a poison to anybody when asked to do so, nor will I suggest such a course." Thus the ability of medicine to hasten or cause death is long known, and the use of this ability by doctors is prohibited. Our current debate over MAiD is thus not about a new technology, but about an old ethical dilemma: Should a doctor poison a patient?

The ethical arguments in favor of assisted dying began from the perspective that people who were dying had little life left to preserve. Such people were seen as entitled to choose the nature and timing of their death to relieve suffering from which they could not otherwise be relieved. This argument involves both respect for the competent autonomous wish to die and compassion for the severity of suffering and death that would follow. From these two origins evolved the legal tests that assert that the person has the legal right to ask a doctor (or nurse practitioner) to assist them in ending their life, with most jurisdictions requiring that they are externally judged to be suffering irremediably. Some jurisdictions have confined this to the end-of-life situation, but the Benelux countries, Switzerland, and now Canada have extended this to non-terminal disorders. Legislation enabling assisted dying relieves health practitioners from criminal liability for causing another person's death under certain circumstances. Thus, the core elements of assisted dying regimes are respect for autonomy, eligibility on the grounds of compassion for suffering, and the designation that ending life is a medical procedure that the state must provide.

We will address each of these core elements and the ethical assumptions that underlie them and argue that all are seriously conceptually flawed. We argue that should the state wish to provide assisted suicide for competent individuals, a different process of assessment and delivery of assisted death is required.

RESPECT FOR AUTONOMY

In medicine, all care should be delivered while cognizant of the person's autonomous wish to accept or reject treatment being offered, a fundamental ethic of medicine and within legal and constitutional frameworks. In relation to the right to choose when and how one should die, the Supreme Court of Canada (SCC) in *Carter v. Canada (AG)* asserted that assisted dying was consistent with the *Canadian Charter of Rights and Freedoms* in the case of a woman who was suffering a degenerative neurological disorder that impaired her autonomous ability to die by suicide.[4] The SCC held that she had the right to suicide, and if she could not physically kill herself then she had the right to ask a doctor to assist. The *Charter* was found to support all competent persons having the right to suicide, a principle in place since suicide was decriminalised many decades ago. Put differently, respect for autonomy argues for the right of competent people to choose whether or not they live. It does not alone argue for the right to assisted death, particularly to medically assisted death. Only if a person is seen as incapable of the physical acts necessary to die by suicide do they have the right to seek assistance, and then only from a medical practitioner.

Assisted dying legislation in Canada greatly expands that argument. It allows medical assistance in a range of clinical situations and makes no reference to the physical ability to kill one's self. But in defining a range of clinical situations (medical condition, irremediability, intolerable suffering), the legislation only provides for assistance to a subgroup of competent persons who want to die by suicide. Only those who have certain defined medical conditions qualify for assisted dying. Another person who autonomously wants to die by suicide may not qualify for assistance if their suffering, or reasoning, does not meet the legal test. Second, assistance is provided regardless of whether the person has the autonomous ability to suicide. Under these regimes, "respect for autonomy" only gives access to assisted dying if the person also has suffering that is deemed irremediable. What is the justification for this distinction? Most people with terminal and non-terminal disorders have the ability to die by suicide, but a subgroup was not selected for assistance in dying based on whether the person has the ability to autonomously end their own life. Is there any logical basis for selecting only some autonomous persons for assistance?

If we respect the autonomy of persons to choose whether they die and provide assistance in their death, logically there is no reason to choose between different types of competent people who request assisted death.[5] If it is autonomy that justifies euthanasia and assisted suicide, then it follows that all autonomous wishes would allow for euthanasia and assisted suicide, not only those wishes of persons with a terminal illness or irremediable suffering. If it is autonomy alone that matters, all competent adults should have the same rights to access assisted dying. This is what we are seeing with the progressive expansion of MAiD from competent adults with terminal disorders to those with non-terminal disorders, mental health disorders, and mature minors. These eventualities are well beyond the arguments of the SCC in *Carter*. Put another way, why do we respect some autonomous decisions to have assisted dying but not others? There is no logic and no ethical basis in separating these two requests. Assisted dying frameworks select only some autonomous persons to receive assistance, and only after they have qualified through forms of state-sanctioned or medically sanctioned approval. With that approval they qualify for medically administered, not autonomously caused, death.

Autonomy argues for a general population's access to assisted dying and not only assisted dying for persons with "irremediable suffering" or at the end of life. Thus, although respect for autonomy is the central pillar of assistance in dying, it is an inadequate basis on its own to argue for assisted dying to be confined to certain subgroups of persons.

The other problem with autonomy is that it is not the only value necessary for human existence or for consideration in medical practice.[6] People exercise autonomy within a social system of relationships, roles, and responsibilities. These relationships, contexts, and responsibilities also nurture people. And the exclusion of these elements from the ethical analysis of the framework for assisted dying ultimately impoverishes our understanding of the nature of human existence and may unwittingly shift the suffering from the person to other members of the person's social network who are left behind after the person's death.

RELIEF OF SUFFERING

The second central component to the ethical case for assisted dying is that of the medical duty to relieve suffering. The World Medical Association notes that two responsibilities, to relieve suffering and to preserve life, are the fundamental ethical bases of medicine.[7] These responsibilities may seem to conflict at times. It has been argued that if a person is dying, is suffering, and is competent to request assistance in dying, it may be ethical to provide assistance in dying as there is little life left to preserve and much suffering to relieve.[8] It appears evident from surveys of medical and public opinion that this is a commonly held view.[9]

Outside the end-of-life situation this argument has been used to extend assisted dying to persons who have a lot of life left to preserve (those with non-terminal disorders). Here the ethical complexity becomes much greater. Understanding why living with a non-terminal disorder may be intolerable for one person and not intolerable for another is a complex process. The definition of what is irremediable can be difficult given the long duration of a non-terminal illness and particularly so for mental disorders for which there are no objective criteria for irremediability.[10] Further, irremediability is also limited to only those remedies that are acceptable to the person, making irremediability subjectively defined. Suffering is also ultimately subjectively defined. This means that the decision to seek assisted death is a values-based and not an evidence-based decision for the person; the provider's judgment that the suffering is intolerable and the condition irremediable is therefore a question of whether the provider agrees with the person. This, again, is a values-based, not evidence-based, judgment.

On what basis then do we decide that a type of human physical or mental suffering is of sufficient severity to qualify for assisted dying? This qualification is deemed one of compassion for the suffering person. This exposes the second central assumption of assisted dying legislation for non-terminal disorders: the unsaid statement that "if I was in that condition I would want access to assisted dying also."[11] The presumption here is that living with some forms of disability are forms of human existence that so stimulate our compassion or pity that we understand why people would want to die, and we are happy, as a society, to assist in their dying.

This is essentially where advocates for persons with disability feel such affront with assisted dying legislation: instead of saying living with disability is deserving of respect and support, this legislation instead says disability should generate compassion and pity that allows people with disability to access assisted dying. Whether said overtly or covertly, this position contains ableist assumptions that resonate with the history of neglect and exclusion that sees states of disability as being inferior. This is a fundamental denigration of those that are referred to as "vulnerable populations" in public policy documents and legislation. The nature of this affront is not always clearly identified or explicitly addressed. It is this presumption that so fuels the concern of the disability sector about the ableist and discriminatory assumptions of this legislation.

What is also clear is that the conditions of life that one finds irremediable are commonly social constructions caused by attitudes, discrimination, underfunding, poor housing, and structural poverty that persons with disability are confronted by. The irony is obvious. The social ills that increase the burden of suffering on persons with disability may qualify the person for state-funded assistance in dying, but state funding to live with dignity with disability is lacking. There are repeated examples of this (grotesque) irony in Canadian media coverage, including with military veterans, that have understandably brought about public shock and opprobrium.[12]

ASSISTANCE IN DYING

As it is clear that the arguments for autonomy and compassion contain deeply concerning assumptions, the next problem is the requirement to have a medical professional or nurse practitioner provide the assistance to die. As already noted, the autonomy to suicide is present in all competent persons. The argument that medical professionals should assist in their dying is to relieve the person of the task of killing themselves. This replaces the autonomous suicide with a medically supervised or medically delivered death. This process of dying is not autonomous but rather something that is done to the person. Because health technologies have the ability to put someone to death (known since the time of Socrates at least), it has been taken for granted that it is necessarily a medical responsibility or duty to provide assisted death. This meant that the provision of assisted dying came to be considered a health care right. It was then argued that should assisted dying be provided to people with a non-terminal physical illness, then it should also be provided for those with a non-terminal mental illness, as to fail to do so would be "discriminatory" against those with mental illnesses.[13]

There are two major problems with this. First, being put to death by a doctor is not autonomy. It is assisted death or suicide by proxy, not self-caused death. Second, assisted dying is not a medical treatment.[14] Health care interventions are to treat or cure a medical condition or relieve the suffering that the person is experiencing from that condition.[15] Instead, the purpose of assisted dying is to kill the patient. No other health care procedure does this. There is one other occasion when a person is put to death using health technology, namely the execution of a person in a capital punishment jurisdiction, but this is clearly not defined as a health care procedure. Providing "a good death" is therefore not a medical procedure, even though it can be delivered with medical technology. Therapeutic abortion does involve the death of a foetus or life in its early stages of development, but for the health considerations of the mother, which is distinct from assisted dying.

Given that putting somebody to death is not a medical procedure, arguments regarding equal access to assisted dying as a health service for persons of varieties of diagnoses (terminal and non-terminal disorders, mental health disorders) have no basis, because this is not a health service.

If it is accepted that respect for autonomy requires the allowance for all competent persons to be able to seek assisted death, then suicide prevention policies at a population level cease to have moral authority. This is because autonomy has now been placed above the other human values of connectedness as mentioned above. The dynamic of distilling and maintaining hope in the face of the temporary if profound distress of a suicidal person becomes especially difficult under an autonomy-driven system. This may be particularly so for vulnerable young adults going through difficult life periods who may have suicidal thoughts and are now getting a societal message that it is possible to choose death and that the state will assist you in doing so. That presents a chilling message to society as a whole, to people with disabilities, to people becoming old and frail, and to young people at vulnerable points in their lives.

Although the Quebec Superior Court in *Truchon* found that it is feasible to separate a desire for suicide from a desire for assisted death, the cognitive and motivational processes that underpin suicide (pain and suffering, loss of hope, and available means of suicide) and the legal criteria for assisted dying (ongoing suffering, irremediability, and capacity to seek and have assisted death delivered) are fundamentally analogous.[16] A desire for suicide and a desire for assisted death overlap significantly. However, the desire for suicide in someone with an acute mental illness may be separated from the more long-term suicidality that is common in the lives of people with serious mental illness, other disabling conditions, or increasing frailty with age. It is clearly possible that a suicidal person is rational, has capacity, and has a desire for suicide or assisted death. While this rational and understandable desire may be expressed as an autonomous wish and is worthy of respect, family members and other loved ones commonly see these decisions as wrong, hurtful, and ultimately impoverished.[17]

To summarize, assisted dying policies started from a desire to relieve the suffering of people with a terminal illness who have little life left to preserve and who make a competent request for assisted death. Many doctors, advocates, and people in the general public see this as a reasonable approach. The principle of respecting a person's autonomous wish to die by non-autonomous means was established and wrongly construed as a medical procedure. Advocates for assisted dying used these principles of autonomy and suffering to extend medically assisted dying to non-terminally ill people including those with mental health disorders. It is now clear that respect for autonomous choice argues that all capable adults should have access to assisted death (if autonomy is all that matters), not only those deemed to be suffering sufficiently to trigger the Canadian legislative standard. The criteria for assisted death in non-terminally ill persons are fundamentally ableist and threaten the collective well-being of many persons such as those with disabilities or vulnerability, and applying these criteria fundamentally undermines suicide prevention policy at a population level. Finally, respect for autonomy and compassion do not make putting a person to death a medical procedure.

POSSIBLE RESOLUTIONS

Should society wish that people should have access to assisted death, there are alternative models that could meet this expectation. One model is the Swiss approach, where a competent person may seek assisted death from a carefully regulated but non-health-care provider.

A second approach is to confine assisted dying to self-administered assisted dying (this is the process for terminal illness in the US jurisdictions, for instance) unless in very rare situations the person is incapable of self-administering the fatal medications.

A third model has been proposed in the United Kingdom entitled legally authorized assisted dying (LAAD). Under this model, approval for assistance in dying would be given by courts who would make orders including providing the required drugs for the procedure. It would establish a pattern of delivery outside of mainstream clinical care analogous to the Swiss model. LAAD courts would require medical reports about the person's medical condition including their capacity to make the request.[18] Such a mechanism would provide for the level of access to assisted dying that society deems appropriate but not construe it as a form of medical or health care. This would also make clear that health care is about hope and recovery for all, which would provide protection for vulnerable persons.

CONCLUSION

We have argued that the ethical bases of respect for autonomy and compassion are inadequate or flawed as they are currently used to justify assisted dying legislation. Further, the fact that putting someone to death can be caused by health technologies is insufficient to argue that this is a health procedure or a medical obligation. Rather, assisted dying meets none of the characteristics of health procedures.

That said, it is clear that there is widespread public support for some form of assisted dying for persons with terminal illness and some people with non-terminal disorders. Alternative models exist or have been proposed that might provide limited assisted dying without undermining the core foundations of clinical practice, suicide prevention, and the support for vulnerable populations.

NOTES

1 Paul S. Appelbaum, "Physician-Assisted Death in Psychiatry," *World Psychiatry* 17, no. 2 (June 2018): 145–6, https://doi.org/10.1002/wps.20548; Roland M. Jones and Alexander I.F. Simpson, "Medical Assistance in Dying: Challenges for Psychiatry," *Frontiers in Psychiatry* 9, no. 678 (December 2018): 1–4.

2 Health Canada, *Third Annual Report on Medical Assistance in Dying in Canada 2021*, July 2022, https://www.canada.ca/en/health-canada/services/medical-assistance-dying/annual-report-2021.html#highlights.
3 Colin Wells, "The Mystery of Socrates' Last Words," *Arion* 16, no. 2 (Fall 2008): 137–48, https://www.bu.edu/arion/files/2010/03/Wells-Mystery-Socrates.pdf.
4 *Carter v. Canada (Attorney General)*, 2015 SCC 5, [2015] 1 SCR 331.
5 Kevin Yuill, "The Unfreedom of Assisted Suicide: How the Right to Die Undermines Autonomy," *Ethics, Medicine and Public Health* 1, no. 4 (November 2015): 494–502.
6 Daniel Callahan, "Reason, Self-Determination, and Physician-Assisted Suicide," in *The Ethics of Suicide*, ed. Margaret Pabst Battin (New York: Oxford University Press, 2015), 706–11.
7 "WMA International Code of Medical Ethics," World Medical Association, April 2023, https://www.wma.net/policies-post/wma-international-code-of-medical-ethics/.
8 Mona Gupta, "A Response to 'Assisted Death in Canada for Persons with Active Psychiatric Disorders,'" *Journal of Ethics and Mental Health* Open Volume (2016): 1–3, http://www.jemh.ca/issues/v9/documents/JEMH_Open-Volume_Commentary_Response_Assisted_Death_in_Canada-June2016.pdf.
9 Skye Rousseau et al., "A National Survey of Canadian Psychiatrists' Attitudes toward Medical Assistance in Death," *Canadian Journal of Psychiatry* 62, no. 11 (2017), 787–94, https://doi.org/10.1177/0706743717711174.
10 Alexander I.F. Simpson, "Medical Assistance in Dying and Mental Health: A Legal, Ethical, and Clinical Analysis," *Canadian Journal of Psychiatry* 63, no. 2 (2018): 80–4; Marie E. Nicolini et al., "Irremediability in Psychiatric Euthanasia: Examining the Objective Standard," *Psychological Medicine* 53, no. 12 (October 2022): 1–19.
11 Yuill, "Unfreedom of Assisted Suicide."
12 Alexander Raikin, "No Other Options: Newly Revealed Documents Depict a Canadian Euthanasia Regime That Efficiently Ushers the Vulnerable to a 'Beautiful' Death," *The New Atlantis* 71 (Winter 2023): 3–24, https://www.thenewatlantis.com/publications/no-other-options.
13 See, for example, Canadian Psychiatric Association, "Position Statement: Medical Assistance in Dying: An Update," October 2021, https://www.cpa-apc.org/wp-content/uploads/2021-CPA-Position-Statement-MAID-Update-EN-web-Final.pdf.

14 Scott Kim, "In Canada, MAID Has Become a Matter of Ideology," *Globe and Mail*, 25 February 2023, https://www.theglobeandmail.com/opinion/article-in-canada-maid-has-become-a-matter-of-ideology/.
15 John Maher, "Assisted Death in Canada for Persons with Active Psychiatric Disorders," *Journal of Ethics and Mental Health* Open Volume (2016): 1–5, https://jemh.ca/issues/v9/documents/JEMH_Open-Volume-Editorial-Assisted%20Death%20in%20Canada-May2016.pdf.
16 *Truchon v. Canada (Attorney General)*, 2019 QCCS 3792; Scott Y.H. Kim, Yeates Conwell, and Eric D. Caine, "Suicide and Physician-Assisted Death for Persons with Psychiatric Disorders: How Much Overlap?" *JAMA Psychiatry* 75, no. 11 (November 2018): 1099–100.
17 Ronald Maris, "Rational Suicide: An Impoverished Self-Transformation," *Suicide and Life-Threatening Behavior* 12, no. 1 (Spring 1982): 4–16.
18 "Assisted Dying and the Role of Mainstream Healthcare," Keep Assisted Dying Out of Healthcare, 2022, https://kadoh.uk/.

4

How Canada's MAiD Law Has Made Death a "First-Line Therapy" for Suffering

Trudo Lemmens, Mary J. Shariff, and Leonie Herx

Bill C-7,[1] which led to amendments to Canada's first medical assistance in dying (MAiD) law,[2] was the Canadian government's response to *Truchon*,[3] a 2019 ruling of the Quebec Superior Court. In *Truchon*, the Quebec court declared that criteria limiting MAiD access to persons whose natural deaths are "reasonably foreseeable" (under the federal law) or who are at the "end of life" (under the Quebec law) were unconstitutional. Neither the Quebec nor the federal attorney general appealed that court decision, even though the case raised several troubling questions about the treatment of evidence, reliance on the concept of discrimination (which no majority of the Supreme Court of Canada had ever done in relation to this end-of-life topic), and the interpretation of rights under the *Canadian Charter of Rights and Freedoms* (the *Charter*).[4] The official reason for not appealing the judgment given by then federal attorney general, minister of justice David Lametti, was that the government "strongly believed legally we would lose on its constitutionality," and that appealing the decision would mean that "so many more Canadians would have had to suffer for so much longer."[5]

But it seems like no coincidence that the decision not to appeal *Truchon* was first announced in the middle of the 2019 election period by Prime Minister Justin Trudeau during a televised debate, whereas such a decision is in fact the prerogative of the attorney general, whose institutional role is to defend the laws of Parliament.[6] The federal government accepted without challenge a single province's court ruling that directly undermined a law the federal government itself had steered through Parliament only three years prior and that had been adopted by a large majority.[7] The failure to appeal *Truchon* signalled a marked departure from the historically careful development of contemporary Canadian medical law and policy, in that the federal government permitted an issue of great ethical complexity involving matters of life and death to be directed by a single superior court judge.

Having received several extensions to the suspension of the "declaration of invalidity" from the *Truchon* ruling, the federal government eventually pushed Bill C-7 through both houses of Parliament in the midst of the COVID-19 pandemic.[8] The resulting law amended the first Canadian MAiD law – the provisions of which are part of Canada's Criminal Code[9] – effective 17 March 2021 (Bill C-7, also known as the "new law" or the "2021 amendments").

The main purpose of the 2021 amendments, as directed by *Truchon*, was to allow people whose natural deaths are not reasonably foreseeable to be able to access MAiD – in Canada, this is now colloquially known as "track 2" MAiD. However, the new law differs in several other respects from the original version of the MAiD law passed in 2016.[10] In particular, the 2021 amendments eliminated key safeguards previously in place for persons whose "natural deaths are reasonably foreseeable" – now known as "track 1" MAiD. For example, it reduced the independent witness requirement at the time MAiD is applied for from two to only one, and the witness can now also be a paid health care worker,[11] and it further eliminated the former mandatory final consent requirement that had required a patient's express consent immediately prior to the physician proceeding with the life-terminating act.[12] This new "waiver of final consent" was introduced for persons who are approaching their natural death (track 1) and allows MAiD to be given to non-capable patients if a capable patient made a verbal agreement with a MAiD provider in advance to waive the final consent requirement.[13] The mandatory ten-day waiting period between a MAiD application and the procedure, which was already flexible since it could be shortened in case of risk of loss of capacity or risk of imminent death, was also removed for track 1.[14] The goals of the law were also slightly different from those of the first law. The preamble, unlike Bill C-14, did not mention, for example, the goal of avoiding a "negative perception of the quality of life of persons who are elderly, ill, or disabled."[15] Interestingly, however, the preamble referred to Canada's obligations under the United Nations Convention of the Rights of Persons with Disability (CRPD) and affirmed "the inherent and equal value of every person's life and the need to take a human rights-based approach to disability-inclusion."[16] It is worth noting that the CRPD imposes on member states an obligation to "promote positive perceptions ... towards persons with disabilities" and to "combat stereotypes, prejudices, and harmful practices."[17] Even though the new law no longer explicitly refers to avoiding negative perceptions as a goal in the preamble, it arguably is indirectly included through references to the CRDP.

As we discuss below, the downgrading of "reasonably foreseeable natural death" from a substantive eligibility criterion to only a procedural consideration not only prioritized the patient's subjective perspective of their condition over objective medical assessment of that condition, but also set the stage for the transformation of medical professional standards and the processes by which those standards are identified.[18]

Additionally, as a result of amendments made by the Senate that were not debated in the House of Commons – a motion submitted by minister Catherine McKenna adopted by a majority of Liberal and Bloc Québécois MPs explicitly closed further debate on the bill[19] – Bill C-7 went even further. It established that within two years of the new law, MAiD was to be permitted for situations where mental illness is the sole medical condition or diagnosis involved.[20] In other words, as of March 2023 in Canada, persons suffering from medical conditions such as schizophrenia, depression, post-traumatic stress disorder, anxiety, obsessive-compulsive disorder, and possibly other disabilities that are also categorized as mental illnesses-were poised to be able to access MAiD for suffering attributable to these illnesses.[21] Following a one-year pause due to concerns about "system readiness,"[22] the federal government passed Bill C-62 in February 2024 to further suspend the expansion of MAiD eligibility to persons suffering solely from mental illness until at least March 2027;[23] yet the current government continues to send a message that it remains fully committed to eventually implementing MAiD for sole reasons of mental illness.[24]

In order to qualify for MAiD under track 2 (i.e., where death is not reasonably foreseeable), the person must still satisfy the other eligibility criteria, including being eighteen years of age, making a voluntary request, and having a "grievous and irremediable medical condition" (defined further below).[25] It should be noted, however, that additional procedural safeguards exist for persons in the second track. There is, for example, an assessment period of ninety days between the first eligibility assessment and the day on which MAiD is provided.[26]

In terms of the scope of medical practice, the imposition of procedural safeguards (whatever they may be) does not change the fact that Canada's track 2 MAiD drills down to the state empowering medical and nurse practitioners to terminate people's lives on the basis of disability.[27] Indeed, the substantive criticism most often voiced by commentators and members of disability rights groups, with which the authors agree,[28] is that the very foundation of this law is discriminatory towards people with disabilities. How so?

The new law has introduced a second access regime to MAiD for persons whose medical conditions meet all the same criteria except for the consideration of "reasonably foreseeable" natural death.[29] Specifically, to receive MAiD, requesting persons must have a "grievous and irremediable" medical condition, meaning they must:

1 have a serious and incurable illness, disease, or disability;
2 be in an advanced state of irreversible decline in capability; and
3 be experiencing intolerable physical or psychological suffering caused by the illness, disease, or disability that cannot be alleviated under conditions acceptable to that person.[30]

By definition, persons with an advanced irreversible decline in capability and who have a serious illness, disease, *or* disability *are* persons with disabilities. Furthermore, "discrimination on the basis of disability" means *inter alia* any distinction on the basis of disability which has the effect of impairing the enjoyment of human rights on an equal basis with others.[31] The new MAiD law thus introduces a death protocol exclusively for persons with disabilities even when their condition is not of a nature that makes them approach their death and even when they may otherwise have years or decades of life left. People with disabilities, which would include persons with any chronic or life-limiting illness, are told by the law that the protections against premature death available to all others in Canadian society (including, for example, suicide prevention initiatives) do not apply to them. Outside of the end-of-life context, they alone will *not* benefit from *all* the state protections working to guard against premature death and suicide applicable to non-disabled members of society. In short, the introduction of the track 2 option is discriminatory towards persons with disabilities since it creates an exclusive fast-track to premature death outside the end-of-life context for people with disabilities.[32]

The law is ableist: by advancing unequal protection it embodies and conveys a societal judgment about the different quality and different inherent value of the lives of people living with disabilities, including persons with chronic illnesses and older persons. This critique of the ableist structure of the new MAiD law has been voiced by all major disability rights organizations, the UN special rapporteur on the rights of persons with disabilities, and other UN human rights rapporteurs and experts.[33] It is therefore understandable, and critical, that the issue of ableism continues to be at the centre of the discussion and debate around MAiD. With this comes yet another critical – and indeed related – question that so far has received scant attention, that is, what the new MAiD law means to the practice of medicine and the effect this has had or will have on patients.

In our view, with its internationally unprecedented MAiD law, Canada has reached one of the most significant junctures in death law reform because of the treatment of and interplay between two key doctrines that all medical practitioners are intimately familiar with, namely the *standard of care* and *informed consent*. Indeed, the general disregard or silence regarding the impact of our MAiD law on how medicine has, up to this point, determined and applied the standard of care constitutes a remarkable instrumentalization of medicine and to some extent even a deconstruction of the medical profession as a learned profession. There is little transparent discussion from all stakeholders in Canadian health care (including health professional organizations or policy scholars who, in principle, endorse the expansion of MAiD outside the end-of-life context) about the impacts of the new law on medical practice and doctrine. Indeed, the concept of introducing "death" as a medical treatment option to persons who are not even dying, from the medical standard of care perspective, is clinically (and legally) suspect. This concern has, in fact, already become an issue in the context of some of the more flexible interpretations and applications of Canadian MAiD law.[34]

It remains a key question as to why the Canadian medical profession is being leveraged, directed, and even compelled to participate in actively and intentionally ending the lives of patients, even in circumstances where evidenced-based medicine suggests there are available treatments that could potentially address the suffering associated with those conditions. While the answer to the *why* question can likely only be answered in the long game, the more targeted question of *how* can be explored – in a preliminary way – within the scope of a chapter.

This chapter therefore explores how medicine has been compelled to shoulder the act of terminating a human life on the basis of suffering that has some nexus (sometimes only remotely) with a "medical" condition, even for conditions for which treatments are available. As part of unpacking how these medical doctrines operate in relation to MAiD, we explain how certain medical doctrines have been engaged (or conversely, disregarded) as Canadian MAiD law reform has proceeded. In addition to providing information that may assist in contemplating how Canadian MAiD reform is impacting medico-legal doctrines and the professional practice of medicine in Canada, the goal of this chapter is to demonstrate how the act of causing death is being medically and legally constructed as a "first-line" therapy for suffering Canadians.

Following a description of the relevant medico-legal doctrines and concepts, this chapter explores the application, operation, and interactions between the standard of care and informed consent within the emergent MAiD law in Canada. More specifically, this discussion describes how:

1 the new MAiD law is dislodging the standard of care;
2 the construction of constitutional or human rights concepts of "right to die" and "effective referral" demonstrates a rejection of the standard of care and a reshaping of the practice of medicine;
3 the (mis)application of informed consent is opening up the standard of care and breaking down the "voluntary request" eligibility criterion;
4 the standard of care is being subsumed into MAiD treatment through the (mis)application of informed consent;
5 informed consent doctrine is replacing standard of care as a result of legal imprecision going back to the *Carter* case; and
6 MAiD is being established as first-line therapy for "suffering."

In our conclusion, we note that unless Canadian medical practice clarifies and reclaims the professional standard of care as key doctrine for medical practice and as distinct from other mechanisms by which new procedures such as MAiD are introduced (in this case through legislation), the role and responsibility of the medical profession in determining what constitutes appropriate health care or appropriate medical practice will become increasingly fragile. With MAiD, Canada is in our view already setting international precedent in fundamentally undermining and altering the very foundations of professional medical practice and the duties of physicians arising out of and in accordance with the standard of care.

DUTY OF CARE, STANDARD OF CARE, INFORMED CONSENT, AND FIDUCIARY DUTY

It is important to clarify from the outset some key, interconnected legal-medical concepts: the duty of care; the standard of care; the concept of informed consent; and fiduciary duty and the fiduciary relationship.

Duty of Care

Whenever a physician-patient relationship exists, the physician has a *duty of care* towards the patient, meaning that a physician has a legal obligation to exercise care that medically benefits the patient and is in the patient's interests.[35] This will include, for example, an obligation to bring a certain level of skill, knowledge, and degree of care when dealing with a patient.[36]

Standard of Care

The actual level of skill, knowledge, and degree of care required of a physician is determined by a different long-standing professional rule and medico-legal doctrine known as the *standard of care*. The standard of care is an objective professional standard that requires every physician to bring to each and every task a reasonable degree of skill, knowledge, and care, with what is reasonable being determined by considering the skills, knowledge, and care of professional peers in similar circumstances. As the Ontario Court of Appeal ruled in *Sylvester v. Crits et al.*, "Every medical practitioner must bring to his task a reasonable degree of skill and knowledge and must exercise a reasonable degree of care. He is *bound to exercise that degree of care and skill which could reasonably be expected of a normal, prudent practitioner of the same experience and standing* and, if he holds himself out as a specialist, a higher degree of skill is required of him than one who does not profess to be so qualified by special training and ability."[37]

Failure to meet and uphold the standard of care is a breach of the doctor's duty of care. It is pursuant to the professional standard of care, then, that a physician identifies the appropriate medical treatment options to be presented to the patient for consideration and discussion. While a physician's duty of care includes obligations to treat the patient in accordance with a patient's best interests and not to abandon a patient, for example, a physician has no duty to provide whatever treatment a patient might request.[38] Again, the scope and limits of what physicians may or may not present to patients as suitable treatment options are circumscribed by the professional standard of care, not the demands of patients. While shared decision-making and patient-centred care are obviously vital, this does not allow patients to insist on procedures that would violate the standard of care. Physicians can only present medical treatment options that are beneficial and reasonably and objectively indicated. This is determined from the perspective of the normal, prudent practitioner.[39] The fact that a patient may ultimately consent to a treatment proposed by a physician does not dislodge this a priori standard.[40] Similarly, the fact that a patient may ultimately refuse a recommended treatment has absolutely no bearing on the identification of appropriate treatment through operation of this a priori standard.

Informed Consent

Once an appropriate treatment option or procedure has been identified (pursuant to the professional standard of care), the physician is obligated to provide the patient with full disclosure in respect of that treatment or procedure. This means that physicians must provide information that a "reasonable" person in the patient's position would want to know in order to allow the patient to make a decision in their best interests and to exercise their autonomy and self-determination. Information to be provided should include the nature of the proposed treatment, material risks and benefits of the proposed treatment and alternatives, as well as the consequences of inaction.[41] Failure of a physician to obtain fully informed consent for a treatment or procedure, regardless of outcome (positive or negative), constitutes a professional violation that can result in physician liability.

Similarly, a competent, capable patient always retains a right to refuse *any* recommended treatment or procedure, even if a treatment is potentially lifesaving.[42] Again, treating without consent or contrary to consent can result in physician liability.

Fiduciary Duty and the Fiduciary Relationship

Physicians have long been described as having a *fiduciary duty* towards their patients based on the fact that physicians occupy a special position of trust and confidence. As such, physicians must act with good faith towards their patients and in their best interests.[43] Canadian courts have explained the fiduciary relationship as having three particular attributes: "(1) the fiduciary has scope for the exercise of some discretion or power; (2) the fiduciary can unilaterally exercise that power or discretion so as to affect the beneficiary's legal or practical interests; and (3) the beneficiary is peculiarly vulnerable to or at the mercy of the fiduciary holding the discretion or power."[44]

With respect to that peculiar vulnerability, the courts have emphasized that a physician holds great power over a patient. As put by Justice McLachlin (as she then was) of the Supreme Court of Canada in the *Norberg v. Wynrib* case: "Whether physically vulnerable or not, however, the patient, by reason of lesser expertise, the 'submission' which is essential to the relationship, and sometimes ... by reason of the nature of the illness itself, is typically in a position of comparative powerlessness. The fact that society encourages us to trust our doctors, to believe that they will be persons worthy of our trust, cannot be ignored as a factor inducing a heightened degree of vulnerability."[45]

The recognized power differential between physicians and patients makes the proper functioning of the standard of care and informed consent doctrines all that more critical. Remarkably, the impact of the power differential between doctors and patients that is so well recognized and established in law is often downplayed or entirely ignored even by legal experts in the debates concerning the proper restrictions on MAiD.

HOW THE NEW MAiD LAW IS DISLODGING THE STANDARD OF CARE

The new MAiD law enables physicians to actively end the life of non-dying people with disabilities or chronic illnesses at their "request."[46] It requires that the medical system ensure that life termination takes place even when physicians in applying their skill and knowledge are aware of medical treatment options, and even when patients may have years or decades to live with potentially good quality of life, if those identified options are explored and pursued. This is because the new MAiD law dislodges or compromises the full application and operation of the doctrine of the standard of care (which again is the mechanism that clarifies the appropriate treatments and interventions) by adding death as a medical treatment option for potentially anyone presenting with a "serious" illness, disease, or disability. Put another way, intentionally ending the life of a patient is elevated to the same level as other treatment options that arise out of the operation of the standard of care and is a homogeneous generic treatment that becomes indicated for any patient who presents with a "serious" illness, disease, or disability.[47]

The application of the standard of care to a particular patient's situation is determined by a complex process involving, for example, medical research, evidence-informed experience, and standards and rules set by the regulatory agencies and professional organizations relevant to the practice of medicine.[48] Less invasive options will typically be explored first, with higher-risk interventions as a last resort. While patients determine which option(s) to proceed with and can of course express their preferences, it is on the basis of the standard of care that physicians insist that first-line treatments be exhausted first, before more invasive interventions with a different risk/benefit profile are offered. For example, total hip or knee replacements for arthritis require that appropriate attempts at non-surgical interventions be tried first, in a gradual shift from lifestyle modifications (diet and exercise) to pain medication. Surgery would be a last resort – and while cost constraints can play a role (health care funders may require that less costly procedures are tried first) this has no bearing on treatments identified through the operation of the standard of care. Likewise, even if the patient requested it, no neurologist would offer deep brain stimulation to a person with epileptic seizures without first trying less invasive treatments such as anti-epileptic medications, in line with evidenced-based practice.

Because physicians cannot offer treatments that run counter to the standard of care, surely they cannot – pursuant to that same standard of care – offer and provide to the patient the ending of their life, an ultimate and irreversible harm, if in their professional opinion other medical interventions could provide relief. Yet, because of how the Canadian MAiD law is drafted (without, for example, explicit language to describe that death is an exceptional last resort intervention[49]), this has been precisely the result. If the MAiD eligibility boxes are successfully checked, the process to determine the proper medical treatment for a particular condition becomes intertwined with the MAiD process. Standard medical practice, requiring the offer of medical treatment options arising out of the standard of care, becomes diminished, if not wholly irrelevant, except perhaps to the extent that treatment options are reformulated as safeguards that the patient requesting MAiD needs to carefully consider, as discussed further below.

The MAiD law's requirement that the condition must also be "incurable" serves, in reality, little to no clinical or legal purpose, given that a patient always retains the right to refuse treatment pursuant to the *no treatment without consent* principle.[50] So here we can observe a shift in the operation of the standard of care, the dilution of the medical professional role, and the instrumentalization of medicine, in that a patient, on the basis of the MAiD law, can demand that a health are professional end their life, even if, pursuant to the standard of care and medical professional judgment, appropriate alternative treatments are available.

HOW CONCEPTIONS OF A CONSTITUTIONAL "RIGHT TO DIE" AND A DUTY OF "EFFECTIVE REFERRAL" IMPLY A REJECTION OF THE STANDARD OF CARE

MAiD has been presented in Canada as a medical treatment option, first to address the suffering of persons whose deaths are "reasonably foreseeable," and then a few years later to also address the suffering of persons whose natural deaths are not "reasonably foreseeable." This has been done on the basis of a questionable construction of a constitutional right to die, not because it constitutes evidenced-informed medical practice through operation of the standard of care. That is, a vague concept of a constitutional "right to die," which has never been expressly recognized in Canada, has resulted in a rejection of the standard of care process that obligates physicians to apply their skills and intricate knowledge to a patient's particular clinical circumstances to identify relevant treatment.[51] Interestingly, in the *Carter* case, which is often invoked in support of such a right, the Supreme Court of Canada rejected the idea that the right to life included a "right to die with dignity."[52]

The political strength of a perceived "constitutional right to die" arising out of the *Carter* and *Truchon* dialogues combined with the designation of MAiD as an insured medical service in Canada conceptualizes MAiD not as a "last resort" option but rather as a potential first-line therapy.[53] Medical regulatory authorities in certain Canadian provinces (e.g., Ontario and Nova Scotia) have further contributed to this construction by imposing "effective referral" or transfer of care policies that require doctors who do not wish to participate in MAiD as a matter of conscience or religion to refer or directly connect MAiD requesting patients to willing physicians or nurse practitioners, or to a service or agency.[54]

A new *Model Practice Standard* developed in 2023 by a task group convened by the federal government as a "resource" for regulators not only includes the effective referral requirement but goes even further.[55] The standard remarkably suggests that if an otherwise willing MAiD provider forms the opinion in a specific case that MAiD is not indicated, this is to be considered as "unwillingness" and a "conscientious objection" and mandates the physician to complete an effective referral.[56]

To require doctors who do not want to provide MAiD in particular circumstances to carry out an effective referral demonstrates abandonment of the professional standard of care to the extent that it would mandate physicians to trigger or facilitate a life-ending procedure even if the professional standard of care mandates other options. It also contributes to a narrative that in not participating in MAiD, an objecting physician (or institution for that matter) is somehow abandoning their patient.

Perhaps even more critically, while MAiD eligibility requires that a medical condition (illness, disease, or disability) be the *cause* of the patient's suffering, the law does not appear to require an actual *clinical nexus* between the condition conferring eligibility and the experience of suffering. This is not only because a patient can refuse treatment that could address their suffering but also because the MAiD law describes that the experience of suffering and its possible relief are to be interpreted and determined entirely from the patient's perspective.[57] The experience of suffering (for purposes of qualifying for MAiD) appears to be disconnected from the medical condition at the basis of the request. Indeed, there have been several reports in Canada of cases where people have described that their motive for requesting MAiD was not their medical condition (which made them eligible for MAiD) but rather their experiences of poverty, homelessness, or lack of support to live and engage in society.[58] As these numerous controversial cases suggest, and as the Health Canada data about what patients consider to be unbearable suffering confirms, the experience of living or trying to survive within a society that fails to ensure the most basic care, housing, and supports has become treated as a source of suffering that can justify MAiD. Even if a physician could tease out what might be non-qualifying "motivations" for MAiD, a doctor's obligation to provide or effectively refer for MAiD squarely rests on the disability-centric eligibility criteria and not on the absence of socially constructed suffering and hardship (except perhaps to the extent that the physician might question consent – and even then there would still be a responsibility to carry out "effective" referral).

It is therefore not only rejecting the role of standard of care that is problematic (the duty to proceed or refer even when physicians are of the professional opinion that other medical interventions are available being a clear example of this), but also its impact, which allows the leveraging of medicine and doctors to end human lives to address suffering that patients themselves attribute to societal shortcomings rather than to an underlying medical condition. This seems to point to a practice or professional philosophy that has very little in common with the practice of medicine and could even be considered completely antithetical to it.

HOW THE (MIS)APPLICATION OF INFORMED CONSENT IS OPENING UP THE STANDARD OF CARE AND BREAKING DOWN THE "VOLUNTARY REQUEST" ELIGIBILITY CRITERION

From the outset, the Canadian MAiD law has also been particularly problematic with respect to the application of another medical doctrine – the doctrine of informed consent.

Within Canadian MAiD law and practice, *informed consent* functions as both:

1 an eligibility criterion or basis for considering MAiD as a treatment option – which takes precedence over the standard of care (as described above); and
2 the principal safeguard to protect "the vulnerable" from MAiD itself – with ambivalence to the fact that those seen to be the beneficiaries of MAiD (i.e., patients) are also those who most require the upholding of the standard of care.[59]

Evidence of the blurring or replacing of the standard of care with informed consent can perhaps be most easily observed in a 2022 guidance document developed by the Canadian MAiD Assessors and Providers (CAMAP), which describes how on the basis of the doctrine of informed consent, a clinician should raise MAiD as an option when a patient appears to meet the eligibility criteria.[60] This MAiD access-focused suggestion by CAMAP was incorporated into the federal government's 2023 *Model Practice Standard*, which should not be surprising given that certain experts invited by the federal government to help develop the *Model Practice Standard* also participated in the development of the CAMAP guidance document.[61]

Thus, through recourse to the concept of informed consent, ending of life or "death treatment" is encouraged and introduced into the physician's general conversation about treatment options, which, as already discussed, should be identified through recourse to the standard of care. In other words, MAiD is being constructed as a global medical treatment option for any chronic medical condition or disability and as such is being layered onto the standard of care in Canada. Thus, as observed by one commentator, MAiD is a "grenade to the fundamental structure and function of medicine."[62]

Furthermore, recourse to informed consent as a multi-purpose vehicle for both determining MAiD treatment eligibility and for directing its process is in turn confronting or narrowing the interpretation of other criteria established in the MAiD law. In addition to impacting the interpretation of suffering as "intolerable" as described above, perspectives on informed consent are impacting the interpretation of another critical eligibility criterion, namely that persons must have made a "request" that is "voluntary" and "not made as a result of external pressure."[63]

For example, certain MAiD proponents and organizations such as CAMAP appear to have rejected a plain-reading interpretation of the "voluntary request" requirement that would appear to require that a MAiD request must first come from the patient. Rather, vocal proponents of MAiD appear to lean on informed consent doctrine to encourage an interpretation that situates the "request" eligibility requirement more like a procedural safeguard to ensure that the practitioner obtain a written request prior to proceeding with the life-terminating act.[64] This also appears to be the result of the federal government's *Model Practice Standard*, which, like the 2022 CAMAP document,[65] describes the following duties:

6.0 Duties to Persons Potentially Eligible for MAID

6.1 [Physicians/Nurse Practitioners] *must* take reasonable steps to ensure persons are *informed* of the full range of treatment options available to relieve suffering.

6.2 [Physicians/Nurse Practitioners] *must not assume* all persons *potentially eligible* for MAID *are aware* that MAID is legal and available in Canada.

6.3 *Upon forming reasonable grounds to believe that a person may be eligible* for MAID, a [physician/nurse practitioner] *must* determine whether MAID is consistent with the person's values and goals of care and:

6.3.1 if consistent,
   (a) *advise the person of the potential for MAID; or*
   (b) *provide an effective [referral/transfer of care]* to another physician, nurse practitioner, or program known to be willing to discuss eligibility for MAID;

6.3.2 if not consistent, do not advise the person of the potential for MAID.[66]

To date, there has been very little analysis of the interplay between the voluntary request eligibility criterion, the informed consent eligibility criterion, and the encouragement of practitioners to introduce MAiD to potentially eligible persons (or effectively refer them) on the basis of the doctrine of informed consent in combination with practitioners' perceptions of a patient's "values." One can only speculate how the common law would actually reconcile the application of informed consent with the potential coercive impact or undue influence of physicians introducing MAiD to patients who have not requested it.[67] This architecture of choice is particularly questionable in light of the well-recognized fiduciary relationship between doctors and patients and characterized by a heightened degree of vulnerability that results in specific obligations for physicians. Regrettably, neither the federal or provincial legislators nor the professional organizations have provided any clarification about how this idea of introducing MAiD to non-requesting persons can be reconciled with the notion of "voluntary request."[68]

HOW THE STANDARD OF CARE IS BEING SUBSUMED INTO MAiD THROUGH INFORMED CONSENT

It is true that the expanded 2021 law retains other qualifying or eligibility criteria. As described, in addition to providing informed consent and making a voluntary request, to qualify for MAiD, patients must be eighteen years of age and "capable" of making health decisions. Patients must also have a "grievous and irremediable medical condition," which is defined as a "serious and incurable illness, disease, or disability," and being in an "advanced state of irreversible decline in capability" causing "enduring" and "intolerable" suffering (physical or psychological).[69]

But it is not clear what might count as "serious" illness, or what is considered an "advanced state of irreversible decline in capability." As already described, with MAiD, "incurable" as an objective clinical term does not have much of a role to play given a patient's right to refuse treatment, and suffering already tends to be interpreted subjectively as determined by the patient.[70] Many, if not most, disabling conditions would seem to fall under the new law. For instance, severe hearing, vision, or mobility loss are all forms of disability that can cause irreversible decline of capability and could thus qualify.[71]

It is therefore easy to observe how informed consent is positioned to replace *in toto* the additional substantive eligibility criteria that currently restricts MAiD access. Perhaps this is why the Canadian MAiD law from the outset positioned informed consent as an eligibility criterion rather than a procedural safeguard. Interestingly, the 2021 amendments include a somewhat "enhanced" informed consent requirement within the procedural safeguards for patients whose deaths are not reasonably foreseeable (i.e., track 2), reflecting, it would seem, the particular gravity of the act of intentionally ending the life of persons who are not even remotely approaching their natural death.

For example, physicians have to agree that patients give "serious consideration" to all other options to relieve their suffering.[72] Additionally, within this second track to MAiD, physicians must not only ensure that patients have been "informed" of the various means to relieve their suffering, such as counselling and disability support services, but they must also ensure that patients have actually been "offered" consultations "with relevant professionals who provide those services or care."[73]

In a way, track 2 procedural safeguards potentially reflect some concept of standard of care in that alternatives to MAiD are offered to a patient. However, it must be noted that this is all subsumed into the MAiD process and falls short of recognizing any need to independently respect and uphold the standard of care and the crucial role it plays in evidenced-based medical practice.

While minimal eligibility criteria theoretically can be maintained (e.g., age, capacity, medical condition, or intolerable suffering), an informed consent-based MAiD regime, even if strengthened procedurally, is dislodging the gold standard required and expected of physicians: the ability to bring to each and every task a reasonable degree of skill, knowledge, and care as determined against the standards observed by their professional peers. The integrity of the standard of care is a critical mechanism that has kept physicians accountable and has held them to the highest level of medical practice. It is key to keeping all patients safe in the hands of their physicians. And it has been within the context of the standard of care exercised by physicians that patients have to exercise their consent to treatment proposed, not the other way around.

Indeed, in the view of the authors, an unadulterated standard of care doctrine remains crucial; when combined with informed consent it makes what is otherwise legally considered assault a justifiable medical intervention. Think about how much more important it is to maintain the role of standard of care as separate and distinct from the doctrine of informed consent when informed consent doctrine itself has been positioned in the law as an eligibility criterion for MAiD death.

HOW INFORMED CONSENT IS REPLACING THE STANDARD OF CARE

To understand how we have come to a point at which informed consent is positioned to dislodge the standard of care doctrine, it is helpful to go back to the Supreme Court of Canada's *Carter v. Canada* (AG) decision.[74]

In *Carter*, the Supreme Court ruled that consenting, competent adults who were suffering intolerably from a grievous and irremediable medical condition should be able to access active support from physicians to bring an end to their life. The Supreme Court invited Parliament to amend the Criminal Code's absolute prohibition against "physician-assisted death" to enable such access and gave Parliament one year to do so.[75] With its confirmation of the role of the criminal law and its emphasis on the need for a strict regulatory regime – a regime unique to MAiD – the Supreme Court acknowledged the exceptional and controversial nature of physician involvement in the intentional ending of patients' lives.[76] Indeed, if MAiD was like any other form of medical practice, why refer to strict regulation, and why intimate, for example, that Canadian Parliament could opt for a regime that allows for much less discretion in the interpretation of safeguards and restrictions than other euthanasia regimes, such as the Belgian regime?[77] The Supreme Court also underlined that the *Charter* rights of patients and physicians would need to be "reconciled" in any legislative and regulatory response.[78]

The Supreme Court further emphasized (and it bears repeating) that "the scope of this declaration is intended to respond to the factual circumstances in this case. We make no pronouncement on other situations where physician-assisted dying may be sought."[79] To briefly recap, the factual circumstances of the case involved a main plaintiff, Gloria Taylor, who was suffering from the progressive, degenerative condition ALS, and who described herself as "terminal."[80] She knew she was approaching her death, and she was actively "seeking" physician-assisted death.[81]

In crafting its decision, the Supreme Court recognized and discussed informed consent, and it felt the need to remind Canadians that in this context as well, patients have a right to refuse treatment even if that refusal results in the patient's death.[82] It reiterated, as it had stated in earlier cases, that the right to medical self-determination is "not vitiated by the fact that serious risks or consequences, including death" may flow from a patient's decision.[83]

But the recognition and protection of this general right to refuse an intervention does not mean that refusal of a recommended treatment on the basis of an informed consent requirement is equivalent to a right to compel a health care provider to provide or support active medical termination of life.[84] Even if the death of a patient with diabetes, for example, can become "reasonably foreseeable" in the event a patient refuses treatment, the distinction is exceptionally clear when viewed from a medical standard of care perspective, in that physicians are always obligated to comprehensively explore with the patient the treatment options that will indeed save their life. They would have to prioritize those treatment options in line with evidenced-based medicine that helps guide clinical options and decision-making.

Furthermore, it is important to note that in the *Carter* case, Ms Taylor was approaching her death and actively seeking physician-assisted dying.[85] Indeed, it is clear throughout the *Carter* decision that the Supreme Court was examining the rights of those "seeking" assistance in dying, which, as far as the *Carter* case goes, positions "seeking" as an eligibility criterion. In terms of informed consent, the court identifies the "informed consent standard" as a possible procedural standard for physicians to use for "patients who *seek* assistance in dying"[86] – in other words, informed consent doctrine is a safeguard procedure that does not substitute for nor satisfy the "seeking" criteria. Unfortunately, when the Supreme Court translated its constitutional analysis into its "declaration of invalidity," the eligibility requirement of *seeking* is expressly absent and seemingly substituted with the words "clearly consents":[87]

> The appropriate remedy is therefore a declaration that s. 241(b) and s. 14 of the Criminal Code are void insofar as they prohibit physician assisted death for a competent adult person who (1) *clearly consents* to the termination of life; and (2) has a grievous and irremediable medical condition (including an illness, disease or disability) that causes enduring suffering that is intolerable to the individual in the circumstances of his or her condition. "Irremediable," it should be added, does not require the patient to undertake treatments that are not acceptable to the individual. The scope of this declaration is intended to respond to the factual circumstances in this case. We make no pronouncement on other situations where physician-assisted dying may be sought.

This is arguably another step (or misstep) provoking the elevation of the doctrine of informed consent beyond a procedural safeguard role.

What also appears to have been lost is that the reference and reiteration of the right to refuse or withdraw treatment in the *Carter* case was made within the factual context of someone approaching her natural death, where it can be seen as consistent with the standard of care. The Supreme Court specifically stated, "We agree with the trial judge. An individual's response *to a grievous and irremediable medical condition* is a matter critical to their dignity and autonomy. The law allows *people in this situation to request palliative sedation, refuse artificial nutrition and hydration, or request the removal of life-sustaining medical equipment,* but denies them the right to request a physician's assistance in dying. This interferes with their ability to make decisions concerning their bodily integrity and medical care and thus trenches on liberty. And, by leaving people *like Ms. Taylor* to endure intolerable suffering, it impinges on their security of the person."[88] Palliative sedation, refusal of artificial nutrition and hydration, or removal of life-sustaining equipment only exist within certain exceptional medical circumstances, and the moral or ethical equivalence with MAiD only arises in those kinds of situations. In our view, it would be improper to interpret the Supreme Court's analysis above as equivalent (whether in morality, ethics, or rights) to circumstances where a patient is not in such extreme circumstances and may have years or decades of life left. Equating the right to refuse treatment with a right to ask for an active intervention explicitly aimed at terminating life from a standard of care perspective is questionable. Outside a factual context like *Carter*, the difference between asking a physician to provide MAiD (in its euthanasia form) – an action that invades one's bodily integrity (even up to the point of death) – and asking a physician to abstain from providing life-sustaining treatment (and thus also abstaining from invading the person's bodily integrity) seems even more obvious.

Whether on the basis of informed consent or conceptions of the constitutional rights arguments involved (i.e., the section 7 *Charter* rights of life, liberty, and security), some may nonetheless take the Supreme Court of Canada's *Carter* decision as a confirmation that MAiD should *always* be considered the standard of care when this is what the patient wants. But this constitutes a wholesale abandonment of the foundational idea that the medical profession has a professional responsibility to carefully consider what constitutes proper medical practice on the basis of evidence, unique knowledge, and expertise. This also operates in tandem with practices consistent with the physician's fiduciary duty to the patient in light of the power dynamic involved. Indeed the above-noted view of MAiD elevates informed consent to the status of sole arbiter of what constitutes proper medical practice.[89] A procedure (i.e., inducing death) that even the other established permissive legal regimes in the world – Belgium, the Netherlands, Luxembourg – recognize as a last resort and available only when no other options remain and is a stunning reversal of the concept of the standard of care that at minimum should be recognized and purposefully discussed.

In our view, it is astonishing that the Canadian Medical Association (CMA) expressed support for this approach when it endorsed the expansion of the MAiD law in 2020.[90] With some regulatory colleges following the CMA's lead, persons in a position to shape the Canadian medical profession are in our view undermining the very reason why society has provided it with self-regulatory powers. The health care professions are thereby also arguably abandoning their commitment towards patients to provide the best evidence-informed care. And it has done all this based on what appears to be a misuse of the concept of informed consent, a concept that is rarely fully realized in practice.[91]

And again, there remains the complicating matter of how the special trust relationship that exists between doctors and patients and the peculiar vulnerability of patients in relation to doctors ought to be reflected in MAiD practice. For example, how should the "voluntary request" eligibility requirement be interpreted given that death treatment for non-dying persons is now firmly established in Canadian health care: Should request mean "seeking," which, though altering the role of standard of care, would at least be consistent with the facts of the *Carter* case and a plain reading of the law? Or is the request requirement to be treated as merely a procedural consideration subsumed under an even more enhanced "informed consent" construction of MAiD whereby, contrary to what the standard of care might identify as possible treatments, physicians are encouraged and possibly even compelled to introduce the topic of MAiD to patients simply on the basis that they appear to be eligible?[92]

HOW MAiD IS BEING ESTABLISHED AS FIRST-LINE THERAPY FOR SUFFERING

While we already believe that the very foundation of the new MAiD law is ableist and discriminatory, we also believe there is no other country in the world that is elevating death into a first-line treatment on demand in the way that Canada has. As described above, our view is that this is occurring because as MAiD has become decriminalized and incorporated into medical practice, there has been a failure to properly respect and apply the distinct doctrines of duty of care, standard of care, informed consent, and fiduciary duty. This failure, in our view, makes the potential impact of an expansion outside the end-of-life context even more problematic and internationally unprecedented.

There are several examples in Canada's MAiD policy that confirm the unprecedented way in which access to MAiD is being promoted as if it were a first-line therapy pursuant to the standard of care.

Some of these examples have been mentioned elsewhere in this volume.[93] Perhaps the most remarkable is a CAMAP guidance document that describes how a track 2 MAiD request by a patient who is not approaching their natural death and who is therefore subject to the safeguard of a longer ninety-day evaluation period (with some additional informed consent procedures) can be transformed into a track 1 request (natural death reasonably foreseeable), thus avoiding the track 2 assessment period: "A person may meet the 'reasonably foreseeable' criterion if they have *demonstrated a clear and serious intent to take steps to make their natural death happen soon or to cause their death to be predictable.* Examples might include stated declarations to refuse antibiotic treatment of current or future serious infection, to stop use of oxygen therapy, to refuse turning if they have quadriplegia, or to voluntarily cease eating and drinking."[94] This explicitly enables the health care provider to fast-track the ending of life of a patient even in situations where the Canadian MAiD law at least recognizes the importance of exploring other options. While the law fails to insist that other options be tried first, which, as we discussed, would be in line with the normal operation of the standard of care, even this most minimal yet critical consideration is intentionally circumvented in policy recommendations. It is worth recalling here that these are recommendations by an organization the federal government is relying on for further MAiD guidance and education. It illustrates how standard of care requirements are deserted and replaced by informed consent procedures. It also illustrates how the work of the legislative branch specifically creating two tracks to MAiD can be circumvented by different actors in (or involved with) a different branch of government.

Another more complex, but not less disturbing, example that reflects the application of the informed consent procedure within MAiD (and Canada's apparent focus on ensuring equal access to MAiD for certain classes of individuals) is another CAMAP guidance document called "Medical Assistance in Dying (MAID) in Dementia."[95]

Ending the life of a person with dementia raises additional, unique concerns, the details of which we will not discuss here but which are discussed in another chapter in this volume.[96] The CAMAP document correctly points out that persons with early-onset dementia mostly retain capacity for health care decision-making. But there are concerns, particularly as dementia progresses, about the person's ability to understand and appreciate the consequences of complex decisions. There is even more controversy around the possibility of stipulating in advance that a person will still want MAiD once the disease progresses, and how to determine whether the person is, at that time in the future, suffering intolerably – an eligibility criterion. Even though a parliamentary committee recommended the introduction of MAiD on the basis of advance request, and Quebec has already formally legalized this practice – and is planning to implement this starting in the fall of 2024 – Parliament explicitly rejected a Senate amendment that would have introduced it with the 2021 expansion. Yet, if CAMAP guidance is followed, MAiD could potentially be provided to dementia patients who are no longer capable of decision-making based on a prior signed "waiver of final consent," which can, according to Canada's MAiD law, be signed by patients whose natural death is reasonably foreseeable under track 1 MAiD.

As mentioned, the option to waive final consent was introduced into the MAiD law in 2021 and arguably focused on situations where a person was approved for MAiD but was worried about an impending loss of capacity that could interfere with their ability to provide the required final consent at the time of the MAiD procedure.[97]

While the CAMAP document does not explicitly recommend using a waiver of final consent for persons diagnosed with dementia, it does provide a remarkably expansive interpretation of the concepts of "reasonably foreseeable natural death" (RFND) and "advanced state of irreversible decline of capability," which if applied, would make a waiver of final consent possible in dementia situations (it also recommends a practice not seemingly supported by a plain reading of the current MAiD law).

How so? First, the guidance document points to the fact that studies of dementia patients indicate a median survival from diagnosis of four to seven years and that "life expectancy of most dementia patients requesting MAiD would likely be less than five years, particularly in older patients."[98] It concludes that the death of persons with an onset of dementia is thus "not too remote" and would therefore fall under the criterion of RFND, which enables MAiD under track 1.[99] Second, the document puts an interesting spin on the requirement of "advanced state of irreversible decline of capability," which is a key requirement for MAiD under both track 1 and track 2. The CAMAP authors admit that it may be hard to determine when persons with dementia are in an "advanced" state of decline. But they argue that the mere risk of imminent loss of capacity is *prima facie* (i.e., in and of itself) an advanced state of irreversible decline."[100]

They put forward two reasons for this view: 1) the removal of MAiD as a permissible option (due to loss of capacity) will prevent them from making decisions about their life in the future, and 2) they will be deemed to have different interests once incapacitated.[101] What the CAMAP authors basically suggest is that the future inability to opt for MAiD causes or meets the advanced state of irreversible decline of capability requirements.

Finally, it is also remarkable how the guidance document recommends that if persons are not yet close to losing capacity, they should be periodically assessed to make sure that the imminent loss of capacity can be caught in time for them to opt for MAiD.[102] The recommendation the CAMAP authors make in this situation is worth reproducing in full, as it reflects a remarkably liberal approach to MAiD assessments, as well as a suggestion that seems to us to come very close to nudging or encouraging patients to proceed with MAiD, which would seem far removed from standard clinical practice and arguably may impact on voluntariness of consent.[103] It states:

> If a person with mild dementia requests MAID and is assessed as eligible except for being in an advanced state of irreversible decline in capability, then they should be reviewed periodically by their primary care provider (if willing to do so and experienced in the assessment of capacity) or by the clinician who is willing to provide MAID. When it is believed that they are close to losing capacity the *clinician should explicitly inform the patient that this is the case*. The provider may wish to have the decision confirmed by the other MAID assessor or the primary care provider, but this is not necessary. The patient may then choose to have MAID as all criteria are satisfied. The patient *is not obliged to accept the provider's advice* and may request continued ongoing review *but should be made aware that they might lose capacity and therefore their right to have an assisted death*.[104]

The CAMAP authors seem to suggest here that MAiD assessors are allowed to sign off on MAiD even when all criteria are not yet fulfilled, and then leave it up to one physician to conclude when MAiD can proceed in the future. There is, however, nothing in the law that explicitly allows this practice. We also draw attention to the remarkable statement that patients are "not obliged to accept" the provider's advice. And, as mentioned, since a waiver of final consent can be signed by persons whose death is reasonably foreseeable, and the CAMAP authors argue that this is the case with a diagnosis of dementia, MAiD could potentially be provided to a patient who has signed a waiver of final consent in the early stages of dementia, potentially several years prior to the procedure.

MAiD AS FIRST-LINE THERAPY AND MENTAL HEALTH

The concerns discussed in this chapter are only heightened with the planned expansion of MAiD for mental illness, a clinical context in which treatment refusal is already a key challenge. Imagine what it will mean for mental health care practice and suicide prevention if, in this new legal context, a severely depressed person who is assessed as capable of decision-making seeks help from a mental health provider. The mental health care provider would, if current recommendations from CAMAP and the federal *Model Practice Standard* are followed, have a duty to talk about treatment options, such as suicide prevention, and MAiD at the same time.[105] Counsellors or navigators would thus introduce, for example, psychotherapy, pharmacological options, *and* MAiD. If a patient refuses to try all available life-focused treatments, they could insist on obtaining MAiD instead, potentially as the first and only intervention. If, as discussed earlier, the approach reflected in some of the regulatory colleges' guidelines and policies is followed, health care providers may even have a professional obligation to facilitate MAiD by ensuring the patient is effectively referred to another health care provider who is "willing" to offer MAiD even if the first provider feels it would be inappropriate in the circumstances.[106] In our view, some existing MAiD practices, based on a flexible interpretation of "reasonably foreseeable death," had already created tensions with the concept of standard of care. Under more flexible interpretations of the original MAiD law, older persons with severe arthritis by virtue of their age, for example, could be deemed eligible for MAiD even if they were expected to live for several years and even when other means existed to alleviate suffering.[107]

The discussion around the adoption of the amended MAiD law (with no requirement that natural death be foreseeable) presented a specific opportunity to consider whether and in what ways the medical profession was being invited to abandon the commitment to the standard of care, given the other means available to address the suffering of patients. Bill C-7 could also have been an occasion to think carefully about the way in which some, including CAMAP, have pushed for a professional duty to put MAiD on the table for all patients who might appear to qualify, even when they have not requested it, and how such a suggestion is prima facie inconsistent with the doctrine of standard of care as well as fiduciary duty.

The implications of allowing the legalization of MAiD and the doctrine of informed consent to blur, ignore, or suspend the role and function of the doctrine of standard of care are grave. In addition to the impact on the profession and practice of medicine, these doctrinal shifts are introducing the following into the emergent MAiD scheme:

- A reasonable apprehension of undue influence or coercion: what would never be raised pursuant to the standard of care doctrine (i.e., causing death as a recommended medical treatment[108]) can now be raised by the physician within a relationship where the imbalanced power dynamic and its attendant potential impact on patient decision-making is well recognized.[109]
- Ableist-informed medical care: as suggested by CAMAP and the *Model Practice Standard*, physicians will be prompted and encouraged to raise death as a treatment option with patients whose conditions the physician perceives may potentially match MAiD eligibility requirements.[110]
- Destabilization of consent, the primary procedural MAiD safeguard aimed at protecting "vulnerable persons": without robust and distinct operation of the standard of care mechanism, consent for MAiD cannot possibly be "informed" against what constitutes appropriate medical treatment and care. In addition, some of the policy recommendations raise serious concerns about how informed consent may be undermined by undue pressure.

CONCLUSION

Canadian physicians should be expected and required to continue to uphold the standard of care regardless of a patient's medical condition or disability and to obtain informed consent – as is always required – before proceeding with *any* treatment. MAiD law and regulation as it attaches itself to the Canadian medical system should also respect the distinct roles of standard of care and informed consent doctrines and should expressly recognize how the MAiD option operates in distinction to treatment options that arise out of application of the standard of care process and evidence-based medicine.

Almost half a century ago, Robert Kouri, one of the éminence grise of Canadian health law, wrote: "Doctors and nurses, by the very nature of their training, are imbued with the idea that their function is to cure or at least to aid the sick or injured. In these circumstances, it is easy to understand how that time-worn adage, 'where there's life, there's hope' now enjoys the status of dogma. So is it with the general public which has come to expect cures, once held miraculous, as a matter of course. We are brought up to believe that life is the most precious 'commodity' we possess."[111]

Kouri wrote this in the context of a heated debate in Canada concerning the rights of religious minorities to refuse medical treatment, in an era when it was sometimes challenging to convince doctors to abstain from intervening or to avoid aggressive interventions aimed at trying to extend the life of a patient, even when such an intervention had little chance of success and came with serious side effects that had a terrible impact on the person's quality of life. How times have changed! Kouri discussed in the same chapter, focusing particularly on Quebec law, how medical law was constructed around three core pillars:

1 the inviolability of the human body;
2 the need to obtain informed consent before any intervention; and
3 the idea that care and treatment has to be identified and provided in a "reasonably diligent, competent and attentive"[112] way.

The last element captures the norm of the standard of care.

When we consider the manner in which professional medical associations and certain doctors have actively pushed for a broad right to request MAiD for disabled persons, it would appear that we are bearing witness to a major paradigm shift, whereby the standard of care pursuant to the third pillar has largely been abandoned, and the door has been opened to a transgression of the first, by overreliance on abstractions of constitutional rights and informed consent. It is a paradigm shift in which the societal role of the medical profession, an institution with a unique responsibility and duty to carefully consider their professional ethical obligations, has fundamentally changed.[113] One could be forgiven for interpreting the new MAiD law as rendering doctors simple agents, executing the will of the patient and contributing to the dogma that the latter – even when in a context of mental, social, or economic oppression and vulnerability – is always able to calmly weigh whether the advantages of death outweigh the advantages of continued life. In our view, it almost seems as if the MAiD law conceives the role of doctors and nurse practitioners as merely procedural, as verifying whether a patient consents to MAiD, whether they have "carefully considered" alternative options, and whether they meet the other criteria set out in the law. If so, the "treatment" is to be either administered or facilitated through effective referral. We also wonder whether health care providers have adequate training to understand how social determinants of health impact on people's experiences of suffering, but even if they do, the law does not appear to allow any space for professional judgment about other options.

Unless and until Canadian medical practice clarifies and reclaims the professional standard of care as a legitimate doctrine in the contemporary practice of evidenced-informed medicine, and distinct from the medicalized act of MAiD, Canada is setting international precedent for changing the very foundations of the profession itself. No other country in the world has elevated the administration of death by health care professionals as a first-line treatment for disability related suffering. It is, in our view, a deeply problematic legacy.

NOTES

This chapter is a significantly revised and expanded English version of Trudo Lemmens, Mary Shariff, and Leonie Herx, "L'Aide Médicale à Mourir et le sacrifice de la norme de qualité de soins de la pratique médicale," in *Mélanges Robert P. Kouri: L'humain au cœur du droit*, ed. Nathalie Vézina, Pascal Fréchette, and Louise Bernier (Cowansville: Éditions Yvon Blais, 2021), 621–44.

1 *Bill C-7, An Act to Amend the Criminal Code (medical assistance in dying)*, 43rd Parliament, 2nd Session (2021), SC 2021, c. 2 (Can.), https://www.parl.ca/DocumentViewer/en/43-2/bill/C-7/royal-assent.
2 See *Bill C-14, An Act to Amend the Criminal Code and to Make Related Amendments to Other Acts (medical assistance in dying)*, 42nd Parliament, 1st session (2016), SC 2016, c. 3 (Can.), https://www.parl.ca/LegisInfo/en/bill/42-1/C-14.
3 *Truchon v. Canada (Attorney General)*, 2019 QCCS 3792.
4 *Canadian Charter of Rights and Freedoms*, Part I of the *Constitution Act, 1982*, being Schedule B to the *Canada Act, 1982* (UK), 1982, c. 11. For a

critical review of the *Truchon* decision, see Trudo Lemmens and Laverne Jacobs, "The Latest Medical Assistance in Dying Ruling Needs to Be Appealed: Here's Why," *Conversation*, 9 October 2019, https://theconversation.com/the-latest-medical-assistance-in-dying-decision-needs-to-be-appealed-heres-why-124955; John Keown, *Euthanasia, Ethics, and Public Policy*, 2nd ed. (Cambridge: Cambridge University Press, 2018). See also chapter 12 (Shariff, Ross, and Lemmens).

5 *House of Commons Debates*, 23 February 2021 (Hon. David Lametti), Edited Hansard Volume 150, No. 064, 2nd Session, 43rd Parliament, 4418, https://www.ourcommons.ca/documentviewer/en/35-2/house/hansard-index.

6 Anne Marie Lecomte, "Aide médicale à mourir: Ottawa et Québec ne vont pas en appel," *Radio Canada*, 3 October 2019, https://ici.radio-canada.ca/nouvelle/1329478/quebec-aide-medicale-mourir-jugement-cour-supreme-pas-appel; John Sikkema, "Federal Leaders Still Don't Seem to Understand the Attorney General's Role," *National Post*, 10 October 2019, https://nationalpost.com/news/politics/election-2019/opinion-federal-leaders-still-dont-seem-to-understand-the-attorney-generals-role.

7 Bill C-14, c. 3.

8 For further discussion of the background to Bill C-7, see "Legislative Background: Bill C-7: Government of Canada's Legislative Response to the Superior Court of Québec *Truchon* Decision," Government of Canada, 1 September 2021, https://www.justice.gc.ca/eng/csj-sjc/pl/ad-am/c7/p1.html#intro-2.

9 *Criminal Code of Canada*, RSC, 1985, c. C-46, s. 241.1.

10 Bill C-14, c.3.

11 Compare amendments to the Criminal Code under *Bill C-14, Act to Amend the Criminal Code* to amendments pursuant to *Bill C-7, Act to Amend the Criminal Code*, s. 241.2 (3)(c).

12 See *Criminal Code of Canada*, ss. 241.2(3) and 241.2(3.2) for provisions related to the final consent waiver whereby an otherwise qualifying patient who may lose the capacity to consent to a MAiD procedure may agree in advance with the MAiD provider to waive the final consent requirement.

13 *Criminal Code of Canada*, ss. 241.2(3) and 241.2(3.2).

14 See *Criminal Code of Canada*, s. 241.2(3).

15 Bill C-14, at Preamble.

16 Bill C-7, at Preamble.

17 See article 8, "Awareness-raising," in "Convention on the Rights of Persons with Disabilities," 13 December 2006, 2515 UNTS 3 (entered into force 3 May 2008), https://www.ohchr.org/en/instruments-mechanisms/instruments/convention-rights-persons-disabilities. See also

the discussion in Gerard Quinn, Claudia Mahler, and Olivier De Schutter to Canada, "Mandates of the Special Rapporteur on the Rights of Persons with Disabilities; the Independent Expert on the Enjoyment of All Human Rights by Older Persons; and the Special Rapporteur on Extreme Poverty and Human Rights," 3 February 2021, ref OL CAN 2/2021, https://t.co/CGNlgjsYFw?amp=1 and our discussion of this letter.

18 Compare *Criminal Code of Canada*, s. 241.2(3), "Safeguards – Natural Death Foreseeable" to Criminal Code s. 241.2(3.1) "Safeguards – Natural Death Foreseeable."

19 *House of Commons Debates*, 11 March 2021, Edited Hansard Volume 150, No. 071, 2nd Session, 43rd Parliament, https://www.ourcommons.ca/DocumentViewer/en/43-2/house/sitting-71/hansard.

20 *Bill C-7, Act to Amend the Criminal Code*, s. 6.

21 Note, however, how the Canadian Association of MAiD Assessors and Providers, citing a governmental background document to Bill C-7, puts forward that assessors can decide on a case-by-case basis whether a serious illness should be considered a mental illness. The governmental document it cites puts forward that "In the context of the federal MAID legislation, the term 'mental illness' would not include neurocognitive or neurodevelopmental disorders, or other conditions that affect cognitive abilities, such as dementias, autism spectrum disorders or intellectual disabilities, which may be treated by specialties other than psychiatry (such as neurology for neurodegenerative or neurodevelopmental conditions) or specialties outside of medicine (such as specialists for intellectual disabilities)." See CAMAP, "Medical Assistance in Dying (MAID) Assessments for People with Complex Chronic Conditions," February 2023, https://camapcanada.ca/wp-content/uploads/CCC-Guidelines-Paper-February-2023-FINAL.pdf.

22 *Bill C-39, An Act to Amend An Act to Amend the Criminal Code (medical assistance in dying)*, 44th Parliament, 1st session (2023), SC 2023, https://www.parl.ca/DocumentViewer/en/44-1/bill/C-39/first-reading. For further discussion, see "Bill C-39: An Act to Amend An Act to Amend the Criminal Code (medical assistance in dying)," Government of Canada, 27 November 2023, https://www.justice.gc.ca/eng/csj-sjc/pl/charter-charte/c39.html.

23 *Bill C-62, An Act to Amend An Act to Amend the Criminal Code (medical assistance in dying)*, No. 2, 44th Parliament, 1st session, SC 2024, https://www.parl.ca/DocumentViewer/en/44-1/bill/C-62/royal-assent. For further discussion, see René Arseneault and Hon. Yonah Martin, MAID *and Mental Disorders: The Road Ahead, Report of the Special Joint Committee Medical Assistance in Dying*, 44th Parliament, 1st Session,

January 2024, https://www.parl.ca/DocumentViewer/en/44-1/AMAD/report-3/.

24 See, for example, Darren Major, "Federal Government Seeking Another Pause on Planned Expansion of Medical Assistance in Dying," CBC, 29 January 2024, https://www.cbc.ca/news/politics/medical-assistance-in-dying-mental-illness-delay-1.7098313.

25 *Criminal Code of Canada*, s. 241.2(1) and (2).

26 *Criminal Code of Canada*, s. 241.2(3.1) (i). Note that this assessment period is a maximum and can be reduced if determined appropriate in the context of an expected loss of capacity.

27 Note that under the MAiD law, both medical and nurse practitioners are permitted to practise MAiD. See *Criminal Code of Canada*, ss 241(2) and 241.2. The vast majority of MAiD providers, however, are physicians. See discussion in Health Canada, *Fourth Annual Report on Medical Assistance in Dying in Canada 2022*, October 2023, 6, 39, https://www.canada.ca/content/dam/hc-sc/documents/services/medical-assistance-dying/annual-report-2022/annual-report-2022.pdf.

28 Trudo Lemmens and Mary J. Shariff, "Brief to the Senate Standing Committee on Legal and Constitutional Affairs; Re. Bill C-7: An Act to Amend the Criminal Code (medical assistance in dying)," 19 November 2020, https://trudolemmens.wordpress.com/2020/11/28/medical-assistance-in-dying-brief-to-the-senate-standing-committee-on-legal-and-constitutional-affairs-by-trudo-lemmens-and-mary-shariff/.

29 Note that the new law positions "reasonably foreseeable" or "*not* reasonably foreseeable" as procedural considerations rather than as "eligibility" requirements. See *Criminal Code of Canada*, ss. 241.2(3) and 241.2(3.1).

30 *Criminal Code of Canada*, s. 241.2(2).

31 *Convention on the Rights of Persons with Disabilities*, 13 December 2006, 2515 UNTS 3 (entered into force 3 May 2008), https://www.ohchr.org/en/instruments-mechanisms/instruments/convention-rights-persons-disabilities.

32 See Michael Bach, Neil Belanger, and Catherine Frazee, "Canada Doesn't Need a Shortcut to Medically Assisted Dying for People with Disabling Conditions," *Hill Times*, 23 November 2020, https://www.hilltimes.com/story/2020/11/23/canada-doesnt-need-a-shortcut-to-medically-assisted-dying-for-people-with-disabling-conditions-2/268159/; Catherine Frazee, "Assisted Dying Legislation Puts Equality for People with Disabilities at Risk," *Globe and Mail*, 17 November 2020, https://www.theglobeandmail.com/opinion/article-assisted-dying-legislation-puts-equality-for-people-with-disabilities/; Isabel Grant, Archie Kaiser, and

Elizabeth Sheehy, "Bill C-7 Shatters Illusions Regarding Canada's Commitments to Persons with Disabilities," *National Newswatch*, 8 December 2020, https://www.nationalnewswatch.com/2020/12/08/bill-c-7-shatters-illusions-regarding-canadas-commitments-to-persons-with-disabilities/#.YMoFvpNKg-Q; Trudo Lemmens and Leah Krakowitz-Broker, "Why the Federal Government Should Rethink Its New Medical Assistance in Dying Law," CBC News, 10 November 2020, https://www.cbc.ca/news/opinion/opinion-medical-assistance-in-dying-maid-legislation-1.5790710.

33 Council of Canadian Disabilities, "Council of Canadians with Disabilities Denounces Trudeau Government's Re-introduction of Unamended Bill C-7 on Medical Aid in Dying as 'Head-in-the-Sand Mentality' that Endangers the Lives of Canadians with Disabilities," 5 October 2020, http://www.ccdonline.ca/en/humanrights/endoflife/Media-Release-Bill-C7-5October2020; United Nations, Human Rights Council, "Rights of Persons with Disabilities: Report of the Special Rapporteur on the Rights of Persons with Disabilities," Doc: A/HRC/43/41, 17 December 2019, https://undocs.org/en/A/HRC/43/41. See, for example, Gerard Quinn, Claudia Mahler, and Olivier De Schutter to Canada, "Mandates of the Special Rapporteur on the Rights of Persons with Disabilities; the Independent Expert on the Enjoyment of All Human Rights by Older Persons; and the Special Rapporteur on Extreme Poverty and Human Rights," 3 February 2021, ref OL CAN 2/2021, http://www.assisteddying.ca/UnitedNationsCommunicationFile(OL_CAN_2-2021)-Feb3rd2021.pdf; see also United Nations Human Rights Office of the High Commissioner, "Disability is Not a Reason to Sanction Medically Assisted Dying – UN Experts," 25 January 2021, https://www.ohchr.org/EN/NewsEvents/Pages/DisplayNews.aspx?NewsID=26687&LangID=E.

34 See, for example, Gabrielle Peters, "Taking MAiD Way Too Far," *Maclean's*, 4 February 2021, https://macleans.ca/opinion/taking-maid-way-too-far/; see also Avis Favaro and Elizabeth St Philip, "Chronically Ill Man Releases Audio of Hospital Staff Offering Assisted Death," CTV News, 2 August 2018, https://www.ctvnews.ca/mobile/health/chronically-ill-man-releases-audio-of-hospital-staff-offering-assisted-death-1.4038841; Geoff Bartlett, "Mother Says Doctor Brought Up Assisted Suicide Option as Sick Daughter Was within Earshot," CBC News, 24 July 2017, https://www.cbc.ca/news/canada/newfoundland-labrador/doctor-suggested-assisted-suicide-daughter-mother-elson-1.4218669; Murray Brewster, "Former Paralympian Tells MPs Veterans Department Offered Her Assisted Death," CBC News, 1 December 2022, https://www.cbc.ca/news/politics/christine-gauthier-

assisted-death-macaulay-1.6671721; Andrea Woo, "Vancouver Hospital Defends Suggesting MAID to Suicidal Patient As Risk Assessment Tool," *Globe and Mail*, 9 August 2023, https://www.theglobeandmail.com/canada/british-columbia/article-maid-suicide-patient-vancouver/; see also "Social Worker Suggests MAID to Woman Seeking Help for Depression," *Global News*, 10 August 2023, https://globalnews.ca/video/9889955/social-worker-suggests-maid-to-woman-seeking-help-for-depression/.

35 Note that this is a common law duty. For discussion on how the duty can arise in the civil code, see Canadian Medical Protective Association, *Medico-Legal Handbook for Physicians in Canada*, version 9.0, May 2021, revised February 2022, https://www.cmpa-acpm.ca/en/advice-publications/handbooks/medical-legal-handbook-for-physicians-in-canada#negligence-civil-responsibility.

36 Philip H. Osborne, *The Law of Torts*, 6th ed. (Toronto: Irwin Law Inc, 2020), 155ff. See also Canadian Medical Protective Association, *Medico-Legal Handbook for Physicians*.

37 *Sylvester v. Crits et al.*, 1956 CanLII 34 (ON CA), [1956] OR 132 (Can.) (affirmed [1956] SCR 991, 1956 CanLII 29 (SCC)), emphasis added.

38 For further discussion, see Canadian Medical Protective Association, *Medico-Legal Handbook for Physicians*. See also discussion of standard of care in *Cuthbertson v. Rasouli*, 2013 SCC 53 (CanLII), [2013] 3 SCR 341 (majority and dissenting judgments).

39 *Wilson v. Swanson*, 1956 CanLii 1 (SCC), [1956] SCR 804 at page 10; see also *Wawrzyniak v. Livingstone*, 2019 ONSC 4900 (CanLII), at para 101, https://canlii.ca/t/j21lm. See also ibid. at para 194: "[In *Rasouli*] McLachlin C.J.C. held that the clinical term 'medical benefit' has implications for the physician's standard of care, and she accepted that a physician may be required to offer a treatment to comply with the standard of care if the treatment would be of medical benefit to the patient. It follows that a physician is not always required to offer a treatment, and whether a physician is required to offer a treatment depends on the physician's professional assessment of whether the treatment offers a *medical* benefit. *Whether a treatment offers a medical benefit requires a contextual assessment of the patient's circumstances, including the patient's condition and prognosis, the expected result of treatment for that patient, and any risks of treatment for that patient* [emphasis added]."

40 Note that we do not suggest here that the "standard of care" is always clear and uncontested. Indeed, as Patrick Garon-Sayegh has eloquently argued, the standard of care often only becomes somewhat fixed through the complex interplay of expert testimony and judicial reasoning in court proceedings. See Patrick Garon-Sayegh, "Medicine at the Bar: Medical

Experts, Lawyers, and the Making of Medical Malpractice in the Courtroom" (PhD diss., University of Toronto, 2022), in particular 230–4. A discussion of this issue exceeds the scope of this chapter. It suffices here to acknowledge that there is within the medical profession an acknowledgment that certain standards must be respected, which are not dislodged by the mere preference or choice of a patient.

41 *Reibl v. Hughes*, [1980] 2 SCR 880, 1980 CanLII 23 (SCC).
42 *B. (R.) v. Children's Aid Society of Metropolitan Toronto*, 1995 CanLII 115 (SCC), [1995] 1 SCR 315; *Malette v. Shulman*, 1990 CanLII 6868 (ON CA), 72 OR (2d) 417 (Can.); *Fleming v. Reid*, 4 OR (2d) 74 (1991) (Can.).
43 *McInerney v. MacDonald*, 1992 CanLII 57 (SCC), [1992] 2 SCR 138, 154.
44 *Norberg v. Wynrib*, 1992 CanLII 65 (SCC), [1992] 2 SCR 226.
45 *Norberg*, 1992 CanLII 65 (SCC), [1992] 2 SCR 226; see also "Professionalism – Professionalism in the Patient-Physician Relationship," Canadian Medical Protective Association, January 2021, https://www.cmpa-acpm.ca/en/education-events/good-practices/professionalism-ethics-and-wellness/professionalism#ref.
46 Note again that nurse practitioners are also permitted to provide MAiD under the Criminal Code. See comment at note 22.
47 For an example of this, refer to Meghan Grant, "Calgary Judge Rules 27-Year-Old Can Go Ahead with MAID Death Despite Father's Concerns," CBC News, 25 March 2024, https://www.cbc.ca/news/canada/calgary/calgary-maid-father-daughter-court-injunction-judicial-review-decision-1.7154794.
48 Admittedly, as mentioned earlier, a final judgment of what constitutes the proper standard of care is in reality only firmly obtained when a court has ruled on what is at times conflicting medical expert evidence in court proceedings. See note 41.
49 See, for example, the discussion of the physician role and how "reasonable alternatives" are interpreted under the Dutch euthanasia law in Regional Euthanasia Review Committees, *Annual Report 2019*, 46, https://english.euthanasiecommissie.nl/binaries/euthanasiecommissie-en/documenten/publications/annual-reports/2002/annual-reports/annual-reports/Annual+report+2019.pdf; see also the discussion in Quebec and comments from the head of the Commission sure le soins de fin de vie in Jacob Serebrin, "Fear of Reprisal Means Some Quebec Doctors Are Afraid to Give MAID, College of Physicians Says," *Global News*, 25 August 2023, https://globalnews.ca/news/9919765/quebec-doctors-maid-worries/.
50 *Criminal Code of Canada*, s. 241.2(2)(a).

51 See also chapter 12 (Shariff, Ross, and Lemmens).
52 *Carter v. Canada (AG)*, 2015 SCC 5, [2015] 1 SCR 331 is the seminal decision of the Supreme Court of Canada that found the Criminal Code's absolute prohibition against "physician-assisted dying" was an infringement on the rights to life, liberty, and security pursuant to section 7 of the *Canadian Charter of Rights and Freedoms* and could not be saved by section 1. Following this decision, Parliament passed *Bill C-14, Act to Amend the Criminal Code*, which decriminalized the practice of medical assistance in dying or MAiD in 2016. See discussion in *Carter* paras. 59–63. Note also with respect to physicians, one of the plaintiffs was described as a physician who would be "willing to participate in physician-assisted dying if it were no longer prohibited." See *Carter* paras. 11 and 23.
53 As an insured service, MAiD treatment is subject to the "five principles" under the *Canada Health Act*, RSC, 1985, c. C-6, namely: administration, comprehensiveness, universality, portability, and accessibility. For further discussion of MAiD as an insured service, see chapter 12 (Shariff, Ross, and Lemmens).
54 "Medical Assistance in Dying," College of Physicians and Surgeons of Ontario (CPSO), June 2016, article 12(e), https://www.cpso.on.ca/Physicians/Policies-Guidance/Policies/Medical-Assistance-in-Dying#endnote02; see also "Professional Standard regarding Medical Assistance in Dying (MAiD)," College of Physicians & Surgeons of Nova Scotia (CPSNS), 26 April 2021, article 4.3, https://cpsns.ns.ca/resource/medical-assistance-in-dying/.
55 Health Canada, "Background Document: The Work of the Medical Assistance in Dying (MAiD) Practice Standards Task Group," March 2023, https://www.canada.ca/en/health-canada/services/publications/health-system-services/background-document-work-medical-assistance-dying-practice-standards-task-group.html; Health Canada, *Model Practice Standard for Medical Assistance in Dying (MAiD)*, March 2023, s 5.2.1, https://www.canada.ca/en/health-canada/services/publications/health-system-services/model-practice-standard-medical-assistance-dying.html#a3.
56 Ibid., s 5.2.1 and footnote 8: "Conscientious objection may be case specific. Some [physicians/nurse practitioners] are conscientiously opposed to all MAID. Some to only certain kinds of MAID (e.g., Track 2). Some to only specific cases given the specific circumstances. The same rules apply no matter the scope of objection – [physicians/nurse practitioners] cannot be compelled to participate but they must follow the steps laid out in 5.2 if they are unwilling to participate."

57 *Criminal Code of Canada*, s. 241.2(2)(c).
58 See, for example, Hannah Alberga, "Toronto Woman Facing Financial Loss of Long COVID Begins Process for Medically Assisted Death," CP24, 11 July 2022, https://www.cp24.com/news/toronto-woman-facing-financial-loss-of-long-covid-begins-process-for-medically-assisted-death-1.5982576?cache=juzexmjvhq; see also Avis Favaro, "Woman with Chemical Sensitivities Chose Medically-Assisted Death After Failed Bid to Get Better Housing," CTV News, 24 August 2022, https://www.ctvnews.ca/health/woman-with-chemical-sensitivities-chose-medically-assisted-death-after-failed-bid-to-get-better-housing-1.5860579; Brennan Leffler and Marianne Dimain, "How Poverty, Not Pain, Is Driving Canadians with Disabilities to Consider Medically-Assisted Death," *Global News*, 8 October 2022, https://globalnews.ca/news/9176485/poverty-canadians-disabilities-medically-assisted-death/; Janine LeGal, "Battle with ALS Brought Overwhelming Struggle for Supports," *Winnipeg Free Press*, 12 November 2022, https://www.winnipegfreepress.com/breaking-news/2022/11/12/battle-with-als-brought-overwhelming-struggle-for-supports; Moira Wyton, "'Jump or burn?': B.C. Woman Is Chronically Ill, But Dying of Poverty," *Tyee*, 14 November 2022, https://www.todayinbc.com/news/jump-or-burn-b-c-woman-is-chronically-ill-but-dying-of-poverty/; Hannah Alberga, "Toronto Woman in Final Stages of MAiD Application After Nearly a Decade-Long Search for Housing," CTV News, 15 November 2022, https://toronto.ctvnews.ca/toronto-woman-in-final-stages-of-maid-application-after-nearly-a-decade-long-search-for-housing-1.6145487; Cynthia Mulligan and Meredith Bond, "Ontario Man Not Considering Medically-Assisted Death Anymore After Outpouring of Support," *City News*, 16 November 2022, https://toronto.citynews.ca/2022/11/16/ontario-medically-assisted-death-support/; Andrew Phillips, "We're All Implicated in Michael Fraser's Decision to Die," *Toronto Star*, 18 November 2022, https://www.thestar.com/opinion/star-columnists/2022/11/18/were-all-implicated-in-michael-frasers-decision-to-die.html; Brooke Kruger, "Regina Resident Applied for Medically Assisted Death after Consistent Surgical Delays," *Global News*, 30 November 2022, https://globalnews.ca/news/9315789/regina-resident-medical-assistance-in-dying-surgical-delay/; Ruth Farquhar, "Farquhar: Are the Disabled Choosing Medically Assisted Death to Escape Poverty?" *Sudbury Star*, 21 November 2022, https://www.thesudburystar.com/opinion/columnists/farquhar-are-the-disabled-choosing-medically-assisted-death-to-escape-poverty; "Canadians Discuss Possible Amendments to Medical Assistance in Dying," CBC News, 2 February 2021, https://www.youtube.com/watch?v=S_ePnz_g4Es.

59 See, for example, *Criminal Code of Canada*, s. 241.2(1)(e) and 241.2(3)(a).
60 Canadian Association of MAiD Assessors and Providers, "Bringing up Medical Assistance in Dying (MAiD) as a Clinical Care Option," 2022, https://camapcanada.ca/wp-content/uploads/2022/02/Bringing-up-MAiD.pdf.
61 See Health Canada, "Background Document," 4.
62 Christopher Lyon (@ChristophLyon), Twitter, 10 December 2022, https://twitter.com/ChristophLyon/status/1601501252751613952.
63 *Criminal Code of Canada*, s. 241.2(1)(d).
64 See Canadian Association of MAiD Assessors and Providers, "Bringing up Medical Assistance in Dying"; see also discussion in Sharon Kirkey, "Canadian Doctors Encouraged to Bring Up Medically Assisted Death Before Their Patients Do," *National Post*, 2 November 2022, https://nationalpost.com/news/canada/canada-maid-medical-aid-in-dying-consent-doctors.
65 The perspective in Canadian Association of MAiD Assessors and Providers, "Bringing Up Medical Assistance in Dying," 6, https://camapcanada.ca/wp-content/uploads/2022/02/Bringing-up-MAiD.pdf.
66 Health Canada, *Model Practice Standard*, section 6 (emphasis added); see also an additional federal document to be read in conjunction with *Model Practice Standard*: Health Canada, "Advice to the Profession: Medical Assistance in Dying (MAID)," section 14, https://www.canada.ca/en/health-canada/services/publications/health-system-services/advice-profession-medical-assistance-dying.html#a19.
67 For two recommendations to bring up MAiD, see the perspective of the Canadian Association of MAiD Assessors and Providers in Canadian Association of MAiD Assessors and Providers, "Bringing up Medical Assistance in Dying," 2–4; see also discussion in Jocelyn Downie, "Can Nurse Practitioners Mention MAID to Patients?," *Impact Ethics*, 3 July 2018, https://impactethics.ca/2018/07/03/can-nurse-practitioners-mention-maid-to-patients/.
68 Compare to assisted dying legislation passed by the state of Victoria in Australia that unambiguously states that a "registered health practitioner who provides health services or professional care services to a person must *not*, in the course of providing those services to the person – (a) initiate discussion with that person that is in substance about voluntary assisted dying; or (b) in substance, suggest voluntary assisted dying to that person." *Voluntary Assisted Dying Act 2017*, No. 61 of 2017 (Victoria, Australia), s. 8(1), emphasis added.
69 *Criminal Code of Canada*, ss. 241.2(1) and (2).
70 See discussion in Thomas McMorrow et al., "Interpreting Eligibility Under the Medical Assistance in Dying Law: The Experiences of

Physicians and Nurse Practitioners," *McGill Journal of Law & Health* 14, no. 1 (2020): 51–108.

71 Some of these conditions have been accepted as a basis for or contributed to euthanasia approvals in Belgium and the Netherlands: see Irene Tuffrey-Wijne et al., "Euthanasia and Assisted Suicide for People with an Intellectual Disability and/or Autism Spectrum Disorder: An Examination of Nine Relevant Cases in the Netherlands (2012–2016)," BMC *Medical Ethics* 19, no. 17 (2018), https://bmcmedethics.biomedcentral.com/articles/10.1186/s12910-018-0257-6; see also Trudo Lemmens, "Charter Scrutiny of Canada's Medical Assistance in Dying Law and the Shifting Landscape of Belgian and Dutch Euthanasia Practice," *Supreme Court Law Review* (2nd Series) 85 (2018): 459–544, 500–1.

72 *Criminal Code of Canada*, s. 241.2(3.1)(h); see also Health Canada, *Model Practice Standard*, s. 10.

73 *Criminal Code of Canada*, s. 241.2(3.1)(g).

74 *Carter*, 2015 SCC 5.

75 Ibid. at paras. 125–32.

76 Ibid. at paras. 131–2.

77 Ibid. at para. 113.

78 Ibid. at para. 132.

79 Ibid. at para. 127. See also ibid., para. 126: "To the extent that the impugned laws deny the s. 7 rights of people *like Ms. Taylor* they are void by operation of s. 52 of the *Constitution Act, 1982*." Emphasis added. See also ibid. at paras. 65 and 66.

80 Ibid. at para. 12.

81 See, for example, ibid., paras. 1, 2, 5, 12, 30, 69, and 98.

82 Ibid., paras. 66–8.

83 Ibid.

84 Ibid. at para. 67.

85 See, for example, ibid. at paras. 1, 2, 5, 12, 30, 69, and 98.

86 *Carter* at para. 106. When applying the informed consent standard "to patients who seek assistance in dying," the trial court further cautioned that "physicians should ensure that patients are properly informed of their diagnosis and prognosis and the range of available options for medical care, including palliative care interventions aimed at reducing pain and avoiding the loss of personal dignity." Ibid. at para. 106.

87 Ibid. at paras. 126 and 127, emphasis added. For further discussion, see Mary J Shariff, "*Carter v Canada*: Exploring the Ebb and Flow of 'Competing' Societal Values through Sections 7 and 1 of the *Canadian Charter of Human Rights and Freedoms*," in *Medical Assistance in Dying in Canada*, ed. Jaro Kotalik and David W. Shannon, vol. 104, The

International Library of Bioethics (Cham, Switzerland: Springer, 2023), https://doi.org/10.1007/978-3-031-30002-8_2.
88 Ibid. at para. 66 (emphasis added).
89 For an example of how this appears to be accepted in one court procedure, see *WV v. MV*, 2024 ABKB 174, and in particular paras. 35–8. See also para. 19, https://www.canlii.org/en/ab/abkb/doc/2024/2024abkb174/2024abkb174.html.
90 See *Carter*, 2015 SCC 5, para. [131]; Canadian Medical Association, "Committee Appearance – Justice and Human Rights: Bill C-7 – Amending the Criminal Code Regarding Medical Assistance in Dying," 5 November 2020, https://policybase.cma.ca/link/politique14374; Ann Collins, "The CMA Calls for a Cautious Approach to Bill C-7," Canadian Medical Association, 9 March 2021, https://www.cma.ca/news-releases-and-statements/cma-calls-cautious-approach-bill-c-7.
91 See Trudo Lemmens, "Informed Consent," in *Routledge Handbook of Medical Law and Ethics*, ed. Y. Joly and B.M. Knoppers (London: Routledge, 2015), 27–51.
92 Canadian Association of MAiD Assessors and Providers' perspective in Canadian Association of MAiD Assessors and Providers, "Bringing up Medical Assistance in Dying," 2022, 6, https://camapcanada.ca/wp-content/uploads/2022/02/Bringing-up-MAiD.pdf.
93 See, for example, chapter 1 (Coelho and Lemmens) in this volume.
94 Canadian Association of MAiD Assessors and Providers, "The Interpretation and Role of Reasonably Foreseeable in MAiD Practice," February 2022, 1, https://camapcanada.ca/wp-content/uploads/2022/03/The-Interpretation-and-Role-of-22Reasonably-Foreseeable22-in-MAiD-Practice-Feb-2022.pdf. Emphasis added. We encourage the reader to think about what this means if this is implemented in the context of MAiD for mental illness as the sole underlying condition.
95 Ellen Wiebe et al., "Medical Assistance in Dying (MAiD) and Dementia," Canadian Association of MAiD Assessors and Providers (sd, sl), accessed 20 March 2024, https://camapcanada.ca/wp-content/uploads/2022/02/Assessing-MAiD-in-Dementia-FINAL-Formatted.pdf.
96 See chapter 14 (Ferrier) in this volume. See also Trudo Lemmens, "Les demandes anticipées de l'aide médicale à mourir (AMM): problématiques du point de vue de l'éthique, du droit constitutionnel, et des droits de l'homme, mémorandum soumis à la commission parlementaire des relations avec les citoyens," 27 March 2023, Assemblée nationale du Québec, https://www.assnat.qc.ca/fr/travaux-parlementaires/commissions/CRC/mandats/Mandat-51109/documents-deposes.html.
97 Criminal Code, Section 241.2(3.2).

98 Wiebe et al. at 11.
99 Ibid.
100 Ibid at 12.
101 Ibid.
102 See, for example, ibid at 6, 12, and 14.
103 We also note here the corollary line of thinking that physicians should introduce MAiD to persons who appear eligible (as discussed above), which appears to be attributable in part to the fact that the MAiD law has not expressly incorporated the "seeking" requirement that was integral to the rights analysis in the *Carter* case.
104 Wiebe et al. at 13. Emphasis added.
105 We again note here that application to persons "seeking" MAiD – as described in the "Explanatory Note" to *Bill C-7, Act to Amend the Criminal Code*, and consistent with the *Carter* decision (see, for example, *Carter*, 2015 SCC 5, para. [68]) – is conspicuously absent from the Criminal Code MAiD provisions. For further discussion, see Mary J. Shariff, "*Carter v. Canada*: Exploring the Ebb and Flow," note 81; see also Mary J. Shariff and Derek Ross, "When Is Suicide Considered Rational?" *Policy Options*, 6 December 2023, https://policyoptions.irpp.org/magazines/december-2023/assisted-suicide-mental-illness/.
106 See CPSO, "Medical Assistance in Dying" and CPSNS, "Professional Standard"; see also discussion of tiebreaker in *WV v. MV*, 2024 ABKB 174, paras. 60–6, https://www.canlii.org/en/ab/abkb/doc/2024/2024abkb174/k2024abkb174.html; see also Health Canada, *Model Practice Standard*.
107 *A.B. v. Canada (Attorney General)*, 2017 ONSC 3779 (Can.); see also Thomas McMorrow et al., "Interpreting Eligibility," note 52.
108 Not to be confused with the death of a patient resulting from a patient's refusal to consent to treatment.
109 *Norberg*, 1992 CanLII 65 (SCC), [1992] 2 SCR 226, 485–6; "Professionalism – Professionalism in the Patient-Physician Relationship," Canadian Medical Protective Association.
110 For examples reported in the media, see note 25.
111 Robert P. Kouri, "Blood Transfusions, Jehovah's Witnesses, and the Rule of Inviolability of the Human Body," *Revue de Droit de l'Université de Sherbrooke* 5 (1974), 156–76.
112 Ibid.
113 On the subject of paradigm shifts in the medical profession, see David Healy, *Shipwreck of the Singular: Healthcare's Castaways* (Samizdat Health, 2021).

5

Conscience and MAiD

Ramona Coelho

The passing of Bill C-14, the federal medical assistance in dying (MAiD) bill, in 2016, with its introduction of the practice of euthanasia and assisted suicide for those whose death was reasonably foreseeable, already constituted for many health care providers a major, in fact unprecedented, shift in health care practice.[1] The March 2021 expansion towards those not dying but living with a disability, and the planned extension to those with mental illnesses in two years, were an unsettling paradigm shift for even more health care professionals.[2]

The legislative preamble of the first bill emphasized that the MAiD law would respect section 2(a) of the *Canadian Charter of Rights and Freedoms*, which protects the freedom of conscience and religion. Bill C-14 added a specific clause to the Criminal Code to clarify that no one could be compelled "to provide or assist in providing medical assistance in dying."[3] The need to respect physicians' right not to participate in MAiD had also been made clear by the Supreme Court justices in the *Carter* case. They stated in their unanimous judgment: "In our view, nothing in the declaration of invalidity which we propose to issue would compel physicians to help in dying. The declaration simply renders the criminal prohibition invalid ... However, we note ... that a physician's decision to participate in assisted dying is a matter of conscience."[4]

Nevertheless, the College of Physicians and Surgeons of Ontario (CPSO), which has significant power when it comes to establishing professional standards that medical professionals in the province must follow, introduced a policy that a physician must create a pathway for MAiD by making "an effective referral to a non-objecting, available, and accessible physician, or the like."[5]

The idea of obliging physicians who are unwilling to provide a specific practice to make "effective referrals" to a physician who is willing is not new. The CPSO's first attempt at passing a general policy on effective referrals occurred in 2008, when it produced a draft policy stating: "there will be times when it may be necessary for physicians to set aside their personal beliefs in order to ensure that patients or potential patients are provided with the medical treatment and services they require." However, the policy was not enacted due to public backlash.[6]

The CPSO chose to interpret a physician declining participation in controversial services as being inherently based on personal beliefs. They failed to understand that some services, though legal, might be unproven in their benefits or potentially unsafe for patients and society at large. Refusal to further a request for services might indeed be based on professional opinion.

In late 2014, before the MAiD bill was enacted, the CPSO held a public consultation on this same matter again. The participation in this consultation was unmatched in CPSO history – well over nine thousand responses. The overwhelming majority supported freedom of conscience for physicians in refusing to provide non-emergency services, and there was little support for a policy of mandatory referral by objecting physicians. Nevertheless, the CPSO adopted its "effective referral" policy. In fact, the final policy was written and endorsed by the CPSO executive before 90 per cent of respondents had submitted their remarks and well before the deadline for the consultation closing.[7]

Before the CPSO's policy was enacted, if I felt that as a physician I couldn't offer a service in good conscience, I could, for example, respectfully let a patient know that the service in question was legal, and that they could contact the local hospital or telehealth (a government information line) for more information. I could provide them with the phone number to these central access resources. But now, according to the CPSO policy, this would no longer be sufficient in many circumstances.

Further, "model practice standards" were published by Health Canada in 2023 to promote provincial practice of MAiD. In addition to recommending that MAiD should be raised to those who might qualify if the practitioner suspects it aligns with a patient's values and preferences, its approach to "conscientious objection" is equally troubling to the CPSO guidelines.[8] Health care providers who object to providing MAiD even in specific cases become conscientious objectors, even when they are MAiD practitioners. The practice standard affirms that physicians must follow the rules set by their provincial regulators but also that effective referral of the patient is the practice standard expectation.

In the pages that follow, I argue that forced participation in MAiD should be reconsidered, and that the CPSO should work to emulate the models for MAiD found in other Canadian provinces as well as in numerous other countries. The arguments against forced participation in MAiD are that it compromises conscience protection, an essential professional tool for doctors; that it will lead to worsened health care access for patients; and that the CPSO's policy will lead the medical profession in Ontario to become less inclusive and less diverse.

THE PROBLEM WITH COMPROMISING CONSCIENCE PROTECTION

Many physicians are unwilling to participate in MAiD or referral for MAiD because of their religious or moral convictions and their adherence to the Hippocratic oath.[9] But there are also many physicians who work with the dying and disabled who could never participate in MAiD for purely pragmatic reasons and also because of their professional opinion on the matter. Death wishes can arise from many sources: because of undiagnosed depression, because a patient's pain has been inadequately treated, because the patient is a victim of abuse, and because of many other factors that take time to address but, more importantly, that could be addressed and mitigated.[10] To ignore these factors and simply refer a patient for MAiD in these cases would be viewed by many physicians as an abandonment of their duty of care. To demand that a physician refer a patient for MAiD in these cases, even if the physician does not believe it to be in the best interest of the patient, is to demand that the physician act against their professional obligations.

Conscience protection in medicine is critical because an ethical decision applies to almost every medical act. As Dr Jaro Kotalik, a physician and bioethicist from Lakehead University, has written:

> if a physician would be forced to act against his or her conscience because of some legal instrument, it would weaken the

physician's commitment to conscientious behaviour in other instances of their clinical practice. One day, he can refer a patient to MAID even if his conscience is telling him that it is wrong. The next day, he or she may act against one's conscience because it would bring about prestige or power or money, or simply because to be true to one's conscience would be just inconvenient. A well-functioning conscience is the best protection – the best guarantee – that society can have that the patients' and society's interests are well served in health care.[11]

Kotalik emphasizes how crucial it is to defend a doctor's ethical integrity, arguing that in the absence of conscience protection, the basis of professionalism and public trust in medicine would be compromised. This demonstrates the wider ramifications of conscience protection for the health care system as a whole, not just for certain practitioners.

One day after a long clinic, I was heading home. My back was turned, but I heard someone enter the clinic who sounded like they were short of breath. I heard my secretary say, "Our doctor has a closed family practice, and the doctor has finished her clinic for the day. Also, your health card has expired." The man responded, "No problem." It might have been within my rights and even within the rules to just head home. Some people have chronic shortness of breath, and I didn't know this man. But I decided to turn around and look at him. He was a young man, maybe a few years older than me, and was struggling for his breath. I examined him, found his vitals to be alarmingly abnormal, and sent him to the hospital immediately. He lost consciousness on the way and he had a subsequent ICU admission, but he survived. Our conscience can hold us to a higher standard than any set of rules.

It is important to note that conscience protection for doctors is also vital because legality cannot always be equated with morality. As an example, during the Nazi occupation of the Netherlands during the Second World War, numerous Dutch doctors turned in their medical licences and proceeded to work in the underground resistance so they could serve the people and not have to work according to government stipulations.[12] These doctors did not follow the government policies meant to regulate them. And while they refused to comply with policy, nonetheless their behaviour was ethical.

There are also examples of doctors acting legally, in accordance with government policy, but through their actions participating in and perpetuating what can only be described as abhorrent crimes. In the Soviet Union, some doctors participated in willfully misdiagnosing political dissenters with mental illnesses to aid the government in discrediting and detaining its opponents.[13] In Nazi Germany, most doctors acquiesced to the government rules and reported people who had disabilities or who were Jewish or Roma to the central authority even when it became known that these patients were being taken for euthanasia or medical experimentation.[14] And during the apartheid era in South Africa, Black patients were systematically neglected and dehumanized by the medical system and by its doctors, who served as participants in their government's cruelty.[15]

It can be assumed that there are numerous instances where doctors have behaved unethically because of their own moral bankruptcy. But it might also be assumed that there are instances when doctors have complied with policy and law and did not dissent not because they completely agreed with their governments, but out of some degree of fear for themselves, their families, and their livelihoods. And while these examples draw from some extreme circumstances, the lessons they hold apply to all times and places: government policy is not always ethical. Doctors who must follow government policy over what is best for their patients' health can be deeply destructive instruments of harm.

This was clearly demonstrated in a training session held by the Canadian Association of MAiD Assessors and Providers (CAMAP) where experts outlined that patients might be driven to MAiD by unmet psychosocial needs. One attending trainee asked, "Given the vulnerability of patients who are maybe requesting MAID because of socioeconomic reasons, do you save yourself that moral and ethical distress by withdrawing?" The expert leading the session responded: "If withdrawing is about protecting your conscience, you have [an] absolute right to do so." But he added: "You'll then have to refer the person on to somebody else, who may hopefully fulfill the request in the end."[16] This video demonstrates precisely how effective referrals can funnel patients towards death despite legitimate professional concerns and obligations that should have instead led to the process being stopped or paused.

Conscience protection, therefore, is not advocating for some kind of unregulated subjectivity and individuality in health care. The moral integrity of physicians matters not only to them but is also crucial for patients. Conscience protection for physicians is about providing medical professionals with an essential safeguard for the practice of their profession and the good of their patients, and this is particularly significant when what is at stake is death. Physicians make decisions and recommendations that often have life-altering consequences for patients and their families. They need to have the freedom to only make the decisions and recommendations that they believe are in patients' best interests based on science and ethics. Telling them they must actively implement government regulation, even when it goes against their conscience, will lead to doctors making health care decisions based on government appeasement instead of patient well-being. Government regulation should aim to not interfere when a doctor has a well-founded and reasoned conscience belief.

Of course, the answer is not some kind of free-for-all, where doctors can simply do what they want with no regulation whatsoever. It is important to note that the American Medical Association, the Canadian Medical Association, and the Ontario Medical Association have all written submissions to the College of Physicians and Surgeons of Ontario saying they disagree with their effective referral policy.[17] The Ontario Medical Association president wrote in a letter to the Ministry of Health that "it is possible to reconcile patient access with physician rights," and that the organization supports a framework that includes both clinician referral and patient self-referral options, which would allow "all physicians to maintain their moral convictions."[18] The Canadian Medical Association said that a forced referral policy creates a false dichotomy, pitting patient access against physicians' conscience when no other jurisdiction has done that, and yet patient access doesn't seem to be a problem in the rest of the world.[19]

There are many health care systems that strike a balance where the physician gives information but is not the direct pathway to MAiD. Alberta, for example, has a model that is respectful and upholds freedom of conscience. Patients in Alberta can contact such services directly through a general telehealth line that all physicians feel comfortable providing. For patients interested in MAiD, teams of health care professionals are available to assess the request for death and can go into the community to evaluate the patient.[20] In many Canadian hospitals, a medical director (who has agreed) can arrange a transfer of care to another facility or practitioner when desired.[21]

Forced referral is not the only way to ensure that patients who desire MAiD can have it. There are other models that allow for patient access and do not jeopardize conscience protection for physicians.

FORCED PARTICIPATION IN MAiD COULD LEAD TO WORSENED ACCESS TO HEALTH CARE FOR PATIENTS

Dr Gerrit Kisma is an associate professor of medical ethics in the Netherlands who first euthanized a patient in 1977. He remarked that there are growing tensions between the increasing demands from the general population and pressure groups to perform euthanasia and physicians who strive to maintain the integrity of their professional role in dealing with requests for help with dying. Although he has not wavered in his belief in euthanasia, he has become critical of the insensitivities of the public regarding what it means for a physician to help someone die in an active way and the media's lack of respect for the physician and their expertise.[22] The consequence of these kinds of pressures are disempowered medical professionals.

The goal of the medical profession is the health and well-being of the patient, and this sometimes can lead doctors to give counsel based on their expertise that patients might not like. It sometimes means disagreeing with patients and in some instances, trying to counsel patients to adopt different choices. We encourage patients who smoke to quit; those who are obese to optimize their diets, get weight loss counselling, and exercise; and those who might be skeptical or scared to get vaccinated. Medicine is ideally based on a collaborative model where both parties work together with the physician only giving the best options based on their professional opinion and the patient then being free to exercise their choice according to their values and preferences.

In circumstances where the practice of medicine becomes more about pleasing customers than treating patients, when the doctor is simply meant to do what the patient wants instead of using their specialized expertise and skills to determine with the patient what will be in the best interests of their health, physicians will easily become demoralized and lose their sense of professional integrity. Such circumstances may lead many physicians to leave the profession, retire early, or burn out. In a society with a shortage of physicians, this can hardly be considered positive and would make access to health care even more strained for patients.

A LESS DIVERSE AND LESS INCLUSIVE HEALTH CARE SYSTEM

Several religious groups, hoping to change the CPSO effective referral policy, brought the issue to the courts and presented the decision not to give a referral for certain services primarily as a matter of religious freedom. They argued that the effective referral requirements obliged them to be complicit in procedures that offend their religious beliefs, and that they discriminated against physicians based on their religions. However, both lower and appellate courts in Ontario sided with the CPSO and rejected both claims. The courts agreed with the plaintiffs that the policy restricts a physician's right to freedom of religion but suggested that practitioners who are opposed to making a referral for MAiD were free to retrain into less controversial areas of medicine or to leave medicine altogether.[23]

The Ontario Medical Association intervened at the appellate level to point out that the conclusions from the lower court were overly burdensome to the physician and that there are numerous difficulties involved in retraining. Further, they argued that there are more respectful systems that would achieve patient access to MAiD without imposing such constraints on physicians, but to no avail.[24] It is worth noting that the Court of Appeal considered that it had no basis to explore whether a broader conscience right was restricted and whether this was justifiable. This was because of how the organizations had constructed their claims. "To the extent the individual appellants raise issues of conscience," the court ruled, "they are inextricably grounded in their religious beliefs."[25]

Subsequently, there have also been protests in Ontario from different religious groups who have argued for conscience protection for their observant members. Hindu, Sikh, Muslim, Jewish, and Christian groups in Ontario have all endorsed a private members' provincial conscience protection bill.[26] What is more, Ontarians support these groups. An Angus Reid poll conducted in November 2019 demonstrated that 82 per cent of Ontario residents would support such provincial legislation.[27]

In February 2021, Indigenous leaders across Canada wrote a joint letter to politicians. It affirmed the need for conscience rights: "Given our history with the negative consequences of colonialism and the involuntary imposition of cultural values and ideas, we believe that people should not be compelled to provide or facilitate in the provision of MAID."[28] Following suit, groups such as the Ontario Medical

Association, the Canadian Society of Palliative Care Physicians, and the Ontario Association of ACT & FACT have asked the government to intervene and create conscience protection legislation.[29]

Likewise, multiple disability groups have echoed that they would feel more comfortable with having a physician who viewed their lives as worth living and would never offer or consider MAiD as a treatment option. As the Council of Canadians with Disabilities wrote, "Given the ubiquity of medical ableism, it is of utmost importance that physicians and other healthcare providers whose views of the quality and worth of lives lived with disability differ from the majority be afforded robust protection of their conscience rights. People with disabilities need to be able to find doctors and other healthcare providers who they know will fight for their lives when necessary."[30]

Further, the Disability Filibuster, a national grassroots initiative formed in opposition to Bill C-7 and the expansion of MAiD, stated:

> Disabled people feel left behind and more so, singled out and targeted by this policy which directly affects disabled people and only disabled people... People spoke of being afraid to seek medical help because they were worried about their physician raising the possibility of MAID. Some even went so far as to say they will be avoiding medical care. Those who struggle or have struggled with suicidal ideation or depression voiced concerns about how the raising of it with them would lead to setbacks and many worried about seeking medical care for a physical emergency if they were at a low point, something that they knew to be temporary but worried they would agree to MAID in that state. We have heard repeatedly from people that they would like to know some way that they might be able to ensure that MAID is not raised with them at all... Many physicians currently are in the practice of hanging signs letting patients know they will not prescribe pain and other medications even if needed. How is that something that a physician can opt out of but advising patients to seek death is not?[31]

When MAiD for sole mental illness is allowed, the CPSO's "effective referral requirement" will further place physicians in a position of being forced to commit professional misconduct given there is no medical standard to guide predictions of irremediability in cases of mental illness.[32] The Canadian Association for Suicide Prevention

(CASP) articulated this risk in a November 2021 letter, writing: "With respect to psychiatrists not willing to provide MAiD being required to make a referral of a patient to a psychiatrist that will, does this not leave the referring psychiatrist open to committing professionally unethical behaviour? If the grounds for not providing MAiD is not based on morality but rather on the fact that there is insufficient evidence to support MAiD as a medical treatment, then the requirement to refer a patient forces them to commit professionally unethical behaviour."[33]

Forced referral inadvertently creates systematic discrimination against practitioners who take seriously their oath to practise good medicine. These physicians are consequently pressured to abandon their professions for less controversial areas of medicine. Many of these practitioners will come from minority religious or cultural traditions. This approach to forced participation is a step backwards in forging a respectful multicultural society. Besides the college policy needlessly disregarding the value of health care practitioners from diverse backgrounds and communities, the policy also reinforces an atmosphere of systematic discrimination in Ontario.

An example of the absurdity of this policy and its consequences is the position of a utilitarian philosopher with no experience as a health care provider. He has stated that conscience objectors should be screened out of medicine by requiring a conscience test before medical school – if people fail, they shouldn't be admitted.[34] As someone who treats numerous refugees who have recently found religious freedom in Canada, I find this position intolerant and painfully distressing.

An Ontario physician I know whose family fled from persecution in the Middle East when she was younger is now concerned about continuing her medical practice. Her family was initially elated at their good fortune in being welcomed into Ontario. She has been very successful and completed her medical training in Canada. Now, her family and friends feel they are reliving their persecution in Ontario, a province where they understood they would be free to practise their religion. She now understands that she will have to leave medicine based on her deeply held religious beliefs, because she could never bring herself to endorse or refer for MAiD.

It follows that when you set an intolerant rule such as effective referral, people and institutions feel justified in furthering isolation and labelling. I have started to hear from doctors at various institutions who feel threatened by their working environments. Physicians have said they no longer feel free to be open about their medical judgement and opinions for fear of reprimand. Medical oncologist Dr Ellen Warner testified before the Legislative Assembly of Ontario: "At my institution, physicians are being bullied into accepting the role of the most responsible physician for MAID patients. This forces these physicians to be legally responsible for the MAID act, even when that goes against their conscience or religious beliefs. It gets worse: at one of our staff meetings, a psychiatrist stood up and announced that any physician who didn't actively support MAID should not be working at our hospital."[35] This does not foster a collaborative working environment and is detrimental to patient care. One of several physicians who have stopped practising in Ontario because of this policy of effective referral shared that "the anxiety, fear, and sadness surrounding my work bled into my family life, and I ultimately felt that I could not manage practising palliative care at this stage of my life."[36]

The importance of diversity and inclusivity within health care cannot be understated. Health care providers should reflect the multicultural society in which Canadians take so much pride, not because it is "nice" but because it is vital that patients can find doctors who understand them, who can deeply empathize with them, and who understand their perspectives, religions, and lives. A less inclusive and diverse health care system will be a consequence of enforced referral, and it will necessarily be a less empathetic health care system.

CONCLUSION

I have argued that forced participation in MAiD will have a detrimental effect on Ontario's health care system in a number of significant ways. It will undermine conscience protection, which is essential to the profession of medicine; it will lead to doctors retraining or leaving the profession, making access to health care, which is already strained, more so; and it will lead to a less diverse and less inclusive health care environment.

The note I wish to end on, though, is that there is a way forward. There are models for balancing patient access to MAiD with conscience protection for physicians who wish to abstain from participation, and these are models that have been implemented in numerous countries and within other provinces in Canada. A balance can be struck; there needs only to be openness and a willingness to work together to achieve this.

NOTES

1 *Bill C-14, An Act to Amend the Criminal Code and to Make Related Amendments to Other Acts (medical assistance in dying)*, 42nd Parliament, 1st Session (2016), SC 2016, c. 3 (Can.), https://www.parl.ca/DocumentViewer/en/42-1/bill/C-14/royal-assent.
2 *Bill C-7, An Act to Amend the Criminal Code (medical assistance in dying)*, 43rd Parliament, 2nd Session (2021), SC 2021, c. 2 (Can.), https://parl.ca/DocumentViewer/en/43-2/bill/C-7/royal-assent.
3 *Criminal Code of Canada*, RSC 1985, c. C-46, s. 241.2 (9).
4 *Carter v. Canada (Attorney General)*, 2015 SCC 5, [2015] 1 SCR 331.
5 College of Physicians and Surgeons of Ontario, "Medical Assistance in Dying," December 2018, https://www.ohchr.org/en/instruments-mechanisms/instruments/convention-rights-persons-disabilities.
6 College of Physicians and Surgeons of Ontario, "Policy Statement #5-08: Physicians and the Ontario *Human Rights Code*," September 2008, https://www.consciencelaws.org/archive/documents/cpso/2008-09-18-cpso-physicians-hrcode.pdf.
7 Protection of Conscience Project, "Medical Regulator Finalized Controversial Policy before Receiving 90% of Invited Public Comment," video, 16 October 2021, https://www.youtube.com/watch?v=sHXuC9MfMXc.
8 Health Canada, *Model Practice Standard for Medical Assistance in Dying (MAID)*, March 2023, https://www.canada.ca/en/health-canada/services/publications/health-system-services/model-practice-standard-medical-assistance-dying.html.
9 Sharon Kirkey, "Majority of Doctors Opposed to Participating in Assisted Death of Patients: CMA Survey," *National Post*, 25 August 2015, https://nationalpost.com/news/canada/0826-na-assisted-death.
10 Trudo Lemmens, Mary Shariff, and Leonie Herx, "How Bill C-7 Will Sacrifice the Medical Profession's Standard of Care," *Policy Options*, 11 February 2021, https://policyoptions.irpp.org/magazines/february-2021/how-bill-c7-will-sacrifice-the-medical-professions-standard-of-care/. See also chapter 4 (Lemmens, Shariff, and Herx).
11 "Testimony of Dr. Jaro Kotalik," in *Meeting of the Standing Committee on Finance and Economic Affairs*, Legislative Assembly of Ontario, 30 March 2017, https://www.ola.org/en/legislative-business/committees/finance-economic-affairs/parliament-41/transcripts/committee-transcript-2017-mar-30#P1418_374500.

12 "Dutch Citizens Resist Nazi Occupation, 1940–1945," Global Nonviolent Action Database, 27 May 2011, https://nvdatabase.swarthmore.edu/content/dutch-citizens-resist-nazi-occupation-1940-1945.

13 Robert van Voren, "Ending Political Abuse of Psychiatry: Where We Are at and What Needs to Be Done," BJPsych Bulletin 40, no. 1 (2016): 30–3, https://doi.org/10.1192/pb.bp.114.049494.

14 United States Holocaust Memorial Museum, "Euthanasia Program and Aktion T4," Holocaust Encyclopedia, 7 October 2020, https://encyclopedia.ushmm.org/content/en/article/euthanasia-program.

15 Anthony B. Zwi, "The Political Abuse of Medicine and the Challenge of Opposing It," Social Science and Medicine 25, no. 6 (1987): 649–57, https://www.sciencedirect.com/science/article/abs/pii/027795368790092X?via%3Dihub.

16 Alexander Raikin, "No Other Options: Newly Revealed Documents Depict a Canadian Euthanasia Regime that Efficiently Ushers the Vulnerable to a 'Beautiful' Death," New Atlantis 71 (Winter 2023): 3–24, https://www.thenewatlantis.com/publications/no-other-options.

17 Ontario Medical Association to the College of Physicians and Surgeons of Ontario, "Professional Obligations and Human Rights Policy," 18 February 2015; Canadian Medical Association, Submission to the College of Physicians and Surgeons of Ontario, Consultation on CPSO Interim Guidance on Physician-Assisted Death, 13 January 2016 (in the author's possession).

18 Virginia M. Walley to Elliott Pobjoy, "Re: Patient Access to Medical Assistance in Dying," 29 June 2016 (in the author's possession).

19 Ontario Medical Association to the College of Physicians and Surgeons of Ontario, 18 February 2015 (in the author's possession).

20 "Patients or Family Members: Medical Assistance in Dying," Alberta Health Services, 2021, https://www.albertahealthservices.ca/info/Page14380.aspx.

21 Michel Bilodeau, "Governments Shouldn't Force Faith-Based Hospitals to Perform Medical Assistance in Dying," Healthy Debate, 1 February 2017, https://healthydebate.ca/opinions/medical-assistance-in-dying-faith-based-hospitals/.

22 Joanne Laucius, "Dutch Lessons: Dr. Gerrit Kimsma on 'a Good Death' in the Netherlands," Ottawa Citizen, 11 October 2016, https://ottawacitizen.com/news/local-news/dutch-lessons-dr-gerrit-kimsma-on-a-good-death-in-the-netherlands.

23 "Ontario Court Decides It's Reasonable to Force Doctors to Refer for Assisted Suicide," Association for Reformed Political Action Canada,

7 February 2018, https://arpacanada.ca/news/2018/02/07/ontario-court-decides-reasonable-force-doctors-refer-assisted-suicide/; Derek Ross and Deina Warren, "The Importance of Conscience as an Independent Protection," in *Medical Assistance in Dying (MAID) in Canada: Key Multidisciplinary Perspectives*, ed. Jaro Kotalik and David W. Shannon (Cham, Switzerland: Springer, 2023), 399–421.

24 Julie Kovacs, "OMA Update," Ontario Rheumatology Association, Summer 2019, https://ontariorheum.ca/newsletter/summer-2019/oma-update-2.

25 *Christian Medical and Dental Society of Canada v. College of Physicians and Surgeons of Ontario*, 2019 ONCA 383, para. 85.

26 *Bill 129, An Act to Amend the Regulated Health Professions Act, 1991 with Respect to medical assistance in dying*, 2nd Session, 41st Legislature, Ontario, 2017, https://www.ola.org/sites/default/files/node-files/bill/document/pdf/2017/2017-05/bill---text-41-2-en-b129_e.pdf (list of endorsers in the author's possession).

27 Angus Reid, "Medical Assistance in Dying: Required Participation of Medical Professionals Study," November 2019 (in the author's possession).

28 CPSO Consultation, "Indigenous Peoples Should Not Be Compelled to Provide or Facilitate Medical Assistance in Dying," February 2021, https://policyconsult.cpso.on.ca/wp-content/uploads/2021/05/Indigenous-Peoples-Should-Not-Be-Compelled-to-Provide-or-Facilitate-MAID_Redacted.pdf.

29 Dr. Samantha Hill (President OMA) to Senator Mobina Jaffer, Chair, Standing Committee on Legal and Constitutional Affairs, 3 February 2020 (in the author's possession); Canadian Society of Palliative Care Physicians, "Submission to the Standing Committee on Justice and Human Rights on Bill C-7: An Act to Amend the Criminal Code (medical assistance in dying)," 30 October 2020, https://www.ourcommons.ca/Content/Committee/432/JUST/Brief/BR10927610/br-external/CanadianSocietyOfPalliativeCarePhysicians-e.pdf; Ontario Association for Act & Fact to the College of Physicians and Surgeons of Ontario, 30 April 2021 (response CPSO public consultation), https://policyconsult.cpso.on.ca/Consultation-Details/?id=80fec0ec-7c04-ee11-8f6e-6045bd5de6d6 (link defunct).

30 Council of Canadians with Disabilities to Minister Jones and the CPSO Policy Department, Regarding Conscience Objection Legislation, 21 November 2022, https://policyconsult.cpso.on.ca/wp-content/uploads/2022/11/POHR-MAID_Response_CCD_20221121_Redacted.pdf.

31 Disability Filibuster to the Ontario Government and CPSO Policy Department, Disability Filibuster, 20 November 2022, https://policyconsult.cpso.on.ca/wp-content/uploads/2022/11/POHR-MAID_Disability-Filibuster_20221128_Redacted.pdf.

32 Marie E. Nicolini, Chris Gastmans, and Scott Y.H. Kim, "Psychiatric Euthanasia, Suicide, and the Role of Gender," *British Journal of Psychiatry* 220, no. 1 (January 2022): 10–13.

33 Sean Krausert to Canadian Psychiatric Association, "RE: CPA's Discussion Paper on Medical Assistance in Dying ('MAiD')," 20 November 2021, https://static1.squarespace.com/static/5ec97e1c4215f5026a674116/t/619bc64ac482815740760931/1637598795070/Letter+to+CPA+re+Discussion+Paper+on+MAiD+%282021+11+20%29.pdf.

34 Tom Blackwell, "Ban Conscientious Objection by Canadian Doctors, Urge Ethicists in Volatile Commentary," *National Post*, 22 September 2016, https://nationalpost.com/health/ban-conscientious-objection-by-canadian-doctors-urge-ethicists-in-volatile-commentary.

35 "Testimony of Dr. Ellen Warner," in *Meeting of the Standing Committee on Finance and Economic Affairs,* Legislative Assembly of Ontario, 23 March 2017, https://www.ola.org/en/legislative-business/committees/finance-economic-affairs/parliament-41/transcripts/committee-transcript-2017-mar-23#P1025_246018.

36 Collectif des médecins contre l'euthanasie, "Alert from a Growing Number of Canadian Physicians: 'We Are Being Bullied to Participate in Medical Assistance in Dying,'" 9 March 2020, https://collectifmedecins.org/en/press-release-2/.

6

MAiD and Palliative Care

Leonie Herx

HISTORY AND DEFINITION OF PALLIATIVE CARE

Palliative care as we know it today originated out of the work of Dame Cicely Saunders, who founded the modern hospice movement in 1967 and opened St Christopher's Hospice in London, England, to improve care for those at the end of their lives. Saunders developed the important concept of "total pain" – that suffering results from a complex interplay of social, psychological, spiritual, and physical factors that require holistic care be provided to the person and their family by an interprofessional team. Her founding philosophy of care is captured in her famous quote: "You matter because you are you, and you matter to the end of your life. We will do all we can not only to help you die peacefully, but also to live until you die."[1]

Dr Balfour Mount, a urologic cancer surgeon, similarly wanted to improve care for patients at the end of their lives here in Canada. After hearing about Saunders's work, he went to study with her in London in 1973 and thereafter coined the term "palliative care" from the Latin *palliare*, meaning "to cloak," to describe whole person-focused care aimed at alleviating suffering. Dr Mount established the first program for palliative care in Montreal at McGill University.[2]

Palliative care is defined by the World Health Organization (WHO) as an approach to care focused on improving the quality of life for patients who are facing problems associated with life-threatening illness and their families.[3] It has five main tenets: (1) it prevents and relieves suffering through the early identification, impeccable assessment, and treatment of pain and other problems, whether physical, psychosocial, or spiritual, through providing an interdisciplinary team-based approach to whole person care; (2) it is applicable early in the course of illness, in conjunction with other therapies that are intended to prolong life; (3) it affirms life and regards dying as a normal process and intends neither to hasten or postpone death; (4) it is applicable to children and adults; and (5) it provides an extra layer of support to help people live as fully as possible until death and to help their families cope during the illness journey and in their own bereavement. The WHO definition of palliative care is endorsed by palliative care organizations around the world and has been adopted by the Health Canada Framework for Palliative Care in Canada.[4]

MYTHS AND STIGMA OF PALLIATIVE CARE AS THE "DEATH SERVICE"

Over the past forty years, palliative care has evolved as a discipline with a growing evidence base for the benefits of early integration of palliative care into serious illnesses, alongside disease-modifying treatments. Early integration of palliative care results in improved quality of life, reduced symptom burden, improved goal-concordant care with fewer unnecessary tests and treatments, less caregiver distress, and lower health care costs, and it can even result in longer life in some cases.[5]

Despite this, palliative care continues to be stigmatized as a "death service," associated with care for those at the very end of their lives, and myths have been perpetuated that palliative care hastens death by giving large doses of medications to manage pain. These misperceptions continue to limit the uptake of palliative care and its early integration within other medical disciplines, resulting in late referrals or fear about involving palliative care at all.[6] It is often seen as "giving up" rather than the active total care that it provides to help people live fully.

Internationally, palliative care organizations have been working for years to educate the general public and health care professionals about the benefits of palliative care – busting myths and destigmatizing palliative care so that it is understood as being about living well even while dying, rather than hastening death. Indeed, the core philosophy, intention, and approach of palliative care is not compatible with hastening death, including the practices of euthanasia and assisted suicide. Rather, it affirms life, seeing dying as a normal part of life, and focuses on living well until natural death. Palliative care intends to alleviate suffering, enhance dignity, and improve quality of life. Its approach is to provide impeccable symptom assessment and management as well as supportive care for the whole person, including addressing physical, psychosocial, emotional, and spiritual issues.

In contrast, the core philosophy of assisted death is that it is ethical to end a person's life at their request. Assisted death intends to end suffering by ending life. The approach is to cause the immediate death of a person through the administration of a lethal dose of drugs.

Unfortunately, during the public and health care professional discourse following the *Carter* case, many expected the discipline of palliative care to provide assisted death. For example, an e-survey by the College of Family Physicians of Canada indicated that many physicians expected palliative care physicians to provide physician-hastened death.[7]

National and international palliative care organizations (including the Canadian Society of Palliative Care Physicians, the Canadian Hospice Palliative Care Association, the World Hospice Palliative Care Association, the International Association of Hospice and Palliative Care, the European Association of Palliative Care, and the Australia New Zealand Palliative Care Association) have excluded termination of life from the practice of palliative care for all of the reasons described above.[8] The World Medical Association has also expressed that assisted death is both distinct from and in conflict with the principles of medical practice that underlies palliative care.[9] Dame Cicely Saunders, the founder of the hospice palliative care movement, has stated that "Palliative and hospice care has its own impetus of care, research and teaching; to include it in part of a drive to make the deliberate shortening of life a legal possibility would be to take a radical change of direction, a denial of the importance of this part of life and I believe should be vigorously resisted."[10]

HOW PALLIATIVE CARE ADDRESSES SUFFERING

Expressing a desire to die and talking about hastening death are most often normal expressions of grief and loss and of coming to terms with one's mortality in the face of a devastating diagnosis or change in condition. Dr Harvey Chochinov's published work in psychiatry and palliative care demonstrates that the desire to die fluctuates and often dissipates within two weeks.[11] Such expressions of distress can be normalized and supported with skilled palliative care interventions to better understand the nature of the suffering and how to address it.

Holistic palliative care interventions such as dignity-conserving therapy, developed by Dr Chochinov, are aimed at restoring purpose, meaning, and hope in the face of the losses and grief that accompany life-threatening illnesses.[12] Such therapies help a person focus on living while dying and provide support to accompany people on their journey so they do not feel abandoned or alone in their suffering.

Evidence demonstrates that most requests for MAiD are motivated by a desire for control, fear of dying, fear of future pain and suffering, and worry about being a burden to others – all existential issues.[13] They are not due to uncontrolled physical symptoms such as pain or shortness of breath. Thus, in palliative care, a request for hastened death is fully and sensitively explored to understand the nature of the person's suffering and to determine what support can be offered to address these existential issues and not only preserve but enhance the dignity of the person so they can get back to focusing on living. Mary J. Shariff and Mark Ginsberg describe this approach as the "life-affirming" pillar of palliative care, "the raison d'être of palliative care is to address the experience of suffering through the development and provision of meticulous whole-person care aimed at 'affirming life' – enhancing its quality and improving its experience."[14]

As Chochinov and Mount beautifully express, "to be clear, palliative care is not a panacea that can eliminate every instance and every facet of end-of life suffering. However, the physician-patient relationship is complex and profound. Preserving dignity for patients at the end of life is comprised of a steadfast commitment to non-abandonment and a tone of care marked by respect, kindness, and an unwavering affirmation of patient worth."[15]

CONFLATION OF MAiD AND PALLIATIVE CARE

Following the *Carter* case in 2015, Canadian national palliative care organizations, including the Canadian Society of Palliative Care Physicians (CSPCP), urged the federal government to use clear language in legislation on assisted death and also to maintain assisted death as a separate service from palliative care, so as not to risk conflating the two.

The CSPCP stated in their submission to the External Panel on Options for a Legislative Response to *Carter v. Canada*, "Without a clear distinction between palliative care and the practice of hastening death, patients' comfort in accessing palliative care could be negatively impacted."[16] At the same time, the Canadian Medical Association (CMA) recognized that the practices of assisted death as defined by the Supreme Court of Canada were distinct from palliative care in a general council motion and in their policy on palliative care.[17]

Despite the clear and strong advocacy from palliative care experts and CMA policy on palliative care, the federal government put forward confusing and euphemistic language for assisted suicide and euthanasia, calling it "medical assistance in dying" in their C-14 legislation.[18] This language, whether intentionally or unintentionally, caused confusion about the difference between MAiD and palliative care. Palliative care provides medical assistance for those who are dying but does not intentionally end life or hasten death.[19] As per Dr Balfour Mount, the father of palliative care in Canada, "Canadian legislation utilizes the euphemism 'medical assistance in dying' (MAiD) to define euthanasia/assisted suicide and that language has caused confusion concerning its distinction from Palliative Care. For over four decades, Palliative Care has been providing expert medical management to assist and support those who are dying without hastening death or administering a lethal dose of drugs to end life. The MAiD euphemism confuses and causes fear in our patients and the general public regarding the practice of Palliative Care and the nature of Palliative Medicine."[20]

Palliative care organizations expressed clear and repeated concerns to the government that this euphemistic language conflated assisted death with palliative care, perpetuating the myth that palliative care hastens death, and that it may prevent patients from seeking timely palliative care. The CSPCP stated that the "Canadian public must be able to continue to trust that the principles of palliative care remain focused on effective symptom management and psychological, social, and spiritual interventions to help people live as well as they can until their natural death."[21] These concerns were completely ignored (or blatantly disregarded) by the federal government.

Following the legalization of MAiD, assisted death advocates continued to co-opt palliative care language so as to place assisted death and palliative care on the same continuum. The CMA, in direct conflict with their own policy on MAiD and palliative care,[22] also misrepresented MAiD as part of palliative care. For example, in a national CMA publication, they chose to showcase a "Physician Changemaker" who described MAiD as "one of the many items in the palliative care basket."[23] And prominent CMA leaders promoted

MAiD as an "extension" of palliative care, romanticizing MAiD on the international stage as the most patient-centered way to relieve suffering and as the "most peaceful death."[24]

Other specialties soon began adopting this problematic misunderstanding. For example, a 2019 *Canadian Guideline for Parkinson Disease* that was published in the *Canadian Medical Association Journal* (CMAJ) commendably presented palliative care as one of five key recommendations for care of persons with Parkinson's disease.[25] Alarmingly, however, they placed MAiD under the pillar of "palliative care" support, and it was the only support they listed. There was no mention of the myriad of evidence-informed palliative care approaches to symptom management or support to enhance quality of life for individuals living with Parkinson's disease (approaches that do not hasten death).

The CSPCP wrote a response to the article, asking for this error to be corrected and the guideline updated by listing MAiD separately from palliative care. CSPCP explained that "confusion ensues when MAiD is seen as part of palliative care. Linking MAiD and palliative care perpetuates the myth that palliative care hastens death and may prevent patients from seeking early palliative care interventions, which improve quality of life and in some cases even enable people to live longer. The Canadian public must be able to continue to trust that the principles of palliative care remain focused on effective symptom management and psychological, social, and spiritual interventions to help people live as well as they can until their death."[26] The Parkinson's guideline was not updated nor have the authors responded to the commentary in the CMAJ.

This misrepresentation of MAiD as an extension of palliative care was not in keeping with the views of the vast majority of Canadian palliative care physicians who did not see euthanasia as part of palliative care and did not provide it.[27] It was also opposed by national and international palliative care associations who endorsed a joint statement by the CSPSP and the Canadian Hospice Palliative Care Association (CHPCA) stating that "hospice palliative care does not seek to hasten death or intentionally end life."[28]

There was a clear systemic failure on the part of both the government and the CMA to correct the erroneous portrayal that MAiD was part of palliative care even after they had been told about this error repeatedly by the national palliative care organizations over many years. This portrayal also contradicted the CMA's own policy that MAiD is distinct from palliative care. This error continues to be perpetuated to this day, and worse, there is an ongoing concerted effort by MAiD proponents to integrate MAiD with palliative care and to require clinicians to raise MAiD as an option to all palliative care patients as part of informed consent.[29]

IMPACT OF MAiD IMPLEMENTATION ON PALLIATIVE CARE RESOURCES

Following the legalization of MAiD in 2016, provinces and territories were tasked with rolling out assisted death practices to ensure MAiD was both available and accessible to those who wanted it, because health care is a provincial and not a federal responsibility. Sadly, the federal government has made no such similar requirement for provinces to make palliative care available and accessible to those who need it. Only about 30 to 50 per cent of Canadians have access to palliative care support, and only about 15 per cent of the population has specialist palliative care support, despite more than 90 per cent of deaths in Canada being thought to benefit from palliative care.[30]

As MAiD implementation was rolled out across Canada, there were significant and deleterious consequences on palliative care resources and funding. In some provinces and territories, MAiD was placed under the umbrella of palliative and end-of-life care programs, using existing palliative care resources to administrate and coordinate MAiD or provide MAiD procedures, despite the clear recommendations of national palliative care organizations to keep them separate.[31]

In Ontario, Canada's most populous province, some local authorities delegated providing MAiD to palliative care nurse practitioners as part of their palliative care role – this created a situation where some nurse practitioners were paid to do palliative care but ended up using their time to provide MAiD, effectively reducing already limited palliative care resources.[32] In addition, palliative care nurses and social workers were tasked with navigating and coordinating MAiD requests, taking time away from their specialized palliative care role. This resulted in an overall reduction in available resources for palliative care.[33] Anecdotally, I as well as my colleagues are aware of some health professionals spending an increasing proportion of their time allocated to palliative care on MAiD, as referrals for MAiD have increased exponentially. A number of nurses and social workers have left their positions because MAiD is now consuming most of their role in palliative care.[34] As a consequence, there are now some communities and hospitals with no dedicated palliative care resources available to patients, and MAiD is the only option to address suffering.

In Ontario, palliative care physician billing codes were designated for use in providing MAiD despite advocacy against this decision by the Ontario Medical Association Section of Palliative Medicine and the CSPCP.[35] Billing codes are used to capture medical work and analyze the use of health care resources – as a result of this, there is no way to separate MAiD from palliative care physician work in Ontario. To this day, palliative care billing codes in Ontario continue to be used to fund MAiD physician work, with further disparity added by allowing MAiD providers to use these palliative codes for indirect patient care work, something that palliative care physicians are not permitted to do. Use of these palliative care codes also allows MAiD providers to access special premiums meant to incentivize family doctors to provide palliative care for their patients.

Why was MAiD placed into some palliative care programs when it goes against the core philosophy and definition of palliative care and was not in keeping with the national and international standards for palliative care? Was it due to ignorance or a lack of understanding of palliative care by health system administrators and leaders? Or was it because of the conflation of MAiD and palliative care through the government's euphemistic language "medical assistance in dying"? Or was it because of the ongoing misrepresentation of MAiD as an extension of palliative care by MAiD advocates? Regardless of the reasons, the implementation and funding of MAiD from within existing palliative care budgets and resources has had significant negative consequences – further reducing both the access to and availability of palliative care, an already scarce resource.

LACK OF ACCESS TO PALLIATIVE CARE AND MAiD REQUESTS

Unfortunately, palliative care is not accessible to the vast majority of Canadians who need it. Access is impacted by the nature of a person's underlying illness, where they live, the language they speak, and other structural determinants of health such as access to housing and extended health care benefits. Palliative care, home care, and disability services have not been deemed essential health care services under the Canada Health Care Act, and thus provinces are not required to ensure they are universally funded or accessible.[36] The disparity in access between support for living and MAiD was openly acknowledged by the federal minister for disability inclusion, Carla Qualtrough, who told the Senate during their study of Bill C-7 that, "we know that in some places in our country, it's easier to access MAiD than it is to get a wheelchair."[37]

Many requests for assisted death are indications of suffering that could be ameliorated by palliative care.[38] Palliative care experts have expressed repeated concerns that the lack of access to palliative care in Canada may lead to some patients choosing MAiD as the only option: "Without access to high quality palliative care, some patients who are suffering may feel that MAID is their only option because their suffering has been inadequately addressed or they perceive that their families or social supports must carry an excessive burden."[39] The International Association for Hospice Palliative Care (IAHPC) has raised similar concerns in their statement that, "no country or state should consider the legalization of euthanasia or PAS (*physician assisted suicide*) until it ensures universal access to palliative care services."[40] Canada falls woefully short on fulfilling universal access to high quality palliative care.

Both the Supreme Court of Canada and the federal government have presented access to palliative care as a safeguard for MAiD.[41] Informed consent for MAiD requires patients to be informed about palliative care options[42] – captured as a check box on the federal MAiD reporting form completed by MAiD assessors and providers. But is it truly informed consent if a service is not well understood by those describing it or experienced by the person suffering? The information a patient gets is only as good as the understanding of the person presenting it, and as we have discussed, many health care professionals continue to misunderstand and stigmatize palliative care.[43]

While palliative care was positioned as a safeguard for MAiD, this role has failed to materialize, and in some regions, we have seen a reduction in palliative care support due to the impacts of MAiD.[44] In Quebec, the number of physicians providing palliative care has dropped since the legalization of MAiD, and palliative care clinicians in other jurisdictions have left the practice or retired early due to the challenges of MAiD, including the emotional and personal impact of MAiD, lack of palliative care resources in the context of expanding MAiD, and other impacts on clinical palliative care practice that have been delineated below.[45]

During the Senate study of Bill C-7, which expanded MAiD to include those without a reasonably foreseeable death, Quebec Senator Julie Miville-Dechene stated that

> The reality is that medical assistance in dying has been available in Quebec since as early as 2015, but palliative care at home has failed to materialize. Yet the Quebec Act respecting end-of-life care reaffirms the right to receive palliative care in institutions or at home. In Quebec, palliative home care teams were supposed to be created throughout the province in 2018 to provide palliative care at home. These teams were to be set up because three quarters of end-of-life patients wanted palliative care at home. However, to date, only one such team has been put in place, in a neighbourhood in Montreal. Meanwhile, access to medical assistance in dying is mandatory everywhere in the province. Obviously, there is a double standard. The Association québécoise des soins palliatifs estimates that 90% of Quebecers at the end of life do not have access to a home care team to provide round-the-clock support at home.[46]

Health Canada has tried to reassure the public that a lack of access to palliative care is not impacting MAiD requests. The *First Annual Report on Medical Assistance in Dying in Canada* stated that 82 per cent of those who received MAiD also accessed "palliative care services" and used this to conclude that "requests for MAID are not necessarily being driven by lack of access to palliative care."[47] The subsequent three annual reports for 2020–22 reported similar findings.[48] The conclusions of these reports have been called into question due to the inadequacies of the data to be able to make such interpretations – Health Canada data relies on self-reports by MAiD providers and lack any meaningful information on the quality or quantity of palliative care and who provided it.[49]

As per the CSPCP, "Although one recent study indicated 82.1 per cent of individuals receiving MAiD reportedly received palliative care services, the adequacy of the services offered was not determined nor was it articulated how palliative care services were defined, what criteria were used to determine the involvement of palliative care, and if these involvements were adequate. Data regarding availability, access, quality, and types of palliative care (e.g. specialist palliative care, primary palliative care or palliative approach) are essential, not only for those requesting or receiving MAID, but in general, in order to better inform areas for improvement."[50]

This lack of objective data was confirmed during a Health Canada presentation to the Special Joint Committee on Medical Assistance in Dying in June 2021, when Health Canada assistant deputy minister Abby Hoffman confirmed that the Health Canada reports rely solely on self-reporting by MAID providers, stating that "what's counted is what providers consider to be palliative care."[51]

A palliative care specialist physician from British Columbia, Dr Romayne Gallagher, examined the Health Canada data more closely and found that "a lack of palliative care is a failure in too many MAID requests," and that an unacceptable number of people who requested MAID received little or no quality palliative care in the months before death.[52]

Dr Gallagher pointed out how the Health Canada report shows that 854 people (15.8 per cent) who got MAID had access to palliative care for *less than two weeks prior to life termination* (so the trigger for referral to palliative care was likely the request for MAID) and that another 874 people (16.2 per cent) received no palliative care. That means over one-third of those who got MAID either had no access to palliative care or received palliative care too late to intervene as MAID had already been requested. Dr Gallagher stated, "This should be considered a failure of our system. Many of these people may have been suffering for months without access to quality palliative care."[53]

Two other reports confirm these findings: (1) Palliative care physician Dr Camille Munro and team in Ottawa examined palliative care involvement in patients requesting MAID in their region. They also found palliative care to be inadequate. In their study, 72.6 per cent of patients requesting MAID had no community palliative care physician and 40 percent had no palliative care involvement prior to requesting MAID.[54] (2) A Quebec study found that in patients requesting MAID, 32 per cent of those who received a palliative care consultation had it requested less than seven days before the provision of MAID, and another 25 per cent were requested the day of or the day after the MAID request.[55]

This raises the important question as to whether a request for MAID can be considered "informed" and "voluntary" if there is limited (too late) or no access to palliative care. The *Final Report of the External Panel on Options for a Legislative Response to Carter v. Canada* stated that "a request for physician-assisted death cannot be truly voluntary if the option of proper palliative care is not available to alleviate a person's suffering,"[56] and Mary J. Shariff and Mark Ginsberg similarly ask, "If there is not a genuine commitment (resource or otherwise) behind an offer of palliative care upon which a patient can rely, can it truthfully be said from a regulatory perspective that a patient has meaningful choice?"[57]

IMPACT OF MAiD ON CLINICAL PALLIATIVE CARE PRACTICE

The impact of legalized MAiD on the day-to-day clinical practice of palliative care and the well-being of the palliative care team has been profound. We are seeing a radical normalization of MAiD as a solution to any form of suffering, a reduced ability to do palliative care work, and pressure for palliative care practitioners to participate in MAiD when it goes against the definition and core philosophy of palliative care practice.

An article by Canadian palliative care experts in the World Medical Journal documented numerous examples of the impacts on palliative care practice, including a "knee-jerk reaction" to consult the MAiD team as a first response to an expression of a desire to die, rather than involving palliative care supports.[58] Since the article was written, colleagues have experienced a further normalization of this approach within clinical settings with "wish to die" statements being interpreted as a request for MAiD, often resulting in a formal referral and assessment for MAiD instead of exploring suffering and providing palliative care supports.[59] This is especially alarming in light of the evidenced-based context that desire to die can fluctuate and often dissipates within two weeks, and that palliative care therapeutic interventions can provide support to enhance dignity, reframe hope, and affirm the inherent value of a person's life.[60]

Establishing therapeutic relationships and providing palliative care interventions takes time and dedicated resources. Unfortunately, time for such interventions to be provided is often missed due to late referrals for palliative care and now with the removal of the ten-day reflection period under the Bill C-7 MAiD legislation. A ten-day reflection period was established as a safeguard in the original C-14 legislation to allow a person time to change their mind on whether to proceed with MAiD.

Evidence that this safeguard was working can be seen within Health Canada's *First Annual Report on Medical Assistance in Dying in Canada*, which shows that in a one-year period, 263

Canadians who had requested MAiD ended up withdrawing their request.[61] Had the ten-day reflection period not been in place then, 263 Canadians who would not have otherwise died may have had their lives ended prematurely.

During the Bill C-7 hearings, the CSPCP told Parliament that they opposed the removal of the ten-day reflection period as palliative care clinicians have front-line experiences consistent with the work of Dr Chochinov, which says that people change their minds about wanting to die.[62] Dr Chochinov himself also testified to Parliament, recommending that the ten-day reflection period remain as it struck an important balance, allowing MAiD to be requested while protecting people who might change their minds and go on to live many weeks, months, or even years.[63]

MAiD advocates, including Dying with Dignity and the Canadian Association of MAiD Assessors and Providers (CAMAP), said that this safeguard should be removed as it only causes unnecessary suffering and excess anxiety.[64] The federal government chose to ignore the evidence and advice of palliative care experts and removed the ten-day reflection period through Bill C-7.[65]

Since Bill C-7 was adopted in March 2021, my colleagues and I have seen MAiD become commonly administered on the same day or within very short days from the initial MAiD assessment for those with a reasonably foreseeable death. A patient's worst day effectively becomes their last day, with no opportunity or time for palliative care supports to be applied or a patient to change their mind. We know that palliative care consults are often requested late, within days of MAiD referral or even at the time of MAiD referral (if requested at all), which reduces any opportunity for meaningful palliative care consultation or impact. This is causing moral distress and moral injury in palliative care clinicians and teams who are unable to provide their expert therapeutic work before a person has their life terminated through lethal drugs.

In cases where palliative care is consulted and a patient requests MAiD, some patients reject ongoing palliative care involvement including suggestions for optimizing symptom management out of misplaced fear that the medications may cause them to lose decisional capacity for MAiD.[66] This might be due to fear of the patient themself or to pressure and concern from family members who want them to get MAiD. This can result in the last days of life being more symptomatic and patients who get MAiD without ever having a proper trial of high-quality palliative care, even where it is available.

PRESSURE FOR PALLIATIVE CARE TO FACILITATE OR PARTICIPATE IN MAiD

MAiD advocates are pushing to make it an obligation for all doctors to inform potentially eligible patients about MAiD.[67] This would mean that palliative care physicians would have to recommend MAiD as an option to all our patients. Palliative care experts have expressed significant concern with such an approach, which may put pressure on a vulnerable patient to choose MAiD. As per the CSPCP, "To safeguard against any possibility of subtle or overt pressure on patients, physicians should not initiate a discussion about MAID or suggest the option of MAID unless brought up by a patient. The expectation that physicians introduce MAID in the absence of a request from a patient, may be all that is needed to push that patient to choose MAID."[68] And that "ultimately, when physicians bring up MAID first, it is likely to be seen as a recommendation by a trusted expert, and coercion becomes a possibility that cannot be ruled out."[69] My colleagues and I regularly see patients who have only requested MAiD because a trusted physician expert "recommended" it to them.[70]

Furthermore, requiring palliative care physicians to bring up MAiD to all of our patients would require us to go against the core philosophy, intention, and approach of palliative care (and its very definition), impacting professional integrity and identity as a palliative care physician. This can cause moral distress and moral injury that can lead to burnout. Sadly, many palliative care clinicians have already left the palliative care practice due to the emotional and moral distress of dealing with MAiD.[71] Many colleagues and I question how we could maintain our professional integrity and identity as palliative care specialists, and in good conscience be able to continue practising palliative care, if a formal requirement to bring up MAiD as part of informed consent for palliative care is put in place.

Palliative care physicians are also facing increasing pressures to directly participate and facilitate MAiD through the provision of eligibility assessments for MAiD. Due to a shortage of MAiD providers, some institutions and administrators are suggesting that attending palliative physicians should complete one of the two MAiD eligibility assessments, under the guise of "knowing the patient best." This results in more and more specialized palliative care resources being diverted to provide MAiD instead of being used for providing palliative care.[72] A qualitative study examining the impact of MAiD on palliative care in Canada found that such consumption of palliative care clinician time by MAiD is creating "additional challenges for already strained palliative care resources."[73]

In addition to pressure on palliative care clinicians to participate in MAiD, there is an ongoing push from MAiD advocates to provide MAiD in all settings of care, including hospices and palliative care units, or lose public funding.[74] The Delta Hospice Society's Irene Thomas Hospice was forced to close in 2021 after refusing to provide MAiD, which was readily accessible next door at the hospital.[75] Along with people who want MAiD, there are also many patients who want hospice and palliative care without fear MAiD might be provided without their consent.[76] I regularly encounter patients who are worried we might hasten their death on our palliative care unit and who are extremely relieved when we say MAiD is not provided there. There are no other publicly funded "medical" procedures that are required to be provided in every single health care setting.

Palliative care facilities (hospices and palliative care units) are also being pressured to use their scarce, highly specialized resources to admit people for the sole purpose of receiving MAiD.[77] This serves to reduce the already limited access to hospice and palliative care units when MAiD can be provided anywhere. Furthermore, forcing MAiD into the delivery of hospice palliative care when it is contrary to the core philosophy of the care provided there can cause distress in palliative care clinicians, worry patients, and continues to conflate MAiD with palliative care.

THE CANARY IN THE COAL MINE

Palliative care has been on the front lines navigating the impacts of the legalization and expansion of MAiD since 2016. We've experienced many challenges and difficulties that other disciplines can learn from as MAiD has now expanded well outside the realm of those with a reasonably foreseeable death.

Our discipline has been misunderstood and its integrity harmed due to intentional choices of euphemistic language by the government and the misrepresentation of MAiD as part of the continuum of palliative care by MAiD advocates. Our expert concerns, evidence, and first-hand experiences of navigating the impacts of MAiD under the C-14 legislation were dismissed by the government during the C-7 legislative process.

The ability to provide palliative care in keeping with the international standards for our discipline is becoming more difficult in Canada due to the impacts and normalization of MAiD as a turnkey solution to suffering. We are seeing reduced availability of already scarce palliative care resources, decreased access to safe spaces such as hospices and palliative care units that can exclusively focus on providing authentic palliative care that does not hasten death, and we are at risk of losing more palliative care professionals due to the emotional impact, moral distress, moral injury, and the resulting burnout from the many impacts of MAiD practice on our work.

With the removal of the reasonably foreseeable death requirement, the experiences in palliative care are likely to be seen in other disciplines as MAiD continues to advance and expand – there are now very few areas of medicine that MAiD does not touch. Palliative care is the canary in the coal mine of MAiD. Our experiences should serve as a warning and give pause to reflect: Is the response to suffering best met in medicine through healing and restorative practices that reframe hope, enhance quality, and affirm life or through intentional termination of life procedures provided with increasing frequency for any illness context, in every place of care, and requiring every clinician to participate?

NOTES

1 Cicely Saunders, *Selected Writings 1958–2004* (Oxford: Oxford University Press, 2006), xxiii.
2 Balfour Mount, *Ten Thousand Crossroads: The Path as I Remember It* (Montreal: McGill-Queen's University Press, 2020), 234.
3 "Palliative Care," World Health Organization (WHO), https://www.who.int/cancer/palliative/definition/en/.
4 Canadian Hospice Palliative Care Association and Canadian Society of Palliative Care Physicians, "Joint Call to Action," November 2019, https://cspcp.ca/wp-content/uploads/2023/02/CHPCA-CSPCP-Endorsed-Statement-on-HPC-MAiD.pdf; Health Canada, "Framework on Palliative Care in Canada," December 2018, https://www.canada.ca/en/health-canada/services/health-care-system/reports-publications/palliative-care/framework-palliative-care-canada.html.
5 Canadian Society of Palliative Care Physicians, "Palliative Care: A Vital Service with Clear Economic, Health and Social Benefits," February 2017, https://cspcp.ca/wp-content/uploads/2023/02/Economics-of-Palliative-Care-Final-EN.pdf.

6   Camilla Zimmermann et al., "Perceptions of Palliative Care Among Patients with Advanced Cancer and Their Caregivers," *Canadian Medical Association Journal* 188, no. 10 (July 2016): E217–27; Megan Johnson Shen and Joseph D. Wellman, "Evidence of Palliative Care Stigma: The Role of Negative Stereotypes in Preventing Willingness to Use Palliative Care," *Palliative and Supportive Care* 17, no.4 (2019): 374–80.

7   College of Family Physicians of Canada, "CFPC ePanel #2: Physician-Assisted Suicide and Euthanasia," 2015, https://www.cfpc.ca/CFPC/media/Resources/Government/ePanel_psa_results_EN.pdf.

8   CHPCA and CSPCP, "Joint Call to Action"; Liliana De Lima et al., "International Association for Hospice and Palliative Care Position Statement: Euthanasia and Physician-Assisted Suicide," *Journal of Palliative Medicine* 20, no. 1 (January 2017): 1–7; Lukas Radbruch et al., "Euthanasia and Physician-Assisted Suicide: A White Paper from the European Association for Palliative Care," *Palliative Medicine* 30, no. 2 (February 2016): 104–16; Canadian Society of Palliative Care Physicians, "Key Messages: Palliative Care and Medical Assistance in Dying (MAiD)," May 2019, https://cspcp.ca/wp-content/uploads/2023/02/CSPCP-Key-Messages-PC-and-MAiD-May-2019-FINAL.pdf; American Academy of Hospice and Palliative Medicine (AAHPM), "Statement on Physician-Assisted Dying," 24 June 2016, http://aahpm.org/positions/pad; Australia New Zealand Society of Palliative Medicine (ANZSPM), "Australian and New Zealand Society of Palliative Medicine Position Statement: The Practice of Euthanasia and Physician-Assisted Suicide," November 2021, https://www.anzspm.org.au/common/Uploaded%20files/Position%20Statements/2%20ANZSPM_Position_Statement_Euthanasia_Physician_Assisted_Dying.pdf; Worldwide Hospice Palliative Care Alliance (WHPCA), "WHPCA Position Paper on Euthanasia and Assisted Dying," May 2016, http://www.thewhpca.org/resources/item/whpca-position-paper-on-euthanasia-and-assisted-dying.

9   World Medical Association, "WMA Declaration on Euthanasia and Physician-Assisted Suicide," October 2019, https://www.wma.net/policies-post/declaration-on-euthanasia-and-physician-assisted-suicide/.

10 Cicely Saunders, "Voluntary Euthanasia," *Palliative Medicine* 6, no. 1 (1992): 1–5, 3–4.

11 Harvey Max Chochinov et al., "Will to Live in the Terminally Ill," *Lancet* 354, no. 9181, (September 1999): 816–9; Harvey M. Chochinov et al., "Desire for Death in the Terminally Ill," *American Journal of Psychiatry* 152, no. 8 (August 1995): 1185–91.

12 Harvey Max Chochinov, "Dignity-Conserving Care – A New Model for Palliative Care: Helping the Patient Feel Valued," *JAMA* 287, no. 17 (May 2002): 2253–60.

13 Ellen Wiebe et al., "Reasons for Requesting Medical Assistance in Dying," *Canadian Family Physician* 64, no. 9 (September 2018): 674–9.
14 Mary J. Shariff and Mark Gingerich, "Endgame: Philosophical, Clinical and Legal Distinctions between Palliative Care and Termination of Life," *Second Series Supreme Court Law Review* 85 (2018): 225–93, 228.
15 Harvey Max Chochinov and Balfour M. Mount, "Physician Hastened Death: Awaiting a Verdict," CMAJ *Blog*, 14 October 2014, https://cmajblogs.com/physician-hastened-death-awaiting-a-verdict/.
16 Canadian Society of Palliative Care Physicians, "Submission to External Panel on Options for a Legislative Response to *Carter v. Canada*," October 2015, 7, https://archive.cspcp.ca/wp-content/uploads/2014/10/CSPCP-Federal-Panel-Submission-Oct-22-2015-FINAL.pdf (link defunct).
17 Canadian Medical Association, "CMA Policy: Palliative Care," 2016, https://www.cma.ca/sites/default/files/2018-11/cma-policy-palliative-care-pd16-01-e.pdf.
18 *Bill C-14, An Act to Amend the Criminal Code and to Make Related Amendments to Other Acts (medical assistance in dying)*, 42nd Parliament, 1st Session (2016), SC 2016, c. 3 (Can.), https://www.parl.ca/DocumentViewer/en/42-1/bill/C-14/royal-assent.
19 CHPCA and CSPCP, "Joint Call to Action."
20 Balfour M. Mount, "Open Letter," December 2019, https://www.archive.cspcp.ca/wp-content/uploads/2019/12/Letter-from-Dr.-Balfour-Mount.pdf (link defunct).
21 CSPCP, "Key Messages."
22 Canadian Medical Association, "CMA Policy: Palliative Care."
23 Matt Kutcher, "Navigating MAiD on PEI," *Canadian Medical Association*, November 2018, https://www.cma.ca/dr-matt-kutcher.
24 Sandy Buchman, "Bringing Compassion to Medicine and to the CMA," *Canadian Medical Association*, October 2019, https://www.cma.ca/dr-sandy-buchman; Jeff Blackmer, "Commentary: How the Canadian Medical Association Found a Third Way to Support All its Members on Assisted Dying," *British Medical Journal* 364 (January 2019): l415; Sandy Buchman, "Why I Decided to Provide Assisted Dying: It is Truly Patient Centred Care," *British Medical Journal* 364 (January 2019): l412.
25 David Grimes et al., "Canadian Guideline for Parkinson Disease," *Canadian Medical Association Journal* 191, no. 36 (September 2019): E989–1004, https://www.cmaj.ca/content/191/36/E989.long.
26 Leonie Herx, "Response to Canadian Guideline for Parkinson Disease – Clarification on Palliative Care & MAID," CMAJ *Group*, October 2019, https://www.cmaj.ca/content/191/36/E989/tab-e-letters#re-canadian-guideline-for-parkinson-disease---clarification-on-palliative-care--maid.

27 Canadian Society of Palliative Care Physicians, "CSPCP Member Survey October 2017 Medical Assistance in Dying (MAiD) – Results," February 2018, https://www.archive.cspcp.ca/wp-content/uploads/2018/02/CSPCP-MAiD-survey-report-Feb-2018.pdf (link defunct).
28 CHPCA and CSPCP, "Joint Call to Action."
29 Canadian Association of MAiD Assessors and Providers (CAMAP), "Key Messages: End of Life Care and Medical Assistance in Dying (MAiD)," February 2020, https://camapcanada.ca/wp-content/uploads/2022/02/FINAL-Key-Messages-EOL-Care-and-MAiD.pdf; Canadian Association of MAiD Assessors and Providers (CAMAP), "Bringing up Medical Assistance in Dying as a Clinical Care Option," February 2022, https://camapcanada.ca/wp-content/uploads/2022/02/Bringing-up-MAiD.pdf.
30 Quality End-of-Life Care Coalition of Canada and Canadian Hospice Palliative Care Association, "The Way Forward National Framework: A Roadmap for an Integrated Palliative Approach to Care," March 2015, https://www.chpca.ca/wp-content/uploads/2024/04/TWF-framework-doc-Eng-2015-final-April1.pdf; Canadian Society of Palliative Care Physicians, "How to Improve Palliative Care in Canada – A Call to Action for Federal, Provincial, Territorial, Regional and Local Decision-Makers," November 2016, https://www.archive.cspcp.ca/wp-content/uploads/2016/11/Full-Report-How-to-Improve-Palliative-Care-in-Canada-FINAL-Nov-2016.pdf (link defunct).
31 CHPCA and CSPCP, "Joint Call to Action"; CSPCP, "Submission to External Panel"; Leonie Herx, Margaret Cottle, and John Scott, "The 'Normalization' of Euthanasia in Canada – The Cautionary Tale Continues," *World Medical Journal* 66, no. 2 (April 2020): 28–39.
32 CSPCP, "CSPCP Member Survey"; Leonie Herx, "Brief to the Special Joint Committee on Medical Assistance in Dying," 24 April 2022, https://www.ourcommons.ca/Content/Committee/441/AMAD/Brief/BR11740612/br-external/HerxLeonie-e.pdf.
33 Herx, "Brief to the Special Joint Committee."
34 Personal communication to author.
35 Ontario Medical Association, "OHIP Payments for Medical Assistance in Dying (MAID)," 23 November 2020, https://www.oma.org/siteassets/oma/media/pagetree/pps/billing/ohip/ohip-payments-for-medical-assistance-in-dying.pdf.
36 CHPCA and CSPCP, "Joint Call to Action."
37 "Remarks by Carla Qualtrough," in *Meeting of the Standing Committee on Justice and Human Rights – Evidence*, 43rd Parliament, 2nd Session (3 November 2020), 11:50, https://www.ourcommons.ca/DocumentViewer/en/43-2/JUST/meeting-4/evidence.

38 CSPCP, "Key Messages."
39 CSPCP, "Submission to External Panel."
40 De Lima et al., "IAHPC Position Statement."
41 *Bill C-14, An Act to Amend the Criminal Code*; *Carter v. Canada (Attorney General)*, 2015 SCC 5, [2015] 1 SCR 331; *Bill C-7, An Act to Amend the Criminal Code (medical assistance in dying)*, SC 2021, c. 2 (Can.).
42 *Bill C-7, An Act to Amend the Criminal Code.*
43 Zimmermann et al., "Perceptions of Palliative Care"; Shen and Wellman, "Evidence of Palliative Care Stigma."
44 Herx, "Brief to the Special Joint Committee."
45 Buchman, "Why I Decided to Provide Assisted Dying"; Herx, "Brief to the Special Joint Committee."
46 "Remarks of Senator M Julie Miville-Dechene," in *Senate Debates, Hansard*, 43rd Parliament, 2nd Session (15 December 2020), Vol. 152, No. 21, 19:50, https://sencanada.ca/en/content/sen/chamber/432/debates/021db_2020-12-15-e#29.
47 Health Canada, *First Annual Report on Medical Assistance in Dying in Canada, 2019*, July 2020, 24, https://www.canada.ca/en/health-canada/services/medical-assistance-dying-annual-report-2019.html.
48 Health Canada, *Second Annual Report on Medical Assistance in Dying in Canada, 2020*, June 2021, https://www.canada.ca/en/health-canada/services/medical-assistance-dying/annual-report-2020.html; Health Canada, *Third Annual Report on Medical Assistance in Dying in Canada, 2021*, July 2022, https://www.canada.ca/en/health-canada/services/publications/health-system-services/annual-report-medical-assistance-dying-2021.html; Health Canada, *Fourth Annual Report on Medical Assistance in Dying in Canada, 2022*, October 2023, https://www.canada.ca/en/health-canada/services/publications/health-system-services/annual-report-medical-assistance-dying-2022.html#.
49 Romayne Gallagher, "Lack of Palliative Care Is a Failure in Too Many MAiD Requests," *Policy Options*, 19 October 2020, https://policyoptions.irpp.org/magazines/october-2020/lack-of-palliative-care-is-a-failure-in-too-many-maid-requests/; Romayne Gallagher, Michael J. Passmore, and Caroline Baldwin, "Hastened Death Due to Disease Burden and Distress that Has Not Received Timely, Quality Palliative Care is a Medical Error," *Medical Hypotheses* 142 (2020): 109727; Canadian Society of Palliative Care Physicians, "Submission to the Standing Committee on Justice and Human Rights on Bill C-7: An Act to Amend the Criminal Code (medical assistance in dying)," 30 October 2020, https://www.ourcommons.ca/Content/Committee/432/JUST/Brief/BR10927610/

br-external/CanadianSocietyOfPalliativeCarePhysicians-e.pdf; Harvey Max Chochinov, "Medical Assistance in Dying, Data and Casting Assertions Aside," *Journal of Palliative Medicine* 26, no. 1 (January 2023): 9–12.
50 CSPCP, "Submission to the Standing Committee."
51 "Remarks of Abby Hoffman," in *Meeting of the Special Joint Committee on Medical Assistance in Dying – Evidence*, 43rd Parliament, 2nd Session (7 June 2021), 20:25, https://parl.ca/DocumentViewer/en/43-2/AMAD/meeting-2/evidence.
52 Gallagher, "Lack of Palliative Care"; Gallagher, Passmore, and Baldwin, "Hastened Death Due to Disease."
53 Gallagher, "Lack of Palliative Care."
54 Camille Munro et al., "Involvement of Palliative Care in Patients Requesting Medical Assistance in Dying," *Canadian Family Physician* 66, no.11 (November 2020): 833–42.
55 Lori Seller, Marie-Ève Bouthillier, and Veronique Fraser, "Situating Requests for Medical Aid in Dying within the Broader Context of End-of-Life Care: Ethical Considerations," *Journal of Medical Ethics* 45, no. 2 (February 2019): 106–11.
56 External Panel on Options for a Legislative Response to *Carter v. Canada*, *Consultations on Physician-Assisted Dying: Summary of Results and Key Findings – Final Report*, 15 December 2015, https://www.justice.gc.ca/eng/rp-pr/other-autre/pad-amm/pad.pdf.
57 Shariff and Gingerich, "Endgame."
58 Herx, Cottle, and Scott, "The 'Normalization' of Euthanasia."
59 Herx, "Brief to the Special Joint Committee"; Jean Jacob Mathews et al., "Impact of Medical Assistance in Dying on Palliative Care: A Qualitative Study," *Palliative Medicine* 35, no. 2 (February 2021): 447–54; Anita Ho et al., "How Does Medical Assistance in Dying Affect End-of-Life Care Planning Discussions? Experiences of Canadian Multidisciplinary Palliative Care Providers," *Palliative Care and Social Practice* 15 (September 2021): 1–14.
60 Chochinov et al., "Will to Live in the Terminally Ill"; Chochinov et al., "Desire for Death in the Terminally Ill"; Chochinov, "Dignity-Conserving Care"; CSPCP, "Submission to the Standing Committee"; Harvey Max Chochinov, "Briefing to the Senate of Canada: Standing Committee on Legal and Constitutional Affairs Regarding Bill C-7," 2021, https://sencanada.ca/content/sen/committee/432/LCJC/Briefs/HarveyMaxChochinov_e.pdf.
61 Health Canada, *First Annual Report on MAID*.
62 CSPCP, "Submission to the Standing Committee."

63 Munro et al., "Involvement of Palliative Care."
64 Dying with Dignity Canada, "Submission to the Standing Committee on Justice and Human Rights – Bill C-7: An Act to Amend the Criminal Code (medical assistance in dying)," 6 November 2020, https://d3n8a8pro7vhmx.cloudfront.net/dwdcanada/pages/4618/attachments/original/1612300823/DWDC_Justice_Committee_submission_110620.pdf?1612300823; Canadian Association of MAiD Assessors and Providers (CAMAP), "Written Brief to the Standing Senate Committee on Legal and Constitutional Affairs," 23 November 2020, https://sencanada.ca/content/sen/committee/432/LCJC/Briefs/CanAssMAiDAssessorsProviders_e.pdf.
65 CSPCP, "Submission to the Standing Committee"; Chochinov, "Briefing to the Senate of Canada."
66 Herx, Cottle, and Scott, "The 'Normalization' of Euthanasia"; CSPCP, "Submission to the Standing Committee."
67 CAMAP, "Bringing up MAiD."
68 Canadian Society of Palliative Care Physicians, "Submission to CPSO Consultation on MAiD and Professional Obligations and Human Rights Policies," 31 March 2021, https://www.archive.cspcp.ca/wp-content/uploads/2021/04/CSPCP-input-to-CPSO-consultation-on-MAiD-and-professional-obligations-Mar-31-2021.pdf.
69 Canadian Society of Palliative Care Physicians, "Submission to Special Joint Committee on Medical Assistance in Dying," April 2022, https://www.archive.cspcp.ca/wp-content/uploads/2022/05/CSPCP-submission-to-Special-Joint-parliamentary-committee-on-expanding-MAiD-Apr-26_.pdf.
70 Herx, "Brief to the Special Joint Committee."
71 Herx, Cottle, and Scott, "The 'Normalization' of Euthanasia"; Herx, "Brief to the Special Joint Committee."
72 Ebru Kaya and Leonie Herx, "Assisted Dying Must Not be Confused for Palliative Care," *Globe and Mail*, 9 May 2022, https://www.theglobeandmail.com/opinion/article-assisted-dying-must-not-be-confused-for-palliative-care/.
73 Mathews et al., "Impact of MAID on Palliative Care."
74 Herx, Cottle, and Scott, "The 'Normalization' of Euthanasia"; Herx, "Brief to the Special Joint Committee."
75 Alexandra Mae Jones and Ben Cousins, "Standoff between B.C. and Hospice Refusing to Offer Assisted Dying," CTV News, 20 January 2020, https://www.ctvnews.ca/health/standoff-between-b-c-and-hospice-refusing-to-offer-assisted-dying-1.4773755.
76 Herx, Cottle, and Scott, "The 'Normalization' of Euthanasia"; Herx, "Brief to the Special Joint Committee"; Gallagher, "Lack of Palliative Care"; CSPCP, "Submission to Special Joint Committee."
77 Herx, "Brief to the Special Joint Committee."

7

Disability and MAiD

Ramona Coelho

Since 2021, medical assistance in dying (MAiD) has been legally offered to Canadians with physical disabilities who are not approaching their death. Disabled patients who fit into track 1 of MAiD, meaning they have a "reasonably foreseeable natural death," can potentially have their life ended the same day as the initial request if all the criteria are met and practitioners are available to approve their request. For those disabled persons who are not approaching their natural death and thus fall under track 2, the law requires a more detailed evaluation, and the timing to die by lethal injection is set at a minimum of ninety days after the start of the first assessment. For both tracks, two assessors need to agree that the patient fulfills the legal criteria: patients must be experiencing intolerable psychological or physical suffering and be in an advanced state of irreversible decline of capability, terms that are not further defined.

The ninety-day period for track 2 is intended to allow health care professionals to explore other available and appropriate means to relieve the person's suffering, including mental health, disability, and community support services, and to enable consultation with other health care and social support professionals. Even in track 2, patients need only be informed about other treatment options.[1] The law does not require that other means of alleviating suffering be accessible to the patient, nor that standard treatments have been appropriately attempted before a lethal injection is administered.[2] This means that a patient who says they are suffering intolerably could access MAiD after having declined treatments that would remediate their condition. This could be because the treatment is inaccessible or unaffordable, or simply because the patient declined therapy.

Although the request must be voluntary, there is no prohibition on suggesting MAiD to a patient and bringing it up as a treatment option. In fact, it is encouraged by the Canadian Association of MAiD Assessors and Providers, an advocacy group that received $3.3 million in funding from Health Canada to guide MAiD assessments and provisions, and by a *Model Practice Standard* published by Health Canada.[3] In contrast, in New Zealand and Victoria, Australia, medical personnel are prohibited from initiating discussions about assisted death to avoid undue influence or pressure.[4]

This is the context in which disabled persons have been receiving offers for MAiD in Canada. As discussed in chapter 1, since the expansion of the law in 2021, more than seven hundred disabled persons not even remotely approaching their natural deaths have had their lives ended by MAiD. All legislation can potentially have unforeseen, detrimental effects. It is a challenge, and some might say an impossibility, to map out all the potential consequences of a law – and this is because no society is a monolith but instead is made up of people with wildly varying histories and with differing access to capital, to political power, to media representation, and so forth. However, considering the entrenched inequalities and the circumstances, disabled persons have clearly been placed at particular risk of wrongful death in the context of Canada's state-funded and medicalized assisted suicide and euthanasia regime, when they would have instead benefitted from greater resources and care.

If the Canadian government truly wants to uphold its citizens' right to life, liberty, and security, it must ensure that all citizens, including those living with and without disabilities, have access to the resources and supports that are necessary to live. They should ensure that disabled lives are not considered as a cost to the system, but rather as those the system is meant to serve.

As it stands now, our current MAiD legislation will result in a disproportionate number of deaths of those living with disabilities, because as discussed below, Canadians with disabilities tend to experience poverty, lack of resources needed to live, and discrimination well above the national average. In the context of these factors, some might see death as their most attractive option, because Canada has not done its part to ensure them the quality of life that should rightfully be theirs.

DISABLED CANADIANS ARE ALREADY CHOOSING MAiD BECAUSE OF UNEQUAL CONDITIONS

United Nations human rights experts, including the special rapporteur on the rights of persons with disabilities, the independent expert on the enjoyment of all human rights by older persons, and the special rapporteur on extreme poverty and human rights have warned our Canadian government that our current MAiD framework could lead to human rights violations.[5] Much of the essential care for those living with disabilities is not available or properly funded, and as a result, many of those living with disabilities are not provided with what they need to live in the community.[6]

As well, access to care in Canada is often not timely, which directly fosters patient suffering. For example, the wait time to see a psychiatrist can exceed four to six times the ninety-day waiting period to access a lethal injection.[7] Thus, persons with intersecting disability (for which they can get MAiD) and mental health challenges will often have more timely access to death than to a psychiatry appointment.

The federal government's failure to address the Canadian health care crisis and provide those with disabilities with adequate resources is already having a substantial impact under the initial MAiD regime. As can be seen from the examples given below, some Canadians with disabilities who seem to have a clear need (and the right to) better living conditions and care are choosing death as their best option.

Jean Truchon lived with cerebral palsy and was a quadriplegic. He was a plaintiff in the *Truchon-Gladu* case that led to the expanded legislation allowing for MAiD for those outside the end-of-life context. Truchon was a resident of Paul-Émile Léger, a long-term care centre in Montreal. He wanted to continue living in the community but was not granted the funding. Long-term care centres across Canada were not equipped to properly cope with the COVID-19 pandemic, and so like countless others, Truchon was forced into further isolation as a consequence.[8]

Because of this, Truchon decided to choose death through MAiD. He left a letter stating: "The coronavirus has literally stolen my time with those I love. Seeing what is coming frightens me the most. Therefore, I made the decision to leave now, and this was well thought out."[9] He was fifty-one. As we see in this example, what Truchon seemed to need most was time with people he loved and the resources to live in community.

Raymond Bourbonnais also chose to die by MAiD and brought media attention to his atrocious situation in a long-term care facility. Bourbonnais reported that his room would reach temperatures as high as thirty degrees Celsius in the summer. He had to leave his door open twenty-four seven to benefit from the air conditioning in the hallway. The noise, coupled with the constant fear of another resident entering and touching him or taking his belongings, led to increased suffering.[10]

A CTV story recounted how "Sophia" was unable to secure affordable housing that was compatible with her chemical sensitivities. Although she had a disability, this was not her reason for choosing MAiD. She chose MAiD because she couldn't find a heathy, affordable place to live. "This person begged for help for years, two years, wrote everywhere, called everywhere, asking for healthy housing," said Rohini Peris, President of the Environmental Health Association of Quebec (ASEQ-EHAQ). "It's not that she didn't want to live ... She couldn't live that way."[11]

Donna Duncan's story is similarly tragic. She suffered from a concussion, and it took over a year to get her the correct specialized care (while she continued to deteriorate), but she received MAiD within four days of her first MAiD assessment.[12]

As we see in all these examples, other options could have and should have been offered to these people. They should have had the right to humane living conditions, to be treated with respect and dignity, and to receive appropriate, timely medical care. But the legal system instead offered a different answer – euthanasia and assisted suicide. Considering the living conditions and lack of care that we as a society allowed them to have, their choices are understandable. But we should ask ourselves if choices made under such inhumane conditions are driven by structural coercion and stem from a lack of other options.

Some reports have pointed out that this is a serious concern. The Canadian government commissioned a University of Guelph study, published in 2021, that was entitled "Disability Inclusion Analysis of Lessons Learned and Best Practices of the Government of Canada's Response to the COVID-19 Pandemic." The researchers shared that some persons with disabilities were encouraged to explore the option of MAiD because of a lack of resources to live when they had not been contemplating this option. The authors noted that Bill C-7 allows a person with a disability to choose death for intolerable suffering. However, they note that a lack of social, economic, and health support increases the perception of intolerable suffering in persons with disabilities.[13]

The fact that several MAiD assessors and providers seem to be perfectly okay with providing MAiD under such inhumane conditions is troubling. Ellen Wiebe testified at the Special Joint Committee on MAiD that if someone had to wait a long time for a service that would remediate their suffering, she would still consider that waiting to be irremediable suffering and grant them MAiD. Therefore, it is not surprising that patients with unaddressed psychosocial suffering are being given MAiD by MAiD assessors like her, especially given that her number of MAiD provisions and assessments far exceeds the average number of that of her MAiD confreres.

She states in her testimony, "I'm also a MAiD provider and, for the last six and a half years, have assessed about 750 people for MAiD, and I've provided about 430,"[14] and then she continues, "For example, if ... I told my patient there was a five-year waiting list for the specialist in their area and asked them whether they were willing to continue suffering for the five years, and they said they weren't, then I would say that was irremediable."[15] As time goes by, an increasing number of MAiD expansionists are openly arguing that MAiD driven by poverty and inequality is supporting choice and is a form of harm reduction.[16]

In speaking of choosing death over waiting for services or poverty, such MAiD assessors show no consideration for how societal actors such as governments create and sustain the predicaments that can make death an attractive choice for those who would have instead benefitted from greater resources and care. The obvious and better solution would be to demand the government provide funding to cut those waiting times.

DISABLED CANADIANS ARE BEING FAST-TRACKED TO DEATH THROUGH INTERPRETATIONS OF RFND

Although the existing track 1 and track 2 pathways have different safeguards, in aiming to allow those near death to have quick access to MAiD with no barriers, CAMAP has created a guidance document that suggests clinicians *can be flexible* as to whether someone fits track 1's reasonably foreseeable natural death (RFND) eligibility criterion, since the law does not require that the person be terminally ill or likely to die within six or twelve months.[17] It also states that a person may meet the reasonably foreseeable criterion if they've demonstrated a clear and serious intent to take steps to "make their natural death happen soon, or to cause their death to be predictable." This could come about if the patient refuses to take antibiotics for an infection, stops accepting oxygen therapy, or refuses to eat and drink.[18]

This means that people with disabilities can *state their intention to or make themselves sick enough* to qualify as having a reasonably foreseeable natural death, as is currently happening with adults who are not dying and yet are having their lives ended within days of their first MAiD assessment.

Some places in Canada have MAiD rates that are the highest in the world. By the end of 2022, there had been almost forty-five thousand MAiD deaths across Canada since legalization – more than thirteen thousand of which took place in 2022 with 463 of those individuals accessing MAiD through track 2.[19] Health Canada and MAiD expansionists have tried to reassure the public that the overwhelming number of MAiD deaths have been track 1 deaths (implying that these patients were already dying), but we do not know how many of those persons were "fast-tracked" and may have had many decades of life left and the potential to recover with time and care.

DISCRIMINATION: ABLEISM LEADING TO MAiD

People with disabilities in Canada experience grave inequalities as a result of myriad factors, but widespread discrimination, and an inequal value placed on the lives of those with disabilities in comparison to those without disabilities, may very well play a role. Doctors are not free from ableism and could be inclined to view those living with disabilities as "good" candidates for MAiD. According to a *Canadian Medical Association Journal* (CMAJ) publication looking at international data where involuntary euthanasia is a reality, people were five times more likely to be involuntarily euthanized if they were over eighty or living with a disability.[20] Further, studies have shown that physicians perceive the quality of life of patients with disabilities as very low.[21]

The numerous parliamentary and media testimonies made by persons with disabilities in relation to the MAiD legislation also shed light on the systemic discrimination faced within the Canadian health care system in particular.

Taylor Hyatt, a young woman with cerebral palsy, testified at the parliamentary hearings for Bill C-7 about her experience after being hospitalized with pneumonia. She recounted how she was offered death and the doctor questioned whether she would really want standard treatments of oxygen and antibiotics. "All the doctors seemed to see was a disabled woman alone, sick, tired, and probably tired of living. This is nothing new," Taylor shared. "I would never want a medical professional to begin the conversation about life-ending initiatives as a result of assumptions they make about what it's like to live with my disability. Otherwise, I would not feel comfortable seeking certain forms of medical treatment. I want to be seen by a doctor who will care for me as a whole person, including taking my status as a disabled woman into account, and who will support me in living and thriving in the only life I have, which is as a disabled woman."[22]

Another witness in the parliamentary hearings was Roger Foley. He shared that "at a time when I was advocating for assistance to live and for self-directed home care, the hospital ethicist and nurses were trying to coerce me into an assisted death by threatening to charge me $1,800 per day or force-discharge me without the care I needed to live. I felt pressured by these staff raising assisted dying rather than relieving my suffering with dignified and compassionate care."[23]

And as Spring Hawes, a woman who has lived with a spinal cord injury for over fifteen years, shared during a press conference: "As disabled people, we are conditioned to view ourselves as burdensome. We are taught to apologize for our existence, and to be grateful for the tolerance of those around us. We are often shown that our lives are worth less than nondisabled lives. Our lives and our survival depend on our agreeableness. A choice to die isn't a free choice when our lives depend on compliance."[24]

The Disability Filibuster, a national grassroots disability community initiative formed in opposition to Bill C-7 and the expansion of MAiD, stated in an open letter that its members have raised fears about seeking health care where death could be offered to them when they are depressed. "People spoke of being afraid to seek medical help because they were worried about their physician raising the possibility of MAiD. Some even went so far as to say they will be avoiding medical care. Those who struggle or have struggled with suicidal ideation or depression voiced concerns about how the raising of it with them would lead to setbacks and many worried about seeking medical care for a physical emergency if they were at a low point, something that they knew to be temporary but worried they would agree to MAiD in that state."[25]

Although these examples suggest that discriminatory attitudes can be behind suggesting MAiD to a patient, health care providers may not realize that they are influenced by stereotypical thinking about disability and may fail to realize how their offer of MAiD may create undue pressure on patients.

When I started doing home care, I realized just how much we can miss in that short encounter with a patient in the office. Abused patients can have feelings of guilt or shame about dependence. Sometimes, it is embarrassment about their situation and loyalty to their families that can make it difficult for the physician to know where the request for death is coming from.

A seventy-year-old woman asked me to die. She had been losing weight dramatically. We did an extensive workup and found no clear cause for her symptoms. It took months to uncover that her son, who had moved in to help her, wasn't feeding her and was stealing her money. If MAiD existed at that time, her death would have been driven by elder neglect and financial abuse. Worse, her death would have been facilitated and approved by the medical community.

PHYSICIANS CAN CONFUSE OTHER TYPES OF SUFFERING WITH PHYSICAL PAIN

Physicians can struggle to differentiate between suffering and physical pain, which can sometimes be mistaken as one and the same, and this can exacerbate patients' suffering. Physicians often make the assumption that suffering and pain are easily distinguishable and identifiable and may have their perspectives coloured by ableism. Doctors who see a medical problem can automatically conclude that it must be the cause of a person's suffering and fail to consider or understand the person's social, situational, and economic variables that may be contributing or in fact be the real source of suffering.[26]

When a person comes to a physician seeking help, they themselves may not know what is actually causing suffering. And because the way that suffering presents and is expressed can be so unique to a person, a health care worker may make assumptions about its source depending on how it is communicated. Interpretations of suffering are influenced by past experiences, family life, culture, personal values, fears, and roles within the life of both the physician and the patient.[27] Identifying suffering can be difficult, and it involves understanding and accepting the patient and their situation as well as an awareness on the physician's part of their own biases, fears, and prejudices and an ability to keep those in check.

One of my patients, Ms A, was in a car accident a few years ago and now has paraplegia.[28] She needs to insert a catheter every three hours to drain her urine and is conscious of how to prevent bed sores. She attends physiotherapy and visits an array of specialists. Her life is different from what it was before the accident. However, the source of her suffering is the fact that people treat her differently. For example, she was shopping for a dress in preparation for an upcoming wedding, and a stranger made a cruel comment about her bothering to dress up at all. It is not her loss of function that she identifies as a cause of unhappiness but the prejudice from others. She says that she almost wishes she had been born with paraplegia because she wouldn't know how differently people treat her now in comparison to before. This example shows how identifying the cause of a person's suffering is not obvious.

All health care workers should try and seek out what is causing a patient's suffering, particularly since not all patients will be as insightful, reflective, and articulate as Ms A. Not all suffering requires a medical cure. Sometimes cures are societal and at the level of the system.

Another one of my patients, Mr Z, had a debilitating neurologic event at the young age of fifty-three.[29] He was initially unresponsive, and his family decided to ask the hospital to pursue every possible option. Within a few weeks he was opening his eyes and looking around, and within months he was speaking, could sit with minimal support, and could converse with visitors. By eight months, he could walk with a walker. His family was very supportive and loving throughout his recovery. He affirmed that he was grateful to be alive and that his quality of life was very good. Understandably, his family was in no way prepared for the financial requirement needed for his equipment and care. The financial stress of trying to bring him home in a time-sensitive manner to avoid him being placed in a long-term care setting proved challenging for them all. Mr Z started to become anxious when he thought he might be burdening his children. In the context of these financial and social stressors, he started asking about receiving MAiD. Many people hearing this request might presume, given his debilitating stroke, that his request was based on intolerable suffering because of his physical disability, but the cause of the suffering was his fear of the burden he had placed on his family, and he wondered if the life insurance policy pay-out would instead leave them a legacy. This is a common perception. The *Fourth Annual*

Report on Medical Assistance in Dying in Canada states that 35 per cent of patients who received MAiD in 2022 identified the perception of being a burden on their family, friends, or caregivers as the source of their unbearable suffering.[30]

Health care workers can sometimes be the source of a patient's suffering by taking a callous approach or failing to acknowledge the patient's concerns and what they are experiencing. Patients may feel they are not validated in their experience and therefore cannot talk about it to anybody else because the doctor has confirmed what they already suspected: that they really are a failure for feeling the way they do and that their life is worthless.

A seventy-one-year-old widower was admitted to hospital after a fall. During his admission, which was geared toward rehab and discharge, he contracted an infectious diarrheal illness, *C. difficile*. The patient was humiliated and ridiculed by staff because of the smell. He also developed new shortness of breath. In the context of this difficult hospital admission, a hospital team member suggested to him that MAiD would be an option to ease his suffering now. While he was vulnerable, depressed, and dealing with unrelenting diarrhea, the team told him he had end-stage chronic obstructive pulmonary disease (COPD). The patient was surprised but trusted his treating team. Within forty-eight hours of his first assessment, he was dead. As a post-mortem MRI showed, and as his family doctor also said, he did not have end-stage COPD, but no one had contacted his family doctor for a collateral history before ending his life. His family felt he was offered MAiD because his admission was proving longer than initially planned and that he chose to die because of how badly the treating team made him feel.[31]

MEDICAL EVIDENCE ON SUICIDALITY AND DISABILITY

It is important to weigh the medical evidence when deciding to offer death for intolerable psychological and physical suffering in those with disability. Suicidality is often present at the outset of chronic illness and disability but is not enduring in the long run. However, it can take time (evidence often suggests two years) for resolution.[32] To repeat what was stated earlier, this legislation proposes a lethal injection can be given within a minimum of ninety days from the first assessment. Remarkably, the legislative timeline of ninety days actually correlates with peak suicidality in new illness or injury.[33]

A Canadian study done by Tchajkova et al. followed patients with spinal cord injuries over time. Half of the participants reported suicidal ideation within the first two years of experiencing a spinal cord injury. However, no participants thought they would have been able to make an informed decision about MAiD in the early years after their injury.[34]

Dr Karen Ethans, who co-authored the paper, shared in a press conference that many people with a new spinal cord injury are suicidal. However, within a few years, these same people rate their quality of life as high, many in fact higher than that of the non-disabled population after rehabilitation and integration back into the community. She also shared that many health care providers in the acute setting can have a profound impact on her patients after injury when they are at their most vulnerable. In her experience, these health care workers do not always have an informed idea about disabilities and may inaccurately present future outcomes to patients.[35]

Kristine Cowley is a person who lives with a spinal cord injury from a motor vehicle accident over thirty-four years ago. She now has a doctorate and is a professor at a university. She was a wheelchair track Paralympian. Following her accident, she got married, had three children, and travelled extensively. But Kristine Cowley shared at a media event that it took her five years after her spinal cord injury to feel great again in the morning. She had to go through rehab, vocational training, and living in the community to feel healed. She shared that if someone suggested MAiD to her in her early years, she may not be here today.[36]

People can presume that spinal cord injury patients do so well and have a high quality of life because the majority are young at the time of injury and therefore have time to rehabilitate and are frequently able to return to work. But the stroke community, who tend to be older, have similar quality-of-life ratings some years post-stroke.[37] And this is true even in the arguably most severe stroke syndromes.

Similarly, studies have also looked at quality of life in survivors of locked-in syndrome. Patients with locked-in syndrome have no voluntary control of muscles, apart from some eye muscles that allow for blinking. They cannot make sounds. The patient is fully conscious and awake, and their cognition is intact. The data collected from the patients themselves serves to question the assumptions made by many who assume this state of life must be intolerable.[38]

Remarkably, quality of life in locked-in syndrome patients is most often in the same range as in age-matched healthy individuals.

The authors conclude that "in opposition to a widespread opinion, locked-in syndrome persons report a satisfactory quality-of-life level that stays stable over time, suggesting that life with locked-in syndrome is worth living."[39]

A man in his seventies experienced a small stroke, affecting his balance and swallowing. While the patient seemed down and had no interest in rehabilitation, the stroke neurologist anticipated the man would likely be able to eat normally and regain most of his balance. He was also isolated due to the COVID-19 pandemic. Psychiatry diagnosed an adjustment disorder but his stroke prognosis for recovery was good, so they opted to monitor him. He then requested MAiD and psychiatry refused to see him again. Neither of his MAiD assessors had any expertise in stroke rehabilitation and recovery. The feeding tube was removed, and he was eating all his food trays without aspiration. He had no comorbidities that were terminal, but due to the fact that he was getting used to a thickened diet and so had a slightly reduced caloric intake, they considered him track 1 eligible – fast-tracking his death and seemingly circumventing the safeguards in place for those not dying. He received MAiD the following week.[40]

The federal government, while considering Bill C-7, asked the parliamentary budget officer to estimate cost savings to our health care system in regard to MAiD. This was done by looking at comparative cost savings of MAiD versus palliative care at the end of life.[41] Through this impoverished lens of valuation, cost savings will actually be even greater when we prematurely end the lives of people who had higher care needs by many years, especially when we factor in social services, disability benefits, equipment, and other costs on top of the direct savings to health care budgets.

Will the medical evidence, skills, and tools we have to accompany patients while they recover no longer be used? Will our society forget that people who suffer an illness or injury with support and good care regain their will to live and share the same quality of life as those who are able-bodied? Will our governments view this loss of life as cost-savings?

CONCLUSION

In expanding MAiD to those whose death is not reasonably foreseeable, we have ignored those who might not be freely choosing to die, those who are neglected or abused or pressured to die by financial constraints or the myriad consequences of systemic discrimination, all which constrain freedom.

Many factors weigh into asking for death. Given the current level of evidence, we know that the overwhelming majority of requests to die in those living with chronic disabilities abate with good care.

The federal government's failure to rectify the Canadian health care crisis and provide those with disabilities with adequate resources will lead to more people choosing death as their best (only) option.

NOTES

1 *Bill C-7, An Act to Amend the Criminal Code (medical assistance in dying)*, 43rd Parliament, 2nd Session (2021), SC 2021, c. 2 (Can.), https://parl.ca/DocumentViewer/en/43-2/bill/C-7/royal-assent.
2 Trudo Lemmens, Mary Shariff, and Leonie Herx, "How Bill C-7 Will Sacrifice the Medical Profession's Standard of Care," *Policy Options*, 11 February 2021, https://policyoptions.irpp.org/magazines/february-2021/how-bill-c7-will-sacrifice-the-medical-professions-standard-of-care/.
3 Canadian Association of MAiD Assessors and Providers, "Bringing up Medical Assistance in Dying (MAiD) as a Clinical Care Option," 2022, https://camapcanada.ca/wp-content/uploads/2022/02/Bringing-up-MAiD.pdf; Minister of Health to Special Committee on Medical Assistance in Dying, "Implementation of Bill C-7," 20 October 2022, https://www.parl.ca/content/Committee/441/AMAD/GovResponse/RP11995101/441_AMAD_Rpt01_GR/DepartmentOfHealth-e.pdf; Health Canada, *Model Practice Standard for Medical Assistance in Dying (MAID)*, March 2023, https://www.canada.ca/content/dam/hc-sc/documents/services/medical-assistance-dying/model-practice-standard/model-practice-standard.pdf.
4 "End of Life Choice Act 2019: Section 10," Parliamentary Counsel Office (New Zealand), 2019, https://www.health.govt.nz/our-work/regulation-health-and-disability-system/assisted-dying-service/about-assisted-dying-service; "About Voluntary Assisted Dying," Department of Health Victoria (Australia), 2019, https://www.health.vic.gov.au/patient-care/general-information-about-voluntary-assisted-dying#can-someone-be-pressured-into-asking-for-voluntary-assisted-dying.
5 "Disability Is Not a Reason to Sanction Medically Assisted Dying – UN Experts," United Nations Human Rights Office of the High Commissioner, 25 January 2021, https://www.ohchr.org/EN/NewsEvents/Pages/DisplayNews.aspx?NewsID=26687&LangID=E.
6 "Vancouver Woman with Disabilities Living in Pain, Forced into Debt Seeks Medically Assisted Dying," *CityNews*, 27 July 2020, https://www.

citynews1130.com/2020/07/27/vancouver-woman-disabilities-medically-assisted-dying/.

7 Mackenzie Moir and Bacchus Barua, "Waiting Your Turn: Wait Times for Health Care in Canada," Fraser Institute, 15 December 2021, https://www.fraserinstitute.org/studies/waiting-your-turn-wait-times-for-health-care-in-canada-2021.

8 Sidhartha Banerjee, "Jean Truchon, Quebecer Who Fought to Expand Medically Assisted Death, Receives Procedure," *Global News*, 8 April 2020, https://globalnews.ca/news/6793568/quebec-jean-truchon-medically-assisted-death/.

9 Tu Thanh Ha, "Jean Truchon, MAID Advocate, Receives Assisted Death Early Because of Coronavirus Fears," *Globe and Mail*, 8 April 2020, https://www.theglobeandmail.com/canada/article-jean-truchon-maid-advocate-receives-assisted-death-early-due-to/.

10 Mélanie Noël, "Dénoncer avant de mourir [VIDÉO]," *Tribune*, 29 November 2019, https://www.latribune.ca/actualites/denoncer-avant-de-mourir-video-6b5b5b9901c42d9660ec5ba19a0eda78.

11 Avis Favaro, "Woman with Chemical Sensitivities Chose Medically-Assisted Death After Failed Bid to Get Better Housing," CTV, 13 April 2022, https://www.ctvnews.ca/mobile/health/woman-with-chemical-sensitivities-chose-medically-assisted-death-after-failed-bid-to-get-better-housing-1.5860579.

12 Penny Daflos, "Police Investigation, Public Outcry Following B.C. Woman's Medically Assisted Death," CTV, 28 April 2022, https://bc.ctvnews.ca/police-investigation-public-outcry-following-b-c-woman-s-medically-assisted-death-1.5881294.

13 Deborah Stienstra et al., *Disability Inclusion Analysis of Lessons Learned and Best Practices of the Government of Canada's Response to the Covid-19 Pandemic*, University of Guelph Live Work Well Research Centre and DAWN Canada, March 2021, https://liveworkwell.ca/sites/default/files/pageuploads/DisabilityInclusionAnalysisCOVID-19_Final_031621_protected.pdf.

14 "Remarks of Ellen Wiebe," in *Meeting of the Special Joint Committee on Medical Assistance in Dying*, 44th Parliament, 1st Session (26 May 2022), https://parl.ca/DocumentViewer/en/44-1/AMAD/meeting-9/evidence#Int-11711664.

15 Ibid.

16 Udo Schuklenk, "Argumenta Ad Passiones: Canada Debates Access Thresholds to MAID," *Bioethics* 36, no. 6 (June 2022): 611–2, https://doi.org/10.1111/bioe.13065; Kayla Wiebe and Amy Mullin, "Choosing Death in Unjust Conditions: Hope, Autonomy and Harm Reduction," *Journal of*

Medical Ethics 50 (26 April 2023), http://dx.doi.org/10.1136/jme-2022-108871.
17 Canadian Association of MAiD Assessors and Providers, *The Interpretation and Role of "Reasonably Foreseeable" in MAID Practice*, February 2022, https://camapcanada.ca/wp-content/uploads/2022/03/The-Interpretation-and-Role-of-22Reasonably-Foreseeable22-in-MAiD-Practice-Feb-2022.pdf.
18 Ibid.
19 Health Canada, *Fourth Annual Report on Medical Assistance in Dying in Canada 2022*, October 2023, 20, https://www.canada.ca/en/health-canada/services/publications/health-system-services/annual-report-medical-assistance-dying-2022.html#a3.1.
20 Kenneth Chambaere et al., "Physician-Assisted Deaths Under the Euthanasia Law in Belgium: A Population-Based Survey," *Canadian Medical Association Journal* 182, no. 9 (June 2010): 895–901, https://pubmed.ncbi.nlm.nih.gov/20479044/.
21 Lisa I. Iezzoni et al., "Physicians' Perceptions of People with Disability and Their Health Care," *Health Affairs* 40, no. 2 (February 2021): 297–306, https://pubmed.ncbi.nlm.nih.gov/33523739/.
22 "Remarks of Taylor Hyatt," in *Meeting of the Standing Committee on Justice and Human Rights*, 43rd Parliament, 2nd Session (10 November 2020), https://www.ourcommons.ca/DocumentViewer/en/43-2/JUST/meeting-6/evidence.
23 "Remarks of Roger Foley," in *Meeting of the Standing Committee on Justice and Human Rights*, 43rd Parliament, 2nd Session (10 November 2020), https://www.ourcommons.ca/DocumentViewer/en/43-2/JUST/meeting-6/evidence.
24 "Testimony of Spring Hawes," Physicians Together with Vulnerable Canadians Press Conference, 2020, https://www.cpac.ca/en/programs/headline-politics/episodes/66298144/.
25 Disability Filibuster to the Ontario Government and CPSO Policy Department, *Disability Filibuster*, 20 November 2022, https://policy-consult.cpso.on.ca/wp-content/uploads/2022/11/POHR-MAiD_Disability-Filibuster_20221128_Redacted.pdf.
26 Geoff MacDonald and Lauri A. Jensen-Campbell, eds., *Social Pain: Neuropsychological and Health Implications of Loss and Exclusion* (Washington, DC: American Psychological Association, 2011), https://doi.org/10.1037/12351-000.
27 J. Makselon, "[The Psychology of Suffering]," *Folia Medica Cracoviensia* 39, nos. 3–4 (1998): 59–66, https://pubmed.ncbi.nlm.nih.gov/10816956/.
28 Name and identifying details changed to preserve anonymity.

29 Name and identifying details changed to preserve anonymity.
30 Health Canada, *Fourth Annual Report*, 20.
31 Michael Cooper, "MAiD Press Conference," Facebook Video (testimony of Erin Smith: 17:10), 10 May 2022, https://fb.watch/eoCh1C_fnq/.
32 Vahé Nafilyan et al., "Risk of Suicide after Diagnosis of Severe Physical Health Conditions: A Retrospective Cohort Study of 47 Million People," *Lancet Regional Health - Europe* 25 (December 2022): 100562, https://pubmed.ncbi.nlm.nih.gov/36545003/.
33 Y. Kishi, R.G. Robinson, and J.T. Kosier, "Suicidal Ideation among Patients with Acute Life-Threatening Physical Illness: Patients with Stroke, Traumatic Brain Injury, Myocardial Infarction, and Spinal Cord Injury," *Psychosomatics* 42, no. 5 (September–October 2001): 382–90.
34 Natalja Tchajkova, Karen Ethans, and Stephen D. Smith, "Inside the Lived Perspective of Life after Spinal Cord Injury: A Qualitative Study of the Desire to Live and Not Live, Including with Assisted Dying," *Spinal Cord* 59, no. 5 (May 2021): 485–92, https://doi.org/10.1038/s41393-021-00619-3.
35 "Testimony of Dr. Karen Ethans," Physicians Together with Vulnerable Canadians Press Conference, 2020, https://www.cpac.ca/en/programs/headline-politics/episodes/66298144/.
36 "Testimony of Kristine Cowley," Physicians Together with Vulnerable Canadians Press Conference, 2020, https://www.cpac.ca/en/programs/headline-politics/episodes/66298144/.
37 C. Woertgen et al., "Quality of Life after Decompressive Craniectomy in Patients Suffering from Supratentorial Brain Ischemia," *Acta Neurochirurgica (Wien)* 146, no. 7 (July 2004): 691–5, https://pubmed.ncbi.nlm.nih.gov/15197612/.
38 D. Lulé et al., "Life Can Be Worth Living in Lock-in Syndrome," *Progress in Brain Research* 177 (2009): 339–51, https://pubmed.ncbi.nlm.nih.gov/19818912/.
39 Marie-Christine Rousseau et al., "Quality of Life in Patients with Locked-in Syndrome: Evolution Over a 6-Year Period," *Orphanet Journal of Rare Diseases* 10, no. 88 (July 2015), https://pubmed.ncbi.nlm.nih.gov/26187655/.
40 "Remarks of Dr. Ramona Coelho," in *Meeting of the Special Joint Committee on Medical Assistance in Dying*, 44th Parliament, 1st Session (30 May 2022), https://parl.ca/DocumentViewer/en/44-1/AMAD/meeting-10/evidence#Int-11717369.
41 Office of the Parliamentary Budget Officer, *Cost Estimate for Bill C-7 Medical Assistance in Dying* (20 October 2020), https://www.pbo-dpb.gc.ca/web/default/files/Documents/Reports/RP-2021-025-M/RP-2021-025-M_en.pdf.

8

Creating a Killable Class and Manufacturing Selective Suicidality: Thoughts of a Past and Future Ironing Board

Gabrielle Peters

SITUATING MYSELF

My lived experience matters always but it especially matters here.

I am a disabled, white, poor woman. I am a non-ambulatory wheelchair user with an autoimmune disease and multiple comorbidities. I am fat and toothless due to a combination of illness, side effects of medications, and the fine print under the words "universal health care." I wear incontinence briefs and live in a tiny improperly adapted unit in social housing that I can't escape in a fire. It's the law. There must be a way for people to independently evacuate in an emergency – except for wheelchair users and other disabled people for whom stairs pose a barrier. For us the emergency plan is not evacuation but to "shelter in place," which is a much too nice way of saying that we are left behind inside a burning building while others flee to safety. We wait and cross our fingers, hoping the fire department gets us out or puts the fire out before we die. I have lived through too many alarms, and it is never my choice to remain inside, but it was someone else's choice to design housing that leaves me with no means of escape. Even when the first sirens are followed by more and more sirens and the fire department uses the PA system to tell everyone to evacuate, I cannot. I call 911 and tell them my unit number and then hang up and hope the fire is many floors away. Unfortunately, policy-makers have also decided to stack disabled people who need emergency evacuation assistance in the same building. When there was a fire in my complex that sent three people to hospital the firefighters told me – and also media – that a large tower full of people who need assistance to evacuate obviously creates a challenge for them. There has since been another fire and this time one of the people had to be resuscitated on scene and was treated in the intensive care unit. There are also no sprinklers in this building. The design of housing worsens our odds of survival – not our choices and not our disability.

In the past I worked multiple jobs and went to university, but now I live on disability benefits in Canada's third-largest city. Somewhere between seven hundred thousand and one million people in my province of just over five million residents do not have a family doctor. I am one of those people. My primary care physician closed her practice and with it her chain of clinics. She sent a letter informing her patients she was pursuing an opportunity to work in addiction treatment. A Google search tells me she is working with a private online company that provides prescriptions for cannabis. I have made several attempts to find a new physician and have set up appointments with doctors who advertised themselves as accepting new patients, only to have this status change when I wheel into their office.

I have no generational wealth or family support.

All of the above – and more – affects my life, health, and the health care I receive – for better or worse.

These things also inform my analysis of medical assistance in dying (MAiD). This is the role lived experience should be playing in discussions of policy. Lived experience is valuable not because it is some sacred text to be regarded as "the truth," but because it plays a vital part in the pursuit of truth.

INTRODUCTION

> If I had my way, I would build a lethal chamber as big as the Crystal Palace, with a military band playing softly, and a Cinematograph working brightly; then I'd go out in the back streets and main streets and bring them in, all the sick, the halt, and the maimed; I would lead them gently, and they would smile me a weary thanks; and the band would softly bubble out the "Hallelujah Chorus."[1]
>
> D.H. Lawrence

D.H. Lawrence wasn't Canadian but there is something very Canadian about this passage – killing people as a form of assistance is just further proof of how nice we are. Surrender is equated with consent.

Canada's MAiD regime asks us to imagine a Canada populated by individuals with private lives and opinions unaffected by the society they live in or by those who run it. In this myth each person functions as an autonomous unit unconstrained by their social or financial situation, unimpacted by the culture, economy, laws, or politics of their era, and uninfluenced by the lobbying, marketing, manipulation, and various means of social persuasion, coercion, and control. The MAiD provider has a modest lethal injection instead of a crystal chamber, though a funeral home in Quebec did create a special MAiD room – to be availed of for a fee of course.[2] They lack a military band, though one can imagine an enterprising provider offering to arrange musical accompaniment as part of their excelsior package.

By promoting the erroneous view that MAiD is merely and exclusively about personal choice and deciding to ignore how choices are made and the society and circumstances they occur in, discussions about MAiD in Canada have blurred important lines about the role of the state around MAiD, in the lives of disabled people, and in general. MAiD proponents like to position euthanasia as a matter of individual rights, specifically the right to die. But leaving aside whether this is fallacious, they conveniently ignore the other real rights that MAiD creates. Specifically, MAiD gives the state the right to involve itself in the killing of certain citizens. And, not insignificantly, MAiD gives certain health care professionals the right to kill. These rights are not part of the talking points or discourse, and therefore the nature of both the state and doctors, and the relationship of each to disabled people, is ignored.

Believing the state has no "right" to "deny" (certain people) the "right" to die does not justify supporting the state changing the Criminal Code to allow itself to fund and regulate a non-culpable homicide program for disabled people. Thus far the proponents have not argued for a universal "right to die" for everyone, but either way this is the opposite of non-intervention on the part of the state.

This chapter invites you to ask yourself to what extent policy is something you shape, and to what extent policy shapes you. And I am guessing that how you answer reflects your position – top and centre or somewhere in the margins.

Research confirms that those who believe they are autonomous also believe they live in a meritocracy. They inaccurately predict the level of inequality in society and likely avoid information that conflicts with the fantastical beliefs about fairness that just so happens to work in their favour. Those who made more accurate judgments about inequality viewed themselves as less autonomous. Having an accurate sense of society, and the degree of choice and power you have within it, is essential to understanding why disabled people oppose MAiD.

When it comes to MAiD I have always felt that those of us on the losing end of an inequitable society are having an argument with those who believe the world is fair and just. But it would also be a mistake to reduce this to an individual level. Even if those who believe themselves to be highly autonomous engage in motivated reasoning, they are not the original authors of the myth. And while it is true that information about inequality is available, it is often presented as if the reasons for it are either a mystery rooted in individual behaviour or one-off instances of institutional misdeeds. None of those things challenge belief in meritocracy or that true individual autonomy is possible let alone typical in our society. This means understanding why inequality exists, not just that it exists, is also essential to understanding MAiD.

Meritocracy and individual autonomy are used to justify structural oppression, not just individual good fortune. They are mutually supporting myths, and challenging the legitimacy of either challenges the claims of the other. Ableism plays an essential role in the construction of both. For this reason, any serious analysis of MAiD must be placed within a proper historical and political context. We need to acknowledge and understand the past that is informing our present.

Belief in these myths is the basis for supporting MAiD. There is also a relationship between these myths and beliefs that lead to a fear of disability. Given that fear of future disability is a big driver of the push for MAiD, we need to understand why people fear disability and why and how the state generates and benefits from that fear.

Disabled people's opposition to MAiD is political but not partisan. It is based on our lives, history, personal experiences, and collective knowledge. While there are undeniably those who deliberately spread false information about us and our reasons for opposing MAiD, they are aided by the fact that they operate within a void of willful ignorance and incuriosity about us. Their failure to understand our opposition to MAiD is rooted in many of the same reasons we oppose MAiD.

This is my attempt to not so much bridge a chasm but achieve the much humbler goal of pointing out one exists between non-disabled and disabled people not just in our lives but in our knowing.

The myth of individual autonomy, and the myths that support it, cannot erase the brutal reality of poverty and ableism, nor should it be allowed to support the lie that MAiD is being offered as an extension of freedom and choice. Grasping for a false feeling of control ultimately denies our humanity and leads away from freedom, not towards it.

The first section, "A Is for Astroturf Autonomy," challenges the liberal notion of independence and the prioritization of individual autonomy that have been used to remove the guardrail prohibiting killing and enabled the creation of state-sanctioned and funded killing. We are a society and interdependence should be understood as a feature, not a bug. Choice does not exist in a vacuum, and in an inequitable and ableist society that choice is very different in quantity and quality for some than others. By flattening autonomy and depriving it of any disability or class context, we are all magically transformed into billionaires (whose false sense of "independence" is built off the exploitation and oppression of others), on a private island just deciding to die because we want to.

The second section, "Rational(ized) Oppression," discusses how disability came to be defined as less human and given the stamp of science. While this section has a lot of history, the examples from the past are intentional due to their ongoing presence and influence, particularly around MAiD.

Using Tanya Titchkofsky's concept of "unintended participant" and "abled-disabled," the third section, "Capitalism and the Making of Disabled People as 'Unintended Participants' in Society," considers how disabled people were designed out of society and why that continues to be the case. Using this concept, it examines how social, cultural, economic, and political motivators and drivers of MAiD operate both systemically and on an individual level. Poverty is a big focus of this section.

The final section, "My Body Is a Map of Policy Decisions," returns to the issue of autonomy. It is the most personal of all the sections although nuggets of lived experience are scattered throughout the chapter and inform the overarching argument.

There are other forces acting against choice. This chapter does not have the space to examine ableist rhetoric, medical ableism, epistemic injustice, bioethics, judicial bias, or the role the media plays in how disabled people are (not) represented and our perspectives (not) presented.[3] Nor does it broach the question of how we should think about autonomy at a time when those seeking to manipulate opinions and manufacture consent, obedience, and desire have fine-tuned their route into our brain, soldering some wires and cauterizing others.

Canada's MAiD program didn't invent discrimination against disabled people. It reified and built onto long-standing, deeply entrenched and entangled beliefs, customs, institutions, and conditions about and around disability and the construction of "other." Understanding their purpose and why they remain in place is essential to understanding the threat posed by MAiD.

Though I will not be delving into the feminist critiques of individual autonomy, I consider this chapter to occupy space with arguments for *constitutively relational* autonomy, which understands people as "socially situated and interdependent."[4] In this context people's "identity-defining beliefs, values, commitments, and reasons for action are shaped by – or, more strongly, are constituted by – the societal positions they occupy and the shared environment they inhabit." Autonomy exists, but it exists within "real-world context of moral, social, and political exchange" and is neither "atomistic or individualistic."[5] It is precisely the value that I place on personal freedom that leads me to my conclusions around MAiD.

There was a time when I made the "choice" to remain in a situation that had become emotionally abusive and felt on the cusp of transitioning to physical violence. I knew that if I reached out for help, I would be forced into a nursing home, which I believed posed at least as much if not more of a threat to my well-being. As a survivor and feminist staying in this situation went against both my personal sense of safety and my political beliefs. At one point this person decided to go on vacation to another country. I had to keep his absence a secret from those coordinating my home care, as I was bedbound and even with the maximum hours allowed through government funding, I would be alone about twenty hours a day. Policies also prevented home care staff from having a key to my apartment. The result was that for ten days I was alone in a rented hospital bed, unable to move other than very limited use of my arms and hands, in an unlocked apartment. I was terrified. Suggesting it was my choice is as much an erosion of the concept of individual rights and freedom as it is a slander against me. Placing responsibility for this "choice" on me is victim blaming.

Others may have more insulation from society and policy – and as a result more illusions – but I would argue the difference between us is less absolute and more a matter of degree. Consider the impacts of the social and political determinants of health. "It is not *inequalities* that kill people ... it is *those who are responsible for these inequalities* that kill people."[6] If we understand health as a collective project, not just a personal responsibility, we must ask ourselves how much autonomy we have over the quality of the air we breathe, the water we drink, or some future environmental disaster that policy decisions of the past and present almost certainly caused or made worse.[7] Even something as seemingly individual as motor vehicle collisions have been shown to reflect road design, vehicle design, and urban planning decisions, not just personal choices.[8] Our personal history, family history, and the history of policy are intertwined.

The crystal palace execution centre D.H. Lawrence imagined is not an act of compassion, but an effort to preserve the class comfort of some at the expense of others. Any real "choice" in this society resides way above my pay grade.

A IS FOR ASTROTURF AUTONOMY

How much of people's sense of independence and choice is attached to a piece of plastic with their name on it that they carry inside their wallet? A study found that "perceiving oneself as highly autonomous is associated with a belief in a meritocratic worldview and the existence of equal opportunities. These individuals are more tolerant of income inequality because they think people tend to get the economic outcomes they deserve." They believe "that income differences stem from differences in effort and ability rather than luck."[9] Those with lowered perceived autonomy had a more accurate sense of income distribution whereas those with greater perceived autonomy underestimated the proportion of lower-income households. And the authors further posited that maintaining such an inaccurate worldview might require avoiding information that conflicts with it: "The belief that income inequality is relatively low can be maintained if one refrains from seeking out information about the actual degree of inequality that may disprove one's belief. We have some initial evidence supporting this explanation."

If one believes there is a high level of autonomy in our society, which they perceive to be fair, then what would their perception of disability be given the status of disabled people in our society? A different US survey found that slightly over half (52 per cent) of Americans said they would rather be dead than disabled.[10] The percentage was almost double among people who had college degrees

(57 per cent) compared with those who had not finished high school (30 per cent). Preferring death to disability was also higher among those with greater income, with 59 per cent of people earning $75,000 or more agreeing compared with 45 per cent among those earning $25,000 or less.

This is also consistent with research that links belief in (the myth of) meritocracy among those with greater wealth.[11] And, in particular, that the greater the inequality where wealthy people lived, the less altruistic and charitable they were.[12] In essence, people on the winning end of inequality appear to believe they are more entitled and deserving of their wealth, power, and privilege and the hoarding of it.[13]

In contrast, working-class culture places greater value on interdependence, "equality, collectivity, and group solidarity"[14] than the middle and upper classes' prioritization of independence.[15] This makes sense given the importance unions, unity, and solidarity in one form or another have played in the working-class struggle to achieve any rights and manage survival. There is also cultural variation in the value placed on independence and choice and the degree to which those are linked to happiness and well-being.[16]

All of this supports the characterization of the original proponents of assisted suicide as white, well-off, and well-educated and explains their continued disinterest in how legalization of it might impact others, whereas the disabled people and activists who oppose this legislation consider the consequences to disabled people as well as society as a whole.

MAiD proponents argue that the obvious class difference between themselves and opponents is reason to assume MAiD poses no risk to others who are not as financially or otherwise privileged. As if the marketing and normalizing of MAiD has no societal impact. Smoking cigarettes began as an upper-class sign of sophistication and, as we know, it spread across class lines, and when the health impacts became known the wealthy stopped smoking but poor people have not.[17] It's never not remarkable how fundamental awareness of *how* our society operates is ignored when discussing MAiD, including (but by no means limited to) that the creation, maintenance, and funding of the support we require to live is dependent on political will that is lessened when another inexpensive "solution" is available.[18] The belief that it is better to be dead than disabled can become "you better be dead if you're disabled" when all routes to dignity are detoured into a duty to die.

A US-to-Canada comparison of the above survey result is imperfect at best, but in this case, I suspect the same survey would only differ for the worse in Canada, with more believing death is preferable to disability and that our quality of life is necessarily lower. I base this on the fact that the US has more enforceable and longer-standing disability rights legislation, which in turn is reflected in, and a cause of, greater public and political presence and understanding of disabled people as a political constituency who are subject to discrimination. Since Canada with its proven track record of incuriosity about itself (leading to major data gaps[19]) is unlikely to ever ask such a question, we may never know if I'm correct.

Among respondents who believed death would be preferable to disability, we should assume they believed they were making the moral and correct choice based on what they have come to believe about disability, and that these opinions would also inform their attitudes towards disabled people and their support for government funding of programs for disabled people. And this gets at one of the core problems – their opinions are not actually well-informed opinions.[20] They are the result of numerous misconceptions about disability, humans, and our society that go unchallenged. Additionally, those assumptions are supported by humans' poor ability to predict how they would feel in hypothetical situations. The latter could be partly a consequence of focalism, which is "the tendency to focus on only one aspect of an experience while disregarding the full picture,"[21] leading people to fixate on symptoms rather than a more holistic imagining of a life fully adapted to them. The thing non-disabled people fixate on about me – not being able to walk – is not something that occupies my thoughts. It's always jarring when a stranger asks what is wrong with me.

Perhaps even more concerning in the immediate decision-making around MAiD is a subgroup of people that also represent a well-off and well-educated demographic – doctors. A 2021 study of over seven hundred US physicians found 82.5 per cent believed people with significant disabilities have worse quality of life compared to non-disabled people. Just over half (56.5 per cent) welcomed disabled people into their practice. Less than half (40.7 per cent) felt confident they could provide quality care to disabled patients.[22]

This is the profession that is now licensed to "assist" disabled people to kill ourselves and is given authority to speak for and about us on this issue. They also have power over whether we receive the support we need to live and, in some cases, where we live and who we live with. Due to the medical model of disability, physicians play a significant role in constructing and carrying out ableism and have been conferred with a level of power over disabled people that far exceeds what they have over non-disabled people, particularly when it comes to disabled people who are poor and require state-funded services or financial assistance of any kind.[23] "When you are forced to realize that other people have more social authority than you do to describe your experience of your body, your confidence in yourself and your relationship to reality is radically undermined. What can you know if you cannot know that you are experiencing suffering or joy; what can you communicate to people who do not believe you know even this?"[24]

Like other prejudices, the harmful and sometimes hateful beliefs about disabled people are learned and absorbed, including by members of the negatively affected group. This learning feeds and is fed by structural oppression. Challenging these beliefs can mean facing the full weight of institutional ableism, which deems disabled people's knowledge, experiences, analysis, perspectives, and lives insignificant, fringe, anecdotal, low value, or outright false or even dangerous. We are not even considered relevant let alone essential in this national discussion about our deaths. The knowledge of devalued people is typically tossed aside.[25]

DIE *FOR* DIGNITY

Invisibilizing us and denying our expertise also works as a subtle but no less effective form of coercive pressure for MAiD, particularly when paired with the resulting material deprivation, social isolation, and exclusion resulting from the state's failure to create the infrastructure necessary to support disabled life. If we don't matter in a life and death debate about us, when would we? Middle-class non-disabled people's wish for their future selves is dangerous for disabled poor and working-class people in the present, in part because we are a society, and the line between personal opinions formulated independently and those shaped and informed by the culture around us is not nearly as impermeable as some would like to imagine.[26]

Even before the invented euphemism of MAiD, when they spoke of "assisted suicide," which is another misnomer since 99.9 per cent of those killed by the MAiD regime in Canada die via euthanasia,[27] there was something about it that always hit me viscerally as upper middle class.

Suicide is highly stigmatized and viewed as an irrational act, but those who sign up for assisted suicide have been lauded as brave, rational, admirably self-sacrificing, and dignified. The act of contracting out killing oneself made it socially acceptable. This division could itself act as a source of social pressure, encouraging a disabled person to apply for MAiD rather than seek support, since being regarded with esteem is certainly preferable to being shamed.[28] In this way MAiD acts as a facade entryway to respectability and middle-class-sanctioned dignity. It's your last shot at climbing the social ladder, even though they'll still put you in a cardboard box.

The repetitive rhetoric about "dying on their own terms," as if MAiD somehow confers control over mortality and makes death a choice not an inevitability, is blatant propaganda. Precious little about the life of a disabled poor person is "on our own terms." We don't live under illusions of rugged individualism. Rather, our lives are spent navigating, relating, and engaging with the world we exist in and the people we exist with. There is never a time when we are far away from feeling the disproportionate consequences of the choices of others, especially those with power.

It could also be argued that someone who says they would rather be dead than disabled does not necessarily think other disabled people would also be better off dead. But this seems like a distinction without a difference. Their reasons for preferring death reflect and contribute to the diminished status of disabled people in society – it is a loop. Notably, calls for empathy would be dangerous to disabled people since most people don't wish worse for themselves than they do for others. It is also reasonable to assume politicians might use these attitudes as a means of gauging the political cost/benefit of addressing the needs of disabled people.

Autonomy is not a simple binary. What is presented as personal choice is rarely if ever a choice arising from that person, but rather that person picking from a limited range of options made available to them. The quality and quantity of those choices depend on the person's circumstances and those circumstances are invariably influenced by the decisions of others past and present. Someone in prison has some degree of autonomy, but it is considerably less than that of the prison guard who, in turn, has less autonomy on duty than off duty. A poor person has far less autonomy than a billionaire. And a billionaire not only has more ability to assert their personal autonomy but the ability to severely limit the autonomy of others. This very imbalanced distribution of power over autonomy of others and the imbalanced distribution of individual autonomy is completely ignored in MAiD discourse. The greater autonomy of the billionaire depends on the lessened autonomy of others. This does not always require overt acts of suppression, and there are many tools of oppression.

It is hardly surprising that non-disabled people live in fear of suffering the indignity of being among the demeaned and devalued. And because attitudes and beliefs about disability are perceived as rational and common sense, people regard the resulting conditions and status of disabled people as pitiable but inevitable. Meanwhile appeals to public emotion are employed regularly by the proponents of MAiD, demanding you justify why you will not help this person die – or as they would phrase it, why you would want to deny them this "right" – using a sleight-of-hand trick they play with the framing, since what they demanded and received was not a lifting of prohibition on suicide but rather a state-funded and state-delivered suicide service for disabled people. Their strategy is successful because empathy "distorts our moral judgments in pretty much the same way that prejudice does" and is at best unreliable, particularly when scaled up to society-wide policy.[29] This means the well-off, white, and well-educated who would rather be dead than disabled are more readily identified with and thus more likely to be on the receiving end of empathy than the disabled poor people who are fighting for housing, health care, and support to live.

We can see evidence of attitudes and perceptions of disability in the reasons given for wanting MAiD, including fear of loss of autonomy, loss of dignity, and fear of being a burden (or a fear of being perceived as one). When people say they fear a loss of dignity, what they may really mean is they fear they will be viewed as less dignified or subjected to undignified treatment. There is no objective reason why someone fed through a tube is less dignified than someone biting down on a hot dog. For all their pretense of science and highbrow rationality, the defenders of MAiD are remarkably shallow in their thinking and transparently bigoted.

We know that many non-disabled people currently support MAiD, but whether disabled people are designated a class of legally killable people should never be a referendum question. What may be a reasonable question to ask is whether the people who say they would rather be dead than disabled would publicly voice that they believe the same should be true for all disabled people. I will concede this is less likely but knowing not to say something out loud because it may not be viewed as socially appropriate is not the same as knowing your opinion is wrong. Measuring discrimination based strictly on whether it is overtly expressed and reaches the level of hate speech is an inaccurate yardstick for whether discrimination exists. This approach ultimately reduces discrimination to a question of etiquette.

Confining the conversation to individual autonomy and ignoring the society MAiD exists in, and the marginalized demographic targeted by it, has been very helpful to proponents of MAiD. Oppression is siloed off to be discussed another day as a separate, unrelated topic. Even when there are publicized MAiD deaths that raise concern about pressure or social coercion, the conversation stays at the individual level, examining specific details of that one person and debating whether it is wrong to tell someone they can't use MAiD to escape terrible conditions of poverty, loneliness, or prison. Once the discussion is kettled within "individual," there is no option to discuss the society or inequitable distribution of freedom within it. Instead, everything about a person's life becomes normalized as part of their inevitable, unchangeable reality, not just whatever diagnosis (or lack of one) they may have had.

YOU'RE COMPETENT, THE STATE IS NOT

As a disabled person I want disabled people (and others) to have greater not less autonomy, and I want to be part of building a society that supports a richer version of that and allows people to make more authentic choices. If someone is choosing MAiD I do not support their choice but neither do I wish to attack the competence of that person (which is currently one of the few legal options available if you are trying to stop a loved one's legalized suicide by MAiD[30]). This is not an issue of competence or capacity. I have certainly made choices that were less than ideal, unaligned with my goals, beliefs, or the best interests of myself or others. Many were made due to the lack of better options; too many reflect previous trauma; others were made in a moment of rebellion, indulgence, anger, passion, underestimation of risk, overestimation of skill, misplaced loyalty, ambition, or simply because they appeared to be good choices at the time and were only recognized as otherwise later. We learn from our choices. The fact I made mistakes is not a reflection of my capacity but of how decision-making is influenced by a multitude of factors internally and externally. Death allows no learning curve. This is also not an argument for removing the humanity from our choices. As Stuart Ewen said, "Our emotions are not our enemies, unless they are used against us."[31] The solution is not to question the competence of a person but to question the competence of the state and ask whether it is fit to become involved in the business of killing its citizens.

MAiD has allowed for a massive increase in the spreading of ableist rhetoric and beliefs, the not subtle broadcasting of key messages and crafted narratives informing us that the noble know when to die – before becoming undignified, burdensome diaper-wearers outliving their use. Suicide with an assist was just different enough for the media to burn the guidebook on how to prevent their coverage from acting as a suicide contagion.[32] Instead, assisted suicide is presented as a solution, and poetic prose is pulled out to describe the method of death in detail.

If people could not be influenced, then marketing, advertising, public relations, and lobbying as professions would not exist and hundreds of billions of dollars would not be spent on them annually. It should be obvious in a consumer society that most of what we assert to be "our choice" reflects the choices provided to us by those who have enormously more wealth and power. But what constitutes choice is not just confined by the very limited range of options that may be available – and affordable and accessible – to us, nor simply by those who work to influence what we think and therefore what we want, though these all have substantial impact. Our "choice" also reflects norms, culture, beliefs, values, interests, knowledge, and desires, some of which we may believe to be our own but in truth are all shaped to varying degrees by the society we live in.

To suggest that disabled people have such a deep, rich, fulsome, and equitably distributed autonomy that even the state's provision of killing as a service to us as a designated group of people (who happen to be a protected class due to the discrimination and oppression and exclusion we face) poses no threat to us is not just fallacious, it's ludicrous. The state and its policies are the reason for the inequity, injustice, and discrimination disabled people face.

When we look at Canada's MAiD, we need to shift from the current focus on individuals to society and contextualize it within long-standing historical and political strategies to construct and manage disability as a category and the resulting "choice" this creates. This is not a conversation about what one individual person does or does not want, because MAiD is public policy. The inequity disabled people – as a group – face in Canada is not a result of what is presented as "natural inequality" playing out in a meritocracy, but choices made by those with power and wealth in the past and present.

In addition to misleading people into thinking that MAiD is merely about personal choice, the state-funded killing of disabled people is presented and absorbed as a component of public health care. The state is not neutral and expanding its role in who lives and dies in an inequitable society means MAiD automatically acquires influence and opportunity to act as a force of persuasion at an individual but even more so at a societal level. We are regularly reminded that budgets are about priorities. At a policy level influence can be blunt and direct or so normalized that it becomes absorbed and integrated into "common sense" and passed along generationally so you are raised with an assumption that goes as unquestioned as the idea that you should never eat before swimming. Policy impacts ripple and influence how people think, feel, and behave, and this impact extends far beyond whether they agree with or follow the policy. Policy shapes our personal and family histories, not just "History."

RATIONAL(IZED) OPPRESSION – INJUSTICE THAT'S OK BECAUSE IT'S SCIENCE!

Since the social and political revolutions of the eighteenth century, the trend in western political thought has been to refuse to take for granted inequalities between persons or groups. Differential and unequal treatment has continued, of course, but it has been considered incumbent on modern societies to produce a rational explanation for such treatment. In recent decades, historians and other scholars in the humanities have studied intensely and often challenged the ostensibly rational explanations for inequalities based on identity – in particular, gender, race, and ethnicity. Disability, however, one of the most prevalent justifications for inequality, has rarely been the subject of historical inquiry. Disability has functioned historically to justify inequality for disabled people themselves, but it has also done so for women and minority groups. That is, not only has it been considered justifiable to treat disabled people unequally, but the concept of disability has been used to justify discrimination against other groups by attributing disability to them.[33]

There's a scene in *Good Will Hunting* where Matt Damon's character, who is poor, is sparring off with Robin Williams's character, who is his psychiatrist. Referencing the books on the shelf in Williams's office, Damon says, "You fuckin' people baffle me. You spend all your money on these fuckin' fancy books. You surround yourselves with 'em. They're the wrong fuckin' books." I find myself regularly thinking a version of this only instead of books, it's that they ask the wrong fuckin' questions. In the case of MAiD the question of why people think it is better to be dead than disabled never comes up. I wonder if people don't ask this question because the answer seems obvious and logical to them. Or do they know that asking this question is like yanking out the Jenga block that will topple the tower?

The question that should be asked is, If killing disabled people is so wrong, why do so many people think it is so right?

The short answer to the question is ableism, and in particular modern Western ableism, was integral to providing a rational(ized) explanation for oppression. And this leads to two questions: what is ableism, and why does it exist? Surprisingly the *why* may be easier to answer than the *what*, because to a certain extent ableism is everything or at least a part of everything – the equivalent of an ideological atom in our economic, political, cultural, and social system.

There are many definitions of ableism. When I use the word, I'm drawing on Fiona Kumari Campbell's definition of the term as "a network of beliefs, processes and practices that produces a particular kind of self and body (the corporeal standard) that is projected as the perfect, species-typical and therefore essential and fully human. Disability then, is cast as a diminished state of being human."[34] I would add that ableism is highly adaptable and malleable, and yet once set, strong and resistant to change. It operates structurally and individually, consciously and unconsciously, to regulate and act as a means of exerting power and controlling access to resources based on a socially constructed, inconsistently applied, arbitrary, and selective definition of normal human, with "normal" further constructed as superior. It is learned, not a reflection of lack of knowledge or awareness, and it asserts itself in our understanding of what it means to be human, and therefore also in how we shape, define, and conceive of human design, human needs, and human relationships with the world as well with as ourselves and each other.

One other definition I will add in full is the updated January 2022 working definition of ableism by @TalilaLewis developed in community with disabled Black and negatively racialized folk. This definition draws important connections to other oppressions and in particular to anti-Black racism. It is not only valuable because it "captures the mutually constitutive nature of racism and ableism,"[35] but because it lights up the runway to show you where it lands in our lives: "able·ism /ābə,lizəm/ noun A system of assigning value to people's bodies and minds based on societally constructed ideas of normalcy, productivity, desirability, intelligence, excellence, and fitness. These constructed ideas are deeply rooted in eugenics, anti-Blackness, misogyny, colonialism, imperialism, and capitalism. This systemic oppression that leads to people and society determining people's value based on their culture, age, language, appearance, religion, birth or living place, 'health/wellness,' and/or their ability to satisfactorily re/produce, 'excel' and 'behave.' You do not have to be disabled to experience ableism."[36]

If you think this sounds like a lot, that's good, because it is. Ableism is presented as being deceptively simple – just don't say the "R" word (a bar I will note a shocking number of people refuse to meet) and build a ramp. But it's the assumptions about yourself as well as us, about what constitutes a good life, and about what it means to be human that influences almost everything.

It should also be mentioned here that prior to colonialism many Indigenous languages lacked even a comparable word for disability as the concept and way of looking at someone was foreign to them. Nicole Inesse-Nash explains that in Anishinaabe culture people's names were chosen to "reflect the gifts that they carry or responsibilities they hold within community," and that "there is not often a discussion about what the child is lacking, or what they cannot do, because of the understanding that all children are gifts to the community."[37]

To distinguish the ableism we are discussing in Canada today from that of pre-Enlightenment history or other cultures (which incidentally is not as one-dimensional as some might predict and does not support the view that all people everywhere at all times in history have just naturally been afraid of or repulsed by disabled people, or viewed them as lesser[38]), I use the term modern Western ableism. Modern Western ableism emerged at a time when a "rational" justification for disproportionate power and wealth was required. "Science" was employed to validate white supremacy, and this also meant any white people deemed inferior posed a threat to the assertion and protection of the "white race" and its claims of racial superiority. The expansive mood of the Enlightenment – the feeling that all men are by nature equal – meant that "an appeal to natural rights could be countered only by proof of natural inequalities ... if social inequalities were to be justified within the framework of Enlightenment thought, scientific evidence would have to show that human nature is not uniform, but differs according to age, race, and sex."[39] These rationalizations were supported by the categorizations and ranking of "scientific ableism,"[40] which defined not only what was normal versus abnormal but an entire range of attributes and behaviours that were ranked as ideal or lesser or degenerate.

When disabled people talk about the social construction of disability, we are referring to the emergence of when "'the disabled' became an interpretive category bureaucratically tracked, counted, managed, and subsequently evocative of a peculiar fascination for thinkers of the time."[41]

This chapter is not a deep dive into history or theory, and all of this is a very broad brush across not just time but continents. But it does seem worthwhile to briefly review how we got here and to take note of some of the ripples and echoes of history. If we are considering the issue of MAiD, we have to have some understanding of ableism and what it is that makes disabled people uniquely killable and a physician deliberately causing our premature and preventable deaths socially acceptable.

One of the reasons ableism might remain so persistent, pervasive, and unexamined is that challenging oppression supported by ableism does not necessarily challenge ableism, and it can have the opposite effect. For example, women assert that our intelligence is equal to that of men. Essentially, in our struggle to achieve equity, women have argued that the ableism directed towards them within sexism is invalid and therefore sexism is invalid. The legitimacy of ableism as a tool for ranking humans remains unchallenged. Proving women's intelligence is equal to men's does not challenge the validity of how we construct and define intelligence or the way we link it to human worth. If anything, it unintentionally legitimizes these concepts further and subtly lends support to the idea that disabled people deemed to be less intelligent have less value and therefore it is not unjust if their diminished rights, social status, and conditions reflect this.

Further expanding and refining Carl Linnaeus's unscientific taxonomy of humans, Charles Darwin's cousin Francis Galton and his theory of eugenics advocated for the use of social and political policy to improve the human race by increasing the amount of preferred inheritable qualities (people) and decreasing or eliminating those qualities (people) that were undesirable. Later Darwin's son George Darwin argued for what is now known as negative eugenics (as opposed to positive eugenics, which focuses on policy that would encourage marriage and procreation among the "superior" humans), by advocating for forced sterilization and denial of the right to marry of those deemed to be "degenerate."[42]

A current policy that eugenicists would laud are spousal clawbacks of disability benefits; that is, when a disabled person who marries or decides to live with a partner loses their benefits and are forced to become financially dependent on their partner. Anecdotally – meaning widely known fact among disabled poor people that is not yet formally documented and written up by someone deemed trustworthy to "interpret" our knowledge and lives for us – this effectively discourages disabled poor people from partnering and from the possibility of becoming parents. Compared to 13.9 per cent of the general population, 20.6 per cent of disabled people live alone.[43] And of course that statistic, like statistics on poverty, does not include those living alone in nursing homes and other institutions.

The emergence of eugenics in England took place against the backdrop of anxiety among the rich and powerful about immigration, "race suicide," and "national degeneration,"[44] as well as fears about expanding suffrage and just how democratic democracy would turn out to be. Eugenicists argued the "poor were not demoralized; they were degenerate,"[45] and that this trait could not be rectified. The upper class was also preoccupied with fears that sympathetic interventions to ease suffering were interfering with natural selection, and as a result "much of the eugenics rhetoric attempted to show that the 'unfit' were a breed apart and, therefore, undeserving of sympathy."[46] When the rich and powerful are fearful, bad things happen to others. The specifics today are different, but the mood feels similar.

Angus McLaren observed that eugenics was comforting to the middle class because it allowed them "to think that poverty and criminality were best attributed to individual weaknesses rather than to the structural flaws of the economy." He suggests that this motivated reasoning explains why so many "humanitarians supported the labelling, the segregation, and ultimately the sterilization of those they designated subnormal."[47] This aligns with the current research referenced earlier that finds correlation between belief in autonomy and meritocracy and that greater education and wealth are associated with an increased belief that it is better to be dead than disabled. We also see similar politics playing out today around the criminalization and human rights abuses of the victims of the housing crisis.[48]

Some retellings of eugenics history limit themselves to the infamous policies of the Nazis, often even excluding their Aktion T4 program of mass murder/involuntary euthanasia of approximately three hundred thousand disabled people. This sometimes appears like a deliberate attempt for other countries, including Canada, to distance themselves from eugenics infamy, especially since forced sterilization continued in Canada long after the end of the Second World War. Others attempt to assuage concerns about the present by focusing strictly on the specific eugenics policy of sterilization, while ignoring that it is difficult to overstate the influence of eugenics in politics, business, labour, science, and culture across the West decades before Hitler rose to power, the fruits of which remain largely in place. The original impetus for eugenics might have been a distortion and misapplication of the theory of evolution, but it became much more. Just as Jim Crow was about more than lunch counters, water fountains, and sundown laws, eugenics was about more than laws governing breeding. It was a philosophy for a future built on less of "those people" and more of "people like us."

Pretending to have the rigour of science while being nothing more than a means to rationalize inequity, injustice, and oppression gave eugenics power, authority, and the ability to be adapted to suit the situation. For example, in writing about how eugenics was applied in the Southern US, Gregory Michael Dore notes that the "harmony between eugenics and public health in the South amplified the 'eugenically disabling' stereotypes of 'born criminality' and 'feeble mindedness.' These new categories allowed doctors to merge class, race, and gender prejudices into a new concept of disability." Dore explains this group of "unfit" was conceived less as a demographic in need of cure or rehabilitation "and more as a dangerous group in need of control."[49] Importantly, by creating entirely arbitrary distinctions and categorizations, eugenics "offered a rationale for distributing scarce medical resources that reinforced the privileges of wealthy and middle-class whites."[50]

One of the reasons it's vital to situate MAiD in this history is that the construction and perimeters of who was fully human during this period necessarily spilled over into whose knowledge, experiences, and perspectives had value. Once another group is established as an expert about you and you are deemed to know nothing of value about yourself, it is very difficult to challenge what they decide to do to you. This period is also when categorizing and counting became a quasi-religion, norms established as "the correct way," and sensibilities about mannerisms that were cultural and class-based came to define "professional" and assumed indications of credibility, reliability, intelligence, and trustworthiness. These ideas also became tangible things and written into policy – and they continue to shape our thinking and choices, especially around MAiD.

I think about Charles Darwin's belief in the "evolutionary superiority" of the affect of wealthy British men and their emotional detachment every time I am simultaneously dismissed and referred to as "passionate" in the MAiD debate by the same people who confer credibility to the people who display not a drop of emotion while plotting out the path to killing us.[51] I would also note that while some are lauded and deemed strong, credible, trustworthy, and of good breeding for their perceived absence of emotion, some neurodivergent people are stigmatized and excluded for the same.

The blending and conflating of what upper class white men considered dignified with evolutionary claims of superiority may also have some relation to the declarations made by senators and MAiD proponents that seem to imply that wearing incontinence briefs or needing assistance in the bathroom are obvious logical reasons for wanting to die by MAiD.[52] There was a time when having personal assistance in the bathroom was a privilege enjoyed by monarchy.[53] Self-categorizing yourself as the highest evolved humans on earth also renders everything you think and do with an air of scientific legitimacy.

Galton was a statistician (as were followers and fellow eugenicists Karl Pearson and R.A. Fisher – Pearson fudged his numbers to "prove" Jewish immigrants intellectually inferior, and Fisher is considered the father of modern statistics).[54] One of Galton's projects was creating a "beauty map" of the British Isles.[55] A high school principal would suspend a student for rating female students based on appearance, but when Galton did this, he called it "science."

> His dictum, "Whenever you can, count," which had a revolutionary impact on biology and psychology, reflected his mystical faith, and one shared by many late Victorians, in the explanatory powers of statistical analysis. Galton even confessed in an autobiographical passage to the habit of secretly counting and categorizing the women he passed in the street: "Whenever I have occasion to classify the persons I meet into three classes, 'good, medium and bad,' I use a needle mounted as a pricker, wherewith to prick holes, unseen, in a piece of paper, torn rudely

into a cross with a long leg. I use the upper end for 'good,' the cross arm for 'medium,' the lower end for 'bad.' The prick holes keep distinct and are readily read off at leisure."[56]

Today Canada prides itself on its "evidence-based policies" while failing to scrutinize what – and who – defines evidence and how inequity factors into what data is collected, how it is measured, and how it is all analyzed. We still seem to have a mystical faith in statistical analysis, perhaps more so. There are many statistics available about the week-long heat dome in 2021 in BC that resulted in the deaths of more than six hundred people. Arguably nothing new was learned. We possessed the knowledge to prevent deaths before the heat dome. What we lacked then and now were policies based on that knowledge, not more statistics of the harm that failing to put them in place causes.[57]

When disabled people testified about our experience and analysis and implored senators and members of Parliament to apply even a minor amount of deductive reasoning skills to their considerations around MAiD, we were dismissed as anecdotal. We received the metaphorical wave of the hand. "There is no evidence," politicians chided, willfully ignoring how power operates in "evidence-based" policy.

In the same 2020 Standing Committee on Justice and Human Rights meeting where NDP MP Randall Garrison urged committee members to include language allowing nurses to raise the topic of MAiD with a patient based on his concern that not doing so would "constrain conversations," he said he was "very cautious about judging the evidence presented to us before the committee" by disabled people about their experiences with the health care system and those working in it.[58] Ironically, he was speaking to a proposed amendment he had brought forward at the urging of the nurses' association who, already protected in initiating discussions about MAiD with patients, wanted additional language to make sure they were extra safe in doing so. On the one hand, he argued that the word of health care professionals about their unsubstantiated fears of possible legal liability should be sufficient for members of the committee to change the wording of the Criminal Code, but evidence presented by multiple disabled people and their organizations about their experiences with health care and their desire for protection from MAiD should be treated with skepticism and not acted upon. On another occasion Garrison seemed to distinguish between non-disabled people and disabled people who testified, thanking "all the witnesses appearing before the committee today," and then adding, "I also thank the members of the disability community and their advocates for their passionate presentations."[59] The list of witnesses included proponents of MAiD whose relatives had received MAiD. Somehow their experiences did not need to be flagged as anecdotal or marked as "passionate." Perhaps if we had poked holes in a piece of paper like Galton did, our experiences with health care would magically transform into science. The committee's arbitrary lines between anecdotal and credible were as openly biased and class-interest-based as those of the original eugenicists.

The past is still present, and some things remain the same. Public support and enthusiasm for eugenics was built the same way euthanasia moved from fringe to mainstream – money.

Galton was a man of inherited wealth,[60] which allowed him the time and means to pursue his "passion," and when eugenics travelled across the ocean from England to North America, it attracted the attention of big capitalists and their charities.

> Eugenics would have been so much bizarre parlor talk had it not been for extensive financing by corporate philanthropies, specifically the Carnegie Institution, the Rockefeller Foundation and the Harriman railroad fortune. They were all in league with some of America's most respected scientists hailing from such prestigious universities as Stanford, Yale, Harvard, and Princeton. These academicians espoused race theory and race science, and then faked and twisted data to serve eugenics' racist aims … The Rockefeller Foundation helped found the German eugenics program and even funded the program that Josef Mengele worked in before he went to Auschwitz … The most commonly suggested method of eugenicide in America was a "lethal chamber" or public locally operated gas chambers.[61]

When eugenics arrived in Canada it wove itself into the fabric of society in such a way as to make itself at once omnipresent and unnoticeable. Education, housing, urban planning, health care, municipal, provincial, and federal policy all bear the evidence of this by excluding disabled people from public life and creating different standards for our lives.[62] Why design any *thing,* place, space, policy, or process to include the range of humanity when you are designing them at a time when disabled people are being institutionalized, sterilized, and, if things go according to plan, eventually eliminated from the human race? At the same time modern cities were being constructed and building codes and design standards set, disabled people were being sent off to institutions in the countryside. This was presented as an act of science and kindness. In reality it was neither.[63] A new world was being built and there was no place for disabled people in it.

CAPITALISM AND THE MAKING OF DISABLED PEOPLE AS "UNINTENDED PARTICIPANTS" IN SOCIETY: "ANY ENVIRONMENT FOR AN IMAGINED POPULATION WILL SURELY SHOW ITS INTENTIONS WHEN THE 'UNINTENDED' SHOW UP"[64]

> Human beings are by nature, weak, vulnerable and physically imperfect. But throughout history people with capabilities have striven for perfection and the more they have managed to intervene in our body structure the more people with impairments have been marginalised. It is as if people with capabilities have deposited their own natural vulnerability, and genuine social dependency, into us so that these attributes of being human are unique to being disabled. Our vulnerability is then seen as a condition that separates us from what is regarded as normal. This transference of vulnerability and consequent dependency into disabled people has not freed people with capabilities from their own dependency upon support systems to ameliorate their essential vulnerability but created a dangerous illusion about the meaning of normality ... In this sense, then, I believe that we cannot understand or deal with disability without dealing with the essential nature of society itself. To do this disabled people must find ways of engaging in the class struggle where the historical direction of society is fought, won or lost. It is in this arena that the boundaries of knowledge that have put disabled people aside from the 'normal' can and have to be openly questioned.[65]

When I was a kid, if my great uncle was visiting, he would thrust five dollars in my hand whenever I was heading outside. Even if I was just going to play, he would look very serious and say, "You keep this on you. This is not for spending. Remember. This is what you show them if they stop you." I had no idea at the time that this was my introduction to disability history.

My uncle was afraid I would be arrested if I did not have sufficient funds on me. That part I understood. I am white, I was not visibly disabled at the time, and while we were working class, we were not poor. My clothes were new. But my uncle's understanding of disability, poverty, and policing was that these things are much more about power than they are about science or facts. "They decide what truth is," he advised.

I knew this meant he loved me, and while I didn't know the details of what happened or to whom – these types of things were mostly hinted at or spoken of cryptically – I knew this was a piece of family history he was passing down. At some point someone in the family had a run-in with a municipal anti-vagrancy law.

In parts of Canada and the United State the laws were not subtle in their disdain for disabled people and came to be referred to as Ugly Laws.[66] And even when the wording was less explicit, it could be used for similar ends. The 1904 Toronto municipal bylaws were clear: "'Nor shall any malformed, deformed, or diseased person expose himself or be exposed in any street or public place in order to excite sympathy or induce help or assistance from general or public charity' (City of Toronto, Municipal By-laws, 1904)."[67]

Pieces of policy history can be found in family photo albums, passed down wisdom, warnings, traditions, behaviours – all shaped by the choices of the state. If you are poor, the wall between the policies of the society you live in and the home and private space you try to create is especially paper thin, if one exists at all. I like Tanya Titchkofskys's exploration of "unintended participants" because it draws focus away from the person and onto the decisions that create belonging for some and exclusion of others, allowing for the discussion of intersections and breaking completely free of the medical model: "Any environment for an imagined population will surely show its intentions when the 'unintended' show up."[68] This section looks at how disabled people have been made unintended participants in society, and as such, the society that made them unintended participants now offering to kill them cannot be reasonably framed as respect for their autonomy.

To fear disability is to fear loss of status, power, and, unless you have exceptionally secure circumstances, poverty. Poverty is both a consequence and a cause of disability in Canada. And poverty is indeed something to fear. Throughout this country's history choices have been made to ensure this fear is realized for a large number of disabled people.

Canada chose not to adopt British Poor Laws, one of the points of which had been to distinguish between deserving and non-deserving poor and grant some (albeit terrible) forms of "relief" to the former. Instead, the federal government was not involved in the provision of social relief, and some provinces such as Ontario off-loaded the responsibility onto local governments.[69]

> This hands-off approach of 'reluctant welfareism' established in the 19th Century guided the direction of providing care and support to people with disabilities well into the 20th Century. The province did establish guidelines for the establishment of poor houses, jails and asylums, but it did not provide direct financial support to these institutions and their inmates. As far as the province was concerned, the care and support of needy populations was first and foremost a family responsibility, and if families could not provide the support, then such support fell onto local charities and municipalities. This system of reluctant support began in the late 1700s and lasted well into the 1900's.[70]

In some parts of the country the hands-off approach also involved the auctioning of poor people to "respectable" people. The "winning bid" went to the farmer offering to take on the poor person, who of course would work for them unpaid, at the "least burden to the taxpayer."[71]

Even after poor auctions were no longer publicly held in Nova Scotia, town overseers would approach "respectable"[72] people in the community to bid on poor people. Similar to the calculations that were developed during chattel slavery for assigning worth,[73] the "old, 'insane,' disabled, or very pregnant... were considered less valuable because they could not work."[74]

The construction of disability became more organized and systematized with the development of capitalism and the Industrial Revolution. Marta Russell applied class analysis and debunked the natural law argument, showing that it "is neither accident nor a result of 'the natural order of things' that disabled persons rank at the bottom of the economic ladder."[75] Disability as a category is a product of wage labour relations, which uses medicalization and the tools of categorization. Russell's work was seminal as she not only made clear that "disability oppression has less to do with prejudicial attitudes than with an accountant's calculation of the present cost of production versus the potential benefits to the future rate of exploitation," but correctly surmised that as a result, under capitalism, "discrimination can be ameliorated, but not eliminated, by changing attitudes."[76]

People who did not fit were part of the surplus population. Disabled people were left behind by design and then blamed for not fitting in. Exclusion was and is a choice. Poverty was and is a choice. But these choices were and are not made by the people who were and are excluded and poor.

In "Disability, and the Helper/Helped Relationship: An Historical View," Vic Finkelstein, a key figure in disability rights activism whose work was influential internationally, describes how disabled people did not fit into the design of modern society and were carved out and left behind.[77] Up to that point some disabled people would have been able to contribute to the family by earning additional income spinning and weaving as well as helping with care of young children and household chores. Finkelstein explains there was proximity and shared circumstance. "Conditions of life were extremely harsh for cripples, but in a context where life was harsh for all the common people, the circumstances of cripples would not have seemed significantly worse."[78]

Of course, this was not the case for all disabled people. It should be noted that disability is not a monolith and ableism is not one-size-fits-all. In addition to intersectionality, multiple factors including the specific condition(s), illness(es), or impairment(s) can affect how ableism presents, and the degree to which it is present in someone's life and relationships. This was true in the past and remains true today. Some are more highly stigmatized and others more infantilized, some feared, some pitied... some, all the above. But as labour relations changed social relations, the proximity Finkelstein refers to was lost, and disabled people were deliberately moved out of sight – anti-vagrancy laws and institutions (which were generally placed outside of cities), segregated schools, and later segregated classrooms are examples of the policy designed to achieve this, along with the policies that defined the design of everything else for everyone who was not disabled. Wage labour placed greater emphasis on the individual. The shift from a rural-agrarian economy to a wage-based economy resulted in "a major shift in the perception of the social importance of the individual, and the individual replaced the collective, as well as the family, as the predominant unit of production."[79] As the "social and economic importance of the individual increased ... greater social value" was placed on non-disabled individuals and less on disabled individuals.[80]

Industrialization and urbanization not only redefined work and workers but also everything about workers' lives and needs – housing, health care, education, city streets, transportation, and, possibly most significantly, community. But while negatively impacting the status of disabled people, creating more disabled people through "unsafe working conditions, child labour, poor sanitation, lack of public health, and poverty," capitalism provided "few suitable resources from which these populations could receive assistance."[81] To this day family support for disabled people is assumed, and without it, a person's circumstance and options become much grimmer.

Initially disabled people were permitted to beg in the streets – to seek relief outdoors. But when the decision was made to move relief indoors it meant alms houses (also known as poor houses), houses of industry (also known as workhouses), asylums, and sometimes prisons. In Ontario and elsewhere, "the old and sick were thrown together with tramps and vagabonds, with the blind, deaf mutes, cripples, idiots, epileptics and insane people. Children, orphans, foundlings, unmarried mothers with children, prostitutes and criminals were put in these houses."[82] The same people were on eugenicists' "hit list" and deemed to be members of the prohibited classes in Canada's early immigration act.

Who is understood as disabled under modern Western ableism has varied over time and could conceivably change in the future. In the context of MAiD, it is useful to understand ableism as a project of constructing and maintaining ideas of what and who is normal or ideal, purportedly premised on reason and science. It's not discrimination if everyone believes it makes sense. It is well-known that doctors invented diagnoses during slavery, such as dysaesthesia aethiopis, the symptom of which was "disrespect for the master's property," and the "cure" was "extensive whipping." More recently, in 1968, "in the prestigious Archives of General Psychiatry," psychiatrists Walter Bromberg and Frank Simon described "schizophrenia as a 'protest psychosis' whereby black men developed 'hostile and aggressive feelings' and 'delusional anti-whiteness' after listening to the words of Malcolm X, joining the Black Muslims, or aligning with groups that preached militant resistance to white society."[83] Hysteria was a made-up diagnosis for women until 1980.[84] I would argue that parental alienation syndrome is a current example of ableism being used to create a completely baseless pseudo-concept "used in family law proceedings by abusers as a tool to continue their abuse and coercion and to undermine and discredit allegations of domestic violence made by mothers who are trying to keep their children safe."[85] These diagnoses are rooted in power, not science.

Disability is a socially constructed category that, as a result of ableism, makes for a profoundly different lived experience. It is separate and additional to an impairment, condition, or illness, and the medical community was charged with categorization, containment, control, and care.[86] While critiques and variations on specifics exist, this general analysis is referred to as the social model of disability (credited in part to the previously mentioned Vic Finkelstein). The social model argues that the oppression, discrimination, and exclusion disabled people face is caused by choices made in the organizing and running of society, not their bodies.[87] This analytical tool is widely adopted in the disability community and stands in contrast to the dominant model, which is the medical model of disability. The medical model maintains that disability is abnormal, and it is the individual that needs to be cured or fixed. It locates epistemic authority – and therefore power – over disabled people in the medical and caregiving community. In essence, the expert on your illness, impairment, or condition is made the expert on you and your life. The medical model is consistent with the natural law argument described earlier and establishes the disproportionate and unique role physicians play in the lives of disabled people and ableism.

The creation of disability as a category was "essential to the development of an exploitable workforce in early capitalism and remains indispensable as an instrument of the state in controlling the labor supply today. By focusing on curing so-called abnormalities and segregating those who could not be cured into the administrative category of 'disabled,' medicine cooperated in shoving less exploitable workers out of the mainstream workforce."[88] Today the government often talks about creating employment programs for disabled people while ignoring that capitalism created disability as a category of unemployability and failing to address its reasons for doing so.

According to the Government of Canada, poverty is *"the condition of a person who is deprived of the resources, means, choices and power necessary to acquire and maintain a basic level of living standards and to facilitate integration and participation in society."*[89] In their own definition the government identifies the absence of choices and means to act on them – important ingredients in autonomy. Poverty is not just being broke, needing a few dollars to tide you over, or dipping into overdraft to avoid being late on a bill and sacrificing your credit rating. It is more than not being able to purchase what you need in a moment or knowing that purchasing one necessity will mean not purchasing another, although that is part of it. The division between the "haves" and the "have nots" is above all else about power. And greater power means greater autonomy, and less power means less and more precarious and conditional choice – though, to be clear, the idea of independence is a myth regardless of class.

Poverty places a person in a state of crisis and cuts off all the lifelines while layering on new and worsening crises. Imagine Sisyphus pushing the rock up the hill, and the rock doesn't just roll down every time but rolls over him – on repeat. And now imagine the boulder keeps growing larger. One year into poverty does not look anything like poverty ten or twenty years later.

When you are poor, even when you have sufficient funds to buy food to eat, you don't have sufficient funds to not be thinking about the consequences of buying and eating food rather than going without and saving money. You are never more than a breath away from the anxiety of not enough. The cognitive load of poverty – the weighing of current needs versus known or possible future ones and having insufficient means for any of them but trying to come up with a formula that will make x = you not dying – is enormous, never mind the emotional load of poverty plus ableism.[90] Ironically – or perhaps intentionally – the rather obvious impact of how the human mind responds to and functions in crisis remains falsely theorized as a cause of poverty. This is obviously the consequence of poverty not the cause of it, but seeking differences in poor people's brains or thought patterns as the cause of poverty and not the consequence of it is also quite obviously consistent with eugenics.[91]

CAPITALISM USES DISABILITY TO TEACH PEOPLE HOW TO THINK OF THEMSELVES AND THEIR LIVES – WHAT IS MAiD TEACHING YOU?

Once established, the division separating disabled people from the non-disabled had to be policed and maintained. In this way ableism is a form of social control that affects the entire population in varying degrees, because even if you are inside the gate of "normal" at some level, you are aware that you are required to behave a particular way to ensure you stay there. *"I didn't sound crazy just now, did I?" "Did that look dumb?"*

Insight into some of the ways the impacts of ableism and eugenics policy spread is captured in devastating detail in "Unheard Voices:

Sisters Share about Institutionalization" by Madeline Burghardt, Victoria Freeman, Marilyn Dolmage, and Colleen Orrick. The paper discusses the depression, confusion, grief, rage, and harm the sisters and other family members experienced after a disabled sibling was sent away to an institution. "It was the 1950s – idealizing perfect families, haunted by eugenics. Having a child 'born wrong' meant our family was tainted; my own future – genetically – was too. Would they abandon me if something went 'wrong' with me? The doctor told my parents that keeping Robert would ruin my life; in effect, he was sacrificed for me. Later, I kept the secret because I felt increasing shame about my parents abandoning a vulnerable child. After I was a mother, it was years before I could tell my own children. So I had abandoned him too."[92]

Absorbing the conditionality of membership in a family, community, and humanity overall has ramifications for our sense of self and security: requiring us to behave in ways that conform to societal expectations but conflict with our own sense of right and wrong is a map to moral injury, not inner peace and happiness. A sister in another family shares: "By the time I was in my teens my mother was clinically depressed and eventually hospitalized. I believe that relinquishing Gerard was a major factor in her depression. My other two brothers got into drugs in their teens, one to a very destructive degree that almost ended in his death. Was it because Gerard was institutionalized?"[93]

Those most negatively impacted by ableism in a direct way are disabled people, but ableism also warns non-disabled people about the conditional nature of their belonging and status should their bodies and minds or behaviour land outside of what is deemed non-disabled. Certainly, it is not difficult to imagine how this would shape fears about becoming disabled and influence people who are newly diagnosed. As to the moral injury MAiD can cause those still alive, we already have many examples of families who are distraught about what they believe to be the unjust deaths of their loved ones by MAiD.[94]

By defining what constitutes human and extending that to human need, policy, and design, not only are disabled people viewed as lesser humans, but also our needs are defined as outside human – "special" – and thus having them acknowledged and met is made more precarious, expendable, and vulnerable to discriminatory barriers and policy. This also informs others to be careful not to need anything beyond or outside "normal." It adds an ever-present contingency clause. Something that is simply assumed by non-disabled people – such as an entrance to a building they can enter through – is instead presented as an "accommodation," a gift, act of charity, or sometimes argued to be too extraordinary, costly, inconvenient, aesthetically unpleasing, or offensive to heritage to provide. We are expected to be grateful when our presence is barely or plausibly permitted and understanding when we are excluded.

This works to limit our access to life and all other things, including friendships. It is also absorbed into our sense of self – if my needs are extra and burdensome, then so am I.

The city I live in shouts, "You aren't human" in a billion tiny but impactful ways. There may not be signs that say, "no disabled people allowed," but the message is conveyed through inaccessible and ableist built environments, practices, and policies that deny, exclude, or omit our needs. These serve to isolate and dehumanize and often, if poor, criminalize. This all has cumulative psychological, emotional, and physiological consequences. Society pushes many of us into the nether regions of the margins where MAiD now awaits, extending a helping hand by yanking us into the grave.

YOU'RE ON YOUR OWN – NEO-LIBERALISM

And just as the emerging capitalism propelled and shaped eugenics, we cannot ignore the emergence of neo-liberalism in Canada and around the Western world at the same time as the rise of euthanasia policies. Neo-liberalism includes, as "a key element" of its "political rationality," "the practice of translating concerns about justice or equity into an economic register, so that all issues must be addressed in terms of fiscal sensibility rather than social or political necessity."[95] Not only has neo-liberalism brought deregulation and privatization, it also delivered these through an ideology and policy approach that off-loads responsibility onto individuals. What was formerly understood as a public good or area of social concern became a personal responsibility. Neo-liberalism reduced to nil the obligations of the state to its citizens. It questions whether the state should bear any responsibility for the well-being of people while tying people's duty to be well (which they define as absence of illness or disability) as part of their obligation to the economy.

Robert Crawford argued in 1980 that this political rationality created a culture of what he called "healthism," and it represented a shift from collective understanding of health to individual choices.[96]

"While working class struggles to shorten the work week, abolish child labor, and change working conditions have historically been in part focused on health, and although occupational health and safety has also generated a new interest in recent years, the current preoccupation with personal health displays a distinctive – although not exclusive – middle-class stamp."[97]

More recently James Davies examines the impact neo-liberalism has had on mental health and mental health care in fundamentally changing our understanding of suffering from an aspect of human experience demanding collective responsibility to an individual pathology by its *d*epoliticizing, privatising, pathologizing, commodifying, and decollectivizing of suffering. He explains that neo-liberalism "introduced a new ideology of individualism, where success was seen as an outcome of exceptional individual qualities (rather than exceptional social privileges and advantages), and failure as rooted in personal deficits (rather than in lack of opportunity, equality or social support)."[98] If this sounds similar to the logic of natural inequality and eugenics it is because it is. And, as Shelley Tremain has pointed out, "an insidious feature of neoliberalism is its capacity to refashion itself in the practice of auto-critique, that is, to co-opt critique as means to achieve its own goals."[99]

While working at a community service group, Tanya Titchkofsky observed that colleagues referred to "the 'abled-disabled.'" The term was used to make "sense of the fact that measures of inclusion that would receive government funding were targeted at young people leaving school, or newly disabled and newly unemployed people." Titchkofsky said the "abled-disabled" was a way to describe those the group deemed "to have the best chance to reflect, desire, or imitate 'normal people' or, at least, 'normal functioning.'"[100] Further, the group believed that servicing this "abled-disabled" "would also attest to the community group's efficacy and thereby secure ongoing government funding."[101] In this way neo-liberalism has provided a sense of greater inclusion and movement towards disability rights while widening and further marginalizing many at the expense of a select few. The "abled-disabled" also communicate the message that poverty, exclusion, and isolation are the fault of the individual not the state and society. With MAiD, the Canadian government has laid out its recommendations for those who are not among "abled-disabled."

The three faces of neo-liberalism in the 1980s were Margaret Thatcher, Ronald Reagan, and Canadian prime minister Brian

Mulroney. Canada has always taken lessons from UK and US politics when developing its own approach. At a time when disability rights movements were growing in all three countries and finding broad support and solidarity that would ultimately lead to the signing of national disability rights legislation in the US and Britain, former prime minister Brian Mulroney teamed up with wheelchair athlete Rick Hansen to instead push a more neo-liberal bootstrap solution to the barriers disabled people face.[102] Mulroney was cutting funding and programs that disabled people needed with one hand and cutting Hansen's Man in Motion mobile telethon a million-dollar cheque for a cure to spinal cord injury with the other. Given Canada's largely unaddressed and undiscussed history of eugenics, it is possibly not coincidental that Mulroney selected someone who became disabled due to injury.

While disabled people in Canada, the US, and Britain were demanding that telethons be shut down, Canadian media were enthralled with Rick Hansen's mobile one. A great deal of rewriting of history takes place, and there has been some attempt to position this event as championing accessibility. But the point of his tour was to raise money for a cure for spinal cord injury, and his message was to disabled people, not governments: "All you have to do is believe and be willing to persevere."[103]

In other words, the message was that the solution to structural oppression is – surprise, there is no structural oppression! The problem is you! You need to be fixed. If you can't be fixed, then you need to overcome! These types of messages – and those who deliver them – are used as a stick against those pointing to the need for structural change. At a societal level, they provide the government and various agencies and organizations with undeserved legitimacy and assure the public through smiling photo ops that disabled people are treated well. And this is what allows them to present MAiD as a "choice."

Yet to live a socially acceptable life as a disabled person, you must be always working to overcome your disability. The unforgiving either/or demands of "overcome champion" or "burden" allow little room to just be. This framing not only causes suffering but informs how we interpret the suffering we experience.

A courier for neo-liberalism's "personal responsibility," the "overcome" mythology places all the glory on those who "overcome their disability" – and thus all the blame on disabled people who fail to reach this realistically impossible, undesirable, and necessarily self-hating bar that is coherently consistent with the belief that it is "better dead than disabled." In contrast, disabled people opposed to MAiD believe disability is not something we live "in spite of" or work to overcome – ableism is.

Disability remains commonly represented as white and middle class and is thus often unconsciously understood through a similar lens.[104] The reality is that labour history overlaps with disability history, and both overlap with the history of Canada's racism. Work-related illness, injury, and death were at the forefront of reasons for early organizing and remain pressing issues today. The myth of Rick Hansen is a page glued over the real Canadian disability history.

Disabled poor and working-class people experience a level of exclusion beyond that of disabled people in general, even more so if they are Indigenous or racialized. What is often characterized as a "difference of opinion" around MAiD is more often a reflection of a difference of position in society. Those with the most access to the microphone are too often those with the most access to resources that enable them to mitigate some of the impacts of ableism. This means we sometimes have the "abled-disableds" speaking in support of MAiD[105] – the people who are least representative of the community but most likely to be listened to by non-disabled people.

One of the biggest harms that Canadian neo-liberalism has caused to disabled people as a group is to deprive us of our own leaders, our own movement, our own goals, our own platform, and our own decisions about what matters – chosen by us.

We no longer have poorhouses – now we have maximum shelter allowances that are one-sixth the amount of an average one-bedroom apartment[106] – but we still have wards on nursing homes and prison cells. There is "public relief" (now called panhandling), and those who rely on it still risk criminalization. The period of slightly less "reluctant welfareism" was replaced by neo-liberalism – reluctant-er welfareism? – effectively dismantling, defunding, or changing the conditions of "relief" and other life-supporting programs.[107]

In 2010 I was discharged from the hospital into a box they call a unit in social housing in a city I had never lived in and where I knew no one. My entire social circle had been obliterated, because that is what often happens when you can no longer work and you don't "get better." My one remaining friend, who unfortunately lived at a distance, paid for a storage locker for things she had packed up from my apartment as my former partner fled town for the life he felt he deserved – one free of a disabled partner. My nurses were not surprised and assured me I was now a member of the club of those whose significant others had left them due to illness or disability.[108] At first the provincial housing authority rejected me – repeatedly – but eventually allowed me to move in without a lease on a "behavioural contract," the condition of which was to determine if I was "too disabled" to live in the community.

It was a five-week month – meaning some months there are five weeks between disability cheques. I had been careful and spent a week eating plain pasta with no sauce. But still I ran short of funds, and I was out of incontinence products. A chaplain from the hospital delivered one package. There are ten diapers in each package, and it was a week until the cheque arrived. I had to save one diaper for the day when it came so I could go out and buy more. That left longer than I care to remember using anything made of fabric in the house. Being hungry was the least bad part of that month, and of course I had no money for the creams to address the skin damage that resulted. I also had to deliberately dehydrate myself, which resulted in a urinary tract infection.

Now let me contextualize this by pointing out that I am not the poorest of the poor, as I live in subsidized housing, which still leaves me with insufficient money on which to live (because 30 per cent less of not enough still leaves not enough), but not to the extent that those who spend virtually their entire disability cheque on rent.[109] A 2018 report by Statistics Canada stated that 283,000 households are on a waiting list for affordable housing, and two-thirds of those have been on the waiting list for more than two years. This, of course, does not include the large number of poor people who have not even applied, either because the length of the waiting list made it seem like a pointless exercise in an existence where tomorrow is a precarious unknown, or because they lack the proper information or tools to do so.[110] To afford an average two-bedroom apartment in 2022 in Vancouver required an income in excess of one hundred thousand dollars per year. BC disability benefits were $1,703.50 per month for a single parent that same year. For someone living on disability benefits who does not have subsidized housing, the options are grim to non-existent, particularly if they require accessible or adapted housing.

Discourse about dignity and autonomy around MAiD has ignored the significant difference disabled poor people experience in this regard. My autonomy is not only unsupported, but also often deemed irrelevant or denied. I am required to regularly choose between my dignity and personal freedom or the support I require to stay alive – not because of my disability, but because of the systems I must engage with as a disabled person. I do not feel my incontinence is undignified, but I do believe the policies that limit my access to the products I need assault my dignity and my autonomy to even decide to go outside. It is hard not to assume ill-intent when the state waves the enticing myth of individual autonomy and middle-class dignity at those who are forced to sacrifice so much of their humanity to access the state assistance they need to live.

The material and social conditions of disabled people in Canada are fundamentally different from those of non-disabled people.[111] Not only are we disproportionately represented below the poverty line, but recent research also provides evidence of a long-known and oft-stated fact shared by disabled people: the poverty line itself has an ableist bias, as it fails to consider the additional costs associated with living as a disabled person. We call these extra expenses Crip Tax. This means both the degree of poverty is worse than currently reflected in statistics, and the rate of poverty among disabled people is actually higher than is reflected. "There are likely several persons with disabilities with income just above the MBM (Market Basket Measure) poverty line but incurring higher costs to participate in society than persons without disabilities."[112]

Many of those extra costs are a result of the ableist bias built into the definition of human and human design, resulting in inaccessible places, spaces, systems, and policies. It's not just the costs of wheelchairs, lifts, mobility scooters, and tech – it's the additional costs for caregiving, items such as incontinence supplies, wound care, medications, transportation, prepared foods, grocery delivery, products suited to your dietary needs and other restrictions, and so on, as well as the costs of adapting or mitigating those things that non-disabled people do not pay for at all in order to make them accessible. For example, some people purchase special cushions to place on public seating that would otherwise be too low. Accessing a beach is free to non-disabled people, whereas a power beach or all-terrain wheelchair is not. And, while the cost of technology and equipment is not all of it, it is a lot, and this also gets tossed aside and ignored or over-simplified by those arguing for universal basic income.

MAID should be understood not as a civil liberties victory but as a further erosion of the already insufficient provision of the essential and necessary conditions for freedom to exist for disabled people.[113] This is evident in inequitable access to housing, education, health care, support necessary for us to live in the community, and in particular the significantly inequitable access to public life disabled people have compared to the general population.[114] The result of this is the often-negligible existence of real choice for disabled people, a lack of social bonds and feelings of alienation and powerlessness resulting from isolation, exclusion, and inaccessibility, and internalized oppression.[115] By every metric of injustice and inequity I am aware of, disabled people are disproportionately represented. By way of example, recent data shows that, among renters experiencing eviction, disability appears at double the rate it does in the overall population.[116]

If you subscribe to the idea of a social contract, the one offered disabled people should be thrown out on grounds of unconscionability. We don't even have the guarantee of freedom to live in the community,[117] and instead we have an unfulfilled promise not to be forced into institutional settings.[118] In 2022, an intellectually disabled woman in the midst of a mental health crisis was placed in a prison due to the lack of hospital beds available.[119] It was other prisoners who notified advocates to express concern for her well-being. Her mother explained that her daughter had been living successfully on her own, but the programs that made that possible had been cut. She was sent to prison for health care.

Most potential routes for attempting to claw oneself out of poverty are inaccessible to many disabled people, and depending on the nature of someone's disability, finding cheap alternatives to save money are as well. Before I was a wheelchair user, I worked two jobs in the summer to save up for the school year, and I could live wherever I could afford and make do. I often walked to work and school to save on transit. I had no dietary restrictions and needed few medications. None of those summer jobs would be accessible to me now, and my housing choices are an adapted apartment with an elevator or the street. As a disabled person, you have more immediate needs and fewer options to hustle for short- or long-term solutions.

Health care under neo-liberalism was declared an extravagance that people recklessly abused – or so we were told while they simultaneously reduced the per capita number of hospital beds.[120] "In 1980, the average number of hospital beds in Canada stood at 6.75 per one thousand inhabitants. By 2021, this rate had decreased to 2.58 per every thousand population."[121] The worried new parent of an infant who brought them to emergency was why we can't have nice things, the articles in the news explained.[122] Then the narrative changed to anxiety about the "grey tsunami,"[123] likening people aging to a natural disaster. It may or may not be the government's motivation, but MAiD does not deviate from the trajectory of the cost-cutting "cult of efficiency."[124] Disaggregated data about disability is in short supply, and ableism is not studied or officially recognized as a cause of health disparity despite being one.[125] Mentions of our existence even on issues specific to us are mostly omitted. My province of BC had a heat dome, and in one week 619 people died from heat. Of these people, 91 per cent had a "comorbidity" – one of the words they use to avoid using the word disability. By mentioning comorbidity and not once using the word disability in the entire BC Coroners report on the mass death event, they manage to avoid discussions of ableism and instead focus entirely on the bodies of those who died. This is the medical model in action. There is no role for disabled people to raise the conditions that put them at risk. In fact, there is no role for disabled people at all. If we are discussing comorbidities the only recognized expertise comes from doctors.

Disability is included as a cause of health disparity in the United States, but not in Canada.[126] However, when it comes to health care spending and the allocation of resources, all the calculators, charts, and number crunchers come out, and disability is highlighted and tracked meticulously. There is no space to discuss this in detail, but the contrast and framing is readily apparent in looking at the number of initialisms. There is the ableist metric of "quality-adjusted life years" (QALY), the obvious judgment of "disability-adjusted life years (DALYs)" or "years of healthy life lost due to disability (YLDs)."[127] We are assured, by the same governments that never stop talking about health care costs, that the monitoring of "high-cost users of health care (HCU)" – the 5 per cent of patients who various studies have estimated account for 61 per cent of hospital and home care spending, 30 per cent of physicians' services, and 41 per cent of prescription expenditures[128] – are never part of the considerations or calculations around MAiD. "Many studies have shown that health care costs in the last year of life (and especially in the last month of life) are disproportionately high, representing between 10% and 20% of total health care costs despite these patients representing about 1% of the population. Nevertheless, this report should in no way be interpreted as suggesting that MAID be used to reduce health care costs."[129] I wonder if the last line comes with a pinky swear promise, because not considering costs runs counter to everything I know about government.

Uncomfortable though it may be for Canadians to accept, D.H. Lawrence's sentiments cited at the beginning of this essay are merely a more proactive version of current public policy even outside of MAiD. Policies for disabled people, particularly those who are poor, easily conform to Frederick Engels's elaboration of the British working-class term "social murder." The workers had coined the term to describe being placed under conditions in which they could "neither retain health nor live long," accumulating conditions they argued hurried "them to the grave before their time." Engels further elaborated that social murder occurs because the society knows how injurious such conditions are and yet does nothing to improve these conditions, stating "that it knows the consequences of its deeds; that its act is, therefore, not mere manslaughter, but murder."[130]

Poverty of disabled people on disability benefits is distinct in that a medical doctor has had to sign a form certifying that this person is not able to participate in the workforce due to disability. The fact that governments maintain benefits at around 50 per cent lower than the poverty line means that our society has chosen a position that either does not believe in science or does not believe in human rights. There is no wiggle room here, because as much as the cause of poverty is always rooted in the system, not the individual, there is much obfuscation about this by governments who blame the unemployed and suggest it is a question of personal responsibility. But in this situation, you simply can't claim a disabled person didn't apply for enough jobs or was insufficiently motivated to seek work.

This also points to the way doctors play a very different role in the lives of disabled people than those of non-disabled people. For many of us, our housing, access to transportation, income, education, recreation, mobility, and other equipment, as well as other aspects of life, not to mention essential medical care, are tethered to a physician's signature that in turn may be dependent upon their perception of us as a "good patient."

For decades the Canadian neo-liberal model of disability stalled the introduction of any legislation comparable to the *Americans with Disabilities Act* (ADA), which was signed into law in 1990. The much narrower *Accessible Canada Act* enacted in 2019 is different in name, scope, and enforceability. It does not even tie receipt of federal funding to adherence to the act. We instead have the privatized Rick Hansen Foundation certification program that gives companies – and governments and public organizations – ratings. Various levels of government have put public money into financing a "problem-ridden private accessibility certification program for buildings" that is "entirely unhelpful for six million people with disabilities in Canada."[131]

An estimated six in ten disabled people in Canada experienced barriers accessing indoor and outdoor public space,[132] and an estimated 60 per cent of public space in three Canadian cities was found to be inaccessible.[133] Praxis, the former Rick Hansen Institute, is based in one of these cities, Vancouver. The Rick Hansen Foundation is based in nearby Richmond. When I was on the City of Vancouver Active Transportation Policy Council, I discovered that eight thousand of the twenty-seven thousand corners in Vancouver had no curb cuts, and they were installing new ones at the rate of approximately forty per year, making the estimated date of completion two hundred years in the future. At the same time, in the nearby US city of Seattle, someone filed an ADA complaint about the condition of curb cuts. The existence of policy instead of a Canadian myth and an inspiring story resulted in a preliminary agreement whereby the city would install 1,250 new curb cuts per year and a total of 22,500 new curb cuts within eighteen years.[134] My motion requesting the city install four hundred per year, moving the date of completion to twenty years instead of two hundred, is on a shelf somewhere gathering dust.[135]

The Canadian model of disability creates conditions that make MAiD even more dangerous than it might be elsewhere due to our lack of political identity, community connections, and authentic leadership. This leaves each disabled person alone to face a society built off an ideology that is vast in its expansiveness and utterly devastating in its capacity to be absorbed into everything and everyone without anyone noticing – like a tasteless, odourless gas that fills our atmosphere.

I agree with Kelly Fritsch, who said that people moving away from "better dead than disabled" requires more than a focus on individualized rights; it requires a reimagining of disability, not as a "something to overcome," but as "part of a life worth living."[136] And with people like Leah Lakshmi Piepzna-Samarasinha, who challenges the fundamental assumption that disabled people are defined by what is absent by highlighting the unique skills and perspectives within the disabled community, notably emotional intelligence.[137]

We have not begun to imagine, let alone create, a society that values disabled life – including our culture and knowledge. Until that happens, we can't realistically pretend to know the choices that would be made by individuals or the extent to which a disabled person's suffering is socially created. Just as ableist definitions of "human" led to ableist human design, an embracing of our bodies/minds and knowledge extends to the design of a society in ways far more radical than adding a ramp. Can you imagine a world where people who are not able to go out live in housing with plenty of room for people to drop by and in communities that encourage and support those kinds of relationships? Or doors large enough to push a bed outside onto a patio and down a path? Or cargo bikes with reclining bed-like attachments so people can recline and enjoy the outdoors? If this seems implausible to you, ask yourself why launching a billionaire's red roadster into space seemed plausible but this does not.

MAiD is killing our elders. A society without elders lacks wisdom and experience. There is also evidence that suggests that people's tolerance for inequality may be shaped by the overall degree of inequality in society when they are between the ages of eighteen and twenty-five – essentially establishing a sort of baseline for expectations. Examining the "effect of inequality experiences on people's demand for redistribution" using an array of large datasets, researchers found that those who "lived through times of higher inequality" held "more positive beliefs about inequality and are less likely to consider the prevailing level of inequality as unfair" and were less likely to support efforts to lessen it.[138] If the degree of inequality is widening and worsening, this would mean that acceptance would be greater with each generation.

It's not just that we need to consider how much we limit some dreams while emboldening others that may be far less worthy, but that we need to look at how this plays out around nightmares, since fear seems to often be the one putting its foot on the gas. We should ask ourselves the reason behind some those nightmares.

MY BODY IS A MAP OF POLICY DECISIONS

In a caring society people would not fear needing to be cared for. The presence – and prevalence – of this fear is an inculpation of our society. We do not live in a caring society; therefore, people are reasonably afraid of what will happen to them if they need care. If needing care is abnormal, shameful, and immorally burdensome on others, better dead than disabled sounds rational. Independence is a myth, but ableism has corralled some needs and declared them normal, marking others as extraordinary and abnormal.

Do people fear loss of independence or fear they won't be provided with the care and support necessary to carry out their wishes? Do they fear isolation, being abandoned and forced to rely on systems that will fail and dehumanize them? Do they fear being left behind and institutionalized, or perhaps worse, resented and despised as a burden? Yes, and these are all valid fears.

The *Fourth Annual Report on Medical Assistance in Dying in Canada 2022* includes a list of twelve of the most frequent types of suffering MAiD providers report in patients they have killed. The MAiD providers were able to give more than one answer. In a ranked list, the top two types of suffering are "loss of ability to engage in meaningful life activities" (86.3 per cent) and "loss of ability to perform activities of daily living" (81.9 per cent). The third most common (59.2 per cent) is an interesting category because it includes both inadequate pain control and "concern" about the potential for inadequate pain control. Who doesn't fear pain? And given the intense politicization of pain medications, it is worth asking whether we may have created a lower bar for state-provided death than accessing sufficient pain control. Fear of loss of dignity (53.1 per cent) is almost as prevalent as fear or presence of insufficiently addressed pain, as is the "inadequate control of symptoms other than pain (or concern)" (47.4 per cent). Other types include perceiving oneself to be a "burden on family, friends or caregivers" (35.3 per cent); "loss of control of bodily functions" – in other words incontinent like me (30.2 per cent); isolation or loneliness (17.1 per cent); "loss of control / autonomy / independence" (4.3 per cent); "emotional distress / existential suffering / fear / anxiety" (3.3 per cent); and "no / poor / loss of quality of life" (1.8 per cent).[139]

Every single one of these types of suffering is a reflection of socially constructed beliefs, inaccessibility, or ableist policy – including that which denies proper pain control while readily supplying lethal IV lines to cause death.[140] They are either a direct consequence of ableism or ableism significantly shapes how they are experienced. This list is an indictment of Canadian society, but one item that I personally find particularly damning and painful is "perceived burden on family, friends, or caregivers." People living in a society of billionaires should not feel like burdens for needing assistance and care.

One of the original plaintiffs to demand that assisted suicide be provided by the Canadian state was Kay Carter. As her illness progressed, she informed her family that she did not wish to live out her life as an "'ironing board,' lying flat in bed."

For a period of time prior to the end of her life, Kay wore diapers because she required assistance to go to the washroom and this assistance was often untimely ... Untimely assistance was unsatisfying and humiliating for my mom and for this reason and others (including getting her out of bed in the morning, brushing her teeth, toiletry issues, getting into the wheelchair, getting down for breakfast, getting assistance to eat, etc.) my mom hired someone to solely care for her six days a week at her expense.

Kay told me that the idea of lying about in an adult diaper was completely repugnant to her. She said and I believe that she was truly horrified by her vision of her future – a vision she said she could see in detail just by looking around her at the care facility. Sometimes when Kay was reading the obituaries, she would express jealousy at the people who had died. "Aren't they the lucky ones," she would say.[141]

Why would the Supreme Court of Canada decide the solution to this testimony about negligent care is a rationale for legalized lethal injections rather than demand that the government create better options? What is interpreted as suffering due to disability is suffering caused by ableism. This suffering is not irremediable.

In the past, I conformed to what she envisioned. I was sometimes transferred via a sling and a ceiling lift to a commode, but at other times that was not possible, and I lay in a rented hospital bed in my rented apartment that my then boyfriend and I had just moved into after being renovicted out of our previous home of several years. I was no longer working and therefore unable to financially contribute, and, as a result of moving, our rent almost doubled. When I was working, we split all expenses fifty-fifty. Due to the regulations around disability benefits, I was not eligible to receive assistance because my boyfriend earned an income. I was made his financial dependent, or, if you prefer the language of ableism, his burden. I served no purpose if you use any of their metrics, and I was a waste of resources if you subscribe to the logic of cost/benefit neo-liberalism.

It was the cheapest apartment we could find. Lab technicians came to my home to take blood. Home care aides flitted in and out, mostly unable to assist me as their time was consumed with the maintenance of things like cleaning catheter bags and disposing of various garbage. Nurses came to my home for wound care and other things home care was not able to perform. All of this happened following multiple hospital admissions. The goal during this time was to keep me comfortable on my way out of life. I didn't have a computer and little contact with the outside world. As part of cutting expenses we also no longer had cable. It was quiet and lonely. By sheer luck and a plot twist that seems more literary than real life, I am still here.

Now armed with a (dying) computer, when I have periods of being an ironing board, I have presented workshops, testified to government committees, spoken at United Nations side events, served as co-chair of the Vancouver City Planning Commission, written numerous reports, created a website for disabled people about the impacts of heat, and set up mutual aid for disabled people in hospital, among other things.

But what if I did not do any of those things? What if I had just listened to music or pondered life while looking at the stains on the popcorn ceiling?

I write this aware of the judgment obliging me to showcase my "productivity" in the hopes that you will decide I and others like me are worthy of life. Ableism slithers in even when we are discussing opposing ableism. It presents in how we think of our value and the way we tether our right to exist to it. Ironing boards have a lot of time for reflection, for thoughts longer than a sound bite, for perspectives formed outside of the frantic pace and urgent demands of "needed yesterday" multi-tasking life. If someone is going to ponder the sound of that tree falling in the forest, we are in a good position to do so. But what if we are just hanging out? What if an ironing board binge-watches multiple seasons of a cooking show while ordering takeout? And then has the sheer audacity to need help with personal hygiene? And uses plastic straws, asthma inhalers, wears disposable adult diapers, and produces other medical waste and plastic garbage.[142] What if we just fill up the cost column and leave the benefit one blank? Are we too much to live? Does the balance sheet compel us to die? Not long ago, on a day when I was very sad thinking about my dreams that were unfulfilled (due to ableism and poverty, not disability), I said to a friend who was complimenting me on the difference she thinks I make, "What have I achieved? All I have done is survive." The friend, Stephanie Allen, who is Black, said to me, "I come from a people for whom surviving *was* achieving."[143]

When an oppressed group lives in spite of – or even on spite – it is achieving. It is the first painful but essential move towards justice.

Right now, surviving is the goal we are striving to achieve. It's not that we don't have dreams. It's just we need some safety around us first and that starts with taking us off the legally killable list.

> In the foreground of the "euthanasia" idea is the "deliverance" of the "sick," though this is much more a "deliverance" of society *from* the "sick." Disabled people allegedly "suffer," and in that sense, it is a charitable act for them and their killing a merciful act on the part of their murderers so that they no longer have to "suffer." The border between killing out of compassion, the destruction of life "unworthy of living," assistance upon death and help to die was and is always fluid ... Non-disabled people would be well advised to deal with their own fears of the above instead of acting out their fears on disabled people. That does not mean accepting unnecessary pain and injury. It is a tightrope walk, at once fighting against injustice and conditions that make a person sick or disable them and at the same time learning to live with sickness and disability.[144]

If – or more likely when – I am bedbound again, I will be a lumpy and bumpy crooked ironing board, larger than I was before prednisone and less streamlined since my leg and foot twisted out of alignment and far less flat as a result of contractures in my hips and knees that were left untreated due to successive neo-liberal governments stripping down to the studs the never fully finished construction of Canada's universal health care system.

I wrote about a snippet of my health story in a piece for *Policy Options* about why we need MAiD-free spaces.[145] If I point to a spot on my body it tells a story – a brain rewired by trauma; the post-IVIG aseptic meningitis that, like the scarring from the pulmonary embolism along with the deep vein thrombosis, was left untreated for days as I made repeated trips to emergency departments pleading for care; the face I don't recognize because it is alternately larger due to prednisone-induced plus poverty-induced – yes, poverty – weight gain and simultaneously sunken due to the absence of teeth thanks to a combination of understaffing of hospital wards and later home care along with side effects of medications, illness, and what qualifies as dental care for poor people; the voice I was told I don't know the sound of – my own voice – and that I must have been imagining things when I noticed it had changed and that it and the pneumonia and choking were unrelated coincidences, not part of my condition, until a specialist heard there were peer-reviewed papers that said the same things I was saying; the shoulders that I am willing to hang in despite the wear and tear they take wheeling and transferring because if I go back to needing to use a ceiling lift in order to transfer they will try to force me – again – into a nursing home, contrary to article 19 of the UN convention this country ratified;[146] the sternum the flustered nurse violently shoved when I tried to point to the dial she'd inadvertently turned that was putting my roommate in danger of coding; the broken ribs; the breath ... no not ready to discuss that; the spine that was fractured when an exhausted nurse on an understaffed ward became frustrated with my limp body and slammed me into the bar on the back of the commode; the urethra that a nurse rammed a cystoscope into minus local anesthetic or warning because she assumed I don't feel things down there and it's more efficient "to catch people off guard"; the cervix that was biopsied with care and respect in an accessible exam room on an accessible table – why is that only available for pap smears and biopsies and not my general health care?; the colon that was the site of so much shitty misogynistic bias that the second chance on life almost never happened; the legs and hips that moved after being unresponsive for years – nine months of physiotherapy and foot surgery had me in the bars and taking steps – all undone when policy decided getting me up and walking would take too long, didn't fit into any of their funding slots, and that I was "going to die soon anyway" (2010); the contractures that have my left foot pointing to the side and my tibia sitting beside it, and the knees and hips that cemented bent and crooked because "physiotherapy is not covered"; the stains on my legs and the two-inch spot on either calf that is pale white, paper thin, and bleeds if rubbed – the final size of much larger wounds that took forever to close. Even when the constant edema subsided and with it the recurring cellulitis, those spots remained open. Dressings were too expensive, so I shoved sanitary napkins into my socks to soak up all the weeping ... the list is long and some stories are for another time.

My body is a map of policy decisions. Disabled poor people understand policy at a cellular level. We understand what happens when the theories of lawyers, ethicists, physicians, and strategists are released into the wild of an inequitable society drunk on delusions of individual responsibility and perverted notions of autonomy. Astroturf autonomy is an intoxicant offered in lieu of genuine freedom and autonomy – feeling "free" to set your own death date is offered in lieu of justice, care, and freedom from being ground into dust for someone else's greed.

The line that defines my body as my own also changed. Disabled people's lives and bodies are The Invisible Man, spectacle, or object to be reviled. It is all at the discretion of others. My first day in my new "home," I went for a stroll/roll. A woman walked into the side of my wheelchair as I waited at the corner for a light to change. She was furious. I was not supposed to be there. Disabled women experience staggeringly high rates of violence – up to ten times that on non-disabled women depending on whether they live in institutional setting or community. Research estimates 83 per cent of disabled women will be sexually assaulted in their lifetime. "The rate of sexual abuse of girls with disabilities is four times greater than the national average," and between 40 to 70 per cent of girls with intellectual disabilities are estimated to be sexually abused before the age of eighteen. In Canada, 80 per cent of psychiatric patients experience physical or sexual abuse.[147] At the same time, it is not uncommon for strangers to put their hands on a disabled person, and we are expected to be appreciative of this. As a wheelchair user I have been pushed by people who I could not see, who did not identify themselves to me, let alone ask my consent before starting to move me. There is a clear social expectation that I be thankful to these people and understand their actions as expressions of kindness. But they are violations of my right to define who touches me or my wheelchair, which, when I am in it, is an extension of me. One day I was stopped on the street and adjusting myself in my wheelchair when a man put his hands on my back. In many ways what followed was an interaction not unlike so many I have had when moving around my city. But this man gave me an extra layer of unsettled, and so I stopped suppressing my instincts just as he started to push me around a corner and off the main street. Later when I got home and was scrolling through social media, I saw his face in a "wanted" tweet. He was a serial sex offender who had not returned to his halfway house. I vowed never to hesitate again, and I have dealt with many indignant non-disabled people as a result. What does it mean when we tell a population of women who are at heightened risk of violence that they must assume strangers touching them mean well? What does it mean around MAiD? There was also the paratransit driver who "joked" about us going out for a date and who insisted he needed to fiddle at the back of my wheelchair as part of his safety protocol and that it was purely accidental when his hands slipped under the waistband of my jeans. And then there is the violence of those who deliver care. The accidental injury caused by a frustrated nurse and the deliberately inflicted bruise by an angry one received the same response: I was a lot of work to take care of, and their jobs are difficult.

I weaved some aspects of my story into this chapter because it too is knowledge, and my reporting of it is evidence. But this chapter, like public policy, is not about me personally even though this policy affects me personally. No policy can or should be written as if I or any other individual exists untouched by and without impact on others around them. "No man is an island," John Donne said, but "a piece of the continent / A part of the main." We are a society. Some of us are extremely marginalized, but even the margins are part of the page policy is written on.

IF WE CONCEDE THAT NO ONE IS AN ISLAND, WHAT DOES IT MEAN TO LIVE A GOOD LIFE OR HAVE A GOOD DEATH?

MAiD and its devaluing of disabled life devalues human life in general.

Distilled down, this legislation is based on whether you are efficient and productive enough to warrant the state being invested in keeping you alive. It is not about suffering. Suffering is the lifeblood of capitalism. Trying to eliminate suffering would be like capitalism shooting itself in the head. It worries me that the state has set up a rights framework that encourages people to demand their suffering be validated as just as "serious" and "MAiD-worthy" as someone else's. I remember those painful years of waiting for someone to put an official name to what was happening to my body. Whatever the motivations of the original conceivers of MAiD – and to be clear, I do believe fewer disabled people was and is a motivator for some – MAiD has been made a marker for suffering. Do you really suffer if the state isn't willing to kill you? Does it mean that your suffering is viewed as less legitimate than someone else's?

It is also a last-minute shot at fame and immortality to put your name on a demand for more expansion, more liberalization of MAiD allowing the lobbyists to argue these thought experiments in court. Nicole Gladu purportedly fought for the expansion of MAiD because of her desire to die with a "flute of pink champagne in one hand and a canape of foie gras in the other."[148] Disabled poor people are being put to death rather than provided with housing, financial support, personal care, and health care that includes all the things science-based medicine can offer, and in the end, Gladu opted not to use the expanded MAiD she had demanded. She just enjoyed having MAiD as an option available in her closet tucked next to her favourite cashmere, and possibly all the attention, recognition, and adoration that came along with being a *cause célèbre*.

THE HEROES OF THE MAiD MOVEMENT ARE MURDERERS

Euthanasia – or as they called it back then, mercy killing – was not always so glamourous. In 1993 Tracy Latimer, who was twelve years old at the time, was put in the front seat of the family pickup truck by her father, who, after running through other methods in his mind, settled on killing his daughter with carbon monoxide by running a hose from the exhaust of the family vehicle. He initially destroyed evidence and lied, claiming Tracy had died in her sleep, but later confessed to killing her, arguing it was justified due to her disability. The Canadian media and public felt this had all the hallmarks of a "a real Canadian hero":[149] a father "only trying to save his family";[150] nobly "sacrificing his needs" in "ending [his daughter's] suffering";[151] as "it is foolish to believe her life could have somehow been less tragic if she had lived."[152] Conflicting facts and inconsistencies and important truths about the case were ignored rather than explored.[153] In contrast, as Dick Sobsey pointed out in his analysis of media coverage, parents who murder their non-disabled children make similar claims about acting out of love and not wishing to see them suffer but are not viewed with same credulity and are universally condemned, not recipients of public sympathy.

The advocates for assisted suicide and euthanasia took full advantage of the media and public interest in the case and used it to promote their cause – which they saw as aligned with Robert Latimer, not the individual rights of Tracy Latimer. Quoted in the *New York Times*, Marilynne Seguin, then executive director of Dying with Dignity, said it was "unconscionable" to sentence the father to a ten-year prison sentence, as the Latimers had already effectively lived a "12 year sentence" by caring for Tracy during her life.[154] Information that conflicted with the storyline, such as Robert Latimer rejecting treatment that might have left his daughter pain-free due to his own views about medicine, was largely ignored.[155] In his book, *The Difference That Disability Makes*, Rod Michalko offers us the concept of disability cast as a "useless-difference." A "useless-difference" is one of no value to society and that "does not, and should not, make a difference in the world." Instead, a "useless-difference" is limited and experienced only on the individual level as a cause of suffering. Thus, "disability as useless-difference and as a personal problem burdensome to both the individual and society, commingles with a specific version of 'help.'" He positions the murder of Tracy Latimer, and I would argue MAiD, as an extreme version of this "help"; and says that her "murder reflects the view that normalcy is the bench-mark for measuring humanity."[156]

There is much to be said about this murder and the role it played in the history of MAiD, but for the purposes of this chapter I will restrict my commentary to pointing out that supporting murder is inconsistent with claiming to prioritize individual autonomy above all else.

The advocacy of Dying with Dignity, ethicists, and others pushing for assisted suicide and euthanasia has always included euthanizing disabled children. As far as I know I still live in a society that has a different legal and ethical understanding of consent when it comes to children versus adults, and regardless we know that Tracy gave no indication of wishing to die. Elke-Henner Kluge, an ethicist at the University of Victoria, and founder of the ethics department of the Canadian Medical Association, said Tracy's life should have been ended by doctors earlier. "By keeping her alive to face a declining quality of life, they were committing what ethicists call 'the injury of continuing existence.' In the end, the parents faced a situation in which they thought they had no choice."[157]

In 2016 when one of his fellow death advocates, albeit a poorer one living in social housing, decided to die by assisted suicide, Kluge paid for his airfare to the clinic located in Switzerland. When asked by media about the reasons for his friend's death, Kluge said, "The major reason was he thought it was unethical to extend his life in an ultimately fruitless way, because he was going to die anyway... It was a violation of the ethics of the Canadian health-care system. Rather than use expensive health-care resources, he was going to engage in deliberate death."[158] This sounds less like an argument for personal autonomy than it is a treatise on the duty-to-die under neo-liberalism.

Derek Humphrey, one of the founders of the Hemlock Society, abruptly left his second wife and co-founder when she decided to seek treatment instead of suicide, for the same cancer his first wife had. Humphrey had "mercy" killed his first wife. These actions do not seem consistent with someone with a high regard for the personal choice of those around him; rather, they align with someone whose support and love is conditional upon the other person making the choices he wishes them to.[159]

Greater media attention garnered better patrons and more money. People who killed their relatives or patients were replaced in the public sphere by philosophy professors and lawyers as the multi-pronged machine of marketing, lobbying, and public relations strategized behind the scenes. Much like how eugenics went from Galton poking holes in paper in his pocket for a beauty map to science-based-sounding categorization that determined your education (some, none, or all) and living situation (home or institution), euthanasia and assisted suicide got a makeover thanks to money. Today, having the state kill you is suddenly a high-demand item flying off the shelves.

The orchestrated death that felt at once real but also very fake – this was the culture of people with wealth. This is not working-class and poor people culture, and it is especially not poor crip culture. We deal. We adapt. We take pride in our hacks. We learn and change and grow, we grieve, and we get pissed off, and we live and are glad of it – not in a peppy trying-too-hard way, but in a way that grounds us solidly in reality, humility, humour, and truth. There is no beating death – if euthanasia gives you a sense of control, it's an illusion. Lying to yourself is bad enough but imposing the resulting threat on the rest of us is much worse.

Trudo Lemmens tackles this in a more cerebral and high-brow manner in his paper "Euthanasia and the Good Life." Referring to the inherent conflict between the version of the good life marketed to us by medicine, and its inability to completely conquer death, he says of euthanasia that "by giving the illusion of control over dying, euthanasia offers us a solution to this conflict."[160]

The need to feel artificially in control extends to many larger problems facing humanity. And it always seems that it is the class of people who suffer the fewest consequences and get their hands the least dirty who have the biggest need to give themselves a feeling of control at the expense of the rest of us.

Maybe you can't live a good life that is built on injustice. Maybe you can't have a good death if it puts marginalized people's lives at risk. If our lives are interconnected, then so too are our deaths. What if none of the timeless questions can be answered at an individual level – maybe they are questions to be solved by humanity, not *a* human.

In a similar vein, I personally find Peter Singer's magic pill scenario odd. Singer argues that a disabled person would take a magic pill to become non-disabled if offered one and cites this as evidence that a disabled life is necessarily worse despite what disabled people claim. It's worth mentioning that he is a leading and influential bioethicist who is known for not only endorsing the euthanizing of disabled children but for suggesting that in some cases it might be ethical to rape disabled people.[161] Aside from the fact that many disabled people would not wish to be non-disabled even if they had the opportunity to be, when I read things like this, I wonder what kind of lives men like Singer have lived. To start, I find it interesting he picked the image of a pill to work from. The things I wish had not happened and things I am glad about are forever mingling and blending into my being, into the person who I was, now am, and will be. Wishing the elimination of one would mean wishing myself out of existence. Perhaps another person would exist, but she would not be me. I know many women who have children who exist because of sex they had with men who (given what followed) it would be reasonable for them to wish they had never met. But they never entertain such a thought because doing so would mean eradicating the existence of their child(ren) and the mother they have become. Life doesn't come with magic pills; it comes with saplings growing out of scorched earth after forest fires. As someone who has experienced pain and suffering of various origins, I make a distinction between that which is part of the human condition and those things which arose as a part of a human-caused injustice and harm. But even then, I do not spend my time wishing the terrible things had not happened to me but rather think about how to prevent them from happening to others. There is a difference between the pursuit of a life of pleasure with the absence of difficulty for oneself and the goal of universal justice, peace, and freedom from violence for all. And, not unlike the dystopian *Minority Report* concept of imprisoning people for possible future crimes they might commit, the project of working to eliminate disability from human existence is a blueprint for genocide, not utopia. Singer's imagining of life feels consumerist. Life is to be lived not shopped for. And one is living even while they are dying. There is living and there is death. As far as disability goes, I am neither proud nor ashamed of being disabled – I just am. For me it is part of being alive, something I would like to continue to be for as long as possible. But if anyone is offering magic pills, I'll take one that makes me able to fly.

Since the passing of MAiD and the push for its expansion, I have been haunted by thoughts of how this could play out in situations of abuse and neglect. I can imagine a spouse urging a disabled person to consider the "better life" possible for their children once they are gone and life insurance pays out. We know that men are more likely to leave female partners who become disabled.[162] We also know that rates of intimate partner violence among disabled people are 50 to 100 per cent higher than among non-disabled people.[163] All these concerns are pushed aside as MAiD proponents tell us that two MAiD assessments would identify any risk of abuse at a time when one in five people don't even have a primary care physician.[164] Never mind that decades of women have had physicians who did not see the signs.

We are at the point where the media has developed an entire new genre of covering death via MAiD. No space is made for disabled people who reject MAiD. We have our own crip, mad, and disability culture, history, politics, and analysis. We are not the same, and we do not seek the "equality of sameness." We struggle and, yes, suffer in a society that was specifically and intentionally constructed to exclude and harm us. Justice is not inclusion, and inclusion is not justice. We want change that we are party to creating, defining, and shaping. At the moment, we mostly want the state to stop killing us slowly or rapidly, by deliberate unknowing omission or with the precision and intention of a sniper.

In the makeup of our society of us and them, we are "them." We are *those people* whose needs must be sacrificed when even the crumbs of pity become too bothersome, tiring, or expensive to perform. *Those people* who fall off the bottom of the bottom line and are triaged to die when systems that were designed to be insufficient unsurprisingly turn out to be so. In our resistance we are "us." This chapter is a declaration for the survival of us. *Us* who have decided to decline your invitation to the Crystal Palace.

When the belief that to be disabled is to be less human, when "better dead than disabled" is common opinion and ableism goes entirely unexamined, the only effective safeguard is to make it illegal to kill us.

On 6 January 1960, the *Toronto Star* published an article by the late Pierre Berton. He wrote about the horrors he saw when visiting the Huronia Regional Centre in Orillia, Ontario, one of Canada's institutions for disabled people. What Berton saw were the conditions disabled people lived in. The violence they suffered in that place was yet to be revealed. But he saw enough to tell readers:

"Remember this: After Hitler fell, and the horrors of the slave camps were exposed, many Germans excused themselves because they said they did not know what went on behind those walls; no one had told them. Well, you have been told about Orillia."[165]

And now, dear reader, you have been told about MAiD.

NOTES

1 D.H. Lawrence to Blanche Jennings, 9 October 1908, in *The Letters of D. H. Lawrence,* ed. James T. Boulton, vol. 1, *September 1901–May 1913* (Cambridge: Cambridge University Press, 1979), 81.
2 Isaac Olson, "Quebec Funeral Homes Offer Space for Families to Gather, Say Goodbye at Assisted Deaths," CBC News, 19 May 2023, https://www.cbc.ca/news/canada/montreal/quebec-funeral-home-assisted-dying-1.6850304.
3 James L. Cherney, "The Rhetoric of Ableism," *Disability Studies Quarterly* 31, no. 3 (2011), https://doi.org/10.18061/dsq.v31i3.1665; Heidi L. Janz, "Ableism: The Undiagnosed Malady Afflicting Medicine," *Canadian Medical Association Journal* 191, no. 17 (2019): E478–E479, https://pubmed.ncbi.nlm.nih.gov/31036612/; David M. Peña-Guzmán and Joel Michael Reynolds, "The Harm of Ableism: Medical Error and Epistemic Injustice," *Kennedy Institute of Ethics Journal* 29, no. 3 (2019): 205–42, https://pubmed.ncbi.nlm.nih.gov/31656232/.

  Shelley Tremain, "Toward an Abolitionist Genealogy of Bioethics," *Biopolitical Philosophy,* 6 February 2023, https://biopoliticalphilosophy.com/2023/02/06/toward-an-abolitionist-genealogy-of-bioethics/. Suggesting that reforming bioethics or educating bioethicists about disabled lives may not be the solution, Tremain says that condemnation of some of the egregious views avoids examination of the "comparatively pernicious ableism that other bioethicists produce." Tremain acknowledges that disability bioethicists are broader in their criticism, focusing also on the systemic ableism within the field with the aim of eliminating bias, but she believes they may unintentionally be solidifying rather than dismantling.

  > Philosophers who self-identify as disability bioethicists regularly participate on panels at bioethics conferences, collaborate with bioethics institutes, support mainstream bioethicists whose views are widely regarded amongst disabled people as detrimental to them, and aspire to publish in bioethics journals that these mainstream bioethicists produce. Disability bioethicists seem not to understand that an insidious feature of neo-liberalism is its capacity to refashion itself in the practice of auto-critique, that is, to co-opt critique as means to achieve

its own goals. Indeed, disability bioethics may be one of the most effective strategic mechanisms to emerge from the apparatus of disability and the biopolitical forms of neo-liberal power that motivated it to coalesce.
Mariah E. MacKay and Katherine Covell, "What about the Rights of the Infant with Disabilities? Responses to Infanticide as Function of Infant Health Status," *Canadian Journal of Disability Studies* 2, no. 2 (2013): 35–57, https://doi.org/10.15353/cjds.v2i2.81; Richard Lucardie and Dick Sobsey, "Homicides of People with Developmental Disabilities: An Analysis of News Stories," *Developmental Disabilities Bulletin* 33, no. 1–2 (2005): 71–98.

4 Marina Oshana, "Relational Autonomy," in *The International Encyclopedia of Ethics*, ed. Hugh LaFollette (Hoboken, NJ: John Wiley & Sons, 2020), https://doi.org/10.1002/9781444367072.wbiee921.
5 Ibid.
6 Vicente Navarro, "What We Mean by Social Determinants of Health," *International Journal of Health Services: Planning, Administration, Evaluation* 39, no. 3 (2009): 423–41, 423, https://pubmed.ncbi.nlm.nih.gov/19771949/.
7 Health Canada, *Health Impacts of Air Pollution in Canada: Estimates of Premature Deaths and Nonfatal Outcomes, Report 2021*, March 2021, https://www.canada.ca/en/health-canada/services/publications/healthy-living/health-impacts-air-pollution-2021.html; Marina I. Salvadori et al., "Factors That Led to the Walkerton Tragedy," *Kidney International – Supplement* 112 (2009): S33–4, https://pubmed.ncbi.nlm.nih.gov/19180129/; Health Canada, *Health of Canadians in a Changing Climate*, February 2022, https://changingclimate.ca/health-in-a-changing-climate/.
8 Michael Branion-Calles et al., "Risk Factors and Inequities in Transportation Injury and Mortality in the Canadian Census Health and Environment Cohorts (CanCHECs)," *Epidemiology* 35, no. 2 (2024): 252–62, https://www.ncbi.nlm.nih.gov/pmc/articles/PMC10836781/; Smart Growth America and National Complete Streets Coalition, "Dangerous by Design 2022," Smart Growth America, July 2022, https://smartgrowthamerica.org/dangeadrous-by-design/; Catherine Berthod, "Land Use Planning Measures Promoting Road Safety," Transportation Association of Canada, 2016, https://www.tac-atc.ca/wp-content/uploads/berthod-e.pdf; Keith Van Ryswyk et al., "Sources of Subway PM2.5: Investigation of a System with Limited Mechanical Ventilation," *Transportation Research Part D: Transport and Environment* 133 (2024): 104164, ISSN 1361-9209, https://www.sciencedirect.com/science/article/pii/S1361920924001214.

9 Abraham Aldama et al., "How Perceptions of Autonomy Relate to Beliefs about Inequality and Fairness," PLOS One 16, no. 1 (13 January 2021): e0244387, https://doi.org/10.1371/journal.pone.0244387.

10 Claire Sibonney, "Americans Would Rather Be Dead Than Disabled: Poll," *Reuters*, 11 July 2008, https://www.reuters.com/article/us-disability-idUSN7B320259200807II/.

11 Anthony W. Orlando, "The Rich Aren't Rich Because They Work Harder. They Work Harder Because They're Rich!," *HuffPost*, 14 February 2014, https://www.huffpost.com/entry/the-rich-arent-rich-becau_b_4791626; Ray Williams, "Social Class, Not Merit, Mostly Determines Success in America," LinkedIn, 7 September 2019, https://www.linkedin.com/pulse/social-class-merit-mostly-determines-success-america-ray-williams; David Labaree, "Pluck Versus Luck," *Aeon*, 4 December 2019, https://aeon.co/essays/pluck-and-hard-work-or-luck-of-birth-two-stories-one-man; Jonathan J.B. Mijs, "The Paradox of Inequality: Income Inequality and Belief in Meritocracy Go Hand in Hand," *Socio-Economic Review* 19, no. 1 (January 2021): 7–35, https://doi.org/10.1093/ser/mwy051.

12 Jason Marsh, "Are the Rich Really Less Generous?," *Greater Good Magazine*, 22 December 2015, https://greatergood.berkeley.edu/article/item/are_the_rich_really_less_generous.

13 Paul K. Piff et al., "Higher Social Class Predicts Increased Unethical Behavior," *Proceedings of the National Academy of Sciences* 109, no. 11 (February 2012): 4086–91, https://doi.org/10.1073/pnas.1118373109; Paul K. Piff, "Wealth and the Inflated Self: Class, Entitlement, and Narcissism," *Personality and Social Psychology Bulletin* 40, no. 1 (August 2013): 34–43, https://doi.org/10.1177/0146167213501699.

14 Kobe De Keere, "Finding the Moral Space: Rethinking Morality, Social Class and Worldviews," *Poetics* 79, no. 101415 (April 2020): 1–15, https://doi.org/10.1016/j.poetic.2019.101415.

15 Antony S. R. Manstead, "The Psychology of Social Class: How Socioeconomic Status Impacts Thought, Feelings, and Behaviour," *British Journal of Social Psychology* 57, no. 2 (April 2018): 267–91, https://www.ncbi.nlm.nih.gov/pmc/articles/PMC5901394/.

16 Hazel Rose Markus and Barry Schwartz, "Does Choice Mean Freedom and Well-Being?," *Journal of Consumer Research* 37, no. 2 (August 2010): 344–55, https://doi.org/10.1086/651242.

> Americans live in a political, social, and historical context that values personal freedom and choice above all else, an emphasis that has been amplified by contemporary psychology. However, this article reviews research that shows that in non-Western cultures and among working-class Westerners, freedom and choice do not have the meaning

or importance they do for the university-educated people who have been the subjects of almost all research on this topic. We cannot assume that choice, as understood by educated, affluent Westerners, is a universal aspiration. The meaning and significance of choice are cultural constructions. Moreover, even when choice *can* foster freedom, empowerment, and independence, it is not an unalloyed good. Too much choice can produce a paralyzing uncertainty, depression, and selfishness. In the United States, the path to well-being may require that we strike a balance between the positive and negative consequences of proliferating choice in every domain of life.

17 William Wan, "America's New Tobacco Crisis: The Rich Stopped Smoking, the Poor Didn't," *Washington Post*, 13 January 2017, https://www.washingtonpost.com/national/americas-new-tobacco-crisis-the-rich-stopped-smoking-the-poor-didnt/2017/06/13/a63b42ba-4c8c-11e7-9669-250d0b15f83b_story.html.

18 Andreas Hechler, "Diagnoses That Matter: My Great-Grandmother's Murder as One Deemed 'Unworthy of Living' and Its Impact on Our Family," trans. Elizabeth C. Hamilton and Leo R. Kalkbrenner, *Disability Studies Quarterly* 37, no. 2 (Spring 2017), https://doi.org/10.18061/dsq.v37i2.5573.

This also concerns the political left, which elevates autonomy, self determination, emancipation, the power to assert oneself, and the liberation from self-imposed immaturity and consequently separates frailty, loss of efficiency, and dependency as the fate of the other and is hard pressed to accept "victims" as well as those who "do not manage well." The worldwide eugenic community prior to National Socialism was predominately socialist-minded and explicitly anti-Nazi; the murderers during National Socialism often saw themselves as reformers and wanted to heal; the legalization of "assisted suicide" today is largely driven by left-leaning liberals. "Euthanasia" is not a fascist project. The differentiation between "worthy" and "unworthy" lives is also present in contemporary discussions about prenatal diagnoses, pre-implantation diagnoses, organ donation, research on those unable to provide consent, and not least of all, assisted suicide, even when it is only in rare case named as such. Whoever is no longer "fit for fun" and only has limited possibilities of optimizing one's fitness level, for that person the justification for existence plunges. Nowadays it is no longer an authoritarian state that makes the decision to end life, but instead the aged and the sick are supposed to dispose of themselves, death is "voluntary" and people are "helped" to it under the auspices of "civic engagement." With insistence on "self-determination," neoliberal trends and ableism meld wonderfully. The cold hospital environment, the horrible specter of high-tech medicine, loneliness; lack of medical, assistive, and financial provisions; social pressure; and the knowledge of the high costs that one's care imposes all do their part for a "dignified" self-disposal. The "right to die" gives way to a duty to die ... The moral indignation about "cost-benefit analyses," "health as a commodity," or the "crisis of health care" fizzles out into vacuity. Whoever does not want all of that cannot get around the need to abolish capitalism. As long as there is an economy that does not produce according to human needs, but is governed by the dictates of maximizing profits, recognizes private ownership of the means of production and makes wage labor a central mode of social organization, then several of the causes will persist that made National Socialist "euthanasia" possible.

19 Eric Andrew-Gee and Tavia Grant, "In the Dark: The Cost of Canada's Data Deficit," *Globe and Mail*, 26 January 2019, https://www.theglobeandmail.com/canada/article-in-the-dark-the-cost-of-canadas-data-deficit/.

20 William J.W. Choi et al., "When Medical Assistance in Dying Is Not a Last Resort Option: Survey of the Canadian Public," *BMJ Open* 14 (2024): e087736, https://doi.org/10.1136/bmjopen-2024-087736.

21 Kathleen R. Bogart, "The Disability Paradox," *Psychology Today*, 14 September 2022, https://www.psychologytoday.com/ca/blog/disability-is-diversity/202209/the-disability-paradox.

22 Lisa I. Iezzoni et al., "Physicians' Perceptions of People with Disability and Their Health Care," *Health Affairs* 40, no. 2 (February 2021): 297–306, https://doi.org/10.1377/hlthaff.2020.01452.

23 The frustration of dealing with physicians became a viral hashtag on Disability Twitter in 2018, centering around the themes of "disbelief in patients' experience and knowledge that contributes to medical errors and harm, the power inequity between patients and providers, and metacommentary on the meaning and impact of the #DoctorsAreDickheads hashtag." Anjana Estelle Sharma et al., "Recommendations from the Twitter Hashtag #DoctorsAreDickheads: Qualitative Analysis," *Journal of Medical Internet Research* 22, no. 10 (October 2020): e17595, https://doi.org/10.2196/17595.

24 Susan Wendell, "Toward a Feminist Theory of Disability," *Hypatia* 4, no. 2 (Summer 1989): 104–24, 121, http://www.jstor.org/slele/3809809.

25 Rachel McKinney, "Extracted Speech," *Social Theory and Practice* 42, no. 2 (2016): 258–84.

26 Anthony M. Mapp, "Modernity, Hegemony and Disability: A Critical Theoretical Exploration of the Historical Determinants of Disability" (PhD diss., York University, 2016).

27 Christopher Lyon, "Words Matter: 'Enduring Intolerable Suffering' and the Provider-Side Peril of Medical Assistance in Dying in Canada," *Journal of Medical Ethics*, published online first, 5 March 2024, https://jme.bmj.com/content/early/2024/03/20/jme-2023-109555.info.
28 Sarah Hemeida et al., "Structural Stigma in Law: Implications and Opportunities for Health And Health Equity," *Health Affairs*, 8 December 2022, https://www.healthaffairs.org/do/10.1377/hpb20221104.659710/.
29 Paul Bloom, *Against Empathy: The Case for Rational Compassion* (New York: Ecco HarperCollins, 2018), 31.
30 Megan Gran, "Father Files Appeal in Continued Effort to Prevent Daughter's MAID Death," CBC News, 2 April 2024, https://www.cbc.ca/news/canada/calgary/calgary-maid-father-daughter-court-injunction-judicial-review-appeal-1.7161377.
31 Chris Hedges, "Stuart Ewen The Power of Persuasion," *On Contact*, RT Media, 12 November 2017, https://www.rt.com/shows/on-contact/409603-power-mass-propaganda-us/.
32 World Health Organization, *Preventing Suicide: A Resource for Media Professionals*, 12 September 2023, https://www.who.int/publications/i/item/9789240076846.
33 Douglas Baynton, "Disability and Justification of Inequality in American History," in *The New Disability History: American Perspectives*, ed. Paul K. Longmore and Lauri Umansky (New York: New York University Press, 2001), 33.
34 Fiona A.K. Campbell, "Inciting Legal Fictions: 'Disability's' Date with Ontology and the Ableist Body of Law," *Griffith Law Review* 10, no. 1 (2001): 42–62, 44.
35 Jamelia Morgan, "On the Relationship Between Race and Disability," *Harvard Civil Rights- Civil Liberties Law Review* (CR-CL) 58 (July 2023), https://ssrn.com/abstract=4519059.
36 Talila A. Lewis, "Working Definition of Ableism – January 2022 Update," 1 January 2022, https://www.talilalewis.com/blog/working-definition-of-ableism-january-2022-update.
37 Nicole Ineese-Nash, "Disability as a Colonial Construct: The Missing Discourse of Culture in Conceptualizations of Disabled Indigenous Children," *Canadian Journal of Disability Studies* 9, no. 3 (2020): 28–51, https://doi.org/10.15353/cjds.v9i3.645.
38 James Gorman, "Ancient Bones That Tell a Story of Compassion," *New York Times*, 17 December 2012, https://www.nytimes.com/2012/12/18/science/ancient-bones-that-tell-a-story-of-compassion.html.
39 Londa Schiebinger, *Nature's Body: Gender in the Making of Modern Science* (Boston: Beacon Press, 1993), 143–5.

40 *Meeting of the Special Joint Committee on Medical Assistance in Dying*, 44th Parliament, 1st session (18 November 2022), Gabrielle Peters, https://www.parl.ca/DocumentViewer/en/44-1/AMAD/meeting-27/evidence.
41 Tanya Titchkosky, "Disability Studies: The Old and The New," *Canadian Journal of Sociology* 25, no. 2 (Spring 2000): 197–224, 200.
42 David M. Levy and Sandra J. Peart, "Experts and Eugenics: 'Science' Privileges a Social Goal," in *Escape from Democracy: The Role of Experts and the Public in Economic Policy* (Cambridge: Cambridge University Press, 2016), 91–109.
43 Jeff Randall and Zachary Thurston, "Housing Experiences in Canada: Persons with Disabilities," Statistics Canada, June 2022, https://www150.statcan.gc.ca/n1/pub/46-28-0001/2021001/article/00011-eng.htm.
44 Angus McLaren, *Our Own Master Race: Eugenics in Canada, 1885–1945*, Canadian Social History Series (Toronto: University of Toronto Press, 1990), chap. 1, Kindle.
45 Ibid.
46 Daniel M. Levy and Sandra J. Peart, "When Linear Models Fail: Two Cases," in *Escape from Democracy: The Role of Experts and the Public in Economic Policy* (Cambridge: Cambridge University Press, 2017), 89–136, https://doi.org/10.1017/9781316499078.006.
47 McLaren, *Our Own Master Race*, chap. 2, Kindle.
48 Canadian Human Rights Commission, "Homeless Encampments in Canada a Human Rights Crisis," Office of the Federal Housing Advocate, 8 December 2022, https://www.housingchrc.ca/en/homeless-encampments-in-canada-a-human-rights-crisis.
49 Gregory Michael Dore, "Defective or Disabled?: Race, Medicine, and Eugenics in Progressive Era Virginia and Alabama," *The Journal of the Gilded Age and Progressive Era* 5, no. 4 (2006): 359–92, http://www.jstor.org/stable/25144454, 360.
50 Ibid., 391.
51 See the discussion in Oksana Yakushko, "Eugenics and Its Evolution in the History of Western Psychology: A Critical Archival Review," *Psychotherapy and Politics International* 17, no. 2 (June 2019): e1495, 3: in his influential book *The Descent of Man and Selection in Relation to Sex*, Darwin, (1888) further proclaimed that, based on scientific evolutionary evidence it is "the western nations of Europe, who now so immeasurably surpass their former savage progenitors, and stand at the summit of civilisation" (p. 141). In his book on emotions Darwin, (1890) routinely contrasted the affective expression of British men (that is, their emotional detachment) with those of women and children,

typically discussed conjointly, and supposedly uncivilized groups (in terms of their lack of emotional control). According to Darwin and subsequent eugenicists, self-control in regard to emotions and thoughts was a mark of superior evolutionary fitness: "The highest stage in moral culture at which we can arrive, is when we recognize that we ought to control our thoughts" (Darwin, 1888, p. 101). Allegedly advanced human groups were viewed as predisposed by their ancient climate-adaptation patterns not only to particular levels of intelligence and health but also to these patterns of emotional expression and self-control.

In his *Descent of Man* Darwin, (1888) stated that the experiences of ancient cavemen meant "the races differ" not only in their physical appearance and functions, but specifically in "their mental characteristics ... chiefly as it would appear in their emotional, but partly in their intellectual faculties ... [such as] the contrast between the taciturn, even morose, aborigines ... and the light-hearted, talkative n*gr**s" [redaction mine] (p. 131). Darwin claimed that these supposed evolutionary racial differences between groups were scientifically proven, repeatedly drawing his evidence from eugenic scholars, contemporary with him, such as Galton, Greg, and Wallace. According to Darwin, (1888) racial and ethnic groups were demonstrated to be suitable or unsuitable for evolutionary progress because of their supposed personality traits and intelligence.

For reference to a study that revealed how women tend to be stereotyped as emotional, see Lindsay Kohler, "New Data Shows That Women Are More Negatively Stereotyped at Work Than Men," Forbes, 24 August 2024, https://www.forbes.com/sites/lindsaykohler/2024/08/28/new-data-shows-women-are-more-negatively-stereotyped-at-work-than-men/. The study found that 78 per cent of women had received feedback describing them as "emotional" compared to only 11 per cent of men.

52 Isabel Grant, "Legislated Ableism: Bill C-7 and the Rapid Expansion of Medical Assistance in Dying in Canada," *McGill Journal of Law and Health* 15, no. 2 (2023): 259–335, 297, https://mjlh.mcgill.ca/wp-content/uploads/2024/04/mjlh-15.2-grant-2024-04-30.pdf.

53 Natalie Zarrelli, "It Was Once Someone's Job to Chat with the King while He Used the Toilet," *Atlas Obscura*, 6 April 2017, https://www.atlasobscura.com/articles/king-toilet-attendant-england.

54 Darcie A.P. Delzell and Cathy D. Poliak, "Karl Pearson and Eugenics: Personal Opinions and Scientific Rigor," *Science and Engineering Ethics* 19, no. 3 (September 2013): 1057–70, https://doi.org/10.1007/s11948-012-9415-2; Walter Bodmer et al., "The Outstanding Scientist, R.A.

Fisher: His Views on Eugenics and Race," *Heredity* 126 (January 2021): 565–76, https://doi.org/10.1038/s41437-020-00394-6; Levy and Peart, "Experts and Eugenics."

55 Stephen Jay Gould, *The Mismeasure of Man*, rev. ed. (New York: W.W. Norton & Company, 1981), 107, Kindle.
56 McLaren, *Our Own Master Race*, chap. 1, Kindle.
57 Gabrielle Peters and Trudo Lemmens, "Climate Change, Vulnerability Theory, and the BC Heat Dome: From Inclusion to Responsive Government," in *Law in a Changing World*, ed. Brenda Cossman, Andrew Green, and Jutta Brunée (Toronto: University of Toronto Press, forthcoming).
58 "Meeting No. 8 JUST – Standing Committee on Justice and Human Rights," Parl VU, video, 17 November 2020, https://parlvu.parl.gc.ca/Harmony/en/PowerBrowser/PowerBrowserV2/20201117/-1/34280.
59 *Meeting of the Standing Committee on Justice and Human Rights – Evidence*, 43 Parliament, 2nd session (10 November 2020), https://www.ourcommons.ca/Content/Committee/432/JUST/Evidence/EV10949494/JUSTEV06-E.PDF.
60 McLaren, *Our Own Master Race.*
61 Edwin Black, "Eugenics and the Nazis: The California Connection," in *Beyond Bioethics: Toward a New Biopolitics*, ed. Osagie K. Obasogie and Marcy Darnovsky (Berkeley: University of California Press, 2018), 52–9, 53, https://doi.org/10.1525/9780520961944-008.
62 Gerald E. Thomson, "Remove from Our Midst These Unfortunates: A Historical Inquiry into the Influence of Eugenics, Educational Efficiency as Well as Mental Hygiene upon the Vancouver School System and Its Special Classes, 1910–1969" (PhD diss., University of British Columbia, March 1999), https://open.library.ubc.ca/soa/cIRcle/collections/ubctheses/831/items/1.0055545; Dustin Galer, "Disability Rights Movement in Canada," *The Canadian Encyclopedia*, 4 February 2015, last edited 23 April 2015, https://www.thecanadianencyclopedia.ca/en/article/disability-rights-movement; Susan Currell, "Breeding Better Babies in the Eugenic Garden City: 'Municipal Darwinism' and the (Anti) Cosmopolitan Utopia in the Early Twentieth Century," *Modernist Cultures* 5, no. 2 (2010): 267–90, https://doi.org/10.3366/mod.2010.0106; Carolyn Strange and Jennifer A. Stephen, "Eugenics in Canada: A Checkered History, 1850s–1990s," in *The Oxford Handbook of the History of Eugenics,* ed. Alison Bashford and Philippa Levine (Online Edition: Oxford Academic, September 2012), https://doi.org/10.1093/oxfordhb/9780195373141.013.0032; Prashan Ranasinghe, "The Refashioning of Vagrancy and the (Re)Ordering of Public Space"

(PhD diss., University of Toronto, 2009), https://www.proquest.com/dissertations-theses/refashioning-vagrancy-re-ordering-public-space/docview/305107441/se-2; *Female Refuges Act*, RSO 1927, c 347, http://digitalcommons.osgoode.yorku.ca/rso/vol1927/iss3/210; Velma Demerson and Scott Piatkowski, "An Honest Woman [Incorrigible]," *This*, July/August 2005, 42, https://www.proquest.com/magazines/honest-woman-incorrigible/docview/203566489/se-2; *An Act Respecting Immigration, Acts of the Parliament of the Dominion of Canada*: passed in the session held in the ninth and tenth years of the reign of His Majesty King Edward VII, vol. 1, *Public General Acts* (Ottawa: C.H. Parmelee, 1910), https://www.canadiana.ca/view/oocihm.9_07184.

63 Dulcie McCallum, *The Need to Know: Woodlands School Report: An Administrative Review*, Ministry of Children and Family Development, August 2001, http://bc-llc.org/index-148.html.

64 Tanya Titchkosky, *Disability, Self, and Society* (Toronto: University of Toronto Press, 2003), 113, https://doi.org/10.3138/9781442673939.

65 Vic Finkelstien, "The Social Model of Disability Repossessed," Manchester Coalition of Disabled People, 1 December 2001, 5, https://disability-studies.leeds.ac.uk/wp-content/uploads/sites/40/library/finkelstein-soc-mod-repossessed.pdf.

66 "Any person who is diseased, maimed, mutilated, or in any way deformed, so as to be an unsightly or disgusting object, or an improper person to be allowed in or on the streets, highways, thoroughfares, or public places in this city, shall not therein or thereon expose himself to public view, under the penalty of a fine of $1 [about $20 today] for each offense. (Chicago City Code 1881)," Susan M. Schweik, *The Ugly Laws: Disability in Public*, Disabilities Histories (New York University Press, 2009), 1–2, Kindle.

67 Roy Hanes, "From Charitable Relief to Social Control: The Criminalization of People with Disabilities in Nineteenth Century Canada," *Review of Disability Studies: An International Journal* 1, no. 2 (2004): 1–15, 10, https://www.rdsjournal.org/index.php/journal/article/view/393.

68 Titchkosky, *Disability, Self, and Society*, 113.

69 Hanes, "From Charitable Relief to Social Control," 11.

70 Ibid., 3.

71 Jordan Gill, "'Farming out the Poor': How Auctions Sold New Brunswickers into the 20th Century," CBC News, 13 January 2024, https://www.cbc.ca/news/canada/new-brunswick/paupers-auctions-roadside-history-1.7081915.

72 Brenda Thompson, *A Wholesome Horror: Poor Houses in Nova Scotia* (Halifax: SSP Publications, 2017), Kindle.

73 Stefanie Hunt-Kennedy, *Between Fitness and Death: Disability and Slavery in the Caribbean*, Disability Histories (Chicago: University of Illinois Press, 2020), 43, Kindle.
74 Thompson, *Wholesome Horror*.
75 Marta Russell, *Capitalism and Disability: Selected Writing by Marta Russell*, ed. Keith Rosenthal (Chicago: Haymarket Books, 2019), 37, Kindle.
76 Ibid.
77 Mike Oliver, "Vic Finkelstein Obituary," *Guardian*, 22 December 2011, https://www.theguardian.com/society/2011/dec/22/vic-finkelstein; Vic Finkelstein, "Disability and the Helper/Helped Relationship: An Historical View," in *Handicap in a Social World Suffolk*, ed. Ann Brechin, P. Liddiard, and J. Swain (UK: Chaucer Press, 1981).
78 Ibid., 2.
79 Hanes, "From Charitable Relief to Social Control," 5.
80 Ibid.
81 Ibid., 6.
82 Ibid., 5.
83 Jonathan Metzl, *The Protest Psychosis: How Schizophrenia Became a Black Disease* (Boston: Beacon Press, 2009), Kindle.
84 Ada McVean, "The History of Hysteria," *McGill Office for Science and Society*, 31 July 2017, https://www.mcgill.ca/oss/article/history-quackery/history-hysteria.
85 Reem Alsalem, *Custody, Violence against Women and Violence Against Children: Report of the Special Rapporteur on Violence against Women and Girls, Its Causes and Consequences*, United Nations General Assembly Human Rights Council, 31 April 2023, https://undocs.org/Home/Mobile?FinalSymbol=A%2FHRC%2F53%2F36&Language=E&DeviceType=Desktop&LangRequested=False.
86 Russell, *Capitalism and Disability*, 32.
87 Mike Oliver, "The Social Model of Disability: Thirty Years On," *Disability and Society* 28, no. 7, 1024–6, https://www.tandfonline.com/doi/full/10.1080/09687599.2013.818773.
88 Russell, *Capitalism and Disability*, 20.
89 *Federal Poverty Reduction Plan: Working In Partnership Towards Reducing Poverty In Canada – Report of the Standing Committee on Human Resources, Skills and Social Development and the Status of Persons with Disabilities* (Ottawa: Government of Canada, 2010).
90 Anandi Mani et al., "Poverty Impedes Cognitive Function," *Science* 341, no. 6149 (August 2013): 976–80.
91 Elliot Berkman, "It's Not a Lack of Self-Control That Keeps People Poor," *Conversation*, 22 September 2015, https://theconversation.com/its-not-a-lack-of-self-control-that-keeps-people-poor-47734.

92 Madeline Burghardt et al., "Unheard Voices: Sisters Share about Institutionalization," *Canadian Journal of Disability Studies* 6, no. 3 (August 2017): 93–117, 104.
93 Ibid., 99.
94 Christopher Lyon, "MAiD Dreams and Nightmares," Christopher Lyon Substack, 26 April 2024, https://christopherlyon.substack.com/p/maid-dreams-and-rituals.
95 Christopher van Veen, Katherine Teghtsoonian, and Marina Morrow, "Enacting Violence and Care: Neo-Liberalism, Knowledge Claims, and Resistance," in *Madness, Violence, and Power: A Critical Collection*, ed. Andrea Daley, Lucy Costa, and Peter Beresford (Toronto: University of Toronto Press, 2019), 63–79, 68.
96 Robert Crawford, "Healthism and the Medicalization of Everyday Life," *International Journal of Social Determinants of Health and Health Services* 10, no. 3 (1980): 365–88, https://doi.org/10.2190/3H2H-3XJN-3KAY-G9NY.
97 Ibid., 365–6.
98 James Barnes, "The Politics of Distress: A Discussion with Dr. James Davies on His New Book Sedated," *Mad in America*, 26 June 2021, https://www.madinamerica.com/2021/06/interview-james-davies/.
99 Shelley Tremain, "Toward an Abolitionist Genealogy of Bioethics," *Biopolitical Philosophy*, 6 February 2023, https://biopoliticalphilosophy.com/2023/02/06/toward-an-abolitionist-genealogy-of-bioethics/.
100 Tanya Titchkosky, *Reading and Writing Disability Differently: The Textured Life of Embodiment* (Toronto: University of Toronto Press, 2007), 159.
101 Ibid.
102 "Is Rick Hansen's Man in Motion Tour of 1986 Doing More Harm than Good?," CBC, video, 6 January 1987, https://www.cbc.ca/player/play/1822264387.
103 Peter Cheney, "PM Gives Hansen $1 Million for Research: [FIN Edition]," *Toronto Star*, 27 October 1986, https://www.proquest.com/newspapers/pm-gives-hansen-1-million-research/docview/435512952/se-2.
104 Kayla Brown, "Dis-course: Disability Representation and the Media, Part One," DO-IT, https://www.washington.edu/doit/dis-course-disability-representation-and-media-part-one.
105 Titchkosky, *Reading and Writing Disability Differently*.
106 "Disability Assistance Rate Table," Government of British Columbia, 1 August 2023, https://www2.gov.bc.ca/gov/content/governments/policies-for-government/bcea-policy-and-procedure-manual/bc-employment-and-assistance-rate-tables/disability-assistance-rate-table; Katie DeRosa, "Average Rent for One Bedroom Apartment in Vancouver Tops $3,000 a

Month," *Vancouver Sun*, 14 August 2023, https://vancouversun.com/news/local-news/average-rent-for-a-one-bedroom-apartment-vancouver-tops-3000-a-month.

107 Hanes, "From Charitable Relief to Social Control," 3.

108 Michael J. Glantz et al., "Gender Disparity in the Rate of Partner Abandonment in Patients with Serious Medical Illness," *Cancer* 115, no. 22 (November 2009): 5237–42, https://doi.org/10.1002/cncr.24577.

109 Julie Gaudet, "And Then There Were the Poorest Amongst the Poor...," *Canadian Poverty Institute*, 26 September 2018, https://www.povertyinstitute.ca/news/2018/9/26/and-then-there-were-the-poorest-amongst-the-poor.

110 "Archived – Waitlist Status Including Length of Time, by Tenure Including Social and Affordable Housing, 2018, Inactive," Statistics Canada, 22 November 2019, https://www150.statcan.gc.ca/t1/tbl1/en/tv.action?pid=4610004201.

111 The Saint John Human Development Council, "Serious Problems Experienced by People with Disabilities Living in Atlantic Canada," Department of Justice Canada, January 2021, https://www.justice.gc.ca/eng/rp-pr/jr/pwdac-phca/docs/RSD_RR2021_Persons_with_Disabilities_Atlantic_Canada_EN.pdf; James L. Charlton, *Nothing About Us Without Us* (University of California Press, 2000), 68–82, Kindle.

112 Craig W.M. Scott et al., "Disability Considerations for Measuring Poverty in Canada Using the Market Basket Measure," *Social Indicators Research* 163 (March 2022): 389–407, https://doi.org/10.1007/s11205-022-02900-1.

113 "End of Mission Statement by the United Nations Special Rapporteur on the Rights of Persons with Disabilities, Ms. Catalina Devandas-Aguilar, on Her Visit to Canada," United Nations Human Rights Office of the High Commissioner, 12 April 2019, https://www.ohchr.org/en/statements/2019/04/end-mission-statement-united-nations-special-rapporteur-rights-persons.

114 Alzheimer Society of Canada et al., *Meeting Canada's Obligations to Affordable Housing and Supports for People with Disabilities to Live Independently in the Community*, 15 May 2017, https://www.ohchr.org/sites/default/files/Documents/Issues/Housing/Disabilities/CivilSociety/Canada-ARCHDisabilityLawCenter.pdf; Gabrielle Peters, "Disabled People More Than 2X as Represented among Recently Evicted Renters as General Population," MsSineNomine Substack, 15 April 2024, https://mssinenomine.substack.com/p/new-disabled-people-are-more-than; "Exclusion Tracker Report 2022/23," BCEdAccess, https://bcedaccess.com/exclusion-tracker/; Matthew B. Downer and Sara Rotenberg, "Disability – A Chronic Omission in Health Equity That Must Be Central

to Canada's Post-Pandemic Recovery," *Health Promotion and Chronic Disease Prevention in Canada* 43, no. 7 (2023): 348–51, https://doi.org/10.24095/hpcdp.43.7.05; Kelly Fritsch and Fady Shanouda, "Warehousing of Disabled People in Long-Term Care Homes Needs to Stop. Instead, Nationalize Home Care," *Conversation*, 12 January 2022, https://theconversation.com/warehousing-disabled-people-in-long-term-care-homes-needs-to-stop-instead-nationalize-home-care-173412; Gabrielle Peters, "Canada Is NOT as Advertised. MAiD Is Eugenics," *mssineomineblog*, 16 June 2022, https://mssineomineblog.wordpress.com/2022/06/16/canada-is-not-as-advertised-maid-is-eugenics/.

115 Meagan Gillmore, "'Catastrophic Pandora's Box': Disabled Ontarians Speak Out against Proposed MAID Law," *TVO Today*, 3 March 2021, https://www.tvo.org/article/catastrophic-pandoras-box-disabled-ontarians-speak-out-against-proposed-maid-law; Fatema Shafiq, Jaque King, and Robyn Ront, "Social Isolation and Loneliness Are Serious Health Concerns for Adults with Disabilities. COVID-19 Has Magnified the Problem," *Health Policy Brief*, 30 November 2020, https://chrt.org/wp-content/uploads/2021/07/SocialIsolationLoneliness_Accessibility.pdf; "Exclusion Tracker Report 2022–23," BCEDAccess Society, 12 September 2023, https://bcedaccess.com/exclusion-tracker/; Canadian Press, "Disabled Blocked from about 60% of Public Spaces in Major Canadian Cities," *Victoria News*, 29 November 2023, https://www.vicnews.com/national-news/disabled-blocked-from-about-60-of-public-spaces-in-major-canadian-cities-7116737; "The Disability Rate in Canada Increased in 2022," Statistics Canada, 3 April 2024, https://www.statcan.gc.ca/o1/en/plus/5980-disability-rate-canada-increased-2022; Charlton, *Nothing About Us Without Us*, 68–82.

116 "Recently Evicted People Tend to be Younger, Have Financial Difficulties, and Report Having Low Trust in Others," Statistics Canada, 12 April 2024, https://www150.statcan.gc.ca/n1/daily-quotidien/240412/dq240412c-eng.htm.

117 Sophie Jin and Megan Linton, "Abolish Long-Term Care," *Briarpatch Magazine*, 25 January 2022, https://briarpatchmagazine.com/articles/view/abolish-long-term-care.

118 Meenakshi Mannoe, "Street Sweeps and Disability Justice," *Pivot*, 4 June 2022, https://www.pivotlegal.org/street_sweeps_disability_justice.

119 Heather Yourex-West, "An Intellectually Disabled Woman Needed Help. She Went to Jail Instead," *Global News*, 20 December 2022, https://globalnews.ca/news/9358863/saskatchewan-intellectually-disabled-woman-jailed/.

120 Diane Francis, "Health-Care Abuse Can Make Your Blood Boil," *Financial Post*, 19 January 1993, LexisNexis. Rebecca Wigod, "Deadly Myths: Don't Blame the Elderly for the High Cost of Health Care, Experts Warn," *Calgary Herald*, 30 June 1997, LexisNexis.

121 Jenny Yang, "Density of Hospital Beds in Canada 1976–2021," Statista, 18 December 2023, https://www.statista.com/statistics/831668/density-of-hospital-beds-canada/.

122 "Taxing Medical Services Could be Illegal: Cote," *Gazette* (Montreal, Quebec), 30 October 1991, https://advance.lexis.com/api/document?collection=news&id=urn:contentItem:3TD8-R2M0-002N-B404-00000-00&context=1516831; "Health-Care User Fees Advised by PC Minister," *Record* (Kitchener-Waterloo, Ontario), 22 April 1991, https://advance.lexis.com/api/document?collection=news&id=urn:contentItem:46YR-3TK0-01GV-M0YR-00000-00&context=1516831.

123 Lorrie Goldstein, "Canada Ill-Prepared for Costly Grey Tsunami," *Sarnia Observer*, 7 May 021, https://advance.lexis.com/api/document?ollection=news&id=urn:contentItem:62M5-PYH1-JC55-D4V1-00000-00&context=1516831.

124 "The 2001 CBC Massey Lectures, 'The Cult of Efficiency,'" CBC Radio, 6 November 2001, https://www.cbc.ca/radio/ideas/the-2001-cbc-massey-lectures-the-cult-of-efficiency-1.2946866.

125 Bonnielin K. Swenor, "Including Disability in all Health Equity Efforts: An Urgent Call to Action," *Lancet* 5, no. 6 (June 2021): E359–60, https://www.thelancet.com/journals/lanpub/article/PIIS2468-2667(21)00115-8/fulltext; Dielle J. Lundberg and Jessica A. Chen, "Structural Ableism in Public Health and Healthcare: A Definition and Conceptual Framework," *Lancet Regional Health Americas* 30, no. 100650 (December 2023), https://www.thelancet.com/journals/lanam/article/PIIS2667-193X(23)00224-7/fulltext; Gloria L. Krahn, Deborah Klein Walker, and Rosaly Correa-De-Araujo, "Persons with Disabilities as an Unrecognized Health Disparity Population," *American Journal of Public Health* 105, Suppl 2 (2015): S198–206, https://pubmed.ncbi.nlm.nih.gov/25689212/.

126 Amanda Morris, "Disability Groups Win Fight to Be Included in Health Equity Research," *Washington Post*, 26 September 2023, https://www.washingtonpost.com/wellness/2023/09/26/disability-groups-win-fight-be-included-health-equity-research/.

127 Paul Schneider, "The QALY Is Ableist: On the Unethical Implications of Health States Worse than Dead," *Quality of Life Research* 31, no. 5 (May 2022): 1545–52, https://pubmed.ncbi.nlm.nih.gov/34882282/; "Disability-Adjusted Life Years," The Global Health Observatory, World Health

Organization, https://www.who.int/data/gho/indicator-metadata-registry/imr-details/158.

128 Sergei Muratov et al., "Regional Variation in Healthcare Spending and Mortality among Senior High-Cost Healthcare Users in Ontario, Canada: A Retrospective Matched Cohort Study," BMC Geriatric 18, no. 262 (November 2018): 1–13, https://bmcgeriatr.biomedcentral.com/counter/pdf/10.1186/s12877-018-0952-7.pdf.

129 Office of the Parliamentary Budget Officer, "Cost Estimate for Bill C-7 'Medical Assistance in Dying,'" 20 October 2020, https://qsarchive-archiveqs.pbo-dpb.ca/web/default/files/Documents/Reports/RP-2021-025-M/RP-2021-025-M_en.pdf.

130 Friedrich Engels, *The Condition of the Working-Class in England in 1844*, trans. Florence Kelley Wischnewetzky (Cambridge: Cambridge University Press, 2011).

131 AODA Alliance, "Disability Coalition Slams Trudeau Government's Giving Millions to Rick Hansen Foundation's Seriously Deficient Building Accessibility Certification Training Program," Accessibility for Ontarians with Disabilities Act, 24 August 2021, https://aoda.ca/disability-coalition-slams-trudeau-governments-giving-millions-to-rick-hansen-foundations-seriously-deficient-building-accessibility-certification-training-program/.

132 "Canadian Survey on Disability, 2017-2022," *Daily*, Statistics Canada, 1 December 2023, https://www150.statcan.gc.ca/n1/daily-quotidien/231201/dq231201b-eng.htm.

133 Canadian Press, "Disabled Blocked from about 60% of Public Spaces in Major Canadian Cities."

134 David Gutman, "Settlement: Seattle to Build Thousands of Sidewalk Curb Ramps over the Next 18 Years," *Seattle Times*, 17 July 2017, https://www.seattletimes.com/seattle-news/transportation/settlement-seattle-to-build-thousands-of-sidewalk-curb-ramps-over-next-18-years/.

135 City of Vancouver, "Active Transportation Policy Council: Minutes," 8 November 2017, https://vancouver.ca/docs/council/atpc20171108min.pdf.

136 Kelly Fritsch, "Desiring Disability Differently: Neoliberalism, Heterotopic Imagination and Intra-corporeal Reconfigurations," *Foucault Studies* 19 (June 2015): 43–66, 43.

137 Leah Lakshmi Piepzna-Samarasinha, *Care Work: Dreaming Disability Justice* (Vancouver: Arsenal Pulp Press, 2018), 69.

138 Christopher Roth and Johannes Wohlfart, "Experienced Inequality and Preferences for Redistribution," 8 August 2018, http://dx.doi.org/10.2139/ssrn.2809655.

139 Health Canada, *Fourth Annual Report on Medical Assistance in Dying Canada 2022*, October 2023, 31, https://www.canada.ca/en/health-canada/

services/publications/health-system-services/annual-report-medical-assistance-dying-2022.html#a4.3.
140 Ibid.
141 Affidavit of Plaintiff at 3-5, *Carter v. Canada (Attorney General)*, No. S112688, Vancouver Registry (BCSC, 24 August 2011).
142 Bronwyn Hemsley et al., "Going Thirsty for the Turtles: Plastic Straw Bans, People with Swallowing Disability, and Sustainable Development Goal 14, Life Below Water," *International Journal of Speech-Language Pathology* 25, no. 1 (2023): 15–19, https://doi.org/10.1080/17549507.2022.2127900; Whitney Lee, "People Who Use Inhalers Aren't Responsible for the Climate Crisis. Corporations and Governments Are," *Rooted in Rights*, 12 November 2019, https://rootedinrights.org/people-who-use-inhalers-arent-responsible-for-the-climate-crisis-corporations-and-governments-are/; Gabrielle Peters, "Pissing and Pooping on The MAiD Parade," mssinenomineblog, 8 March 2023, https://mssinenomineblog.wordpress.com/2023/03/09/pissing-and-pooping-on-the-maid-parade/.
143 Stephanie Allen, "Fight the Power: Redressing Displacement and Building a Just City for Black Lives in Vancouver," Simon Fraser University Summit Research Depository, 12 June 2019, https://summit.sfu.ca/item/19420.
144 Andreas Hechler, "Diagnoses That Matter."
145 Gabrielle Peters, "Reality Not Religion Is Why People Need MAiD-Free Health-Care," *Policy Options*, 26 April 2024, https://policyoptions.irpp.org/magazines/april-2024/maid-free-healthcare/.
146 *Convention of the Rights of Persons with Disabilities*, 13 December 2006, 2515 UNTS 3, https://www.ohchr.org/en/instruments-mechanisms/instruments/convention-rights-persons-disabilities.
147 Government of Canada, "Violence Against Women with Disabilities," National Clearinghouse on Family Violence, 2004, https://publications.gc.ca/collections/Collection/H72-22-9-2004E.pdf.
148 *Meeting of the Standing Senate Committee on Legal and Constitutional Affairs – Evidence*, 43rd Parliament, 2nd Session (3 February 2021), https://sencanada.ca/en/Content/Sen/Committee/432/LCJC/12ev-55130-e.
149 Peter L. Cossingham, "Robert Latimer Hailed as Hero," *Winnipeg Free Press*, 13 February 1997, cited in Council of Canadians with Disabilities, "Chilling Quotes," 15 October 1998, http://www.ccdonline.ca/en/human-rights/endoflife/latimer/1998/10d.
150 Dorothy Duncan, *The News-Optimist*, 7 December 1994, cited in CCD, "Chilling Quotes."
151 Patrick Conroy, *Macleans*, 12 December 1994, cited in CCD, "Chilling Quotes."

152 David Cooper, *Without Restraint*, 1998, cited in CCD, "Chilling Quotes." For these full quotes and more chilling citations, see CCD, "Chilling Quotes."
153 Dick Sobsey, "The Latimer Case – The Reflections of People with Disabilities – Media," *Council of Canadians with Disabilities*, August 1995, http://www.ccdonline.ca/en/humanrights/endoflife/latimer/reflections/media.
154 Clyde H. Farnsworth, "Mercy Killing in Canada Stirs Calls for Changes in Law," *New York Times*, 22 November 1994, https://www.nytimes.com/1994/11/22/world/mercy-killing-in-canada-stirs-calls-for-changes-in-law.html.
155 The Council of Canadians with Disabilities provided extensive fact versus myth breakdowns and analysis. Dick Sobsey, "The Latimer Case."
156 Rod Midchalko, *The Difference That Disability Makes* (Philadelphia: Temple University Press, 2002): 93–111, 102, 103, 110.
157 D'arcy Jenish, "What Would You Do? In Saskatchewan, a Wrenching Verdict of Murder Re-Ignites a Long-Simmering Debate about Mercy-Killing," *Maclean's*, 28 November 1994.
158 Louise Dickson, "Victoria Right-to-Die Activist Felt Pressure to Take His Own Life," *Times Colonist*, 9 April 2016, https://www.timescolonist.com/local-news/victoria-right-to-die-activist-felt-pressure-to-take-his-own-life-4635166.
159 Cal McCrystal, "Love, Death & Loathing on the Road to Windfall Farm; Derek Humphry Helped His First Wife to Die. His Second Wife, Ann, Helped Her Parents to Die. Together They Formed the Hemlock Society. Dying Was Their Business. And Then They Fell Out ...," *Independent*, 8 April 1990.
160 Trudo Lemmens, "Euthanasia and the Good Life," *Perspectives in Biology and Medicine* 39, no. 1 (Autumn 1995): 15–27 at 19.
161 Nathan J. Robinson, "Now Peter Singer Argues That It Might Be Okay to Rape Disabled People," *Current Affairs*, 4 April 2017, https://www.currentaffairs.org/2017/04/now-peter-singer-argues-that-it-might-be-okay-to-rape-disabled-people; Jeff McMahan and Peter Singer, "Who Is the Victim in the Anna Stubblefield Case?," *New York Times*, 3 April 2017, https://www.nytimes.com/2017/04/03/opinion/who-is-the-victim-in-the-anna-stubblefield-case.html.
162 Glantz et al., "Gender Disparity in the Rate of Partner Abandonment."
163 "Fact Sheet on Women with Disabilities and Violence," Dawn Canada, https://www.dawncanada.net/issues/women-with-disabilities-and-violence/.

164 "After a 'Decade of Decline' in Health Care, Canadians not Convinced that Money Is Enough to Solve the Crisis," Angus Reid Institute, 17 August 2023, https://angusreid.org/cma-health-care-access-priorities-2023/.

165 Pierre Burton, "Huronia: Pierre Berton Warned Us 50 Years Ago," Remember Every Name, 12 September 2023, https://www.remembereveryname.ca/huronia-pierre-berton-warned-us-50-years-ago.

9

Indigenous Peoples and MAiD

Hon. Graydon Nicholas

Bill C-7, which expanded medical assistance in dying (MAiD) legislation, removed most of the MAiD safeguards enacted just five years prior and expanded eligibility to those whose death is not foreseeable but who live with chronic illness, disability, and, in future, mental illness. As well, the government enacted a Special Joint Parliamentary Review Committee to immediately study additional expansions to MAiD, such as including mature minors and allowing advance requests, among other issues.[1]

Bill C-7 has no legal stipulation that standard of care treatments be provided to patients before accessing MAiD. This despite the fact that most patients who qualify for MAiD under Bill C-7 will recover their will to live if they can receive good medical care (as discussed in other chapters). Since MAiD is legislated on a federal level, it will be delivered in a sweeping manner across the whole country to all Canadians who qualify – including Indigenous communities.[2]

The United Nations Declaration on the Rights of Indigenous Peoples, along with other international documents, and the Canadian Truth and Reconciliation Commission's report of 2015 outline Indigenous peoples' beliefs about health. These beliefs incorporate spiritual, intellectual, emotional, and physical dimensions as well as sustainable environmental stewardship. Importantly, these documents emphasize that Indigenous peoples have a right to self-governance and self-determination in regard to their own health care delivery.[3]

As is their right, many Indigenous leaders, Elders, and healers have therefore expressed grave concern to the Canadian government and medical regulators regarding Bill C-7 and MAiD, which will affect their communities.

> As Indigenous people in Canada, we have grave concerns over the implications of Bill C-7 on our communities... Not only has the consultation of Bill C-7 with our leaders been inadequate, it has not taken into account the existing health disparities and social inequalities we face compared to non-Indigenous people. As sovereign nations in Canada, we have a right in determining how health services will be delivered in our communities, and the Government of Canada has a responsibility to respect this relationship... Given our history with the negative consequences of colonialism and the involuntary imposition of cultural values and ideas, we believe that people should not be compelled to provide or facilitate in the provision of MAID. Furthermore, our population is vulnerable to discrimination and coercion in the healthcare system, and should be protected against unsolicited counsel regarding MAID.[4]

Indigenous communities are struggling with high suicide rates. In the last Canadian census report published in 2019, the rate of suicide among First Nations people was three times higher than the rate among non-Indigenous people, and twice as high on reserves compared to those First Nations people not living on reserves. The rate among Métis was twice as high as the suicide rate of non-Indigenous people, and the suicide rate was nine times higher among the Inuit than the non-Indigenous.[5]

The Canadian Association of Suicide Prevention (CASP) has written in regard to the expansion of MAID, "It is important to be perfectly clear that when considering MAID in the context of someone who is not dying as a result of their particular condition, we are talking about suicide. By the very definition of suicide, i.e., the act of killing oneself, if the condition from which they are suffering is not killing them then the act of providing MAID is doctor assisted suicide."[6] Bill C-7 and the expansion of MAiD outside the end-of-life context now offers doctor-assisted suicide and euthanasia to communities already struggling with high rates of suicide.

LEGISLATION OF BILL C-7: INADEQUATE INDIGENOUS CONSULTATION

In February 2020, justice minister David Lametti and his parliamentary secretary, Arif Virani, held round table discussions on MAiD with various stakeholders. During a round table that explored

Indigenous perspectives, Indigenous individuals and practitioners expressed concerns about the pervasive history of generational trauma and spoke of the harmful experiences that Indigenous peoples have faced within the health care system, including procedures done on them against their will. Moreover, limited access to health care resources and discriminatory treatments within the health care system were cited as current barriers to physical and mental wellness. There were serious concerns over MAiD being expanded outside the end-of-life period within Indigenous communities. Some were worried that Indigenous patients may choose MAiD because they do not have access to adequate health care and resources, while some highlighted the differences in how Indigenous peoples view death and dying. They emphasized a need for guidance from Elders and spiritual leaders in these matters. Overall, the consensus amongst the Indigenous leaders present was that Indigenous consultation on MAiD had been inadequate.[7]

Neil Belanger, executive director of the British Columbia Aboriginal Network on Disability Society, commented about the round table:

> I was in Ottawa with both my colleagues here – it was an Indigenous-focused meeting. At that meeting, there was quite a lengthy list of people and organizations who were invited, but in all reality, very limited participation. I would be confident in saying that I don't believe the Government of Canada has reached out to Inuit peoples, to Métis or to First Nations in a substantive way on MAID or Bill C-14 or Bill C-7… I don't believe there has been any engagement in a proper way. Furthermore, there were no Indigenous stakeholders invited to the House Justice committee hearings on Bill C-7 despite requests from Indigenous leaders to attend.

Mr Belanger also explained this: "Where is the voice of the Indigenous peoples of Canada in Bill C-7 and their membership living with disabilities? It wasn't at the Justice Committee. Our organization asked to present, but we were declined."[8]

Member of Parliament Chris Lewis, one of the House Justice committee members, pointed out the blatant lack of Indigenous consultation. Mr Lewis asked for another session to consider input from Indigenous stakeholders, but the Liberals, NDP, and Bloc voted against his motion.[9]

At the level of the Senate, there was minimal Indigenous representation. Scott Robertson, a Mohawk from Six Nations of the Grand River, represented the Indigenous Bar Association. During his testimony on 2 February 2021, he shared: "Health care providers who work within Indigenous communities need to be consulted to ensure MAiD is implemented and administered in a respectful and culturally appropriate manner. Failing to do so may lead to further harm and racism towards Indigenous peoples. There is much work to be done by this committee in order to reconcile this law with Indigenous people's perspectives and interests. It remains to be seen how this will be accomplished within the time frame set out by Parliament."[10] Despite Mr Robertson's warning that was echoed by many other Indigenous leaders, Parliament pushed through legislation expanding MAiD in March 2021.

A brief discussion of the effects of colonialism and racism on Indigenous populations, current conditions on reserves, as well as the lack of political action to rectify the deep-rooted injustices will be helpful to understand the concern about MAiD expansion outside the end-of-life context. It is necessary to state that the pages below provide only a cursory examination of what is a deeply complex and nuanced subject.

INDIGENOUS SUICIDE RATES AND GOVERNMENT INACTION

Stories from Indigenous communities and gathered evidence from historians suggest that before colonialization, suicide rates of Indigenous persons were low. Many knowledge-keepers and historians recount that suicide was foreign to their communities prior to colonialization.[11]

This is clearly no longer the case. The tragedy of each suicide and the suicide epidemic among Indigenous communities is an ongoing public health crisis in Canada. Many traditional healers who work across Canada on reserves can attest to the contagion of suicide in families and among teenagers. Suicide deaths are often clustered in time, with one suicide triggering additional tragedies in the days to come.[12]

Mary is from an Ontario First Nations community.[13] Mary's family has suffered much. Growing up, the family endured her father frequently beating her mother and her siblings. Several of her family members committed suicide, all by hanging themselves in the span of a few weeks. The suffering was overwhelming for her, and one year later she also tried to take her life, except that a neighbour happened to drop in and helped by staying with her for many hours. The community rallied to support her until she recovered. These events took place many years ago, but Mary states that her life is marked by this loss, and she devotes her time to teaching the younger members on her reserve that suicide is not a solution to their problems.

In the midst of a vast suicide crisis, one would expect immediate attention from the government and an urgent remedy. Notwithstanding multiple government commitments to act and several Canadian reports undertaken to create a strategy for action, very little has actually been done in terms of providing the funding and resources needed for change in these communities. Some Indigenous leaders have pointed out that the lack of government funding is in itself a form of systemic racism.[14]

The Indigenous suicide epidemic is a tragedy that the government contributes to by their lack of effective action. This inaction allows the cycle of desperation to perpetuate and is in itself a social injustice in the history of Indigenous peoples.

ORIGINS OF SOCIAL INJUSTICES THAT INDIGENOUS PEOPLES FACE: COLONIALISM, COERCED STERILIZATION, RESIDENTIAL SCHOOLS, AND MISSING PERSONS

Colonialism and the losses that followed play a major part in the suffering of Indigenous peoples across the entire globe.[15] The Indigenous people of Canada have endured the loss of their land and their way of life when they were moved onto reserves. The imposition of new cultural values has led to a loss of identity and the demoralization of their communities. All these are crucial aspects of Canada's history.

Law and policies since colonialism have also not favoured Indigenous people. There was formal legislation in Alberta and British Columbia that led to thousands of Indigenous women and girls being sterilized, either through coercion or without their knowledge, while they were delivering their babies in hospitals and therefore vulnerable. Similar practices, without legislative support, were present across Canada up until the 1970s and even more recently.[16]

In 2018 the United Nations Committee Against Torture acknowledged that "forced or coerced sterilization of Indigenous women and girls dating back to the 1970s and including recent cases" in

Canada is a form of torture. Canada has yet to apologize or respond to these statements.[17]

As well, from the 1880s right up until the 1990s, many Indigenous children were separated from their parents and sent to residential schools where they were disconnected from their families, community traditions, language, and values.[18]

Jonah is from an Alberta First Nation and shared his story.[19] Jonah was sent to a residential school and separated from his family at a very young age. He has many traumatizing memories, but the worst involve sexual abuse that was repeated over many years. When Jonah returned home, he reunited with his siblings, and they formed a circle of support to help each other reintegrate into society. After some time, Jonah's sister died by suicide, giving no warning and leaving many unanswered questions. Jonah himself had a seemingly happy and stable life. He supported his wife and children. But he admits that because he had a gun in his possession, he came very close to killing himself at four different times during his adult life. He would sit in his car with his gun, contemplating escape. These desires for death intensified when there was community news of sexual abuse that involved minors. The trauma and aftermath of the residential schools still haunt most Indigenous families, and Jonah's story is one of many.

The Kamloops Indian Residential School, which operated between 1890 and 1969, was once the largest Canadian residential school. In May 2021, 215 First Nations bodies were found buried on its grounds.[20] These unmarked graves were located using special radars. More graves of children have been found since, in other residential school grounds.[21] Even with this discovery, those children's identities will forever be erased for posterity.

Such examples of historical disregard for Indigenous people only adds insult to injury in the Indigenous community. Those who had believed their family members had run away are now re-traumatized in learning of their loved ones' true fate.

Grand Chief Stewart Phillip, president of the Union of British Columbia Indian Chiefs, lamented: "This is the reality of the genocide that was, and is, inflicted upon us as Indigenous peoples by the colonial state. Today we honour the lives of those children, and hold prayers that they, and their families, may finally be at peace."[22]

The Truth and Reconciliation Commission report in 2015 estimated that 3,200 Indigenous children died from abuse or neglect while attending Canadian institutions. The report called on the federal government to fund Indigenous healing centres to address the physical, mental, emotional, and spiritual harms caused by the legacy of the residential schools.[23]

And the 2014 Royal Canadian Mounted Police report on missing and murdered Indigenous women (MMIW) noted more than 1,200 victims spanning from 1980 to 2012.[24] However, Indigenous groups report the true number to be closer to 4,000.[25] The National Inquiry into MMIW, which concluded in 2019, found that the legacy of missing and murdered Indigenous females amounted to race-based genocide.[26]

POVERTY, UNEMPLOYMENT, FOOD SCARCITY, CONTAMINATED WATER, AND CRAMPED LIVING CONDITIONS

Indigenous peoples also suffer from many negative social determinants of health. In Canada, they experience the highest levels of poverty, with 25 per cent overall and 40 per cent of Indigenous children living in poverty.[27] Besides poverty, many of those living on reserves struggle with unemployment, cramped living quarters, food scarcity, and inadequate drinking water. The levels of crime and drug abuse are also much higher than national averages.[28]

Canada is gifted with one of the world's largest freshwater supplies in the world. Despite this, Indigenous communities often have boil-water advisories and warnings of contaminated water supplies. As an example, Lytton First Nation has been under a boil-water advisory for over twenty years. "You would have flu-like symptoms and have diarrhea and vomiting from drinking the water [without boiling]," says one resident.[29]

The Six Nations of the Grand River Indigenous reserve in Ontario had been without access to running water for many years. In 2018, there was excitement about a project to get potable water to its residents. Chief Ava Hill stated at that time, "In early 2018, only nine per cent of Six Nations residents, the most populated First Nation in Canada, had access to safe, treated potable water from our water treatment plant… I am very happy to state that since that time we have secured enough funds to more than triple our water distribution coverage. This means that approximately 4,000 of our Six Nations residents will have access to a safe and reliable water source."[30]

And yet in 2021, 89 per cent of its residents still did not have access to clean water because there was no money to operate their "state-of-the-art" water treatment plant. Meanwhile, Nestlé has been able to extract millions of litres of water from Six Nations treaty land daily.[31]

Similarly, many Indigenous communities are still struggling with the same lack of access to water due to inadequate funding. In May 2021, Indigenous services minister Marc Miller said that his department was working hard to keep Prime Minister Justin Trudeau's word to end all boil-water advisories on Indigenous territory.[32] At the time of this writing, this issue has not been rectified across Canada.[33]

In a 2021 national news broadcast covering the effects of COVID-19 on Indigenous peoples, Minister Marc Miller also admitted that securing a reliable, affordable supply of food is always a challenge in remote areas during the winter months for Indigenous communities, and that it will be even harder this year due to COVID-19.[34]

How can such basic needs remain unaddressed year after year?

Mumilaaq Qaqqaq was elected at the age of twenty-five as the member of Parliament for Nunavut in 2019.[35] She decided to tour her riding to see first-hand the living conditions of her constituents. She was traumatized by witnessing the inequalities of her constituents and experienced "extreme burnout, anxiety and depression." "I couldn't begin to fathom how many Inuit were clearly struggling, so obviously struggling, and it seemed like the rest of the country was relatively OK with this ... Inuit continue to die due to a lack of basic human rights, due to a lack of safe spaces and affordable food," she said. "While families in Ottawa and Toronto are told to stay home, wash their hands, and stay physically distanced, Nunavummiut are packed inside overcrowded and mouldy homes that are falling apart. How can they stay in their homes when their houses are full of mould, they live with 14 other people in a four-bedroom, and their house is full of broken pipes?"[36]

In 2021, she announced she would not be seeking re-election and characterized Canada as a country that was "created off the backs, trauma and displacement of Indigenous People."[37]

RACISM AND DISCRIMINATION IN ACCESSING HEALTH CARE

Indigenous people continue to face racism even in seeking basic health care. In June 2020, British Columbia's minister of health requested that a report be conducted to review Indigenous-specific racism in the provincial health care system. In that recent British

Columbia report, *In Plain Sight*, Mary Ellen Turpel-Lafond found that "84 per cent of Indigenous peoples described personal experiences of racism and discrimination that discouraged them from seeking necessary care and that reduced access to care, negatively affecting their health."[38]

The British Columbia health minister further shared that health care workers were involved in "a game that was being played to investigate the blood alcohol level of patients in the emergency rooms, in particular with Indigenous people... [;] if true, it is intolerable and racist and of course [has] affected profoundly patient care."[39]

Incidents like this occur across the country. Another tragic story that played out in southwestern Quebec is that of Joyce Echaquan, a thirty-seven-year-old Atikamekw Nation mother of seven. She died while being mistreated and prematurely and she streamed the hospital staff racially abusing her on Facebook Live as she was dying. The hospital staff told Echaquan she was stupid, only good for sex, and that she would be better off dead.[40] This led to Atikamekw Nation submitting a brief to the Government of Canada, entitled "Joyce's Principles." The brief laments the lack of enforcement of previous commitments to Indigenous persons on the part of the Canadian government and calls for real action.[41]

CONSEQUENCES OF MULTIPLE INEQUALITIES

Colonialism, residential schools, coerced sterilization, systemic racism, and social inequality coupled with a disruption of language, culture, and values have negatively impacted the lives of Indigenous peoples. These external assaults have led to increased addictions and emotional and collective struggles in these communities, and that in turn has exposed many children of these communities to adverse childhood experiences and family instability.[42]

Common childhood experiences include living through emotional or sexual abuse; domestic violence; witnessing someone they love struggle with substance abuse or criminal behaviours; and grieving after family members or friends commit suicide. There are also higher rates of foster care and disrupted family life. As these children grow up, these exposures contribute to hopelessness, addiction, and suicidal behaviour, and so the cycle of violence continues intergenerationally.

With this understanding of social inequality and intergenerational trauma, it is understandable that suicide rates in some Indigenous communities are substantially higher than the national Canadian average – in some areas, the leading cause of death among those under eighteen in Indigenous populations is suicide.[43]

Indigenous people live with higher levels of cancer, chronic illness, mental illness, and disability – all directly related to the many negative social determinants of health that have been thrust upon them.[44] Because Indigenous persons face racism in seeking health care and are often funded for treatments that are not rooted in their own values and beliefs, they often have suboptimal clinical outcomes, which delays and stifles their healing. The Inuit, Métis, and First Nations have a life expectancy that is ten to fifteen years less than non-Indigenous Canadians.[45]

INDIGENOUS COMMUNITIES AND MAiD

Indigenous peoples of Canada are systematically disadvantaged and neglected. Providing access to a lethal injection, a decidedly Western solution to the problem of pain, risks exploiting rather than helping them.

The relationship between the history of intergenerational trauma, a lack of resources, and high levels of physical and mental illness, coupled with a suicide crisis, are afflicting Indigenous peoples. Combined with the government's idleness in implementing the calls to action by the Truth and Reconciliation Commission, how will ushering in MAiD factor into all this? Dr Rod McCormick, a Mohawk psychotherapist, has many years of clinical experience with Indigenous peoples. He shared:

> A few common messages emerged from those who recovered from being suicidal. The first was that youth shared how their thinking was very distorted when they were suicidal. Other distorted beliefs were that there was no hope of helping with their suffering and no chance of ending the pain. They believed life wasn't worth living and that others wouldn't care if they killed themselves.
>
> In recovery, they realized how inaccurate these beliefs were. In hindsight, they shared the message that they thought suicide was a permanent solution to a temporary problem. The message that MAID presents to those who are suffering is that when the suffering becomes more than they can tolerate, they can have medical professionals end their lives for them. This message undermines the whole concept of suicide prevention.

> The proposed change [Bill C-7] would mean that the act should more aptly be called medical assistance for dying versus medical assistance in dying ... From an Indigenous perspective, it seems ironic to discuss these new opportunities to die when we are second class citizens in Canada with regard to medical assistance in living ...
>
> Our friends and family die of preventable diseases. We watch many prematurely end their lives and experience death in custody, in the care of social services and the justice system. Our people die of complex and higher rates of disease than the general population. So, when we're already overrepresented at every stage of this health system, it seems ironic to provide yet another path to death.
>
> Lastly, in terms of disabilities, roughly one third of Indigenous peoples in Canada have a disability that limits them in their daily activities, and about 40% of those have a severe or very severe disability. Bill C-7 seems to open the door to anyone with disabilities to seek MAID. This is not going to make things any better for our people given the high rates of disabilities.
>
> Given our history with coerced sterilizations and other strategies for cultural genocide, it is understandable that Indigenous peoples would be distrustful of this proposed bill.[46]

Dr Lisa Richardson is mixed Anishinaabe Kwe. She is the strategic lead for the Centre for Wise Practices in Indigenous Health at Women's College Hospital. She states:

> I express my concerns about expanding MAID to include people whose natural death is not reasonably foreseeable. Why is this? This is because Indigenous peoples are not secure in our health system. Racism exists in health care.
>
> In an environment where both systemic and interpersonal racism exists, I don't trust that Indigenous people will be safe. I don't trust that anti-Indigenous prejudice and bias will not affect the decision making and counselling about MAID for Indigenous people, no matter how much education is given.
>
> In my opinion, a bill that does not actually take into account how social inequities disproportionately affect Indigenous peoples is highly problematic.
>
> Any legislation related to health care that involves Indigenous peoples must be done in partnership with us. This is in

accordance with our Indigenous rights, as well as the United Nations Declaration on the Rights of Indigenous Peoples. There is a need for more meaningful partnership and input from Indigenous peoples – First Nations, Inuit, Métis of different backgrounds and different traditional territories. There is a huge diversity amongst us in terms of our belief systems and our approaches. Unless adequate consultation is done, we are not upholding the right to respect the needs of Indigenous peoples.[47]

And François Paulette, an Elder and a chair of Yellowknife Stanton Territorial Health Authority Elders' Advisory Council, shared:

In this world view of the Dene, there is no description or word for "medical assistance in dying" or suicide ... Today, suicide runs rampant in our communities. It's become like a way of life. As I said, we have no word for suicide. It's totally against the spiritual laws of how we live.

I look at this Bill C-7 as not belonging to us. I know that Western people, the way they do business, is quite different, very different. I am asked now in the late stages to amend this act. I should have been asked right from the beginning. You should have had Indigenous people sitting down with government people and designing this legislation.

... if you're going to proceed with this law, you should carefully design it where First Nations who want to opt out of it stay out of it by default of their own laws and their own rules that have been given to them for thousands of years. Do not think that everyone is assimilated so we will be part of this change.

I know that Bill C-7 to amend the Criminal Code (medical assistance in dying) for our people is out of touch with our involvement in this process. That goes with any other legislation that comes along by the Government of Canada.[48]

Indigenous consultation was insufficient and inadequate in regard to the legalization and expansion of MAiD. Even the Government of Canada's Expert Panel on MAiD and Mental Illness admitted this in its document.[49] Of those who testified in the Senate and in more recent hearings, all Elders and leaders expressed concerns about MAiD expansion.[50]

CONCLUSION

Indigenous communities, which have a diversity of languages and customs, values, belief systems, and sacred teachings, should have culturally based solutions while also drawing on evidence-based suicide prevention frameworks to help their communities and members heal.

Despite multiple government commissions and working groups to create plans and recommendations for change, very little has been done in terms of providing the actual funding and resources for these communities. Funding is key to successfully running comprehensive suicide prevention and programs promoting community life.

The expansion of MAiD will work to contradict the efforts that are currently being made to prevent suicide among First Nations, Metis, and Inuit peoples. It will be introduced in the context of health care practice that is already often characterized by discrimination and by pervasive biases against and stereotypes about Indigenous people. MAiD is arguably the worst kind of aid to provide to Indigenous communities, which are unanimously calling for helpful solutions not to die, but to live well.

NOTES

1 *Bill C-7, An Act to Amend the Criminal Code (medical assistance in dying)*, 43rd Parliament, 2nd Session (2021), SC 2021, c. 2 (Can.), https://parl.ca/DocumentViewer/en/43-2/bill/C-7/royal-assent.
2 Trudo Lemmens, Mary Shariff, and Leonie Herx, "How Bill C-7 Will Sacrifice the Medical Profession's Standard of Care," *Policy Options*, 11 February 2021, https://policyoptions.irpp.org/magazines/february-2021/how-bill-c7-will-sacrifice-the-medical-professions-standard-of-care/.
3 Truth and Reconciliation Commission of Canada, *Final Report of the Truth and Reconciliation Commission of Canada*, July 2015, https://web.archive.org/web/20200513112354/https://trc.ca/index-main.html.
4 "Indigenous Peoples Should Not Be Compelled to Provide or Facilitate Medical Assistance in Dying," CPSO Consultation, February 2021, https://policyconsult.cpso.on.ca/wp-content/uploads/2021/05/Indigenous-Peoples-Should-Not-Be-Compelled-to-Provide-or-Facilitate-MAiD_Redacted.pdf.
5 "Suicide Prevention Framework," Government of Canada, November 2016, https://www.canada.ca/en/public-health/services/publications/healthy-living/suicide-prevention-framework.html.

6 Sean Krausert to Canadian Psychiatric Association, "Re: CPA's Discussion Paper on Medical Assistance in Dying," Canadian Association for Suicide Prevention, 20 November 2021, https://static1.squarespace.com/static/5ec97e1c4215f5026a6741l6/t/619bc64ac482815740760931/1637598795070/Letter+to+CPA+re+Discussion+Paper+on+MAiD+%282021+11+20%29.pdf.

7 "What We Heard Report: A Public Consultation on Medical Assistance in Dying (MAID)," Government of Canada, March 2020, https://www.justice.gc.ca/eng/cj-jp/ad-am/wwh-cqnae/access/p3.html.

8 *Meeting of the Standing Senate Committee on Legal and Constitutional Affairs*, 43rd Parliament, 2nd Session (2 November 2020), https://sencanada.ca/en/Content/Sen/Committee/432/LCJC/o5ev-55075-e.

9 *Meeting of the Standing Committee on Justice and Human Rights*, 43rd Parliament, 2nd Session (12 November 2020), https://www.ourcommons.ca/DocumentViewer/en/43-2/JUST/meeting-7/evidence.

10 *Meeting of the Standing Senate Committee on Legal and Constitutional Affairs*, 43rd Parliament, 2nd Session (2 February 2021), https://sencanada.ca/en/Content/Sen/Committee/432/LCJC/11ev-55129-e.

11 Laurence J. Kirmayer et al., *Suicide Among Aboriginal People in Canada* (Ottawa: Aboriginal Healing Foundation, 2007).

12 "Indigenous Suicide Prevention Resources," Centre of Suicide Prevention, 2020, https://www.suicideinfo.ca/indigenous/.

13 Name and identifying details changed to preserve anonymity.

14 Federation of Sovereign Indigenous Nations, *Saskatchewan First Nations Suicide Prevention Strategy*, 24 May 2018, https://www.suicideinfo.ca/wp-content/uploads/gravity_forms/6-191a85f36ce9e20de2e2fa3869197735/2018/07/Saskatchewan-First-Nations-Suicide-Prevention-Strategy_oa.pdf.

15 United Nations, *State of the World's Indigenous Peoples* (New York: United Nations, 2009), https://www.un.org/esa/socdev/unpfii/documents/SOWIP/en/SOWIP_web.pdf.

16 Penny Smoke, "UN Committee Recommends Canada Criminalize Involuntary Sterilization," CBC, 7 December 2018, https://www.cbc.ca/news/indigenous/un-committee-involuntary-sterilization-1.4936879.

17 Alisa Lombard and Samir Shaheen-Hussein, "Coerced and Forced Sterilization of Indigenous Women and Girls: This Is What Genocide Looks Like in Canada," *Toronto Star*, 9 March 2021, https://www.thestar.com/opinion/contributors/2021/03/08/coerced-and-forced-stereilization-of-indigenous-women-and-girls-this-is-what-genocide-looks-like-in-canada.html.

18 "Residential Schools in Canada," *The Canadian Encyclopedia*, last modified June 2022, https://www.thecanadianencyclopedia.ca/en/article/residential-schools.

19 Name and identifying details changed to preserve anonymity.

20 Tristin Hopper, "Why So Many Children Died at Indian Residential Schools," *National Post*, 29 May 2021, https://nationalpost.com/news/canada/newly-discovered-b-c-graves-a-grim-reminder-of-the-heartbreaking-death-toll-of-residential-schools.

21 Sarah Grochowski, "104 'Potential Graves' Detected at Site of Former Residential School in Manitoba," *Abbotsford News*, 12 June 2021, https://www.abbynews.com/news/104-potential-graves-detected-at-site-of-former-residential-school-in-manitoba/.

22 Regan Hasegawa, "'This Is the Reality of the Genocide That Was,' B.C. Chief Says of Discovery of Remains at Residential School Site," CTV, 28 May 2021, https://bc.ctvnews.ca/this-is-the-reality-of-the-genocide-that-was-b-c-chief-says-of-discovery-of-remains-at-residential-school-site-1.5447116.

23 Truth and Reconciliation Commission of Canada, *Final Report*.

24 "Missing and Murdered Aboriginal Women: A National Operational Overview," Royal Canadian Mounted Police, last modified 27 May 2014, https://www.rcmp-grc.gc.ca/en/missing-and-murdered-aboriginal-women-national-operational-overview.

25 "Missing and Murdered Indigenous Women and Girls in Canada," *The Canadian Encyclopedia*, last modified 8 July 2020, https://www.thecanadianencyclopedia.ca/en/article/missing-and-murdered-indigenous-women-and-girls-in-canada.

26 National Inquiry into Missing and Murdered Indigenous Women and Girls, *Reclaiming Power and Place: The Final Report of the National Inquiry into Missing and Murdered Indigenous Women and Girls*, 2019, https://www.mmiwg-ffada.ca/final-report/.

27 "Poverty in Canada," Canadian Poverty Institute, 2022, https://www.povertyinstitute.ca/poverty-canada.

28 Department of Justice, "Indigenous Overrepresentation in the Criminal Justice System," Government of Canada, May 2019, https://www.justice.gc.ca/eng/rp-pr/jr/jf-pf/2019/may01.html.

29 "Canada's Water Crisis: A Fight for Safe Water in Lytton First Nation," BBC News, accessed 6 December 2022, https://globalreportingcentre.org/lytton-water/.

30 Simran Chatta, "Mississaugas of the Credit and Six Nations of the Grand River Launch Watermain Project," *Water Canada*, 12 August 2019,

https://www.watercanada.net/mississaugas-of-the-credit-and-six-nations-of-the-grand-river-launch-watermain-project/.

31 Alexandro Shimo, "While Nestlé Extracts Millions of Litres from Their Land, Residents Have No Drinking Water," *Guardian*, 4 October 2018, https://www.theguardian.com/global/2018/oct/04/ontario-six-nations-nestle-running-water.

32 Rachel Aiello, "Feds Break Promise to Eliminate All Drinking Water Advisories in 2021, Vow Work Will Continue," CTV, 2 December 2020, https://www.ctvnews.ca/politics/feds-break-promise-to-eliminate-all-drinking-water-advisories-in-2021-vow-work-will-continue-1.5213658.

33 Indigenous Services Canada, "Ending Long-Term Drinking Water Advisories," Government of Canada, May 2022, https://www.sac-isc.gc.ca/eng/1506514143353/1533317130660.

34 Maan Alhmidi, "Feds Detail $100 Million Pledged to Fight Food Insecurity during COVID-19 Pandemic," *National Post*, 18 December 2020, https://nationalpost.com/pmn/news-pmn/canada-news-pmn/feds-detail-100-million-pledged-to-fight-food-insecurity-during-covid-19-pandemic.

35 Zi-Ann Lum, "NDP MP Mumilaaq Qaqqaq Says 'Extreme' Burnout Was a Reason for Leave of Absence," *HuffPost*, 5 January 2021, https://www.huffingtonpost.ca/entry/mumilaaq-qaqqaq-mpburnout_ca_5ff492b7c5b61817a53a1217.

36 Mélanie Ritchot, "Nunavut MP Calls Federal Housing Funding 'Laughable,'" *Nunatsiaq News*, 14 May 2021, https://nunatsiaq.com/stories/article/nunavut-mp-calls-federal-housing-funding-laughable/.

37 Sheena Goodyear, "Nunavut MP Mumilaaq Qaqqaq on Leaving Politics, and Why She Feels No Pride in Canada," CBC Radio, 16 June 2021, https://www.cbc.ca/radio/asithappens/as-it-happens-the-wednesday-edition-1.6067864/nunavut-mp-mumilaaq-qaqqaq-on-leaving-politics-and-why-she-feels-no-pride-in-canada-1.6068158.

38 "'In Plain Sight' Report: Systemic Racism in B.C. Healthcare," School of Population and Public Health, University of British Columbia, 18 December 2020, https://spph.ubc.ca/in-plain-sight/, citing Government of British Columbia, *In Plain Sight – Addressing Racism Review Summary Report*, November 2020, https://engage.gov.bc.ca/app/uploads/sites/613/2020/11/In-Plain-Sight-Summary-Report.pdf.

39 Rhianna Schmunk, "B.C. Investigating Allegations ER Staff Played 'Game' to Guess Blood-Alcohol Level of Indigenous Patients," CBC, 19 June 2020, https://www.cbc.ca/news/canada/british-columbia/racism-in-bc-healthcare-health-minister-adrian-dix-1.5619245.

40 Mélissa Godin, "She Was Racially Abused by Hospital Staff as She Lay Dying. Now a Canadian Indigenous Woman's Death Is Forcing a Reckoning on Racism," *Time Magazine*, 9 October 2020, https://time.com/5898422/joyce-echaquan-indigenous-protests-canada/.

41 Council of the Atikamekw of Manawan, "Joyce's Principle," November 2020, https://principedejoyce.com/sn_uploads/principe/Joyce_s_Principle_brief___Eng.pdf.

42 Federation of Sovereign Indigenous Nations, *Saskatchewan First Nations Suicide Prevention Strategy*.

43 Ibid.

44 Paul J. Kim, "Social Determinants of Health Inequities in Indigenous Canadians Through a Life Course Approach to Colonialism and the Residential School System," *Health Equity* 3, no. 1 (25 July 2019): 378–81, https://www.ncbi.nlm.nih.gov/pmc/articles/PMC6657289/.

45 "Life Expectancy of First Nations, Métis, and Inuit Household Populations in Canada," Statistics Canada, 18 December 2019, https://www150.statcan.gc.ca/n1/pub/82-003-x/2019012/article/00001-eng.htm.

46 *Meeting of the Standing Senate Committee* (2 February 2021).

47 *Meeting of the Standing Senate Committee on Legal and Constitutional Affairs*, 43rd Parliament, 2nd Session (3 February 2021), https://sencanada.ca/en/Content/Sen/Committee/432/LCJC/55130-e.

48 *Meeting of the Standing Senate Committee* (2 February 2021).

49 Health Canada, *Final Report of the Expert Panel on MAID and Mental Illness*, 13 May 2022, https://www.canada.ca/en/health-canada/news/2022/05/final-report-of-the-expert-panel-on-maid-and-mental-illness.html.

50 "Testimony of Neil Belanger, Indigenous Disability Canada," in *Meeting of the Special Joint Committee on Medical Assistance in Dying*, 44th Parliament, 1st Session (4 November 2022), https://parl.ca/DocumentViewer/en/44-1/AMAD/meeting-25/evidence.

10

Ableism in Canada: Why Track 2 MAiD Violates the *Canadian Charter of Rights and Freedoms*

Isabel Grant

Early in 2022 a thirty-one-year-old woman in Ontario (using the pseudonym "Denise") was approved for a medically assisted death.[1] Denise, who uses a wheelchair due to a spinal cord injury, was diagnosed with multiple chemical sensitivity (MCS), which causes rashes, difficulty breathing, and severe headaches.[2] Denise applied for medical assistance to die in part because she could not tolerate her smoke- and chemical-filled apartment and could not afford accessible housing on the monthly $1,169 she received from the Ontario Disability Support Program. In response to media coverage, disability organizations and private citizens rallied to raise enough money to keep Denise alive in the short term. Denise was able to move to a hotel temporarily to continue her search for appropriate housing.[3] "Sophia," who was diagnosed with MCS and had spent years searching and pleading with all levels of government for safe housing, had received a medically assisted death only months earlier. In a video Sophia made eight days before her death, she stated: "the government sees me as expendable trash, a complainer, useless, and a pain in the ass."[4]

This chapter examines how medical assistance in dying (MAiD) has been transformed into a solution for the suffering of people like Denise and Sophia, who have disabilities but are not at the end of their lives. This chapter challenges the argument that Denise and Sophia were simply exercising their individual autonomy in seeking MAiD. Rather, I suggest that the state offering death as a solution to the suffering of disability for those not at the end of life is inherently ableist and based on the discriminatory premise that disability can be worse than death and, therefore, that death is a benefit for this group of Canadians. This is not to deny that some people with disabilities support MAiD, and of course that disabled individuals were the face of court challenges leading to expanded MAiD. I take no position on the difficult decision made by any individual to die through MAiD. Rather, I argue that the state, through the medical profession, should not participate in ending the lives of people who are not otherwise dying.

In 2021, the federal government expanded MAiD to provide medically assisted deaths for people who are not facing death but are suffering intolerably from an irremediable medical condition or disability and are in an advanced state of decline.[5] This legislative process took place at the height of a global pandemic, which had taken a particularly harsh toll on people with disabilities.[6] Thousands of disabled Canadians died during the pandemic due to the inadequacies of long-term care, while others were left neglected and uncared for.[7] Some even accessed MAiD to escape the misery of lockdown in long-term care.[8] People with intellectual disabilities were more likely to die of COVID-19 yet were not consistently prioritized for vaccines unless they were immunocompromised or institutionalized.[9] COVID-19 triage protocols did not just consider whether patients would survive the acute illness but rather whether mortality overall was impacted, which clearly had a disproportionate impact on people with disabilities.[10] Mask mandates were dropped before it was safe for those with "pre-existing conditions," forcing many people with disabilities into further social isolation in order to survive the ongoing pandemic. Government benefits were provided least and last to those with disabilities living in poverty.[11] A long-promised federal disability support program was repeatedly delayed by the Trudeau government.[12] Most recently, Ontario passed Bill 7 that allows hospitalized patients to be sent to long-term care facilities without their consent, sometimes far from family members, under the threat of daily fees if they refuse.[13] These realities for people with disabilities highlight their social inequality in Canada and provide a context for understanding why MAiD is an existential threat to disabled lives.

As has been discussed elsewhere in this book, in *Carter v. Canada* the Supreme Court reversed its earlier decision in *Rodriguez v. British Columbia (Attorney General)* and held that the absolute prohibition on aiding suicide violated the *Canadian Charter of Rights and*

Freedoms.[14] *Carter* precipitated Bill C-14, which introduced Canada's first MAiD regime and became law in 2016 and was limited to people whose natural deaths were reasonably foreseeable.[15] In 2019, the Superior Court of Quebec's decision in *Truchon v. Canada* prompted a significant expansion of the initial MAiD regime, enacted through Bill C-7 in 2021, by striking down the requirements that natural death be reasonably foreseeable.[16]

This chapter explores why this legislation has raised such profound concerns among disability organizations and activists, many of whom have denounced this expansion of MAiD. The first part of this chapter sets out the context of systemic ableism in Canada as a lens through which track 2 MAiD must be assessed. The second part turns to an argument that track 2 MAiD in fact violates both section 7 and section 15 of the *Charter*, the very sections that were used to bring about the decisions in *Carter* and *Truchon*. Track 2 devalues and endangers disabled lives by making suicide more readily available than the social supports people need to alleviate their intolerable suffering. Track 2 MAiD unduly medicalizes the suffering associated with disability, portrays death as a form of medical treatment, and ignores the social and political contributors to suffering. The fact that a medical condition is irremediable does not necessarily mean that intolerable suffering cannot be alleviated.

Through Bill C-7, the government has abdicated its responsibility to respond to that suffering through means other than helping people die.[17] Many Canadians with disabilities are suffering intolerably, and much of that suffering could be at least reduced through government action such as, for example, accessible housing, home care, decreased reliance on institutional care, and improved financial support. To suggest that the state, through the medical profession, has an obligation to provide access to death but no obligation to make life tolerable for a *Charter*-protected group positions MAiD as a cheaper and quicker escape route rather than as true equality.

THE LEGISLATIVE SCHEME

Bill C-7 repealed the reasonable foreseeability of death requirement from the 2016 MAiD laws and set up what are now referred to colloquially as two tracks to access MAiD. Track 1 applies to those for whom natural death is reasonably foreseeable, and track 2 applies to those who are not at the end of their natural lives. Track 2 has a few additional safeguards, including a ninety-day period between the first assessment and the provision of MAiD. Bill C-7 originally denied MAiD on the sole basis of mental illness but, following a Senate amendment, was drafted with a sunset clause such that on 17 March 2023, intolerable suffering from irremediable mental illness would be a sufficient basis to obtain MAiD. That sunset clause has since been extended twice such that MAiD for mental illness is scheduled to become available on 17 March 2027.

The purpose of Bill C-7 was to provide access to MAiD for people with disabilities who are suffering intolerably and to decriminalize the medical practitioners who cause or assist in their deaths. The underlying premise was that a medically assisted death was preferable to requiring such individuals to continue suffering. The phrase "death with dignity" is often used to describe MAiD, whereas a life of suffering is depicted as undignified.[18] The assumption is that making MAiD available somehow brings dignity to these lives and, potentially, reduces suicide by giving people an easier path to a death within their control.

PRELIMINARY DATA ON MAiD

In 2022 there were 13,241 MAiD deaths in Canada, totalling 4.1 per cent of all deaths.[19] This was an increase from 10,064 MAiD deaths in 2021.[20] Of those deaths, 463 were track 2 deaths, 3.5 per cent of all MAiD deaths.[21] While we had only nine months of data from 2021 under track 2, this is more than double the 219 reported for that year.[22] In 2022, people accessing track 2 were generally younger than those accessing track 1, with 41.5 per cent between the ages of eighteen and seventy as compared to 28.9 per cent falling into this age group for the overall MAiD population.

For the first time we have data on track 2 and gender indicating that "there was a greater percentage of females than males (59.0 per cent vs 41.0 per cent) whose death was not naturally foreseeable in 2022."[23] This disproportionate number of women is not seen in track 1 where there are slightly more men than women accessing MAiD (51.8 per cent versus 48.2 per cent). There is very little information on diagnosis, with 50 per cent of cases attributed to "neurological conditions," 37.1 per cent to "other conditions," and 23.5 per cent to "multiple comorbidities,"[24] which include things like chronic pain, diabetes, and "frailty."[25] The number of MAiD requests where the applicant is found ineligible have gone consistently down, with 8 per cent in 2019 and a low of 3.5 per cent in 2022.[26]

It is important to bear in mind when looking at MAiD statistics that, for many categories of statistics, track 1 and track 2 are not disaggregated. Because there are so many more deaths classified as track 1, those deaths will inevitably overshadow the track 2 deaths in terms of numbers alone. For example, when looking at the nature of the suffering for people who received MAiD in 2022, both tracks are combined together. Thus, it is impossible to say with any certainty what the nature of the suffering was for those 463 individuals killed under track 2 specifically. Similarly, with respect to the individuals who received palliative care or disability supports, the annual report does not provide data on track 2 specifically. We know that 19.6 per cent of people who accessed MAiD did not receive palliative care, although 87.5 per cent of this number had access to palliative care.[27] And 89.5 per cent percent of people received disability support services, but 39.8 per cent of those people received these services for less than six months.[28] Again, track 1 and track 2 are not disaggregated.

Experience from other jurisdictions would suggest that the equivalent of track 2 cases tend to increase over time, which is consistent with the early Canadian data. In Belgium, for example, where medical assistance in dying is available for those not at the end of life, there has been a steady increase in the number of cases where death was not reasonably foreseeable. In 2003, death was not foreseeable in 8.1 per cent of deaths.[29] In 2013, death was not foreseeable in 14.7 per cent of the deaths.[30] There was also a steady increase during that time period of cases linked to a neuropsychiatric disorder diagnosis, such as major depressive disorder, schizophrenia, or bipolar disorder. In 2005, for example, 0.8 per cent of medically assisted deaths were linked to a neuropsychiatric disorder, whereas in 2013, 3.9 per cent of cases were linked to such a disorder.[31]

Experience from other jurisdictions also suggests that women will be especially overrepresented in track 2 cases involving psychiatric disabilities. In one study, researchers found that of a sample of one hundred patients who requested MAiD in Belgium on the sole basis of at least one psychiatric disorder, 77 per cent were women.[32] Those psychiatric patients were also, on average, forty-seven years old.[33] Other researchers have demonstrated that the preponderance of women seeking MAiD for mental illness is a consistent finding with "women [accounting] for the majority (69–77 per cent) of persons who request and receive euthanasia based on a psychiatric condition."[34] One study found that 36 per cent of those who died from psychiatric MAiD had a history of trauma.[35] We are already seeing an overrepresentation of women in track 2 deaths in Canada (59 per cent). It is likely that this overrepresentation will increase if and when MAiD for mental illness becomes available.

Track 2 MAiD has galvanized disability organizations and disability activists across the country. The bill was described by Krista Carr, executive director of Inclusion Canada, as the disability community's "worst nightmare."[36] Disability organizations and advocates argue that this law violates the rights of disabled Canadians by devaluing and stigmatizing disabled lives, portraying disability as something to be avoided at all costs – even death. A group of disabled Canadians started a "Disability Filibuster" – an online forum to celebrate disability culture and to talk about the impact of the expansion of MAiD on disabled lives.[37] To understand these critiques it is necessary to understand why these organizations and advocates see Bill C-7 as a function of widespread and systemic ableism in Canada.

ABLEISM IN CANADA

Despite the growing awareness of systemic racism and sexism in mainstream social and political life, ableism has not yet received the same level of attention in public discourse. Yet it is impossible to examine the disability community's concerns about MAiD without understanding the pervasive nature of ableism in Canada and the degree to which the medical profession has been complicit in that ableism. The former UN special rapporteur on the rights of persons with disabilities described ableism as follows in her report drafted after her visits to Canada and Norway: "[Ableism is] a value system that considers certain typical characteristics of body and mind as essential for living a life of value. Based on strict standards of appearance, functioning and behaviour, ableist ways of thinking consider the disability experience as a misfortune that leads to suffering and disadvantage and invariably devalues human life."[38] Fiona Kumari Campbell goes further and suggests that ableism includes the view that being disabled is being "less than" and therefore having a disability is "tolerated" but ultimately "inherently negative."[39]

Ableism is so deeply embedded in our social structures as to be largely unrecognizable or invisible. As Dr Heidi Janz argues, what makes ableism so insidious is that it has been transformed into "common sense."[40] James Cherney posits that the rhetoric of ableism has become so reified and accepted as common sense that it "denies its own rhetoricity."[41] Ableism does not exist outside of our laws and legal processes but rather is a deeply embedded part of them. Ableism often intersects with racism, as can be seen in the sterilization of (disproportionately Indigenous) women and girls with disabilities.[42] Other laws and policies that sustain and promote systemic ableism include the institutionalization of people with intellectual disabilities or mental illness, limits on the ability to immigrate to this country based on disability, welfare rates that force disabled people to live below the poverty line, removal of children from parents with disabilities, and prioritizing able-bodied people for access to medical care. Disabled writer and policy analyst Gabrielle Peters describes ableism as the "rebar in our economy, politics and culture."[43]

The medical model of disability is central to sustaining ableism both in medicine and in legislative policy.[44] The medical model of disability constructs disability as a medical shortcoming or a flaw, and as something needing to be fixed or ameliorated.[45] If the medical profession's raison d'être is to cure or eradicate illness and disability, those living with chronic disabilities represent their failures: those they have not been able to fix or make whole. Thus, it is not surprising that doctors consistently rate the quality of life of their disabled clients as lower than the ratings disabled individuals give their own lives.[46]

The medical model also puts doctors in a central role as gatekeepers to resources and supports, which gives them enormous power to name and label who is included in and excluded from particular categories that are linked to resources.[47] These labels also affect other legal statuses such as who is capable of making medical decisions, marrying, entering a contract, or consenting to sexual activity. When doctors are the gatekeepers, we tend to insist on fewer safeguards than when, for example, police or judges are making these profound decisions about life and death. The benevolence we implicitly attribute to doctors obscures the need for procedural safeguards.

Professor Joel Reynolds identifies one way in which the medical model has maintained its pre-eminence through what he describes as the ableist conflation of disability, suffering, and death. Reynolds asks the critical question: "What if a vast range of medical thinking and communication about disability is based not in its lived experience, but in misguided aversion to and fear of it?"[48] As he identifies, "it is this bold-faced linking of disability with pain, of which death is ultimately a species, that achieves such a spectacle of uncritical thinking about disability."[49]

Nowhere has the conflation between disability and suffering been more starkly illustrated than in the Joint Committee hearings reviewing Canada's MAiD laws. Committee members and witnesses described that they would rather be dead than become incontinent, live in long-term care, or lose their mental acuity.[50] Disabled Canadians have listened to their legislators discuss whether it would be better to be dead than like them.[51] Gabrielle Peters, for example, tweeted that the MAiD hearings "broke her in new and terrible ways."[52] Peters started the Twitter hashtag "#whileincontinent," where disabled Canadians tweeted about their many accomplishments while experiencing incontinence after a witness suggested that incontinence might be a reason to access MAiD.[53]

In contrast to the medical model, the social model of disability highlights the social and political realities of living with a disability in a world where ableism is the common-sense norm.[54] Much of the suffering associated with disability is imposed by stigma, discrimination, and exclusion from full participation in social and political life. These models are not necessarily mutually exclusive, nor is either a comprehensive description of disability. A person with a disability may experience both the actual physical impairments and the social barriers and stigmatization of disability as negative.[55] But the pro-MAiD movement relies exclusively on the medical conception of disability and of suffering while ignoring the social components. Only when something is characterized as medical in nature, and medically unfixable, is MAiD available.

The medical model foregrounds the medicalization of suffering as if it can be compartmentalized and distinguished from the social and political factors contributing to suffering. Professor Ameil Joseph has criticized the ableist way these realities of disability have been obscured in the MAiD debate: "Historical context is critical to this discussion yet almost nowhere is it being included in the debates. In the Senate hearings, in the media coverage and even in the advocacy, much of it has ignored the long history of eugenics and discrimination of persons with disabilities in Canada ... If we listen to persons with disabilities, we'll learn that so much of their day-to-day suffering is a result of systemic discrimination that denies them the basic needs for robust living. Disability itself is not a consignment to suffering and misery. That's an ableist lens."[56] Joseph continues by explaining that this medicalization of disability and suffering is not an accident but rather part of a coherent historical trajectory of ableism and eugenics. Peters similarly argues that MAiD is a rebranding of the eugenics movement.[57]

Ableism underlies the idea that the suffering associated with disability is not only inherent to disability but is also distinct from other human suffering. Only the intolerable suffering of people with disabilities is responded to with an offer of death. Yet if one examines the reasons people give for seeking MAiD, many of them are neither directly caused by disability nor unique to disabled suffering: loneliness and isolation, loss of dignity, and being a burden on loved ones are not unique to disability. The suggestion that the dignity of a life is diminished if one lacks full independence is also ableist. Many people with disabilities depend on family or caregivers to manage various aspects of their lives. Their dignity is not diminished through this dependence; rather, their dignity is diminished because society repeatedly tells them it should be and often denies them the supports to ensure that their basic needs are met.

Recognizing the degree to which ableism is embedded in law and social policy is a necessary step to understanding the *Charter* arguments against Bill C-7. In the MAiD case law, these arguments are pitted against more traditional liberal autonomy and formal equality arguments, which are wrongly portrayed as being neutral when it comes to race and disability. These arguments presume that everyone has the same access to the same opportunities to alleviate intolerable suffering. The concept of choice in the abstract is prioritized without any scrutiny given to the range of choices available to people with disabilities. The medical model is co-opted to obscure the degree to which intolerable suffering is socially enabled and facilitated.

The next part of this chapter uses an analysis of ableism as a lens through which to assess track 2 MAiD under section 15 and section 7 of the *Charter*. The intention is not to provide a comprehensive constitutional analysis but rather to lay the groundwork for others to build on these arguments.

CHARTER ARGUMENTS AGAINST BILL C-7

The constitutional analysis in this part of the chapter is premised on the basic assumption that everyone who can access track 2 MAiD has a disability, as that term is understood in law. While this point should be obvious, it has been obscured by attempts to draw artificial lines between disability and, for example, a chronic illness or a mental illness.[58] Whether someone chooses to identify as disabled is a separate question from whether the law would recognize their irremediable chronic illness that causes intolerable suffering and an advanced state of decline as a disability. While not every disabled person will meet the criteria for track 2 MAiD, this constitutional analysis proceeds from the starting point that everyone who meets those criteria would be considered legally disabled in the sense that they would, for example, have access to human rights legislation if they were denied basic services because of that illness. More importantly, they are disabled for the purposes of section 15 of the *Charter*.

Section 15 Argument

Section 15 of the *Charter* guarantees everyone equal protection and benefit of the law without discrimination based on grounds that include physical and mental disability. Canada's MAiD regime operates as an exemption from the crimes of aiding suicide and murder. Is it discriminatory to decriminalize the ending of life for people based on their disabilities?

There are two steps to an analysis under section 15 of the *Charter*. To prove a prima facie violation of section 15(1), a claimant must demonstrate that the impugned law or state action:

- *on its face or in its impact, creates a distinction based on enumerated or analogous grounds; and*
- *imposes burdens or denies a benefit in a manner that has the effect of reinforcing, perpetuating, or exacerbating disadvantage.*[59]

STEP 1: DOES THE LAW MAKE A DISTINCTION BASED ON ENUMERATED OR ANALOGOUS GROUNDS?

The MAiD legislation makes a distinction based on a subset of people with disabilities, which is an enumerated ground under section 15. The legislation decriminalizes ending the lives of people with irremediable medical conditions or disabilities, a decline in capability, and intolerable psychological or physical suffering, even if they are not otherwise dying. As described above, all the individuals who qualify for track 2 MAiD come under the enumerated ground of physical disability as protected by section 15. In March 2027 the law will allow for MAiD for people whose intolerable suffering is based solely on mental illness, also a protected ground under section 15. Members of other groups who are suffering intolerably but not disabled do not qualify for MAiD. The Supreme Court of Canada has made it clear that one need not establish discrimination against every member of a class to establish a section 15 violation and that violating the rights of a subset of that class will suffice.[60]

STEP 2: IS THE DISTINCTION DISCRIMINATORY?

The discrimination inquiry is based on whether a law has "'the effect of reinforcing, perpetuating or exacerbating ... disadvantage,' including 'historical' disadvantage."[61] The impugned law need not be the primary source of the social or political disadvantage: "If the law reinforces, perpetuates, or exacerbates [a group's] disadvantage, it violates the equality guarantee and thereby gives discrimination the force of law."[62] If the law furthers the gap between people with disabilities and the rest of society, it is discriminatory: "The root of s. 15 is our awareness that certain groups have been historically discriminated against, and that the perpetuation of such discrimination should be curtailed. If the state conduct widens the gap between the historically disadvantaged group and the rest of society rather than narrowing it, then it is discriminatory."[63]

The lived reality for people with disabilities in Canada continues to be one of marginalization and the devaluing of disabled lives. In *Eldridge*, the court identified how discrimination against people with disabilities has been perpetuated by portraying disability as a flaw or something that needs to be fixed: "This historical disadvantage has to a great extent been shaped and perpetuated by the notion that disability is an abnormality or flaw. As a result, disabled persons have not generally been afforded the 'equal concern, respect and consideration' that s. 15(1) of the *Charter* demands. Instead, they have been subjected to paternalistic attitudes of pity and charity, and their entrance into the social mainstream has been conditional upon their emulation of able-bodied norms."[64]

More recently in G, the Supreme Court of Canada recognized the ongoing systemic discrimination based on disability: "In our society, persons with disabilities regrettably 'face recurring coercion, marginalization, and social exclusion' ... As this Court has recognized, '[t]his historical disadvantage has to a great extent been shaped and perpetuated by the notion that disability is an abnormality or flaw.'"[65] Justice Karakatsanis went on to describe the role of section 15 in alleviating this disadvantage: "Section 15's promise of respect for 'the equal worth and human dignity of all persons' requires that those with disabilities be considered and treated as worthy and afforded dignity in their plurality. And s. 15's guarantee that discrimination not be given the force of law requires careful attention to the diverse impacts that government action will have on those with disabilities."[66]

Singling out the suffering associated with disability in a way that portrays it as different from all other human suffering, and as the only suffering that warrants death as a solution, is based on an ableist stereotype that life with a disability may be worse than death.

Criminal law plays an important expressive function in the messaging about what behaviour is acceptable in society and what behaviour is condemned. By allowing medical professionals to provide death to people with disabilities, the Criminal Code sends the message to disabled and non-disabled Canadians alike that these lives are less worthy of saving through suicide prevention efforts. The expressive role of this legislation goes well beyond those who actually access MAiD. This legislation risks normalizing death as a response to the suffering associated with disability, which is stigmatizing for all people with disabilities.

There is research that demonstrates that when suicide is more accessible, suicide rates increase.[67] Contrary to the assumptions referenced in *Carter* that restricting MAiD could force people to take their own lives,[68] recent studies demonstrate that access to MAiD does not in fact reduce suicide rates in jurisdictions that allow it; rather there is some suggestion those rates might even increase, particularly among women.[69]

Further discriminatory impacts will likely be felt by other groups such as women and Indigenous people with disabilities, demonstrating the intersectional inequalities of track 2 MAiD. Even in its first full year, track 2 MAiD was disproportionately accessed by women (59 per cent).[70] Similarly, as described above, the international experience tells us that psychiatric MAiD is disproportionately accessed by women. One explanation for the gender paradox in suicide – the fact that more women attempt suicide but more men complete it – is that men choose more violent means that are more likely to be successful (e.g., the use of firearms) whereas women, at least in Western countries, tend to choose less violent methods (e.g., drug ingestion), which are less likely to be fatal. Often those attempts are followed by treatment and the woman survives. One recent study suggests that the data on the gender divide for psychiatric MAiD maps almost exactly onto the data on gender relating to attempted suicide. By providing women with a non-violent means that is socially acceptable and 100 per cent effective, the provision of MAiD for mental illness ensures that these women succeed in ending their lives.[71]

It is also notable that Indigenous witnesses before the Senate opposed this expansion of MAiD. Many Indigenous communities are already experiencing a crisis in suicides, particularly among youth, and Indigenous people have significantly higher rates of disability than other communities in Canada.[72] Indigenous witnesses urged fulsome consultation with Indigenous communities before the enactment of Bill C-7.[73] However, the federal expert report on MAiD for mental illness acknowledges that "to date, engagement with Indigenous peoples in Canada concerning MAID has yet to occur."[74]

The discrimination in Bill C-7 is both direct, as disability is singled out explicitly as a basis for death, and indirect by having an adverse impact on disabled lives. The law deliberately targets a subset of people with disabilities for whom the aiding of suicide and even the intentional killing will be decriminalized, thus denying them the protection of criminal law. But the discrimination is also indirect, by depicting MAiD as a form of "treatment." This depiction permits medical professionals to offer MAiD to persons who are not otherwise seeking it, which may undermine a person's trust in their doctor and send a signal that the physician has lost hope. This change in the relationship between doctors and persons with disabilities may deter people from either seeking medical support in their most vulnerable moments or from fully disclosing the extent of their suffering. It also could discourage doctors from pursuing every possible treatment option where MAiD is an easier, fully funded, and less time-consuming option. We are starting to see cases emerge, for example, where people are being offered or are accessing MAiD because the wait times for needed medical treatment are contributing to intolerable suffering.[75]

The trial judge in *Carter* talked about MAiD as "an insurance policy" that brings comfort to dying Canadians such that if the dying process gets too difficult, they have the emotional security of knowing that there is an escape route.[76] This language needs to be contested for those who are not dying. Rather than an insurance policy, some perceive it as an albatross constantly hanging over them during the struggle to deal with the realities of chronic illness and disability in Canada. They are put in a position of having to re-evaluate whether their lives are worth living in a social context where the state is offering to end those lives. That is a burden other Canadians do not bear.

IS MAiD A BENEFIT FOR PEOPLE WITH DISABILITIES?
Advocates of extending the MAiD regime to those not at the end of their lives argue that it provides a benefit to people with disabilities, rather than discriminating against them. It allows them to exercise a choice to die when their lives are perceived as no longer worth living. This is the essence of the government's *Charter* statement justifying Bill C-7 and is the language used to justify extending MAiD to people with mental illness – that is, that it would be discriminatory to deny this "benefit" to people on the basis of mental illness.[77]

To portray MAiD as a benefit, proponents work to distinguish it from suicide because most people agree that easier access to suicide is not generally a benefit and that suicide prevention is an important social goal. Characterizing MAiD as a benefit for people with disabilities who are not dying is the legislative entrenchment of the "I would rather be dead than disabled" narrative that Reynolds identifies as being at the heart of ableism. There is no context in which we characterize death as a benefit for any other person who is not dying. Presenting MAiD as a benefit in these circumstances allows society to deny the actual benefits that might reduce the intolerable suffering experienced by Canadians with disabilities.

If the state has an obligation to alleviate intolerable suffering and to decrease the risk of people taking steps to end their own lives in more violent ways, why is this only a benefit for people with disabilities? Disabled people are not the only people who suffer intolerably, nor are they the only people who contemplate ending or attempt to end their lives. For others, we assume that people can and should be dissuaded from suicide, that with adequate resources and supports, life can be made tolerable.

Section 15(2) of the *Charter* does allow for legislation that targets disability to ameliorate conditions of disadvantage. Thus, for example, a financial benefit that is only available to people with disabilities could be insulated from challenge by a non-disabled person through section 15(2). However, the Supreme Court has held that this section is meant to protect ameliorative state action only from claims of reverse discrimination by those who are not included in the legislation.[78] In other words, section 15(2) "cannot bar s.15(1) claims by the very group the legislation seeks to protect."[79] Section 15(2) cannot insulate legislation from claims that it violates the rights of people with disabilities.

The UN special rapporteur on the rights of persons with disabilities, the special rapporteur on extreme poverty and human rights, and the independent expert on the enjoyment of all human rights by older persons formally wrote to Canada expressing "grave concern that provisions contained in the Bill may be contrary to Canada's international obligations to respect, protect and fulfil the core right of equality and non-discrimination of persons with disabilities."[80] They noted a real risk "that those without adequate support networks of friends and family, in older age, living in poverty or who may be further marginalized by their racialized, indigenous, gender identity or other status will be more vulnerable to being induced to access MAID."[81]

Section 7 Argument

Section 7 of the *Charter* guarantees the right not to be deprived of life, liberty, and security of the person except in accordance with the principles of fundamental justice. These principles are found in the basic tenets of our legal system and reflect "basic values underpinning our constitutional order."[82] In *R v. Bedford*, the court described section 7 as "concerned with capturing inherently bad laws: that is, laws that take away life, liberty, or security of the person in a way that runs afoul of our basic values."[83]

Section 7 has played an important role in the development of MAID; it was both the basis on which the *Carter* court struck down the absolute prohibition on MAID, and one of the grounds on which the *Truchon* court struck down the reasonable foreseeability of natural death requirement.[84] Thus, the scope of *Carter* is particularly important for assessing the constitutionality of Bill C-7.

The *Carter* court was not clear on the scope of its judgment. The court did not explicitly limit access to MAID to people at the end of life, but referred throughout the judgment to those "during the passage to death"[85] or at the "end-of-life."[86] For example, the court acknowledged that "s. 7 recognizes the value of life, but it also honours the role that autonomy and dignity play at the end of that life."[87] The court explicitly limited its judgment to the named plaintiffs: "the scope of this declaration is intended to respond to the factual circumstances in this case. We make no pronouncement on other situations where physician-assisted dying may be sought"[88] and indicated that the declaration "simply renders the criminal prohibition invalid" and does not go further.[89] There is nothing in *Carter* that speaks to the constitutionality of extending that access to those not at the end of life, but the court was explicit that its judgment does not extend to MAiD for mental illness.[90] *Carter* says nothing about whether a MAiD regime could go too far or whether Bill C-7 does just that.

Unlike in *Carter*, the section 7 analysis in *Truchon* is so expansive that it is difficult to see how any limit on MAiD could be upheld if that decision were followed. *Truchon* found, at least for people with disabilities, a "right to decide the time of [one's] death"[91] is part of the right to life. The *Truchon* court held that it would be paternalistic to deny people with disabilities the right to make choices about ending their lives. Yet it is always "paternalistic" to intervene in suicide, not just when a person has a disability. Nonetheless we invest significant resources to deter and intervene in suicide, because we believe that saving people's lives is a social good that justifies the paternalism of intervention.

LIFE, LIBERTY, AND SECURITY OF THE PERSON

Life   In *Carter*, the Supreme Court of Canada established that "the right to life is engaged where the law or state action imposes death or an increased risk of death on a person, either directly or indirectly."[92] Providing MAiD to persons with disabilities outside of end-of-life circumstances and exempting medical practitioners from the criminal offences of murder and aiding suicide directly increases the risk of death of disabled individuals. It is reasonable to assume that most medical practitioners would not help people die without this immunity from prosecution, and that at least some disabled people will choose MAiD who would not have attempted suicide because the option of MAiD is presented as a pain-free and infallible path to ending one's life.

The court in *Carter* found a deprivation of life on the basis that the absolute prohibition forced people "to take their own lives prematurely, for fear that they would be incapable of doing so when they reached the point where suffering was intolerable."[93] Almost seven hundred people with disabilities who were not at the end of their lives have died through track 2 MAiD in the first year and nine months since passing this legislation in March 2021. Some of those people might have ended their own lives through suicide, but many would not. Some of these deaths, including Sophia's, could have been prevented if the state provided the resources people need to live. Track 2 MAiD undoubtedly increases the risk of death for a subset of people with disabilities.

Liberty and Security of the Person   In *Carter*, liberty and security of the person were interpreted together and construed in negative terms, focusing on the right to be left alone by the state and the right to make choices about one's bodily integrity and medical decision-making independent of state interference. This negative conception of liberty does not create a constitutional entitlement to MAiD, but rather limits the state's ability to prohibit it through criminal sanction.

Laws that increase the risk of death also implicate physical security of the person by denying persons with disabilities the protection provided by the law of murder and aiding suicide. Psychological security of the person is also implicated through the severe psychological stress that is imposed on people with disabilities through the stigmatization of their lives. When a person asks for support, they may be met with an offer of MAiD. News stories of war veterans being offered MAiD when they seek supports or MAiD being suggested to a woman seeking urgent psychiatric care illustrate the impact of this law on people who simply want the supports they need to live.[94]

While some persons with serious and irremediable disabilities may welcome the choice to die because of lack of access to resources to alleviate their suffering, others find this choice deeply stressful and stigmatizing. Offering death as an option for people who are suffering and struggling to live may lead them to constantly reassess whether their lives are worth living. They lose the benefit of living in a society (and dealing with a medical profession) that takes for granted that their lives are worth saving. As Professor Martha Minow has noted, "the option of medical assistance in dying would alter the menu for all involved. It would turn the continuation of living into a question, open for debate, doubt, and persuasion."[95] Dr Joshua Briscoe describes this in terms of how the person "even if they never face the overt inquiry from others, must nevertheless settle the matter in their own mind: why am I still trying to live? Can I come up with sufficient reasons? Is society helping me find a reason to live? The mere offer – even the existence – of [MAiD] forces them out of default territory. Now they *must* choose ... This exacerbates suffering rather than relieves it. It adds to the burdens of those who already perceive themselves to be a burden. The desiccated imagination of our modern age does not offer to help bear this burden; rather, it offers reasons why some have a duty to die."[96]

PRINCIPLES OF FUNDAMENTAL JUSTICE

The principles of fundamental justice have developed in a way that focuses on arbitrariness, overbreadth, and disproportionality. None of these existing principles work particularly well in the context of a law that decriminalizes the killing of people with disabilities who are not at the end of life. In this chapter, I focus only on the established principle of gross disproportionality.

Gross Disproportionality Gross disproportionality targets laws that may be rationally connected to their stated purpose but whose *effects* are so disproportionate that they cannot be supported. Gross disproportionality applies only in extreme cases where "the seriousness of the deprivation is totally out of sync with the objective of the measure."[97] Gross disproportionality does not consider the beneficial effects of the law for society, since balancing the law's beneficial and deleterious effects is a function more properly reserved for section 1 of the *Charter*.[98]

Gross disproportionality requires an assessment of the government's purpose in enacting the law. This chapter suggests that the government's purpose in enacting Bill C-7 was to provide people with disabilities who are not at the end of their lives the option to escape intolerable suffering through death, while immunizing medical practitioners from criminal responsibility for assisting them.

It is difficult to imagine a more grossly disproportionate effect than a death that could have been avoided had proper supports been provided. In explaining why the death penalty is contrary to our fundamental values, the Supreme Court of Canada in *United States v. Burns* stressed the fallibility of existing systems to prevent wrongful convictions and correspondingly, wrongful deaths: "what is important is the recognition that despite the best efforts of all concerned, the judicial system is and will remain fallible and reversible whereas the death penalty will forever remain final and irreversible."[99] A medical system that is under-resourced to the breaking point, with far fewer safeguards than a judicial system, is fallible in the extreme.

Because MAiD is portrayed as beneficent for people with disabilities not at the end of life, and because we trust doctors implicitly, we fail to recognize the fallibility of the systems in place to ensure wrongful deaths do not happen. It may be easier to describe a wrongful death in the context of the death penalty than in the context of track 2 MAiD. At the very least, a death where the intolerable suffering could be made tolerable through adequate social supports, such as housing in Sophia's case or better home care for Sathya Dhara Kovac, fits the criterion for a "wrongful death." Bill C-7 does not require that resources be made available to alleviate intolerable suffering – instead, it simply requires that the individual be informed of and consider what resources are already available. Given our imperfect medical and social support systems, wrongful deaths are inevitable.

The *Burns* court made no exception for the convicted offender who wanted to choose the death penalty over life in prison – the death penalty was seen as morally repugnant to the values protected by the *Charter*. This clarity about the death penalty begs the question of why Canadians are so comfortable with doctors ending the lives of people with disabilities who are not otherwise dying? No court would uphold MAiD if it were only available to alleviate the intolerable suffering of Indigenous or racialized persons in Canada, or members of any other group protected by section 15. The Supreme Court in the death penalty context highlighted that one wrongful death was one too many. How many wrongful deaths of people with disabilities are we willing to tolerate to provide able-bodied Canadians the "insurance policy" of knowing that if they become disabled, they will have an exit ramp?

The Centrality of Choice in the Section 15 and 7 Analysis

Proponents of Bill C-7 stress that all the legislation does is provide one more choice in the arsenal of treatment options available to a person with a disability. How could legislation that simply gives people more choices be in violation of their rights? The concept of choice presupposes the social conditions that are prerequisites to making a non-coerced choice and a choice between options. Because the choice argument is central to both the section 15 and the section 7 analysis, I will combine that discussion in this section.

Choice is complicated in the MAiD context where the only choice provided by the legislation is between intolerable suffering and death. Looking at the story of Sophia, she exercised her choice to die, but that choice, like her intolerable suffering, was shaped by her inability to obtain what she needed to live: accessible housing. Sophia's disability may have been irremediable, but her suffering could have been reduced through adequate government supports to help her escape poverty. By conflating her suffering with her disability, rather than with her poverty, we obscure the state's obligation to provide the bare necessities of life. The fact that Denise ultimately obtained the money to live in a hotel temporarily and delay MAiD demonstrates the starkness of this choice. Sathya Dhara Kovac chose MAiD because she was denied adequate home care to manage her ALS.

Where choices are driven by inescapable poverty, social isolation, stigma, loneliness, or perceiving oneself to be a burden on others, it is problematic to construct state-inflicted death as an autonomous choice.[100] Such marginalization in this context may be a form of coercion.[101] While no one can access MAiD solely on the basis of poverty, for many Canadians, disability, social marginalization, and poverty are inextricably linked.[102]

A recent article by bioethicists Kayla Wiebe and Amy Mullin argues that even where people live in "unjust" social conditions, and where those conditions impact a decision to seek MAiD, autonomy requires that we respect that choice if they meet the eligibility requirements for track 2 MAiD. They go so far as to label track 2 MAiD in unjust social conditions a form of "harm reduction." A harm reduction approach "acknowledges that the recommended solution is necessarily an imperfect one: a 'lesser evil' between two or more less than ideal options."[103] The authors completely fail to engage with the role of the state in the creation of the unjust social conditions, the refusal to remediate those conditions, and the ready availability of a state-funded death.[104] We go beyond individual autonomy when the state gets involved in funding, approving, and providing death through the use of its criminal law power and its health care system. In other words, by making death the only solution to intolerable suffering, the state is facilitating, encouraging, and in fact causing disabled deaths, not just leaving people alone to exercise their own autonomy.

The importance of putting the choice argument in context finds support in the majority decision of Justice Abella in *Fraser*, where she acknowledged that the courts have consistently held that "differential treatment can be discriminatory even if it is based on choices made by the affected individual or group."[105] This is particularly the case where those choices are constrained by the kinds of systemic inequalities faced by people with disabilities. Justice Abella explained the importance of understanding constrained choices when applying a standard of substantive equality: "In contrast to formal equality, which assumes an 'autonomous, self-interested and self-determined' individual, substantive equality looks not only at the choices that are available to individuals, but at 'the social and economic environments in which [they] pla[y] out.'"[106] She cited with approval the scholarship of Professors Margot Young and Sonia Lawrence, who have both demonstrated that the choice narrative has impeded women's equality.[107] As Lawrence indicates, "[A] contextual account of choice produces a sadly impoverished narrative, in which choices more theoretical than real serve to eliminate the possibility of a finding of discrimination ... The result is a jurisprudence which almost mocks a more nuanced version of the what and how of discrimination, through frequent recourse to the idea that any harm to the claimant was actually the result of her choice, or her unwise exercise of her own judicially protected liberty."[108]

Justice Abella emphasized Lawrence's argument that the structural conditions in which people exist mean that some choices are made more often by people with "particular 'personal characteristics.'"[109] This is especially true with MAiD where the only people to whom MAiD is accessible are those with the personal characteristic of disability.

A central weakness of a formal equality model is its failure to recognize the particularities of disabled people's lives. Young explains how formal equality is underpinned "by an idealized vision of the liberal individual: autonomous, self-interested and self-determined. The individual is otherwise unencumbered by particularity of history, social location or circumstance."[110] This vision of formal equality posits maximizing the choice of the individual as paramount and, correspondingly, the individual becomes responsible for those choices. Substantive equality, by contrast, requires us to interrogate the range of choices available and the social and economic contexts in which they play out.

An understanding of section 7 that focuses on unencumbered autonomy ignores the role of social location and the corresponding constraints put on the range of available choices. The choice to live in woefully inadequate institutional care, isolated from loved ones, or to die is no choice at all.

Consider what choice looks like in the context of people with disabilities who are incarcerated through the criminal justice system. The correctional investigator testified before the Senate that he opposed making MAiD available to anyone who is living behind prison walls, indicating that Canada is an outlier in allowing MAiD in prisons: "Hopelessness, despair, lack of choice, denial of community alternatives are all conditions imposed by the reality of incarceration. A prisoner's ability to choose how, when and where to end one's life is mediated through the exercise of state power."[111]

Yet MAiD is available to incarcerated individuals with disabilities even when compassionate release may not be.[112] Their so-called autonomous choice may be between a life of intolerable suffering at the hands of the state or death at the hands of the state. This "choice" will be particularly problematic when MAiD becomes available for mental illness in March 2027, given the very high rates of mental illness and the overrepresentation of Indigenous persons in prisons.

Involuntary detention through the civil or forensic mental health systems raises similar concerns. The expert panel reviewing MAiD for mental illness has recommended that MAiD be available to persons who are involuntarily detained in psychiatric facilities for six months or longer, or for those who face repeated periods of detention of less than six months. The only additional safeguard recommended is that the assessment be conducted by persons outside of the institution. In all Canadian jurisdictions, those who are civilly detained cannot leave the facility at will and may lose the right to refuse psychotropic medication. They may be held in seclusion or restrained physically or chemically. They may have no choice about what treatment to undergo, whether to leave the facility, what clothes to wear, or who they are allowed to see or contact. Yet we feel safe offering them the "choice" of death. These examples highlight the fraught nature of choice in the lives of people who have no tolerable choices available to them and the very tenuous line between coercion and choice.

CONCLUSION

If suffering is cast as an entirely medical matter, and medical practitioners say it cannot be fixed, they inevitably become the gatekeepers to determine whose lives are worth saving and whose lives are not. The suffering of disability is exceptionalized as different and inherently worse than other suffering. This medicalization of suffering and the atomized construction of autonomy obscures the coercive role of the state and its own wilful failure to address the social inequalities that many people with disabilities face on a daily basis in Canada.

This chapter has argued that track 2 MAiD is unconstitutional, and that it should be repealed or struck down by a court. It is true that if Bill C-7 were found to be unconstitutional or repealed, some disabled people who are suffering would be unable to access a medically administered death if their natural death was not reasonably foreseeable. Able-bodied Canadians who are worried about future disability will lose the benefit of an "insurance policy." As Catherine Frazee has noted: "to walk in solidarity with disability rights defenders on the issue of medically hastened death, most of us will have to accept some limits on our privileged autonomy. Many will have to abandon the hubris of full control in life."[113]

It is equally true that if Bill C-7 is ultimately upheld, disabled people will die even though their suffering could have been rendered tolerable through adequate supports. For Sophia, state-sanctioned poverty and social marginalization led to MAiD; her disability was simply the gateway through which she accessed it.

As a country, we need to decide which results in a graver injustice: denying state-provided death to disabled Canadians who are suffering but not at the end of life or facilitating state-provided death for someone whose suffering could have been alleviated. How we answer that question says a lot about the kind of country in which we live and the value we put on each disabled life. It is not the role of the state to ensure that those individuals have access to death when the state is not willing to ensure that they have access to a life without intolerable suffering.

It is very important to give people with disabilities more choices and more autonomy in how they live their lives. But offering autonomy over death to those who may not have access to what they need to live does not enhance equality or autonomy; it simply provides an exit ramp from the state-sanctioned misery of their lives – an exit ramp that will save the state millions of dollars in health care and social supports. It is striking that access to MAiD is fully covered by state-provided health care in Canada when so many of the supports needed to live are not.

We must cede to the lessons of history that, even with the best of intentions, the altruism of the medical profession can be invoked to carry out the eugenic policies of the state. Any law that authorizes the killing of people with disabilities must therefore be subjected to the highest level of scrutiny. Quite simply, there is no safe way for the state or the medical profession to be in the business of killing people who are not otherwise dying. I end with the words of Gabrielle

Peters: "In many ways it comes down to whether you believe in the infallibility and absolute integrity of the institutions of our society or not. If you don't, then – at minimum – you draw the line at the state delivering lethal injections to people not near the end of life."[114]

NOTES

A longer version of this chapter was first published as Isabel Grant, "Legislated Ableism: Bill C-7 and the Rapid Expansion of MAiD in Canada," *McGill Journal of Law and Health* 15, no. 2 (2023): 259–335.

1 Avis Favaro, "Woman with Disabilities Approved for Medically Assisted Death Relocated Thanks to 'Inspiring' Support," CTV News, 28 May 2022, https://www.ctvnews.ca/health/woman-with-disabilities-approved-for-medically-assisted-death-relocated-thanks-to-inspiring-support-1.5921893 (https://perma.cc/VYU9-Z2W6).
2 Ibid.
3 See, for example, Avis Favaro, "Woman with Disabilities Nears Medically Assisted Death After Futile Bid for Affordable Housing," CTV News, 4 May 2022, https://www.ctvnews.ca/health/woman-with-disabilities-nears-medically-assisted-death-after-futile-bid-for-affordable-housing-1.5882202 (https://perma.cc/KB66-PYBH). For further discussion of these cases, see also Kayla Wiebe and Amy Mullin, "Choosing Death in Unjust Conditions: Hope, Autonomy and Harm Reduction," *Journal of Medical Ethics*, published online first (2023): 1, 10.1136/jme-2022-108871; Avis Favaro, "Woman with Chemical Sensitivities Chose Medically-Assisted Death After Failed Bid to Get Better Housing," CTV News, 13 April 2022, https://www.ctvnews.ca/health/woman-with-chemical-sensitivities-chose-medically-assisted-death-after-failed-bid-to-get-better-housing-1.5860579 (https://perma.cc/G6QE-P3EV).
4 Ibid. (The video was shared with CTV News before Sophia's death.) See also Leyland Cecco, "Are Canadians Being Driven to Assisted Suicide by Poverty or Healthcare Crisis?," *Guardian*, 11 May 2022, https://www.theguardian.com/world/2022/may/11/canada-cases-right-to-die-laws (https://perma.cc/6C7Z-9RAF).
5 Bill C-7, *An Act to Amend the Criminal Code (medical assistance in dying)*, 43rd Parliament, 2nd Session (2021), cl. 1(2.1), SC 2021, c. 2, preamble (Can.), https://parl.ca/DocumentViewer/en/43-2/bill/C-7/royal-assent.
6 See generally "Impacts of COVID-19 on Persons with Disabilities," Statistics Canada, 27 August 2020, https://www150.statcan.gc.ca/n1/en/daily-quotidien/200827/dq200827c-eng.pdf?st=h3nLZlwe (https://perma.

cc/JWA8-HASK); Tom Shakespeare, Florence Ndagire, and Queen E. Seketi, "Triple Jeopardy: Disabled People and the COVID-19 Pandemic," *Lancet* 397, no. 10282 (2021): 1331–3, 1331.

7 See, for example, Ontario's Long-Term Care COVID-19 Commission, *Final Report* (Toronto: Queen's Printer for Ontario, 2021), 1, 16–20, 40, 212, https://wayback.archive-it.org/17275/20210810150133/http://www.ltccommission-commissionsld.ca/report/pdf/20210623_LTCC_AODA_EN.pdf (https://perma.cc/HQ7Q-USDR); Nora Loreto, "The COVID Outbreaks that Ontario Wasn't Counting," *Maclean's*, 1 July 2021, https://macleans.ca/news/canada/the-covid-outbreaks-that-ontario-wasnt-counting/ (https://perma.cc/VY3P-HDFK); Taylor Blewett, "COVID-19 Death Rate More than Double for Ontarians with Intellectual, Developmental Disabilities, Study Finds," *Ottawa Citizen*, 17 August 2021, https://ottawacitizen.com/news/local-news/covid-19-death-rate-more-than-double-for-ontarians-with-intellectual-developmental-disabilities-study-finds (https://perma.cc/3WSB-4XZT).

8 See, for example, Avis Favaro, Elizabeth St Philip, and Alexandra Mae Jones, "Facing Another Retirement Home Lockdown, 90-year-old Chooses Medically Assisted Death," CTV News, 19 November 2020, https://www.ctvnews.ca/health/facing-another-retirement-home-lockdown-90-year-old-chooses-medically-assisted-death-1.5197140 (https://perma.cc/HJ9G-DRXQ); see also Sera Whitelaw, Trudo Lemmens, and Harriette G.C. Van Spall, "The Expansion of Medical Assistance in Dying in the COVID-19 Pandemic Era and Beyond: Implications for Vulnerable Canadians," *Canadian Journal of General Internal Medicine* 17, no. 2 (2022): 17–21, 19.

9 Scott D. Landes, Julia M. Finan, and Margaret A. Turk, "COVID-19 Mortality Burden and Comorbidity Patterns among Decedents with and without Intellectual and Developmental Disability in the US," *Disability and Health Journal* 15, no. 4 (2022): 1–7, 3. This American study found that people with intellectual disabilities were more likely to die of COVID than others; COVID was the leading cause of death for people with intellectual disabilities in 2020 and the third leading cause of death for those without intellectual disabilities.

10 See Roxanne Mykitiuk and Trudo Lemmens, "Assessing the Value of a Life: COVID-19 Triage Orders Mustn't Work against Those with Disabilities," CBC News, 19 April 2020, https://www.cbc.ca/news/opinion/opinion-disabled-covid-19-triage-orders-1.5532137 (https://perma.cc/LFS3-WQSJ); see also Gabrielle Peters, "Dying for the Right to Live," *Maclean's*, 12 November 2020, https://macleans.ca/opinion/dying-for-the-right-to-live/ (https://perma.cc/N3YY-EMDS).

11 See also Rosa Saba, "CERB and CRB Discriminated against Canadians with Disabilities, New Charter Challenge Claims," *Toronto Star*, 26 November 2021, https://www.thestar.com/business/cerb-and-crb-discriminated-against-canadians-with-disabilities-new-charter-challenge-claims/article_deff4d4b-9a23-5b8c-8824-5c10351c960a.html (https://perma.cc/Y9S3-8457). While the CERB benefit provided thousands of dollars to many Canadians, including university students, people with disabilities who were unemployed received a one-time $600 benefit, and only if they qualified for the federal disability tax credit.

12 Bill C-22 has now been passed into law and given royal assent: see *Bill C-22, Canada Disability Benefit Act*, 44th Parliament, 1st Session (22 June 2023) (Can.). This is after the Liberal government rejected a Senate amendment which would prevent clawbacks from private insurance companies: see Bill Curry, "Employment Minister Carla Qualtrough Rejects Key Senate Amendment to Government's Disability Bill," *Globe and Mail*, 15 June 2023, https://www.theglobeandmail.com/politics/article-bill-c-22-disability-benefit-act-amendment/ (https://perma.cc/J2WY-PV5D). It is important to note that Bill C-22 is a framework for developing a disability benefit with details like "who qualifies" and "how much" to be worked out over the coming year: see *Bill C-22, Canada Disability Benefit Act*, cl. 11(1.1)(1.2).

13 See *Bill 7, An Act to Amend the Fixing Long-Term Care Act, 2021 with Respect to Patients Requiring an Alternate Level of Care and Other Matters and to Make a Consequential Amendment to the Health Care Consent Act, 1996*, 43rd Legislature, 1st Session (31 August 2022), SO 2022, c. 16, s. 2(3) (Ontario, Can.). See also Desmond Brown, "Ontario Hospital Patients Who Refuse Pre-Arranged Long-Term Care Spot Will Now Be Charged $400 a Day," CBC News, 20 November 2022, https://www.cbc.ca/news/canada/toronto/ontario-more-beds-better-care-act-1.6658350.

14 *Carter v. Canada (Attorney General)*, 2015 SCC 5, [2015] 1 SCR 331, para. 147; *Rodriguez v. British Columbia (Attorney General)*, 1993 CanLII 75 (SCC), [1993] 3 SCR 519 (Can.). *Canadian Charter of Rights and Freedoms*, Part I of the *Constitution Act, 1982*, being Schedule B to the *Canada Act, 1982* (UK), 1982, c. 11.

15 See *Bill C-14, An Act to Amend the Criminal Code and to Make Related Amendments to Other Acts (medical assistance in dying)*, 42nd Parliament, 1st Session (2016), SC 2016, c. 3 (Can.), https://www.parl.ca/DocumentViewer/en/42-1/bill/C-14/royal-assent.

16 *Truchon c. Procureur général du Canada*, 2019 QCCS 3792.

17 See, for example, Bryce Hoye, "Winnipeg Woman Who Chose to Die with Medical Assistance Said Struggle for Home Care Help Led to Decision,"

CBC News, 4 October 2022, https://www.cbc.ca/news/canada/manitoba/sathya-dharma-kovac-als-medical-assistance-in-death-1.6605754 (perma.cc/YN5D-LSGJ). Sathya Dhara Kovac accessed MAiD in October 2022 when she was unable to get the additional home care she needed to live with ALS. In an obituary she wrote before her death, she stated, "It was not a genetic disease that took me out, it was a system." Reports of Kovac's death surfaced at the same time a Montreal man announced he was applying for MAiD after changes were made to his home care: see Lillian Roy and Angela MacKenzie, "'I Can't Live That Way': Montreal Man Seeking Medically Assisted Death Due to Home Care Conditions," CTV News, 3 October 2022, https://montreal.ctvnews.ca/i-can-t-live-that-way-montreal-man-seeking-medically-assisted-death-due-to-home-care-conditions-1.6090165 (https://perma.cc/V59X-WZPZ).

"Of particular concern are persons with disabilities who choose MAiD, the worry being that such persons might choose MAiD for social, rather than strictly medical reasons, because they cannot access alternative means of reducing their suffering, such as housing compatible with their condition or sufficient hours of paid care." Wiebe and Mullin, "Choosing Death," 4.

18 See, for example, Anna Vargo, "Death with Dignity in Canada: No Longer Limited to the Terminally Ill," *Voices in Bioethics* 8, no. 1 (May 2022): 1–4, 1.

19 See Health Canada, *Fourth Annual Report on Medical Assistance in Dying in Canada 2022*, October 2023, 21, https://www.canada.ca/content/dam/hc-sc/documents/services/medical-assistance-dying/annual-report-2022/annual-report-2022.pdf. In response to the more than 30 per cent increase in the number of MAiD deaths in 2022, the *Globe and Mail* editorial board has called on the government to take a step back on MAiD, concluding that "Ottawa needs to withdraw its amendments that include mental illness in the law for MAID. There are too many uncertainties, most crucially the inability to determine who is suffering from a truly irremediable mental disease and who will recover given enough time, treatment – and hope." Editorial Board, "It's Time to Take a Step Back on Assisted Death," *Globe and Mail*, 4 November 2023, https://www.theglobeandmail.com/opinion/editorials/article-its-time-to-take-a-step-back-on-assisted-death/.

20 Health Canada, *Third Annual Report on Medical Assistance in Dying in Canada 2021*, July 2022, 18, https://www.canada.ca/content/dam/hc-sc/documents/services/medical-assistance-dying/annual-report-2021/annual-report-2021.pdf.

21 Health Canada, *Fourth Annual Report*, 34.

22 Health Canada, *Third Annual Report*, 28. The *Fourth Annual Report* actually reports the number of track 2 deaths for 2021 at 223, but the *Third Annual Report* reports the number of track 2 deaths as 219.
23 Health Canada, *Fourth Annual Report*, 35.
24 Ibid., 34. This is particularly striking given that very detailed information is provided on gender and diagnosis for the overall sample.
25 Ibid., 27. Chart 4.1D shows other comorbidities including very common conditions such as osteoarthritis, osteoporosis, and hearing and vision loss. These numbers led the *Globe and Mail* editorial board to ask whether "Canadians [are] being approved for a medically assisted death simply because they are old." Editorial Board, "It's Time to Take a Step Back."
26 Health Canada, *Fourth Annual Report*, 48. See chart 7.1.
27 Ibid., 32.
28 Ibid., 33. Note that being a recipient of provincial social assistance qualifies as receiving disability support services.
29 See Sigrid Dierickx et al., "Euthanasia in Belgium: Trends in Reported Cases Between 2003 and 2013," *Canadian Medical Association Journal* 188, no. 16 (2016): E407–14, E410; for an examination of Canadian law in the context of Belgium and the Netherlands prior to Bill C-7, see also Trudo Lemmens, "Charter Scrutiny of Canada's Medical Assistance in Dying Law and the Shifting Landscape of Belgian and Dutch Euthanasia Practice," *Supreme Court Law Review* (2nd Series) 85 (2018): 459–544.
30 Lemmens, "Charter Scrutiny."
31 Ibid.
32 See Lieve Thienpont et al., "Euthanasia Requests, Procedures and Outcomes for 100 Belgian Patients Suffering from Psychiatric Disorders: A Retrospective, Descriptive Study," *BMJ Open* 5, no. e007454 (2015): 1–8, 6. The researchers point out at 6 that having a majority of women in their sample "is in line with other reports in the literature, which indicate that women fulfil the diagnostic criteria for mental disorders more often than men, except in the case of substance use disorders."
33 Ibid., 6–7.
34 See Marie E. Nicolini, Chris Gastmans, and Scott Y.H. Kim, "Psychiatric Euthanasia, Suicide and the Role of Gender," *British Journal of Psychiatry* 220, no. 1 (2022): 10–13, 10. It has been suggested that women in coercively controlling and otherwise abusive relationships may be particularly vulnerable to coercion in this context and that a history of violence may contribute to accessing psychiatric MAiD. See also Sonia Sodha, "Assisted Dying Seems Humane, But Can We Protect the Vulnerable from the Malign?," *Guardian*, 1 January 2023, https://www.theguardian.com/

commentisfree/2023/jan/01/assisted-dying-seems-humane-but-can-we-protect-the-vulnerable-from-the-malign (perma.cc/QP45-H3KS).

35 See Marie E. Nicolini et al., "Euthanasia and Assisted Suicide of Persons with Psychiatric Disorders: The Challenge of Personality Disorders," *Psychological Medicine* 50, no. 4 (March 2020): 575–82, 577.

36 *Meeting of the Standing Committee on Justice and Human Rights – Evidence*, 43rd Parliament, 2nd Session (10 November 2020), 4 (Krista Carr), https://www.ourcommons.ca/Content/Committee/432/JUST/Evidence/EV10949494/JUSTEV06-E.PDF (perma.cc/PB4L-HM57).

37 See "Homepage," Disability Filibuster, https://disabilityfilibuster.ca/ (perma.cc/PF8W-3AYY).

38 Special Rapporteur on the Rights of Persons with Disabilities, *Rights of Persons with Disabilities*, United Nations General Assembly, 43rd Session, 24 February–20 March 2023, UN Doc A/HRC/43/41 (2020), para. 9, https://documents-dds-ny.un.org/doc/UNDOC/GEN/G19/346/54/PDF/G1934654.pdf (perma.cc/U3C7-UFPG), citing Ron Amundson, "Disability, Ideology, and Quality of Life: A Bias in Biomedical Ethics," in *Quality of Life and Human Difference*, ed. David Wasserman, Jerome Bickenbach, and Robert Wachbroit (New York: Cambridge University Press, 2005).

39 See, for example, Fiona A. Kumari Campbell discussing the concept of internalized ableism in "Exploring Internalized Ableism Using Critical Race Theory," *Disability and Society* 23, no. 2 (2008): 151–62, 151.

40 Heidi L. Janz, "Ableism: The Undiagnosed Malady Afflicting Medicine," *Canadian Medical Association Journal* 191, no. (2019): E478–9, E479.

41 James L. Cherney, "The Rhetoric of Ableism," *Disability Studies Quarterly* 31, no. 3 (2011), https://dsq-sds.org/index.php/dsq/article/view/1665/1606 (perma.cc/WMU5-2BRR).

42 See, for example, Susan M. Brady, "Sterilization of Girls and Women with Intellectual Disabilities: Past and Present Justifications," *Violence Against Women* 7, no. 4 (2001): 432–61, 432; Robert A. Wilson, "Eugenics, Disability, and Bioethics," in *The Disability Bioethics Reader*, ed. Joel Michael Reynolds and Christine Wieseler (London: Routledge, 2022), 21; Special Rapporteur, *Rights of Persons with Disabilities*, para. 10; *E. (Mrs.) v. Eve*, 1986 CanLII 36 (SCC), [1986] 2 SCR 388 (Can.), 393–4.

43 Peters, "Dying for the Right to Live."

44 See Joel Michael Reynolds, "'I'd Rather Be Dead than Disabled': The Ableist Conflation and the Meanings of Disability," *Review of Communication* 17, no. 3 (2017): 149–63, 153; Justin Anthony Haegele and Samuel Hodge, "Disability Discourse: Overview and Critiques of the Medical and Social Models," *Quest* 68, no. 2 (2016): 193–206, 196;

Bradley A. Areheart, "When Disability Isn't Just Right: The Entrenchment of the Medical Model of Disability and the Goldilocks Dilemma," *Indiana Law Journal* 83, no. 1 (2008): 181–232, 193.

45 See Areheart, "When Disability Isn't Just Right," 186; Reynolds, "Rather Be Dead than Disabled," 153.

46 See Lisa I. Iezzoni et al., "Physicians' Perceptions of People with Disability and Their Health Care," *Health Affairs* 40, no. 2 (2021): 297–306, 304. For a description of physicians' perspectives on caring for people with disability, see Tara Lagu et al., "'I Am Not the Doctor for You': Physicians' Attitudes about Caring for People with Disabilities," *Health Affairs* 41, no. 10 (October 2022): 1387–95, 1391.

47 See Haegele and Hodge, "Disability Discourse," 195–6.

48 See Reynolds, "Rather Be Dead than Disabled," 150.

49 See ibid., 152–3. Reynolds also argues at 150 that the reason that the medical model remains "so gallingly entrenched is because of what [he calls] the 'ableist conflation': the conflation of disability with pain and suffering."

50 This evidence was given by British Columbia psychiatrist Derryck Smith, who stated that "if you wait too long to apply for MAID, you're going to become incompetent. If you become incompetent, then you are sentenced to five years of sitting around in a home in adult diapers." See *Meeting of the Special Joint Committee on Medical Assistance in Dying – Evidence*, 44th Parliament, 1st Session (25 May 2022), 9 (Derryck Smith), https://www.parl.ca/Content/Committee/441/AMAD/Evidence/EV11814179/AMADEV08-E.PDF (perma.cc/KA8M-5N7Q).

Alistair MacGregor noted that "we've often heard during this committee about the stigma that many people have – i.e., 'Oh, my goodness, if I were to get a diagnosis of Alzheimer's, my life would essentially be over.' They look at the state of long-term care in Canada, and there's a very real fear there." See "Remarks of Alistair MacGregor," in *Meeting of the Special Joint Committee on Medical Assistance in Dying – Evidence*, 44th Parliament, 1st Session (9 May 2022), 28 (Alistair MacGregor), https://www.parl.ca/Content/Committee/441/AMAD/Evidence/EV11767828/AMADEV06-E.PDF (perma.cc/E9G6-L9MF). See also Audrey Baylis, who states: "I haven't nursed for a number of years, because I had three careers, but I am a registered nurse. Most of the people whom I have been knowledgeable with are 100% behind MAID, because none of us are going to go into a nursing home, one way or another. Right now I still do not qualify to have MAID in Canada because I don't have anything really medically serious at the moment. I don't qualify." *Committee on Medical Assistance in Dying – Evidence*, 44th Parliament, 1st Session (25 April

2022), 25 (Audrey Baylis), https://www.parl.ca/Content/Committee/441/AMAD/Evidence/EV11721028/AMADEV03-E.PDF.

In asserting the importance of enacting advance directives for MAiD, Senator Kutcher described people with dementia as "smear[ing] their feces on the wall or eat[ing] them" and "spend[ing] their whole day sitting in front of a television set, laughing and singing, clapping at TV shows, and moving their body in time to the music." *Meeting of the Special Joint Committee*, 9 May 2022, 28 (Senator Kutcher).

51 See *Meeting of the Special Joint Committee on Medical Assistance in Dying – Evidence*, 44th Parliament, 1st Session (25 November 2022), 09:01 (Isabel Grant), 08:54 (testimony of Catherine Frazee), https://www.parl.ca/DocumentViewer/en/44-1/AMAD/meeting-29/evidence.

52 Gabrielle Peters (@mssinenomine), "In case you don't know, the MAID hearings in 2021 broke me in new and terrible ways and this Description was/is very much me," Twitter, 25 November 2022, https://www.twitter.com/mssinenomine/status/1596174154163982336.

53 See Gabrielle Peters (@mssinenomine), "If it feels safe to you – and I completely understand why it might not – and you have or have ever been incontinent, could you consider tweeting #WhileIncontinent and what you did?," Twitter, 25 May 2022, https://twitter.com/mssinenomine/status/1529552586445008896 (perma.cc/3TSD-5K9V).

54 The Supreme Court has acknowledged the importance of the social model in understanding disability, exclusion, and marginalization in *Granovsky v. Canada (Minister of Employment and Immigration)*, 2000 SCC 28, [2000] 1 SCR 703, paras. 30, 34.

55 See Sara Goering, "Rethinking Disability: The Social Model of Disability and Chronic Disease," *Current Reviews Musculoskeletal Medicine* 8, no. 2 (June 2015): 134–8, 135. Tom Shakespeare rejects what he describes as a "strong" social model of disability that rejects the reality of actual impairment in favour of what he calls an agenda for disability equality that recognizes "both the diversity of illness and impairment experiences and contexts, and the breadth of everyday life." Tom Shakespeare, *Disability Rights and Wrongs Revisited*, 2nd ed. (London: Routledge, 2013), 1, 4.

56 Ameil Joseph, "Expanding Medical Assistance in Dying Could Worsen Discrimination against People with Disabilities," *QUOI Media*, 22 February 2021, https://quoimedia.com/expanding-medical-assistance-in-dying-could-worsen-discrimination-against-persons-with-disabilities/ (perma.cc/TB6Z-FU4E).

57 Gabrielle Peters, "Canada Is NOT as Advertised. MAiD Is Eugenics," mssinenomineblog, 16 June 2022, https://mssinenomineblog.wordpress.

com/2022/06/16/canada-is-not-as-advertised-maid-is-eugenics/ (perma.cc/E9BK-S2SX).

58 See Jocelyn Downie and Udo Schuklenk, "Social Determinants of Health and Slippery Slopes in Assisted Dying Debates: Lessons from Canada," *Journal of Medical Ethics* 47 (2021): 662–9, 665.

59 *Fraser v. Canada (Attorney General)*, 2020 SCC 28, [2020] 3 SCR 113, para. 27.

60 See *Brooks v. Canada Safeway*, 1989 CanLII 96, [1989] 1 SCR 1219, 1247–8; *Eldridge v. B.C. (Attorney General)*, 1997 CanLII 327 (SCC), [1997] 3 SCR 624 (Can.), paras. 56–8; *Fraser*, 2020 SCC 28, para. 72.

61 *Ontario (Attorney General) v. G.*, 2020 SCC 38, [2020] 3 SCR 629 (Can.), para. 40.

62 Ibid., para. 42.

63 *Quebec (Attorney General) v. A.*, 2013 SCC 5, [2013] 1 SCR 61 (Can.), para. 332.

64 *Eldridge*, [1997] 3 SCR 624, 668.

65 *G.*, para. 61.

66 Ibid.

67 See, for example, N. Kreitman, "The Coal Gas Story: United Kingdom Suicide Rates, 1960–71," *British Journal of Preventive and Social Medicine* 30, no. 2 (June 1976): 86–93, 92; Shu-Sen Chang et al., "Factors Associated with the Decline in Suicide by Pesticide Poisoning in Taiwan: A Time Trend Analysis, 1987–2010," *Clinical Toxicology* 50, no. 6 (July 2012): 471–80, 471; D. Gunnell et al., "The Impact of Pesticide Regulations on Suicide in Sri Lanka," *International Journal of Epidemiology* 36, no. 6 (December 2007): 1235–42, 1240.

68 See *Carter*, 2015 SCC 5, para. 30; *Carter v. Canada (Attorney General)*, 2012 BCSC 886, [2012] BCJ No. 1196 (QL), para. 17.

69 See, for example, Anne M. Doherty, Caitlyn J. Axe, and David A. Jones, "Investigating the Relationship between Euthanasia and/or Assisted Suicide and Rates of Non-Assisted Suicide: Systematic Review," *British Journal of Psychiatry Open* 8, no. 4 (July 2022): 1–8, 7, https://www.ncbi.nlm.nih.gov/pmc/articles/PMC9230443/ (perma.cc/GGE6-XTKM); see also Silvia Sara Canetto and John L. McIntosh, "A Comparison of Physician-Assisted/Death-with-Dignity-Act Death and Suicide Patterns in Older Adult Women and Men," *American Journal of Geriatric Psychiatry* 30, no. 2 (February 2022): 211–20.

70 See Health Canada, *Fourth Annual Report*, 35.

71 Nicolini, Gastmans, and Kim, "Psychiatric Euthanasia, Suicide, and Gender," 12. The authors note that women's social and economic inequality includes high rates of gender-based violence, which is a risk factor for

women's mental illness and suicidality and could contribute to these alarming numbers.

72 See Tara Hahmann, Nadine Badets, and Jeffrey Hughes, *Indigenous People with Disabilities in Canada: First Nations People Living off Reserve, Métis and Inuit Aged 15 Years and Older* (Ottawa: Statistics Canada, 12 December 2019), 3, https://www150.statcan.gc.ca/n1/en/pub/89-653-x/89-653-x2019005-eng.pdf?st=HIZ2g423 (perma.cc/G3Y4-KHV3).

73 See *Meeting of the Special Joint Committee on Medical Assistance in Dying – Evidence*, 44th Parliament, 1st Session (4 November 2022), 9:45 (Neil Belanger).

74 Ontario's Long-Term Care COVID-19 Commission, *Final Report*, 72.

75 Katie DeRosa, "Cancer Treatment Delayed, B.C. Man Opts for Medically Assisted Death," *Vancouver Sun*, 5 December 2023, https://vancouversun.com/health/local-health/bc-cancer-radiation-wait-times-worsen.

76 *Carter*, 2012 BCSC 886, para. 1329.

77 Department of Justice, *Charter Statement: Bill C-7: An Act to Amend the Criminal Code (medical assistance in dying)*, 21 October 2020, https://justice.gc.ca/eng/csj-sjc/pl/charter-charte/c7.html (perma.cc/D6CC-2JQ2).

78 Jonnette Watson Hamilton and Jennifer Koshan, "The Supreme Court of Canada's Approach to the Charter's Equality Guarantee in Its Pay Equity Decisions," *ABlawg*, 12 July 2018, https://ablawg.ca/wp-content/uploads/2018/07/Blog_JWH_and_JK_Pay_Equity_Cases_SCC_July2018.pdf (perma.cc/5D9N-7AK6), 10, citing *Centrale des syndicats du Québec v. Quebec (Attorney General)*, 2018 SCC 18, [2018] 1 SCR 522 (Can.), paras. 37, 39.

79 See *Quebec (Attorney General) v. Alliance du personnel professionnel et technique de la santé et des services sociaux*, 2018 SCC 17, [2018] 1 SCR 464 (Can.), para. 32.

80 Gerard Quinn, Claudia Mahler, and Olivier De Schutter to Canada, "Mandates of the Special Rapporteur on the Rights of Persons with Disabilities; the Independent Expert on the Enjoyment of Human Rights by Older Persons; and the Special Rapporteur on Extreme Poverty and Human Rights," 3 February 2021, ref OL CAN 2/2021, 4, https://spcommreports.ohchr.org/TMResultsBase/DownLoadPublicCommunicationFile?gId=26002 (perma.cc/H2QR-VCGC).

81 Ibid., 3.

82 *Re B.C. Motor Vehicle Act*, 1985 CanLII 81 (SCC), [1985] 2 SCR 486 (Can.), para. 31; *Canada (Attorney General) v. Bedford*, 2013 SCC 72, [2013] 3 SCR 1101, para. 96.

83 See *Carter*, 2015 SCC 5, para. 95, citing *Bedford*, 2013 SCC 72, para. 96.
84 *Carter*, 2015 SCC 5, para. 147; *Truchon*, 2019 QCCS 3792, para. 638.
85 *Carter*, 2015 SCC 5, para. 63.
86 Ibid., paras. 10, 11, 22, 23, 106, 115. See also *Canada v. F.E.*, 2016 ABCA 155, [2016] AJ No. 505 (QL), para. 41 (where the Court of Appeal of Alberta held that *Carter* did not require the applicant to be terminally ill to benefit from an exemption during the suspension of the declaration of invalidity).
87 *Carter*, 2015 SCC, para. 68.
88 Ibid., para. 127.
89 Ibid., para. 132.
90 Ibid., para. 111.
91 *Truchon*, 2019 QCCS 3792, para. 582.
92 See *Carter*, 2015 SCC 5, para. 62.
93 See *Carter*, 2015 SCC 5, para. 57.
94 See, for example, Jessica Doria-Brown, "'Horrifying' That Veterans Affair Worker Raised Assisted Suicide with Troubled Veteran, Group Says," CBC News, 24 August 2022, https://www.cbc.ca/news/canada/prince-edward-island/pei-veterans-affairs-maid-counselling-1.6560136 (perma.cc/BS4Z-KRYF). See also Tom Yun, "Paralympian Trying to Get Wheelchair Ramp Says Veterans Affairs Employee Offered Her Assisted Dying," CTV News, 2 December 2022, https://www.ctvnews.ca/politics/paralympian-trying-to-get-wheelchair-ramp-says-veterans-affairs-employee-offered-her-assisted-dying-1.6179325 (perma.cc/FE33-VD3A). Kathrin Mentler went to Vancouver General Hospital in the midst of a psychiatric crisis seeking support. Instead, she was asked if she had ever considered MAiD, because the psychiatric system was "completely overwhelmed"; see Michelle Gamage, "She Sought Help in Crisis and Was Suggested MAID Instead," *Tyee*, 9 August 2023, https://www.thetyee.ca/News/2023/08/09/Medical-Assistance-Dying-Slippery-Slope-Mental-Illness-Disabled/; Andrea Woo, "Vancouver Hospital Defends Suggesting MAID to Suicidal Patient as Risk Assessment Tool," *Globe and Mail*, 9 August 2023, https://www.theglobeandmail.com/canada/british-columbia/article-maid-suicide-patient-vancouver/.
95 Martha Minow, "Which Question? Which Lie? Reflections on the Physician-Assisted Suicide Cases," *Supreme Court Review* 1997 (1998): 1–30, 22.
96 Joshua C. Briscoe, "Affirming Dignity: Arguments Against Medical Aid in Dying," *Psychiatric Times*, 21 December 2022, https://www.psychiatrictimes.com/view/affirming-dignity-arguments-against-medical-aid-in-dying (perma.cc/5WPK-TX8K).

97 *Bedford*, 2013 SCC 72, para. 120; see also *Canada (Attorney General) v. P.H.S. Community Services Society*, 2011 SCC 44, [2011] 3 SCR 134, para. 133.
98 See *Bedford*, 2013 SCC 72, paras. 120–2.
99 *United States v. Burns*, 2001 SCC 7, [2001] 1 SCR 283, para. 129.
100 See Health Canada, *Fourth Annual Report*, 31. Of the people who requested MAiD in 2022, 35.3 per cent cited being a burden to their families as one of the causes of their intolerable suffering.
101 See Brennan Leffler and Marianne Dimain, "How Poverty, Not Pain, Is Driving Canadians with Disabilities to Consider Medically-Assisted Death," *Global News*, 8 October 2022, https://globalnews.ca/news/9176485/poverty-canadians-disabilities-medically-assisted-death/ (perma.cc/2WCT-CVZ8). As palliative care physician Dr. Naheed Dosani told *Global News*: "When people are living in such a situation where they're structurally placed in poverty, is medical assistance in dying really a choice or is it coercion? That's the question we need to ask ourselves."
102 See "Poverty and Low-Income Statistics by Disability Status," Statistics Canada, 7 September 2022, https://doi.org/10.25318/1110009001-eng (perma.cc/3JQU-EURA). According to Statistics Canada, the percentage of persons with disabilities who are considered to be low income is nearly double that of persons without disabilities in 2019 and 2020.
103 Wiebe and Mullin, "Choosing Death," 5.
104 Mullin herself accepts that it is a refusal to remediate these conditions. "The public 'may be shocked to realize that some people's lives become intolerable to them – not simply because of their health condition, but because of something that, as Canadians, we have the power to change,' Mullin said." Sharon Kirkey, "Canada Shouldn't Deny Assisted Suicide If Social Conditions Made Life Intolerable: Bioethicists," *National Post*, 9 May 2023, https://nationalpost.com/news/canada/canada-medical-aid-in-dying (perma.cc/4P2Z-PF9V).
105 *Fraser*, 2020 SCC 28, para. 86.
106 Ibid., para. 88 (emphasis in original), citing *Nova Scotia (Attorney General) v. Walsh*, 2002 SCC 83, [2002] 4 SCR 325 (Can.), para. 342.
107 Margot E. Young, "Unequal to the Task: 'Kapp'ing the Substantive Potential of Section 15," *Supreme Court Law Review* 50, no. 2 (2010): 183–219, 190–1, 196, cited in *Fraser*, 2020 SCC 28, para. 89.
108 Sonia Lawrence, "Choice, Equality and Tales of Racial Discrimination: Reading the Supreme Court on Section 15," in *Diminishing Returns: Inequality and the Canadian Charter of Rights and Freedoms*, ed. Sheila McIntyre and Sanda Rodgers (Markham, ON: LexisNexis Canada, 2006), 115–6, cited in *Fraser*, 2020 SCC 28, para. 90.

109 Ibid., 124–5, cited in *Fraser*, 2020 SCC 28, para. 90 (emphasis removed).
110 Young, "Unequal to the Task," 190–1.
111 See *Meeting of the Standing Committee on Public Safety and National Security – Evidence*, 43rd Parliament, 2nd Session, (2 November 2020), 20:05 (Shannon Stubbs), where it was noted that "in the latest correctional investigator's report, he raised serious concerns about euthanasia in prisons. He called on the government to stop the practice altogether. Today he was at the committee and said he is deeply disturbed by three instances that he said should never have happened." See also Kathleen Martens, "MAiD in Prison: Inmates Are 'Dying to Get Out' Says Senator," *APTN News*, 15 May 2023, https://www.aptnnews.ca/national-news/maid-in-prison-inmates-are-dying-to-get-out/ (perma.cc/H4YZ-PDMX); Avis Favaro, "The Number of Medically-Assisted Deaths in Canada's Prisons a Concern for Some Experts," CTV News, 3 May 2023, https://www.ctvnews.ca/health/the-number-of-medically-assisted-deaths-in-canada-s-prisons-a-concern-for-some-experts-1.6380440 (perma.cc/Y8BQ-DJUZ); Office of the Correctional Investigator, "Standing Senate Committee on Legal and Constitutional Affairs – Remarks for Dr. Ivan Zinger," 2 February 2021, https://oci-bec.gc.ca/en/content/standing-senate-committee-legal-and-constitutional-affairs-2021-02-02 (perma.cc/TQ82-AGML).
112 See generally Alexander I.F. Simpson, Jason Tran, and Roland M. Jones, "Ethical Considerations Regarding Mental Disorder and Medical Assistance in Dying (MAiD) in the Prison Population," *Medicine, Science, and the Law* 63, no. 1 (January 2023): 3–5; Adelina Iftene, "The Case for a New Compassionate Release Statutory Provision," *Alberta Law Review* 54, no. 4 (2017): 929–54, 929.
113 Isabel Grant, Janine Benedet, Elizabeth Sheehy, and Catherine Frazee, "A Conversation on Feminism, Ableism and Medical Assistance in Dying," *Canadian Journal of Women and the Law* 34, no. 3 (2023): 31–72.
114 See Gabrielle Peters, "MAiD – Marginalized Against Institutionalizing Death – The Opposition to the Expansion of MAiD Is About Faith – But Just Not the Religious Kind," mssinenomineblog, 7 September 2022, https://mssinenomineblog.wordpress.com/2022/09/07/maid-marginalized-against-institutionalizing-death-the-opposition-to-the-expansion-of-maid-is-about-faith-but-just-not-the-religious-kind/ (perma.cc/3CDK-SNCC).

11

Mental Illness, Health Care, and Assisted Death: Part I – Examining Parameters for Expanding or Restricting MAiD under Canada's *Charter*

Mary J. Shariff, Derek B.M. Ross, and Trudo Lemmens

In 2021, the federal government of Canada amended the Criminal Code to eventually allow medical assistance in dying (MAiD) for persons whose sole underlying condition is a mental illness (MAiD MI-SUMC). This expansion was recently postponed until March 2027. Many, including the former minister of justice, have suggested that this expansion is, or inevitably will be, required by the courts. This has led advocates to insist that both the federal and provincial governments must take immediate action to facilitate MAiD MI-SUMC. The following two chapters address these issues as follows.

Part I, this chapter, "Examining Parameters for Expanding or Restricting MAiD under Canada's *Charter*," examines the relevant case law, including *Carter v. Canada (Attorney General)*, 2015 SCC 5; *Truchon v. Canada (Attorney General)*, 2019 QCCS 3792; and *Canada (Attorney General) v. E.F.*, 2016 ABCA 155. This chapter concludes that no Canadian court has recognized a *Charter* right to MAiD where mental illness is the sole underlying condition, nor is this necessarily a conclusion the courts will reach in the future given the complex social, medical, ethical, and legal considerations engaged.

Part II, the next chapter, "Examining Parameters for Expanding or Restricting MAiD under Canada's Federal System," explores a number of jurisdictional considerations that have yet to be resolved surrounding MAiD, including the extent to which provinces can potentially develop their respective provincial regulatory schemes in a manner that is more restrictive than that which the federal Criminal Code permits (as Quebec has done). Drawing guidance from the Supreme Court of Canada's recent decision *Murray-Hall v. Quebec (Attorney General)* 2023 SCC 10, the chapter concludes that there is significant constitutional room for the provinces to more actively regulate MAiD practice and considers the implications for provincial legislation such as Quebec's.

INTRODUCTION

In 2021, the federal government of Canada amended the Criminal Code to allow MAiD for persons whose sole underlying condition is a mental illness (MAID MI-SUMC),[1] a change now scheduled to come into effect in March 2027.[2] This is further to the government's overall expansion of MAiD in Bill C-7, which removed the law's previous eligibility requirement that a person's natural death be "reasonably foreseeable."[3]

The move to decriminalize MAiD MI-SUMC has been controversial, insofar as MAiD could potentially be offered as a publicly funded medical treatment option for conditions such as clinical depression, chronic anxiety, eating disorders, obsessive compulsive behaviour, and post-traumatic stress disorder[4] – all of which can include among their symptoms, for example, hopelessness, despair, and suicidality (even if considered "rational").[5] It has also been suggested that substance use disorders and addictive disorders may also give rise to MAiD eligibility.[6] And though there is significant controversy over whether such conditions are to be considered mental disorders, MAiD MI-SUMC could arguably be interpreted to apply to, or expand the provision of MAiD for, neurodevelopmental disorders, such as cognitive or intellectual disabilities and autism spectrum disorder.[7]

All of this has raised a number of questions among medical professionals,[8] mental health specialists,[9] legal and human rights experts,[10] disability scholars,[11] and many others who are particularly concerned about the prospect of offering MAiD in such contexts.[12] Some of these questions relate to the practice of evidence-informed medicine: for example, can mental illness be confidently predicted as being "irremediable" in specific cases?[13] A number of mental health experts and organizations have emphasized that there is no reliable scientific basis to determine, in advance, whether a person will be effectively treated or will sufficiently recover to cope with their illness.[14] Other concerns relate to systemic ableism and the need to uphold equality rights as well as the right to life and security of the person for persons with disabilities (including mental illness) – especially in the Canadian context where many basic mental health supports and services are lacking.[15] *Charter* concerns have been raised in connection with the government offering "death as a solution to the suffering of disability for those not at the end of life" in this context, as it perpetuates the "discriminatory premise that disability can be worse than death and therefore, death is a benefit for this group of Canadians."[16]

There are also significant questions relating to broad social and public health policy goals. Is mental illness a context that points to a different "line in the sand" in relation to MAiD?[17] For many, when it comes to MAiD, mental illness is a paradigmatic example that more clearly reveals the problem of dealing with MAiD as a "medical treatment" for various forms of suffering and symptoms associated with illness. Realistically, can MAiD MI-SUMC actually be reconciled with the public health goal of suicide prevention?[18] Is it possible to do so without undermining the massive efforts many have undertaken to address stigmatization and structural vulnerability to improve mental health and well-being, and to promote meaningful participation in Canadian life?[19] And to what extent might extraneous factors such as systemic inequality, societal barriers, or unmet needs be influencing a person's request to die in these contexts?[20] Would addressing these factors as a priority after careful balancing and consideration of competing considerations be patently unconstitutional?[21] Would it be unreasonable to argue that MAiD in these situations is ultimately irreconcilable with efforts to address these challenges?

Addressing such questions has, in the view of the authors, been largely side-stepped by lawmakers and others who call for urgent MAiD expansion. Instead, they have suggested that legislators have no other choice, constitutionally speaking. For example, when asked to explain why Parliament was intent on moving forward with MAiD for mental illness, then minister of justice David Lametti stated: "We do have to respect decisions of the courts. They have said that medical assistance in dying is a right that Canadians have."[22] When asked if there was a chance that Parliament would not proceed with allowing MAiD for mental illness, the minister replied, "I think that would run us afoul of the courts."[23] Similarly, the minister was asked,

"How can you ethically, in good conscience, go ahead and provide this [MAiD for mental illness] to people when you know that they may not have had the ability to get proper treatment?" He replied, "Well again, it is something that our courts, and the highest court in Canada, has said is a Charter right that Canadians have."[24]

In fairness, Minister Lametti did not stand alone in asserting this view.[25] Several medical professionals and professional organizations appear to have embraced this argument as the primary reason to support its legalization.[26] However, based on our review of existing constitutional jurisprudence, the claim that the courts require a MAiD MI-SUMC regime is not accurate. As examined in detail below, no court has stated that Canadians have a "*Charter* right" to MAiD where mental illness is the sole underlying condition.[27] Nor is this necessarily a conclusion that courts will automatically reach in the future. Whether section 7 or section 15 of the *Charter* can be interpreted to require the government to allow MAiD for mental illness remains, at the very least, an unadjudicated question. So too is the question of whether the government could justify a legislative decision not to offer MAiD MI-SUMC as a "reasonable limit" in a "free and democratic society" under section 1 of the *Charter*. No Canadian court has examined the constitutionality of a regulatory regime that specifically excludes MAiD for mental illness, as representatives of the Department of Justice recently acknowledged.[28] And only one trial-level court has specifically adjudicated on the constitutionality of limiting access to MAiD outside the end-of-life context at all.[29]

It is also important to consider the compelling human rights arguments that might *restrict* the government from offering death as a medical solution for mental illness, as well as other conditions.[30] For example, multiple United Nations experts have repeatedly warned that Canada's existing MAiD regime undermines international human rights law obligations, including those Canada has committed to uphold such as article 3 (right to life, liberty, and security) of the Universal Declaration of Human Rights, article 6(1) (protection of right to life in law) of the International Covenant on Civil and Political Rights, and article 10 (right to life on an equal basis with others) of the Convention on the Rights of Persons with Disabilities.[31] UN experts have concluded that Bill C-7's expansion of MAiD outside of the end-of-life context (i.e., for disability-related suffering and *only* for disability-related suffering) is "contrary to Canada's international obligations to respect, protect and fulfil the core right of equality and non-discrimination of persons with disabilities," as it creates and reinforces negative, ableist social assumptions – including that "it is better to be dead than to live with a disability."[32] They have also expressed concern that Canada's approach singles "out the suffering associated with disability as being of a different quality and kind than any other suffering," and results "in a two-tiered system in which some would get suicide prevention and others suicide assistance, based on their disability status and specific vulnerabilities."[33] These concerns apply equally in the context of advancing medicalized death as a solution for suffering experienced by Canadians with mental health disorders as for those with physical disabilities.[34]

With all of this said, the only two cases that have invalidated federal restrictions on MAiD – *Carter* and *Truchon* – considered just one legislative purpose in their deliberations: the protection of vulnerable persons from being induced to end their lives in a moment of weakness.[35] This narrow framing of the criminal law's objective drove the courts' constitutional analyses in both cases.[36] In the *Truchon* case, the court did so even by rejecting the new and very specific legislative objectives framed by Parliament only one year earlier in relation to Bill C-14, the government's new MAiD legislation enacted in response to *Carter*.[37]

But the enactment of a new regime – for example, one that expressly excludes mental illness as a basis for MAiD eligibility in furtherance of a distinct purpose or objectives – would require a fresh constitutional analysis and would not necessarily be governed by the reasoning employed in *Carter*. This was made clear in *Lamb v. Canada*, where the BC Supreme Court rejected the argument that *Carter* was dispositive of Bill C-14 because each law needs to be assessed based on its specific and unique legislative objectives.[38]

Similarly, it is far from a foregone conclusion that constitutional arguments against such an exclusion would be successful. As will be discussed further, comments from the courts intimate that should Parliament, after rigorous study of medical, social, ethical, and human rights considerations, decide to exclude MAiD MI-SUMC through a "complex regulatory regime," such a regime may be upheld.[39]

With the foregoing in mind, the cases that some have cited to support the assertion that the courts, including the Supreme Court of Canada, have identified a *Charter* right to MAiD MI-SUMC are examined in detail below. Our main conclusion is this: no court has mandated Parliament to introduce a MAiD MI-SUMC regime.[40]

CANADIAN COURTS HAVE NOT RECOGNIZED A CONSTITUTIONAL RIGHT TO MAID FOR MENTAL ILLNESS

Carter v. Canada (Supreme Court of Canada)

In *Carter v. Canada* (*Carter* or *Carter 2015*), the Supreme Court of Canada was (exceptionally) presented with "fresh" expert evidence and argument.[41] This evidence and argument, based on the experience of permissive countries like Belgium, examined how legalizing assisted suicide or euthanasia[42] for persons like the claimant Gloria Taylor, who was suffering from ALS, would lead to its expansion in other, more controversial contexts.[43] Concerns were specifically raised about "the potential for a slippery slope" leading to the legalization of assisted suicide or euthanasia for, among other conditions, mental illness.[44] The Supreme Court dismissed these concerns, specifically stating that "euthanasia for minors or persons with psychiatric disorders" would "not fall within the parameters suggested in these reasons" ("paragraph 111").[45]

The Supreme Court went on to strike down Canada's ban of physician-assisted death housed within the Criminal Code,[46] but only to the extent that it prohibited physician-assisted death for "competent adult person who (1) clearly consents to the termination of life; and (2) has a grievous and irremediable medical condition (including an illness, disease or disability) that causes enduring suffering that is intolerable to the individual in the circumstances of his or her condition,"[47] as described in the court's declaration of invalidity.

Although the declaration of invalidity itself did not explicitly include or exclude mental illness, it must be read in conjunction with the court's previous comments that euthanasia for persons with psychiatric disorders did not fall within the decision's parameters.[48] And as many continue to also point out, the declaration of invalidity was also accompanied by these comments immediately following it: "The scope of this declaration is *intended to respond to the factual circumstances in this case. We make no pronouncement on other situations where physician-assisted dying may be sought.*"[49]

Indeed, it is a basic premise of *Charter* jurisprudence that cases cannot be decided in a factual vacuum and the "presentation of facts ... is essential" to the court's consideration of the constitutional issues.[50] Accordingly, the Supreme Court's clear boundary around the scope of the declaration of invalidity requires careful examination: exactly what were the "factual circumstances" of the *Carter* case?[51]

Carter involved the claimant Gloria Taylor, who was terminally ill,[52] diagnosed with ALS (a fatal neurodegenerative disease[53]), and proactively seeking a physician-assisted death at a time of her own choosing.[54] The court and the claimant described how the unavailability of physician-assisted dying in light of the claimant's deteriorating physical condition, along with her desire to obtain a physician-assisted death, presented her with "the 'cruel choice' between killing herself while she was still physically capable of doing so, or giving up the ability to exercise any control over the manner and timing of her death."[55] As succinctly put by the court, whether it be in the context of "progression of degenerative illness" or a "gruesome death from advanced-stage cancer," "running through the evidence of all the witnesses is a constant theme – that they suffer from the knowledge that they lack the ability to bring a peaceful end to their lives at a time and in a manner of their own choosing."[56]

The court further emphasized that its conclusions were based on the circumstances of the plaintiff "and of *persons in her position.*"[57] Even if "persons in her position" could be interpreted to include persons not yet in the terminal phase of the irremediable medical condition, it is clear that the factual circumstances in *Carter* pertain to medical conditions involving a progressive physical decline towards death, making that death potentially protracted and painful, and potentially rendering a person incapable of ending their own life.[58]

The *Carter* decision said nothing about physician-assisted dying for persons whose sole underlying condition was a mental illness, other than its express assurance in paragraph 111 that psychiatric disorders fell outside the decision's scope in response to "slippery slope" concerns and data from other jurisdictions.[59]

MENTAL ILLNESS NOT A BASIS, NOR AUTOMATIC
DISQUALIFIER, FOR MAiD ELIGIBILITY: *CARTER*

It should also be noted that while mental illness was not part of the plaintiffs' claim, nor was it analyzed in terms of providing a basis upon which to permit assisted death in Canada, mental illness was discussed in another context – namely, impact on capacity and capacity assessment.

In finding that the infringement of the claimant's freedom to "seek" physician-assisted death pursuant to section 7 of the *Charter* (life, liberty, and security) was not minimally impairing (and therefore could not be justified under section 1), the court examined the concept of capacity and the argument that factors such as "cognitive impairment, depression or other mental illness" "could escape detection or give rise to errors in capacity assessment."[60] The court, however, dismissed this argument, agreeing with the trial judge that it is "possible for physicians, with due care and attention to the seriousness of the decision involved, *to adequately assess decisional capacity*"[61] using the same "procedures" that they apply "in the context of medical decision-making more generally."[62]

The court's conclusion that physicians are able to assess decisional capacity – even if other factors like depression or mental illness are present – thus pertains specifically to the feasibility and efficacy of safeguards and not the medical condition(s) that would qualify for access to assisted death.[63] In other words, the court maintained that the presence of a mental illness would not automatically *disqualify* an otherwise eligible application for assisted death – but it did not say that a mental illness as a sole condition would itself render someone *eligible for* assisted death. Rather, the qualifying medical condition(s) were constructed on the basis of Ms Taylor's specific claim and turned on the case's "factual circumstances."[64]

To better understand those "factual circumstances" in *Carter*, it is helpful to study some additional aspects of the trial judge's discussion of the evidence and facts, since the Supreme Court relied on and adopted much of her reasoning and conclusions.[65]

THE TRIAL DECISION IN *CARTER V. CANADA* (BC SUPREME COURT)

In delineating eligibility criteria for MAiD, the trial judge in *Carter* (Justice Lynn Smith) rejected the plaintiffs' argument that "the term 'grievously and irremediably ill persons' should incorporate reference to 'psychosocial suffering.'"[66] While Justice Smith did not define "psychosocial" factors, she did refer to expert evidence "that suicide related to mental illness ... and other psychosocial factors *is different from end-of-life decision making* by grievously and irremediably ill individuals."[67] Justice Smith further observed: "I accept ... that it is *problematic to conflate decision-making by grievously and irremediably ill persons about the timing of their deaths*, with *decision-making about suicide by persons who are mentally ill.*"[68]

When Justice Smith addressed concerns that the legalization of MAiD would send the message that suicide is an answer to suffering, she repeated the plaintiffs' rejoinder that there is "a *difference between assisted death in response to intolerable suffering at the end of life*, and suicide arising out of mental illness."[69] The *Carter* case was concerned with the former, as the plaintiff also explicitly recognized, and not the latter.

This is made clear in Justice Smith's decision to limit the definition of "grievous and irremediable" "to those who are also in an *advanced state of weakening capacities*, with *no chance of improvement.*"[70] This limitation helps to underscore that access to physician-assisted death for psychiatric conditions was simply not part of the claim or judicial calculus in *Carter*. Again, the only thing the court was discerning in terms of mental illness was not the medical condition or grounds for *granting access* to physician-assisted suicide in Canada, but rather the extent to which mental illness could potentially impact *decisional capacity*, and the court appropriately concluded that it did not automatically or necessarily do so in every case.

CARTER CONSIDERED MAiD ONLY FOR "IRREMEDIABLE"/"INCURABLE" CASES

While the Supreme Court of Canada (SCC) did not ultimately include the trial court's specific limitation "in a state of advanced weakening capacities with no chance of improvement" in its declaration of invalidity, an exchange between plaintiffs' lead counsel and the SCC regarding the meaning of "irremediable" further accentuates the point that eligibility on the basis of psychiatric illness was not before the courts in *Carter*.

> MADAM JUSTICE ABELLA: One of the qualities that you said we should look at in permitting assisted dying is irremediable medical conditions.
> MR ARVAY, Q.C.: Yes.
> MADAM JUSTICE ABELLA: How is that consistent with your argument that an individual has the right to decide the quality of his or her life based on a dignity interest?
> MR ARVAY, Q.C.: *Because our argument is founded on what Professor Battin sort of described as both principles of autonomy and the value of mercy.* Because we are seeking to constitutionalize or to strike down the law that criminalizes assistance in suicide, *we don't rely on autonomy alone, we rely on autonomy and suffering.*

MADAM JUSTICE ABELLA: *But that can exist whether or not the medical condition is irremediable.* I'm just asking why you think that has to be a condition that you impose in the decision to strike down when somebody wants the assistance of a doctor. *Why can it not be a medical condition period? What is there about the ability of somebody to choose that should be restricted by the longevity or the fatality, the expected fatality of the illness?*
MR ARVAY, Q.C.: Well, first of all, we do not limit our claim to the terminally ill. People like Tony Nicklinson who had locked-in syndrome, which means he was going to live for 20 years.
MADAM JUSTICE ABELLA: So what do you mean by –
MR ARVAY, Q.C.: So we had people like that in mind as to say that *we are not limiting our case to the terminally ill, but we are limiting our case to people whose condition is irremediable or incurable, if you want to use that language, because assisted dying should only be allowed in the most serious cases and not just because somebody wants to, it's because their condition is not going to get any better.*
MADAM JUSTICE ABELLA: Thank you.
MR ARVAY, Q.C.: Okay.
MADAM JUSTICE ABELLA: *That's what I wanted your clarification on.*
MR ARVAY, Q.C.: Yes. Thank you.[71]

Notwithstanding that "irremediable," according to the SCC, "does not require a patient to undertake treatments that are not acceptable to the individual,"[72] the above exchange points to an objective evaluation of what an irremediable medical condition is for the purposes of physician-assisted death eligibility, namely that the condition is "incurable" and is "not going to get any better," rather than eligibility hinging solely on whether or not individuals will accept evidence-based, recommended medical treatment(s).

As for Gloria Taylor, the claimant in the *Carter* case, the trial court accepted, based on the attestation of her physician, that there was "no hope of her recovering."[73] The same cannot be determinatively concluded in cases of mental illness.[74]

It is also noteworthy and bears repeating that the Supreme Court explicitly situated its section 7 *Charter* analysis within a particular context: "*during the passage to death*" (as opposed to *any* stage of life), where "in certain circumstances" (as opposed to *all* circumstances) "an individual's choice about the *end of her life* is entitled to respect."[75]

Ultimately, the trial court in *Carter* was satisfied that the risks associated with physician-assisted suicide and euthanasia could be limited by making physician-assisted death a "stringently-limited" exception, subject to "an almost-absolute prohibition."[76] In support of this conclusion, the trial judge specifically pointed to "the low numbers of persons in Oregon who have availed themselves of physician-assisted suicide."[77]

Oregon's "death with dignity" (DWD) regime, both then and now, does not allow assisted death for mental illness or, for that matter, any medical condition other than a "terminal disease," that is, an incurable and irreversible disease that, as medically judged, "will produce death within six months."[78] The *Carter* trial judgment noted that in 2010, there were sixty-five assisted deaths in Oregon, amounting to 0.209 per cent of deaths in that jurisdiction.[79] In 2022, Oregon's DWD numbers rose to 278, amounting to an estimated 0.6 per cent of total deaths in that state.[80] And since the Oregon DWD law was passed in 1997, the total number of DWD deaths in Oregon is 2,454.[81] In contrast, 13,241 people died by MAiD in Canada in 2022 alone, amounting to 4.1 per cent of total deaths that year.[82] This rate is 583 per cent higher than the 2022 Oregon rates and 1860 per cent higher than the 2010 per capita rates in Oregon that appeared to reassure the trial court in *Carter*.[83] This single year total also amounts to 10,787 more deaths, nearly 440 per cent higher, than the total DWD deaths in Oregon (2,454) over the span of 25 years.[84]

The large discrepancy in the use of MAiD in Canada when compared with other jurisdictions such as Oregon can be explained in part by euthanasia (in which a physician administers lethal drugs to the patient) being permitted in Canada, whereas only assisted suicide (in which the patient self-administers the lethal drugs) is permitted in Oregon.[85] The rapid expansion of MAiD in Canada, with numbers equalling or bypassing the most liberal euthanasia regimes in a short period of time, is likely also related to the lack of explicit requirement in Canadian law that physicians need to agree that there are no other medical options left to address a patient's suffering, which is a requirement under Belgian and Dutch law.[86]

In the end, pursuant to the section 7 infringement, Justice Smith issued a declaration allowing "physician-assisted suicide or consensual physician-assisted death," but only for (among other criteria) "a fully-informed, non-ambivalent competent adult person who … *is not clinically depressed.*"[87] The court also required that Ms. Taylor's physician attest that she was "*terminally ill and near death*, and there is *no hope of her recovering.*"[88]

It is difficult to see how these conditions (terminally ill, near death, and no hope of recovery) could be met where the sole underlying condition is a mental disorder.

In sum, the trial court did not declare – or even suggest – that MAiD should be offered as a medical treatment for mental illness. Quite the opposite, the court was explicitly concerned that a mental illness (specifically, clinical depression) should *not* be a factor driving the request for MAiD. Based on the *Carter* cases, then, it is difficult to interpret the Supreme Court's decision as in any way *mandating* Parliament to legally introduce the practice of termination of life for mental illness.

Two additional lower court cases, however, are relevant to this discussion, as both have been referenced by MAiD-MI-SUMC proponents as confirming or establishing the right to MAiD for mental illness. These decisions are discussed below.

At the outset, however, it is important to note that neither of these decisions have been reviewed by the Supreme Court of Canada. The first case, *E.F.*, is a decision of the Alberta Court of Appeal, which explicitly stated that its opinion did *not* represent a constitutional analysis of any kind.[89] The second case, *Truchon*, is a decision of a single judge of the Quebec Superior Court, which was not appealed.[90] Neither decision is binding on the Supreme Court of Canada, and neither is binding outside of their respective provinces.[91]

Canada (Attorney General) v. E.F. (Alberta Court of Appeal)

Pursuant to *Carter*, the Supreme Court's declaration of invalidity was suspended for twelve months (until 6 February 2016) to allow time for Parliament to respond, meaning the absolute prohibition against physician-assisted death remained in place while awaiting new federal legislation.[92] Failing to pass legislation within that time frame, Parliament received a four-month extension from the Supreme Court (until 6 June 2016) and eventually passed Bill C-14 on 17 June 2016.[93] That bill amended the Criminal Code to allow the practice of "medical assistance in dying" or MAiD.[94]

During the four-month extension period, however, individuals who wished to seek "termination of life" were granted an exemption that allowed them to "apply to the superior court of their jurisdiction for relief *in accordance with the criteria set out in para. 127*" of *Carter*.⁹⁵ Accordingly, the task of the judges hearing these applications was to determine whether applicants came "within the class of people" who had been granted a constitutional exemption during that four-month period.⁹⁶

Approximately fifteen applications for judicial authorization were brought before the provincial courts, only one of which involved a psychiatric illness as the underlying medical condition, namely, *E.F.*⁹⁷

E.F. involved a patient suffering from "severe conversion disorder," a psychogenic disorder causing physical symptoms. For E.F., the disorder caused involuntary muscle spasms that, among other things, affected E.F.'s vision (her eyelid muscles spasmed shut) and digestive system, rendered her non-ambulatory, and caused severe and constant pain.⁹⁸ Because the medical condition had "at its root a psychiatric condition," the motions judge's decision authorizing E.F.'s application was challenged, and the Alberta Court of Appeal (ABCA) was called on to determine *inter alia* whether "persons suffering psychiatric conditions and who otherwise comply with the criteria in *Carter 2015* [are] excluded from the ambit of the constitutional exemption."⁹⁹

Again, *E.F.* was not considering an individual constitutional challenge, nor the constitutionality of a legislative regime that explicitly excluded assisted death in cases where mental illness is the sole underlying medical disorder.¹⁰⁰ As put by the court in *E.F.*: "the constitutional dimensions and debate inherent in the granting of a personal constitutional exemption *do not form part of the inquiry in an application* under *Carter 2016*. The authorization hearings are not intended as requests for exemptions. *These are not individual constitutional challenges.* The question the Supreme Court has directed the superior courts to answer in these applications is *whether the applicant falls within the identified group. This limited inquiry* is individual and fact-specific."¹⁰¹

Accordingly, the comments in *E.F.* regarding assisted death for psychiatric illness reflect an interpretation of the Supreme Court's words in *Carter*. Furthermore, the court in *E.F.* was only tasked with determining the scope of the Supreme Court's declaration in *Carter* because Parliament had not yet passed a new law in response.¹⁰² As the Quebec Superior Court later affirmed in the *Truchon* case (discussed further below), what *Carter* said and what the *Charter* ultimately requires in terms of curative legislation after a constitutional challenge are not necessarily equivalent.¹⁰³

Keeping the foregoing in mind, the ABCA concluded *inter alia* that the declaration in *Carter* did not exclude or preclude psychiatric conditions from MAiD eligibility.

With respect to the Supreme Court's comment in *Carter* at paragraph 111 that high-profile cases of assisted dying in Belgium (i.e., psychiatric cases) "would not fall within the parameters suggested in [its] reasons," the ABCA asserted that it was made in the limited context of clarifying that "slippery slope" concerns arising out of Belgium were "addressed by the safeguards put in place in the court's description of the declaration of invalidity."[104]

However, this assertion overlooks the fact that MAiD MI-SUMC (along with MAiD for minor medical conditions or MAiD for minor children), as earlier alluded to, was *itself* one of those substantive "slippery slope" concerns. In the expert evidence affidavit from Professor Etienne Montero (an expert on euthanasia practice in Belgium) – the evidence underlying the Supreme Court's paragraph 111 statement – Professor Montero described the difficulty in maintaining boundaries around the statutory conditions in Belgium and cited, *inter alia*, examples of conditions that were "officially eligible" under the Belgian law due to "loose interpretation of the statutory conditions"[105] – namely:

- euthanasia for psychological pain (e.g., an inmate with long-term incarceration and a transgender individual with a "botched sex change surgery");
- euthanasia in anticipation of future pain that is also a form of psychological pain (e.g., a cancer diagnosis, Alzheimer's, or diagnosis of glaucoma and future blindness);
- euthanasia for psychiatric patients (e.g., anorexia nervosa); and
- euthanasia for multiple but non-serious disorders (e.g., conditions that might arise in relation to older age).[106]

Professor Montero also described the more recent legislative developments in Belgium, such as euthanasia for children, as well as emerging developments such as euthanasia for persons with dementia and disabled newborns.[107] When describing euthanasia for psychiatric patients, Professor Montero also noted the confusion that exists between psychological pain and psychiatric illness.[108]

Again, the expert evidence at issue identified specific concerns about euthanasia for particular types of conditions or circumstances (for example, psychiatric illness, non-terminal conditions, or psychological pain) or particular classes of persons (for example, minors). Equally important at this point in the Supreme Court's analysis was the question of whether the absolute prohibition against MAiD could be justified and thus retained (pursuant to section 1) notwithstanding the limitation of the claimant's section 7 rights.

With this added information, let's look at the SCC's paragraph 111 in full, and in context:

> [110] ... Canada says that Professor Montero's evidence demonstrates *that issues with compliance and with the expansion of the criteria granting access to assisted suicide inevitably arise, even in a system of ostensibly strict limits and safeguards.* It argues that this "should give pause to those who feel very strict safeguards will provide adequate protection: paper safeguards are only as strong as the human hands that carry them out" (R.F., at para. 97).
>
> [111] Professor Montero's affidavit *reviews a number of recent, controversial, and high-profile cases of assistance in dying in Belgium which would not fall within the parameters suggested in these reasons, such as euthanasia for minors or persons with psychiatric disorders or minor medical conditions.* Professor Montero suggests that *these cases* demonstrate that a slippery slope is at work in Belgium. In his view, "[o]nce euthanasia is allowed, *it becomes very difficult to maintain a strict interpretation of the statutory conditions.*"
>
> [112] *We are not convinced that Professor Montero's evidence undermines the trial judge's findings of fact*. First, the trial judge (rightly, in our view) noted that the permissive regime in Belgium is the product of a very different medico-legal culture. Practices of assisted death were "already prevalent and embedded in the medical culture" prior to legalization (para. 660). *The regime simply regulates a common pre-existing practice. In the absence of a comparable history in Canada, the trial judge concluded that it was problematic to draw inferences about the level of physician compliance with legislated safeguards* based on the Belgian evidence (para. 680). This distinction is relevant both in assessing the degree of physician compliance *and in considering evidence with regards to the potential for a slippery slope.*
>
> [113] Second, the cases described by Professor Montero *were the result of an oversight body exercising discretion in the*

interpretation of the safeguards and restrictions in the Belgian legislative regime – a discretion the Belgian Parliament has not moved to restrict. These cases offer little insight into how a Canadian regime might operate.[109]

A plain reading of these paragraphs from *Carter* seems to point to the SCC generally rejecting Professor Montero's evidence of slide or eligibility expansion into, for example, MAiD for children, psychiatric disorders, or minor medical conditions, based on two main reasons or observations: (1) that these types of cases are simply not relevant to the scope of the decision at hand, and (2) that evidence of slide within the Belgian regime (due to a "different medico-legal culture," interpretive discretion, non-compliance, and so forth) provides little-to-no insight with respect to assessing Canadian physician compliance with eventual Canadian safeguards and criteria and how a Canadian regime might ultimately operate.

Implicit in both of these reasons is an acknowledgment that the *Charter* question at hand does not concern assisted death for children, psychiatric disorders, or minor conditions. Even more explicitly, the Supreme Court makes clear, both here and in confining its scope to the "factual circumstances in the case," that its declaration clearly does not encompass such cases or circumstances.[110] The Supreme Court also suggests that, contrary to the Belgian legislature, Canada's Parliament could enact stronger safeguards and restrictions, reducing the level of "discretion" compared to that allowed under Belgian law.[111] It is therefore remarkable that the opposite appears to have occurred.[112]

In *E.F.*, the ABCA (agreeing with the motions judge's interpretation) maintains that paragraph 111 "does not serve to exclude all psychiatric conditions from the court's declaration of invalidity."[113] According to the ABCA, the SCC rejected Professor Montero's concerns not on the basis of the irrelevance of the Belgian scheme and experience to Canada's eventual scheme, but on the basis that the SCC has identified specific "safeguards" – safeguards that the Supreme Court later articulates in the declaration paragraph (paragraph 127), namely:

- that a medical condition be "grievous and irremediable" and causing enduring and intolerable suffering (a requirement that excludes minor medical conditions and potentially also indicates "incurable");[114]

- that a person be an "adult" (a requirement to exclude *and* safeguard minors because of their "vulnerability"); and
- that a person be "competent" and "clearly consents" (requirements to safeguard the vulnerability of persons who have psychiatric disorders).

So instead of excluding MAiD for psychiatric illness, the ABCA's interpretation of *Carter*'s paragraph 111 is that concerning or problematic issues related to psychiatric disorders (such as "vulnerability" or lack of consent) are addressed by safeguards contained in paragraph 127.[115] In other words, the ABCA effectively reads language into paragraph 111 to say something like this: "controversial ... cases of assistance in dying ... such as [assistance in dying] for ... persons with psychiatric disorders ... would not fall within the parameters suggested in these reasons *because the 'competent adult' and 'clearly consents' safeguards exclude any problematic cases of mental illness; otherwise, euthanasia for persons with psychiatric disorders as the sole underlying medical condition fall within the parameters of the Declaration, so long as all the criteria are met.*"

This is one interpretation of the Supreme Court's language, but in our respectful view, it is a strained and implausible one – such an approach is hardly explicit in the reasons themselves, and the Supreme Court could have used much clearer language if that was its intent.

In *E.F.*, the ABCA was also presented with the federal government's argument that psychiatric conditions were inferentially excluded from MAiD by the Supreme Court's statement that its declaration was "intended to respond to the *factual circumstances* in this case," and *Carter* did not involve a claimant with a psychiatric condition.[116] The ABCA also rejected this argument, stating that "in *Carter 2015* the issue of whether psychiatric conditions should be excluded from the declaration of invalidity *was squarely before the court;* nevertheless the court *declined to make such an express exclusion* as part of its carefully crafted criteria."[117]

Again, this conclusion seems strained. One might ask: what is paragraph 111 of *Carter* if not an "express exclusion" of psychiatric conditions from the court's "carefully crafted criteria"? And regardless, why assume that psychiatric conditions are *included* unless they are "expressly excluded"? Why not conclude that they are *excluded* unless they are "expressly included"?[118]

Nevertheless, the ABCA concluded that persons "with a psychiatric illness are not explicitly or inferentially excluded if they fit the criteria."[119] In doing so, the ABCA seemed to read *Carter*'s declaration as restricting or colouring the scope of the clarifying statements surrounding it (including paragraph 111), rather than the other way around.

In terms of psychiatric conditions being "squarely before the court" in *Carter*,[120] as discussed above, this is true only in respect of evidence and analysis regarding the potential impacts of mental illness or psychological suffering on *decision-making capacity to consent* to MAiD, but not in respect of whether psychiatric disorders as the sole medical condition would qualify *as a condition for* MAiD *eligibility* in Canada.

For these reasons, it appears that the court in *E.F.* was conflating (or collapsing the distinction between) criteria aimed at ruling out psychiatric disorders potentially affecting or likely to affect the decision-making process with the types of medical conditions that would qualify for MAiD access.

Ultimately, however, the *E.F.* decision did not involve any interpretation of *Charter* rights, nor a declaration of the constitutionality of a specific legislative provision. It was simply an interpretation of the scope of *Carter*'s declaration for the purpose of determining whether a specific applicant to the court met the criteria for a constitutional exemption for physician-assisted death during the interim period in which Parliament had not yet implemented a legislative response. The ABCA acknowledged this point, recognizing that there was no legislation before it that was the subject of constitutional review, stating: "Issues that might arise regarding the interpretation and constitutionality of eventual legislation should obviously wait until the legislation has been enacted."[121]

E.F. therefore does not and cannot stand for the proposition that the *Charter* requires MAiD for mental illness. As the Quebec Superior Court later affirmed in *Truchon*, even if legislative requirements are inconsistent with *Carter*'s parameters, they are not "*de facto* unconstitutional."[122] The question is whether legislation complies with the *Charter*, which requires a case-specific, contextual analysis of the legislative regime in question.[123] Indeed, in a 2021 decision, the Supreme Court described *Carter 2016*'s constitutional exemptions for physician-assisted death as "guidelines" and noted: "Of course, *the legislature can always legislate a different approach*, including retroactively, within the confines of the Constitution."[124]

Moreover, *E.F.* does not speak to the legislature's ability to introduce additional safeguards around MAiD in connection with psychiatric conditions, such as (for example) the exclusion of cases in which a plaintiff is suicidal or clinically depressed. In fact, the ABCA emphasized evidence before it that the plaintiff was not "depressed or suicidal."[125] Like the trial decision in *Carter*, this points to the complexity of mental illnesses such as depression and how related symptoms may necessitate additional considerations.[126] Certainly, *E.F.* does not state or even suggest that MAiD must be available where clinical depression is a patient's sole underlying condition.

In short, while the *E.F.* case rejected the government's argument that *Carter* categorically excluded psychiatric conditions from its declaration, it remains that *Carter* did not issue a specific legislative mandate to Parliament to decriminalize or permit MAiD *for* mental illness, nor did it assert that the *Charter* prohibits a legislative response that might exclude it. The mere conclusion that the *Carter* declaration did not specifically exclude mental illness does not mean that Parliament must include it.[127] As Justice Moldaver acknowledged during the Supreme Court's hearing of *Carter* 2016, Parliament "might want *other conditions beyond what we talked about* ... they might want to put in measures that ensure so far as possible that we are not killing people who really ought not to be killed."[128] This statement was cited by the BC Supreme Court in concluding that a fresh constitutional analysis was merited in assessing Parliament's legislative response to *Carter*.[129]

Ultimately, *E.F.*'s comments on *Carter* pertain to a limited factual and legal context and have not yet been addressed, let alone affirmed, by the Supreme Court of Canada.

A WORD ON "GRIEVOUS AND IRREMEDIABLE" CRITERIA
Though not related to the immediate question of whether the Canadian courts have established a *Charter* right to MAiD MI-SUMC, and notwithstanding that *E.F.* was not considering legislated safeguards around MAiD for psychiatric conditions,[130] it is noteworthy that the ABCA implicitly imposed its own procedural safeguard in respect of the applicant's psychiatric illness being considered "irremediable" – one of the eligibility requirements under the declaration.[131] The ABCA explained that while some patients with conversion disorder might be "successfully treated," others like the applicant might not respond to treatment even over a significant amount of

time.[132] Here, the applicant had undergone both traditional and non-traditional treatments for over nine years, none of which had remedied the applicant's condition, which included physical symptoms that had resisted treatment and interfered with the applicant's quality of life.[133] On this basis, the ABCA agreed with the conclusion of the motions judge, that the applicant's psychiatric condition met the grievous *and* irremediable criteria.[134]

It is further worth pointing out that psychiatric experts have criticized the evidentiary basis and procedures followed in *E.F.* to establish the claimant's eligibility even according to the broad criteria the court set out. In an article in the *Journal of Ethics in Mental Health*, Dr Trevor Hurwitz, one of Canada's specialists on this rare disorder, expressed concern that E.F. was unlikely to have been assessed by someone with special expertise in the disorder, and that this was particularly problematic for a condition that is often misdiagnosed and confused with other neurological disorders, and for which more appropriate treatment may be available. He further pointed out that the court-appointed expert confirmed the diagnosis without meeting the patient in person. One could, therefore, invoke the *E.F.* decision to highlight the dangers of allowing MAiD in complex situations like the *E.F.* case, and at least the need for additional safeguards, instead of as support for the existence of a constitutional right to MAiD for mental illness.[135]

Truchon (Quebec Superior Court)

As described earlier, in June 2016, federal Bill C-14 amended the Criminal Code to permit the practice of MAiD.[136] Quebec's end-of-life (EOL) law was already in effect as of December 2015.[137] The 2019 Quebec Superior Court's decision in *Truchon* struck down Bill C-14's requirement that in order to access MAiD, a person's natural death must be "reasonably foreseeable" (RFND), as well as the "end-of-life" criterion contained in the Quebec EOL law.[138]

The *Truchon* case involved applicants Jean Truchon and Nicole Gladu, both of whom were seeking access to MAiD but were considered ineligible because their respective physical medical conditions did not meet the RFND/EOL criteria.[139] The applicants successfully challenged the federal RFND criterion on the basis of the section 7 *Charter* right to life, liberty, and security of the person and the section 15 *Charter* right to equality, as well as the Quebec EOL criterion on the basis of section 15 only.[140]

Although a closer examination of MAiD jurisdictional issues is the subject of the following chapter, it should be pointed out here that the distinction with respect to the section 7 and section 15 *Charter* arguments in *Truchon* relates in part to the different objectives of the statutory provisions at issue (as identified by the Quebec court). The court (Justice Baudouin) observed that while the federal MAiD law under the Criminal Code was a response to a court decision (i.e., *Carter 2015*), the Quebec EOL legislation was enacted pursuant to provincial jurisdiction over health as a "social response" and "paradigm shift" based on Quebec medical community initiatives that desired a "holistic approach" to appropriate "end-of-life" care.[141] Therefore, the court identified the objective of the federal legislation and RFND criterion as the protection of "vulnerable persons who might be induced to end their lives in a moment of weakness, *by preventing errors when assessing requests for medical assistance in dying.*"[142] Note here that the object of the federal law (as identified by the Quebec court) is no longer in relation to the absolute prohibition of assisted suicide (the issue in *Carter*), but rather in relation to Bill C-14's new MAiD scheme pursuant to the Criminal Code. Thus, as later stated by the Quebec court, "*The object of the legislation is precisely to allow people who meet the state-imposed conditions to request medical assistance in dying.* It is admitted that the applicants, having been examined and assessed by several experts, *meet every legal requirement except for the one regarding end of life. There is no question of a potential error regarding their eligibility or of protecting them as vulnerable persons due to their medical condition.*"[143]

On the other hand, the court identified the purpose of the Quebec legislation with its EOL requirement as having a "twofold" purpose, namely, end-of-life care and the "recognition of dignity and autonomy."[144] The court also stated that in terms of purpose, "medical aid in dying" under the Quebec EOL law was considered appropriate care not because of it being provided at end of life, but because it related to suffering and decision-making autonomy.[145] Consequently, the court focused on the effects of the EOL provision on the applicants in relation to their section 15 equality rights.[146]

The main point here is that in *Truchon* the court was tasked with determining whether the RFND and EOL criteria were constitutionally valid. And again, MAiD MI-SUMC was not part of this question. Justice Baudouin did recognize early in the judgment that despite decriminalization, MAiD continued to prompt concerns and raise questions that remained unanswered, including, for example, MAiD in respect of minor children and incapable persons.[147] However, Justice Baudouin clarified that the sole question before the court was to "determine the constitutional validity" of the RFND and EOL requirements, and that this was "the *only question* that it will answer."[148]

The court agreed to hear some expert evidence concerning MAiD-MI-SUMC in connection with "the impact that the removal of the reasonably foreseeable natural death requirement would have on the vulnerable persons that the government wants to protect."[149] Ultimately, however, the court stressed that, because neither of the plaintiffs in that case had "a psychiatric illness that could be related to their request for medical assistance in dying,"[150] the "relevance of any evidence adduced by the Attorney General of Canada on the subject of people who might avail themselves of medical assistance in dying based solely on a psychiatric illness is doubtful, to say the least."[151] With this caveat, *Truchon*'s limited discussion of MAiD MI-SUMC, summarized below, should be considered *obiter dicta*.

TRUCHON'S LIMITED DISCUSSION OF MAiD MI-SUMC
Because the *Charter* analysis in *Truchon* involved consideration of the "vulnerable person," as well as physicians' ability to assess the capacity of patients,[152] the court allowed and considered, to a limited extent, evidence regarding "vulnerable persons whose psychiatric illness is the only medical condition underlying their request for medical assistance in dying."[153] Specifically, the court contemplated evidence and arguments led by Canada in relation to the "the danger of extending access to medical assistance in dying to patients suffering from a psychiatric condition."[154] For the court, the only relevance of this evidence boiled down to the issue of whether a person could have the capacity to consent in "the presence of any illness" including a "psychiatric illness," whatever the legislative provisions in force.[155] The court concluded that, whether or not a patient is suffering from a psychiatric or physical condition, the question of capacity and vulnerability can and must be assessed on an individual, case-by-case basis. Justice Baudouin was satisfied on the evidence before her that the process for assessing capacity in Canada by health care professionals was sufficient.[156]

The court's observations around capacity in the potential presence of mental illness or psychological suffering say nothing about whether MAiD-MI-SUMC is *required* by the *Charter*. The court made no such declaration.[157] The court was not asked to opine on whether Parliament could specifically exclude psychiatric conditions from the MAiD regime based on a variety of other factors. Rather, Justice Baudouin concluded that, for the purposes of determining eligibility, patients who *otherwise meet the statute's requirements* cannot be presumed to be ineligible based solely on collective assumptions related to mental illness or psychiatric conditions. In the view of the authors, Justice Baudouin's discussion is best understood as dealing with safeguards and whether mental illness or psychiatric condition precludes an *otherwise eligible person* from receiving MAiD, not whether the *Charter* requires Parliament to include psychiatric conditions within the eligibility criteria for granting MAiD in the first place.

Again, it is important here not to conflate *eligibility* for MAiD solely on the basis of a psychiatric illness with how the court tackled issues of *decisional capacity* and *vulnerability* when a person has psychological pain or suffering associated with the somatic medical condition or if psychiatric illness is concurrently present. For example, although the applicants' respective somatic medical conditions caused them psychological suffering in various forms, including in relation to dependency, fear of dependency, being bedridden, loss of autonomy, and loss of meaning in life,[158] neither had any psychiatric illness affecting their capacity to consent[159] or in relation to their respective requests for medical assistance in dying.[160]

It should, however, also be pointed out that the court's analysis seemed to assume that, other than the "reasonably foreseeable death" qualifier, MAiD for certain "mental" conditions (for example, intellectual disability) might already be included in Parliament's existing legislative regime.[161]

For its part, the federal government (which chose not to appeal *Truchon*, despite calls from numerous commentators and disability rights organizations to do so)[162] evidently did not interpret *Truchon* as requiring MAiD for mental illness,[163] as its initial legislative response to *Truchon* (i.e., Bill C-7 as introduced) specifically excluded mental illness as a sole underlying condition from MAiD's eligibility criteria.[164] Furthermore, no court has considered the constitutionality of the government's initial legislative proposal to exclude mental illness in Bill C-7, nor, for that matter, the amended version that followed, which removed the mental illness exclusion through a sunset clause.[165] Finally, we note that, even if the courts had issued an opinion on the constitutionality of a mental illness exclusion, that would not necessarily be the end of the matter. As the

Supreme Court has acknowledged, "it does not follow from the fact that a law passed by Parliament differs from a regime envisaged by the Court in the absence of a statutory scheme, that Parliament's law is unconstitutional. Parliament may build on the Court's decision, and develop a different scheme as long as it remains constitutional. Just as Parliament must respect the Court's rulings, so the Court must respect Parliament's determination that the judicial scheme can be improved. To insist on slavish conformity would belie the mutual respect that underpins the relationship between the courts and legislature that is so essential to our constitutional democracy."[166]

CONCLUSION

Contrary to what some have argued, the courts have not directed legislatures to permit MAiD for mental illness. Instead, they have expressed some caution and an inclination to defer to legislative deliberations on this issue. Canadian courts *have* declined to allow MAiD for patients who are clinically depressed or suicidal, by ruling out the presence of certain psychiatric conditions or suicidality,[167] and *have* stated that assisted death should be subject to an "almost-absolute prohibition."[168] Canadian courts have also affirmed that a high degree of deference is owed to legislators regarding MAiD, especially in the context of a "complex regulatory response," which is better created by the legislature than by the courts.[169] In our view, a degree of deference that the *Carter* decision recognized should already have been a reason to defend the original end-of-life focused MAiD law (Bill C-14). This call for deference would certainly need to be taken into account if Parliament or the provinces were to decide to prohibit or restrict MAiD for mental illness based on complex medical, clinical, ethical, and social considerations, including those related to provincial jurisdiction over health care.[170]

Thus far, the federal government has chosen not to seek a reference to the Supreme Court of Canada for its opinion with respect to some of these issues. Similarly, the attorney general refused to appeal the *Truchon* decision, which would have permitted the Supreme Court to opine on whether a safeguard of reasonably foreseeable natural death was indeed unconstitutional and irreconcilable with the parameters it issued in *Carter*. Expanding MAiD now further, shouldering the "obviously irreversible and heavy"[171] consequences of a MAiD MI-SUMC regime on the basis that advocates have simply *argued* that the *Charter* requires it, is in our view an abdication of the constitutional role bestowed upon legislators: to wrestle with "complex issues of social policy and a number of competing societal values" to determine the appropriate boundaries of *everyone*'s rights in accordance with the principles of a free and democratic society.[172]

Simply asserting that the *Charter* requires Canada to offer MAiD for mental illness, when in fact no court has stated so, and with the arguments remaining untested, not only risks misleading the public – it pre-empts their opportunity to contribute, through the democratic process, to the determination of what justice actually requires in this context. Similarly, it suppresses meaningful medical and ethical discourse on what constitutes appropriate health care and what services are – and are *not* – clinically appropriate medical solutions to mental disorders.

The determination of what is "clinically appropriate" should not be dictated by what is merely projected (by some) as "constitutionally required." Rather, clinical experience and medical expertise must help *inform* the constitutional analysis of what constitutes a reasonable legislative regime in a free and democratic society under section 1 of the *Charter*. As the trial judge noted in *Carter*, ethical principles appropriately help shape the law and enter into constitutional analysis,[173] and "both legal and constitutional principles are derived from and shaped by societal values."[174]

Thus, health care professionals and their organizations should not feel pressured to embrace certain practices as "good medicine" simply because some have asserted that the Constitution "requires" it.[175] What the Constitution actually requires is that decision-makers carefully consider all of the evidence, including the insights and recommendations of health care professionals with clinical experience and expertise in supporting those with disabilities and mental disorders, in determining what is "reasonable" in a "free and democratic society."[176]

The Constitution of Canada is not a governmental tool for political expedience. It does not excuse governments from justifying contentious policies nor is it a political shortcut to bypass challenging work – it is a mandate requiring legislators to meaningfully engage in it.

For the Constitution (and for that matter medicine as well) to work effectively, it requires courage: courage from professionals and their organizations to challenge prevailing narratives where necessary – even when doing so is unpopular – and to offer decision-makers, the courts, and society insights based on their special knowledge, experience, and expertise. It also requires courage from political decision-makers to wrestle with that evidence and to develop legislative and regulatory regimes that offer adequate protection within the context of constitutional constraints. It sets a precarious precedent when policy changes with major societal implications are pushed through on the basis of self-imposed, fictitious, or even prematurely perceived legal constraints.

NOTES

This chapter is, combined with the next chapter, a slightly revised version of an article that was originally published in the *Manitoba Law Journal*, under the title "Mental Illness, Health Care, and Assisted Death: Examining Parameters for Expanding or Restricting MAID under Canada's Charter and Federal System," *Manitoba Law Journal* 47, no. 2 (forthcoming 2025): preprint. The authors are grateful to the *Manitoba Law Journal* for permission to republish the article here as two slightly revised chapters.

1 *Mental illness* is the term used in federal MAiD legislation, including Bill C-14, Bill C-7, and Bill C-39, but it has not yet been defined in such statutes. None use the term *mental disorder*, although this terminology is used elsewhere in the *Criminal Code of Canada*, RSC 1985, c. C-46 (where it is defined as "disease of the mind" and is largely used in relation to determining whether an accused is criminally responsible). The term *mental illness* was described by the Expert Panel on MAID and Mental Illness as referring to "a subset of mental disorders, but lack[ing] a standard clinical definition." The term *mental disorder* appears to be favoured in the clinical context and "is the term used in both major diagnostic classification schemes relied upon in Canadian psychiatric practice." It is also the term used in *Quebec's Act Respecting End-of-Life Care*, CQLR c. S-32.001 (Can.) (in French, *trouble mental*). The terms *mental illness* and *mental disorder* are often used interchangeably in discussions around MAID policy. Because federal MAID legislation has only used the former term to date, we generally use the term *mental illness* throughout this paper, although *mental disorder* and *psychiatric disorder* are also used, particularly when describing cases, statutes, or sources that use those terms. Whether there is a substantive difference between the terms as a matter of statutory interpretation remains to be seen; we note, however, that even in legislation, the terms *mental illness* and *mental disorder* often appear to be interchangeable. Section 2 of the French version of Criminal Code ("definitions"), for example, simply uses the former term (*maladie*

mentale) to define the latter term (*trouble mental*). Other statutes, such as the *Youth Criminal Justice Act,* SC 2002, c. 1 (Can.), employ them both (using the term *mental illness or disorder*).

2 Initially, this change was set to come into effect in March 2023, pursuant to amendments introduced in *Bill C-7, An Act to Amend the Criminal Code (medical assistance in dying)*, 43rd Parliament, 2nd Session (2021), cl. 1(2.1), SC 2021, c. 2 (Can.). In December 2022, the federal government announced that it would seek to delay the March 2023 start date, but stressed that it would only be *delaying* and not *cancelling* the implementation of MAiD MI-SUMC. On 2 February 2023, then minister of justice David Lametti introduced Bill C-39, which was passed on 9 March 2023. Bill C-39 delays the repeal of the exclusion from eligibility for MAiD MI-SUMC until 17 March 2024. For the text of the bill, see *Bill C-39, An Act to Amend An Act to Amend the Criminal Code (medical assistance in dying)*, 44th Parliament, 1st Session (2023), SC 2023, c. 1 (Can.).

Bill C-314, a private member's bill introduced by MP Ed Fast, proposed to halt this expansion; it was defeated on 18 October 2023 by a vote of 167–150. Immediately after the vote, Parliament referred the matter to a special joint committee to assess the degree to which Canada is prepared for this expansion and to report back with a final recommendation by 31 January 2024. See *Bill C-314, An Act to Amend the Criminal Code (medical assistance in dying)*, 44th Parliament, 1st Session (22 November 2021), last modified 2023, https://www.parl.ca/legisinfo/en/bill/44-1/c-314.

Further to that study, the Special Joint Committee on Medical Assistance in Dying concluded that "the medical system in Canada is not prepared for medical assistance in dying where mental disorder is the sole underlying medical condition," and recommended that it "should not be made available in Canada until the Minister of Health and the Minister of Justice are satisfied, based on recommendations from their respective departments and in consultation with their provincial and territorial counterparts and with Indigenous Peoples, that it can be safely and adequately provided." Special Joint Committee on Medical Assistance in Dying, MAID *and Mental Disorders: The Road Ahead*, 44th Parliament, 1st Session (29 January 2024), https://www.parl.ca/Content/Committee/441/AMAD/Reports/RP12815505/amadrp03/amadrp03-e.pdf.

In response to the committee's report, Parliament adopted Bill C-62, which delays the expansion of MAiD MI-SUMC until (at least) 17 March 2027 and also requires a "comprehensive review relating to the eligibility of persons whose sole underlying medical condition is a mental illness to receive medical assistance in dying" to be commenced by a joint committee by 29 February 2026. See *Bill C-62, An Act to Amend An Act to Amend the Criminal Code (medical assistance in dying)*, No. 2, 44th Parliament, 1st Session (2024).

3   See *Bill C-7, An Act to Amend the Criminal Code*, cl. 1(1).

4   Depending on one's interpretation, all of these conditions could meet the statutory definition of a "grievous and irremediable medical condition," and thus give rise to MAiD eligibility, if: (1) their manifestation is "serious and incurable"; (2) the patient is "in an advanced state of irreversible decline in capability"; and (3) the condition "causes them enduring physical or psychological suffering that is intolerable to them and that cannot be relieved under conditions that they consider acceptable." See *Criminal Code of Canada*, s. 241.2(2)(a-c). Although the "irremediability" of a particular case of mental illness is a matter of debate and disagreement among many experts and specialists (discussed further below), according to the federal government, after Bill C-7's exclusion of mental illness expires, MAiD will be available for those solely struggling with mental disorders including depression and personality disorders. See "Canada's Medical Assistance in Dying (MAID) Law," Department of Justice, last modified 19 June 2023, https://www.justice.gc.ca/eng/cj-jp/ad-am/bk-di.html (perma.cc/B76D-CBZU).

5   See Lars Mehlum et al., "Euthanasia and Assisted Suicide in Patients with Personality Disorders: A Review of Current Practice and Challenges," *Borderline Personality Disorder & Emotion Dysregulation* 7, no. 15 (2020): 1–7; Aiste Lengvenyte et al., "'Nothing Hurts Less Than Being Dead': Psychological Pain in Case Descriptions of Psychiatric Euthanasia and Assisted Suicide from the Netherlands," *Canadian Journal Psychiatry* 65, no. 9 (2020): 612–20; Mary J. Shariff and Derek Ross, "When Is Suicide Considered Rational?" *Policy Options*, 6 December 2023, https://policyoptions.irpp.org/magazines/december-2023/assisted-suicide-mental-illness/; see generally Expert Panel Working Group on MAiD Where a Mental Disorder Is the Sole Underlying Medical Condition, *The State of Knowledge on Medical Assistance in Dying Where a Mental Disorder is the Sole Underlying Medical Condition* (Ottawa: Council of Canadian Academies, 2018), chap. 4, https://rapports-cac.ca/wp-content/uploads/2018/12/The-State-of-Knowledge-on-Medical-Assistance-in-Dying-Where-a-Mental-Disorder-is-the-Sole-Underlying-Medical-Condition.pdf (perma.cc/HX8U-J548).

   For a discussion that distinguishes between the concepts of "rational" or "understandable" suicide versus "true" suicide within the MAiD context, see Ellen R. Wiebe et al., "Suicide vs Medical Assistance in Dying (MAiD): A Secondary Qualitative Analysis," *Death Studies* 44, no. 12 (2020):

802–7. However, a clear distinction between "MAID" and "suicide" in our view remains implausible. For example, a report from the Canadian Association for Suicide Prevention states as follows: "when considering MAID in the context of someone who is *not* dying as a result of their condition, such as a mental disorder alone, we are talking about suicide. By the very definition of suicide, which is the act of killing oneself, if the condition from which they are suffering is not killing them, then the act of providing medical assistance in dying is doctor-assisted suicide." See "CASP Issues Statement About MAID for Mental Illness," Canadian Association for Suicide Prevention, 14 December 2022, https://suicide prevention.ca/media/casp-issues-statement-about-maid-for-mental-illness/ (perma.cc/9DHY-AUMT).

6 The *Diagnostic and Statistical Manual of Mental Disorder*s (DSM-5) includes alcohol use disorder, stimulant use disorder, and gambling disorder. See discussion in "Substance-Related and Addictive Disorders," American Psychiatric Association, 2013, https://www.psychiatry.org/ file%20library/psychiatrists/practice/dsm/apa_dsm-5-substance-use-disorder.pdf.

7 See the discussion in the report of the Association des Médecins Psychiatres du Québec, *Accès à l'aide médicale à mourir pour les personnes atteintes de troubles mentaux: Document de réflexion*, 2020, 44–5, https://ampq.org/wp-content/uploads/2020/12/ampqdocreflexionammfinal.pdf (perma.cc/Y9S4-HJW8). In Belgium and the Netherlands (until recently the only other countries with a significant euthanasia practice for persons with mental illness), several persons with such cognitive disabilities have been approved for and have had their life ended by euthanasia. For a discussion of this practice, see Irene Tuffrey-Wijne et al., "Euthanasia and Physician-Assisted Suicide in People with Intellectual Disabilities and/or Autism Spectrum Disorders: Investigation of 39 Dutch Case Reports (2012–2021)," *BJPsych Open* 9, no. 3 (2023) 1–8, https://www.cambridge.org/core/journals/bjpsych-open/article/euthanasia-and-physicianassisted-suicide-in-people-with-intellectual-disabilities-andor-autism-spectrum-disorders-investigation-of-39-dutch-case-reports-20122021/93B38EAE616E0A6C378BE308C87253A2 (perma.cc/FZ97-G2KA). See also the discussion in Timothy Stainton and Trudo Lemmens, "Intellectual Disability, Euthanasia, and Assisted Suicide," in *Intellectual Disability and Autism: Ethics and Practice*, ed. Andria Bianchi and Janet A. Vogt, vol. 108, The International Library of Bioethics (Cham, Switzerland: Springer, 2024), 351–63, https://doi.org/10.1007/978-3-031-61565-8_26.

In Canada, because "mental illness" is not defined in federal MAiD legislation, it has generated some debate about whether it extends to neurodevelopmental disorders. In 2021, the federal government issued a statement on its website specifying that "the term 'mental illness' would not include neurocognitive or neurodevelopmental disorders, or other conditions that may affect cognitive abilities, such as dementias, autism spectrum disorders or intellectual disabilities, which may be treated by specialties other than psychiatry." See "Legislative Background: Bill C-7: Government of Canada's Legislative Response to the Superior Court of Québec *Truchon* Decision," Department of Justice, last modified 1 September 2021, https://www.justice.gc.ca/eng/csj-sjc/pl/ad-am/c7/p3.html.

Some seem to have interpreted this to mean that such conditions are *not currently* excluded and could *already* qualify for MAiD. We note that in 2022, 12.6 per cent of the 13,102 reported MAiD deaths listed "neurological conditions" as the main underlying condition, of which 9 per cent were listed as "dementia." Autism was not named in the annual report (although "other neurological conditions," which were not specified, accounted for 28.5 per cent of this category): see Health Canada, *Fourth Annual Report on Medical Assistance in Dying in Canada 2022*, October 2023, https://www.canada.ca/content/dam/hc-sc/documents/services/medical-assistance-dying/annual-report-2022/annual-report-2022.pdf.

We also note that a recent Alberta case generated controversy when a father requested a judicial review of the MAiD approval of his twenty-seven-year-old daughter, who he claimed had only autism, ADHD, and other undiagnosed mental health conditions. After an interim injunction was granted, the injunction was set aside by the Court of King's Bench. The judge recognized that the father had a reasonable cause of action for potential violation of procedural requirements but ruled that the potential harm to the daughter because of not having immediate access to MAiD outweighed the potential harm of grief to the parents. The judge refused to make any inquiry into the substantive basis of the approval, which he ruled was a purely medical matter and not open to judicial review. There is therefore no explicit confirmation of what the basis of the MAiD approval was, but the case raises concerns that persons with neurocognitive disorder are already being approved for MAiD. The father's appeal of this decision was later withdrawn due to mootness. *WV v. MV*, 2024 ABKB 174. For a brief discussion of the case, see Trudo Lemmens, "How Canada's Medical Assistance in Dying Law Turned Euthanasia and Assisted Suicide into a Quasi-Universal Therapy for Suffering," *Journal de Droit de La Santé et de l'Assurance Maladie* 39 (2024): 110–22, at 121–2.

The Criminal Code itself does not specifically state whether neurodevelopmental conditions are included in the definition of "mental illness" (and therefore excluded from Canada's MAiD regime). An amendment put forward by the Senate would have specified that the MAiD MI-SUMC exclusion did *not* apply to "a neurocognitive disorder," but this amendment was rejected by the House of Commons because "this matter, including questions of most appropriate precise definitions, whether those definitions should be included in the Criminal Code or elsewhere, and whether any consequential amendments or protections relating to issues such as consent and capacity are necessary in relation to such an amendment, will also be addressed by the expert panel and the upcoming parliamentary review, and the Government will collaborate with provincial and territorial health authorities to ensure a consistent approach": House of Commons, *Notice Paper*, 43–2, no. 67 (26 February 2021), at 13. On the other hand, Quebec's "medical aid in dying" legislation, discussed in the following chapter, specifically excludes "a mental disorder *other than a neurocognitive disorder*" from its regime (neither term being further defined).

An Expert Panel on MAiD and Mental Illness was established by the federal government in August 2021. That panel's final report stated it "was constituted to look at safeguards appropriate to MAiD for mental illness, and not for neurodevelopmental or other intellectual disabilities even if many of the same issues arise in such cases. Given the lack of subject matter expertise for this topic amongst the Panel membership, there is a need for the particular issues related to MAiD for persons with intellectual disabilities to be considered further and addressed in collaboration with people with lived experience and their supporters." *Final Report of the Expert Panel on MAID and Mental Illness* (Ottawa: Health Canada, 2022).

Practically speaking, the end result is that the determination of whether a particular condition meets the eligibility requirements is largely left to medical professionals to determine on a case-by-case basis, with little if any judicial review or oversight (at least before the patient's death), based on the current case law. All of this raises a number of concerns – beyond the scope of this chapter – about a lack of clarity, intelligibility, and transparency surrounding the application of Canada's existing and expanding MAiD framework to conditions such as autism spectrum disorder and intellectual disabilities, among other conditions.

8 See Ramona Coelho et al., "Bill C-7, From MAiD to MAD: Medical Assistance in Dying Becomes Medically Administered Death," MAiD to MAD, last modified 2022, https://maid2mad.ca/#DeclarationEnglish (perma.cc/N2WX-U66J); K. Sonu Gaind, "Assisted Suicide: We Are

Poised to Soon Be Ending Lives of Non-Dying People," *Toronto Star*, 24 February 2020, https://www.thestar.com/opinion/contributors/assisted-suicide-we-are-poised-to-soon-be-ending-lives-of-nondying-people/article_6628e869-dbaf-58d5-a3a8-f56c93dc4eb3.html (perma.cc/TG8B-9M9W).

9 See the report of the Expert Advisory Group on MAiD: K. Sonu Gaind et al., *Canada at a Crossroads: Recommendations on Medical Assistance in Dying and Persons with a Mental Disorder: An Evidence-Based Critique of the Halifax Group IRPP Report* (Toronto: Expert Advisory Group on Medical Assistance in Dying, 2020), https://www.eagmaid.org/report (perma.cc/XXX3-SFLT). See also the discussion in Gaind et al., "Canada's Medically Administered Death (MAD) Expansion for Mental Illness: Targeting the Most Vulnerable," *World Medical Journal* 71, no. 4 (2022): 72–82, 77–8, https://www.wma.net/publications/world-medical-journal/ (perma.cc/3LXK-Q2J6).

10 See discussion in Gerard Quinn, Claudia Mahler, and Olivier De Schutter to Canada, "Mandates of the Special Rapporteur on the Rights of Persons with Disabilities; the Independent Expert on the Enjoyment of All Human Rights by Older Persons; and the Special Rapporteur on Extreme Poverty and Human Rights," 3 February 2021, ref OL CAN 2/2021, https://spcommreports.ohchr.org/TMResultsBase/DownLoadPublicCommunicationFile?gId=26002 (perma.cc/ER9E-3Z93); see also Isabel Grant and Elizabeth Sheehy, "Focus on Dignified Lives, Not Facilitated Deaths," *Law360 Canada*, 24 March 2021, https://www.law360.ca/articles/25576 (perma.cc/6PS2-R2HA); Trudo Lemmens and Laverne Jacobs, "The Latest Medical Assistance in Dying Decision Needs to Be Appealed: Here's Why," *Conversation*, 9 October 2019, https://theconversation.com/the-latest-medical-assistance-in-dying-decision-needs-to-be-appealed-heres-why-124955 (perma.cc/MX6V-NECR); Jonas-Sébastien Beaudry, "The Way Forward for Medical Aid in Dying: Protecting Deliberative Autonomy is Not Enough," *Supreme Court Law Review (2d)* 85 (2018): 335–85, 361.

11 See Catherine Frazee, "Assisted Dying Legislation Puts Equality for People with Disabilities at Risk," *Globe and Mail*, 17 November 2020, https://www.theglobeandmail.com/opinion/article-assisted-dying-legislation-puts-equality-for-people-with-disabilities/ (perma.cc/HW3D-XFKS); Heidi Janz, "We Must Ensure Revised Assisted Dying Law Will Not Threaten Lives of People with Disabilities," *Calgary Herald*, 26 October 2020, https://calgaryherald.com/opinion/columnists/opinion-we-must-ensure-revised-assisted-dying-law-will-not-threaten-lives-of-people-with-disabilities (perma.cc/7PH5-KEY9); Jonas-Sébastien Beaudry, "Somatic Oppression

and Relational Autonomy: Revisiting Medical Aid in Dying through a Feminist Lens," UBC *Law Review* 53, no. 2 (December 2020): 241–98, 283–7; see also Jaro Kotalik and David W. Shannon, eds., *Medical Assistance in Dying (MAiD) in Canada: Key Multidisciplinary Perspectives* (Cham, Switzerland: Springer, 2023). Note that disability scholars and advocates have expressed serious concern about the overall expansion of MAiD outside the context of an approaching natural death, thus not just MAiD MI-SUMC. We share this broader concern as well.

12 *Bill C-39, An Act to Amend An Act to Amend the Criminal Code (medical assistance in dying)*, 3rd reading, *Senate Debates*, 44-1, No. 105 (9 March 2023), 3088–90 (Hon. Fabian Manning) (Can.); see also Special Joint Committee on Medical Assistance in Dying, *Medical Assistance in Dying and Mental Disorder as the Sole Underlying Condition: An Interim Report*, 44th Parliament, 1st Session, June 2022, 35–42, https://www.parl.ca/DocumentViewer/en/44-1/AMAD/report-1.

According to a recent poll conducted by the Angus Reid Institute, 51 per cent of Canadians surveyed were opposed to allowing MAiD MI-SUMC, 31 per cent were in favour, and 18 per cent were unsure: "Mental Health and MAID: Canadians Question Looming Changes to Canada's Assisted-Death Law," Angus Reid Institute, 13 February 2023, https://angusreid.org/assisted-dying-maid-mental-health/ (perma.cc/A4CJ-KL55).

13 For discussion, see Gaind et al., *Canada at a Crossroads*, 9–14; Karandeep Sonu Gaind, "What Does 'Irremediability' in Mental Illness Mean?," *Canadian Journal of Psychiatry* 65, no. 9 (September 2020): 604–6, citing Sisco M.P. van Veen, Andrea M. Ruissen, and Guy A.M. Widdershoven, "Irremediable Psychiatric Suffering in the Context of Physician-Assisted Death: A Scoping Review of Arguments," *Canadian Journal of Psychiatry* 65, no. 9 (September 2020): 593–603; see also "Medical Assistance in Dying (MAiD) and Mental Illness – FAQs," Centre for Addiction and Mental Health, February 2023, https://www.camh.ca/en/camh-news-and-stories/maid-and-mental-illness-faqs (perma.cc/5HW4-EAEA); Association des Médicins Psychiatres du Québec, *Accès à l'aide médicale à mourir*, 28–31; compare to recommendations in Health Canada, *Final Report of the Expert Panel*, 12–13, which differentiates between "irremediable" and "incurable" and describes that whether a psychiatric illness is ultimately "incurable" requires assessment on a case by case basis and furthermore "cannot be established in the absence of *multiple attempts* at interventions with therapeutic aims" (emphasis added). Note how this appears to run contrary to interpretations of "irremediability" that incorporate a patient's refusal of evidence-based treatments. See also discussion in

Special Joint Committee on Medical Assistance in Dying, MAID and *Mental Disorder Interim Report*, 37–9.

14 See note 13.

15 Canadian Human Rights Commission, "MAID cannot be an answer to systemic inequality," 10 May 2022, https://www.chrc-ccdp.gc.ca/en/resources/maid-cannot-be-answer-systemic-inequality.

16 Isabel Grant, "Legislated Ableism: Bill C-7 and the Rapid Expansion of MAID in Canada," *McGill Journal of Law and Health*, 15, no. 2 (2024) 259–335; https://mjlh.mcgill.ca/wp-content/uploads/2024/04/mjlh-15.2-grant-2024-04-30.pdf; and chapter 10 (Grant) in this volume. See also Heidi Janz, "MAID to Die by Medical and Systemic Ableism," in Kotalik and Shannon, eds., *MAID in Canada*, 299–308.

17 This is, in our view, an issue that arises broadly in the context of MAID, and particularly in situations where death is not approaching, and also in situations where mental illness and physical illness and disability intersect. But it is perhaps most starkly presented in situations of mental illness where suicidality is often a key component of the illness that underlies the request for MAID. We note that "No other country permits MAID MD-SUMC where one of the eligibility criteria is based on an individual's personal assessment of what conditions for relief of their intolerable suffering they consider acceptable. If Canada were to expand MAID MD-SUMC using this criterion, it could become the most permissive jurisdiction in the world with respect to how relief of suffering is evaluated." Expert Panel Working Group, *The State of Knowledge*. For discussion of disability being the "line in the sand," ableism, and eugenics perspectives, see, for example, Ameil J. Joseph, "Expanding MAID Could Worsen Discrimination against People with Disabilities," *iPolitics*, 19 February 2021, https://www.ipolitics.ca/news/expanding-maid-could-worsen-discrimination-against-people-with-disabilities (perma.cc/S7F9-6GSB); Shelley Tremain, "Disaster Ableism, Assisted Suicide, and Bioethics," Biopolitical Philosophy, 3 June 2022, https://biopoliticalphilosophy.com/2022/06/03/my-virtual-presentation-to-philosophia-june-3-2022-disaster-ableism-assisted-suicide-and-bioethics/ (perma.cc/X23U-8EKB).

18 When Bill C-14, the federal government's new MAID law, was introduced in 2016, the government emphasized that its restrictions on eligibility were needed, in part, to prevent MAID from being used as a means for suicide more generally. The Justice Department also emphasized that "restricting access to only those individuals whose death is reasonably foreseeable" was designed, in part, to further "the objective of suicide prevention." See

"Legislative Background: Medical Assistance in Dying (Bill C-14, as Assented to on 17 June 2016)," Department of Justice, https://www.justice.gc.ca/eng/rp-pr/other-autre/adra-amsr/p4.html (perma.cc/BM3X-CHNJ). This was affirmed in the text of the final bill; its preamble states that "suicide is a significant public health issue that can have lasting and harmful effects on individuals, families and communities": *Bill C-14, An Act to Amend the Criminal Code and to Make Related Amendments to Other Acts (medical assistance in dying)*, 42nd Parliament, 1st Session (2016), preamble para. 5, SC 2016, c. 3 (Can.).

19 "Structural vulnerability refers to the impacts of the interaction of demographic attributes (i.e., sex, gender, socioeconomic status, race/ethnicity), with assumed or attributed statuses related to one's position in prevailing social, cultural, and political hierarchies. Negative perceptions of these characteristics may lead to difficult social circumstances such as unstable housing and lack of employment opportunities. It can also affect self-perception and have an impact on how people interact with and are treated by health care systems. These types of circumstances can influence suffering and contribute to viewing death as one's only option." Health Canada, *Final Report of the Expert Panel*, 11.

20 "Data related to specific topics (eligibility, supported decision-making, means available to relieve suffering, refusal of means available, and residence and legal status) should be collected in the MAID monitoring system in addition to data already collected under the 2018 Regulations. These data can be used to assess whether key areas of concern raised about MAID MI-SUMC and complex Track 2 cases discussed in this report are being addressed by the clinical practices recommended." Health Canada, *Final Report of the Expert Panel*, 17. See Expert Panel Working Group, *The State of Knowledge*, 148–9; see also Bill C-39, *Senate Debates*, 3091 (Hon. Julie Milville-Dechêne).

21 See Expert Panel Working Group, *The State of Knowledge*, 148–9; see also Bill C-39, *Senate Debates*, 3091 (Hon. Julie Milville-Dechêne).

22 Sidney Cohen, "N.W.T. Senator Questions Territory's Ability to Offer Medical Assistance in Dying," CBC News, 5 January 2023, https://www.cbc.ca/news/canada/north/maid-expansion-on-hold-nwt-1.6704124 (perma.cc/VAJ8-QCP7); see also Stephanie Levitz, "Government Seeks Delay in Expanding Medical Access in Dying to Those with Mental Illnesses," *Toronto Star*, 15 December 2022, https://www.thestar.com/politics/federal/government-seeks-delay-in-expanding-medical-access-in-dying-to-those-with-mental-illnesses/article_2625015a-4153-5eb8-b1be-411156f203f.html (perma.cc/CX5T-Q327).

23 Cohen, "N.W.T. Senator Questions Territory."

24 "Is It Too Easy to Die in Canada? Surprising Approvals for Medically Assisted Death," CBC, *The Fifth Estate*, video, 19 January 2023, at 00:37:02, https://www.youtube.com/watch?v=plinQAHZRvk&t=2176s (perma.cc/ZUN7-5XPG).

25 See, for example, "Senate Briefing Note re Bill C-7," British Columbia Civil Liberties Association, 17 December 2020, 2–4, https://sencanada.ca/content/sen/committee/432/LCJC/Briefs/Supportdoc_BCCivilLibertiesAss_e.pdf (perma.cc/ZBU2-8AV7).

26 See, for example, Association des Médecins Psychiatres du Québec, *Accès à l'aide médicale à mourir*, 26, 45, which discusses in detail the legal context, including the *Carter* and *Truchon* decisions, and emphasizes the need to avoid "discrimination" and to recognize "le même droit à l'autodétermination" (the same right to self-determination). For a critical discussion of the Canadian Psychiatric Association position, see Gaind et al., "Canada's Medically Administered Death," 74–5 and references therein.

27 This conclusion was also reached by thirty-one law professors in a joint letter submitted to the federal government: "We disagree as law professors that providing access to MAID for persons whose sole underlying medical condition is mental illness is constitutionally required, and that *Carter v. Canada AG* created or confirmed a constitutional right to suicide, as Minister Lametti repeatedly stated. Our Supreme Court has never confirmed that there is a broad constitutional right to obtain help with suicide via health-care provider ending-of-life." Trudo Lemmens, "Parliament Is Not Forced by the Courts to Legalize MAID for Mental Illness: Law Professors' Letter to Cabinet," *University of Toronto Faculty of Law Blog*, 2 February 2023, https://www.law.utoronto.ca/blog/faculty/letter-federal-cabinet-about-governments-legal-claims-related-maid-mental-illness (perma.cc/T564-RVDR).

28 See *Meeting of the Special Joint Committee on Medical Assistance in Dying – Evidence*, 44th Parliament, 1st Session (21 November 2023), https://www.parl.ca/DocumentViewer/en/44-1/AMAD/meeting-39/evidence. Myriam Willis (counsel, Department of Justice) stated that "No court has ruled on whether or not the charter requires MAID for mental illness" and noted that the Department of Justice has issued *Charter* statements "supporting the charter consistency of both prohibiting MAID for mental illness and permitting MAID for mental illness."

29 *Truchon v. Canada (Attorney General)*, 2019 QCCS 3792. *Truchon* is discussed further below.

30 See Grant, "Legislated Ableism"; André Schutten, "Lethal Discrimination: A Case Against Legalizing Assisted Suicide in Canada," *Supreme Court Law Review (2d)* 73 (2016), 143, paras. 61–3; see also Beaudry, "Somatic

Oppression," 283–7. The argument here includes the idea that by expanding MAiD, while not adequately funding other options such as palliative care and disability support services, the government is actually undermining "genuine" autonomy because the only "choice" left to patients is really a choice of a premature death they may not actually want. See also the discussion of assisted death, "meaningful choice," and the "right to highest attainable standard of health" in Mary J. Shariff, "Navigating Assisted Death and End-of-Life Care," *Canadian Medical Association Journal* 183, no. 6 (2011): 643–4, https://www.ncbi.nlm.nih.gov/pmc/articles/PMC3071380/.

31 See Quinn, Mahler, and De Schutter, "Mandates of the Special Rapporteur," 4.
32 Ibid.
33 Ibid., 7.
34 Ibid.; see also United Nations Human Rights Office of the High Commissioner, "Visit to Canada: Report of the Special Rapporteur on the Rights of Persons with Disabilities," Doc: A/HRC/43/41/Add.2, 19 December 2019, https://www.ohchr.org/en/documents/country-reports/ahrc4341add2-visit-canada-report-special-rapporteur-rights-persons (perma.cc/GTA2-WCJJ).
35 *Carter v. Canada (Attorney General)*, 2015 SCC 5, [2015] 1 SCR 331; *Truchon c. Procureur général du Canada*, 2019 QCCS 3792; compare to *Rodriguez v. British Columbia (Attorney General)*, 1993 Canlii 75 (SCC) (Can.), paras. 140, 149, 162, 186, the previous Supreme Court of Canada precedent on assisted suicide. *Rodriguez* upheld the law on the basis that it had as one of its objectives the goal of "preserving life," which was grounded in "the policy of the state that human life should not be depreciated by allowing life to be taken," as well as the principle that "the active participation by one individual in the death of another is intrinsically morally and legally wrong." The later 2015 Supreme Court of Canada decision, *Carter*, 2015 SCC 5, agreed that "the sanctity of life is one of our most fundamental societal values" (para. 63). However, it articulated the law's object as having "the narrow goal of preventing vulnerable persons from being induced to commit suicide at a time of weakness" (para. 78). As the Supreme Court later summarized, the prohibition was deemed "overbroad *to the extent it applied* to individuals who were not vulnerable" (*R. v. Ndhlovu*, 2022 SCC 38, at para 106, emphasis added). This finding of overbreadth in relation to the law's (deemed) objective is not tantamount to a recognition of a freestanding constitutional right to MAiD.

For a critique of *Carter*'s narrow framing of the legislative purpose, and its departure from the *Rodriguez* precedent, see John Keown, "*Carter*: A Stain on Canadian Jurisprudence?," in *Assisted Death: Legal, Social and Ethical Issues After Carter*, ed. Derek B. M. Ross (LexisNexis Canada, 2018), 14–16; John Sikkema, "The 'Basic Bedford Rule' and Substantive Review of Criminal Law Prohibitions Under Section 7 of the Charter," *Supreme Court Law Review* (2d) 85 (2018): 49. For a discussion of the court's lack of consistency when articulating and applying the legislative purpose through the *Charter* analysis, see also Mary J. Shariff, "*Carter v. Canada*: Exploring the Ebb and Flow of 'Competing' Societal Values through Section 7 and Section 1 of the *Canadian Charter of Rights and Freedoms*," in Kotalik and Shannon, eds., MAID *in Canada*, 25–54.

In the 2019 decision of the Quebec Superior Court, *Truchon*, 2019 QCCS 3792, paras. 555–6, the court rejected arguments that Bill C-14's "reasonably foreseeable natural death requirement" had the objective of affirming the inherent and equal value of every person's life and the importance of preventing suicide (despite clear language in the preamble of the law). Rather, the court determined that the provision's sole purpose was to "protect vulnerable persons who might be induced to end their lives in a moment of weakness, by preventing errors *when assessing requests for medical assistance in dying*" (emphasis added). For critiques of this analysis, see Grant, "Legislated Ableism," and Derek Ross, "What's the Purpose of Canada's MAID Law?," 10 October 2019, https://www.christianlegalfellowship.org/blog/2019/10/10/whats-the-purpose-of-canadas-maid-law (perma.cc/4G6Y-T229).

36 See *Carter v. Canada (Attorney General)*, 2012 BCSC 886, para. 16; *Carter*, 2015 SCC 5, para. 78; *Truchon*, 2019 QCCS 3792, para. 556. In a judgment on a preliminary motion in *Truchon*, the court also refused to admit certain evidence on the competing interests considered by Parliament in drafting Bill C-14 and the objectives of the law. The court noted that its role was not to examine all of the criteria or objectives of the "nouveau régime législatif" (new legislative regime) – rather, its sole function was to decide whether the reasonably foreseeable death requirement is contrary to the *Charter*: see *Truchon c. Procureur général du Canada*, 2018 QCCS 317, paras. 19–26.

As such, the attorney general was restricted from bringing evidence on the general objectives of the law and was instead limited to "la seule et unique question du critère de la mort devenue raisonnablement prévisible" (the sole and unique question of the criterion for death having become reasonably foreseeable) (para. 31). While the court was understandably concerned with admitting excessive evidence, this restrictive approach (combined with the court's ultimate dismissal of the preambular statements of purpose as mere "vehicles used to affirm social values or stakes," (*Truchon*, 2019 QCCS 3792, para. 556) seems difficult to reconcile with principles articulated by the Supreme Court of Canada: namely, that "determining legislative purpose requires us to consider *statements of legislative purpose* together with the words of the provision, *the legislative context*, and *other relevant factors*," and that an impugned provision "must also be read harmoniously *with other provisions of the statute.*" See *R. v. Appulonappa*, 2015 SCC 55 (Can.), paras. 33, 46. See also *R. v. Moriarty*, 2015 SCC 55 (Can.), para. 31, *and R. v. N.S.*, 2022 ONCA 160 (Can.), para. 47 (emphasis added).

Most recently, in "Reference re *An Act respecting First Nations, Inuit and Métis Children, Youth and Families*," 2024 SCC 5, the Supreme Court specifically emphasized the importance of preambular language, both in determining a law's purposes (paras. 39, 42), and in furthering Parliament's ability to engage in "dialogue with both courts and society" (para. 81, quoting Kent Roach, "The Uses and Audiences of Preambles in Legislation," *McGill Law Journal* 47, no. 1 (2002): 159).

37 See Lemmens and Jacobs, "The Latest MAID Decision." The legislative goals that were rejected by Justice Baudouin as mere "vehicles used to affirm social values or stakes" included the affirmation of the inherent and equal value of every person's life, combined with the prevention of negative perceptions of the quality of life of persons who are elderly, ill, or disabled and the prevention of suicide.

38 See *Lamb v. Canada (Attorney General)*, 2017 BCSC 1802, para. 70: "I find that while medical assistance in dying is the general subject of both *Carter* and the present case, *the constitutional issues in each case differ because the respective claims challenge two different pieces of legislation with arguably different objectives, purposes and effects [...]* These objectives, purposes and effects are consequential in determining the legislation's constitutional validity in both the s. 7 *Charter* analysis and s. 1 *Charter* analysis. *As a result, the constitutionality of the eligibility criteria in Canada's newly permissive regime remains to be decided.*" Emphasis added.

This finding was endorsed by the BC Court of Appeal, which affirmed that "the assessment of the constitutionality of the new legislation should proceed 'on relevant, current evidence that is specific to the objectives and effects of the legislation'": *Lamb v. Canada (Attorney General)*, 2018 BCCA 266, para. 100, citing Hinkson J. in *Lamb*, 2017 BCSC 1802, para. 107. The *Lamb* case was discontinued by the plaintiffs before proceeding to a hearing on its merits; thus, the BC courts never issued a decision on the constitutionality of Bill C-14. And although the Quebec Superior Court in *Truchon* did find Bill C-14 unconstitutional, its analysis was premised on its finding that the bill had essentially the same legislative purpose as the law impugned in *Carter*. Thus, nothing in *Truchon* challenges the principle in *Lamb* that the outcome *could* be different where a different law is found to further a *different* objective. See also Sikkema, "The 'Basic Bedford Rule,'" paras. 1, 6, 70; see also discussion in *Truchon*, 2019 QCCS 3792, paras. 503–4.

39 See, for example, *Carter*, 2015 SCC 5, para. 125; see also Peter W. Hogg and Ravi Amarnath, "Understanding Dialogue Theory," in *The Oxford Handbook of the Canadian Constitution*, ed. Peter Oliver, Patrick Macklem, and Nathalie Des Rosiers (New York: Oxford University Press, 2017), 1053–72, 1068–9. Hogg and Amarnath describe how in the *Carter* case, "the Supreme Court recommended how the legislative scheme could be fixed, without compelling such a solution," leaving the "ultimate modification of the legislation" to the legislature.

40 It also bears repeating that only one lower Quebec court has ruled that the reasonably foreseeable death safeguard, which protects the life of those not approaching their natural death, is unconstitutional, making it even more questionable to defend, as the government has done, the main expansion under Bill C-7 as constitutionally required.

41 *Carter*, 2015 SCC 5, para. 110. Typically, appellate courts do not consider new evidence that was not before the lower courts whose decisions are being reviewed. In this case, the government was granted special permission to file "fresh evidence on developments in Belgium since the time of the trial." Note the reference to *Carter* or *Carter 2015* is to distinguish from the later decision, *Carter*, 2016 SCC 4 (in which the government sought an extension to introduce a new law to respond to the 2015 *Carter* decision).

42 Note that terms *physician-assisted dying* and *physician-assisted death* are used interchangeably throughout the *Carter* decision and were defined by the trial court to include *both* the acts of "physician-assisted suicide" or PAS (whereby the patient intentionally kills themselves with assistance of a physician or someone acting under a physician's direction) and "voluntary euthanasia" (whereby the patient's life is intentionally terminated by a physician or someone acting under a physician's direction). In its "declaration of invalidity" (discussed further below), the Supreme Court uses the term *termination of life*. See *Carter*, 2012 BCSC 886, paras. 23, 37–9. See also *Carter*, 2015 SCC 5, paras. 127, 147. Following the passage of *Bill C-14, An Act to Amend the Criminal Code*, these terms were

statutorily superseded by the term *medical assistance in dying* or MAiD. Bill C-14 received royal assent 17 June 2016.

43 See, for example, *Carter*, 2015 SCC 5, paras. 8, 11–12, 110–12. The assisted dying regimes reviewed by the court in *Carter* included models from the Netherlands, Belgium, Luxembourg, Switzerland, Oregon, Washington, Montana, and Colombia.

44 *Carter*, 2015 SCC 5. For the trial court's findings on fundamental distinctions between the reasoning of a terminally ill person (whose judgment is not impaired by mental illness) to end their life and that of decision-making about suicide by persons who are mentally ill, see *Carter*, 2012 BCSC 886, paras. 812–14.

45 See also discussion in Department of Justice, *Charter Statement: Bill C-7: An Act to Amend the Criminal Code (Medical Assistance in Dying)*, 21 October 2020, justice.gc.ca/eng/csj-sjc/pl/charter-charte/c7.html. A different interpretation of paragraph 111 in the subsequent case, *Canada (Attorney General) v. E.F.*, 2016 ABCA 155 is discussed further below. See also the discussion of *Carter* in Trudo Lemmens, Heeso Kim, and Elizabeth Kurz, "Why Canada's Medical Assistance in Dying Legislation Should Be C(h)arter Compliant and What It May Help to Avoid," *McGill Journal of Law and Health* 11, no. 1 (2018): 61–148, 100–19.

46 Specifically, ss. 241(b) and 14. For a full discussion of the *Charter* arguments, see *Carter*, 2015 SCC 5, paras. 54–92.

47 *Carter*, 2015 SCC 5, para. 127.

48 Note that this particular point was emphasized by the attorney general of Canada in support of its position that mental disorders fell outside the declaration's scope, but its argument was rejected by the Alberta Court of Appeal in *E.F.*, 2016 ABCA 155. Respectfully, however, the ABCA's reasons for doing so are contestable in our view and, in any event have never been addressed by the Supreme Court. See further discussion below.

49 *Carter*, 2015 SCC 5, para. 127 (emphasis added).

50 *MacKay v. Manitoba*, [1989] 2 SCR 357 at 361, 1989 CanLII 26 (SCC) (Can.).

51 Note that a different interpretation of these qualifying words is discussed below.

52 See, for example, *Carter*, 2015 SCC 5, para. 12. See also *Carter*, 2012 BCSC 886, paras. 14, 1414(b).

53 See *Carter*, 2015 SCC 5, para. 11.

54 Ibid., paras. 12–13.

55 Ibid., paras. 1, 13.

56 Ibid., para. 14 (emphasis added).

57 Ibid., para. 56 (emphasis added); see also para. 66: "people like Ms. Taylor."
58 Ibid., paras. 14–18, 57. We note that within the *Charter* analysis the SCC attached the inability to end one's life due to physical decline to the section 7 right to life and attached the right to choose and exercise control over bodily integrity free from state interference to section 7 rights to liberty and security of the person.
59 Ibid., para. 111. For discussion of interpretation in the Alberta case, *E.F.*, 2016 ABCA 155, see below.
60 See *Carter*, 2015 SCC 5, at paras. 54, 121 and 114.
61 Ibid., para. 116 (emphasis added).
62 Ibid., para. 115.
63 Ibid., paras. 114–17.
64 For the importance of factual circumstances to *Charter* analyses, see *MacKay*, [1989] 2 SCR 357. See also *Carter*, 2012 BCSC 886, para. 1386.
65 See, for example, *Carter*, 2015 SCC 5, paras. 3, 66, 98, 117, 119.
66 *Carter*, 2012 BCSC 886, para. 1390.
67 Ibid., para. 813 (emphasis added).
68 Ibid., para. 814 (emphasis added).
69 Ibid., para. 1262 (emphasis added).
70 Ibid., para. 1391 (emphasis added); see also para. 1393. Note also how this limitation aligns with the statutory eligibility criterion "advanced state of irreversible decline in capability." See *Criminal Code of Canada*, s. 241.2 (2)(b).
71 Joseph J. Arvay, QC, "Written Submissions to the Standing Senate Committee on Legal and Constitutional Affairs: In View of Its Study on Bill C-14, An Act to Amend the Criminal Code and to Make Related Amendments to Other Acts (medical assistance in dying)," Senate of Canada, 5 May 2016, 5–6, https://sencanada.ca/content/sen/committee/421/LCJC/Briefs/LCJC_May5_2016_Arvay_J_e.pdf (perma.cc/Y9ZE-2QAJ) (emphasis added).
72 *Carter*, 2015 SCC 5, para. 127.
73 *Carter*, 2012 BCSC 886, para. 1414(b).
74 See Gaind, "Irremediability in Mental Illness."
75 *Carter*, 2015 SCC 5, para. 63.
76 *Carter*, 2012 BCSC 886, paras. 1283; see also *Carter*, 2015 SCC 5, paras. 16, 1243, 1267.
77 *Carter*, 2012 BCSC 886, para. 1284.
78 See *Death with Dignity Act*, ORS 127.800 § 101.12, 127.805 § 2.01.
79 *Carter*, 2012 BCSC 886, paras. 398–400.

80 Public Health Division, Center for Health Statistics, *Oregon Death with Dignity Act: 2022 Data Summary* (Portland: Oregon Health Authority, 8 March 2023), 6, https://www.oregon.gov/oha/PH/PROVIDER PARTNERRESOURCES/EVALUATIONRESEARCH/DEATHWITH DIGNITYACT/Documents/year25.pdf.
81 Ibid.
82 Health Canada, *Fourth Annual Report*, 5; see also ibid., 21.
83 See *Carter*, 2012 BCSC 886, paras. 398–400, 626.
84 It might also be noted that Canada's 10,064 MAiD deaths in 2021 surpass Belgium's euthanasia deaths for 2020–21 combined (5,145 total, including 2,445 or approximately 1.93 per cent of total recorded deaths in 2020 [126,850] and 2,700 or approximately 2.4 per cent of total recorded deaths [112,291] in 2021). See Commission fédérale de Contrôle et d'Évaluation de l'Euthanasie, *Dixième rapport aux Chambres législatives (années 2020-2021)* (Brussels: Secrétariat de la Commission, 2021), https://organesdeconcertation.sante.belgique.be/sites/default/files/documents/10_rapport-euthanasie_2020-2021-fr_1.pdf (perma.cc/8F54-VWEM); "112,291 Inhabitants Died in Belgium in 2021," Statbel, 16 June 2022, https://statbel.fgov.be/en/news/112291-inhabitants-died-belgium-2021 (perma.cc/A6JC-DFNP). Canada's MAiD numbers appear to be closer to those of the Netherlands, where its euthanasia law came into effect in 2002. In 2021, there were 7,666 euthanasia deaths representing approximately 4.5 per cent of all deaths (170,839) in the Netherlands. See Regional Euthanasia Review Committees, *Annual Report 2021*, April 2022, 4, https://english.euthanasiecommissie.nl/the-committees/documents/publications/annual-reports/2002/annual-reports/annual-reports (perma.cc/MCV4-TB8W).
85 See Gian Domenico Borasio, Ralf J. Jox, and Claudia Gamondi, "Regulation of Assisted Suicide Limits the Number of Assisted Deaths," *Lancet* 393, no. 10175 (March 2019): 982–3. In Canada, almost all MAiD deaths are by euthanasia (administered by a health care practitioner), not self-administration; in 2022, of the 13,241 MAiD deaths, "fewer than seven" were self-administered, "a trend consistent with previous years" (see Health Canada, *Fourth Annual Report*, 21). This distinction perhaps reflects another way in which Justice Smith may have had a much narrower regime in mind as a potential option than the one Parliament ultimately implemented with Bill C-14. See also Daryl Pullman, "Slowing the Slide Down the Slippery Slope of Medical Assistance in Dying: Mutual Learnings for Canada and the US," *American Journal of Bioethics* 23, no. 11 (2023): 64–72, https://www.tandfonline.com/doi/full/10.1080/1526516 1.2023.2201190 (perma.cc/83C3-2Y98), where the author compares the

numbers of Canada with the assisted suicide numbers in California and discusses the potential reasons.

86 For discussion see Trudo Lemmens, Mary J. Shariff, and Leonie Herx, "L'Aide Médicale à Mourir et le sacrifice de la norme de qualité de soins de la pratique médicale," in *Mélanges Robert P. Kouri – L'humain au cœur du droit*, ed. Nathalie Vézina, Pascal Fréchette, and Louise Bernier (Montreal: Yvon Blais: 2021), 621–64; Ramona Coelho et al., "The Realities of Medical Assistance in Dying in Canada," *Palliative and Supportive Care* 21, no. 5 (October 2023): 871–8, https://pubmed.ncbi.nlm.nih.gov/37462416/ (perma.cc/ZK6L-MC7U).

87 *Carter*, 2012 BCSC 886, para. 1393(b).

88 Ibid., para. 1414(b).

89 See *E.F.*, 2016 ABCA 155.

90 See *Truchon*, 2019 QCCS 3792.

91 One other potentially relevant decision is *A.B. v. Canada (Attorney General)*, 2017 ONSC 3759, which maintained, as did the attorney general, that Bill C-14's "reasonably foreseeable" death criterion did not "require that people be dying from a terminal illness, disease or disability" (para. 82). However, that decision does not state that Parliament is constitutionally prohibited from introducing such a restriction, nor that Parliament must legalize MAiD MI-SUMC – it simply concluded that, for the claimant in that case, their "natural death was reasonably foreseeable" and met the applicable legislative requirements.

92 See *Carter*, 2015 SCC 5, para. 128. Note that the trial judge had initially granted Gloria Taylor a constitutional exemption permitting her to obtain physician-assisted death under certain conditions, but she passed away before the Supreme Court's decision and thus the court declined to "create a mechanism for exemptions during the period of suspended validity." See *Carter*, 2012 BCSC 886, para. 1414; see also *Carter*, 2015 SCC 5, para. 129.

93 See *Carter v. Canada (Attorney General)*, 2016 SCC 4, [2016] 1 SCR; see also *E.F.*, 2016 ABCA 155, para. 3.

94 See *Bill C-14, An Act to Amend the Criminal Code*.

95 *Carter*, 2016 SCC 4, para. 7 (emphasis added); see also para. 1; note that the SCC also granted Quebec an exemption from the extension, allowing the provincial MAiD legislation to operate notwithstanding the ongoing Criminal Code prohibition, and making no pronouncement on the validity of the Quebec legislation. See para. 4.

96 *E.F.*, 2016 ABCA 155, para. 5.

97 These cases include: *H.S. (Re)*, 2016 ABQB 121 (Can.); *A.B. v. Canada (Attorney General)*, 2016 ONSC 1912; *Patient v. Attorney General of*

Canada, 2016 MBQB 63; *A.B. v. Ontario (Attorney General)*, 2016 ONSC 2188 (Can.); *A.A. (Re)*, 2016 BCSC 570 (Can.); *W.V. v. Canada (Attorney General)*, 2016 ONSC 2302; *C.D. v. Canada (Attorney General)*, 2016 ONSC 2431; *E.F. v. Canada (Attorney General)*, 2016 ONSC 2790; *E.F.*, 2016 ABCA 155; *Patient 0518 v. R.H.A. 0518, Physician A0518 and Physician C0518*, 2016 SKGB 176 (Can.); *M.N. v. Canada (Attorney General)*, 2016 ONSC 3346; *I.J. v. Canada (Attorney General)*, 2016 ONSC 3380; *H.H. (Re)*, 2016 BCSC 971 (Can.); *Tuckwell (Re)*, 2016 ABQB 302 (Can.); *O.P. v. Canada (Attorney General)*, 2016 ONSC 3956; see also discussion in Health Canada, *Final Report of the Expert Panel*, 23.
98 *E.F.*, 2016 ABCA 155, para. 7.
99 Ibid., para. 11. A second and related issue in *E.F.* concerned whether the constitutional exemption only applied to terminal illness, which the ABCA concluded it did not. See paras. 11, 27–42. This is discussed further below.
100 See discussion in ibid., para. 5.
101 Ibid., para. 24 (emphasis added).
102 Ibid.
103 See, for example, *Truchon*, 2019 QCCS 3792, paras. 502–3 (emphasis added): "Even if they are inconsistent with the *Carter* parameters, are [legislative requirements] *de facto* unconstitutional, as the applicants submit? The Court does not think so. *The mere fact that the federal statute includes additional requirements or conditions not found in* Carter *does not render it unconstitutional*, as such. The applicants' burden of proving that their section 7 and 15 *Charter* rights have been infringed is not lesser simply because the impugned provisions are not in perfect harmony with *Carter*."
104 *E.F.*, 2016 ABCA 155, para. 49.
105 *Carter v. Canada (Attorney General)*, 2015 SCC 5, Affidavit, Professor Etienne Montero, MAID in Belgium, sworn 23 April 2014 – English translation, para. 30.
106 Ibid., paras. 30–43.
107 Ibid., paras. 79–88.
108 Ibid., paras. 32–34, 40ff.
109 *Carter*, 2015 SCC 5, paras. 110–3.
110 Ibid., para. 127; see also note 54 et seq and associated text.
111 See *Carter*, 2015 SCC 5, para. 113: "the cases described by Professor Montero were the result of an oversight body exercising discretion in the interpretation of the safeguards and restrictions in the Belgian legislative regime – a discretion the Belgian Parliament has not moved to restrict.

These cases offer little insight into how a Canadian regime might operate."
112 For a discussion regarding why the Canadian regime is providing broader access and contains weaker safeguards, see Lemmens, Shariff, and Herx, "L'Aide Médicale à Mourir," 621–44; Coelho et al., "Realities of MAiD." See also note 93 and accompanying text data related to Canadian MAiD numbers surpassing those of Belgium.
113 *E.F.*, 2016 ABCA 155, paras. 49–50.
114 See the exchange between J. Arvay and Madame Justice Abella in *Carter*: Arvay, "Written Submissions," at note 79 and accompanying text.
115 *E.F.*, 2016 ABCA 155, para. 49.
116 Ibid., para. 29 (emphasis added); see also *Carter*, 2015 SCC 5, para. 127.
117 *E.F.*, 2016 ABCA 155, para. 57 (emphasis added).
118 For further discussion, see Dianne Pothier, "Doctor-Assisted Death Bill Falls Well Within Top Court's Ruling," *Policy Options*, 29 April 2016, https://policyoptions.irpp.org/2016/04/doctor-assisted-death-bill-falls-well-within-top-courts-ruling/ (perma.cc/4PAC-XXXZ); see also Dianne Pothier, "The Parameters of a Charter Compliant Response to Carter v. Canada (Attorney General), 2015 SCC 5," unpublished article, 20 March 2016, archived at SSRN, https://papers.ssrn.com/sol3/papers.cfm?abstract_id=2753167 (perma.cc/7DXE-ECFZ); see also discussion above regarding relevance of the facts to *Charter* analysis at note 56 and associated text.
119 *E.F.*, 2016 ABCA 155, para. 59.
120 Ibid., para. 54.
121 Ibid., para. 72. This point is also emphasized in Lemmens, Kim, and Kurz, "*C(h)arter* Compliant," 105.
122 *Truchon*, 2019 QCCS 3792, para. 502.
123 Ibid., paras. 502–8.
124 *R. v. Albashir*, 2021 SCC 48, at para 58 (emphasis added).
125 *E.F.*, 2016 ABCA 155, para. 7.
126 See, for example, discussion in Gaind, "Irremediability in Mental Illness"; "MAiD and Mental Illness," Centre for Addiction and Mental Health; Association des Médecins Psychiatres du Québec, *Accès à l'aide médicale à mourir*; Health Canada, *Final Report of the Expert Panel*, 39–41; see also Lemmens, Kim, and Kurz, "*C(h)arter* Compliant," 108 and associated references, discussing how complex clinical issues may not have been adequately dealt with in the *E.F.* case.
127 See also notes 40–2 and surrounding discussion.

128 This quote is from the transcript of the hearing of *Carter*, 2016 SCC 4 (in which the government sought an extension to introduce a new law to respond to the 2015 *Carter* decision).
129 *Lamb*, 2017 BCSC 1802, para. 27.
130 See *E.F.*, 2016 ABCA 155, para. 72.
131 Note that the requirement that a condition be "irremediable" in addition to "grievous" is an eligibility criterion that continued into the current legislated MAiD law. See *Criminal Code of Canada*, s. 241.2(1)(c); note that whether a psychiatric illness can actually be considered "irremediable" continues to be a source of major controversy and debate. For further discussion, see references at note 14.
132 *E.F.*, 2016 ABCA 155, para. 64.
133 Ibid., para. 65.
134 Ibid., para. 66.
135 See Trevor A. Hurwitz, "Euthanasia in Mental Illness: A Four Part Series. Part 1: The Case of EF," *Journal of Ethics Mental Health* 10 (2018), perma.cc/YZL7-RVLE.
136 See *Bill C-14, An Act to Amend the Criminal Code*.
137 See *Act Respecting End-of-Life Care*, CQLR c. S-32.0001 (Quebec, Can.).
138 See *Truchon*, 2019 QCCS 3792, para. 12; see also *Act Respecting End-of-Life Care*, s. 26(3); see also *Bill C-14, An Act to Amend the Criminal Code*, cl. 3.
139 See *Truchon*, 2019 QCCS 3792, paras. 5, 35, 69–70. Mr Truchon suffered from "spastic cerebral palsy with triparesis since birth" and was later also diagnosed with "severe spinal stenosis (narrowing of the spinal canal) as well as myelomalacia (spinal cord necrosis)" – causing constant physical and psychological pain due to complete dependency for daily activities; see paras. 17–50. Ms Gladu contracted polio at age four and was later diagnosed with "degenerative muscular post-polio syndrome" as well as osteoporosis and pulmonary disease – causing constant physical pain and discomfort, psychological suffering due to loss of functional autonomy, and a fear of complete dependency; see paras. 51–73.
140 Ibid., paras. 12–14.
141 Ibid., para. 120.
142 Ibid., para. 556 (emphasis added). Note, however, the broader objectives of the new MAiD legislation as described in the House of Commons during the debate over amending Bill C-14: "to recognize the significant and continuing public health issue of suicide, to guard against death being seen as a solution to all forms of suffering, and to counter negative perceptions about the quality of life of persons who are elderly, ill or disabled ... C-14 strikes the right balance for Canadians between protection of vulnerable

individuals and choice for those whose medical circumstances cause enduring and intolerable suffering as they approach death." See discussion at para. 118.

See also para. 244 where Canada describes the objective in relation to vulnerability: "affirming the inherent and equal value of vulnerable persons' lives and of addressing and preventing suicide and would put vulnerable individuals at risk," and compare to para. 252 where the court rejects the concept of "collective vulnerability." See also para. 551, where Canada formulates the objective of the legislative regime, including the RFND provision, into three categories: 1) to affirm inherent and equal value of every life and avoid encouragement of negative perceptions of quality of life for persons who are elderly, ill, and disabled; 2) to address suicide, a significant public health issue that has lasting, harmful effects on individuals, families, and communities; and 3) to protect vulnerable persons from being induced to end their lives in moments of weakness.

143 Ibid., para. 576 (emphasis added).
144 Ibid., para. 725.
145 Ibid., paras. 724–5. Compare to discussion of the purpose of the *Quebec Act Respecting End-of-Life Care* in parliamentary discussion. See, for example, discussion in *Bill C-14, An Act to Amend the Criminal Code and to Make Related Amendments to Other Acts (medical assistance in dying)*, 2nd reading, *Senate Debates*, 42-1, No. 41 (1 June 2016) (Can.).
146 See *Truchon*, 2019 QCCS 3792, paras. 691–704.
147 Ibid., para. 16.
148 Ibid. (emphasis added).
149 See discussion in ibid., paras. 230–2.
150 Ibid., para. 386; see also para. 232: "the issue of psychiatric illness as the only underlying medical condition for a request for medical assistance in dying, concern neither Mr. Truchon nor Ms. Gladu, who are not suicidal and do not suffer from any psychiatric condition."
151 Ibid., para. 387.
152 Ibid., para. 239.
153 Ibid., para. 237 (emphasis original).
154 Ibid., para. 388.
155 Ibid., para. 406: "The Attorney General is mistaken on the importance to be assigned to the issue of the presence of psychiatric illnesses *under the legislative provisions currently in force*, because the Attorney General confuses the person's capacity to consent with the presence of a diagnosed mental illness. The only thing that is relevant for the Court's purposes is *the determination of capacity* taking into consideration the presence of any illness. Once again, the overwhelming evidence, on a balance of

probabilities, does not at this time raise any doubt as to the quality of the process for assessing the capacity of a patient who has requested medical assistance in dying in Canada, whether or not the patient is suffering from a psychiatric condition [emphasis added]."

156 See, for example, ibid., paras. 420–2.
157 Ibid., para. 16.
158 See, for example, ibid., paras. 25, 39, 42, 45, 47, 58, 67, and 68.
159 See, for example, ibid., paras. 39, 42, 45, 66, 68, and 69.
160 Ibid., para. 387.
161 See, for example, ibid., paras. 304–6, noting that, under the existing regime, a "mental condition might possibly, in some cases, correspond to the legislative requirement of a grievous and irremediable medical condition," but that this is only one of the regime's statutory conditions. See also ibid., paras. 406, 421.
162 See, for example, Council of Canadians with Disabilities et al., "Advocates Call for Disability-Rights Based Appeal of the Quebec Superior Court's Decision in Truchon & Gladu," 4 October 2019, https://inclusioncanada.ca/2019/10/04/advocates-call-for-disability-rights-based-appeal-of-the-quebec-superior-courts-decision-in-truchon-gladu/ (perma.cc/83P5-XL5N); Lemmens and Jacobs, "The Latest MAID Decision"; see also discussion in Tim Stainton, "Disability, Vulnerability and Assisted Death: Commentary on Tuffrey-Wijne, Curfs, Finlay and Hollins," BMC Medical Ethics 20, no. 89 (2019), https://bmcmedethics.biomedcentral.com/articles/10.1186/s12910-019-0426-2 (perma.cc/UK8P-82E3); see also discussion in Department of Justice, What We Heard Report: A Public Consultation on Medical Assistance in Dying (MAID) (Ottawa: Government of Canada, March 2020), https://www.justice.gc.ca/eng/cj-jp/ad-am/wwh-cqnae/access/rep-rap.pdf (perma.cc/J3GU-GTXW).
163 See discussion in Department of Justice, Charter Statement, at "Excluding Eligibility for MAID Where Mental Illness Is the Sole Underlying Medical Condition."
164 See Bill C-7, An Act to Amend the Criminal Code; see also Department of Justice, Charter Statement.
165 See Bill C-7, An Act to Amend the Criminal Code, cl. 6, and Bill C-62, An Act to Amend An Act to Amend the Criminal Code (medical assistance in dying), No. 2, 44th Parliament, 1st Session (2024).
166 R. v. Mills, [1999] 3 SCR 668, para 55. see also paras 56–60 and R. v. Brown, 2022 SCC 18, para 140.
167 See, for example, Truchon, 2019 QCCS 3792, para. 232 and E.F., 2016 ABCA 155, para. 7.
168 Carter, 2012 BCSC 886, para. 1283 and para. 1393.

169 Ibid., para. 1174, citing *Alberta v. Hutterian Brethren of Wilson Colony*, 2009 SCC 37 (Can.), para. 37.
170 For a survey of some of these considerations, see Ramona Coelho et al., "Normalizing Death as 'Treatment' in Canada: Whose Suicides Do We Prevent, and Whose Do We Abet," *World Medical Journal* 68, no. 3 (2022): 27–35; see also Alexander I.F. Simpson, Jason Tran, and Roland M. Jones, "Ethical Considerations Regarding Mental Disorder and Medical Assistance in Dying (MAID) in the Prison Population," *Medicine, Science and the Law* 63, no. 1 (January 2023): 3–5.
171 This was the language used by the Quebec Superior Court to describe medical assistance in dying in *Truchon*, 2019 QCCS 3792, para. 156.
172 *Carter*, 2015 SCC 5, para. 98; see also *Canadian Charter of Rights and Freedoms*, s. 1, Part I of the *Constitution Act*, 1982, being Schedule B to the *Canada Act* 1982 (UK), 1982, c. 11.
173 See *Carter*, 2012 BCSC 886, para. 165.
174 Ibid., para. 317.
175 This point was also made in Scott Kim, "In Canada, MAID Has Become a Matter of Ideology," *Globe and Mail*, 25 February 2023, https://www.theglobeandmail.com/opinion/article-in-canada-maid-has-become-a-matter-of-ideology/ (perma.cc/H3BT-N3L7). The fact that professional organizations, political decision-makers, and even individual practitioners are seemingly uncritically accepting this claim is in our view a serious issue. It raises fundamental questions about how expert evidence should inform policy-making and about inherent limitations of judge-made law in relation to complex policy and medical questions. It also seems to us difficult to reconcile an arguably all-too-easy invocation of "the courts require us to do so" with the doctrine of "constitutional dialogue," which has been firmly embraced in Canadian constitutional law. See Peter W. Hogg and Allison A. Bushell, "The Charter Dialogue between Courts and Legislators (Or Perhaps the Charter of Rights Isn't Such a Bad Thing After All)," *Osgoode Hall Law Journal* 35, no. 1 (1997): 75–124.
    This is particularly so when a single lower court decision is used to shape such an important area of new social policy-making for the entire country. For further discussion, see Paul Yowell, *Constitutional Rights and Constitutional Design: Moral and Empirical Reasoning in Judicial Review* (Oxford: Hart Publishing, 2018). As one of us formulated it elsewhere: "Proportionality review embedded in constitutional or human rights-analysis must be informed by evidence-informed clinical, policy and ethical arguments. Yet, in Canada, rights rhetoric largely replaced evidence-informed debate." Trudo Lemmens, "When Death Becomes Therapy: Canada's Troubling Normalization of Health Care Provider

Ending of Life," *American Journal of Bioethics* 23, no. 11 (2023): 79–84, 80. We cannot discuss these questions here in detail, but our analysis could also inform further debate about these broader questions.

176 As discussed above, many mental health experts maintain that it is impossible to confidently predict irremediability in individual cases. The claim of the "right to access MAiD" is thus invoked in the context of the ongoing debate between psychiatric experts. The explicit authorization embedded in the legislation to allow MAiD for mental illness seemingly also includes an acceptance of the argument that its "irremediability" can be assessed. This makes it so much more important to critically examine the claim that "the courts oblige us to."

12

Mental Illness, Health Care, and Assisted Death: Part II – Examining Parameters for Expanding or Restricting MAiD under Canada's Federal System

Mary J. Shariff, Derek B.M. Ross, and Trudo Lemmens

As explained in the previous chapter, "Examining Parameters for Expanding or Restricting MAiD under Canada's *Charter*," despite assertions or intimations to the contrary:

1 No Canadian court has stated that Parliament must make MAiD available for individuals whose sole underlying condition is a mental illness (MAiD MI-SUMC), nor is there any clear indication that such a conclusion will necessarily be reached in the future as a jurisprudential *fait accompli*; and
2 No Canadian court has specifically examined the constitutionality of a legislative regime that explicitly excludes mental illness as a sole basis for MAiD eligibility, nor the range of policy, legal, medical, and other considerations that might lead Parliament to exclude MAiD MI-SUMC.

Parliament has nonetheless decided that the practice of MAiD MI-SUMC is to be made permissible under the Criminal Code as of 17 March 2027.[1] But what impact would the *decriminalization* of MAiD MI-SUMC have on Canadian provinces, who bear responsibility for *administering health care regimes* within their jurisdictions? This is a particularly germane question, as not all provinces have embraced MAiD MI-SUMC. Alberta's premier, for example, has voiced opposition to the federal government proceeding with it without provincial agreement.[2] Furthermore, in 2023, the province of Quebec expressly excluded mental disorders (other than neurocognitive disorders) from eligibility for MAiD through amendments to its own provincial end-of-life care statute, *Act Respecting End-of-Life Care* (also known as the Quebec EOL law), which establishes the practice of "medical aid in dying" within that province.[3] The Quebec EOL law was adopted by Quebec in 2014 pursuant to its provincial jurisdiction over health care and approximately two years prior to Parliament decriminalizing MAiD under the Criminal Code.[4] At the time, the Quebec EOL law was not challenged on the basis of it being, for example, ultra vires or conflicting with the federal prohibition. In fact, in *Carter*, the Supreme Court, though not providing any view on the validity of the Quebec EOL law, recognized that "aspects of physician-assisted dying may be the subject of valid legislation by both levels of government, depending on the circumstances and focus of the legislation."[5]

This, in turn, raises additional constitutional questions, including:

- Which aspects of MAiD practice fall within provincial health care jurisdiction?
- To what extent can a provincial MAiD scheme be constructed differently from that which the federal Criminal Code permits?

Clarity around these questions is critical. This chapter thus attempts to frame some of the jurisdictional considerations, including where a line might be drawn between the federal MAiD framework and provincial zones of competence, drawing guidance from the Supreme Court of Canada's recent decision in *Murray-Hall v. Quebec (Attorney General)*.[6]

The *Murray-Hall* decision indicates that when the federal criminal law permits an act, it does not create a positive right to that act and the provinces can potentially still, in certain contexts, regulate or even restrict it pursuant to their jurisdiction. Indeed, the Supreme Court of Canada affirmed unanimously that "the making of exceptions or exemptions under a criminal law scheme cannot serve to confer positive rights to engage in the activities covered by those exceptions or exemptions" and "provinces can legitimately undertake regulatory initiatives to provide a framework for decriminalized activities."[7]

This chapter concludes that there is significant constitutional room for the provinces to more actively regulate MAiD and considers the implications of these conclusions for provincial legislation like Quebec's.

The use of *Charter* rights to argue for MAiD decriminalization and access might legally justify the delivery of MAiD through the health care system. But it does not automatically follow that MAiD is a "medically necessary" or "medically required" health care service, *per se* – particularly when the acts that have been decriminalized stray from other established medical doctrines such as standard of care that also operate within an integrated medical ethical framework. This, many maintain, is the situation for MAiD-MI-SUMC, as it would be for any situation where other medical or support options that preserve life or alleviate suffering are available, and is therefore relevant to the question of provincial jurisdiction.[8]

CONSTITUTIONAL JURISDICTION

MAiD as a Medicalized Act – Preliminary Considerations

In Canada, national MAiD law reform was advanced on the basis of a *Charter* challenge to the criminal law in relation to a practice framed as a medical act and thus from the outset has involved consideration of the intersection between federal (criminal) and provincial (health) law.[9] As the Supreme Court of Canada observed in *Carter*, "Health is an area of concurrent jurisdiction; both Parliament and the provinces may validly legislate on the topic ... This suggests that aspects of physician-assisted dying may be the subject of valid legislation by both levels of government, *depending on the circumstances and focus of the legislation*."[10]

Following that *Charter* challenge, Parliament created an exemption in the Criminal Code to permit medical personnel to practise MAiD, and pursuant to that exemption, the delivery and further regulation of MAiD fell to provincial health jurisdiction.[11]

To date, however, with the exception of Quebec, provinces generally have not enacted legislation substantively regulating MAiD beyond the baseline requirements imposed by the Criminal Code. Pursuant to the Criminal Code MAiD exemption, provincial MAiD law and policy has been predominantly focused on implementation and regulation, addressing, for example, matters related to the regulation of health professions; insurance; access and delivery;

reporting, registering, and monitoring MAiD deaths; limitation of liability; vital statistics and investigation; and codes of medical ethics and practice directions.[12] Indeed, following the *Carter* decision and in light of federal government limitations with respect to regulating health care, a conversation regarding achieving a "pan-Canadian" approach to MAiD to avoid a "patchwork" of MAiD regimes across the provinces and territories emerged, with certain committees, panels, and advisors encouraging cooperation between federal and provincial or territorial governments.[13]

Nevertheless, there appears to be significant constitutional room for the provinces to more actively legislate matters regarding MAiD within the provincial zone of competence with respect to health, notwithstanding an early argument by some that "[p]rovinces and territories cannot ... *restrict* the circumstances in which physician-assisted dying is permitted beyond those validly provided for by Parliament."[14] But to what degree and for what purposes? If provincial regulations do take a more restrictive approach to MAiD in the delivery of health care based on legitimate provincial considerations, would they frustrate the purpose of the federal law and be struck down? When might provincial legislation in this area create conflict or inconsistency with federal law such that it might be deemed "inoperative"? To try to find answers to these types of questions, it is helpful to review the Constitution's division of powers between the provincial and federal governments in relation to matters of health care and the Supreme Court of Canada's interpretation of same.

Jurisdiction Over "Health"

CONCURRENT, OVERLAPPING, AND "AMORPHOUS"
Not only is health an area of *concurrent* jurisdiction (whereby both Parliament and the provinces may validly legislate on the topic),[15] the Supreme Court of Canada has recently reiterated in *Murray-Hall v. Quebec (Attorney General)* (discussed further below) that "health, as a matter not assigned in the *Constitution Act, 1867*, is an area of *overlapping* jurisdiction."[16] The court, quoting Justice Karakatsanis's decision in the 2020 *Reference re Genetic Non-Discrimination Act*, further described this jurisdiction as "amorphous": "Health is an '*amorphous*' *field of jurisdiction, featuring overlap* between valid exercises of the provinces' general power *to regulate health* and Parliament's criminal law power *to respond to threats to health.*"[17]

FEDERAL JURISDICTION: A PROHIBITION, A LEGITIMATE "EVIL," AND ESTABLISHING A "BASELINE"

The federal government has legislative competence in the area of health pursuant to its criminal powers (section 91(27)) as well as its federal spending power, which has been said to be inferred from its jurisdiction over public debt and property (section 91(1A)) and its general taxing power (section 91(3)).[18]

With respect to its criminal law jurisdiction, the federal power to legislate must be in the form of a prohibition and directed at legitimate criminal law purpose. Thus, as stated by the Supreme Court in the 1995 decision *RJR-MacDonald*, "The scope of the federal *power to create criminal legislation with respect to health matters* is broad, and is circumscribed only by the requirements that the legislation *must contain a prohibition accompanied by a penal sanction and must be directed at a legitimate public health evil.*"[19] And as further explained by the Supreme Court in 2011 in the later *PHS* decision (and reiterated in *Carter*): "Parliament has power to legislate with respect to federal matters, notably criminal law, that touch on health. *For instance, it has historic jurisdiction to prohibit medical treatments that are dangerous, or that it perceives as 'socially undesirable' behaviour.*"[20]

In the context of assisted death, MAiD can thus be validly regulated by the federal government because it involves activities that would otherwise be considered culpable homicide, aiding suicide, or administering a noxious thing under the Criminal Code[21] – practices that are not only inherently dangerous in that they involve the intentional ending of life (or the intentional endangerment to life) but also practices historically perceived as, in the words of Justice Sopinka in *Rodriguez*, "intrinsically morally and legally wrong."[22] Notwithstanding that there are different views on the morality and ethics of MAiD, it is for these kinds of reasons – i.e., threats to health, morality, public safety, and security – that the acts of administering or providing a substance to a person to intentionally cause that person's death are legitimate subjects for criminal prohibition. Accordingly, the federal Criminal Code continues to prohibit the offences of aiding suicide, culpable homicide, and administering a noxious thing but carves out an exemption from these offences for physicians and nurse practitioners (and individuals assisting them) who actively and knowingly cause a consenting patient's death in accordance with the specific requirements set out in the Criminal Code MAiD provisions.[23]

In short, pursuant to its criminal law jurisdiction, the federal government sets out the criminal law framework and the "legal conditions under which MAID can be provided."[24] Thus, as put by one senator during the Bill C-14 Parliamentary debates, "Essentially, what we as federal lawmakers can do is say, 'Yes, *you can be exempt from our law, but only if you do it according to our framework.*' ... We are not imposing how the provinces will regulate their health care service delivery. We are sending them the message that if you want to break our federal law, you have to meet a *minimum standard.*"[25]

And as explained by then minister of justice Jody Wilson-Raybould, when describing the interface between the federal MAID provisions pursuant to the criminal law and provincial jurisdiction over MAID as a health matter, "The views of the provinces and territories, the attorneys general and the health ministers across the country and the view of our government is that there should be and needs to be a *uniform criminal law* across the country. That's what we have sought to do in terms of Bill C-14, *to ensure that there is a baseline of safeguards which exist, to ensure there is consistency in terms of eligibility.*"[26]

PROVINCIAL JURISDICTION: HEALTH CARE, FLEXIBILITY, AND LOCAL CONSIDERATIONS

Generally speaking, the provinces have broad jurisdiction over matters of health care, "grounded primarily in broad and plenary jurisdiction over property and civil rights (s. 92(13)) and residual jurisdiction over matters of a merely local or private nature in the province (s. 92(16))."[27] In addition, s. 92(7) expressly grants the provinces jurisdiction over the "Establishment, Maintenance, and Management of Hospitals, Asylums, Charities and Eleemosynary Institutions."[28]

Accordingly, when it comes to matters of health care policy, administration and delivery of medicine or health care services, and the regulation of the health care profession, it is generally agreed that the provinces have been constitutionally endowed with primary jurisdiction.[29] So, while the federal government has decriminalized MAID as a matter of criminal law policy and established specific "baseline" standards to render health care professionals exempt from criminal liability in certain circumstances, it is the provinces who ultimately decide on MAID implementation and the extent to which it is to be incorporated into the provincial health care system as a *medical* treatment option.[30]

Thus in 2016, when asked during the Bill C-14 parliamentary debates whether Quebec's EOL law was potentially in conflict with the forthcoming federal MAiD law (the latter of which was understood to be more permissive in scope than the former[31]), minister of justice Jody Wilson-Raybould again explained as follows:

> There are some differences between what is in place in the Province of Quebec and what is being put forward within Bill C-14. As you rightly point out, senator, the Quebec legislation *is around end of life and care at the end of life by medical practitioners.* ...
>
> We have purposefully – and this is where there is a distinction between the Quebec law and Bill C-14 – *put in place reasonable foreseeability in terms of "death has become reasonably foreseeable," to inject the flexibility* to enable medical practitioners, based on the close relationship they have with their patients, to determine whether or not their patient is eligible to receive medical assistance in dying. I have been in close contact with the Province of Quebec and the Attorney General, *and what we're doing in terms of Bill C-14 is exercising the criminal law power.*
>
> The legislation in place in the Province of Quebec is under the health jurisdiction of the province, and we do not see a conflict necessarily between those two laws ... there is no conflict in terms of the laws ...
>
> So there are *standards of safeguards and eligibility which exist in the criminal law context.* The provinces and territories, including as I said with respect to Quebec, have the ability to work with the federal Minister of Health, *but working within their own jurisdictions to put in place other regulatory provisions they deem appropriate in terms of medically assisted dying.*[32]

In other words, the Quebec law did not conflict with the federal provisions in that Quebec's narrower provincial criteria (end of life) fit within the broader and more permissive federal standard (reasonably foreseeable natural death), and this was also not contested in *Truchon*.[33] Additionally, the quote above reflects the recognition that the goal of uniformity in terms of the criminal law must be balanced with facilitating flexibility and respecting the provinces' ability to tailor their laws to address local needs and concerns. As described in the 2022 *Final Report of the Expert Panel on MAID and Mental Illness*:

A major advantage of federal legislation for MAID is uniformity across the country, which ensures important measures, like safeguards, are implemented everywhere and in all cases. However, *some desirable measures* might fall within the provincial rather than federal legislative powers. *An advantage of provincial legislation is that it can be tailored to reflect local needs and concerns.* Variation in the organization and delivery of MAID between provinces and territories may in certain cases, reflect appropriate responses to needs of patients, families and practitioners. *Legislative uniformity, particularly in health care organization and delivery, may constrain appropriate flexibility in frontline care.* Other matters may be better left to regulatory authorities to develop and enforce through self-regulatory processes.[34]

Furthermore, in terms of the legitimate scope of provincial regulation pursuant to the federal exemption, the Provincial-Territorial Expert Advisory Group on Physician-Assisted Dying had previously acknowledged in 2015, post-*Carter*:

Provided that provincial/territorial laws were not inconsistent with valid federal legislation or with the Charter, provinces and territories *could regulate aspects of physician-assisted dying not prohibited by federal law. For example, provinces and territories could enact legislation to regulate in relation to at least*:

- *eligibility* (including rules regarding who may determine eligibility);
- determining competency and obtaining consent;
- *safeguards* to protect the vulnerable;
- settings in which physician-assisted dying is permitted;
- provider participation, including health institutions and both physicians and non-physician health professionals;
- means of delivery of physician-assisted dying;
- insurance (life and professional liability);
- certification of death; and
- reporting requirements and quality review.[35]

THE CANADA HEALTH ACT, INSURED SERVICES, AND "MEDICALLY NECESSARY"

There appear to be three principal lines of reasoning behind arguments that provinces do not have the ability to narrow or restrict the circumstances in which MAiD is permitted: the first is that to do so would be contrary to *Charter* rights (but as discussed in the preceding chapter, there is no recognized *Charter* right to MAiD-MI-SUMC); the second is that it could "frustrate" or intrude on valid federal law (discussed further below); and the third relates to federal cash transfers pursuant to the *Canada Health Act* (CHA), the federal legislation for publicly funded health care insurance.[36]

This third argument is fairly straightforward: MAiD's classification as a "medically necessary" and thus "insured health service" makes provinces accountable to the principles of the CHA, including satisfying the five criteria of public administration, comprehensiveness, universality, portability, and accessibility.[37]

Accordingly, as the argument goes, if provinces deviate from the federal MAiD framework – for example, by narrowing eligibility or increasing safeguards – this would potentially fall afoul of CHA requirements by creating barriers to access, for example. This argument may also be shored up by reference to the preamble of Bill C-14, which describes the new MAiD law in the context of the Canadian government's commitment to uphold the principles set out in the CHA.[38]

With all of this said, however, it may be relevant to first note that the main statutory consequence of provincial non-compliance with the criteria and conditions of the CHA is that the federal government can withhold a portion of its federal cash contribution to the province(s) at issue.[39] The CHA is not a constitutional statute that can enforce practical conformity on the part of the provinces. It is simply a federal law that governs federal transfer payments. As the Nova Scotia Court of Appeal has explained, even if provincial action "fails to meet the standards or objectives of the Canada Health Act," it does not necessarily follow that there would be any entitlement to a *judicial* remedy: "Jurisdiction over health care is exclusively a provincial matter. Failure of a province to comply with the *Canada Health Act* may result in the Government of Canada imposing a financial penalty on the province. It raises a political, not a justiciable issue. *It does not render the provincial legislation unconstitutional.*"[40]

Perhaps of more significance is that while the CHA requires provinces to provide insured health services (to receive federal transfers), the term "insured health services" is quite fluid, being described as "medically necessary" hospital services or "medically required" physician services.[41] In turn, the terms "medically necessary" and "medically required" are not defined in the CHA, meaning the

CHA has "left it open to the provinces and territories to interpret and determine what services are medically necessary or medically required. As a result, the list of insured services varies from one jurisdiction to another across Canada."[42]

Accordingly, a province may decide not to sponsor a particular service at all, on the basis that it is not considered medically necessary or required (particularly in comparison to other services and in the context of a publicly funded system with limited resources that must respond to multiple competing priorities).[43] This was affirmed by the Nova Scotia Court of Appeal, which noted:

> A very important limitation in the policy [of the *Canada Health Act*] is that insured services be medically necessary or medically required. Of necessity, what is or is not medically required must be judged by those placed in charge of the administration of the policy. The judgment call requires an appreciation not only of medical procedures, but the availability of funds to finance them. The exercise of such judgment is not a function of this Court. Our role is limited to requiring that those who make and administer the policy follow their own rules – in particular, the Act and the Regulations – in doing so. We are not accountable for the raising and expenditure of public monies. The persons who make these decisions under the policy are persons who are directly or indirectly so accountable. Charter considerations aside, as long as their decisions are reached in good faith and are not shown to be clearly wrong, we have no power to overturn them.[44]

This is not to say that we are asserting a position on whether MAiD or only certain categories of MAiD should be an insured health service or not. Rather, we simply point out that what is ultimately deemed medically necessary or required and in turn an insured health service is a determination largely left to the provinces, as a matter of health care policy.

PRELIMINARY SUMMARY RE: JURISDICTION

Both the federal and provincial governments have constitutional authority to legislate matters related to assisted death. The federal government can, subject to the *Charter*, prohibit or restrict the practice in connection with its criminal law authority to "suppress some evil or injurious or undesirable effect upon the public," while the provinces may also regulate assisted death "in order to protect the health and security of the public" from harm pursuant to its jurisdiction over health care.[45]

While it may be less contentious to assert that provinces pursuant to their health jurisdiction cannot permit that which is prohibited by the criminal law,[46] it is not a foregone conclusion that provinces could not legitimately restrict or limit the circumstances in which MAiD is permitted pursuant to specific provincial objectives including those responsive to local needs and concerns. In short, and in the view of the authors, "Parliament can create a regulatory baseline but not a ceiling for how activities that are approved by the provinces as health care are delivered."[47]

As previously noted, the provinces have generally not exercised their jurisdiction to regulate MAiD beyond the baseline regime set out in the Criminal Code. As described by legal scholar Brian Bird, "the prevailing view on how the provinces should handle assisted death seems to be that they must robotically and robustly integrate into their health-care systems whatever Parliament decriminalizes in this area."[48] As discussed above, however, it is the authors' opinion that this "prevailing view" is simply not accurate – an opinion shared by Bird,[49] and which finds support in the recent decision of the Supreme Court of Canada, *Murray-Hall v. Quebec (Attorney General)*. This decision offers helpful guidance on the contours of the respective zones of competence of the provincial and federal governments. Most significantly, it affirms that the provinces can not only *regulate* certain practices or treatment options but could potentially even *restrict* them in furtherance of public health and security purposes, even when the practices at issue have been decriminalized by Parliament. A close examination of that case is therefore merited.

Murray-Hall: Provinces Can Restrict What Parliament Permits ... In Certain Circumstances

Murray-Hall involved a constitutional challenge to a Quebec law that completely prohibited the possession and cultivation of cannabis plants at home. The claimant argued that this law conflicted with federal law, which permitted an individual to possess or cultivate up to four cannabis plants in their home. The question for the Supreme Court was whether "the more 'permissive' federal approach and the more 'restrictive' Quebec approach [could] coexist from a legal standpoint within the Canadian federation."[50] The court unanimously answered this question in the affirmative.

The court noted that merely prohibiting a practice does not necessarily constitute an intrusion into the federal government's criminal law power.[51] According to the court, in characterizing the impugned provisions, the court must read the impugned provisions in the context of the scheme, meaning that the court must not look just at the fact that a prohibition exists, but rather at the *purpose* of the prohibition as distinct from the *means* for achieving that purpose.[52] The driving question is: What are the *ends* or *purposes* which the *means* (i.e., the restrictions) seek to achieve? In the present case, the court found that the purpose of the impugned provisions was to establish a provincial scheme to "protect the health and security of the public, *and of young persons in particular, from cannabis harm.*"[53] This was a proper legislative purpose related to public health, grounded in the provincial heads of power in ss. 92(13) and (16).

Part of the claimant's argument was that the province was effectively recriminalizing what Parliament sought to decriminalize,[54] in part evidenced by comments made by members of the Quebec legislature that, according to the claimant, demonstrated intent to thwart Parliament's chosen approach.[55] This argument was rejected by the court. Although the court reiterated "[t]he guiding principle ... that the provinces may not invade the criminal field by attempting to stiffen, supplement or replace the criminal law ... or to fill perceived defects or gaps therein," there was no evidence that Quebec had attempted to do so in this case.[56] The Quebec government was not seeking to condemn or eliminate an act deemed morally reprehensible or a "public evil" (such would be a matter for exclusive federal jurisdiction); rather, it was concerned "about the *risks* arising from cannabis consumption, particularly for younger individuals."[57] Furthermore, ministerial statements expressing uneasiness or concerns were not taken by the court as demonstrating any intention to recriminalize but rather were statements that simply showed "that concerns about the harmful effects of cannabis on health did not disappear merely because this substance was decriminalized."[58] The court thus determined that "The impugned provisions do not represent a colourable attempt to re-enact the criminal law prohibitions repealed by Parliament ... while the impugned provisions do bring otherwise decriminalized conduct into the sphere of penal law, the consequences flowing from a contravention are very different from those arising under the provisions of the [federal law] ... Prohibiting the possession and cultivation of cannabis plants is not in itself the *purpose* of the impugned provisions, but rather a *means* of steering consumers to the only source of supply considered to be reliable and safe."[59]

Thus, because the prohibitions were an integral part of a larger scheme anchored in an area of legitimate provincial competence, the purpose of which was to protect the public from harm for health and security reasons rather than to suppress an act (solely for the sake of suppressing it), they were deemed an acceptable use of the provincial legislative power and not a "colourable attempt to re-enact the criminal law prohibitions repealed by Parliament."[60]

With respect to classifying the law (i.e., whether the impugned provisions fell under the federal criminal law power or within the powers conferred on the provinces),[61] the court first explained the space for provincial regulation with respect to conduct decriminalized by Parliament: "Parliament's decision to decriminalize conduct *leaves the field clear for the provinces to enact their own prohibitions accompanied by penalties in relation to that conduct, as long as the prohibitions serve to enforce laws relating to matters within provincial jurisdiction.* ... It follows that penal regulatory measures adopted by the provinces with regard to decriminalized activities are not necessarily attempts to legislate in criminal matters."[62]

Second, the court clarified that that the provinces do have "jurisdiction to make laws in relation to several matters that touch on purposes that otherwise constitute valid criminal law purposes," including touching on "moral aspects" and the consideration of risk cannabis consumption poses to certain vulnerable populations.[63] The provincial scheme at issue was advancing the objectives of public health and security, which are clearly related to provincial heads of power: property and civil rights (s. 92(13)) and residual jurisdiction over matters of a merely local or private nature (s. 92(16)).[64]

Third, it was also significant that, in the court's view, the impugned prohibitions ultimately did not have a punitive purpose: "the Quebec legislature saw the possession and personal cultivation of cannabis not as a social evil to be suppressed, but rather as a practice that should be prohibited in order to steer consumers to a controlled source of supply ... the purpose of the legislation was not to punish persons with a drug addiction, but *rather to regulate their medical treatment and ensure their safety* ... In the instant case ... the prohibitions ... do not have punitive purposes as such, but instead reflect an approach based on regulating and supervising access to the substance."[65]

APPLYING THE *MURRAY-HALL* ANALYSIS TO QUEBEC'S EOL LAW

Applying this analysis to Quebec's EOL law, we can see how it contains similar elements to the legislation upheld in *Murray-Hall*. Bill 11 does not restrict MAiD MI-SUMC to punish those who participate in it, nor because the provincial government deems it to be a social or public "evil" to be suppressed. Rather, it excludes mental disorders as a basis for MAiD eligibility in the context of a larger statutory regime regulating "end-of-life care," which has a broader *medical* purpose, including:

- ensuring "patients are provided care that is respectful of their dignity and their autonomy" and
- establishing "the rights of such patients as well as the organization of and a framework for end-of-life care, including medical aid in dying, so that everyone may have access, throughout the continuum of care, to quality care that is appropriate to their needs, including prevention and relief of suffering."[66]

The Quebec government's express exclusion of MAiD for mental disorders is rooted in a legislative committee's extensive study of various clinical and medical-ethical considerations.[67] That committee identified the difficulties associated with determining whether mental disorders are incurable and irreversible, distinguishing between suicidal ideation and a desire to obtain MAiD, balancing the right to self-determination with the protection of vulnerable persons, and the adverse impacts that MAiD MI-SUMC would have on suicide prevention and therapeutic relationships.[68] All of these considerations are directly related to public health and security. At the conclusion of this study, Quebec's Select Committee on the Evolution of the Act respecting end-of-life care expressed concern about the "differences of opinion that persist within the medical profession about the incurability of mental disorders and the irreversible decline in capability that may be associated with them" and "therefore recommended that access to medical aid in dying not be made available to persons whose only medical condition is a mental disorder."[69]

This exclusion, like the impugned provisions in *Murray-Hall*, is part of a larger legislative scheme within the province's constitutional competence. And like the impugned provisions in *Murray-Hall*, it reflects health and safety concerns about an act (MAiD MI-SUMC) that do not disappear with its decriminalization.

It should be noted here that when the Quebec Superior Court in *Truchon* found the Quebec EOL law's "end-of-life" restriction unconstitutional, it was *not* on the basis that the Quebec law deviated from or was narrower than the federal MAiD law (which the court also found unconstitutional).[70] Additionally, it is worth recalling that the court identified that the respective laws had different objectives. That is, according to the Quebec Superior Court, the objective of the federal MAiD law was the protection of "vulnerable persons who might be induced to end their lives in a moment of weakness, by preventing errors when assessing requests for medical assistance in dying";[71] whereas the provincial EOL legislation was identified as having a twofold purpose: end-of-life care (because it relieves suffering at the end of life) and the "recognition of dignity and autonomy."[72] Although the Quebec Superior Court ultimately struck down certain provisions contained in that law for *Charter* reasons (pertaining to the end-of-life criterion), the constitutional validity of these provincial *objectives* were never questioned.

One can see how Quebec's exclusion of mental disorders from MAiD eligibility would actually *further* these valid provincial objectives. It would be reasonable to conclude, for example, that the purpose of the exclusion is not the restriction itself, but a *means* of steering patients towards health care that the province has deemed medically efficacious and clinically appropriate in relieving suffering and affirming the dignity and autonomy of patients, in a way that also supports provincial suicide prevention efforts and the prevention of harm to patients' health and security. In other words, the legislature, after a careful study of complex policy considerations, may choose to prioritize life-affirming mental health care and supports – not death – as the best model and therapeutic medical response to suffering associated with mental disorders.

Depending on the evidence and context, it would be open to a court to conclude that a legislative exclusion of mental illness for MAiD eligibility is not punitive, nor aimed at "morally suppressing [it] as such."[73] Rather, a court could find the provincial regulatory scheme to be, like the law upheld in *Murray-Hall*, concerned with protecting the health and security of the public – including vulnerable persons – from harm and of advancing the legitimate legislative purposes recognized in *Truchon*: relieving suffering (in this case, by means *other* than by their premature death) and the recognition of dignity and autonomy.

WHEN DOES A PROVINCIAL LAW "FRUSTRATE" A FEDERAL LAW?

But even if a provincial law restricting MAiD is grounded in a legitimate provincial head of power, another question remains: by restricting MAiD or introducing additional safeguards that have the effect of making it less immediately accessible than it otherwise would be, are the provinces unconstitutionally frustrating the Criminal Code's more permissive approach? It has been argued that the provinces cannot "restrict the circumstances in which physician-assisted dying is permitted beyond those validly provided for by Parliament."[74] Is this accurate?

The Supreme Court's analysis in *Murray-Hall* indicates that the answer to this question is "no," at least in appropriate circumstances. The provinces have a clear constitutional basis for legislative action in the field of public health, even where such matters "touch on purposes that otherwise constitute valid criminal law purposes."[75] As earlier described, when Parliament partially decriminalizes a practice – be it the cultivation of cannabis plants or physician-assisted suicide – it "open[s] the door to provincial legislative action" and "leaves the field clear for the provinces to enact their own prohibitions," as long as they "serve to enforce laws relating to matters within provincial jurisdiction."[76] Under the "double aspect doctrine," provincial legislation may apply and operate concurrently with federal legislation, because there are a number of matters – including MAiD – that "by their very nature, have both a federal aspect and a provincial aspect."[77]

This doctrine has application even where a provincial law is more restrictive than an overlapping federal criminal law. This is because the criminal law power has an "essentially prohibitory nature" and it cannot create positive rights immune from any and all provincial limits.[78] As the Supreme Court explains, "when exceptions are carved out for practices that Parliament does not wish to prohibit, this 'only means that a particular practice is not prohibited, not that the practice is positively allowed by the federal law'...the creation of positive rights is not a valid exercise of the criminal law power."[79]

The Supreme Court's thorough analysis on this point in *Murray-Hall* is worth reproducing at length:

> The purpose of the federal Act's provisions is not to create a positive right to self-cultivate cannabis as part of a broader objective of limiting the influence of organized crime. *Such a purpose*

would be inconsistent with the fact that "the criminal law power is essentially prohibitory in character" (*Rothmans*, at para. 19), a fact that has been recognized in Canadian law since the leading case of *Proprietary Articles Trade Association v. Attorney General for Canada*, [1931] A.C. 310 (P.C.). As McLachlin C.J. noted in *Reference re AHRA*, "[t]he federal criminal law power may only be used to prohibit conduct" (para. 38).

The guidance provided in *Rothmans* is relevant for the purposes of this appeal. In my view, the principles arising from that case are determinative of the issue of the operability of the impugned provisions. The question in *Rothmans* was whether provincial legislation that prohibited the promotion of tobacco products in any place accessible to young persons frustrated the purpose of federal legislation that prohibited the promotion of tobacco products except in retail businesses. The Saskatchewan Court of Appeal had found that the provincial legislation negated the authorization otherwise afforded by the federal legislation for the promotion of tobacco in retail businesses. This Court came to a different conclusion, stating that "Parliament did not grant, and could not have granted, retailers a *positive entitlement* to display tobacco products" (para. 18 (emphasis added)). In addition, statutes enacted pursuant to the criminal law power "do not ordinarily create *freestanding rights* that limit the ability of the provinces to legislate in the area more strictly than Parliament" (para. 19 (emphasis added)).

The principle to be drawn from these excerpts is that the making of exceptions or exemptions under a criminal law scheme cannot serve to confer positive rights to engage in the activities covered by those exceptions or exemptions. This is an important point in a case like the one before us. The provinces can legitimately undertake regulatory initiatives to provide a framework for decriminalized activities without thereby frustrating a purpose – the creation of positive rights – that by definition is outside the scope of the federal criminal law power.

I cannot accept that exceptions or exemptions made under a scheme of criminal offences may give rise to positive rights, even where the exceptions or exemptions are closely related to the achievement of criminal law purposes. [...] The recognition of positive rights created out of exceptions or exemptions closely related to a valid criminal law purpose would improperly extend the scope of the federal criminal law power.[80]

The Supreme Court's analysis here is noteworthy for a few reasons. First, it articulates an important principle: the removal of a criminal prohibition does not establish a positive right. This must be borne in mind when contextualizing various elements of the "rights rhetoric" surrounding MAiD.[81] To the extent that a legal "right" to access a decriminalized service exists – including MAiD – it is not as a freestanding, positive right. In other words, there is no automatic corollary right to demand that a third party or the state provide it. The Criminal Code only regulates criminal liability, and in this regard, its MAiD provisions simply specify the circumstances in which a willing medical or nurse practitioner can voluntarily participate in the termination of another person's life, at their request and with their consent, without risk of criminal sanction. The criminal law does not – and can not – mandate any practitioner to terminate a patient's life, nor does it – or can it – require provinces to implement and incorporate such a procedure as part of its provincial health care program. To the extent that the *Charter* is engaged, it is as a shield against unconstitutional state *restrictions* on a practitioner's voluntary participation in MAiD in certain circumstances, not as a sword to *compel* medical or nurse practitioners, hospitals, or provincial health care systems to actively provide and finance it. As Chief Justice McLachlin emphasized, "[t]he Charter does not confer a freestanding constitutional right to health care" – even for procedures that aren't criminally regulated like MAiD.[82] The Criminal Code is also explicit that nothing in its provisions "compels an individual to provide or assist in providing medical assistance in dying."[83] Similarly, it has "never been the case that all hospitals must provide all health services."[84] Contrary to popular rhetoric, then, there is no positive "right" to MAiD – or any other procedure – at least not as a publicly funded health care service.

Second, *Murray-Hall* does not attach any exceptions to the basic rule that the criminal law cannot create a *positive* right to an activity or service. This principle is not limited to certain *kinds* of criminal law provisions, nor to the specific facts of *Murray-Hall* (unlike the declaration in *Carter*).[85] Thus, while one might point to certain differences between the impugned law in *Murray-Hall* and Quebec's Bill 11, for example, the legal principles enunciated by the court are what must govern the analysis. Those legal principles make clear that decriminalizing an act or service does not, in itself, prevent a province from regulating or even potentially restricting it, provided it is doing so for a constitutionally legitimate purpose.

Third, nowhere in *Murray-Hall* does the Supreme Court suggest that a province can only regulate a decriminalized service so long as it does not ultimately restrict *access* to it.[86] Quebec was found constitutionally competent to completely prohibit an act that Parliament had decriminalized (self-cultivation of marijuana). In affirming this, the Supreme Court cited another case where Saskatchewan was also found constitutionally competent to completely prohibit an act that Parliament had decriminalized (promotion of tobacco in retail businesses accessible to young persons).[87]

If it were otherwise – if the federal government's decriminalization of a procedure *required* provinces to provide it – this would undercut the provinces' jurisdiction and autonomy to, for example, regulate health care in a manner consistent with local needs. This point was made by Chief Justice McLachlin in the *Assisted Human Reproduction Act Reference*:

> In my view, the requirement that a criminal law contain a prohibition prevents Parliament from undermining the provincial competence in health. The *federal criminal law power may only be used to prohibit conduct, and may not be employed to promote beneficial medical practices.* Federal laws (such as the one in this case) may involve large carve-outs for practices that Parliament does not wish to prohibit. However, *the use of a carve-out only means that a particular practice is not prohibited, not that the practice is positively allowed by the federal law.* This has important implications for the doctrine of federal paramountcy. *If a province enacted stricter regulations than the federal government, there would be no conflict in operation between the two sets of provisions since it would be possible to comply with both.* Further, there would be no frustrations of the federal legislative purpose since federal criminal laws are only intended to prohibit practices. *A stricter provincial scheme would complement the federal criminal law.*[88]

Therefore, provincial regulation or restriction of MAiD would not be deemed inoperative for conflicting with the Criminal Code simply because it has the *effect* of limiting access to MAiD that might otherwise be more accessible pursuant to permissive criminal law. There must be a conflict of *purposes*. The purpose of a criminal law exception can never be to create a *positive entitlement* to something, but simply to *allow* it, subject to limits that other levels of government are constitutionally authorized to impose and maintain.

Application to MAiD

The above principles as discussed in *Murray-Hall* demonstrate how a province may, as Quebec has done, exclude assisted death for mental disorders from its health care regime. Whether such an exclusion will unconstitutionally conflict with federal law will depend on its *purpose*, which courts will assess based on "the actual text of the law, including its preamble and purpose clauses, as well as extrinsic evidence, such as parliamentary debates and minutes of parliamentary committees."[89]

If the purpose of the provincial law is to protect health and security as part of a larger health care regime (one aimed at suicide prevention and life-affirming care and support, for example), it will very likely not be seen as conflicting with federal purposes. On the other hand, if the purpose were, by contrast, to condemn or suppress an act as a public or social "evil," it would likely be seen as conflicting with the federal criminal power.[90]

To summarize, the Supreme Court has made it clear that the decriminalization of an act – in this case, MAiD – does not, in itself, create a positive right to it. The criminal law may only *prohibit* conduct – it cannot *compel* provinces to allow or facilitate it. Furthermore, provinces may potentially restrict activities that Parliament has decriminalized, provided they do so for purposes clearly grounded in their heads of power set out in s. 92 of the *Constitution Act, 1867*. Regulating health care services and protecting the health and security of the public are clear examples of such purposes within provincial zones of competence.

All of this supports the conclusion that provinces may restrict the circumstances in which MAiD is performed as a publicly funded health care service. In the authors' view, this authority potentially allows provinces to exclude, as a matter of public health policy, MAiD MI-SUMC from their respective health care systems. Provinces might also wish to introduce new and additional safeguards. This could include, for example, a specific legislative or regulatory regime requiring independent review of all MAiD cases reported under the law or requiring mandatory review of cases in which serious questions have been raised regarding whether eligibility criteria or safeguards have been met. Some provinces, such as Quebec and Ontario, have already introduced specific additional review at the provincial level.

Excluding MAiD MI-SUMC is still subject to the *Charter*, of course, and would likely face future arguments that such an exclusion infringes section 7 right to life or section 15 equality rights – whether the exclusion arises out of federal or provincial legislation.[91] However, as discussed in the preceding chapter, no Canadian court has yet ruled on this question; there is no court ruling dictating that Parliament must decriminalize assisted death for mental illness as a sole underlying condition, much less that provinces must offer it as a publicly funded health care service. Additionally, there is no guarantee that such challenges would be successful. Indeed, it is just as likely that a law *introducing* MAiD for mental disorders could be constitutionally challenged, on the basis that it undermines the equal protection of the right to life for individuals with mental illness, for example.[92] And even short of a complete exclusion from their health care systems, as discussed above, provinces nonetheless have wide constitutional authority to *regulate* MAiD MI-SUMC including adding additional substantive eligibility criteria and procedural safeguards as a matter of health care policy.[93]

It is important to note that, to date, the federal government has opted not to introduce any additional requirements to the Criminal Code MAiD provisions if and when MAiD MI-SUMC becomes permitted, despite concerns and calls to the contrary.[94] To borrow from the words of *Murray-Hall*, concerns about MAiD MI-SUMC simply do not disappear merely because it has been decriminalized.

FUTURE CONSIDERATIONS

The above discussion has focused on MAiD MI-SUMC as a case study, but the reasoning discussed herein may also apply to other contexts where provinces wish to prioritize medical supports other than termination of life in furtherance of their larger health care schemes. The effect of doing so may be to more strictly regulate MAiD than the federal law, but that would not necessarily be fatal to the provincial regime in question.

For example, in the same way that Quebec has excluded mental disorders (again, with the exception of neurocognitive disorders) as a basis for MAiD eligibility, another province might decide to exclude MAiD for non-terminal illnesses from its provincially sponsored health care system and adopt something similar to Bill C-14's "reasonably foreseeable death" safeguard. While that safeguard was invalidated by a single judge in Quebec, that decision (*Truchon*) is not binding on other provinces, and because the federal government declined to appeal it, its reasoning has yet to be reviewed by the Supreme Court of Canada (or any appellate court, for that matter). And, as mentioned in the previous chapter, several scholars have put forward, in the very opposite direction, reasonable arguments in support of the claim that the expansion outside of the end-of-life context itself is open to a *Charter* challenge.[95]

Furthermore, the purpose of new provincial legislation in respect of MAiD would be different from that of the federal MAiD provisions and as such, with the exception of Quebec's specific provisions reviewed in *Truchon*, has not been judicially examined. Similarly, as Parliament considers expanding MAiD in cases of diminished capacity (i.e., via "advance request") or for mature minors,[96] provinces might also decide to adopt a more restrictive approach, based on medical, public health, and security considerations.[97]

Similar to MAiD in cases of mental illness, we note that there is no court directive compelling Parliament to introduce MAiD for mature minors or through advance requests. *Carter*'s paragraph 111, discussed in detail in the previous chapter, stated that "euthanasia for minors" would "not fall within the parameters suggested in these reasons," and the Supreme Court referred only to "*adults*" throughout the decision, including the final declaration. Similarly, the court's reasons only discussed MAiD in cases where a *competent* adult "*clearly consents*" (present tense) to the termination of life. The court made no reference to the possibility of MAiD for patients who have lost competence (and therefore can't provide contemporaneous consent), based on a prior request. No subsequent court decision has suggested that safeguards that limit MAiD eligibility to competent, contemporaneously consenting adults are unconstitutional. To the contrary, the BC Court of Appeal interpreted *Carter* to require that "when assisted suicide is legalized, it must be conditional on the on the 'clear consent' of the patient," and noted that courts should be "assiduous in seeking to ascertain and give effect to the wishes of the patient in the 'here and now,' even in the face of prior directives."[98] In *Truchon*, the court emphasized that the questions of whether MAiD should be made available for minors, or for incapable persons based on prior requests, were "not at issue" in the case.[99]

A full discussion of potential *Charter* issues in these areas is beyond the scope of this chapter, but we would note that much of the discussion herein with respect to MAiD for mental illness has equal relevance to the matters of MAiD for minors or for advance requests. Subject to *Charter* considerations, these practices are within the jurisdictional scope of Parliament to criminally prohibit, and, even if decriminalized, would be within the power of the provinces to potentially restrict or further regulate in the health care context accordance with their jurisdiction over health care.

We would also observe that the analysis in *Murray-Hall* could also support new possibilities for *federal* regulation. The Supreme Court confirmed that a federal law may have, as its legitimate constitutional objective under s. 91(27), the prohibition of an act *for the purpose of prohibiting it* – be it as an "evil" or an act having an "injurious or undesirable effect on the public."[100] Thus, it potentially remains open for Parliament to re-enact a restriction on MAiD for individuals who are not dying, not only for "the narrow goal of preventing vulnerable persons from being induced to commit suicide at a time of weakness,"[101] but to suppress consensual homicide in such contexts because it has been deemed inherently "injurious or undesirable" for individuals and for society. Such a conclusion may, for example, be informed by the concerns of disability advocates, human rights experts, and health care professionals, who have pointed to the harms of offering death as a "solution" for – and only for – disability-related suffering,[102] as well as current data indicating that "the Canadian MAID regime is lacking the safeguards, data collection, and oversight necessary to protect Canadians against premature death."[103] It could also be supported by international human rights instruments Canada has signed, including the Convention on the Rights of Persons with Disabilities, as discussed in the previous chapter.

One can see how the suppression of an injurious act is the purpose of existing Criminal Code provisions like s. 14 (which states that no person can "consent to have death inflicted on them") – a provision that was partially invalidated by the Supreme Court *Carter* decision without any discussion as to its purpose in that case. Why does the Criminal Code prohibit inflicting death upon another person, even with their consent, if not to suppress it as an inherently injurious act?

Of course, if such a prohibition were federally re-enacted with a clearly stated purpose of suppressing MAiD in cases where a patient is not already dying, it could still be challenged under the *Charter*. But a fresh analysis would be required to determine whether it is overbroad, arbitrary, or grossly disproportionate contrary to section 7. And unlike the purpose examined in *Carter* – "the protection of vulnerable persons from being induced to commit suicide at a time of weakness" – it is difficult to see how a prohibition of termination of life outside the end-of-life context goes further than necessary to achieve its purpose, namely, *suppressing it as such* as an individual, public, or social harm.[104] There may be other grounds to challenge such a law – under section 15, for example – and a full discussion of its constitutionality is beyond the scope of this paper. But it is worth noting that this too is an area in which Parliament may have more room to legitimately legislate than some might suggest.

CONCLUSION

Certain assumptions appear to be driving current Canadian law and policy as it relates to MAiD. This and the previous chapter have sought to identify and challenge some of these assumptions with the hopes of providing increased clarity with respect to the constitutional parameters surrounding MAiD. In so doing, we hope this work might help ensure that further dialogue and decision-making concerning MAiD is more fully informed.

NOTES

This chapter is, combined with the previous chapter, a slightly revised version of an article that was originally published in the *Manitoba Law Journal*, under the title "Mental Illness, Health Care, and Assisted Death: Examining Parameters for Expanding or Restricting MAID under Canada's Charter and Federal System," *Manitoba Law Journal* 47, no. 2 (forthcoming 2025): preprint. The authors are grateful to the *Manitoba Law Journal* for permission to republish the article here as two slightly revised chapters.

1 See *Bill C-39, An Act to Amend An Act to Amend the Criminal Code (medical assistance in dying)*, 44th Parliament, 1st Session (2023), SC 2023, c.1 (Can.). See also *Bill C-62, An Act to Amend An Act to Amend the Criminal Code (medical assistance in dying)*, No. 2, 44th Parliament, 1st Session (2024).
2 See David Fraser, "Alberta Premier Danielle Smith Opposes Assisted-Dying Expansion as Ottawa Seeks Further Delay," *Canadian Press*, 30 January 2023, https://www.theglobeandmail.com/canada/article-alberta-premier-danielle-smith-opposes-assisted-dying-expansion-as/ (perma.cc/GR2C-ATJ8); see also the reservations expressed by Senator Margaret Dawn Anderson of the Northwest Territories about whether MAiD MI-SUMC can be provided in light "of the barriers residents face in

accessing adequate, consistent and culturally-appropriate health care and mental health services," reported in Sidney Cohen, "N.W.T. Senator Questions Territory's Ability to Offer Medical Assistance in Dying," CBC News, 5 January 2023, https://www.cbc.ca/news/canada/north/maid-expansion-on-hold-nwt-1.6704124 (perma.cc/VAJ8-QCP7).

3 The *Act Respecting End-of-Life Care*, CQLR c. S-32.0001 (Quebec, Can.) was assented to 10 June 2014 and has been in effect since 10 December 2015. Various provisions of the act (including with respect to mental disorders) were amended in 2023 through *Bill 11, An Act to Amend the Act Respecting End-of-Life Care and Other Legislative Provisions*, 44th Legislature, 1st Session (2023) CQLR 2023, c. 15. The relevant provision states that "a mental disorder other than a neurocognitive disorder cannot be an illness for which a person may make a request." See *Act Respecting End-of-Life Care (Quebec, Can.)*, s. 26 and *Bill 11, An Act to Amend the Act Respecting End-of-Life Care (Quebec, Can)*, explanatory note and cls. 16(1), 20. Medical aid in dying under the act is currently defined as: "care consisting in the *administration by a competent professional* of medications or substances to a patient, at the patient's request, in order to relieve their suffering by hastening death." See *Act Respecting End-of-Life Care (Quebec, Can.)*, s. 3(6) as amended by Bill 11, cl. 3(2) (emphasis added). In this chapter, the term MAiD will be used generally to refer to the practice of physician-assisted death under both the federal Criminal Code and Quebec regimes, except where a distinction is required for purposes of legal clarity.

4 See *Bill C-14, An Act to Amend the Criminal Code and to Make Related Amendments to Other Acts (medical assistance in dying)*, 42nd Parliament, 1st Session (2016), SC 2016, c. 3 (Can.).

5 *Carter v. Canada (Attorney General)*, 2015 SCC 5, [2015] 1 SCR 331, para. 53; compare to *Carter v. Canada (Attorney General)*, 2016 SCC 4, [2016] 1 SCR, para 4; see also discussion in *Truchon v. Canada (Attorney General)*, 2019 QCCS 3792, paras. 691–733.

6 See *Murray-Hall v. Quebec (Attorney General)*, 2023 SCC 10 (Can.).

7 Ibid., para. 97.

8 See discussion in Trudo Lemmens, Mary J. Shariff, and Leonie Herx, "L'Aide Médicale à Mourir et le sacrifice de la norme de qualité de soins de la pratique médicale," in *Mélanges Robert P. Kouri – L'humain au cœur du droit*, ed. Nathalie Vézina, Pascal Fréchette, and Louise Bernier (Montreal: Yvon Blais, 2021), 621–64. For a shorter discussion, see Trudo Lemmens, Mary Shariff, and Leonie Herx, "How Bill C-7 Will Sacrifice the Medical Profession's Standard of Care," *Policy Options*, 11 February 2021, https://policyoptions.irpp.org/magazines/february-2021/

how-bill-c7-will-sacrifice-the-medical-professions-standard-of-care/ (perma.cc/XAJ3-2YQA).
9 See, for example, *Carter*, 2015 SCC 5, paras. 10, 23, 30, 66–7.
10 Ibid., para. 53, citing *RJR-MacDonald Inc. v. Canada (Attorney General)*, 1995 CanLII 64 (SCC), [1995] 3 SCR 199, para. 32; *Schneider v. The Queen*, 1982 CanLII 26 (SCC), [1982] 2 SCR 112, 142 (Can.) (emphasis added). The court made this comment in the context of rejecting the claimant's claim of a core provincial jurisdictional power over health on the grounds of interjurisdictional immunity.
11 See, for example, the preamble of *Bill C-14, An Act to Amend the Criminal Code*: "Whereas it is desirable to have a consistent approach to medical assistance in dying across Canada, while recognizing the provinces' jurisdiction over various matters related to medical assistance in dying, including the delivery of health care services and the regulation of health care professionals, as well as insurance contracts and coroners and medical examiners."
12 Note that the federal government introduced reporting obligations (including reporting obligations for physicians, nurse practitioners, preliminary assessors, pharmacists, and pharmacy technicians) to which provincial regulatory bodies or health authorities may add. See *Regulations Amending the Regulations for the Monitoring of Medical Assistance in Dying*, SOR 2022-222, s. 10(1). For regulation of health professionals, see, for example, College of Physicians and Surgeons of Nova Scotia, "Professional Standard Regarding Medical Assistance in Dying," 5 May 2021, cpsns.ns.ca/wp-content/uploads/2021/04/Professional-Standard-Regarding-Medical-Assistance-in-Dying-April-26-2021-amended-May-5-2021.pdf. For effective referrals for physicians who object to MAiD, see, for example, "Human Rights and the Provision of Health Services," College of Physicians and Surgeons of Ontario, September 2023, https://www.cpso.on.ca/en/Physicians/Policies-Guidance/Policies/Human-Rights-in-the-Provision-of-Health-Services. Regarding nurses, see, for example, College of Registered Nurses of Manitoba, "Medical Assistance in Dying (MAID): Guidelines for Manitoba Nurses," April 2024, https://www.crnm.mb.ca/wp-content/uploads/2024/04/TriCollege-MAID-guideline-April-2024.pdf. Regarding pharmacists, see, for example, *Pharmacists Regulation*, BC Reg. 417/2008, s. 4.1(2) (BC, Can.). Regarding MAiD and insurance, see, for example, *The Insurance Act*, SS 2015, c. I-9.11, s. 8-118.1(4) (Sask., Can.), which states that a medically assisted death, provided it was administered lawfully, is not to be considered a suicide under a life insurance policy; see also *Workplace Safety and Insurance Act*, 1997, SO 1997, c. 16, Sch A. (Ont., Can.).

Regarding physicians and MAiD access, see, for example, "Human Rights and the Provision of Health Services," College of Physicians and Surgeons of Ontario, September 2023, https://www.cpso.on.ca/en/Physicians/ Policies-Guidance/Policies/Human-Rights-in-the-Provision-of-Health-Services, ss. 12–16; compare to Manitoba's *The Medical Assistance in Dying (Protection for Health Professionals and Others) Act*, CCSM c. M92 (Can.). For reporting, registering, and monitoring MAiD deaths see, for example, *Medical Assistance in Dying Statute Law Amendment Act*, 2017, SO 2017, c. 7 (Ont., Can.); see also *The Fatality Inquiries Amendment and Vital Statistics Amendment Act*, SM 2016, c. 21 (Man., Can.); see also *The Coroners Amendment Act*, 2020, SS 2020, c. 21 (Sask., Can.). Regarding immunity or limitation of liability, see, for example, *Excellent Care for All Act*, 2010, S.O. 2010, c. 14 (Ont., Can.), s.13.8. Regarding vital statistics and investigation see, for example, *Vital Statistics Act*, R.S.O. 1990, c. V.4, s. 21(7) (Ont., Can.); see also *The Fatality Inquiries Act*, (Man.). For codes of medical ethics and practice directions, see, for example, College of Physicians and Surgeons of Nova Scotia, "Professional Standard Regarding Medical Assistance in Dying," 26 April 2021, https://cpsns.ns.ca/wp-content/uploads/2021/04/ Professional-Standard-Regarding-Medical-Assistance-in-Dying.pdf; see also College of Physicians and Surgeons of British Columbia, "Practice Standard: Medical Assistance in Dying," 26 February 2024, https://www.cpsbc.ca/files/pdf/PSG-Medical-Assistance-in-Dying.pdf; College of Physicians and Surgeons of Manitoba, "Standard of Practice: Medical Assistance in Dying (MAiD)," 20 March 2024, https://cpsm.mb.ca/assets/ Standards%20of%20Practice/Standard%20of%20Practice%20Medical% 20Assistance%20in%20Dying%20(MAID).pdf.

13 See, for example, External Panel on Options for a Legislative Response to *Carter v. Canada*, *Consultations on Physician-Assisted Dying: Summary of Results and Key Findings: Final Report*, Department of Justice, 15 December 2015, iv–vii, 18–19, https://www.justice.gc.ca/eng/ rp-pr/other-autre/pad-amm/pad.pdf (perma.cc/4NDB-ZFFW); see also Provincial-Territorial Expert Advisory Group on Physician-Assisted Dying, *Final Report*, 30 November 2015, 2–4, 19, https://novascotia.ca/ dhw/publications/Provincial-Territorial-Expert-Advisory-Group-on-Physician-Assisted-Dying.pdf (perma.cc/GXU5-2KE3); see also Special Joint Committee on Physician-Assisted Dying, *Medical Assistance in Dying: A Patient-Centered Approach*, 42nd Parliament, 1st Session, February 2016, 2, 6, 58, https://www.parl.ca/Content/Committee/421/ PDAM/Reports/RP8120006/pdamrp01/pdamrp01-e.pdf (perma.cc/7ZH5-GLKJ); see also *Bill C-14, An Act to Amend the Criminal Code*, preamble.

14 See Provincial-Territorial Expert Advisory Group, *Final Report*, 16 (emphasis added).
15 *Carter*, 2015 SCC 5, para. 53.
16 *Murray-Hall*, 2023 SCC 10, para. 73 (emphasis added).
17 *Murray-Hall*, 2023 SCC 10, para. 73 (emphasis added); see also *Reference re Genetic Non-Discrimination Act*, 2020 SCC 17, [2020] 2 SCR 283, para. 93; see also *Chaoulli v. Quebec (Attorney General)*, 2005 SCC 35, [2005] 1 SCR 791, 2005 SCC 35 (Can.), para. 16.
18 For discussion see, for example, Special Joint Committee, *Patient-Centered Approach*, 4.
19 *RJR*, 1995 CanLII 64 (SCC), para. 32 (emphasis added).
20 *Canada (Attorney General) v. PHS Community Services Society*, 2011 SCC 44, [2011] 3 SCR 134, para. 68, citing *R v. Morgentaler*, 1988 CanLII 90 (SCC), [1988] 1 SCR 30 (Can.); *Morgentaler v. The Queen*, 1975 CanLII 8 (SCC), [1976] 1 SCR 616 (Can.); *R v. Morgentaler*, 1993 CanLII 74 (SCC), [1993] 3 SCR 463 (Can.). This passage was quoted by the court in *Carter*, 2015 SCC 5, para. 51 (emphasis added).
21 See *Criminal Code of Canada*, RSC 1985, c. C-46, ss. 222(4), 229 (re. culpable homicide), ss. 245(1)-(3) (re. administering noxious thing), and ss. 241(2)-(7), 241.1, 241.2, 241.3 (re. aiding suicide).
22 *Rodriguez v. British Columbia (Attorney General)*, 1993 CanLII 75 (SCC) (Can.), para. 162.
23 See discussion and comments in *Bill C-14, An Act to Amend the Criminal Code and to Make Related Amendments to Other Acts (medical assistance in dying)*, 2nd reading, House of Commons Debates, 42-1, No. 62 (31 May 2016), 3797 (Hon. Jody Wilson-Raybould) (Can.).
24 Expert Panel Working Group on MAID Where a Mental Disorder Is the Sole Underlying Medical Condition, *The State of Knowledge on Medical Assistance in Dying Where a Mental Disorder Is the Sole Underlying Medical Condition* (Ottawa: Council of Canadian Academies, 2018), chap. 4, https://rapports-cac.ca/wp-content/uploads/2018/12/The-State-of-Knowledge-on-Medical-Assistance-in-Dying-Where-a-Mental-Disorder-is-the-Sole-Underlying-Medical-Condition.pdf (perma.cc/HX8U-J548), 54.
25 *Bill C-14, An Act to Amend the Criminal Code and to Make Related Amendments to Other Acts (medical assistance in dying)*, 2nd reading, Senate Debates, 42-1, vol. 150, No. 46 (9 June 2016), 1016 (Hon. Tobias C. Enverga J.) (Can.).
26 *Bill C-14, An Act to Amend the Criminal Code and to Make Related Amendments to Other Acts (medical assistance in dying)*, 2nd reading, Senate Debates (in Committee of the Whole), 42-1, vol. 150, No. 41 (1 June 2016), 750 (Hon. Jody Wilson-Raybould) (Can.) (emphasis added).

27 *Murray-Hall*, 2023 SCC 10, para. 71, citing *Chaoulli*, 2005 SCC 35, para. 18.
28 *Constitution Act*, 1867 (UK), 30 & 31 Vict., c. 3, s. 92(7), reprinted in RSC 1985, Appendix II, No. 5.
29 Ibid., ss. 92(7), 92(13), 92(16); see *Eldridge v. British Columbia (Attorney General)*, 1997 CanLII 327 (SCC), [1997] 3 SCR 624, para. 24: "the hospital insurance and medicare programs in force in this country come within the exclusive jurisdiction of the provinces under ss. 92(7) (hospitals), 92(13) (property and civil rights), 92(16) (matters of a merely local or private nature)." See also Howard Leeson, *Constitutional Jurisdiction Over Health and Health Care Services in Canada – Discussion Paper No. 12 of Commission on the Future of Health Care in Canada* (Ottawa: 2002), v.
30 A basic example of this is that while the Criminal Code MAiD provisions permit both physician and nurse administration as well as patient self-administered MAiD, the Quebec EOL law, for example, only permits physician administration. See *Criminal Code of Canada*, ss. 241.1(a) and (b) and compare to *Act Respecting End-of-Life Care (Quebec, Can.)*, s. 3(6). Furthermore, Quebec's medical regulator, while providing a protocol for physician administration, has not provided one for self-administration as of 2019. See Collège des médecins du Québec et al., *L'aide Médicale à Mourir: Mise à Jour 11/2019: Guide D'Exercice et Lignes Directrices Pharmacologiques*, November 2019, 5.1, https://cms.cmq.org/files/documents/Informations-cliniques/amm/AideMedicaleAMourir-FR-2019-11-28-v-def-revo1.pdf, perma.cc/X4GY-GFG8; see also discussion in C. Harty et al., "The Oral MAiD Option in Canada, Part 1: Medication Protocols, Review and Recommendations," Canadian Association of MAiD Assessors & Providers, 18 April 2018, 21, https://camapcanada.ca/wp-content/uploads/2022/02/OralMAiD-Med.pdf (perma.cc/Q5ER-S9M4); C. Harty et al., "The Oral MAiD Option in Canada, Part 2: Process for Providing, Review and Recommendations," Canadian Association of MAiD Assessors & Providers, 18 April 2018, 5, https://camapcanada.ca/wp-content/uploads/2022/02/OralMAiD-Process.pdf (perma.cc/SYT4-QKG4); Igor Stukalin et al., "Medications and Dosages Used in Medical Assistance in Dying: A Cross-Sectional Study," *CMAJ Open* 10, no. 1 (January 2022): E19–E26, E19; *Cameron v. Nova Scotia (Attorney General)*, 1999 NSCA 14 (CanLII), [1999] NSJ No. 297 (QL) (Can.), leave to appeal to dismissed, [1999] SCCA No. 531 (QL), discussed below.
31 That is, "reasonably foreseeable natural death" under Federal *Bill C-14, An Act to Amend the Criminal Code*, versus "end of life" under the Quebec *Act Respecting End-of-Life Care (Quebec, Can)*, ss. 3(3), 3(6).

32 Bill C-14, 2nd reading, *Senate Debates (in Committee of the Whole)*, 749 (Hon. Jody Wilson-Raybould).
33 It is interesting to point out here how this makes it all the more remarkable that the *Truchon* decision was not appealed by the federal attorney general. As others have pointed out (Thomas McMorrow, Sabrina Tremblay-Huet, and Michaela Kelly, "Interpreting Eligibility under the Medical Assistance in Dying Law: The Experiences of Physicians and Nurse Practitioners," *McGill Journal of Law and Health* 14, no. 1 [2020]: 51–108, 57), the plaintiffs in *Truchon* would have had immediate access to MAiD in other provinces. Indeed, a reason that the plaintiff in *Lamb* abandoned her challenge to the MAiD law was precisely because an expert witness for the AG testified that she (Ms Lamb) would likely qualify under a broad interpretation of "reasonable foreseeable natural death." Arguably, the plaintiffs in *Truchon* did not qualify for MAiD in Quebec due to the more narrow Quebec law criterion of "end of life," which resulted in a more narrow application of the federal RFND requirement. A declaration of unconstitutionality of the Quebec law could thus arguably have sufficed to provide the plaintiffs access to MAiD.
34 Health Canada, *Final Report of the Expert Panel on MAiD and Mental Illness*, May 2022, 32–3, https://www.canada.ca/en/health-canada/corporate/about-health-canada/public-engagement/external-advisory-bodies/expert-panel-maid-mental-illness/final-report-expert-panel-maid-mental-illness.html.
35 Provincial-Territorial Expert Advisory Group, *Final Report*, 16–17 (emphasis added).
36 See *Canada Health Act*, RSC 1985, c. C-6.
37 Ibid., ss. 2, 7.
38 See *Bill C-14, An Act to Amend the Criminal Code*, preamble.
39 See *Canada Health Act*, ss. 15–17. For further discussion, see Colleen M. Flood and Bryan Thomas, "Modernizing the *Canada Health Act*," *Dalhousie Law Journal* 39, no. 2 (Fall 2016): 397–411, 399.
40 *Cameron*, 1999 NSCA 14, para. 97 (emphasis added).
41 *Canada Health Act*, s. 2; see also Flood and Thomas, "Modernizing the CHA," 403.
42 See Marlisa Tiedemann, *The Canada Health Act: An Overview – Publication No 2019-54-E* (Ottawa: Library of Parliament, 2020), 3, https://lop.parl.ca/sites/PublicWebsite/default/en_CA/Research Publications/201954E (perma.cc/CR3M-S9YH), citing J.C. Herbert Emery and Ronald Kneebone, "The Challenge of Defining Medicare Coverage in Canada," *SPP Research Papers* 6, no. 32 (October 2013): 1–23; see also Commission on the Future of Health Care in Canada, *Medically*

Necessary: What Is It, and Who Decides? (Ottawa: Government of Canada, 2002); Timothy A. Caulfield, "Wishful Thinking: Defining 'Medically Necessary' in Canada," *Health Law Journal* 4 (1996): 63–85.

43 See Brian Bird, "The Provinces Could Pass on Expanding Assisted Death – Regardless of the Federal Government's Wishes," *Hub*, 7 March 2023, https://thehub.ca/2023-03-07/brian-bird-the-provinces-could-pass-on-expanding-assisted-death-regardless-of-the-federal-governments-wishes/ (perma.cc/TK2D-DA4C): "Regardless of whether the Charter is said to require the decriminalization of assisted death, provinces are not necessarily obliged to integrate assisted death into their health-care systems. Provinces cannot criminalize assisted death, as criminal law is federal jurisdiction. But pursuant to their jurisdiction over the delivery of health care, provinces could have potentially declined to sponsor assisted death as health care and could potentially decline to sponsor other forms or features of assisted death that may be decriminalized in the future."

44 *Cameron*, 1999 NSCA 14, para. 101; see also ibid., paras. 93–7; see also discussion in John J. Morris and Cynthia D. Clarke, *Law for Canadian Health Care Administrators*, 2nd ed. (Toronto: LexisNexis Canada, 2011), 32–3.

45 *Murray-Hall*, 2023 SCC 10, paras. 77, 80.

46 But note that Quebec proceeded with regulating assisted death prior to federal decriminalization.

47 Bird, "Provinces Could Pass."

48 Ibid.

49 Ibid.

50 *Murray-Hall*, 2023 SCC 10, para. 2.

51 Ibid., para. 68. The court also cited *Siemens v. Manitoba (Attorney General)*, 2003 SCC 3, [2003] 1 SCR 6 (Can.), para. 25, Major J: "the mere presence of a prohibition and a penalty does not invalidate an otherwise acceptable use of provincial legislative power."

52 See *Murray-Hall*, 2023 SCC 10, para. 33.

53 Ibid., para. 28 (emphasis added); see also para. 60.

54 Ibid., para. 54.

55 Ibid., para. 51.

56 Ibid., para. 55, citing *Morgentaler*, [1993] 3 SCR 463, 498.

57 *Murray-Hall*, 2023 SCC 10, para. 54 (emphasis added).

58 Ibid.

59 Ibid., paras. 57–64 (emphasis original).

60 Ibid., para. 57.

61 Ibid., para. 65.

62 Ibid., para. 68 (emphasis added).
63 Ibid., para. 69.
64 Ibid., paras. 71–2. *Murray-Hall* was recently followed in a Manitoba case (the only other province, along with Quebec, to completely prohibit home cultivation of cannabis). The Manitoba Court of King's Bench affirmed the constitutionality of Manitoba's prohibition, noting that, although its legislation differed from the Quebec regime upheld in *Murray-Hall* (it did not create a provincial monopoly on cannabis and did not explicitly mention "health and safety"), it was within the jurisdiction of the province to enact. The court was satisfied, following *Murray-Hall*, that the statute's purposes were valid, as it was intended to advance the objectives of public health and safety: see *Lavoie v. The Government of Manitoba*, 2023 MBKB 146 (Can.), paras. 74–6.
65 *Murray-Hall*, 2023 SCC 10, para. 74, citing *Schneider*, [1982] 2 SCR 112, 132–3 (emphasis added).
66 *Act Respecting End-of-Life Care (Quebec, Can.)*, s. 1. Note that, following *Bill 11, An Act to Amend the Act Respecting End-of-Life Care (Quebec, Can)*, "medical aid in dying" was expressly added to the purpose of the act text.
67 See Assemblée Nationale du Québec, *Report of the Select Committee on the Evolution of the Act Respecting End-of-Life Care*, December 2021, https://www.assnat.qc.ca/en/travaux-parlementaires/commissions/cssfv-42-1/index.html (perma.cc/678F-CHUD).
68 Ibid., 47, 49–50, 54–5.
69 Ibid., 61.
70 That said, the court did consider the distinction between the two laws as part of the legal context for the purposes of the section 15 analysis in respect of the Quebec EOL law. See *Truchon*, 2019 QCCS 3792, para. 703. See also discussion in the previous chapter at note 153 et seq and accompanying text as well as notes 210, 216 and accompanying text.
71 *Truchon*, 2019 QCCS 3792, para. 556 (emphasis added). For further discussion of *Truchon* and the court's views on the different objectives of the statutory provisions at issue, see previous chapter.
72 Ibid., paras. 724–5.
73 *Murray-Hall*, 2023 SCC 10, para. 15.
74 Provincial-Territorial Expert Advisory Group, *Final Report*, 16.
75 *Murray-Hall*, 2023 SCC 10, para. 69.
76 Ibid., paras. 68, 71.
77 Ibid., para. 76 citing *Desgagnés Transport Inc. v. Wärtsilä Canada Inc.*, 2019 SCC 58, [2019] 4 SCR 228, paras. 84–5; *Reference re Securities Act*, 2011 SCC 66, [2011] 3 SCR 837, para. 66.

78 *Murray-Hall*, 2023 SCC 10, para. 83.
79 Ibid., paras. 90, 95, quoting *Reference re Assisted Human Reproduction Act*, 2010 SCC 61, [2010] 3 SCR 457, para. 38.
80 *Murray-Hall*, 2023 SCC 10, paras. 90, 96–7, 99 (emphasis added).
81 For further discussion on "rights rhetoric" surrounding MAiD, see Trudo Lemmens, "When Death Becomes Therapy: Canada's Troubling Normalization of Health Care Provider Ending of Life," *American Journal of Bioethics* 23, no. 11 (2023): 79–84.
82 *Chaoulli*, 2005 SCC 35, para. 104; see also *Auton (Guardian ad litem of) v. British Columbia (Attorney General)*, 2004 SCC 78, [2004] 3 SCR 657 (Can.); *Flora v. Ontario (Health Insurance Plan, General Manager)*, 2008 ONCA 538, 91 OR (3d) 412, para. 108 (Can.). Of course, the *Charter* may become engaged in other ways if and when the government decides to provide a service, for example by requiring it to do so in a non-discriminatory manner (see, for example, *Chaoulli*, 2005 SCC 35, para. 24: "where the government puts in place a scheme to provide health care, that scheme must comply with the Charter"; *Eldridge v. British Columbia (Attorney General)*, 1997 CanLII 327 (SCC), [1997] 3 SCR 624, para. 66 (Can.)).
83 *Criminal Code of Canada*, s. 241.1(9). Some provincial physicians' colleges have, however, introduced policies requiring health care professionals to participate through the provision of "effective referrals." For discussion on these types of policies and concerns about their impact on medical conscience and independent clinical and ethical decision-making, see Derek Ross and Deina Warren, "The Importance of Conscience as an Independent Protection," in *Medical Assistance in Dying (MAID) in Canada: Key Multidisciplinary Perspectives*, ed. Jaro Kotalik and David W. Shannon (Cham, Switzerland: Springer, 2023); Mary Ann Waldron, "Conscientious Objections to Medical Aid in Dying: Considering How to Manage Claims of Conscience in a Pluralistic Society," *Supreme Court Law Review* (2d) 85 (2018): 77–106; Brian Bird, "The Call in *Carter* to Interpret Freedom of Conscience," *Supreme Court Law Review* (2d) 85 (2018): 107–41.
84 John Morris, Cynthia Clarke, and Anna L. Marrison, "Consent to Treatment," *Law for Canadian Health Care Administrators*, 3rd ed. (Toronto: LexisNexis Canada, 2020), chap. 6.12.
85 Indeed, as Jesse Hartery observes, even prior to *Murray-Hall*, the Supreme Court unanimously held that that the criminal law power "does not allow Parliament to create positive entitlements. Rather, it is properly limited to the suppression of an 'evil or injurious or undesirable effect upon the public,' and is not a license to regulate intra-provincial trade and health." See

Jesse Hartery, "Federalism and the Paramountcy Doctrine," *Constitutional Forum* 32, no. 1 (2023): 9–24, quoting *Reference re Validity of Section 5(a) of the Dairy Industry Act*, [1949] SCR 1 at 49.
86 *Murray-Hall*, 2023 SCC 10, para. 78: "many regulatory prohibitions are absolute in nature without being considered criminal law prohibitions."
87 See *Rothmans, Benson & Hedges Inc. v. Saskatchewan*, 2005 SCC 13, [2005] 1 SCR 188 (Can.).
88 *Reference re AHRA*, 2010 SCC 61, para. 38 (emphasis added).
89 *Murray-Hall*, 2023 SCC 10, para. 25.
90 Provinces may also want to regulate where and how MAiD could be offered. For example, private funeral homes have started to offer MAiD in Ontario and Quebec, and the Quebec legislature debated whether this should be permitted. Conflict of interest concerns may arise in the context of funeral homes renting out space for MAiD, which the provinces can legitimately regulate. There has also been discussion about offering MAiD in public spaces, for example in public parks. Rules about use of such property and public spaces fall under provincial jurisdiction, even if some of the rules may touch on issues of public morality.
91 *Murray-Hall*, 2023 SCC 10, para. 25.
92 See, for example, Isabel Grant, "Legislated Ableism: Bill C-7 and the Rapid Expansion of MAiD in Canada," *McGill Journal of Law and Health* (2023), http://dx.doi.org/10.2139/ssrn.4544454. See also human rights lawyer Julius Grey's analysis in Anna Farrow, "Lawyer to Challenge MAiD for Mentally Ill," *Catholic Register*, 22 November 2023, https://www.catholicregister.org/item/36153-lawyer-to-challenge-maid-for-mentally-ill.
93 The division of jurisdictional responsibility over assisted death between the federal and provincial governments was recently summarized by the Alberta Court of King's Bench in *WV v MV*, 2024 ABKB 174 (para. 8) as follows:
> The federal government has some control over the provision of MAiD through its criminal law power. The MAiD provisions of the Criminal Code articulate a set of criteria and safeguards that, if followed, exempt doctors, nurse practitioners, and pharmacists who participate in MAiD from criminal liability. The MAiD provisions of the Criminal Code establish a minimum standard that medical professionals must adhere to if they are to avoid criminal liability; *higher standards of practice may be imposed by tort law, professional governing bodies, AHS policies, or provincial legislation.* Alberta has jurisdiction over health care, professions, and the relevant areas of private law. Concurrent provincial jurisdiction over MAiD is expressly recognized in Criminal Code s

241.2(7) which provides "Medical assistance in dying must be provided with reasonable knowledge, care and skill and in accordance with any applicable provincial laws, rules or standards." *Should Alberta wish, subject to limits imposed by the Constitution, it may shape the contours of* MAID *within the province* [emphasis added].

94 The repeal of the exclusion from eligibility for MAiD MI-SUMC is to take place on 17 March 2027. See *Bill C-62, An Act to Amend An Act to Amend the Criminal Code (medical assistance in dying)*, No. 2, 44th Parliament, 1st Session (2024). For discussion of concerns regarding MAiD MI-SUMC, see previous chapter, especially notes 7–10.

95 See chapter 11 (Shariff, Ross, Lemmens). See also the submission of Professor Kerri Froc, "Re: Extension of MAiD Where the Sole Underlying Condition is Mental Illness," submission to the Joint Committee on Medical Assistance in Dying, 17 November 2024.

96 See Special Joint Committee on Medical Assistance in Dying, *Medical Assistance in Dying in Canada: Choices for Canadians*, 44th Parliament, 1st Session, February 2023, 61, 73, https://www.parl.ca/DocumentViewer/en/44-1/AMAD/report-2, which recommended that the federal government "amend the eligibility criteria for MAID set out in the *Criminal Code* to include minors deemed to have the requisite decision-making capacity upon assessment" and also "to allow for advance requests following a diagnosis of a serious and incurable medical condition disease, or disorder leading to incapacity." But see the federal government's response to the report, which noted that these proposals "require further consideration, consultation, and study" and that any specific reform "would require a significant amount of work with provinces and territories to implement." The government response also acknowledged that "MAID crosses federal, provincial, and territorial jurisdictions. Certain aspects of MAID fall under federal jurisdiction, such as the criminal law dimensions, whereas others fall under provincial and territorial jurisdiction, such as health care delivery." Hon. Jean-Yves Duclos to Hon. Yonah Martin and Hon. Marc Garneau, "Government Response to the Second Report of the Special Joint Committee on Medical Assistance in Dying," 13 June 2023, 1, 7, https://www.parl.ca/content/Committee/441/AMAD/GovResponse/RP12536195/441_AMAD_Rpt02_GR/DepartmentOfHealth-2023-06-15-b.pdf (perma.cc/QFY5-4ZBJ).

97 Note that Quebec, while excluding mental disorders from assisted death eligibility, expanded its EOL law to permit assisted death pursuant to advance request. See *An Act Respecting End-of-Life Care (Quebec, Can)*, s. 3. We note, however, that to the extent that Quebec's law is more *permissive* than the federal Criminal Code's prohibitions, it would likely be

rendered inoperative for offending the constitutional doctrine of paramountcy. See, for example, *Québec (Procureur général) c. D'Amico*, 2015 QCCA 2138 (Can.). There, although the Quebec Court of Appeal upheld Quebec's more permissive EOL law in the face of a total criminal prohibition on MAiD, it did so because the federal law had recently been found unconstitutional in *Carter*, and therefore, in the court's view, there was no conflict with a "valid" federal law. This decision generated some criticism as the federal law was technically still in effect at the time (*Carter*'s declaration of invalidity had been suspended for one year). That dimension of the decision aside, we note that *D'Amico* did state that "if Parliament eventually enacts valid federal legislation with respect to medical aid in dying that applies to Quebec, the provisions of the *Act respecting End-of-Life Care* that concern medical aid in dying *will need to be re-examined to determine whether they are in conflict with that legislative framework*" (para. 44, emphasis added). This comment was made in the context of conflicts created by a more *permissive* Quebec regime. In the case of a more *restrictive* provincial regime, as discussed in this paper, there may not be any conflict of purposes, since the purpose of the criminal law cannot be to create positive rights. It is also noteworthy that the Court of Appeal in *D'Amico* emphasized the provinces' jurisdiction to legislate around MAiD (para. 41) and described Quebec's *Act Respecting End-of-Life Care* as "legislation with respect to health which falls within Quebec's legislative jurisdiction" (see para. 42). Thus there is support, from at least one appellate court, for provincial jurisdiction to implement its own "strong framework for controlling medical aid in dying, thereby limiting the risks involved" (para. 42).

98 *Bentley v. Maplewood Seniors Care Society*, 2015 BCCA 91, para. 18.
99 *Truchon*, 2019 QCCS 3792, para. 16.
100 *Murray-Hall*, 2023 SCC 10, para. 77.
101 *Carter*, 2015 SCC 5, para. 78.
102 See in general chapter 10 (Grant), and chapter 11 (Shariff, Ross, and Lemmens), notes 8–11 and 34.
103 Ramona Coelho et al., "The Realities of Medical Assistance in Dying in Canada," *Palliative and Supportive Care* 21, no. 5 (October 2023): 871–8, https://pubmed.ncbi.nlm.nih.gov/37462416/ (perma.cc/ZK6L-MC7U).
104 For further discussion, see John Sikkema, "The 'Basic Bedford Rule' and Substantive Review of Criminal Law Prohibitions Under Section 7 of the Charter," *Supreme Court Law Review* (2d) 85 (2018): 49.

13

Evaluating the Existing Scientific Evidence for Physician-Assisted Death for Mental Illness

Mark Sinyor and Ayal Schaffer

SCIENTIFIC EVIDENCE AS A QUINTESSENTIAL ASPECT OF MEDICAL DECISION-MAKING

The debate about physician-assisted death (PAD) for mental illness is complex, and other chapters in this book delineate a variety of key concerns about the ethical and philosophical justifiability of this practice. This chapter, however, will focus on the specific issue of whether the scientific justifications for PAD for mental illness followed standards that would be considered acceptable within the field of medicine and health care in general.

The most important point of contention is clearly expressed by the November 2020 discussion paper released by the Association des Médecins Psychiatres du Québec (the Quebec Psychiatry Association or AMPQ), in which they wrote that "whether to permit [medical assistance in dying] ... is not an empirical question, it is an ethical one."[1] This idea – that scientific evidence is irrelevant – was repeated during the Canadian government's Senate hearings on the matter,[2] was self-evidently used as a crucial justification for Canada's decision to amend the law without the requirement for further research, and has since been extensively challenged, including by a 2022 statement from the Association of Chairs of Psychiatry in Canada.[3] It is also counter to any standard understanding of medical science and the delivery of health care. To be clear, there is no such thing as an ethical question that is separable from empirical fact.

Consider the so-called "trolley problem," different versions of which are often used to teach basic principles of ethics.[4] For example, five people are standing on train tracks and are about to be struck by an oncoming locomotive. You have the power to pull a lever that will divert the train away onto a different track where only one person is standing. Ethicists typically agree that this is permissible for utilitarian reasons – because you are reducing the number of deaths from five to one. From that ethical perspective, under these circumstances, it is your obligation to pull the lever.

But what if the details of the scenario change? What if there is one person standing on the train tracks and five people standing on the alternate set of tracks who will all die if you pull the lever (i.e., the inverse of the way the original trolley problem was framed)? Is it ethical to save the single individual if it will kill the five others? In this case, most ethicists will likely conclude that saving the single individual is unethical.

One can introduce many further nuances to the trolley problem that can influence the ethics of different decisions, but the key point is that changes to the precise empirical facts are important and often decisive in determining the ethics of an action.

Medical ethics, and indeed all ethics, can be broadly divided into teleology or consequentialist theory (judging an action based on its consequences) and deontology or non-consequentialist theory (judging an action based on its intrinsic virtue or morality).[5] As mentioned, there are many disparate views regarding the deontological moral question as it applies to PAD in mental illness, which are discussed elsewhere in this book. But decisions grounded in medical ethics place extraordinary emphasis on the *consequences* of actions. The randomized controlled trial (RCT), a bedrock of medical scientific evidence, can be thought of as an effort to carefully delineate the consequences of applying an intervention.[6] The efficacy (positive consequences) and safety or tolerability (negative consequences) of treatments measured in RCTs are used to identify numbers needed to treat (NNT) and numbers needed to harm (NNH) that are then routinely relied upon to determine whether an intervention is medically justifiable.[7]

Such calculations must go beyond benefits and harms to individual patients, as they also need to account for the potential impact on other individual patients, the health care system, and society in general. Among individuals, for example, ethics dictate that we must weigh evidence of harm and benefit for different groups in deciding who is at the front of the line to receive a vaccine or an organ transplant.[8] Likewise, we must consider harms and benefits to everyone in the health care system when determining whether some treatments may be so expensive that public funders ought to refuse to provide them given the opportunity cost.[9] Patients with severe mental illnesses that manifest in homicidal ideation with intent to act or with actual violence are sometimes involuntarily confined to hospital for prolonged periods, an intervention that often causes them substantial harm but is nevertheless widely regarded as ethically permissible, if not required, because it protects society at large.[10]

Health care providers and bioethicists routinely carefully consider how to interpret empirical evidence when making decisions. For the examples above, relevant evidence includes the number of serious adverse events in a RCT, survival rates post-transplant in specific populations, the economic impacts of an expensive treatment on the viability of a public health care system, and calculations about risk of violence. Once we have this high-quality evidence, vigorous debate is healthy. Health care providers, bioethicists, and policy-makers universally adhere to the notion that such evidence is critical to medical decision-making. Under usual circumstances, that evidence is often considered determinative in resolving questions of medical ethics.

The notion that the consequences of delivering a medical intervention are irrelevant is, at best, terribly misguided. At worst, it is itself an abrogation of responsibility and a sharp deviation from norms established over centuries and across jurisdictions. The fact that physicians and other advocates chose to take this view in the case of PAD for mental illness, which would never be acceptable anywhere else in health care, is baffling. That the Canadian government accepted that position is extraordinary and reckless.

MISSING SCIENTIFIC EVIDENCE

Advocates for PAD for mental illness successfully argued that making the practice available to Canadians is the "right thing" to do, and that no evidence could change that fact.[11] This position is fundamentally anti-scientific. Karl Popper, the famous science philosopher, noted that for a theory to qualify as science, it must "falsifiable."[12] That is, we must be able to articulate the kind of experimental evidence that would lead us to judge the theory false.

The position that providing PAD for mental illness is ethical irrespective of any evidence is therefore not a scientific one and should never have been presented as science. As described above, positioning evidence as irrelevant is an untenable stance that flies in the face of both common sense and how modern medicine actually operates. But what sort of evidence was missing and why does it matter?

INTOLERABLE SUFFERING

Arriving at a Definition

As of March 2021, the Canadian medical assistance in dying legislation listed having "enduring and intolerable ... psychological suffering that cannot be alleviated under conditions the person considers acceptable" as a criterion for eligibility.[13] Yet intolerable suffering is an ambiguous scientific construct that has never been clearly operationalized, let alone rigorously studied. Some researchers, clinicians, and patients themselves have advocated for an entirely subjective definition (i.e., if a person says that his or her suffering is intolerable to them then a physician should accept that without question).[14] However, this notion leads to potentially absurd conclusions wherein literally any symptom or circumstance could potentially be eligible for being remedied by death. Likewise, there is no accepted definition for what constitutes "enduring" suffering.[15] Does that indicate suffering lasting for at least one month, one year, or ten years? Would suffering need to be continuous during that period, occur for at least most of the time, or only be present sufficiently often to cause the subjective sense that when it is present it is intolerable? These important questions have never been subject to systematic inquiry by the scientific community.

WHAT SHOULD HAVE HAPPENED

There are well-established scientific processes for arriving at consensus expert opinion in medicine. One recognized strategy in the case of establishing parameters for a complex concept such as "enduring and intolerable suffering" would be a Delphi study.[16] In this design, researchers would convene a panel of experts with broad knowledge of and experience in relevant subject areas including psychiatry, palliative care, bioethics, and suicide prevention, ideally including both national and international experts. This group would be joined by representatives from relevant stakeholders including patient advocacy groups, mental health associations, and people with lived experience of mental illness and disabilities, as well as members of the general public.

Once convened, this group would conduct questionnaires and discussions about possible definitions in iterative rounds to allow the opportunity for individuals to comment in response to ideas raised by other members. The results would then be synthesized into consensus criteria that operationalize what suffering would meet the threshold of "enduring and intolerable" in the context of an application for PAD. This would establish a common starting point from which all research in the area could move forward.

WHAT DID HAPPEN

Nothing. The phenomenon of enduring and intolerable suffering has yet to be the subject of any rigorous scientific study. In Canada, it was proposed that expert committees sort out these issues now that the law has passed;[17] however, there was no requirement that this process adhere to the rigorous approach described above, and as of this writing there has been no indication that it will. To the contrary, committee reports have recommended that determinations of enduring and intolerable suffering be made between PAD assessors and PAD requestors (with a call for "Periodic, Federally Funded Research ... on questions relating to the practice of MAID").[18]

Demonstrating Its Applicability to Patients with Sole Mental Illness and Quantifying Its Prevalence in Clinical Samples (If Applicable)

Because intolerable suffering has never been adequately defined or studied in psychiatry, people advocating for PAD for mental illness have had to rely on proxy indicators for that outcome. The indicators that have generally been used are the prevalence of symptoms in clinical samples and research trials.[19] The problem with this kind of extrapolation will be discussed in more detail below in relation to the identification of "irremediable" suffering. For now, the key point is that it is a substantial logical error to conflate the idea of the *presence* of a circumstance with its intolerability. Let us imagine that 12 per cent, 7 per cent, and 3 per cent of the general population suffer from headaches, back pain, and depression at some point in time. That information tells us absolutely nothing about whether and how often those circumstances are experienced as intolerable according to any definition. It could be true in every case, in some cases, or in no cases.

So prevalence estimates of illness and symptoms are of no use to us in quantifying the phenomenon of intolerable suffering. This is especially problematic when considering the notion of suffering, which is not only a feature of mental illness but also an intrinsic component of human experience at various points in life. Yet the prevalence of symptoms was the main scientific data presented to the Government of Canada for consideration in their deliberations on this matter.

Note that whether a clinical circumstance is rare or common cannot necessarily, in and of itself, be used as a justification for determining which medical intervention should be offered for it. However, there are certainly important practical implications if enduring and intolerable suffering exists, for example, in 5 per cent, 1 per cent, 1 in one thousand, or 1 in one million people with mental illness, and a basic foundational step for those proposing an intervention for it must be to demonstrate to what specific degree it exists in the first place. Arriving at a precise quantification is also crucial as a baseline for further research into how often intolerable suffering may be remediable. It would also be necessary for monitoring whether implementation of this intervention in the future may be occurring appropriately and that it is not being offered to far more people than prevalence estimates suggest could be eligible.

WHAT SHOULD HAVE HAPPENED

After the scientific community arrived at a consensus definition for enduring and intolerable suffering (as discussed), if that had happened, measurement and evaluation tools should have been developed and validated through established methods for such research to have a reliable way to identify people who meet criteria for that phenomenon.[20] Those tools should then have been used in research studies involving clinical and population samples to quantify the degree to which enduring and intolerable suffering exists in those samples of people with sole mental illness, as defined by consensus.

WHAT DID HAPPEN

Nothing. No rigorous definition of enduring and intolerable suffering has ever been used to identify the prevalence in Canada of the phenomenon in any sample of people with mental illness. And, to our knowledge, there is no plan to do so prior to implementation of the new law. In other words, those experts proposing PAD as a treatment for intolerable suffering in mental illness did not take even basic scientific steps to determine to what degree it exists in the first place. They have instead taken an entirely unscientific approach, something unheard of within a modern health care system.

Note that many advocates will likely argue that the issues raised here and elsewhere in this chapter are irrelevant. They will suggest that the decision about whether suffering is intolerable is entirely subjective and that if people ask for this intervention, it should simply be provided. It must be acknowledged that the primacy of autonomy is a defensible philosophical position. It just isn't a scientific one (i.e., it does not adhere to the bedrock of modern health care). This raises the question of whether the medical profession or some medical professionals are entitled to seek an exemption from the usual expectations of science and evidence-based medicine in this one specific instance and, if so, how that can possibly be justified.

IRREMEDIABILITY

Demonstrating Irremediability and (If Applicable) Quantifying Its Prevalence

As discussed, the existence and prevalence of enduring and intolerable suffering in mental illness has never been adequately scientifically characterized. However, for the purposes of this section, let us assume that we can identify a baseline prevalence of people with mental disorders who meet a definition for that circumstance (at least *prior* to treatment). Again, experts advocating for this intervention have used proxies to infer how often such suffering might persist following treatment. And again, these proxies are mainly enduring symptoms of the mental health condition (and, sometimes, functional impairment). As described, the persistence of symptoms or impairment tells us nothing about whether these are experienced as intolerable.

To illustrate the substantial conceptual problems with these arguments, let us examine what may have been the most frequently cited research study in hearings on the matter in Canada – the Sequenced Treatment Alternatives to Relieve Depression (STAR*D) Study. STAR*D was the largest psychiatric clinical trial ever conducted, providing sequential pharmacological or psychotherapeutic treatment to 2,876 patients with depression.[21] It found that, after a sequence of up to four treatments over the course of up to one year, two-thirds of participants had achieved full remission. On its face, that may seem like strong evidence that depression remains intolerable for some people (up to one-third) even after high-quality care. After all, this was the biggest and, by implication, "best" study available. Indeed, the results were repeatedly presented that way by those seeking to expand PAD to people with mental illness in Canada.

But that analysis and conclusion requires one to actively avoid a close, scientific examination of the precise strengths and limitations of the STAR*D trial and their implications for interpreting the results. STAR*D included a talk therapy treatment option under some circumstances, but only 6 per cent of all patients in the trial ultimately received cognitive behavioural therapy (CBT), the talk therapy offered, with 94 per cent receiving only medication(s).[22] So STAR*D is almost exclusively a medication trial. The most treatment that anyone in the trial could receive was a sequence of four randomly assigned medicines (with limited patient and physician choice) that were not tailored to their specific symptoms or needs, and more than 80 per cent of those enrolled in the trial only received one or two medicines.[23] Furthermore, nearly 40 per cent of the participants never saw a psychiatrist and were prescribed those medications by their family doctor, who followed an algorithm.[24] Crucially, interpreting the results also requires an understanding of the meaning of the term remission, the primary outcome of the trial.[25] Remission is the absence (or at least near absence) of symptoms, and therefore two-thirds of patients in STAR*D achieved remission by this fairly limited, stepped medication treatment strategy often without even seeing a specialist. The STAR*D interventions were always conceptualized as providing an average, community-based first layer of treatment for depression. They were never proposed as the only interventions to be contemplated before giving up and considering someone's depression to be irremediable. That is a gross misrepresentation of the study and any reasonable understanding of the current, modern state of treatment for patients with depression.

The STAR*D study participants who did not achieve remission included a mixture of responders (people whose symptoms were at least 50 per cent better with treatment), partial responders (people whose symptoms improved but by less than 50 per cent) and non-responders (people whose symptoms were unchanged or worse). So, the pool of *potential* candidates for enduring and intolerable suffering is difficult to estimate but certainly much, much smaller than one-third, and that was after relatively modest treatment efforts. Those seeing family doctors were not offered specialist follow-up. No patients received individually tailored medication treatment, almost none received CBT, and none received the myriad of other talk therapies that have strong evidence in mood disorders. Nor did any patients receive help with an exercise program, dietary counselling, or biological complementary and alternative medicine treatments such as omega-3 fatty acid supplementation. None received light therapy. None received ketamine, a medication that has shown promise for rapid relief of depressive symptoms in a large proportion of people who do not respond to other treatments.[26] And none received any of the growing arsenal of neuromodulation strategies that are available for depression.[27]

Understood in that context, STAR*D is a useful trial that showed that relatively non-specific medication treatments often delivered by generalists in non-hospital settings performed quite well as a first effort in ameliorating depression. And this is, in fact, the story of most psychiatric intervention trials. A single intervention or *narrow* set of interventions is applied and improves *symptoms* in some but not all patients. The key point is that we cannot infer from such results that applying a *broad* range of interventions will likewise fail to improve *suffering* and make it tolerable. This is an apples to oranges comparison that involves a substantial and rather obvious error in logic. Yet this data and similar data was used to present the concept of irremediability in mental illness to the Canadian government as a *fait accompli*. As in the other sections of this chapter, we again find a problematic inference used as a substitute for actual scientific evidence to inform critical legislative decisions that affect the future of Canadians. From an evidence-based medicine standpoint, this is the most important omission of all of the research gaps described in this chapter. It is unlikely that careful research will show that suffering without treatment is always tolerable. But showing that all suffering can be made tolerable is a legitimate possibility that deserved to be studied *before* legislative decisions were made.

There is overwhelming evidence that existing psychiatric treatment is unable to cure all mental illness or result in remission of most or all symptoms. It has been established that some of our patients remain symptomatic even with excellent treatment, a fact that is true in every area of medicine, for instance for diabetes, osteoarthritis, and severe asthma. Whether currently available comprehensive and individualized care is able to make all suffering in mental illness tolerable nevertheless remains a fundamental and unanswered scientific question. While we do not have the capacity to remove all suffering, there is at least a reasonable possibility that outstanding care can always make suffering *tolerable*. Any honest appraisal of the existing literature and its limitations must allow for that possibility. In other words, careful study might determine that the scenario of irremediable suffering in the context of mental illness identified in Canadian medical assistance in dying legislation *never exists*. That information would seem important to have had before making law and before striking a committee to determine how to apply this irreversible intervention in this population.

WHAT SHOULD HAVE HAPPENED

Researchers in this area should have contacted researchers conducting large studies such as STAR*D and asked to add ancillary studies using their validated measures of intolerable suffering, had they been developed (see "Arriving at a Definition"), to quantify the proportion of patients who were positive on that measure at baseline and after treatment in each larger study.

They should then have devised follow-up studies enrolling subjects from a single or multiple such trials whose suffering remained intolerable at endpoint, if they existed. These studies would offer that much-smaller group a more robust and comprehensive series of treatments to determine whether those interventions could make their suffering tolerable.

This approach could and should have also been undertaken naturalistically with interviews of patients entering treatment in specialty mental health care centres as well as during and after treatment. A subgroup of patients with continued intolerable suffering could again be enrolled in an enhanced care trial to quantify remediability.

Even if these trials and the very best mental health care efforts at ameliorating intolerable suffering were found not do so in every case, this work would still estimate the true prevalence of the phenomenon of intolerable suffering after proper mental health care. It should be expected that after a rigorous approach such as this, the number would, at a minimum, be quite low.

WHAT DID HAPPEN

Nothing. Experts and advocates relied on inference and a selective and unsuitable interpretation of prior studies, conflating the presence of residual symptoms with irremediability. At the time of writing, there is no indication that this mischaracterization of the evidence has been addressed or that advocates have identified an adequate research plan to obtain new data that more accurately examines the remediability of intolerable suffering in mental illness.

Quantifying the Reliability of Ascertaining Cases of Irremediability (If It Is Shown to Exist)

TRUE POSITIVES AND FALSE POSITIVES

For this section, let us assume that all of the above careful research had been undertaken and that, despite the best efforts of mental health providers, a small proportion of people with mental illness experience enduring and intolerable suffering that is truly irremediable (i.e., the hypothesis advanced as fact by advocates for PAD for mental illness in Canada). One might think that this would be sufficient scientific justification to proceed with this intervention; however, it is not.

Even if physicians have strong evidence for a condition that merits intervention and a proposed remedy, their obligation is first to understand whether they can correctly identify the population to whom that treatment ought to be offered. In medical research we call this group the "true positives" (people who are correctly identified as having the condition, in this case enduring and intolerable suffering in mental illness).[28] But in medicine we also have "false positives" (people incorrectly identified as having the condition).[29] Before applying treatments, we are obliged to quantify rates of true and false positives to understand whether our diagnostic constructs are safe and adequate.[30] We could have the best chemotherapy in the world, for example, but it would be a serious problem if we give it to many people who were suspected of having cancer but ended up having only benign tumours. A life-saving surgical amputation procedure would likewise seem less miraculous if most of the time it mistakenly removed a limb that would have returned to health. This is not a trivial issue in the context of evaluating the safety of Canada's medical assistance in dying laws for people with mental illness. False positives quite literally mean ending the life of a person who was going to later experience relief from their mental suffering. It is putting it charitably to say that medicine frowns on that. To use an analogy from another area of society, it would be akin to broad use of capital punishment without considering the possibility of incorrect convictions.

WHAT SHOULD HAVE HAPPENED

Returning to the controlled and naturalistic studies described in the section "Demonstrating Irremediability and (If Applicable)

Quantifying Its Prevalence" above, psychiatric assessors for medical assistance in dying should have been included to assess a large prospective cohort of patients and their charts to capture predictions about which patients' symptoms are likely to remain irremediable even after treatment or over time. The primary outcome could have been the true positive:false positive ratio of predictions of irremediability, for example, two years later. Advocates for the practice would hope that this "positive likelihood" ratio might be high (10:1 or greater), such that the overwhelming majority of those identified have the true condition and thus leading to confidence that the practice will be applied appropriately and not cause "unnecessary deaths" that might outweigh any potential benefits.

Note, however, that careful research as described above is likely to determine that the phenomenon of irremediability in mental illness, if it exists, is relatively rare. Let's say for the sake of argument, since this has never been investigated, that it is as common as one case in every five hundred patients with mental illness. To arrive at a 10:1 ratio, assessors would have to evaluate five thousand cases, correctly identify ten patients with true irremediable illness, and only misidentify one with remediable illness as irremediable.

Here it may be helpful to say more about two of the most important metrics in evaluating whether doctors proceed with medical interventions: the "number needed to treat" (NNT: how many patients must be treated before, on average, one patient receives the intended benefit) and the "number needed to harm" (NNH: how many patients must be treated before, on average, harm occurs to one patient).[31]

NNT = how many patients must be treated before, on average, one patient receives the intended benefit
NNH = how many patients must be treated before, on average, harm occurs to one patient

In the scenario above, our NNT is about 1 – an excellent value. That is, you confer the expected benefit in nearly every patient treated. The NNH would be eleven (i.e., an incorrect application of PAD once for every eleven patients). Even those values would probably lead to some debate over the ethics of the practice, but certainly they would lend support to the notion that benefits may outweigh harms. However, this seems a highly unlikely outcome. We should expect many false positives. And a positive likelihood ratio in the opposite direction – e.g., 1:2, 1:5, or 1:10 – would be of great concern. The 1:10 value, for example, would mean the opposite calculus of the above – harming nearly every patient treated and benefiting only one in eleven. Such a finding would, at a minimum, call into question the ethics of the practice and quite probably lead bioethicists to a consensus that it is not justifiable to offer this intervention under these conditions.

Such trials could also be used to measure false negative rates. Note also that if expediency was crucial, this research could have been done retrospectively with guesses made by assessors based on chart reviews alone and follow-up phone calls to participants. This would have been a weaker methodology but would at least have allowed for some estimation of the quality of predictions.

WHAT DID HAPPEN

Nothing. The concepts of true and false positives, false negatives, NNT, and NNH have not been investigated in this area and therefore were not included in the medical assistance in dying hearings in Canada.

Note that one option for making a determination of irremediability that is being considered in Canada is to have two physicians assess an applicant for PAD who has mental illness and require that they agree that the person's condition is irremediable. However, this is a poor safeguard. It is well known in science that improved precision (agreement between multiple tests) is not evidence of good accuracy. Without the above information, we should expect clinicians to frequently agree incorrectly, since they would be relying on their opinion, rather than empirical evidence, and thus be at risk of group think. The history of medicine is riddled with examples of physicians agreeing on an intervention that we would now consider untenable, with changes in care only spurred by scientific discovery.

QUANTIFYING OTHER POTENTIAL HARMS

As described above, there are numerous potential ancillary harms related to PAD for mental illness that deserved careful scientific study prior to legalization. This section will focus on four important ones – the effects on suicide and its prevention, societal attitudes toward disability, psychiatric care, and investments into mental health care.

Suicide Contagion and Societal Attitudes Toward Suicide

The deliberations in Canada about PAD for mental illness included substantial debate about the degree to which this practice may be the same as suicide.[32] That discussion almost exclusively focused on whether psychiatrists are able to distinguish an irrational desire to be dead from one that may be rational – yet another area that has not been rigorously studied and therefore relied on expert opinion and conjecture.

Human decision-making is a complex process and is rarely entirely rational or irrational. Rather than treating a suicidal wish as a binary, present or absent phenomenon, it is probably more helpful to consider the degree of overlap between a specific person's wish for PAD and the phenomenon of suicide.[33] The original iteration of the Canadian medical assistance in dying legislation restricted its use to those with a foreseeable death and, in effect, positioned it as a treatment to remedy a painful death.[34] Although some people at the end of life may be suicidal, in the standard meaning of that term, that circumstance has limited overlap with suicide. Most people who die by suicide are not facing an imminent painful death, and most people facing a painful death would not wish to be dead if that outcome could be averted.

The more recent iteration of the legislation alters those conditions to allow PAD as a remedy for a painful life.[35] That circumstance has a much higher potential for overlap with suicide, particularly in the case of people with mental illness. This is because suicide almost always arises in people with mental illness who develop suicidal thoughts and view acting on them as a remedy for a painful life. Anecdotally, many clearly suicidal patients have already stated that they are "waiting for March" (when PAD for mental illness was scheduled to start), in order to request medical assistance in dying.

For the moment, let us make the potentially dubious assumption that mental health experts are able, with a high degree of precision, to distinguish people with mental illness whose thinking has substantial overlap with suicide from those whose wish to be dead is rational. If this is true, then it may mitigate some of the potential for harm in the clinical application of PAD in people with mental illness. However, it tells us nothing about the effects on the lay public who certainly will not have the same understanding of such finely nuanced distinctions as experts in the area.

Social learning has emerged as a crucially important issue in suicide prevention. There is now ample evidence that public dissemination of stories of identifiable people taking their lives is frequently associated with large increases in suicides in subsequent months.[36] This is likely because some vulnerable people exposed to that content identify with the person who died and emulate their behaviour.[37] This phenomenon can occur in response to news media reports about suicide deaths, suicide attempts, the topic of suicide in general, social media, or online exposures to suicide-related content or exposures in one's life to suicide or suicidality in family, friends, and acquaintances. As a result, numerous international and national recommendations caution against public messaging depicting suicide as a useful or desirable means of responding to painful lives (and indeed, they suggest modelling mastery and healthy coping given emerging evidence that this may lower suicide rates).[38]

Whether exposures to stories of death in those with mental illness via medical assistance in dying may confer a similar risk is unknown. The only study to examine the impact of stories about PAD on actual suicide rates was conducted in Toronto and found a possible association with more subsequent suicides following newspaper stories about these deaths, estimating a 13 per cent increase in suicides, with the true change anywhere from a 1 per cent reduction to a 28 per cent increase in suicides being correct nineteen times out of twenty.[39] Note that these newspaper stories were focused on the prior iteration of the legislation with an emphasis on people with physical illness at the end of life. Whether stories of people accessing PAD for mental illness might be likely to lead to increased identification with the deceased among people at risk of suicide and more subsequent suicide deaths is an open question.

Regardless, it is plainly true that the Canadian government's endorsement of death as a means of responding to suffering in mental illness is diametrically opposed to the evidence-based messages that the suicide prevention community are trying to promulgate. And this leads to the second, related, potential harm – the impact on societal views about the acceptability and rationality of suicide. The above discussion focused on the risks that we may observe *short-term* imitative acts of suicide or contagion events following exposure to media highlighting death as a means of coping with mental illness. However, there is also a question of whether shifting attitudes as this practice becomes normalized may result in more suicides in the long term. This legislative change is likely to alter the way that people think about suicide and that could certainly affect suicide rates.

WHAT SHOULD HAVE HAPPENED

Suicide rates from countries that have legalized this practice, such as the Netherlands and Belgium, should have been subjected to rigorous statistical methodologies accounting for changes in factors associated with suicide rates such as age and sex distributions, marital rates, cost of living (e.g., consumer price indices), unemployment rates, social safety net programs, access to mental health care, lethal means restriction efforts, and suicide prevention campaigns. These techniques should have been used to estimate the independent contribution of legalization of the practice on suicide rates and whether it resulted in no change, increases, or decreases.

To evaluate acute contagion effects, systematic searches ought to have been conducted for media reporting on PAD in mental illness, particularly those that were of a higher profile and may have led to more substantial exposure across a population. These reports should have been coded for content and that data should have been subject to standard statistical tests, such as time-series and regression analyses, to determine whether all or certain kinds of such reports were associated with increased subsequent suicide rates.

To evaluate the long-term impact on attitudes, ideally mixed-method approaches involving surveys would have been conducted before and after legalization to identify whether the legislation resulted in more people considering suicide to be a rational option for coping with mental illness. Those surveys should have included questions to test one of the key hypotheses put forth by medical assistance in dying advocates – that the public will see this practice as fundamentally different from suicide. Since no such research occurred before the legislative change, a true before-and-after study is likely impossible. However, it would still have been of use to conduct these surveys and focus groups asking people about how they think that their perceptions of suicide have changed since the legislation was enacted. Controls could be added – the same research methods could be applied to people from neighbouring countries where the practice remains illegal and the two groups compared.

WHAT DID HAPPEN

Advocates for PAD for mental illness attempted to assuage any concerns that legalizing the practice might inadvertently lead to more suicides by presenting data that suicide rates have been stable or have declined in Benelux countries that have already legalized the practice.[40]

Even if we accept this as true, which it is not for every country and epoch, it is still a finding of dubious scientific significance.

To see why, consider the following example: rates of youth cigarette smoking increased substantially (27.5 per cent to 36.4 per cent) in the United States from 1991 to 1997, yet despite that increase, rates of lung cancer have diminished in the intervening decades.[41] One can find any number of examples of surprising associations like this one in public health. But it would be a mistake to conclude based on this data that smoking does not cause (or may actually lower rates of) lung cancer. That is obviously false. In scientific language, it mistakes correlation for causation. Instead, the issue is that rates of lung cancer are affected by many factors, all of which need to be accounted for to make such calculations remotely valid.

If that were done for smoking, we would almost certainly discover that the increase in the behaviour contributed to higher current rates of lung cancer than would have been observed had it not happened (i.e., there would be even fewer cases of lung cancer than we have now had youth not increased their smoking habits in the 1990s). Given this issue, presenting suicide data from Benelux countries with no correction for trends arising from other factors is scientifically flawed. That fact was not highlighted by (and possibly unknown to) those presenting that data as evidence.

No studies of media reporting about PAD in mental illness or potential changes to societal attitudes on suicide were undertaken or presented.

The Societal Value of People Living with Disabilities

In January 2021, the United Nations Office of the Commissioner for Human Rights released a statement opposing the use of PAD as a remedy for people with disabilities (both physical and mental).[42] In part, it read, "Under no circumstance should the law provide that it could be a well-reasoned decision for a person with a disabling condition who is not dying to terminate their life with the support of the State...even when access to medical assistance in dying is restricted to those at the end of life or with a terminal illness, people with disabilities, older persons, and especially older persons with disabilities, may feel subtly pressured to end their lives prematurely due to attitudinal barriers as well as the lack of appropriate services and support."

One of the provisions of the Canadian medical assistance in dying legislation is that the intervention arises following "a voluntary request that is not the result of external pressure."[43] Evidently the goal of this criterion was to prevent a circumstance where, for example, a family member coerces a patient to petition to receive physician assisted death. However, that does not constitute the only potential form of external pressure.

Let us imagine a circumstance where we shift societal attitudes about the appropriateness of death as a remedy for a painful life (see the section "Suicide Contagion and Societal Attitudes Toward Suicide") in the context of inadequate access to high-quality mental health care (see the section "Investment in Mental Health Care"). If, in parallel, we change public perceptions of the value of lives lived with disabilities and whether they are even worth living, then that confluence of factors is likely to fundamentally alter attitudes of some people with disabilities in general and mental illness in particular. Specifically, it may create a form of societal peer pressure that could influence some to seek out death as a remedy when they would not otherwise consider that a viable or desirable option. Many of these people who have illnesses that require substantial care from their loved ones may even believe they have a "duty to die" to alleviate the burden of their life and disability on others.[44]

Stated slightly differently, advocates for expansion in medical assistance in dying legislation in Canada argued that it was important to allow Canadians to make their own choices about their lives with the implicit premise that those decisions would be free and unbiased. However, it is likely that the existence of the legislation itself and the government's tacit endorsement of death as a remedy for disability will influence both how people view their lives and their decision-making. That concern deserved scientific scrutiny.

WHAT SHOULD HAVE HAPPENED

As in the case of societal attitudes toward suicide, mixed-method research with surveys and focus groups ought to have been conducted in countries and regions where PAD for mental illness has been legalized, along with control regions where it has not (ideally before and after legalization). The aim of this research would be to characterize how the legislation may have impacted attitudes about disability and whether disabled lives are worth living.

If it was found that this legislation creates more negative attitudes toward people with disabilities, additional studies could also investigate societal changes in metrics of support for them, for example, funding and charitable donations to public and private institutions with mandates to assist those with disabilities. Evidence of harm in either case would then need to be considered as a key negative externality and factored into calculations related to the bioethics of this legislative change.

WHAT DID HAPPEN

Nothing. Whether these potential harms exist in reality and, if so, at what magnitude has been left uninvestigated.

Attitudes toward Psychiatric Care and Changes to the Physician-Patient Relationship

As has been described in detail, people who may be experiencing truly irremediable suffering due to mental illness even after receiving high-quality mental health care are likely, at most, to represent a small fraction of all of those people with mental illness who present for care with an initial report that their mental suffering is intolerable. That is because most of those people likely have symptoms that can be made tolerable provided they receive truly adequate treatment. So what happens when some mental health advocates take the position that "sometimes it really is hopeless and you can't feel better," which then receives the endorsement of the federal government?

It introduces the worry that this will contribute to changing attitudes about psychiatric care and specifically nihilism on the part of patients, physicians, or both. The results could include more people who believe that psychiatric care is ineffective or futile, fewer people seeking out psychiatric care, and fewer people persisting with psychiatric treatment. This is an additional mechanism that could even theoretically contribute to more suicides. Psychiatric care also routinely involves care for people whose illnesses lead them to experience cognitive distortions ("thinking errors")[45] that in turn make them believe that a situation is hopeless when in fact it is not.[46] The mental health care provider's job is to use the various treatments at their disposal to help patients perceive their situation in a more balanced and realistic manner. Medical assistance in dying advocates acknowledged this reality of psychiatric care with an emphasis on the idea that patients with this kind of suicidal ideation would be deemed ineligible for PAD if they applied.[47]

But that narrow argument neglects the fact that such patients will continue to represent a substantial proportion of all patients in psychiatric care. Until now, the usual public messaging about psychiatric care is that there is always hope and that, even if symptoms may not fully abate, treatment can always help to make mental illnesses tolerable. We can choose to ignore the extraordinary dearth of scientific evidence about whether mental illnesses are ever irremediable. But, regardless, the notions that, for some people, treatment is a lost cause may result in substantial harm to the mental health care field and to patients in general. Returning to the concept of "false positives," there ought to be concern that such a message will lead more patients and physicians to incorrectly judge treatment to be hopeless. That may interfere with the mental health care models in general as well as with some provider-patient relationships, and it could also lead to circular reasoning resulting in more people accessing PAD whose suffering could have been remediated with further treatment.

WHAT SHOULD HAVE HAPPENED

Again, mixed-method approaches, as described above, surveying and interviewing people in different countries and regions should have been conducted to characterize the impact of legalizing physician-assisted death for mental illness. The emphasis of these studies should have been on public, physician, and patient attitudes towards mental health care, its utility or lack thereof, and if and when it is appropriate to render treatment futile and to discontinue it. Once again, ideally, these studies would have tested how attitudes have evolved over time in areas where the practice has been made legal and in ones where it has not.

As above, if harms are detected these would need to be factored into ethical calculations.

WHAT DID HAPPEN

Nothing. Whether these potential harms exist in reality and, if so, at what magnitude has been left uninvestigated.

Investment in Mental Health Care

The decision to legalize PAD for mental illness has some fundamental economic consequences. They arise because provision of high-quality mental health care to complex patients is often very expensive.[48] In contrast, ending their lives is comparatively inexpensive for the health care system.[49] This situation, at least theoretically, sets up two key, interrelated perverse incentives. The first is that health care systems are incentivized to favour PAD regardless of whether it is good for patients. This is because investment in the practice drives down both the demand for and cost of mental health care for a whole population by removing some of its most expensive users. Viewed strictly through an economic lens, that might seem like a benefit. This brings us to the second potential perverse incentive: by continuing to underfund mental health care and maintain substandard systems of care despite overwhelming evidence of increased need in a growing population, more patients are likely to be deemed "irremediable" for practical reasons (i.e., because they cannot access the care required to remediate their symptoms) and therefore more people are likely to die unnecessarily through this mechanism. That is the option that results in the greatest cost saving, which we know that markets are most likely to gravitate towards, although, self-evidently, it would not be the circumstance that leads to the best care for patients. This concern is also impacted by current inequalities in the system, especially for certain high-need populations.

WHAT SHOULD HAVE HAPPENED

Mixed-method studies should again have been undertaken to characterize this phenomenon in countries where PAD has been legalized for mental illness. Patterns of health care expenditures and other objective markers of a more robust system of care such as waiting times and access to more scarce treatments such as talk therapy and neurostimulation should have been compared before and after the legislative change. Qualitative interviews ought to have been conducted with patients, physicians, and members of the general public to understand whether their experience suggests an improvement, a deterioration, or no change in the provision of mental health care.

WHAT DID HAPPEN

Nothing. The consequences of legalization of PAD for mental illness on mental health care systems have never been rigorously investigated.

OTHER ARGUMENTS PRESENTED TO THE GOVERNMENT THAT DEVIATED FROM USUAL MEDICAL STANDARDS

The Issue of "Choice"

It is important to note that one of the key arguments from advocates supporting PAD for mental illness in Canada was that autonomy and patient choice are, for all practical purposes, unassailable rights that are immune to challenges.[50] While autonomy and patient choice are indeed crucial aspects of patient care, this argument involves a rather fundamental misunderstanding of the principles of medical care.

It is true that medicine is a service industry. But it is important to understand that medicine is a special kind of service and that there are key constraints on choice that exist in medical settings compared to other service industries where client preference is often sacrosanct. If someone walks into a convenience store and sees a banana or a carton of cigarettes, they can choose to buy one, the other, or both, and it would be wrong for the proprietor to refuse sale of either item to anyone for whom it is legal. However, once physicians and other health care providers are introduced into the calculation, they are bound by ethical frameworks and principles.

The freedom to choose any intervention at all is not actually part of the framework of medical ethics. It might be quite appropriate for a physician to prescribe a banana to a patient who has a potassium deficiency. However, it would be unethical for a physician to prescribe a cigarette. This discrepancy and fundamental difference from a convenience store clerk arises because physicians are obliged to offer only treatments where the *benefits outweigh the risks*. All physicians take the Hippocratic oath that specifies the fundamental principle that we must first do no harm (*primum non nocere*). So positioning this as a question of "choice" is really a misunderstanding. It is a physician's responsibility to offer all effective treatments to patients *after* it has been established that their benefits outweigh the risks. As described throughout this chapter, that scientific groundwork has not been undertaken. As a result, it is really inappropriate for physicians to consider this intervention, whether it has been made legal or not.

Typically, a novel medical intervention in this country would be subject to the stringent requirements of Health Canada approval (similar to the Food and Drug Administration in the United States).[51] Pharmaceutical companies and other manufacturers of health technologies spend years and many millions or even billions of dollars carefully characterizing risks and benefits of their proposed treatments. And doctors cannot simply prescribe these experimental treatments outside of highly regulated research trials until they have received Health Canada approval. Patient "choice" begins to enter the conversation after safety and effectiveness have been established. In this way, the public can be confident that they are only receiving treatments from their physicians that have a proven scientific track record. This is why doctors did not dispense, or encourage patients to take, potentially dangerous treatments such as ivermectin (or drinking bleach) during the COVID-19 pandemic when there was no data supporting their safety or efficacy.[52] This was not a matter of patient choice but of basic medical ethics.

PAD for mental illness is a novel intervention that represents a quantum shift in health care, but it does not involve a new pharmaceutical agent or device. As such, its advocates exploited a loophole in which Health Canada oversight was not mandated and therefore there was no requirement for research to be conducted on its potential negative consequences. This despite the fact that potential harms that could arise from misapplication of PAD are analogous to the most severe adverse outcomes in pharmaceutical clinical trials (i.e., inappropriate death). Returning to the COVID-19 pandemic, at its height in October 2020, when more than one million deaths had already occurred worldwide, Johnson & Johnson paused their crucial vaccine trial of sixty thousand subjects for eleven days because of "a serious medical event experienced by *one study participant.*"[53] People desperate to be vaccinated were not given a choice, and in fact when we first began writing this chapter in the spring of 2021, Health Canada was still considering whether to recommend use of this vaccine due to emerging safety concerns (it was later approved in November 2021).[54] They had to wait for this thoughtful and careful research process to be completed before their choice became a medical option. The push for expansion of medical assistance in dying legislation in Canada was unique in bypassing those considerations entirely. It was akin to having the government endorse a new antidepressant on philosophical grounds without any rigorous process quantifying its risks and benefits.

The Issue of "Discrimination"

The misunderstanding of "choice" in health care presented to the Canadian government was compounded by further confusion about the related issue of "discrimination." To be clear, it is never appropriate for physicians or the health care system to discriminate against anyone. The issue is that scientific processes to weigh risks and benefits were bypassed. As above, physicians are obliged to offer treatments to patients when the benefits outweigh the risks and are ethically permitted to withhold treatments where the risks outweigh the benefits. The words in medicine for these situations are when a treatment is "indicated" or "contraindicated."

The MedlinePlus Medical Encyclopedia defines a contraindication as "a specific situation in which a drug, procedure, or surgery should not be used because it may be harmful to the person."[55] Those advocating for PAD in mental illness in Canada conflated the idea of contraindication (a standard aspect of medical care) with the notion of discrimination (something that is ethically forbidden in medical care). This helped them to inaccurately portray those experts calling for more and better science as somehow prejudiced against people with mental illness, which, to be fair, is a clever rhetorical move. It just isn't in keeping with how medical science works.

Let us take a simple example to understand the distinction between discrimination and contraindication more clearly. What if two patients – one man and one woman – have bipolar disorder and are seeking treatment with valproic acid, an antiepileptic mood stabilizer. This treatment is indicated for acute and long-term management of bipolar disorder and is effective in both men and women. In this vignette, it would be discriminatory and highly unethical to offer valproic acid to only one patient, the man for example, and deny it to the woman. But what if we change the conditions of the scenario slightly (as in the trolley problem described at the beginning of the chapter)? What if the woman has just become or is trying to become pregnant? In this case, valproic acid is contraindicated due to a high risk of serious birth defects in infants born to mothers who have taken it. In this scenario we give the medication to the man and refuse it to the woman according to typical medical standards, not because we are discriminating, but because of our ethical duty to do no harm. This kind of scenario is exceedingly common across medicine because many treatments are contraindicated in specific populations when evidence shows that harms outweigh benefits.

So it was never appropriate to frame the debate before the Canadian government as one about discrimination. The key question was this: Is there evidence to suggest that the risks of PAD in mental illness outweigh the benefits? In other words, should it be "contraindicated"? The answer to this question is quite clear – *we don't know*. The reason we don't know is because of all of the missing research described in this chapter. Here, again, we see how two devastating logical errors allowed the debate to bypass medical norms. The first, as discussed at length, was that evidence does not matter. But when you are missing all of the requisite evidence, you can no longer have an informed or intelligent discussion about whether a treatment may be indicated or contraindicated. This leads into the second error, which is to exit from science entirely and fall back on an ethical mandate to avoid discrimination. In the absence of evidence and with no clear plans to generate it, we can certainly take the stance that people with mental illness should not be discriminated against – that is correct. But this tells us nothing about whether it is safe to provide this intervention to that population and whether it ought to be indicated.

Parenthetically, it is worth noting that PAD advocates were strategic in their use of nomenclature that emphasized seemingly unimpeachable ideas such as "choice," opposition to "discrimination," and even the sanitized term MAiD. These words maximized the political strength of their arguments, but they are highly medically imprecise and were exceedingly effective at shifting the conversation away from science. Even the term MAiD itself literally describes assistance "in" death, a wording that was coherent when it was used in the context of end-of-life care. Yet it loses any precise meaning when applied to people not at the end of life. In that situation physicians are not assisting "in" death but rather inducing a death that is not occurring. While precision may not be of paramount importance in politics and rhetoric, in science it matters. And the lack of care in precise terminology is simply further evidence of the comprehensive failure of those advancing this intervention to adhere to the standard scientific approach expected in medical care.

THE IMPERATIVE TO AVOID "PREMATURE" DEATH

Suicide is legal in Canada and, despite the best efforts of suicide prevention experts, information about how to end one's life and the means to die by suicide are both readily available to able-bodied people in this country. The major rationale of the Supreme Court in legalizing medical assistance in dying in Canada in the first place was that without this option some people facing incapacitation would choose to end their lives "prematurely" while they were still physically capable.[56] That circumstance was considered a violation of Canadians' rights to have "life, liberty and security."[57]

Yet the physical capacity to end one's life differs between people with serious physical and mental illnesses. Some people with serious physical illnesses lack the corporeal capability to take steps to end their lives. Leaving aside whether death is an ethically justifiable intervention for people with chronic, non-life-threatening physical illnesses, it is a practical fact that many people with these conditions could not end their lives without assistance from someone else.

This is simply not the case for people who suffer solely from mental illnesses. That important distinction did not appear to be a factor in the Canadian government's decision-making regarding this legislation. Yet it is important to point out that the Supreme Court's calculus is reversed. We should expect that some, perhaps even many, Canadians with mental illnesses (it is impossible to estimate how many without adequate data) will abandon care that would remediate their suffering in favour of accessing PAD. Thus, a key feature of the new version of the medical assistance in dying legislation in Canada is, quite ironically, to help people with mental illness die prematurely. That situation already occurs with alarming frequency in the context of suicide in Canada. The proposed expansion of the law would permit premature death in people with mental illnesses to be induced by physicians without any acknowledgment of the practical differences between this situation and that faced by those with physical illnesses (i.e., that suicide is already widely available to people with mental illness) and none of the scientific groundwork required to quantify harms that may arise.

"SCIENCE TAKES TOO MUCH TIME"

It should be acknowledged that scientific experts were given an opportunity before the Canadian government to briefly summarize many of the concerns outlined in this chapter. In response, advocates for PAD noted that the research described would take years and took umbrage at the notion that Canada might even consider delaying access to this intervention while waiting to have the science.[58]

This argument was evidently accepted by the government, yet it really is an outrage. Imagine this scenario with any other medical intervention. If a pharmaceutical company had been hoping to release a new medication onto the market for a decade and failed to use that time to conduct the basic, standard research necessary to receive regulatory approval, would any government entity possibly take seriously the argument "but that would take years!" as reasonable grounds to bypass that process? No. To the contrary, policy-makers would likely be openly outraged that a company would fail to perform usual due diligence and then have the temerity to demand approval anyway since addressing that problem would involve substantial work.

The idea that science takes a long time is an exceedingly weak argument for bypassing it, made especially so because there were many years in which the research described above could have and should have been conducted. It may have been unreasonable to expect anyone to conduct every single study described in this chapter, but we should have expected those advancing this intervention to do something, and there are mechanisms within Canadian funding agencies to spur on such efforts. These mechanisms, however, were not used.

CONCLUSION

This chapter aimed to outline a valid scientific approach, adhering to usual practices in health care, to evaluate whether PAD should ever be offered to people with mental illness. As described, no such process was followed. While the dearth of scientific evidence in this area is unprecedented, particularly in view of the consequences of a false positive approval of a request for PAD, there are other examples in the history of medicine in which treatments were rushed out before all of the potential harms were properly characterized and understood, to disastrous effect. The opioid epidemic stands as a cautionary example.[59] In that case, doctors were seduced by partial evidence about the powerful pain-relieving effects of opioids and prescribed these treatments widely when ultimately their risks proved dramatically greater than their benefits. Had the medical community insisted on more careful research and data up front, it is likely that many thousands of deaths could have been averted in recent decades.

Providing PAD to people who experience what they perceive to be intolerable suffering may, in theory, seem like a humane practice that respects patient autonomy, but describing any medical intervention as "indicated" without evidence is simply inappropriate, dangerous, and wrong. If and when PAD becomes legally accessible for Canadians with sole underlying mental illness, we must assume that many individuals whose conditions could be remediated with outstanding mental health care will be deemed to have an irremediable illness as a result of an assessment error and flaws in our system of mental health care provision. They will die unnecessarily and prematurely as a result. The only uncertainty is how many will die inappropriately as well as why the field has not laid the scientific groundwork to inform adequately policy decisions.

As also described in other chapters, many people with scientific degrees and leadership positions argued for expansion of PAD for mental illness in government hearings, but they did so taking a non-scientific and even an anti-scientific stance. In those hearings, different hypotheses were presented about how this intervention might impact Canadians. Happily, we have a mechanism for resolving competing hypotheses in science: data and rigorous scientific study. Yet the government was largely presented with deontological arguments with the assumption not only that they may supersede consequential and utilitarian considerations but indeed that the latter are of no importance at all. That was an extraordinary position made all the more stunning by the fact that its audacity went almost entirely unchallenged and seemingly unnoticed by the Canadian government during their deliberations.

The lack of robust research literature in this area means that many questions have quite literally been left unanswered. But perhaps the most important question is why the Canadian government accepted the arguments of people presenting themselves as scientific experts who did not actually undertake scientific investigations and were openly hostile to the notion that evidence matters. These red flags were ignored. It is hard to imagine a government (or any entity) relying on the expertise of historians who choose not to consult the historical record, lawyers who avoid case law, or architects and engineers who oppose pre-construction land surveys. Yet here, with lives hanging in the balance, a decision was reached on the basis of counsel from experts who shunned and even rebuffed the very concept of science.

Earnest people are entitled to differing beliefs about medical ethics and how best to shape the practice of medicine. The problem in this situation is not that experts advocating for PAD for mental illness had bad intentions or were not trying to help Canadians. The problem is that, by failing to take any of the typical steps required in preparation for advancing a new medical intervention, or even to demand that these steps be taken, it is clear that they were terribly flawed in their approach. By accepting their arguments, the Government of Canada was complicit, leading to a catastrophic failure of understanding and duty that leaves all Canadians, and particularly those with mental illness, in a scientific wilderness where doctors may soon be offering them death as a remedy for their suffering without any adequate scientific justification. And that's not fair. We owe them better.

NOTES

1 Association des médecins psychiatres du Québec, *Access to Medical Assistance in Dying for People with Mental Disorders: Discussion Paper*, November 2020, 14, https://ampq.org/wp-content/uploads/2020/12/mpqdocreflexionammenfinal.pdf.
2 *Meeting of the Standing Senate Committee on Legal and Constitutional Affairs*, 43rd Parliament, 2nd Session (3 February 2021), https://sencanada.ca/en/Content/Sen/Committee/432/LCJC/55130-e.
3 Erin Anderssen, "Medical Experts Call on Government to Delay Expansion of MAID for Mental Illness," *Globe and Mail*, 1 December 2022, https://www.theglobeandmail.com/canada/article-maid-delay-mental-illness-medical-experts/.
4 Judith Jarvis Thomson, "The Trolley Problem," *Yale Law Journal* 94, no. 6 (1985): 1395–415.
5 Peter Vallentyne, "The Teleological/Deontological Distinction," *Journal of Value Inquiry* 21, no. 1 (1987): 21–32.
6 A.K. Akobeng, "Understanding Randomised Controlled Trials," *Archives of Disease in Childhood* 90, no. 8 (July 2005): 840–4; A.K. Akobeng, "Principles of Evidence Based Medicine," *Archives of Disease in Childhood* 90, no. 8 (August 2005): 837–40.
7 Chittaranjan Andrade, "The Numbers Needed to Treat and Harm (NNT, NNH) Statistics: What They Tell Us and What They Do Not," *Journal of Clinical Psychiatry* 76, no. 3 (March 2015): e330–3.
8 Nancy S. Jecker, Aaron G. Wightman, and Douglas S. Diekema, "Vaccine Ethics: An Ethical Framework for Global Distribution of COVID-19 Vaccines," *Journal of Medical Ethics* 47 (February 2021): 308–17; Govind Persad, Alan Wertheimer, and Ezekiel J. Emanuel, "Principles for Allocation of Scarce Medical Interventions," *Lancet* 373, no. 9661 (January 2009): 423–31.

9 Mark Sculpher, Karl Claxton, Steven D. Pearson, "Developing a Value Framework: The Need to Reflect the Opportunity Costs of Funding Decisions," *Value in Health* 20, no. 2 (February 2017): 234–9.
10 Manne Sjöstrand et al., "Ethical Deliberations about Involuntary Treatment: Interviews with Swedish Psychiatrists," BMC *Medical Ethics*, 16 (May 2015): 37.
11 *Meeting of the Standing Senate Committee*, 3 February 2021.
12 Stephen Thornton, "Karl Popper," *Stanford Encyclopedia of Philosophy*, ed. Edward N. Zalta and Uri Nodelman, Winter 2022 ed., https://plato.stanford.edu/archives/win2022/entries/popper/.
13 "Canada's Medical Assistance in Dying (MAID) Law," Government of Canada, 2021, https://www.justice.gc.ca/eng/cj-jp/ad-am/bk-di.html.
14 Kees D.M. Ruijs et al., "Unbearability of Suffering at the End of Life: The Development of a New Measuring Device, the SOS-V," BMC *Palliative Care* 8 (November 2009): 16; Justine Dembo, "We Need to Understand that Psychological Suffering Can Be Unbearable, Too," *Policy Options*, 26 February 2020, https://policyoptions.irpp.org/fr/magazines/february-2020/we-need-to-understand-that-psychological-suffering-can-be-unbearable-too/; Amelia Nuhn et al., "Experiences and Perspectives of People who Pursued Medical Assistance in Dying: Qualitative Study in Vancouver, BC," *Canadian Family Physician* 64, no. 9 (September 2018): e380–6.
15 Paul Kioko and Pablo Requena, "Towards a Definition of Unbearable Suffering and the Incongruence of Psychiatric Euthanasia," *British Journal of Psychiatry* 212, no. 4 (April 2018): 247–8.
16 Marlen Niederberger and Julia Spranger, "Delphi Technique in Health Sciences: A Map," *Frontiers in Public Health* 8 (2020): 457.
17 "Expert Panel on MAID and Mental Illness," Government of Canada, 2021, https://www.canada.ca/en/health-canada/corporate/about-health-canada/public-engagement/external-advisory-bodies/expert-panel-maid-mental-illness.html.
18 Health Canada, *Final Report of the Expert Panel on MAID and Mental Illness*, May 2022, https://www.canada.ca/en/health-canada/corporate/about-health-canada/public-engagement/external-advisory-bodies/expert-panel-maid-mental-illness/final-report-expert-panel-maid-mental-illness.html.
19 *Meeting of the Standing Senate Committee*, 3 February 2021.
20 Chinyereugo M. Umemneku Chikere et al., "Diagnostic Test Evaluation Methodology: A Systematic Review of Methods Employed to Evaluate Diagnostic Tests in the Absence of Gold Standard – An Update," *PLOS One* 14, no. 10 (October 2019): e0223832.

21 Bradley N. Gaynes et al., "What Did STAR*D Teach Us? Results from a Large-Scale, Practical, Clinical Trial for Patients with Depression," *Psychiatric Services* 60, no. 11 (November 2009): 1439–45; Mark Sinyor, Ayal Schaffer, and Anthony Levitt, "The Sequenced Treatment Alternatives to Relieve Depression (STAR*D) Trial: A Review," *Canadian Journal of Psychiatry* 55, no. 3 (March 2010): 126–35.
22 Gaynes et al., "What Did STAR*D Teach Us?"; Sinyor, Schaffer, and Levitt, "The Sequenced Treatment Alternatives."
23 Gaynes et al., "What Did STAR*D Teach Us?"; Sinyor, Schaffer, and Levitt, "The Sequenced Treatment Alternatives."
24 Bradley N. Gaynes et al., "A Direct Comparison of Presenting Characteristics of Depressed Outpatients from Primary vs. Specialty Care Settings: Preliminary Findings from the STAR*D Clinical Trial," *General Hospital Psychiatry* 27, no. 2 (March–April 2005): 87–96.
25 Gaynes et al., "What Did STAR*D Teach Us?"; Sinyor, Schaffer, and Levitt, "The Sequenced Treatment Alternatives."
26 Luke A. Jelen and James M. Stone, "Ketamine for Depression," *International Review of Psychiatry* 33, no. 3 (May 2021): 207–28.
27 Hao Li et al., "Comparative Efficacy and Acceptability of Neuromodulation Procedures in the Treatment of Treatment-Resistant Depression: A Network Meta-Analysis of Randomized Controlled Trials," *Journal of Affective Disorders* 287 (May 2021): 115–24.
28 Don van Ravenzwaaij and John P. A. Ioannidis, "True and False Positive Rates for Different Criteria of Evaluating Statistical Evidence from Clinical Trials," BMC *Medical Research Methodology* 19, no. 1 (2019): 218.
29 Ravenzwaaij and Ioannidis, "True and False Positive Rates."
30 Li et al., "Comparative Efficacy and Acceptability of Neuromodulation Procedures."
31 "Number Needed to Treat (NNT)," Centre for Evidence-Based Medicine, University of Oxford, 2022, https://www.cebm.ox.ac.uk/resources/ebm-tools/number-needed-to-treat-nnt.
32 *Truchon c. Procureur général du Canada*, 2019 QCCS 3792.
33 Scott Y. H. Kim, Yeates Conwell, and Eric D. Caine, "Suicide and Physician-Assisted Death for Persons with Psychiatric Disorders: How Much Overlap?," JAMA *Psychiatry* 75, no. 11 (November 2018): 1099–100.
34 *Bill C-14, An Act to Amend the Criminal Code and to Make Related Amendments to Other Acts (medical assistance in dying)*, 42nd Parliament, 1st Session (17 June 2016), https://www.parl.ca/DocumentViewer/en/42-1/bill/C-14/royal-assent.

35 Mark Sinyor and Ayal Schaffer, "The Lack of Adequate Scientific Evidence Regarding Physician-Assisted Death for People with Psychiatric Disorders Is a Danger to Patients," *Canadian Journal of Psychiatry* 65, no. 9 (September 2020): 607–9.

36 Thomas Niederkrotenthaler et al., "Association Between Suicide Reporting in the Media and Suicide: Systematic Review and Meta-Analysis," *BMJ* 368 (March 2020): m575; Thomas Niederkrotenthaler et al., "Systematic Review and Meta-Analyses of Suicidal Outcomes following Fictional Portrayals of Suicide and Suicide Attempt in Entertainment Media," *EClinicalMedicine* 36 (June 2021): 100922; Thomas Niederkrotenthaler et al., "Role of Media Reports in Completed and Prevented Suicide: Werther v. Papageno Effects," *British Journal of Psychiatry* 197, no. 3 (2010): 234–43.

37 Benedikt Till et al., "Personal Suicidality in Reception and Identification with Suicidal Film Characters," *Death Studies* 37, no. 4 (April 2013): 383–92.

38 Mark Sinyor et al., "Media Guidelines for Reporting on Suicide: 2017 Update of the Canadian Psychiatric Association Policy Paper," *Canadian Journal of Psychiatry* 63, no. 3 (March 2018): 182–96; Samaritans, *Media Guidelines for Reporting Suicide*, April 2020, https://media.samaritans.org/documents/Media_Guidelines_FINAL.pdf.

39 Mark Sinyor et al., "The Association between Suicide Deaths and Putatively Harmful and Protective Factors in Media Reports," *CMAJ* 190, no. 30, (July 2018): E900–7.

40 Justine Dembo, Udo Schuklenk, and Jonathan Reggler, "'For Their Own Good': A Response to Popular Arguments Against Permitting Medical Assistance in Dying (MAID) Where Mental Illness Is the Sole Underlying Condition," *Canadian Journal of Psychiatry* 63, no. 7 (July 2018): 451–6.

41 US Cancer Statistics Working Group, "U.S. Cancer Statistics: Data Visualizations," US Centers for Disease Control and Prevention and National Cancer Institute, based on 2019 submission data (1999–2017), www.cdc.gov/cancer/dataviz; "Overall Smoking Trends," American Lung Association, 2022, https://www.lung.org/research/trends-in-lung-disease/tobacco-trends-brief/overall-tobacco-trends.

42 "Disability Is Not a Reason to Sanction Medically Assisted Dying – UN Experts," United Nations Human Rights Office of the High Commissioner, 25 January 2021, https://www.ohchr.org/EN/NewsEvents/Pages/DisplayNews.aspx?NewsID=26687&LangID=E.

43 "Canada's Medical Assistance in Dying (MAID) Law," Government of Canada.

44 B.B. Ott, "Physician-Assisted Suicide and Older Patients' Perceived Duty to Die," *Advanced Practice Nursing Quarterly* 4, no. 2 (Fall 1998): 65–70.
45 Ricardo Cáceda, Charles B. Nemeroff, and Philip D. Harvey, "Toward an Understanding of Decision Making in Severe Mental Illness," *Journal of Neuropsychiatry and Clinical Neurosciences* 26, no. 3 (Summer 2014): 196–213.
46 Laura L. Fazakas-DeHoog, Katerina Rnic, and David J. A. Dozois, "A Cognitive Distortions and Deficits Model of Suicide Ideation," *Europe's Journal of Psychology* 13, no. 2 (May 2017): 178–93.
47 Justine Dembo, Sisco van Veen, and Guy Widdershoven, "The Influence of Cognitive Distortions on Decision-Making Capacity for Physician Aid in Dying," *International Journal of Law and Psychiatry* 72 (September–October 2020): 101627.
48 David Labby et al., "Drivers of High-Cost Medical Complexity in a Medicaid Population," *Medical Care* 58, no. 3 (March 2020): 208–15.
49 E.J. Emanuel and M.P. Battin, "What Are the Potential Cost Savings from Legalizing Physician-Assisted Suicide?," *New England Journal of Medicine* 339, no. 3 (July 1998): 167–72; Aaron J. Trachtenberg and Braden Manns, "Cost Analysis of Medical Assistance in Dying in Canada," *CMAJ* 189, no. 3 (January 2017): E101–5.
50 *Meeting of the Standing Senate Committee*, 3 February 2021; *Truchon c. Procureur général du Canada*, 2019 QCCS 3792.
51 "Drug and Health Product Review and Approval," Government of Canada, 2022, https://www.canada.ca/en/health-canada/services/drug-health-product-review-approval.html.
52 "Why You Should Not Use Ivermectin to Treat or Prevent COVID-19," US Food and Drug Administration, December 2021, https://www.fda.gov/consumers/consumer-updates/why-you-should-not-use-ivermectin-treat-or-prevent-covid-19 (link defunct).
53 "Johnson & Johnson Prepares to Resume Phase 3 ENSEMBLE Trial of its Janssen COVID-19 Vaccine Candidate in the U.S.," Johnson & Johnson, October 2020, https://www.jnj.com/our-company/johnson-johnson-prepares-to-resume-phase-3-ensemble-trial-of-its-janssen-covid-19-vaccine-candidate-in-the-us (emphasis added).
54 "Johnson & Johnson COVID-19 Vaccine Fully Approved by Health Canada to Prevent COVID-19 in Individuals 18 Years and Older," Johnson & Johnson, November 2021, https://www.jnj.com/johnson-johnson-covid-19-vaccine-fully-approved-by-health-canada-to-prevent-covid-19-in-individuals-18-years-and-older.

55 "Contraindication," MedlinePlus, 2021, https://medlineplus.gov/ency/article/002314.htm.
56 *Carter v. Canada (Attorney General)*, 2015 SCC 5.
57 *Carter*, 2015 SCC 5.
58 *Meeting of the Senate Standing Committee*, 3 February 2021.
59 Lisa Belzak and Jessica Halverson, "The Opioid Crisis in Canada: A National Perspective," *Health Promotion and Chronic Disease Prevention in Canada* 38, no. 6 (June 2018): 224–33.

14

MAiD by Advance Request: Vulnerability, Stigma, and the Myth of Free and Informed Advance Consent

Catherine Ferrier

Despite the repeated affirmations of medical assistance in dying (MAiD) advocates that their purpose is to promote autonomous decision-making about one's death, the question of MAiD for persons not able to consent to it has been on the horizon since the beginning of the debate in Canada. The possibility of MAiD by advance request for people who have lost decision-making capacity has rapidly gained in popularity, due to fear of a future with dementia in a social environment where stigma and neglect are common.

The claim that the death by MAiD of such persons can become an autonomous choice through written consent to MAiD before they lose decision-making capacity is philosophically and ethically flawed, as I will demonstrate in this chapter.

CANADIAN LAWS

The 2016 MAiD law did not allow for MAiD without concurrent consent. It required, as stated in article 9.1 (1) of Bill C-14, that "the Minister of Justice and the Minister of Health must, no later than 180 days after the day on which this Act receives royal assent, initiate one or more independent reviews of issues relating to requests by mature minors for medical assistance in dying, to advance requests and to requests where mental illness is the sole underlying medical condition."[1]

The independent review was carried out by an expert committee convened by the Council of Canadian Academies (CCA). The report, which was released on 12 December 2018, contains an extensive review of the literature but did not have a mandate to give recommendations. It documented, however, a lack of evidence and knowledge gaps in all three areas of possible extension.[2] With regard to MAiD by advance request, the panel concludes: "Consensus on which situations, if any, are suitable for allowing ARs [advance requests] for MAID is unlikely."[3]

Nevertheless, in Bill C-7, which received royal assent on 17 March 2021, the government permits a waiver of final consent for patients at the end of life who had requested and been found eligible for MAiD if, in a written arrangement, "they consented to the administration ... of a substance to cause their death on or before the day specified in the arrangement if they lost their capacity to consent to receiving medical assistance in dying prior to that day."[4] It is now lawful to give a lethal injection to someone who cannot consent to it.

There is evidence that many people who request MAID and retain decision-making capacity change their minds: 14 per cent did so in one Quebec study,[5] and 15 per cent did so according to the 2023 report of Quebec's *Commission sur les soins de fin de vie*.[6] The law thus puts people at risk of dying prematurely by MAiD contrary to their wishes. Advocacy for this provision is based on the unproven assumption that death by lethal injection is preferable to natural death with skilled, respectful, and empathetic palliative care. There is no data that compares these two options with regard to suffering or any other parameter.

The 2021 Canadian law required the immediate creation of a parliamentary review to consider MAiD through other types of advance request, as well as other extensions.[7] The Special Joint Committee on Medical Assistance in Dying was created and tabled its report in February 2023.[8] It recommends "that a person of full age and capacity be permitted to make an advance request for medical aid in dying following a diagnosis of a serious and incurable illness leading to incapacity." A group of forty-five expert witnesses to the committee, including eight experts in the area of advance requests, decried the many biases in the committee hearings and the report. The committee dismissed grave concerns expressed by witnesses about the validity of advance consent and about the serious ethical and practical challenges of implementing such requests in the Netherlands, the only jurisdiction where it is legal for people who are not permanently unconscious. The group concluded, "The recommendations on MAID by advance request reflect the activism of witnesses and politicians, not the prudence and knowledge necessary in considering such a life and death matter."[9]

A Senate bill to authorize MAiD by advance request was tabled on 2 June 2022 and reached second reading in the Senate on 6 June 2023.[10] Quebec's *Act to Amend the Act Respecting End-of-Life Care and Other Legislative Provisions* (Bill 11), adopted on 7 June 2023, authorizes persons diagnosed with a serious and incurable illness expected to lead to a loss of decision-making capacity to formulate an advance request for MAiD that would be implemented after they become incapable of consenting to it.[11] The person would include in their request the specific manifestations of the illness for which he or she wishes to receive MAiD. The law foresees a delay of a maximum of two years for its implementation, presumably because the government hopes during that time to obtain federal consent to a measure that is illegal in Canada. Several experts communicated grave concerns about the law, including the fact that it violated the *Canadian Charter of Fundamental Rights and Freedoms* and international human rights law, particularly the International Convention on the Rights of Persons with Disabilities.[12]

OTHER COUNTRIES

What can be learned from the few jurisdictions that permit MAiD by advance request (AR)? According to the CCA report,

> Little empirical evidence exists on how well ARs for MAID work in practice. Belgium, Colombia, Luxembourg, and the Netherlands permit some form of AR for MAID (referred to in these countries as advance euthanasia directives or AEDs), though their use is rare. Of the four countries that allow AEDs, two (Belgium and Luxembourg) only allow them when a person is irreversibly unconscious, and one (Colombia) allows them only in the context of imminent death ... Belgium and the Netherlands are the only two countries with any substantial practical experience with AEDs ... nearly all of the information about implementation of AEDs is from the Netherlands, due to a lack of detailed case information (from either the review commission or academic studies on AEDs) in Belgium.[13]

In the Netherlands MAiD is rarely used for patients with dementia, despite being legal if the physician considers the patient's suffering unbearable, because of the difficulty in evaluating suffering in this population. At the time of the CCA report, there were only six reported cases of euthanasia by advance request of incapable patients in the country. The panel observed that in the Netherlands, both physicians and relatives of people with dementia "are more positive about respecting AEDs in principle than in practice. Relatives of patients with dementia generally support euthanasia if an AED exists ... but when they are faced with the decision to follow an AED, most decide against it."[14]

> A 2007 to 2008 survey of 434 Dutch elderly care physicians revealed that, while 110 indicated that they had treated a patient with dementia who had an AED, only 3 physicians had actually performed euthanasia in such a case ... The top reason given for lack of compliance with an AED was that in the physician's opinion the patient experienced "no unbearable suffering" or "no hopeless suffering" ... More than half ... believed that it was "impossible to determine whether an incompetent person experiences his/her 'dementia' as unbearable and hopeless suffering" ... Most ... felt that it was "impossible to determine at what moment an advance directive for euthanasia of a person with dementia is to be carried out" ... *All patients with dementia who received euthanasia ... were "deemed competent and able to communicate their wishes."*[15]

It becomes evident that even the country with the most data on euthanasia by advance request has no useful information to offer. The practice is supported by some Dutch in theory, but it is rarely applied because of its contentious nature. When it is, the decision is based on the doctor's or the family's subjective impression of the patient's suffering. As the CCA report concludes, "The practical application of AEDs, the details of professional judgments in these cases, and the societal impacts of allowing AEDs remain significant knowledge gaps. In addition, the transferability of international evidence to the Canadian context is complicated by differences in legislative approaches to MAID, and may be affected by differences in healthcare systems and professional practices."[16]

The first case ever referred to a criminal court after euthanasia became legal in the Netherlands in 2002 was precisely one of euthanasia by advance request.[17] In 2016, a seventy-four-year-old woman with Alzheimer's disease was euthanized a few weeks after she moved to a nursing home. Mrs A's cognition had been declining for nine years. Four years before her death, she was diagnosed with Alzheimer's disease, and shortly afterwards she wrote an advance directive stating that she wanted euthanasia "when I am still at all mentally competent and when I am still able to live at home with my husband."[18] Three years later she revised it to state: "I want to make use of the legal right to undergo euthanasia whenever I think the time is right for this. Trusting that at the time when the quality of my life has become so poor, I would like for my request for euthanasia to be honored."[19]

Later that year she often said she wanted to die, "but not yet." When she arrived at the nursing home, her husband asked the doctor for euthanasia according to her advance directive. Mrs A was generally well in the mornings but was restless and unhappy in the afternoons. She missed her husband, was sad when he left, and wandered around looking for him. She regularly said she wanted to die, but when asked about it, would answer, "But not just now, it's not so bad yet!" After seven weeks, the treating physician concluded that the woman was suffering unbearably and decided in consultation with her family to euthanize her. She put a sedative drug into the woman's coffee without telling her, "because she would have asked questions about it and refused to take it," and "to prevent a struggle during the euthanasia."[20] Later she was given another sedative, and an IV was put into her arm to inject thiopental. During the injection, the patient suddenly tried to get up. Her family helped hold her down and the remaining drugs to cause her death were injected.

Unsurprisingly, this case generated much discussion in the bioethics literature because of the force and deception used to euthanize the patient. Supporters of the doctor's actions, while agreeing that the advance request lacked clarity, leading to doubts about the patient's consent, left no doubt as to their low opinion of life with dementia and embraced the doctor's acquittal in 2019 as a triumph of autonomy and beneficence.[21]

Dutch journalist Gerbert van Loenen, in his book *Do You Call This a Life?*, explains how circumstances changed him from "an average Dutchman who thought of euthanasia as one of the crowning achievements of our liberal country into someone who was shocked by the harsh tone used by the Dutch when they talk about handicapped life."[22] After his partner became disabled following surgery for a brain tumour, a friend referred to him as being "better off dead." Another told his partner he had "no right to whine," since he had chosen to go on living. Both statements haunted van Loenen and led to his book as well as his advocacy in favour of respect and support for those who live with disabilities and against the rampant ableism (discrimination against those who live with disabilities) that leads to support for hastening their death.

Dutch academic Boris Brummans wrote in his 2007 article "Death by Document" of his father's euthanasia death through an advance directive.

> I used to be in favor of euthanasia ... As so often, actual experience altered my point of view in such a way that I now no longer know where I'm standing. Although the euthanasia was meant to liberate my dad from the conventional constraints of suicide, its textual, declarative form turned him into a prisoner of himself (and us into his cellmates). By signing the euthanasia declaration ... my father created a persona of, and for, himself that transcended space and time, based on the person he thought he would be. On what were these thoughts based? Hollow images of a self not yet lived; meager ideas about a life not yet fleshed out. Similarly, we signed the declaration ... ready to act on his behalf ... In retrospect, it seems that our writing projected our past selves into the future in ways that deprived us, especially my dad, from the very liberty we thought to have signed for.[23]

Brummans underlines the absurdity of deciding for one's future self based on the illusion that one's perspective and ideas will never change. He shows how freedom is lost, not gained, through such attempts to determine one's death in advance by a legally binding document.

In Belgium, euthanasia is only authorized if the patient is unconscious. In 2022, several Belgian academics examined the Dutch regime to consider the wisdom of applying it in their country.[24] They concluded that the Dutch model creates serious difficulties and might create more problems than it solves.

CONSENT

The requirement of obtaining a patient's consent before undertaking any medical examination or treatment is undisputed in contemporary Western medical ethics. In fact, treatment without consent is a crime of assault.[25] Consent must be given voluntarily, the patient must have capacity to consent, and the patient must be informed.[26]

The Canadian Medical Protective Association, on the basis of Canadian legal judgments, lists the information that must be given to the patient for consent to be considered informed:[27]

- Inform the patient of the diagnosis, when possible. If some uncertainty exists about the diagnosis, mention this uncertainty, the reason for it, and what other possibilities you are considering.
- Explain the proposed investigations or treatments.
- Indicate the chances of success and/or anticipated outcome, covering both material and special risks.
- Inform the patient about available alternative treatments and their risks. It is important not to neglect addressing the possibility of not treating and its associated risks. There is no obligation to discuss what might be clearly regarded as unconventional therapy, but patients should know there are other accepted alternatives and why the recommended therapy has been proposed.
- Offer print material or electronic resources to support the consent discussion, but be mindful they are only an adjunct and do not replace the discussion.

Note the great emphasis on providing the patient with detailed knowledge of the medical condition for which treatment is being proposed and of all reasonable treatment options and their potential risks and benefits. This cannot be provided in advance for an unknown future health condition.

There is nevertheless an important role in health care for advance care planning, defined as a process of reflection and communication of one's values and wishes related to health and personal care, to prepare for a situation in which a decision about care must be made while the person concerned is unconscious or incapable of consenting to it for other reasons.[28]

These two statements, seemingly contradictory, can be reconciled by examining the different ways one can undertake advance care planning.

Advance directives to accept or refuse (but never demand) specific burdensome but potentially life-saving interventions are especially applied to technological interventions such as cardiopulmonary resuscitation and mechanical ventilation that must be decided upon quickly, carry a high burden, and may in some instances offer only a precarious extension of the dying process. Since there is little or no time to reflect when a possible need for these interventions arises, the alternatives are a decision made by the patient in advance, taking into account his or her state of health, personal circumstances, and preferences about the intensity of technological intervention or a decision made by a proxy decision-maker, preferably named by the patient and aware of the patient's values and preferences.

Directives that give detailed instructions on other specific interventions, often lists of interventions, are limited in their applicability. Regardless of how well-informed a person might be on the nature of the interventions under consideration, it is impossible to know in advance the medical situation for which they might be considered, the probability of their success in that situation, and the alternatives. This may vitiate consent because it is not informed in terms of diagnosis, proposed investigations, proposed and alternative treatments and their expected benefits and risks, and the consequences of not treating.

The Council of Canadian Academies Expert Panel Working Group on Advance Requests for MAID, after examining all the provincial laws on advance directives, observes that:

> Their application [of instructional directives] depends on how relevant the written instructions are to the specific medical situation. In British Columbia, for example, an advance directive does not apply if a healthcare practitioner reasonably believes that the instructions do not pertain to the decision at hand; the instructions are unclear; the directive does not reflect significant changes that have occurred in the maker's wishes, values, or beliefs; or, since the directive was written, there have been significant medical advances that might benefit the maker. Furthermore, in emergencies, healthcare practitioners are not required to locate and consult advance directives before providing life-saving treatments.[29]

Instead of a directive giving detailed instructions, many experts in advance care planning favour a process of reflection on broad health care goals, conversations with loved ones about the type and degree of intervention one would want, and the designation of a proxy decision-maker. The proxy would use the person's preferences as guidelines, without being bound by them, and make at each crossroads the best possible decision that is consistent with the sick person's values and known wishes.

Limited as they are, directives to refrain from certain treatments contrast starkly with directives ordering MAiD, in that they indicate a wish to be left alone, not a wish to have something actively done to end one's life. No jurisdiction in the world requires physicians to obey an advance directive mandating any specific medical intervention, much less the ending of life. J.J.M. van Delden observed that:

> There are two sorts of advance directives: negative ones, containing a treatment refusal, and positive ones, containing a wish that something be done – for example, the termination of life ... Is there a morally relevant difference between these sorts of advance directives? I think there is and by providing reasons for this I hope to show that, irrespective of the value of negative directives, positive ones are "a bridge too far."
>
> It is one thing to be free from controlling influences by others and from limitations that prevent choice. It is something else to be able to act in accordance with a self chosen plan ... The positive form of respecting patient autonomy ... does not imply that someone else is obligated to act according to your wishes ... Therefore I think people have more reason to refrain from action according to the negative claim than to act according to the positive one.[30]

For both sorts of directives, the question remains as to what sort of consent the patient gave at the time he or she signed it. As discussed, full discussion of the potential risks and burdens, and determination of patient decision-making capacity and freedom from coercion, is required for contemporaneous consent to request, accept, or refuse medical treatment. I am aware of no jurisdictions that require any such discussion at the time of signing an advance directive to withhold medical interventions. Fully informed consent is in any case impossible in advance. Directives are often signed at home, with family, using a pre-printed form or a text provided by a legal professional.

I am often asked to review texts proposed to patients by their lawyers or notaries that include statements such as: "I am opposed to all heroic therapeutic measures, namely disproportionate measures or treatment, given my condition, that merely increase or prolong my suffering needlessly [list of examples of interventions] when my condition is deemed irreversible ... I am opposed to any operation or treatment that could cause serious after-effects or leave me in a vegetative state."[31]

What is heroic? Disproportionate to what sort of benefit? What is needless prolongation of suffering? What is irreversible, that is, does it refer to no chance of returning to complete health or to some limited but acceptable state of health? To answer this would require reflection on what is an acceptable state of health and what is not, an estimation that often changes through the lived experience of illness. What are serious after-effects of a procedure, and what degree of benefit would justify each degree of after-effects?

Other texts, in the form of checklists of interventions one wants or does not want in a situation of incapacity and critical illness, may be so precise about specific choices that they could tie the doctor's hands and forbid treatments that are exactly what the patient needs to get better.

It soon becomes clear that consent to a hypothetical future treatment decision, in the context of a hypothetical future medical condition, life experience, and personal values, cannot be free and informed as ethics and law require. However, my patients, unversed in medical complexities, are often perfectly willing to sign such vague and dangerous documents because they are proposed by someone in authority and use words that sound important.

These risks are multiplied in the case of an advance request for MAiD, in which the outcome is certain death, and the requirement is to act to cause that death, not to refrain from acting.

Every individual's wishes change over time. This relates to the well-known concept of the changing self. This is also true for persons with dementia, as a written directive locks them into their expressed pre-illness wishes, however deeply or lightly determined at the time and maybe altered over the years.[32]

Miller et al., commenting on the Dutch law, express their concern about a low threshold of decisional capacity for preparing AEDs and presumption of capacity in early Alzheimer's disease, as well as "the law's failure to require an independent consultation for patients preparing AEDs, as it does for physicians implementing AEDs and physicians assessing requests for contemporaneous EAS [euthanasia or assisted suicide]. But this presents a paradox: given that the patient's desire for EAS is expressed at the time of writing the AED, rather than when EAS occurs, a particularly controversial form of EAS request by a cognitively vulnerable patient receives less scrutiny than does a contemporaneous request by a cognitively intact person."[33]

If even a fully capable patient finds it impossible to untangle the web of hypothetical future events, conditions, and decisions, what of a person with even mildly impaired decision-making capacity?

What of someone caught up in the emotional whirlwind of a recent diagnosis of a neurocognitive disorder? Receiving such a diagnosis is a major life crisis. Those of us who have been through even lesser crises know that our judgment is not at its best when flooded with emotions, fears, and questions. Most would be sensible enough to defer life-changing decisions until we are calm enough to think clearly. But for the person diagnosed with dementia, the clock is ticking, and the advance directive must be signed sooner rather than later.

For my patients, the existence of an option to choose death in this situation would not lead to peace, but rather to anxiety, conflict, and, in some cases, elder abuse.[34] And ultimately, by definition, all decisions to implement an advance request for MAiD, and to directly cause the death of the patient, are made by a third party, who may or may not have the patient's interest at heart.

COMPETING INTERESTS

A few years ago, there was a story in the *Montreal Gazette* about a patient of mine who lost her freedom and life's savings after an enduring power of attorney, later found to be forged, stripped away her rights without anyone speaking to her or questioning the validity of the document.[35] To advocate, as some have done, for legally binding advance requests for MAiD for patients with dementia betrays a naive and shocking ignorance of the many subtle and unrecognizable ways in which fragile seniors, even those who are cognitively intact, can be manipulated and abused.[36]

I often assess the decision-making capacity of patients caught in the middle of family disagreements, usually over money. One party of the disagreement may question the patient's capacity at the time of signing a legal document, rightly or wrongly. I have often seen even legitimately signed powers of attorney used contrary to the interests of the patient.

There are many competing interests in the lives of dependent elders. Families are microcosms with competing interests; the same can be said of the patient-physician relationship. Conflicts of interests are not rare. The risks are high when a physician deliberately ends the life of a person who is not autonomously asking for it to be ended.[37]

Putting aside situations of flagrant abuse, many united and well-intentioned families are torn between the needs of a sick relative, typically a parent, and other responsibilities, including attention to spouses and children and to their work and necessary leisure. They may feel their attention is not appreciated if the parent no longer recognizes them, takes their efforts for granted, or is aggressive or accusatory because of the effects of the illness. They may even withdraw from close attention to the parent in such a situation.

They may experience guilt and fear related to "placing" the parent in a long-term care centre, all amplified by the experience of the recent COVID-19 pandemic and the excess burden of illness on residents of such centres, as well as the isolation and physical and cognitive decline caused by the confinement measures.

There may be financial burdens related to paying for necessary care, whether at home or in a residential setting. Even in families with abundant means to pay for such care, there can be conflicts over how much of the children's hoped-for inheritance should be spent on it. Such considerations are inevitably present, often unconsciously, in all decisions related to the needs of the dependent senior.

The state has interests too. Funding for home and residential care depends on many political and budgetary factors unrelated to the needs of the people concerned. Indeed, one of the reasons for the disproportionate effect of the pandemic on seniors in residential care in Canada was the chronic underfunding that was present for years before it began.

Health professionals who care for people with dementia also experience distress, especially in situations of understaffing. If a patient has difficult behaviour, it becomes easy to blame the patient instead of reflecting on the nature of the illness and trying to understand the motivation behind the behaviour.

These interests would unavoidably be factors in decisions to implement advance requests for MAiD, whether by distressed families or health care providers who project their suffering onto the patient or by health care administrators in need of beds.

DIGNITY, STIGMA, AND VULNERABILITY

As we saw in chapter 7 on marginalization, ableism, the stigmatization of persons with disabilities, and the "I wouldn't want to live like that" mentality are constantly present in discourse promoting MAiD. The emphasis on autonomy gives way to "life not worth living" when discussing MAiD for dementia.

In his book *La responsabilité de protéger les personnes âgées atteintes de démence* (The responsibility to protect older persons with dementia), geriatrician Dr Félix Pageau reflects on the "error of loss of dignity." He differentiates between a "decorative" dignity or propriety, often invoked to justify MAiD when it is lacking because one has become dependent on others for personal care, and true human dignity, which everyone possesses. Another false understanding of dignity, as he writes, is social utility, implying that "a person who does not buy, sell or produce anything is no longer of value and should be eliminated. It considers a human person as a means rather than an end, the only end being to consume and keep the economy rolling."[38]

Pageau observes: "The intrinsic value of a toddler who is incontinent and needs help to eat, dress and wash, is never contested by his parents. This child is worthy of consideration and care, even if he has not yet acquired propriety. What about those who live their whole life with a mental or physical disability that limits their access to this type of dignity? Should these people be euthanized? This constitutes a eugenic mentality that must be avoided at all costs."[39]

A group of two hundred geriatricians and other health professionals caring for elderly patients wrote in an open letter to Canadian members of Parliament:[40]

> Throughout our careers caring for frail elderly patients, we have been confronted with ageist and ableist biases against our patients, especially those with neurocognitive disorders (dementia). They are referred to with derogatory language, blamed for occupying space in emergency rooms and hospital wards, and often discharged prematurely, to their detriment and resulting in return visits to the ER. A large percentage of seniors living in nursing homes receive few or no visitors. The effect of the COVID-19 pandemic on this population is well known, highlighting the deficiencies in the way frail seniors are cared for in Canada in the 21st century compared to their younger counterparts. Systemic ageism is everywhere, especially in the healthcare system.
>
> The natural evolution of this discrimination against our patients is enthusiasm for MAID by advance request. Why would anyone want to be part of such a marginalized and neglected group? Kill me first!

The demographic seeking MAiD, and specifically MAiD by advance request, is composed primarily of the worried well. Kill me first!

The letter goes on to affirm:

> This fear-driven attitude ignores the many positive aspects of aging and of caring for those who are aging. We have witnessed, repeatedly, positive evolution in family relationships, as roles are reversed in families and the adult children of our patients have an opportunity to "pay back" the care they received from their parents in the early years of their lives. As geriatricians, we experience on an everyday basis the beauty of caring for the elderly.

Indeed, seniors with dementia often rate their quality of life higher than proxies rate it.[41]

Psychiatrist Dr Harvey Max Chochinov, distinguished professor of psychiatry at the University of Manitoba and officer of the Order of Canada, has dedicated his career to promoting the dignity of patients approaching the end of their life, who may feel they have lost it through illness. His approach, dignity therapy, will be discussed below. Ultimately, we are all vulnerable, even those who are presently healthy and strong. Bioethicist Cory Andrew Labrecque observes, "embodied beings are vulnerable; etymologically speaking, this means that we are all woundable." This fact, as he notes, was rendered indisputable by the COVID-19 pandemic, especially when we saw young healthy people become critically ill and even die. He proceeds to observe, with legal theorist Martha Albertson Fineman, that "this pairing of vulnerability and weakness, however, has often been an impetus for 'othering' and for the perpetuation of an us-versus-them way of thinking that ultimately forms chasms between the (ostensibly) strong and weak, young and old, abled and disabled, as well as between patient and health-care provider."[42] Pageau, citing philosopher Gaëlle Fiasse's essay "Amour et fragilité," uses the term "fragility."[43] He deplores the criterion permitting MAiD for the reason of "an advanced state of irreversible decline in capability" as discriminatory, devaluing people based on disability and glorifying functional autonomy.[44] He recalls that we are all interdependent, and that this dependence constitutes one of the pillars of human nature.

Instead of rejecting our shared vulnerability, we must accept it as part of the human condition, unavoidable but beautiful, as it draws us to interdependence and connectedness instead of unrealizable radical autonomy.

Labrecque goes on to remind us that: "Love and vulnerability ... are sources of relationship, challenging the socially constructed dichotomies that seek to divide the world between poor and rich, weak and strong, old and young, ill and healthy. Solidarity, in itself a moral virtue, is not a feeling of vague compassion or shallow distress at the misfortunes of so many people, both near and far. On the contrary, it is a firm and persevering determination to commit oneself to the common good. That is to say to the good of all and of each individual, because we are all really responsible for all."[45]

BUILDING COMMUNITY

If vulnerability is universal, and solidarity to support and affirm the dignity of those currently vulnerable is the answer, how can that solidarity be expressed?

It is constantly expressed by countless Canadians who care for sick and aging family members and friends. I see it daily in my clinic, in the spouses, children, nieces, nephews, siblings, and friends of my patients. I see it in many individuals working in health care settings who go beyond strict duty to care for patients. I see it in non-profit organizations created to provide companionship and all kinds of help to people who are alone and aging or sick. But of course more is always needed.

Health care for vulnerable Canadians, and supports to enable families to care for them at home, must be adequately funded. Non-institutional housing that celebrates individuality should be available for those who choose it.

Behavioural and psychological symptoms in dementia, such as Mrs A experienced, are a well-known phenomenon, especially in the context of a change of environment causing disorientation, or of illness, medication side effects, pain, fear, poor sleep, or any other source of distress. The symptoms can be eased by adapting one's approach to the needs of each individual, using interventions such as music therapy, and in many other ways.[46] To do so requires time and education of the caregivers, both professionals and family. It is easily neglected when there is insufficient staff in nursing homes. MAiD is quick and cheap, compared to creative approaches to behavioural and psychological symptoms that support each person's dignity and individuality.

Dr Chochinov's dignity therapy seeks to promote the dignity of every sick person. As explained on the Dignity in Care website:[47]

> There is an intimate connection between every person's self-image and the way they feel they are seen by the people working in the health care system. Whether they realize it or not – and whether

they desire it or not – patients and families look to them as they would to a mirror, seeking a positive reflection of themselves.

Attitudes and behaviours can shape those all-important reflections. It's important to reflect back an appreciation of the whole person, and not just the illness or affliction. No one wants to feel invisible, and no one wants to be seen as a tumour or a defective part. Patients want to be seen as people who are seeking help with a medical concern.

Research with the terminally ill showed that a personal sense of dignity can literally make the difference between a person's wish to live or die.

The dignity model includes the following principles for care:[48]

- Affirm the person's value
- View people apart from their disease
- Safeguard the person's privacy
- Address pain and discomfort
- Deal with fears and anxieties
- Help people maintain a feeling of control and independence
- Offer or bolster social support

Beyond the individual level, there are initiatives in many places to build compassionate cities or compassionate communities. Based on the work of Dr Allan Kellehear and others, these communities promote networks of social support around those facing illness and death. As stated by Compassionate Kingston, "We are a voluntary network of people who are passionate about actively improving the experiences of those coping with life-limiting conditions, dying and death. We are dedicated to creating a community in which people are better able to help each other in times of need. Our purpose is to help our citizens who are dealing with aging, a variety of health issues or loneliness and socialization. We want everyone to live as well as they can for as long as they can. We hope our community will become more and more kind and compassionate."[49] Other cities all over the world, including Ottawa, have taken up the challenge.[50] Pallium Canada continues to create tools to facilitate development of compassionate communities.[51]

Initiatives specifically focused on people with dementia include the Carpe Diem approach, created by Nicole Poirier of Trois-Rivières, Quebec.[52] Centred on a home open to both residents and day visitors, Carpe Diem also offers support to persons with cognitive disorders and their caregivers by telephone, in their homes, or in other locations. It is guided by the following principles:

- Favour the creation of a *relationship* of trust between the person and the people who accompany him/her;
- Aim to maintain autonomy and self-esteem by promoting a flexible framework that allows the person to decide on his or her own schedule and activities, and by offering multiple opportunities to feel useful by participating in domestic tasks, according to his or her tastes and interests;
- Respect the person's links with his or her family and friends and encourage the family's involvement in their relative's daily life, without any time constraints;
- Create a unique response to each situation, offering services adapted to each person and family throughout the illness.[53]

The Carpe Diem Resource Centre offers education to individuals and groups seeking to implement the model in other settings.

We could go on, but these few examples suffice. Many initiatives exist in Canada to support people who face cognitive and other limitations. Much remains to be done, but help can be found.

CONCLUSION

There is a very vocal lobby in Canada for MAiD by advance request of adults incapable of decision-making. It is composed mainly of healthy people who fear future dementia and its associated vulnerability and stigma. Kill me first! Such a policy, if implemented, will be based on fear, not on thoughtful consideration of the needs of each person and of the common good. The campaign ignores the many ethical problems inherent in the proposal and the deaths without consent that would occur should it be adopted.

We are often told, in the context of the MAiD debate, that if lethal injection were legal it would be for those who choose it, and it would not be imposed on anyone. This is doubtful in any situation and is clearly false in the one under discussion. By definition the person dying through MAiD would be unable to consent to it, and the so-called advance consent would not be informed. Third-party decision-makers, with their own agendas and interests, would inevitably make the final decision.

In the forty years I have been caring for people with dementia, patient requests for MAiD have been virtually non-existent. My patients and their families have many other concerns. But I have no doubt that, if MAiD by advance request becomes legal, people will start asking, not because they suddenly need it, but because it will be marketed to them, as MAiD is now, by lobby groups, the media, the government, and health care organizations.

Seniors will sign documents they do not understand, as they are doing already, relinquishing the right to change their mind, because the documents are proposed by their lawyer, their notary, or their doctor, whom they trust. They will not fully understand that these documents will lead to their death instead of to humane care.

Their life with dementia will be devalued in the public view. Their vulnerability will be considered a burden to their family and to society instead of a sign of our radical interdependence and a call to solidarity. Lethal injections will replace truly humane measures, which they will be denied because of the document they signed.

If MAiD by advance request becomes legal, people with dementia, our elders, our parents, will be held down and injected with poison to end their life when they are happy and not asking for it. If such requests are legally binding, Canada will be the only place in the world where a state agency is obliged by law to kill an innocent and defenceless person. To our shame if we ever take that fateful step.

NOTES

The author is grateful to Dr Félix Pageau for constructive criticism of the manuscript.

1 *Bill C-14, An Act to Amend the Criminal Code and to Make Related Amendments to Other Acts (medical assistance in dying)*, 42nd Parliament, 1st Session (2016), SC 2016, c. 3, art. 9.1 (1) (Can.), https://www.parl.ca/DocumentViewer/en/42-1/bill/C-14/royal-assent.
2 Expert Panel on Medical Assistance in Dying, *Medical Assistance in Dying* (Ottawa: Council of Canadian Academies, 2018), https://cca-reports.ca/reports/medical-assistance-in-dying/.
3 Expert Panel Working Group on Advance Requests for MAiD, *The State of Knowledge on Advance Requests for Medical Assistance in Dying* (Ottawa: Council of Canadian Academies, 2018), 176, https://cca-reports.ca/wp-content/uploads/2019/02/The-State-of-Knowledge-on-Advance-Requests-for-Medical-Assistance-in-Dying.pdf.

4 *Bill C-7, An Act to Amend the Criminal Code (medical assistance in dying)*, 43rd Parliament, 2nd Session (2021), cl. 1(2.1), SC 2021, c. 2 (Can.), https://parl.ca/DocumentViewer/en/43-2/bill/C-7/royal-assent.
5 Lori Seller, Marie-Ève Bouthillier, and Véronique Fraser, "Situating Requests for Medical Aid in Dying within the Broader Context of End-of-Life Care: Ethical Considerations," *Journal of Medical Ethics* 45, no. 2 (February 2019): 106–11, https://pubmed.ncbi.nlm.nih.gov/30467196/.
6 Commission sur soins de fin de vie, *Rapport annuel d'activités du 1er avril 2022 au 31 mars 2023*, 2023, https://csfv.gouv.qc.ca/fileadmin/docs/rapports_annuels/rapport_annuel_dactivites_2022-2023.pdf.
7 "Special Joint Committee on Medical Assistance in Dying," Parliament of Canada, https://www.parl.ca/Committees/en/AMAD.
8 Special Joint Committee on Medical Assistance in Dying, *Medical Assistance in Dying: Choices for Canadians*, 44th Parliament, 1st Session, February 2023, https://www.parl.ca/Content/Committee/441/AMAD/Reports/RP12234766/amadrp02/amadrp02-e.pdf.
9 Harvey Max Chochinov et al., *Expert Witnesses Speak Out Against Bias in Medical Assistance in Dying Report*, March 2023, https://static1.squarespace.com/static/61db373a8e4e00423c117825/t/640739a3f6062c0b00236bbe/1678195107898/MAID+Report+Response+March+7+2023.pdf.
10 *Bill S-248, An Act to Amend the Criminal Code (medical assistance in dying)*, 44th Parliament, 1st Session (2021) (Can.), https://www.parl.ca/legisinfo/en/bill/44-1/s-248.
11 *Bill 11, An Act to Amend the Act Respecting End-of-Life Care and Other Legislative Provisions*, 44th Legislature, 1st Session (2023) CQLR 2023, c. 15, cls. 16(1), 20 (Quebec, Can.), https://www.publicationsduquebec.gouv.qc.ca/fileadmin/Fichiers_client/lois_et_reglements/LoisAnnuelles/en/2023/2023C15A.PDF.
12 See, for example, Trudo Lemmens, "Les demandes anticipées de l'aide médicale à mourir (AMM): problématiques du point de vue de l'éthique, du droit constitutionnel, et des droits de l'homme. Mémorandum soumis à la Commission parlementaire des relations avec les citoyens," Assemblée nationale du Québec, 23 March 2023, https://www.assnat.qc.ca/fr/travaux-parlementaires/commissions/CRC/mandats/Mandat-51109/documents-deposes.html.
13 Expert Panel on Medical Assistance in Dying, *The State of Knowledge on Medical Assistance in Dying for Mature Minors, Advance Requests, and Where a Mental Disorder Is the Sole Underlying Medical Condition – Summary of Reports* (Ottawa: Council of Canadian Academies, December 2018), 21: https://cca-reports.ca/wp-content/uploads/2018/12/MAID-Summary-of-Reports.pdf.

14 Expert Panel on Medical Assistance in Dying, *State of Knowledge on Advance Requests*, 122.
15 Ibid. Emphasis added.
16 Expert Panel on Medical Assistance in Dying, *State of Knowledge on Medical Assistance in Dying for Mature Minors – Summary of Reports*, 22.
17 David Gibbes Miller, Rebecca Dresser, and Scott Y.H. Kim, "Advance Euthanasia Directives: A Controversial Case and its Ethical Implications," *Journal of Medical Ethics* 45, no. 2 (February 2019): 84–9, https://pubmed.ncbi.nlm.nih.gov/29502099/.
18 Ibid.
19 Ibid.
20 Ibid.
21 "Watching children's television or smearing shit on the wall ..." Eva Constance Alida Asscher and Suzanne van de Vathorst, "First Prosecution of a Dutch Doctor since the Euthanasia Act of 2002: What Does the Verdict Mean?," *Journal of Medical Ethics* 46, no. 2 (February 2020): 71–5, https://pubmed.ncbi.nlm.nih.gov/31806678/.
22 Gerbert Mark Van Loenen, *Do You Call This a Life? Blurred Boundaries in the Netherlands' Right-to-Die Laws*, trans. Maggie Oates (London, ON: Ross Latner Educational Consultants, 2015), 159.
23 Boris H.J.M. Brummans, "Death by Document: Tracing the Agency of a Text," *Qualitative Inquiry* 13, no. 5 (July 2007): 711–27, 722, https://doi.org/10.1177/1077800407301185.
24 Jan Versijpt et al., "Euthanasie bij dementie middels een voorafgaande wilsverklaring: een reflectie vanuit België en Nederland," *Tijdschrift voor Geneeskunde* 4, no. 18 (February 2022), https://doi.org/10.47671/TVG.77.21.199.
25 "Consent: A Guide for Canadian Physicians," Canadian Medical Protective Association, 4th ed., updated June 2016, https://www.cmpa-acpm.ca/en/advice-publications/handbooks/consent-a-guide-for-canadian-physicians#assault.
26 "Informed consent," Canadian Medical Protective Association, revised November 2022, https://www.cmpa-acpm.ca/en/education-events/good-practices/physician-patient/informed-consent?panel=checklist-obtaining-a-valid-consent.
27 Ibid.
28 Advance Care Planning Canada (website), accessed 18 November 2023, https://www.advancecareplanning.ca/.
29 Expert Panel on Medical Assistance in Dying, *State of Knowledge on Advance Requests*, 92.

30 J.J.M. van Delden, "The Unfeasibility of Requests for Euthanasia in Advance Directives," *Journal of Medical Ethics* 30, no. 5 (October 2004): 447–52, https://pubmed.ncbi.nlm.nih.gov/15467074/.
31 Email to author, 4 July 2021.
32 José A. Morais, Pierre J. Durand, and Félix Pageau to Canadian Parliament, "Warning against the Dangers of MAID by Advance Request, from Professionals Who Care for Canadians with Dementia: Open Letter to Canadian Members of Parliament," 23 February 2021, French version published in *Le Devoir*, 26 February 2021, https://www.ledevoir.com/opinion/idees/595951/notre-inquietude-face-a-l-aide-medicale-a-mourir.
33 Miller et al., "Advance Euthanasia Directives," 87.
34 Geriatric Clinic of the McGill University Health Centre, focused on neurocognitive disorders and decision-making capacity assessment.
35 Jesse Feith, "92-Year-Old Woman Says People Took Control of Her Life Using a Mandate That Was Forged," *Montreal Gazette*, 12 March 2016, https://montrealgazette.com/news/veronika-piela.
36 *Meeting of the Standing Senate Committee on Legal and Constitutional Affairs – Evidence*, 43rd Parliament, 2nd Session (24 November 2020) (Dr Alain Naud), https://sencanada.ca/en/Content/Sen/Committee/432/LCJC/03EV-55073-E: "Une fois le diagnostic posé, après un certain temps, après avoir bien étudié la question, un individu pourrait faire une demande en signant un formulaire devant témoin. On pourrait répéter la demande après trois ou six mois en sachant que le malade est toujours apte à donner son consentement. Cette demande aurait une valeur contraignante." ("Once the diagnosis has been made, after some time and careful consideration, an individual could make a request by signing a form in front of a witness. The request could be made again after three or six months if the patient is still capable of giving consent. This request would be binding.")
37 Morais et al., *Warning against the Dangers*.
38 Félix Pageau, *La responsabilité de protéger les personnes âgées atteintes de démence – Manifeste* (Quebec: Les Presses de l'Université Laval, 2020), 8, my translation, https://www.pulaval.com/produit/la-responsabilite-de-proteger-les-personnes-agees-atteintes-de-demence-manifeste.
39 Ibid., 9, my translation.
40 Morais et al., *Warning against the Dangers*.
41 Divyansh Dixit et al., "Quality of Life Assessments in Individuals with Young-Onset Dementia and Their Caregivers," *Journal of Geriatric Psychiatry and Neurology* 34, no. 5 (July 2020): 426–33, https://doi.org/10.1177/0891988720933348; Laura Dewitte, Mathieu Vandenbulcke, and Jessie Dezutter, "Cognitive Functioning and Quality of Life: Diverging

Views of Older Adults with Alzheimer and Professional Care Staff," *International Journal of Geriatric Psychiatry* 33, no. 8 (August 2018): 1074–81, https://pubmed.ncbi.nlm.nih.gov/29869400/.
42 Cory Andrew Labrecque, "Vulnerability, Dependency, and Trust in the Shadow of Medical Aid in Dying," *Cardus*, 30 September 2020, https://www.cardus.ca/research/health/reports/vulnerability-dependency-and-trust-in-the-shadow-of-medical-aid-in-dying/.
43 Pageau, *La responsabilité de protéger*, 38; Gaëlle Fiasse, *Amour et fragilité: Regards philosophiques au cœur de l'humain* (Quebec: Presse de l'Université Laval, 2015), https://www.pulaval.com/produit/amour-et-fragilite-regards-philosophiques-au-coeur-de-l-humain.
44 *Criminal Code of Canada*, RSC 1985, c. C-46, s. 241.2, accessed 19 November 2023, https://laws-lois.justice.gc.ca/eng/acts/C-46/section-241.2.html.
45 Labrecque, "Vulnerability, Dependency, and Trust."
46 Gill Livingston et al., "Non-Pharmacological Interventions for Agitation in Dementia: Systematic Review of Randomised Controlled Trials," *British Journal of Psychiatry* 205, no. 6 (December 2014): 436–42, https://pubmed.ncbi.nlm.nih.gov/25452601/.
47 Dignity in Care (website), accessed 10 November 2023, https://www.dignityincare.ca/en/approach.html#dignity_model.
48 Ibid.
49 Compassionate Communities Kingston Canada (website), accessed 19 November 2023, https://compassionatekingston.ca/about/.
50 Compassionate Ottawa (website), accessed 19 November 2023, https://compassionateottawa.ca/.
51 "Compassionate Communities," Pallium Canada, accessed 19 November 2023, https://www.pallium.ca/compassionate-communities/.
52 Carpe Diem, Centre de Ressources Alzheimer (website), accessed 19 November 2023, https://alzheimercarpediem.com/.
53 "L'approche Carpe Diem," Carpe Diem, Centre de Ressources Alzheimer, accessed 19 November 2023, https://alzheimercarpediem.com/lapproche-carpe-diem/lapproche-carpe-diem/, translated with https://www.DeepL.com/Translator (free version).

15

Mature Minors and MAiD

Ramona Coelho

Bill C-14 introduced medical assistance in dying (MAiD) as an exceptional medical act to administer a lethal injection to consenting adults with intolerable suffering and whose natural death was reasonably foreseeable.[1] Bill C-7 extended MAiD to offer death based on intolerable suffering (psychological or physical) for adults living with any disability or chronic disease. MAiD will soon also be offered to those living with psychiatric disease.[2]

In April 2022, the Special Joint Committee on Medical Assistance in Dying (AMAD) was reconvened after the 2021 federal election. The AMAD federal parliamentary committee held its first meeting on 8 April 2022, with its final report made public in February 2023.[3] The committee, consisting of members of Parliament and senators, made recommendations regarding advance directives for MAiD, the regulation of psychiatric MAiD, the state of palliative care in Canada, the protection of persons with disabilities, and MAiD for mature minors.[4] Tasked with covering an unrealistic amount of evidence in a very short time frame, the committee did not provide a thorough review of the evidence regarding any of these five topics, let alone MAiD for mature minors. Regardless, and given the federal government's clear appetite for expansion, the Special Joint Committee on MAiD recommended studying various factors in offering MAiD for children and to expand MAiD to mature minors where their natural death is reasonably foreseeable (RFND).[5] They recommended that, when appropriate, parents be consulted, but that the capacity to consent and the decision would ultimately rest with the child. They glossed over the lack of safeguards and the abuses arising from the current MAiD regime, despite these being raised in committee meetings.[6]

This chapter will review several considerations in regard to MAiD for mature minors and will examine a legal perspective on the issue of capacity to consent to MAiD, coupled with a scientific understanding of brain maturation and the impact on mature minors' decision-making capacity. I will explore parental/child roles in family life and how allowing MAiD for mature minors might undermine parental roles. As well, the research on suicide contagion among teenagers will be reviewed. I will consider how coercion or factors such as bullying, discrimination, or growing up as a child in poverty or violence can affect young peoples' choices to die. Lastly, as Canadian evidence obviously does not yet exist in this domain, I will review the limited international evidence on MAiD for mature minors.

THE LAW

The Supreme Court of Canada decision in the *Carter* case (2015) is the only high court ruling that decriminalized MAiD in Canada. It explicitly restricted its decision to the factual circumstances before it and made "no pronouncement on other situations where physician-assisted dying may be sought."[7] The ruling stated clearly that MAiD should be voluntary and for adults: "While there is no clear societal consensus on physician-assisted dying, there is a strong consensus that it would only be ethical with respect to voluntary adults who are competent, informed, grievously and irremediably ill, and where the assistance is 'clearly consistent with the patient's wishes and best interests, and provided in order to relieve suffering.'"[8]

Further, the justices clearly excluded minors from their judgement when they responded to an affidavit that reviewed controversial and high-profile cases of assistance in dying in Belgium, stating these cases "would not fall within the parameters suggested in these reasons, such as euthanasia for minors or persons with psychiatric disorders or minor medical conditions."[9]

Despite serious red flags raised regarding the recklessness of the current MAiD legislation, which is presently available only to adults, proponents of the legalization of euthanasia and assisted suicide continue to argue that it is unfair to withhold MAiD from mature minors. They also argue that mature minors already have decision-making capacity to withdraw life support, and being so capable, should not be deprived the right to access MAiD.

In the *A.C. v. Manitoba* case, the Supreme Court recognized that the capacity for decision-making of minors must be evaluated by taking into consideration the child's mental, emotional, and physical needs; state of development; and potential unique views and preferences including the religious heritage of the child.[10] The court applied a sliding scale to the concept of capacity, recognizing that the more serious the consequences of the choice, the more heightened the scrutiny that must be applied in assessing a child's capacity. The Supreme Court has also recognized "heightened concerns about younger adolescents' maturity and vulnerability to subtle and overt coercion and influence."[11] Therefore, under our legal system's mature minor doctrine, minors' capacity for decision-making is not based on age but on a determination of their ability to understand and appreciate the consequences of specific health care decisions.

In some cases, a total prohibition on choices that would cause harm to the child, such as the use of marijuana, alcohol, and cigarettes, is considered necessary. It is important, in this regard, to emphasize the finality of invoking MAiD: mature minors would not be consenting to potential future health problems, such as would be the case when consenting to using marijuana, alcohol, or cigarettes, but rather to having no future at all.

REASONABLY FORESEEABLE NATURAL DEATH (RFND) AND FUTURE EXPANSION

The MAiD expansion proposed by the Special Joint Committee on MAID will also qualify minors who aren't imminently dying for MAiD. The Canadian Association of MAiD Assessors and Providers (CAMAP), a group which received 3.3 million dollars from Health Canada to educate MAiD assessor and providers,[12] has written a document on interpreting MAiD requests and RFND criteria.[13] It emphasizes, for example, that clinicians can be flexible when it comes to determining whether someone fits the RFND criterion, since "the law does not require ... that the person must be terminally ill" or that they will die within "6 or 12 months."[14] Remarkably, the document also states: "A person may meet the 'reasonably foreseeable' criterion if they have demonstrated a clear and serious intent to take steps to make their natural death happen soon or to cause their death to be predictable. Examples might include stated declarations to refuse antibiotic treatment of current or future serious infection, to stop use of oxygen therapy, to refuse turning if they have quadriplegia, or to voluntarily cease eating and drinking."[15]

Using CAMAP's criteria, a child indicating intent, for example, to refuse to eat and drink, such as a fifteen-year-old disabled child, could be found eligible by MAiD assessors under the current MAiD RFND framework, if the law was expanded to mature minors.

Further, MAiD for adults has expanded quickly from reasonably foreseeable natural death to include those with any type of chronic illness or disability, and now soon for those solely with mental illness. Though it is not within the current recommendations, it isn't hard to imagine a similar progression of MAiD for children.

PARENT/CHILD CONSIDERATIONS

If Canada allows MAiD for children, MAiD could undermine the parents' role of guardianship. The child has not internalized the parental role of managing their welfare or making decisions that are beneficial to them, meaning they cannot yet rightfully act as their own parent with respect to serious decision-making. The law is not meant to interfere when the parents are fulfilling their role of caring for the welfare and best interests of their children. If Canada allows MAiD for mature minors to become legal, MAiD could undermine the parents' role of guardianship and become an abuse of government power. Given that the committee recommendations are already calling for parent involvement only if appropriate, it is clear that cases will be approved without parents' agreement.

Do we want a future where parents of a depressed fifteen-year-old are helpless to stop their child from completing assisted suicide or euthanasia, while the government supports and facilitates it?

It is of concern that parents' knowledge of their children's maturity and emotional drivers could be ignored by MAiD assessors in the Canadian context. In most non-Western cultures, including among members of other cultures transplanted to Canada,[16] the family often makes medical decisions together as a group; there is no "I," just an "us." While not an expressed Canadian value, many functioning families operate this way. Parents will be devastated when their child's request for MAiD is granted against their wishes, and despite their knowledge that the suffering is transient and reflects temporary drivers over authentic choice.

BRAIN DEVELOPMENT

Current medical evidence confirms that adolescents' judgment continues to develop well into adulthood. The American Academy of Pediatrics states:

> Newer insight into brain structure and function now makes the determination of which minors possess the maturity for decision-making much less clear-cut ... Although the size of the brain nearly reaches its adult size in early childhood, we know ... that much of the brain has continued dynamic changes in gray matter volume and myelination into the third decade of life. The prefrontal cortex, where many executive functions are coordinated, including the balancing of risks and rewards, is among the last areas of the brain to mature, with these functions continuing to develop and mature into young adulthood.[17]

The long time frame for full brain development explains the risky behaviours that can be observed in adolescence. This is also why exploration of risky behaviours and preventive counselling are prioritized in health care checkups for adolescents, with the goal of mitigating the risk of injury and preventing premature death. The phenomenon of adolescents demonstrating more risk-taking behaviours could also lead to choosing MAiD without due deliberation, death being the greatest risk and unknown of all.

Later brain development also means that mature minors may lack the developmental capacity to imagine their future selves, and therefore lack fulsome appreciation of their opportunity horizons. Ask a fifteen-year-old what they want to do in life and await the shrug. Not only can there be an inability to imagine their future but also there may be limited ability to imagine coping or living with disability or disease. Yet over time, many will learn as adults that they can accept living with all kinds of disabilities.

One can imagine that this limited ability to visualize their future makes it is more likely that a mature minor could get caught up in and act upon a reunion fantasy that may drive a MAiD request (e.g., with deceased parents, grandparents, boyfriends or girlfriends who completed suicide or died, friends who have overdosed, or celebrities or others with whom they have identified). Similarly, adolescent bravado and defying parents they are angry with because the parents failed to protect them from disease or suffering could drive a

MAiD request. Rage-driven MAiD could also be fuelled by emotional immaturity.

Now imagine the opposite scenario. Instead of blaming their parents for their illness, children may fear being a burden and want to protect their parents. A well-known phenomenon of "mutual pretense" exists whereby sick children protect their parents by pretending that they are doing better than they are. This could also be expressed as a MAiD choice because they don't want their parents to suffer due to their own suffering. Mature minors who undergo long courses of chemotherapy misunderstand their parents' present distress as an immediate parental desire to have that distress end, not understanding that the child's death would cause far greater and inconsolable distress.

Even beyond the scientific or legal framework, a mature understanding of our mortality is a lifelong process. MAiD before maturity is an affront to the primary human task of finding purposeful, existential meaning to our lives in the face of suffering and sorrow.

MENTAL HEALTH CHALLENGES AND TEENAGE SUICIDE CONTAGION

Evidence from the Benelux (Belgium-Netherlands-Luxemburg) countries indicates that psychiatric MAiD is often chosen by those who have experienced early childhood trauma, including abuse.[18] Childhood trauma can be internalized and lead to devaluing of the self. Suicidality is also an expression of self-loathing. MAiD offered to youth would therefore be an affirmation of this internalized aggression, devaluing of the self, and self-loathing.

Consider how bullying, discrimination, or growing up in the child welfare system might affect a mature minor's views of life and influence their choice to die. The disability rights organization Toujours Vivant–Not Dead Yet (TV-NDY) expresses concern: "ill and disabled children often grow up in families where non-disabled parents see their lives as burdensome, tragic, a disappointment of their hopes for the future, and 'not worth living.'"[19] The group points to blogs of those living with disabilities who recollect a lack of positive role models and feelings of shame as children. Yet this despair resolved in adulthood, replaced by the understanding that it is actually the views of society that need to change. In this context, allowing MAiD for mature minors would be the cruelest offering to those who have already suffered so much injustice.

As a result of the myriad of harms associated with colonialism and intergenerational trauma perpetuated by systemic discrimination and policies that oppress Indigenous persons, Indigenous youth have higher suicide rates on average and higher rates of mental illness. It is therefore unethical for our federal government to expand MAiD to mature minors but ignore recommendations from Indigenous stakeholders across Canada to implement strategies for youth suicide prevention and the promotion of mental wellness. According to the *First Nations Mental Wellness Continuum Framework Summary Report*, the definition of mental wellness is a balance of the mental, physical, spiritual, and emotional. This balance is enriched when individuals have "purpose in their daily lives whether it is through education, employment, care-giving activities, or cultural ways of being and doing; hope for their future and those of their families that is grounded in a sense of identity, unique Indigenous values, having a belief in spirit; a sense of belonging and connectedness within their families, to community, and to culture; and finally a sense of meaning and understanding of how their lives and those of their families and communities are a part of creation and a rich history."[20]

In terms of suffering, Rod McCormick, a Mohawk psychologist, pointed out in his brief to the Special Joint Committee on MAID the injustice of offering MAiD to minors while so many resources, supports, and medical care are not remotely accessible:

> I can clearly see the Residential School from the windows of my house and can make out a glimpse of the fields in which at least 215 children have been buried in shallow graves. This attempt to conceal the bodies is in some ways symbolic of the numerous historical attempts by Canada to deal with what Duncan Campbell Scott referred to as the need to get rid of the Indian problem. Those attempts have consisted of forced starvation; forced sterilization; forced relocation to reserves with unsafe, unhealthy, crowded housing; the Introduction of liquor; smallpox blankets; forced residential schooling; experimentation with malnutrition in residential schools; Ignoring the contagion of tuberculosis in residential schools; the ongoing child welfare seizure of children; excessive imprisonment of Indigenous peoples in the penal system and the list goes on ...
>
> I have worked with many Indigenous youth in emotional pain who were able to recover from being suicidal. The common reflection they had was one of relief that they did not choose a permanent solution to what proved to be a temporary problem. Getting the proper and timely help is the key to survival.

There are many barriers to attaining that help. Among them are a lack of accurate diagnosis and corresponding treatment; a racist health care system; a mistrust of the health care system which does not always have our "best interest" in mind; jurisdictional ambiguity and the abdication of responsibility by various governments; and the big factor: remoteness of our communities. Living on reserve and/or in a remote location often means that health services are provided by nurses or nurse practitioners who are often overworked and ill prepared to provide the range of services that are required. This is especially the case in the near total absence of palliative care services for Indigenous children and youth.[21]

In considering how MAiD offered to mature minors will affect this peer group's collective mental suffering, it is important to consider mature minors' high rates of depression and the medical evidence documenting the phenomenon of teenage suicide clustering.[22] Risk factors for suicide include being exposed to messages promoting suicide and knowing someone who has engaged in self-harm.[23] Mature minors are still learning and must trust their community, their educators, and other adults in their life to teach them and to help shape their values and life prospects. The suicide messaging of "you have the right to choose death" presented by the Canadian government and the medical establishment to minors before they have the ability to discern power imbalances, and the reality that doctors and government employees can be mistaken, corrupt, or not acting in their best interest, is inherently dangerous.

Consider also that there are no statistics on access to palliative care for children. Pediatric palliative care centers do exist (Calgary, Vancouver, Toronto, Ottawa, and Montreal), but most places have little to no resources. Advice over the telephone from a team in one of those centers for children in rural and remote areas is probably the best "care" many are getting in Canada. For example, there is no trained pediatric palliative care doctor on the east coast, and so McGill (Quebec) pediatric palliative care provides phone support to Nova Scotia. The first subspecialty program in pediatric palliative care was only launched in Ottawa in 2021.[24] Canada does not have the resources in place to offer real choices to children; normalizing death through MAiD is putting the cart before the horse.[25]

The Canadian Association of Suicide Prevention has pointed out that MAiD outside the end-of-life context is actually assisted suicide.[26] Therefore, increased suicide messaging in offering MAiD to minors and trying to normalize this practice, coupled with the increased likelihood of knowing someone who has completed suicide through MAiD, may impact teenager suicide contagion and increase the overall suicide rate.

EXPERT AND INTERNATIONAL EVIDENCE

The 2018 report by the Expert Panel Working Group on MAiD for Mature Minors at the Council of Canadian Academies noted a lack of evidence on how MAiD for mature minors would affect families. There is no robust evidence that captures the voices of youth, including the views of minors with disabilities, Indigenous youth, and those in the child welfare system, and these voices are not adequately captured in the literature on MAiD. The report also cites a paucity of international evidence on which to draw conclusions.[27]

The working group based its recommendations on MAiD for mature minors using a surrogate form of evidence: withdrawal of life support.[28] Yet, as stated by the Canadian Medical Association, MAiD "does not encompass ... withdrawing or withholding life-prolonging treatment."[29] The withdrawal of life support has a long tradition and certainty of application in very specific situations, mostly when cure is impossible. It allows natural death, but it does not kill the patient; rather the patient succumbs to their disease. Allowing mature minors to choose death is not a well-studied or understood concept and therefore not comparable at all to treatment refusal. Allowing death to occur versus choosing it must remain an important distinction. Furthermore, since the release of this 2018 CCA document, Bill C-7 has been adopted in Canada. MAiD is now being used in all kinds of situations, including for disability and chronic pain, and is soon to be expanded further to psychological suffering. Each of these situations leads to new problems that have been addressed in other chapters of this book.

It is also important to note that we have no precedent of allowing children to refuse all therapy and choose assisted suicide and euthanasia outside the end-of-life context. No jurisdiction in the world allows this. Belgium, which amended its law to allow euthanasia for mature minors, does not allow it for mental illness and restricts access significantly. For example, under the Dutch and Belgian laws, physicians must agree that no other options are left to relieve suffering. However, in Canada, MAiD laws thus far allow a patient to refuse treatment and choose MAiD even outside the end-of-life context. As well, in Belgium, parents need to consent to a child's request for euthanasia for terminal illness. Our Canadian legal framework already allows mature minors to make decisions without parental consent.

Kasper Raus, a bioethicist working in Belgium, summarizes the requirements for mature minor euthanasia in that country in this abbreviated quote:

> The amendment provides that euthanasia is legalized for minors who request euthanasia and are judged to display a capacity of discernment ("oordeelsbekwaamheid" in Dutch) when they are in a "medically futile condition of constant and unbearable physical suffering that cannot be alleviated and that will, within a short period of time, result in death, and results from a serious and incurable disorder caused by illness or accident" (Act amending the Act of 28 May 2002 on euthanasia, sanctioning euthanasia for minors 2014) ... The amendment clearly states that for minors, only physical suffering can be an indication for euthanasia ... The new amendment further provides that the minor's death has to result within a short period of time. The scope of the euthanasia law is thus more restricted for minors. For example, a nineteen-year-old patient suffering from early-stage amyotrophic lateral sclerosis who has a good life-expectancy is entitled to receive euthanasia (provided all other criteria are met), whereas for a (non-emancipated) sixteen-year-old, this would be legally impossible.
>
> It is also important to note that euthanasia is only legal for minors who themselves make multiple and sustained requests that are both voluntary and free of pressure ...
>
> Finally, the new amendment provides that the minors' legal representatives should also consent to the euthanasia, and this consent should be written down and stored in the medical file together with the patients' written consent.[30]

The Belgian law requires parents' written consent and reserves this practice to cases of physical suffering, after all treatments have been exhausted and where death is the expected result of the illness. Given our current framework for MAiD, the current Canadian law regarding mature minors, and the Special Joint Committee recommendations, it is unlikely to be so applied in Canada.

The Canadian government is already planning a legislative rollout of MAiD for mental illness with no changes to the safeguards for this practice in legislation; MAiD for chronic disability and mental illness along with the end-of-life context would likely eventually be included in any extension to mature minors. All the problems related to allowing MAiD in each of these scenarios is discussed in other chapters and would also apply here. And given their young age, mature minors' lives would be prematurely cut short, especially since treatments might be developed that could have extended and improved their quality of life and function in their lost future.

CONCLUSION

Despite serious red flags raised in previous chapters regarding the recklessness of the current MAiD legislation available only to adults, proponents of assisted suicide and euthanasia continue to argue that it is unfair to withhold MAiD from mature minors.

Due to delayed brain maturation, mature minors might not have the demonstrated ability to choose death with sufficient understanding to provide true, informed consent. In terms of relationships to peers and family, MAiD could interfere with parental and guardianship roles and is likely to raise the rate of suicide among Canadian teenagers. Coupled with a lack of international and Canadian evidence on how such an expansion will impact the lives of young people who struggle with ill health, disability, mental health challenges, and suicidality, this extension of MAiD to mature minors is ill-conceived.

While those who urge caution and express concern are told by the government that they must produce evidence of the risks inherent in MAiD for mature minors before it is legalized, the same demand for evidence is not made of the proponents of MAiD for mature minors, even though the consequences of legalization will be irrevocable loss of life. Surely these factors must be considered before involving the state in assisted suicide and euthanasia for mature minors.

NOTES

1 *Bill C-14, An Act to Amend the Criminal Code and to Make Related Amendments to Other Acts (medical assistance in dying)*, 42nd Parliament, 1st Session (2016), SC 2016, c. 3 (Can.), https://www.parl.ca/DocumentViewer/en/42-1/bill/C-14/royal-assent.
2 *Bill C-7, An Act to Amend the Criminal Code (medical assistance in dying)*, 43rd Parliament, 2nd Session (2021), cl. 1(2.1), SC 2021, c. 2 (Can.), https://parl.ca/DocumentViewer/en/43-2/bill/C-7/royal-assent.

3 Special Joint Committee on Medical Assistance in Dying, *Medical Assistance in Dying in Canada: Choices for Canadians*, 44th Parliament, 1st Session, February 2023, https://www.parl.ca/DocumentViewer/en/44-1/AMAD/report-2.
4 "Special Joint Committee on Medical Assistance in Dying," 44th Parliament, 1st Session, 8 April 2022, https://www.parl.ca/Committees/en/AMAD.
5 *Meeting of the Special Joint Committee on Medical Assistance in Dying – Evidence*, 44th Parliament, 1st Session (4 November 2022), https://parl.ca/DocumentViewer/en/44-1/AMAD/meeting-25/evidence.
6 "Remarks by Dr. Ramona Coelho," in *Meeting of the Special Joint Committee on Medical Assistance in Dying – Evidence*, 44th Parliament, 1st Session (30 May 2022), 19:40 (Ramona Coelho), https://parl.ca/DocumentViewer/en/44-1/AMAD/meeting-10/evidence#Int-11717369.
7 *Carter v. Canada (Attorney General)*, 2015 SCC 5, [2015] 1 SCR 331, para. 127.
8 Ibid., para. 24.
9 Ibid., para. 111.
10 *A.C. v. Manitoba (Director of Child and Family Services)*, 2009 SCC 30, [2009] 2 SCR 181 (Can.).
11 Ibid., para. 143.
12 Minister of Health to Special Committee on Medical Assistance in Dying, "Implementation of Bill C-7," 20 October 2022, https://www.parl.ca/content/Committee/441/AMAD/GovResponse/RP11995101/441_AMAD_Rpt01_GR/DepartmentOfHealth-e.pdf.
13 Canadian Association of MAiD Assessors and Providers, *The Interpretation and Role of "Reasonably Foreseeable" in MAiD Practice*, February 2022, https://camapcanada.ca/wp-content/uploads/2022/03/The-Interpretation-and-Role-of-22Reasonably-Foreseeable22-in-MAiD-Practice-Feb-2022.pdf.
14 Ibid., 1.
15 Ibid.
16 Mark Tan Kiak Min, "Beyond a Western Bioethics in Asia and Its Implication on Autonomy," *New Bioethics* 23, no. 2 (July 2017): 154–64, 157–8.
17 Aviva L. Katz, Sally A. Webb, and AAP Committee on Bioethics, "Informed Consent in Decision-Making in Pediatric Practice," *Pediatrics* 138, no. 2 (August 2016): e20161485, e7, http://pediatrics.aappublications.org/content/early/2016/07/21/peds.2016-1485.
18 Marie E. Nicolini et al., "Euthanasia and Assisted Suicide of Persons with Psychiatric Disorders: The Challenge of Personality Disorders,"

Psychological Medicine 50, no. 4 (March 2020): 575–82, https://pubmed.ncbi.nlm.nih.gov/30829194/.

19 Amy Hasbrouck, "NDY Canada Explains the Dangers to Disabled Children of 'MAID' Expansion to Minors," Not Dead Yet, 25 August 2017, https://notdeadyet.org/2017/08/ndy-canada-explains-the-dangers-to-disabled-children-of-maid-expansion-to-minors.html.

20 Health Canada, *First Nations Mental Wellness Continuum Framework Summary Report*, January 2015, preamble, https://www.sac-isc.gc.ca/DAM/DAM-ISC-SAC/DAM-HLTH/STAGING/texte-text/mh-health-wellness_continuum-framework-summ-report_1579120679485_eng.pdf.

21 Rod McCormick, "Submission to the Special Joint Committee on MAID re: Bill C-7," 17 May 2022, https://www.ourcommons.ca/Content/Committee/441/AMAD/Brief/BR11765340/br-external/McCormickRoderick-e.pdf.

22 "Child and Youth Mental Health," Canadian Mental Health Association, accessed 6 December 2022, https://ontario.cmha.ca/mental-health/child-and-youth-mental-health/; Madelyn S. Gould et al., "Newspaper Coverage of Suicide and Initiation of Suicide Clusters in Teenagers in the USA, 1988–96: A Retrospective, Population-Based, Case-Control Study," *Lancet* 1, no. 1 (June 2014): 34–43, https://www.thelancet.com/journals/lanpsy/article/PIIS2215-0366(14)70225-1/fulltext.

23 Thomas Niederkrotenthaler et al., "Association of Increased Youth Suicides in the United States with the Release of *13 Reasons Why*," *JAMA Psychiatry* 76, no. 9 (May 2019): 933–40, https://jamanetwork.com/journals/jamapsychiatry/fullarticle/2734859; Becky Mars et al., "Predictors of Future Suicide Attempt among Adolescents with Suicidal Thoughts or Non-Suicidal Self-Harm: A Population-Based Birth Cohort Study," *Lancet Psychiatry* 6, no. 4 (March 2019): 327–37, https://www.thelancet.com/journals/lanpsy/article/PIIS2215-0366(19)30030-6/fulltext.

24 Mike Vlasvled, "Canada's First Pediatric Palliative Care Residency Program Housed at CHEO," *CityNews*, 17 November 2021, https://ottawa.citynews.ca/2021/11/17/canadas-first-pediatric-palliative-care-residency-program-to-be-housed-at-cheo-4767176/.

25 "Canadian Network of Palliative Care for Children," Canadian Hospice Palliative Care Association, 2020, accessed 6 December 2022, https://www.chpca.ca/projects/canadian-network-of-palliative-care-for-children/.

26 Canadian Association of Suicide Prevention to Canadian Psychiatric Association, "CPA's Discussion Paper on Medical Assistance in Dying 'MAID,'" 20 November 2021, https://static1.squarespace.com/static/5ec97e1c4215f5026a674116/t/619bc64ac482815740760931/

1637598795070/Letter+to+CPA+re+Discussion+Paper+on+MAiD+%282021+11+20%29.pdf.
27 The Expert Panel Working Group on MAID for Mature Minors, *The State of Knowledge on Medical Assistance in Dying for Mature Minors* (Ottawa: Council of Canadian Academies, 2018), https://cca-reports.ca/wp-content/uploads/2018/12/The-State-of-Knowledge-on-Medical-Assistance-in-Dying-for-Mature-Minors.pdf.
28 Ibid.
29 Canadian Medical Association, "CMA Policy – Medical Assistance in Dying," 2017, 6–7, https://policybase.cma.ca/flipbook?pdfUrl=%2Fmedia%2FPolicyPDF%2FPD17-03.pdf.
30 Kasper Raus, "The Extension of Belgium's Euthanasia Law to Include Competent Minors," *Journal of Bioethical Inquiry* 13, no. 2 (June 2016): 305–15, 307, https://pubmed.ncbi.nlm.nih.gov/26842904/.

CONCLUSION

Insights on Canada's MAiD Expansion: Is This About Autonomy or Privilege?

K. Sonu Gaind, Ramona Coelho, and Trudo Lemmens

Canada has often been seen (and likes to see and present itself) as a beacon of thoughtful deliberation and balance in a turbulent world. The "made in Canada" brand aims to reflect a strong commitment to human rights and social justice and a measured yet forward moving sensibility as we embrace an evolving society responsive to our shared humanity and ideals. Yet as the numerous authors of this volume have attested to, it is questionable whether "MAiD in Canada" lives up to these aspirations, or abandons them.

As co-editors of this volume, we each bring different perspectives and personal belief systems to the complex issue of societally sanctioned assisted or hastened death. This should be expected when it comes to societal topics as complex and multifactorial as facilitated suicide and euthanasia, or as Canada reframed the term in 2016, medical assistance in dying (MAiD). Notwithstanding our varied perspectives, we all agree that the path to MAiD in Canada has not followed the robust process most would expect "made in Canada" policies to emerge through, resulting in serious flaws in our MAiD regime with literal life or death consequences. Unfortunately, as detailed by many of this book's authors, these flaws disproportionately endanger the lives of the most marginalized and vulnerable Canadians, raising serious social justice and human rights concerns.

EVER-EXPANDING EXPANSION

A recap of the evolution of Canada's MAiD framework shows the gaps in process that have propelled us to where we are now.

As explored through the chapters of this book, Canada's assisted dying regime has seen a remarkable expansion in an unusually short time. Canada's first assisted dying law came into place in 2016 under Bill C-14, and for the first few years included a safeguard requiring the person's natural death to be reasonably foreseeable. Even with this initial safeguard, Canada immediately became one of the most liberal assisted dying regimes in the world, since, under the regulations that are unique to Canada, people did not need to have had access to "due care" or standard treatments prior to receiving MAiD, and physicians did not have to agree that there were no other options left to relieve suffering. While the foreseeable death safeguard alluded to some element of terminality, even this requirement was quite broad and interpreted even more broadly, allowing those with several years of life (even up to a decade) left to receive MAiD. Under this regime, some Canadians were already receiving MAiD for age and frailty.

Canada's initial liberal MAiD policies under Bill C-14 were quickly mirrored in our country's rising MAiD numbers (which Health Canada has termed "growth"). This dramatic "growth" was unprecedented and unparalleled, with no other country on the planet showing such a rise of assisted dying numbers in the first few years after introduction of their assisted death laws. With the law in place for less than half a dozen years, by 2021 over ten thousand Canadians were receiving MAiD annually.

In 2021, the Liberal government chose to expand national MAiD law further under Bill C-7, after declining to appeal the 2019 *Truchon* case in which a single Quebec judge ruled that the reasonably foreseeable death safeguard breached the *Canadian Charter of Rights and Freedoms* (a ruling that would not have had force outside that province and had primarily persuasive authority in the province). Expansion under Bill C-7 created a "track 2" for those whose deaths were not reasonably foreseeable, opening assisted death pathways for any adult with a disability and an irreversible decline of capability. At the same time, the government removed some key safeguards (including eliminating any reflection period for those whose death is reasonably foreseeable – which includes people with otherwise still years left to live), and committed to providing assisted suicide and euthanasia for sole mental illness conditions by 2023. This further expansion to mental illness was subsequently twice delayed at the last minute, first until 2024, and subsequently to the currently planned date of 2027.

With Bill C-7's removal of the initial reasonably foreseeable death safeguard in 2021, the term "MAiD" that Canada coined in 2016 became a misnomer. While "medical assistance in dying" could describe the process of aiding those in the process of dying to induce death, it is not an apt description for providing death to those who are not otherwise dying. Following Bill C-7's expansion of assisted death to those with disabilities who are not dying, Canada's regime more accurately became a medically administered death or medically assisted suicide regime.

The assisted death numbers continued to rise in 2022, showing another over 30 per cent increase. By 2022, less than a decade after assisted death laws were first introduced, over thirteen thousand Canadians were receiving state-facilitated deaths annually, reflecting 4.1 per cent of all Canadian deaths and 5.5 per cent and 6.6 per cent of all deaths in British Columbia and Quebec, respectively. Over one-third of those receiving assisted death cited feeling like a burden on families as a cause of the suffering fuelling their requests, over half cited loss of dignity, and almost one-fifth cited loneliness. A concerning gender gap also started to emerge, with disproportionate numbers of women receiving MAiD on the newly created track 2.

We expect this high-level overview and unparalleled rise in numbers alone would give many pause or at least reason to reflect prior to considering even further expansion of assisted dying laws, given concerns some were already receiving MAiD fuelled by social suffering. Yet at this time, the Canadian government seems intent on pushing ahead with even further expansion to legalize assisted suicide and euthanasia for sole mental illness conditions by 2027. Meanwhile, it continues to consider introducing assisted death for mature minors (potentially with no lower age limit) and further expanding assisted death based on advance requests, particularly for persons with Alzheimer's disease. And as discussed, the option of a waiver of final consent, combined with expansive interpretation in professional guidance, already introduced some form of advance request in 2021.

Rather than modelling a beacon of thoughtful deliberation and balance, Canada has become the proverbial canary in the coal mine, a cautionary tale for the rest of the world to avoid.

PROPELLED BY IDEOLOGY

How, and why, has this happened?

From 2016 to present we have seen three different ministers of justice and three different ministers of health, and changes in the minister of mental health and addictions. The policies planning MAiD expansions to those with disabilities and those with sole mental illness, with Bill C-7 initially drafted in 2020, were passed as Canadians and the world were adjusting to a worldwide pandemic. From what we have seen and our intimate knowledge of the process, Canada's assisted death expansion has been driven by ideology verging on zealotry, often with the explicit rejection or denial of evidence, as has been documented in this volume.

Hints of this can be seen through unusually broad national decisions, like the federal government's decision to neither appeal, nor refer to the Supreme Court, the question of whether the initial reasonably foreseeable natural death safeguard was constitutional. This includes inexplicable changes in federal policy direction that were not based on any new evidence nor demonstration of safety regarding assisted death expansion.

For example, on a now archived Government of Canada Department of Justice webpage defending the safeguards contained in Bill C-14, the Justice Department previously explained that "although Carter was the impetus for Bill C-14 and sets out the constitutional principles that have informed the development of the legislation, the question is not whether the Bill 'complies with Carter' but rather, whether it complies with the Charter."[1] Regarding reasonably foreseeable death in particular, the authors write: "Bill C-14, through the definition of 'grievous and irremediable medical condition' in s. 241.2(2), restricts medical assistance in dying to individuals whose 'natural death has become reasonably foreseeable'... While some constitutional experts have taken the position that the restriction is constitutional, others have expressed the opposite view based on the fact that the words in s. 241.2(2)(d) do not appear in the Carter decision. The Government's position is that Bill C-14 is fully consistent with the Charter."

At the time, the Department of Justice explicitly rejected a broad assisted death regime, writing: "The first category, which represents the majority of the regimes, restricts medical assistance in dying to individuals whose natural death is approaching...most of these regimes limit eligibility to terminally ill patients who have less than 6 months to live. The second category is based more broadly on providing relief from unbearable suffering, without regard to whether the person is on a path towards death. Only three jurisdictions in the world have enacted this latter type of regime – the Netherlands, Belgium and Luxembourg (Benelux). Based on the range of views on the relative risks and benefits of the two types of regimes, the Government has concluded that a Benelux-style model would frustrate its objectives."

The department acknowledged expert opinion about "the wide range of circumstances that can cause suffering and that can render individuals vulnerable – social isolation, poverty, grief, discrimination, fears about the future and about being burden on others, etc. Because of the subtle and hard-to-detect ways in which vulnerability can compromise autonomy, these experts have argued that permitting medical assistance in dying as a response to suffering in life would pose unacceptable risks that could not be adequately addressed through any system of safeguards. Experts from Benelux jurisdictions have pointed to recent developments in those jurisdictions, including increasing rates of euthanasia, the expansion of eligibility and increases in suicide rates, and have argued that permitting medically assisted dying outside the end-of-life context leads to the normalization of suicide."

Finally, the Department of Justice concluded that they were "adopting an approach that is closer to existing end-of-life models than to the Benelux approach – a model that restricts eligibility to individuals who are declining toward death, allowing them to choose a peaceful death as opposed to a prolonged, painful or difficult one. At the same time, the flexible 'reasonably foreseeable death' standard, and the absence of a specific 'time remaining before death' requirement, make Bill C-14 broader than existing end-of-life regimes. *This represents the best and most responsible model for Canada unless and until robust and reliable data, gathered in the Canadian context, can offer sufficient assurance that expansion beyond this approach would not put vulnerable Canadians at risk.*"[2]

It is hard to know what to make of such a drastic change in position, when in the absence of any such evidence that expansion "would not put vulnerable Canadians at risk," and in fact despite known evidence of vulnerable Canadians getting MAiD, the same government chose not to appeal *Truchon* and, without any case of mental illness being before the courts in either *Carter* or *Truchon*, chose to push for even further expansion to assisted suicide for sole mental illness, now planned for 2027.

Our only explanation is that ideology has pushed our present and planned assisted death expansions, to the disregard of evidence and caution.

NOT EVERYONE'S AUTONOMY

A narrowing echo chamber of prominent expansion promoters can be seen increasingly guiding national policy decisions over recent years. As discussed earlier, some of them had already been pushing for broad legalization of assisted dying prior to *Carter,* in support of the plaintiffs in *Carter,* and then immediately following the case.

After introducing Bill C-14 in 2016, the government tasked the Council of Canadian Academies (CCA) with issuing reports on three key areas: MAiD for mental illness, mature minors, and advance directives. These CCA panels included approximately fifty experts between them, with a range of expertise and views. The 2018 CCA report on mental illness explicitly identified five key areas of continued disagreement and continued lack of evidence. After hastily deciding in 2021 to add a last minute "sunset clause" to Bill C-7, to ensure assisted suicide and euthanasia for sole mental illness would be legal by 2023 (first extended to 2024 and now extended to 2027), the government selected a twelve-member expert panel (which did not include any former CCA panelists who had expressed caution about expansion) to provide guidance on protocols for implementing assisted suicide for mental illness. This panel recommended no additional legislative safeguards prior to expanding MAiD to mental illness. Two members of this 2022 expert panel resigned and publicly cited the panel chair's known activism for MAiD expansion as a process flaw.

After facing pressure and being forced to delay the planned 2023 mental illness expansion to 2024 (now pushed further back to 2027), the government appointed a six-member panel, again composed largely of prominent MAiD expansion promoters, to construct a MAiD *Model Practice Standard.* Unlike virtually everywhere else in the world, where practitioners are restricted or discouraged from raising the option of assisted dying unless it is raised by the patient to avoid unduly pressuring suffering patients' decisions for death, the standard adopted by Health Canada requires every practitioner to "advise the person of the potential for MAID, or provide an effective referral/transfer of care to another practitioner or program known to be willing to discuss eligibility for MAID" unless they have somehow already determined that MAiD is not "consistent with the person's values and goals of care."

The messaging and consequences are clear. Rather than being an option of last resort to compassionately help Canadians avoid painful deaths, the ideology fuelling Canada's assisted death expansion reflects a zealous, narrow vision that assisted suicide and euthanasia should be offered as broadly as possible as an "autonomous choice" of the individual. Rather than seeing the remarkably rapid rise in MAiD numbers in a few short years – close to 7 per cent of some province's total deaths – as a potential reason to reflect or pause prior to further expansion, some expansion activists have suggested the lower percentages in other provinces are the problem. This may explain Health Canada's blasé description of Canada exceeding thirteen thousand annual deaths in 2022 as reflecting a "steady" growth rate of over 30 per cent year over year. This push to the broadest possible "access" for MAiD is echoed by MAiD expansion promoters, reflecting the sentiment that "there can be better and worse deaths and that we can and should fight to ensure the best death possible for everyone."[3] This focus on "dying with dignity" embeds highly privileged assumptions that the person is making a fully autonomous choice, having had options to live with dignity, in seeking MAiD.

Those promoting broad MAiD expansion have acknowledged that "people getting MAID are actually very privileged. They're white. They're well off. They're highly educated. They're not in institutions. They have families. The picture is one of privilege."[4] When faced with pending death, we know that some people do view MAiD as an autonomous choice to avoid a painful death. Unfortunately, these same expansion proponents perpetuate systemic discrimination by turning a blind eye to other life suffering that fuels MAiD requests in those who have not had the chance to live a life of privilege.

There are many reasons people may request assistance to die. As assisted suicide expands further and further away from near end-of-life situations, more and more life suffering, including poverty, homelessness, isolation, other social distress, and elder and financial abuse may drive motivations for MAiD. As illustrated through the chapters of this book, ableism, ageism, sexism, and racism risk fuelling assisted dying requests of the most marginalized and disenfranchised Canadians who are not otherwise dying. Whether Canadians think it appropriate for our national policies to provide state-facilitated death to escape such life and social suffering is a question for each reader to reflect upon for themselves; for our part, we are concerned about the blind spots displayed in Canada's MAiD expansion to date, which largely ignore or actively deny that our most vulnerable fellow Canadians' lives are risked by our policies of MAiD expansion. And we are concerned that policy-makers and parliamentarians have allowed the process to be hijacked by overly zealous promoters of MAiD as a cure-all for suffering, while remaining silent about the obvious conflicts of interest facing politicians attempting to balance budgets when assisted suicide generates savings compared to health care and social support.

FINALLY A PAUSE TO REFLECT: TIME TO STEP BACK?

At this time the Canadian government remains intent on expanding MAiD further to sole mental illness by 2027. With more Canadians learning about the complex issues involved with wide MAiD provision and understanding that different people seek MAiD for different reasons, many more are raising concerns about this expansion. As one of us (Gaind) testified in November 2023 in the AMAD Special Joint Parliamentary Committee hearings reviewing whether Canada was ready for expanding MAiD to mental illness, Canada's MAiD expansion has been less of a slippery slope and more of a runaway train. Like the Lac-Mégantic disaster, the warning signs are there; the question is whether policy-makers will put the brakes on this runaway train.[5] And for the first time since Canada legalized MAiD, the AMAD parliamentary committee recommended against further expansion and concluded Canada should indefinitely pause its planned MAiD expansion to mental illness (note that while the committee recommended an indefinite pause, the Canadian government legislated a three-year delay, until 2027, before expanding MAiD to mental illness).

The AMAD committee made its recommendation due to concerns regarding the inability to predict irremediability of mental illness, inability to distinguish suicidality from other motivations fuelling psychiatric MAiD requests, and risks posed to marginalized populations seeking MAiD for social suffering or lack of access to care. While these concerns were most clearly demonstrable and undeniable related to mental illness, the Canadian experience shows that these same issues are also cause for concern in track 2 cases already being conducted under Canada's existing Bill C-7 expansion. Even prominent MAiD expansion activists acknowledge this, but instead of advising caution as a result they use this to support their contention that MAiD should be further expanded to mental illness since the areas of concern already exist for track 2. For example, the mental illness expert panel chair, Mona Gupta, explicitly acknowledged in her testimony that "there are many medical conditions for which prognostication is difficult, if not impossible" under track 2, but suggested the fact that "no physician has been prosecuted and not a single successful college complaint has been made" implied there were no problems and that Canada should proceed with expansion of MAiD for mental illness.[6] Meanwhile, the social suffering and lack of access to care fuelling motivations leading to some Canadians being provided state-facilitated suicide through our MAiD regime is drawing increasing international scrutiny.[7]

In countries that are now debating or contemplating the introduction of some form of assisted suicide or euthanasia, those supporting legalization increasingly feel the need to distinguish their proposals from the Canadian approach, while those opposed hold it up as a mirror for what happens when these practices become normalized. For example, when the Jersey government recently requested that its legislative assembly approve plans for two forms of assisted dying, the state assembly members firmly rejected a Canadian-style second route of assisted dying for suffering outside the end-of-life context, opting to only move forward with a narrow terminal illness model.[8] And in other jurisdictions, commentators and parliamentarians have also indicated they want to stay away from what is happening in Canada.

This all begs the provocative question: As we expand and continue to broaden eligibility for assisted suicide in Canada, are we expanding autonomy, or are we perpetuating privilege? The insights of the authors of this book suggest that the answer is perhaps different for different people and groups. The main drivers pushing MAiD expansion have been persons of privilege trying to remove what they consider "barriers" to more accessible and easier state-facilitated "painless death." However, these "barriers" act as safeguards to prevent other more vulnerable people from being enticed to state-facilitated death through MAiD as a way to escape demoralization, internalized oppression, being perceived as a burden, and other social distress, sometimes because of problems with access to timely care and support.[9] As Canada has been pushing further and further expansion of state-sponsored and facilitated suicide through its expanding "MAiD" policies, it might have been catering to the privileged few, while providing state-sanctioned death to vulnerable and marginalized Canadians under the guise of false autonomy. It is time to consider whether Canada's MAiD expansion has already gone too far and is, in some cases, a form of "social murder."[10]

Fortunately, there are signs that Canadians are slowly realizing this. Particularly in the last couple of years, we have witnessed a shift in the media reporting on MAiD, with more and more critical reports coming out about some of the problematic components of Canada's MAiD practice, many of which have been discussed in this volume. The AMAD parliamentary report's recommendation was, in fact, the first time since 2016 that a federal committee explicitly recommended restraint, rather than full-steam expansion. This may suggest that there is a momentum for a more thoughtful reflection and reconsideration. An entire issue of the *Canadian Journal of Disability Studies* was recently dedicated to memorialize testimonies of experts and those with disabilities cautioning against track 2 MAiD expansion, with professor emerita, disability advocate, and former chief human rights commissioner of Ontario Catherine Frazee providing insightful commentary emphasizing that "future historians will have to probe well below the surface veneer of MAiD to offer an accurate rendering of disability rights opposition, which, although vigorously discounted as hyperbolic and irrational, has instead been substantive, consistent, principled and evidence-based."[11]

It would, indeed, reveal remarkable hubris for our policy-makers and professional organizations not to take stock of the growing national and international critique of our untrammeled MAiD practice. We hope our book contributes to a much-needed critical reflection, reorientation, and resetting of our national policies.

NOTES

1 "Legislative Background: Medical Assistance in Dying (Bill C-14) – Addendum," Government of Canada, 2016, https://www.justice.gc.ca/eng/rp-pr/other-autre/addend/index.html.
2 Ibid. Emphasis added.
3 Jocelyn Downie, "From Prohibition to Permission: The Winding Road of Medical Assistance in Dying in Canada," *HEC Forum* 34 (2022): 321–54, 322, https://link.springer.com/article/10.1007/s10730-022-09488-6.
4 "Testimony of Jocelyn Downie," *Meeting of the Special Joint Committee on Medical Assistance in Dying – Evidence*, 44th Parliament, 1st Session (21 November 2023), 39, https://www.parl.ca/DocumentViewer/en/44-1/AMAD/meeting-39/evidence.
5 "Testimony of K. Sonu Gaind," *Meeting of the Special Joint Committee on Medical Assistance in Dying – Evidence*, 44th Parliament, 1st Session

(28 November 2023), 40, https://www.parl.ca/DocumentViewer/en/44-1/AMAD/meeting-40/evidence.

6 "Testimony of Mona Gupta," *Meeting of the Special Joint Committee on Medical Assistance in Dying – Evidence*, 44th Parliament, 1st Session (7 November 2023), 38, https://www.parl.ca/documentviewer/en/44-1/AMAD/meeting-38/evidence.

7 Gemma Ware and K. Sonu Gaind, "Assisted Dying: Canada Grapples with Plans to Extend Euthanasia to People Suffering Solely from Mental Illness," *Conversation*, 16 May 2024, https://theconversation.com/assisted-dying-canada-grapples-with-plans-to-extend-euthanasia-to-people-suffering-solely-from-mental-illness-230129.

8 Zhara Simpson and Ammar Ebrahim, "Assisted Dying Plans for Terminally Ill Approved," BBC, 22 May 2024, https://www.bbc.com/news/articles/c6ppl7e551do. This vote is in line with the recommendation of an ethics report that was commissioned by the Jersey government to evaluate its proposed models, and which one of us co-authored: Richard Huxtable, Trudo Lemmens, and Alex Mullock, *Assisted Dying in Jersey: Ethical Review* (Jersey: Strategic Policy, Performance and Population, 2023), https://www.gov.je/government/pages/statesreports.aspx?reportid=5744.

9 Ramona Coelho, "Canada's Assisted Dying Regime Should Not Be Expanded to Include Children," *Al Jazeera*, 16 February 2024, https://www.aljazeera.com/opinions/2024/2/16/canadas-assisted-dying-regime-should-not-be-expanded-to-include-children.

10 Karandeep Sonu Gaind, "Rapid Response Re: Assisted Dying: (Un)balancing Safety with Access," *British Medical Journal* 387 (2024): q2382, https://www.bmj.com/content/387/bmj.q2382/rr.

11 Canadian Disability Studies Association, "Medical Assistance in Dying: Resistance in Canada," *Canadian Journal of Disability Studies* 13, no. 2 (August 2024): 1–300, https://cjds.uwaterloo.ca/index.php/cjds/issue/view/47.

Contributors

RAMONA COELHO, MDCM, CCFP, practises family medicine in London, Ontario. She was a home care physician in Montreal, Quebec, before relocating to London. Currently, she cares for a family practice largely composed of people living with disabilities, as well as refugees and groups that suffer marginalization. She was an expert witness before the House and Senate committees examining Bill C-7 as well as an expert before the federal Special Joint Committee on MAID. She is a founding member of Physicians Together with Vulnerable Canadians. She is a senior fellow with the Macdonald-Laurier Institute. She is also a member of the MAiD Death Review Committee, a multidisciplinary committee that assists the Office of the Chief Coroner with the evaluation of public safety issues in relation to MAiD deaths in Ontario.

CATHERINE FERRIER, MD, CCFP (COE), FCFP, is a family physician and holds a certificate of special competence in care of the elderly from the College of Family Physicians of Canada. She has worked for over forty years in the Division of Geriatric Medicine of the McGill University Health Centre (MUHC), where she sees patients suffering from ailments related to aging, especially neurocognitive disorders, as well as specializing in assessment of decision-making capacity. She is assistant professor in the Department of Family Medicine at McGill University.

K. SONU GAIND, MD, FRCP(C), DFAPA, is a professor and governor at the University of Toronto and chief of psychiatry at Sunnybrook Health Sciences Centre. His clinical expertise is psycho-oncology, and he was physician chair of the MAiD team at his former hospital (Humber River Hospital). Dr Gaind sat on the Council of Canadian Academies Expert Panel on MAID and Mental Illness and was retained as an expert in the *Truchon* and *Lamb* cases. He has testified before numerous House and Senate committees on MAID over the past decade. He is a former president of both the Canadian Psychiatric Association and Ontario Psychiatric Association and an honorary member of the World Psychiatric Association.

ISABEL GRANT, BA, LLB, LLM, FRSC, is a professor at the Peter A. Allard School of Law, University of British Columbia. She specializes in criminal law and has published extensively on topics including homicide, violence against women and people with disabilities, and medical assistance in dying. She appeared as an expert witness before the Senate committee examining Bill C-7 and the federal Special Joint Committee on MAID. She is the chair of the Strategic Litigation Committee for Inclusion Canada, a national disability organization, and a fellow of the Royal Society of Canada.

LEONIE HERX, MD, PhD, CHE, CCFP (PC), FCFP, is a clinical professor of palliative medicine in the Cumming School of Medicine, University of Calgary, section chief of pediatric palliative medicine, Alberta Health Services – Calgary Zone, and director of the Rotary Flames House, Children's Hospice and Palliative Care Services in Calgary, Alberta. She is a former president of the Canadian Society of Palliative Care Physicians and was an expert witness before the House and Senate committees examining Bill C-7 and the federal Special Joint Committee on MAID. She is a founding member of Physicians Together with Vulnerable Canadians.

ROLAND M. JONES, PhD, MSc, MBChB, BSc, FRCPsych, is an associate professor in the Division of Psychiatry, University of Toronto. He is a forensic psychiatrist and medical lead for research and fellowships at the Division of Forensic Psychiatry at the Centre for Addiction and Mental Health (CAMH) in Toronto, Canada. He has provided consultation to the Ontario Ministry of Community Safety and Correctional Services and has led research on the measurement of severity of mental disorder in prison settings, factors associated with recidivism, and an appraisal of need for inpatient mental health services in provincial jails in Ontario. His clinical role involves the assessment and treatment of people in forensic mental health and correctional settings, and he serves as an expert witness in criminal courts in Ontario.

TRUDO LEMMENS, LicJur, LLM (*bioethics*), DCL, is a professor and Scholl Chair in Health Law and Policy at the Faculty of Law and the Dalla Lana School of Public Health of the University of Toronto. He was a member of the Council of Canadian Academies Expert Panel on Medical Assistance in Dying and an expert witness for the federal attorney general in the *Truchon* and *Lamb* cases, and he has testified before Canadian, UK, Irish, and Jersey parliamentary committees on issues related to the legalization of euthanasia and assisted suicide. In 2023, he co-authored a report for the Jersey government on the ethical implications of legislative options for assisted dying. He is a member of the MAiD Death Review Committee, a multidisciplinary committee that assists the Office of the Chief Coroner with the evaluation of public safety issues in relation to MAiD deaths in Ontario.

HONOURABLE GRAYDON NICHOLAS, CM, ONB, LLD, is an attorney, judge, and politician who served as the appointed 30th lieutenant governor of New Brunswick (2009–14). He is the first Indigenous person to hold the office, to be appointed as a provincial court judge (in 1991), and to obtain a law degree in Atlantic Canada. Graydon was appointed co-chair of the New Brunswick Stakeholder Advisory Council to review youth suicide prevention and mental health services in 2021. He is a member of the Wolastoqey Nation.

GABRIELLE PETERS is a disabled writer, researcher, consultant, and policy analyst whose areas of work have included health, urban planning, poverty elimination, housing, and climate change. She is co-founder of Dignity Denied and the Disability Filibuster, two groups formed around opposition to the expansion of MAiD. Gabrielle was lead author of the Broadbent Institute's submission for BC Accessibility legislation. Her map of the development of modern Western ableism is a work in progress and part of the materials she creates for those interested in developing anti-ableist practice and policy. Gabrielle's writing has been published in *Maclean's* magazine, CBC, and other publications. She does most of this work while reclining, propped up on her collapsing couch in social housing. She is guided by the enormous debt she feels to disabled people who fought before her and a sense of obligation to those who will come after her.

DEREK B.M. ROSS, LLB, LLM, is the executive director and general counsel for Christian Legal Fellowship (CLF), a national association of legal professionals that intervened in the *Carter* and *Truchon* litigation. He has acted for public interest interveners in a number of cases involving the *Canadian Charter of Rights and Freedoms*, appearing at all levels of court including the Supreme Court of Canada. He has also appeared before legislative and parliamentary committees to present on legal and constitutional issues related to assisted death. He is a centre associate with the University of British Columbia's Centre for Constitutional Law and Legal Studies and has published a number of articles on freedom of conscience, law and religion, human rights, and assisted death.

AYAL SCHAFFER, MD, FRCPC, is a psychiatrist at Sunnybrook Health Sciences Centre and a professor in the Department of Psychiatry at the University of Toronto. His research mainly focuses on bipolar disorder, suicide prevention, and their intersection. Dr Schaffer is the vice president of research of the International Society for Bipolar Disorders, board member of the Canadian Network for Mood and Anxiety Treatments, and deputy editor of the *Canadian Journal of Psychiatry*.

MARY SHARIFF, BSC, LLB, LLM, PhD, is a professor in the Faculty of Law at the University of Manitoba, where she also held two associate dean positions. She has written numerous scholarly and popular articles on physician-assisted death (including MAiD) and the right to palliative care and has particular expertise in assisted death from a comparative law perspective. She was an expert witness in the *Carter* case and has presented on assisted death to numerous organizations and expert committees. She sits as a commissioner on the Manitoba Law Reform Commission and is the director of the Master of Human Rights program, housed within the Faculty of Law at the University of Manitoba.

ALEXANDER SIMPSON, MBChB, BMedSci, FRANZCP, FCPA, is a professor in the Department of Psychiatry at the University of Toronto and the chair in Forensic Psychiatry at UofT/CAMH. He was co-chair of the MAiD Committee at CAMH from 2016 to 2021. He has written extensively on MAiD, with particular emphasis on MAiD and mental illness, and the impact of MAiD in correctional settings. He is a co-investigator in a qualitative study of patient and family perspectives on MAiD and mental illness.

MARK SINYOR, MSC, MD, FRCPC, is a psychiatrist at Sunnybrook Health Sciences Centre and an associate professor in the Department of Psychiatry at the University of Toronto. His research mainly focuses on population-level strategies for suicide prevention with an emphasis on how media messaging impacts suicide. Dr Sinyor is the International Association for Suicide Prevention's "Partnerships for Life" lead for the Americas and lead author of the Canadian Psychiatric Association (CPA) guidelines on responsible media reporting about suicide.

Index

abandonment: of children with disabilities, 234; fear of, 246; of patient, 118, 122, 169; of standard/duty of care, 79, 122, 131, 135–7, 153

abled-disabled, 208, 236, 238

ableism: assumptions about inferiority, 105; "better dead than disabled," 257, 295, 305, 307, 334; definitions of, 219–20, 299; among doctors, 159, 193–5; and health disparity, 242; invisibility of, 299–300; in MAiD law, 115; and medical care, 136; modern Western, 219, 220, 231; scientific, 221; and suffering, 246–7, 301–2

abortion and MAiD, 106

abuse: of children, 478; and death wishes, 153, 195; financial, 195; of persons with disabilities, 251, 257; in residential schools, 282; of seniors, 195, 461

access: to care and irremediability/intolerable suffering, 188, 437; to care and MAiD requests, 44, 81, 88, 494–5; to health care, 157; to health care for children, 480; to health care for Indigenous peoples, 279, 285, 479–80; to health care in remote communities, 284, 480; to housing, 32, 173, 240; to MAiD, 38, 41–2, 156, 399, 495; to mental health/psychiatric care, 62, 87, 190; to palliative care, 32–3, 39–40, 172–80, 298, 480; to public life, 241; to resources and supports, 189, 219, 238, 310; to standard care, 39, 488; to state assistance, 240; to treatment and choice, 78. *See also* accessibility

accessibility: and alienation, 241; and costs, 240; in housing, 239, 294, 296, 312; in jobs, 241; in public spaces, 244; and suffering, 246

Accessible Canada Act, 243

accommodations, 41, 235

accountability: of doctors, 127; of provinces, 389, 390

Act Respecting End-of-Life Care, 175, 382, 394, 416, 453. *See also* Bill 11; Quebec EOL law

A.C. v. Manitoba, 475

addiction, 285, 331

adolescents, 475, 477. *See also* mature minors; teenagers

advance care planning, 457–8
advance directives: and consent, 459; and dementia, 461; for MAiD, 44, 324n50; in the Netherlands, 454–6; positive versus negative, 459; provincial laws on, 458; use of, 457–8. *See also* advance care planning; advance requests
advance requests: for MAiD, 133, 415n96, 451–8, 460–3, 468; and waiver of consent, 35, 44. *See also* advance care planning; advance directives
ageism, 89, 463
aiding or abetting suicide: impact of decriminalizing, 306, 309, 310; and MAiD, 13, 26, 303, 385; unconstitutionality of prohibition on, 19
Aktion T4 program, 223
Alberta, 156, 281–2, 381
Alberta Court of Appeal (ABCA), 341–3, 345–9
altruism, 211, 316
Alzheimer's disease, 323n50, 343, 354–5, 460. *See also* dementia
AMAD Special Joint Parliamentary Committee. *See* Special Joint Committee on Medical Assistance in Dying (AMAD) (2021)
ambiguity, 420
American Academy of Pediatrics, 477
American Medical Association, 156
American Psychiatric Association, 80–1, 85
Americans with Disabilities Act (ADA), 243–4
Angelou, Maya, 88

Anishinaabe culture, 220
Annual Report on Medical Assistance in Dying, 175, 177, 246
assault, 127, 456
assessment period, 35–6, 42, 132
assessments: arbitrariness in, 82, 89; and capacity, 134, 336–7; of irremediability, 66–7; by palliative physicians, 179; requirement for two, 27, 35, 188. *See also* assessment period
assisted dying: terminology, 13, 100, 369n42
Assisted Human Reproduction Act Reference, 399
assisted suicide (as distinct from euthanasia), 13, 100
Association des médecins psychiatres du Québec (AMPQ), 72, 75, 82, 417
Association of Chairs of Psychiatry in Canada, 85, 417
Association québécoise des soins palliatifs, 175
Australasia, 100
Australia, 42, 189, 147n68
autism, 140, 331, 359–60n7
autonomy: as basis for MAiD, 101–3, 313; beliefs about, 206–8, 210, 222; constitutively relational, 209; degrees of, 214–15; as discussed in *Carter*, 129–30, 308, 338; as discussed in *Truchon*, 350, 395; and formal equality, 314; and informed consent, 118; limits on, 316; myth of, 206, 240; and oppression, 207; and power, 233; and principles of medical care, 438; prioritization of, 254,

423, 462; and privilege, 487, 493; and vulnerability, 464

Baudouin, Christine, 28, 63–4, 350–2

Belgium: advance euthanasia directives in, 453, 456; euthanasia as a last resort, 130; euthanasia for mature minors in, 481–2; euthanasia for psychiatric disorders in, 298, 478; euthanasia when death not reasonably foreseeable, 298, 490; as inspiration for Canadian MAiD regime, 3–4, 14; problems with euthanasia practice in, 14, 19, 21, 343–4

Benelux countries, 100, 101, 432, 478, 490–1. See also Belgium; Luxembourg; Netherlands

Bill 7, 295

Bill 11, 394, 398, 453. See also *Act Respecting End-of-Life Care*; Quebec EOL law

Bill C-7: and choice, 312–15; and cost savings, 199; and Disability Filibuster, 159, 194; goals of, 112–13; impact on Indigenous peoples of, 286–8; Indigenous engagement on, 277–80; and MAiD tracks, 35–6, 488; and mental illness, 12, 67–9, 72, 113, 297; and number of deaths, 44; parliamentary hearings on, 193–4; passing of, 33–5, 84; and reflection period, 38, 177–8; and removal of safeguards, 277, 488; and RFND criterion, 296–7, 488–9; and risk of premature death, 12; and s. 1 of the *Charter*, 311–12; and s. 7 of the *Charter*, 308–11; and s. 15 of the *Charter*, 302–8; and *Truchon*, 111–12; and United Nations obligations, 333–4; and waiver of consent, 452

Bill C-14, 26–7; and *Carter*, 334; constitutionality of, 368–9n38, 490; and federalism, 386–7; and freedom of conscience/religion, 152; goals of, 26; and Indigenous engagement, 279; and mental illness, 61, 64; no requirement to access treatments to alleviate suffering in, 488; and number of deaths, 43; and RFND requirement, 28, 363n18, 376–7n142, 488, 491; and *Truchon*, 349–50, 367n35

Bill C-62, 113, 356–7n2

Bill C-314, 86, 356n2

billing, 173

Bloc Québécois, 32, 34, 35, 113, 279

bodily integrity, 130, 310

Bourbonnais, Raymond, 191

brain maturation, 474, 483

British Columbia: advance directives in, 458; percentage of euthanasia deaths in, 43, 489; and Provincial-Territorial Expert Advisory Group on Physician-Assisted Dying, 23; racism in health care in, 284–5; sterilization legislation in, 281

British Columbia Aboriginal Network on Disability Society, 279

British Columbia Civil Liberties Association, 18

British Columbia Court of Appeal, 21, 402

British Columbia Supreme Court, 18, 334, 337, 348
British Poor Laws, 229
budgets, 84, 173, 199, 218, 494
bullying, 474, 478
burden, perception of being a: and ableism, 217; and children, 478; and disabled people, 194, 235, 237, 254, 302; impact of MAiD on, 310–11, 434; as motivation for MAiD, 169, 196, 215, 245–6, 313; and prohibition against assisted suicide, 16; as source of suffering, 197, 489; and vulnerability, 468
burnout, 179, 181, 284

California, 44
Canada (Attorney General) v. E.F., 341–2
Canada (Attorney General) v. PHS Community Services Society, 385
Canada Health Act, 388–90
Canada Health Care Act, 173
Canadian Association for Suicide Prevention (CASP): and call for pause on MAiD expansion, 85; and criticism of Canadian Psychiatric Association, 70; and effective referrals, 159–60; position on MAiD as assisted suicide, 278, 358n5, 480
Canadian Association of MAiD Assessors and Providers (CAMAP): and bringing up MAiD, 42, 189; and defining mental illness, 140n21; and distinguishing suicidality from MAiD requests, 87; and effective referrals, 155; funding of, 42; and interpretation of RFND, 42, 475; and reflection period, 178
Canadian Bar Association, 35–6
Canadian Journal of Disability Studies, 496
Canadian Medical Association (CMA): and effective referral policy, 156; endorsement of MAiD expansion, 130–1; and Latimer case, 254; and policy change, 37; recognition of distinction between MAiD and palliative care, 170; recognition of distinction between MAiD and withdrawing life support, 481
Canadian Medical Association Journal, 171, 193
Canadian Medical Protective Association, 457
Canadian Psychiatric Association (CPA): advocacy group responses, 78–9; input on Bill C-7, 71–2, 75; input on Bill C-14, 61; member engagement, 60–1, 62–3, 65–6, 70–1; member proposals, 71, 80–1; member survey, 69, 73–4, 82; and Ontario Medical Association survey, 76–7, 80–1; policies of privilege, 78; position statements, 65–7, 69, 70, 71, 77–9; suicide facilitation, 78; support of MAiD for mental illness, 70, 85, 87; task force on MAiD, 61, 62–3; view of MAiD as a constitutional right, 37, 70
Canadian Society of Palliative Care Physicians (CSPCP): and billing, 173; and bringing up MAiD, 179; and conscience protection, 159;

and data on palliative care access, 175; and distinction between MAiD and palliative care, 168, 169–71; position on removing reflection period, 178
Canadian Truth and Reconciliation Commission, 277, 282, 286
capability, irreversible decline of, 114, 126, 133–4, 394, 464
capacity: and advance requests, 402, 451–3, 460; assessments, 79, 461; and consent, 456, 459; and dementia, 132; impact of mental illness on, 336–7, 338, 347, 351–2; influences on, 216; loss of, 27, 112, 133–4, 178; and minors, 473–5, 477, 482; and suicidality, 107. *See also* capability, irreversible decline of; competence
capitalism, 220, 229–32, 252
capital punishment, 16, 106, 427
Carter, Kathleen/Kay, 18, 246–7
Carter v. Canada (AG): assumption about MAiD and suicide, 305; and concurrent jurisdiction, 383; and consent, 127–9, 402; description of MAiD as insurance policy, 306; and doctors' freedom of conscience and religion, 151; evidence before court, 20, 30, 335, 340, 343–5; factual circumstances, 336; justification for overturning *Rodriguez*, 19; and legislative objective, 334, 404; and MAiD for mental illness, 60, 74–6, 336–8, 341, 343–8; and MAiD for minors, 402, 474; and MAiD terminology, 13; and right to die, 102, 121; and s.

7 of the *Charter*, 308–10. *See also* Carter, Kathleen; External Panel on Legislative Options to *Carter v. Canada*; Taylor, Gloria
Catholicism, 24
Centre for Addiction and Mental Health (CAMH), 65
Centre for Wise Practices in Indigenous Health, 287
change of mind, 31, 38, 177–8, 452, 468
Charter of Rights and Freedoms: and *Carter*, 335–41, 343–5, 348; and *E.F.*, 341–2, 347, 348; and right to MAiD, 333–4, 398, 400–1; and *Rodriguez*, 15–16; section 1, 311, 333, 337, 344, 354; section 2(a), 151, 158; section 7, 15, 308–12, 333, 339, 349–50; section 15, 15, 303–8, 312, 333, 349–50; and *Truchon*, 349–52
children: and brain development, 477–8; capacity of, 475; and consent, 254; Indigenous, 220, 282–3, 285, 479–80; MAiD for, 44, 254, 343, 345, 473–4; MAiD in other jurisdictions for, 481–2; and palliative care, 480; relationship with parents, 476; and RFND criterion, 476; and trauma, 478; and violence, 474. *See also* adolescents; mature minors; teenagers
child welfare system, 478, 479, 481
Chochinov, Harvey: Bill C-7 hearing testimony, 178; and dignity therapy, 168–9, 464, 465; and Expert Panel on Options for a Legislative Response to *Carter*, 23; on Royal Society report, 20

choice: and advance requests, 451, 459–60; and capacity, 216–18; and children/young people, 474–80; as a concept, 302, 438–9; and cultural variation, 211; detailed discussion on, 206–10; as discussed in *Carter*, 310, 340; and doctor-patient relationship, 125, 157; influence of mental health on, 39; and limited options, 191–2, 214, 312–15; and MAiD expansionists, 44, 192, 434, 438, 441; and medical ethics, 102, 438–9; and palliative care, 177; and paternalism, 309; and persons with disabilities, 194, 302, 313–14, 316; and poverty, 78, 232–3, 313
chronic illness: in Indigenous people, 286; and MAiD, 31, 119, 302–3; and suicidality, 197; value of lives of persons with, 115, 306
clinical trials, 423, 439
coercion: and adolescents, 475; and doctors bringing up MAiD, 125, 136, 179; and Indigenous people, 278; and MAiD, 34, 194, 213, 216, 313; and section 15 of the *Charter*, 304; structural, 191
cognitive behavioural therapy (CBT), 424
cognitive distortions, 435
collective responsibility, 236
College of Family Physicians of Canada, 168
College of Physicians and Surgeons of Ontario (CPSO), 7, 151–3, 156, 158–9
Colombia, 370n43, 453

colonialism, 158, 220, 278, 281, 285; and suicide rates, 478
Commission on End-of-Life Care (Quebec), 40
Commission spéciale sur la question de mourir dans la dignité (Quebec), 17
Commission sur les soins de fin de vie, 452
community: living, 84, 190, 239, 241; supports, 80, 189
compassion, 16, 101–2, 104–5, 249
compassionate communities, 466
compassionate homicide, 17. *See also* mercy killings
competence: and autonomy, 102–3; and *Carter*, 346, 402; and dementia, 454–5; of the individual versus the state, 216–17; regulation of determinations of, 388; and right to refuse treatment, 119. *See also* capacity
competing interests, 461. *See also* conflicts of interest
conflicts of interest, 84, 461, 494. *See also* competing interests
connectedness, 106, 464, 479
conscience, freedom of: advocacy for protection of, 159; and bringing up MAiD, 152; and discrimination, 160–1; and effective referrals, 122, 152–6, 158–61; importance of, 153–4, 155–6, 159, 161; and patient access to MAiD, 156, 161; protected by the *Charter*, 151; recognized in *Carter*, 151; and religion, 158. See also *Charter of Rights and Freedoms*
conscientious objection, 25, 41, 76, 122, 152–3

consent: and advance requests, 451–3, 457–60; and *Carter*, 402; and children, 473–4, 475, 482; doubts about, 455; elements of, 456–7; manufactured, 70; no treatment without, 119, 121, 456; parental, 482; requirements under track 2, 35; and role of doctors, 138; as a safeguard, 346; and section 14 of *Criminal Code*, 403; waiver of under track 1, 35, 44, 112, 452. *See also* capacity; informed consent
consequences, ability to understand and appreciate, 132, 475
consequentialist theory, 418
Conservative Party, 23, 25, 32, 35
Constitution Act 1867: division of powers, 384; section 91, 403; section 92, 386, 393, 400
Constitution Act 1982. See Charter of Rights and Freedoms
constitutional right to MAiD, 36–7, 41, 121, 310, 398. *See also Charter of Rights and Freedoms*
Convention on the Rights of Persons with Disabilities (United Nations), 112–13, 250, 333, 403, 453
conversion disorder, 342, 348
coroner: British Columbia, 242; Ontario chief, 40, 88
cost/benefit analysis, 214, 229, 247, 248
cost savings, 84, 199, 437
Council of Canadian Academies (CCA): Expert Panel on MAiD for Sole Reasons of Mental Illness, 30, 62, 492; Expert Panel Working Group on Advance Requests for MAID, 452–4, 458;

Expert Panel Working Group on MAiD for Mature Minors, 481; mandate to study MAiD, 27, 62, 492
Council of Canadians with Disabilities, 78, 159
COVID-19: impact on suffering, 190, 199, 284, 295, 462–3; and passage of Bill C-7, 31, 90, 112
Cowley, Kristine, 198
Criminal Code: and Bill C-7, 288, 331; and Bill C-14, 151, 341; definition of MAiD, 13; exemption to, 3, 22, 26, 385; expressive function of, 305; and MAiD for mental illness, 331, 401; and provincial law, 18, 382, 383, 391, 399; role of, 22, 398; section 14 (consensual homicide), 129, 403; section 222.4 (culpable homicide), 13, 385; section 241 (aiding or abetting suicide), 13, 129; section 245 (provision of noxious substance), 13, 385; voiding of provisions, 22, 129. *See also* aiding or abetting suicide; Bill C-7; Bill C-14; *Charter of Rights and Freedoms*
criminal court, 454
criminal law power: and Bill C-14, 387; and health, 384; intrusion on, 392–3; prohibitory nature of, 396–7, 399; and rights, 397, 413n85. *See also* jurisdiction
criminal liability, 101, 386, 398, 414–15n93

Darwin, Charles, 221, 224, 264–5n51
Darwin, George, 221

death: better than disability, 210–11, 219, 222, 301, 334; Indigenous views on, 279; irreversibility of, 120, 311, 426, 475; penalty, 311–12; as a remedy, 434–5; risk of, 309–10; service, 167. *See also* premature death; wrongful death
decision-making: influences/impact on, 136, 216, 434; and maturity, 477; and mental disorders/illness, 79, 337, 347; process, 430; shared, 118. *See also* autonomy; capacity
decriminalization, 396–401. *See also* criminal law power
deference to legislators, 353
dementia: and advance directives, 453–5, 460–2, 468; and capacity, 132–4; and Carpe Diem initiative, 466–7; description of people with, 324n50; fear of, 452, 467; MAiD data on, 359n7; not a "mental illness" for purposes of MAiD, 359n7; and quality of life, 464; and RFND criterion, 133; and stigma, 462; symptoms of, 465; and waiver of final consent, 133–5
Dene world view, 288
deontology, 418, 444
dependence, financial, 222, 247
dependency: and abuse, 195; and dignity, 302, 463; as a human experience, 227, 464; and MAiD tracks, 88; and suffering, 352, 376n139. *See also* independence; interdependence
depression: and Bill C-7, 113, 159; and capacity, 337; court commentary on MAiD for, 341, 348; influence of on choice to die, 39, 153; rates of in mature minors, 480; symptoms of, 331; treatment of, 423–5
design of society, 230, 245
dignity: and Bill 11/Quebec EOL law, 350, 394, 395; and disability, 239–40; as discussed in *Carter*, 129, 308, 338; as discussed in *Truchon*, 350, 395; dying with, 18, 297, 493; and "euthanasia" terminology, 38; false understandings of, 463; living with, 105, 191, 493; loss of, 215, 246, 302, 463, 489; and MAiD, 214; and palliative care, 167, 169, 177; right to die with, 121; and section 7 of the *Charter*, 308; and section 15 of the *Charter*, 304; therapy, 169, 464–6. *See also* Dignity Denied; Dying with Dignity
Dignity Denied, 78
disabilities, persons with: and Bill C-7, 297; and choice, 302, 313–14, 316; and COVID-19, 295; discrimination against, 114–15, 193, 301, 304–6; and formal vs substantive equality, 313–14; institutionalization of, 226–7, 234, 246, 295, 300; and MAiD for lack of resources, 44, 191–2; and poverty, 78, 189, 240; and pressure to end lives, 433; relationship with doctors, 159, 306; and RFND criterion, 193; and right to life and security of the person, 332; and risk of death, 309–10; and section 7 of the *Charter*, 309–12; and section 15 of the *Charter*, 303–7;

Index

and support for MAiD, 295; and track 2, 114–15; and UN obligations, 113, 333–4; value of lives of, 16, 26, 115, 244, 434; violence against, 251–2, 257. *See also* ableism; disability

disability: as abnormality or flaw; 221, 232, 304; advocates, 28–9, 32, 105, 299, 403; benefits, 205, 222, 239, 243, 247; community, 16, 25, 34, 232, 299; fear of, 207, 215, 228, 234, 300; inclusion, 113, 236; medical model of, 213, 228, 232, 242, 300–2; misconceptions about, 212; rights, 29, 212, 236–7, 496; rights activism, 230; rights defenders, 316; rights groups/organizations, 114, 115, 352, 478; social construction/model of, 221, 232, 301; support services, 32, 35–6, 126, 295, 298

Disability Filibuster, 159, 194, 299

disabled, better dead than, 210–11, 219, 222, 301, 334

disabled people. *See* disabilities, persons with

discrimination: and capitalism, 230; and choice, 313–14; versus contraindication, 440–1; against doctors, 158, 160; by excluding MAiD for mental illness, 33, 66, 106, 307, 440–1; in health care, 193–5, 278, 284–5; against Indigenous people, 278, 279, 285, 289, 478; by limiting MAiD access, 28–9, 38; against people with disabilities, 189, 209, 217, 218, 301; against people with mental illness, 62; protections under international law, 113,

333–4; and track 2 of MAiD, 34, 114, 303–6, 308, 464. *See also* ableism; ageism; racism

doctors: beliefs about quality of disabled lives, 212, 300; duty of care of, 117–18, 131, 153; ethical duties of, 101, 104, 137, 154, 438–41; as gatekeepers to resources, 300; impact of MAiD on, 174, 179, 181; integrity of, 76, 154–5, 157, 179; power over disabled people, 212–13; primary care, 134, 205, 257; relationship with patients, 119, 125, 131, 306; role in lives of disabled people, 243; shortage of, 157, 179. *See also* ableism; conscience, freedom of; doctors; duty of care; effective referrals; fiduciary duty; geriatricians

double aspect doctrine, 396

Downie, Jocelyn, 24, 75

due diligence, 74, 90, 443

Duncan, Donna, 191

duty to die, 211, 254, 311, 434

Dying with Dignity, 30, 88, 178, 253–4

Echaquan, Joyce, 285

economic considerations. *See* cost savings

economy, 222, 230, 235, 463

effective referrals: and discrimination, 158, 160; and freedom of conscience, 152–3, 155–6, 158–61; impact on working environment, 160–1; Ontario court challenge to, 158; opposition to, 25, 152–3, 156, 158; policy on, 41, 122–3, 151, 155

efficiency, 242, 252
elder abuse/neglect, 195, 461, 493
elderly people, 463–4; perceptions about quality of life of, 26, 29, 112. *See also* Alzheimer's disease; dementia; seniors
elders, 245, 461, 468
Elders (Indigenous), 70, 277, 279, 288
Eldridge v. BC (Attorney General), 304
eligibility for MAiD: under Bill C-7, 126, 331; under Bill C-14, 26; and dementia, 133–4; grievous and irremediable, 337, 348; informed consent, 126, 129; intolerable suffering, 420; jurisdiction to regulate, 388; and mature minors, 473–4; meaning of irremediable, 339; medical condition as cause of suffering, 122–3; for mental illness, 338, 343, 347, 352, 382; for neurocognitive disorders, 140n21, 359–60n7, 382; potential, 125, 179; reasonably foreseeable natural death, 135, 192–3; removal of reasonably foreseeable natural death criterion, 349; under track 1, 188, 199; under track 2, 113–14; voluntary request, 124, 131. *See also* assessments
empirical evidence, 417–19, 428–9, 435
end-of-life. *See* reasonably foreseeable natural death
Enlightenment, 220–1
equality: formal, 302, 314; right to, 15, 303–8, 312, 333, 349–50; substantive, 313–14. See also *Charter of Rights and Freedoms*; discrimination; inequality
ethical bases of medicine, 104, 108
ethicists, evidence of in *Carter* trial, 19
ethics: and consent, 456, 460; and freedom to choose, 102, 438–9; principles of, 418; relationship to empirical facts, 417–19, 428–9, 435
eugenics, 220–6, 233–4, 255, 301, 463; and medical profession, 316
euthanasia, 13, 38, 100
existential issues, 169
Expert Advisory Group (EAG) on MAiD, 64–5, 84
expert opinion, 420, 430, 491
Expert Panel on MAiD and Mental Illness, 41, 288, 315, 360n7, 387
External Panel on Options for a Legislative Response to *Carter v. Canada*, 23, 60, 169, 176

fallibility of systems to prevent wrongful deaths, 311, 317
false neutrality, 70
false positives, 427–9, 436, 443
falsifiability, 419
family instability, 285
family responsibility, 229
federalism. *See* jurisdiction; paramountcy
fiduciary duty, 117, 119; and MAiD, 125, 130, 131, 136
Fineman, Martha Albertson, 464
Finkelstein, Vic, 230, 232
First Nations Mental Wellness Continuum Framework Summary Report, 479

Index 515

First Nations peoples, 278, 280, 282, 288. *See also* Indigenous peoples
Fisher, R.A., 224
focalism, 212
Foley, Roger, 194
food insecurity, 233, 283–4
foster care, 285. *See also* child welfare system
forced participation in MAiD, 153, 160, 161. *See also* conscience, freedom of; effective referrals
Fraser v. Canada (Attorney General), 313
Frazee, Catherine, 23, 316, 496
free and democratic society, 333, 354. *See also* Charter of Rights and Freedoms
freedom of choice. *See* choice
freedom of conscience and religion. *See* Charter of Rights and Freedoms; conscience, freedom of; religion, freedom of
frustration of federal law, 384, 389, 396–9
funding of MAiD, 39, 105, 172–3, 313

Gallagher, Romayne, 176
Galton, Francis, 221, 224–6, 255. *See also* eugenics
gender, 72, 87, 297, 305
generational trauma, 279. *See also* intergenerational trauma
genocide, 256, 282–3, 287
geriatricians, 34, 463–4
Gibson, Jennifer, 23
Ginsberg, Mark, 169, 177
Gladu, Nicole, 28, 33, 252–3, 349. See also *Truchon v. Canada (Attorney General)*

Goba, Ruth, 24
good faith, 119, 390
good life, what constitutes, 220, 255
Green Party, 32, 35
grey tsunami, 241
grief, 168–9, 359n7, 491
grievous and irremediable medical condition: as described in MAiD legislation, 26, 113–14, 126, 490; as discussed in *Carter*, 22, 129, 335, 338, 345; as discussed in *E.F.*, 348–9
group think, 429
guardianship, 476, 483
guilt, 195, 462
Gupta, Mona, 41, 82, 85, 87, 495

Halifax Group, 64, 82
Hansen, Rick, 237–8, 243–4
harm/benefit analysis, 43, 418–9, 428, 440. *See also* cost/benefit analysis; risk/benefit analysis
harm reduction, 44, 192, 313
Hawes, Spring, 194
heads of power, 392–3, 396, 400
Health Canada: data, 123, 175–6; public reassurances of, 175, 193, 488, 493; report on MAiD, 38, 39–40, 177. *See also* Canadian Association of MAiD Assessors and Providers; *Model Practice Standard*
Health Canada Framework for Palliative Care in Canada, 167
health care: access, 157; access for Indigenous peoples, 279, 285, 479–80; costs, 199, 242; discrimination in, 193–5, 278, 284–7, 480; diversity in, 161; and hope, 108, 137; inclusivity

of system, 153, 161; MAiD as, 105–6; medically necessary, 383, 388–90; oversight, 438–9; right to, 398; systems, differences in, 454; universal, 204, 249. See also *Canada Health Care Act*; mental health care; palliative care; psychiatric care; treatment

health disparities, 242, 278

hemlock, 100–1

Hemlock Society, 254

Hippocrates, 101

Hippocratic Oath, 153, 438

holistic care, 166, 169

home care: and choice for MAiD, 312, 313; limitations in, 209, 247–8; need for, 17, 175, 194, 296; not an essential service, 173; as prerequisite for MAiD eligibility, 32; underfunding of, 462

homelessness, 122, 493

homicide, 13, 206, 208, 385, 403. See also Criminal Code; compassionate homicide

hope: and colonialism, 285; in doctors, 306; and health care, 108, 137; and incarceration, 315; and mental illness, 89, 331, 435–6; and mental wellness, 479; and palliative care, 169, 177, 181; and suicidality, 106–7, 286

hospice, 166, 168, 171, 180–1

housing: affordable, 191, 239; crisis, 222; design of, 204–5; lack of, 78; quality of, 105. See also access; accessibility

human, less than, 208, 221, 257

human, what constitutes, 234

human rights: under international law, 113, 190, 333, 403, 453; and Inuit, 284; and MAiD, 114, 487. See also *Charter of Rights and Freedoms*; rights

Humphrey, Derek, 254

Huronia Regional Centre, 257

Hyatt, Taylor, 193–4

hypothetical future, 460, 475

ideological basis of MAiD, 59, 66, 75, 89–90, 490–1

immigration, 222, 231, 300

incarceration, 314–15, 343. See also prison

incentivization: of health care system, 437; of MAiD providers, 173

Inclusion Canada, 299

income: inequality, 210–11; support, 32. See also disability: benefits; poverty

incontinence, 224, 240, 246, 301, 463

incurability, 26, 114, 345, 362n13; and mental illness, 85, 126, 339, 394. See also irremediability

independence: loss of, 245–6; myth of, 208, 210–11, 233, 245. See also dependency

independent expert on the enjoyment of all human rights by older persons (United Nations), 190, 308

independent physician, 27

independent witness, 27, 112

Indigenous Bar Association, 280

Indigenous peoples: beliefs about health, 277, 286, 479; children, 220, 282–3, 285, 479–80; conceptions of disability, 220; consultation with, 25, 33,

278–9, 288, 306; leaders, 78, 84, 158, 277–80, 281; life expectancy of, 286; suicide rates in, 278, 280, 285, 479. *See also* discrimination; Elders
individualism, 209, 214, 236
individual responsibility, 250
inequality: beliefs about, 206–7, 210–11; disability as justification for, 218; natural, 218, 221, 236; systemic, 313, 332; tolerance for, 245
Inesse-Nash, Nicole, 220
influence. *See* choice; decision-making; undue influence
informed consent: and bringing up MAiD, 124–5, 131, 172; and children, 483; and dementia, 132–5; and palliative care, 172, 174, 179, 180; as a pillar of medical law, 137; requirements of, 118–19, 456–7; and standard of care, 123–31, 132, 136
inhumane conditions, 191–2, 284
injury of continuing existence, 254
institutionalization, 226–7, 234, 246, 295, 300
insurance policy, MAiD as an, 306, 312, 316. *See also* life insurance
insured health service (under *Canada Health Act*), 122, 389–90
interdependence, 208, 209, 211, 464, 468
intergenerational trauma, 285–6, 286, 478–9. *See also* generational trauma
International Association for Hospice and Palliative Care (IAHPC), 168, 174

International Covenant on Civil and Political Rights (United Nations), 333
intersectionality, 40, 78, 230, 305
intolerable suffering: and access to care, 188; ambiguity of criterion, 420–3; conflation with presence of suffering, 421–2; and lack of care and supports, 123; and mental illness, 421–2, 435–6; quantifying prevalence of, 423–6; and wait times, 306
Inuit, 278, 284. *See also* Indigenous peoples
invalidity, declaration of, 22, 129, 151, 335–46; suspension of, 23, 112, 341
involuntary detention, 315
irremediability: and AMAD Special Joint Committee recommendations, 87, 494; AMPQ findings on, 72; CCA Expert Panel on MAiD and Mental Illness findings on, 62; definition of, 104–5, 339; EAG findings on, 64–5; and effective referrals, 159; grievous and irremediable, 114, 121, 337, 348; and incurability, 362n13; lack of objective standards for assessing in mental illness, 66–7, 104; prediction of in mental illness generally, 38, 75, 89, 331, 423–9; values-based judgments on, 104. *See also* grievous and irremediable medical condition; incurability
irreversible decline of capability, 114, 126, 133–4, 464; and mental disorders, 65, 394
isolation: due to COVID-19, 190, 199, 295, 416; and decisions to

seek MAiD, 246, 302, 313, 314; of people with disabilities, 213, 235, 236, 241

jurisdiction: concurrent, 383, 384; federal, 18, 385–6, 392, 415n96; provincial, 18, 350, 381–4, 386–403. *See also* frustration of federal law; paramountcy

Kenny, Nuala, 24
Kimsma, Gerrit, 157
Kluge, Elke-Henner, 254
Kotalik, Jaro, 40, 153–4
Kouri, Robert, 137
Kumari Campbell, Fiona, 219, 299
Kutcher, Senator Stan, 75, 86

Labrecque, Cory Andrew, 464
Lac-Mégantic, 494
Lamb, Julia, 28. See also *Lamb v. Canada*
Lamb v. Canada, 28, 29, 63, 334, 368n38
Lametti, David: appointment as minister of justice and attorney general, 63; assertion that there is right to MAiD, 332–3; and Bill C-7, 31–3, 38, 278; and decision not to appeal *Truchon*, 29, 111; and MAiD for mental illness, 67, 83. *See also* minister of justice
Lamoureux, Kevin, 68
last resort, 18, 120–2, 130, 492
Latimer: Robert, 16, 253; Tracy, 16–17, 253–4
Lawrence, D.H., 205, 210, 243
Lawrence, Sonia, 314
legislation, purpose/object of, 334, 350, 392, 395; uniformity of, 386, 387–8

legislators, constitutional role of, 354
Lewis, Talila, 219
liberal individual, 314
Liberal Party: and access to MAiD, 26; and Bill C-7, 31–5, 488; and Indigenous consultation, 279; and MAiD for mental illness, 68, 82, 113; and MAiD terminology, 38; and mandate of Expert Panel on Options for a Legislative Response to *Carter v. Canada*, 23
liberty. See *Charter of Rights and Freedoms*
life: doctors' beliefs about quality of, 193, 300; necessities of, 313; perceptions of quality of, 26, 29, 112, 212; preservation of, 104, 107, 366n35, 383; quality of for people with dementia, 464; quality of among people with disabilities, 189, 196, 198–9, 199; quality of if treatment pursued, 120, 483; role of palliative care in improving quality of, 166–7, 171; value of disabled, 16, 26, 115, 244, 434; value of under the *Charter*, 308
life-affirming care, 169, 395, 400
life expectancy, 133, 286, 482
life insurance, 196, 257
life support, 19, 474, 481
life-threatening illness, 166, 169, 442
Linnaeus, Carl, 221
lived experience: of disability, 41, 232, 300; of illness, 460; of mental illness, 64, 84, 420; and pursuit of truth, 204–5
locked-in syndrome, 198–9, 339

loneliness: and compassionate communities, 466; and COVID-19, 31; ethics of allowing MAiD for, 216, 313; as reason for MAiD, 72, 246, 302, 489
long-term care, 190–1, 196, 295, 301, 462
Luxembourg, 130, 453, 490. *See also* Benelux countries

magic pill, 256
MAiD: access to, 31, 38, 41–2, 156, 399; alternative models to, 107–8; arguments in favour of, 101–7; assumption that preferrable to natural death or suicide, 309, 452; as a benefit, 307; calls for evidence-based policy on, 80, 82, 84–5; data, 297–9; definition of, 13; for dementia, 133–4; effective referrals for, 41, 122–3, 151–61; eligibility under Bill C-7, 126, 331; eligibility under Bill C-14, 26; eligibility under track 1, 188, 199; eligibility under track 2, 113–14, 188; in funeral homes, 206; ideological basis of, 59, 66, 75, 89–90, 490–1; impact on suicide rates, 22, 305, 431–2, 481, 491; informed consent criterion, 126, 129; interpretation of criteria, 29, 42, 192, 343, 420; intolerable suffering criterion, 420; jurisdiction to regulate, 388; as a last resort, 18, 120–2, 130, 492; for mature minors, 473–83; meaning of grievous and irremediable, 337, 348; meaning of irremediable, 339; meaning of reasonably foreseeable natural death, 27, 42, 135, 192–3; medical condition as cause of suffering, 122–3; as medical treatment, 106; misnomer, 63, 213, 489; motivations for, 123, 169, 493, 494–5; and palliative care, 169–73, 177–80, 199; public support for, 37; rates, 3, 43, 340, 493; removal of reasonably foreseeable natural death criterion, 349; right to, 102, 333–4, 398, 400–1; and suicide, 106–7, 394, 430–3, 480–1; terminology, 13–15, 38, 63–4, 100, 369n42; as treatment for life suffering, 83, 177, 181, 305, 495; voluntary request criterion, 124, 131. *See also* MAiD for mental illness; track 1; track 2
MAiD for mental illness: AMAD Special Joint Committee recommendations on, 87, 494; and AMPQ findings on irremediability, 72; and Bill C-7, 67–9, 72, 113; and Bill C-14, 64; and Bill C-62, 113; and capacity, 336–8, 347, 351–2; and CCA Expert Panel findings on irremediability, 62; CPA survey on, 73–4; discriminatory to exclude, 33, 66, 106, 307, 440–1; and EAG findings on irremediability, 64–5; eligibility, 338, 343, 347, 352, 382; evidence-based input on, 61–2, 64, 70–2, 74–6, 89; and intolerable suffering, 421–2, 435–6; and irremediability, 38, 75, 89, 331, 423–9; OMA survey on, 76–7; public opinions on, 39; in Quebec, 395; and standards for assessing irremediability,

66–7, 104; and substance use disorders, 331; and suicide, 106–7, 337–8, 394, 430–3; and women, 298–9, 305. *See also* constitutional right to MAiD; mental illness

MAiD MD-SUMC (MAiD for mental disorder as the sole underlying medical condition), 75, 91–2n8, 363n17. *See also* MAiD for mental illness; MAiD MI-SUMC

MAiD MI-SUMC (MAiD for mental illness as the sole underlying medical condition): conditions included under "mental illness," 331; and constitutional role of legislators, 353; to be legalized in March 2027, 330; provincial regulation of, 381–3, 400–1; and Quebec EOL law, 394; right to, 333–4, 341, 351; and slippery slope, 343; and suicide prevention, 332; and *Truchon*, 350–1. *See also* MAiD for mental illness; MAiD MD-SUMC

manufactured consent, 70

mature minors: arguments in favour of MAiD for, 474, 483; and brain maturation, 477–8; and capacity, 474–5, 477; February 2023 recommendation on MAiD for, 473; and MAiD in other jurisdictions, 481–2; no court directive to introduce MAiD for, 335, 344, 346, 402; relationship with parents, 476; and RFND criterion, 476; study of MAiD for, 25, 27; and suicide contagion, 480–1; and trauma, 478–80. *See also* adolescents; children; teenagers

maturity. *See* adolescents; children; mature minors

McCormick, Rod, 286, 479

McLachlin, Beverley, 16, 119, 397, 398, 399

McLaren, Angus, 222

medical justifiability, 418

medically necessary health care service, 383, 388–90

medical profession, goal of, 157

medical responsibility, 105

medicine, evidence-based, 137, 423, 425

mental health care: access to, 25, 62, 333, 434; cost of, 436–7; impact of MAiD on, 135, 435–6; underfunding of, 437

mental illness: definition of, 359–60n7; and incarceration, 315; and Indigenous peoples, 286, 479; and minors, 480; and psychosocial suffering, 62, 66; symptoms of, 62, 67, 331. *See also* depression; MAiD for mental illness; schizophrenia

mental wellness, Indigenous conception of, 479

mercy killings, 16, 253. *See also* compassionate homicide

meritocracy, beliefs in, 206–7, 211, 218, 222

Michalko, Rod, 253–4

minister of employment, workforce development, and disability inclusion, 32, 33. *See also* Qualtrough, Carla

minister of health: of British Columbia, 284; of Canada, 25, 33, 61, 387; of Quebec, 18. *See also* Philpott, Jane minister of justice: and Bill C-7, 33; and Bill C-14, 25–6; comments on jurisdiction over MAiD, 386–7; comments on MAiD for mental illness, 83, 330, 332; decision not to appeal *Truchon*, 29, 75, 111; and SNC-Lavalin affair, 63. *See also* Lametti, David; Wilson-Raybould, Jody; Virani, Arif

minor medical conditions, 343–5, 474

minors. *See* adolescents; children; mature minors; teenagers

misnomer, 63, 213, 489

missing and murdered Indigenous women (MMIW), 283

Miville-Dechêne, Julie, 32, 175

Model Practice Standard: and conscientious objection, 41–2, 122, 152–3; and duty to bring up MAiD, 42, 124–5, 135, 189, 492; and effective referrals, 122, 124–5, 152–3, 492

Moldaver, Michael, 348

Montero, Etienne, 343

moral distress, 178, 179, 181

moral injury, 178, 179, 181, 234

morality: versus legality, 154; of MAiD, 70, 385, 418. *See also* ethics

Mount, Balfour, 15, 166, 169, 170

mourir dans la dignité, 17

multiple chemical sensitivity, 294

Munro, Camille, 36–40, 176

murder. *See* compassionate homicide; Criminal Code; homicide; Latimer; social murder

Murray-Hall v. Quebec (Attorney General): conflict of purposes versus effects, 399; decriminalization versus positive right, 382, 396–8; doctrine of frustration, 396–9; factual circumstances, 391; federal vs provincial jurisdiction, 384, 391–5, 399; legitimate federal law objective, 403; purpose of criminal law, 396–7, 399, 400; purpose of provincial law, 392–3, 395, 398, 399, 400

mutual pretense, 478

Nazi, 154–5, 223

negligence of hospital, 285

Neo-liberalism, 235–8, 241, 243

Netherlands: and advance requests for euthanasia, 452–4; concerns about euthanasia practice in, 14, 19, 21; judicial consideration of evidence from, 30; Nazi occupation of, 154; percentage of euthanasia deaths in, 43; pressure to perform euthanasia in, 157; and right to refuse treatment, 130; study of experiences with euthanasia in, 23, 25. *See also* Benelux countries

neurocognitive disorders: and MAiD eligibility, 140n21, 359–60n7, 382; people with, 461, 463. *See also* Alzheimer's disease; dementia

neurodevelopmental disorders, 140n21, 331, 359–60n7

neurological disorders, 102, 297, 349

neuropsychiatric disorders, 298

New Democratic Party (NDP), 25, 32, 35, 225, 279

New Zealand, 3, 42, 189

nihilism, 435

non-ambivalence safeguard, 64–5
Norberg v. Wynrib, 119
normalization of MAiD: impact of on suicide rates, 431, 480–1; as treatment for life suffering, 83, 177, 181, 305, 495
Nova Scotia, 122, 229, 480
Nova Scotia Court of Appeal, 389–90
novel medical interventions, 438
number needed to harm (NNH), 418, 428–9
number needed to treat (NNT), 418, 428–9
Nunavut, 284
nursing homes: forcing of people into, 209, 250; insufficient staffing in, 465; and visitors, 463. *See also* long-term care

Ontario: and Bill C-14, 25; and delegation of MAiD provision to palliative care nurses, 172; and effective referral policy, 41, 122, 153, 158, 160–1; Indigenous communities, 280, 283; and MAiD billing, 173; and MAiD in funeral homes, 414n90; notable MAiD case in, 294; and Provincial-Territorial Expert Advisory Group on Physician-Assisted Dying, 23; and review of MAiD cases, 400; and treatment of marginalized people, 229, 231, 257, 295
Ontario Association for ACT & FACT (OAAF), 70, 78, 79
Ontario Court of Appeal, 117, 158
Ontario Disability Support Program, 294
Ontario District Branch of American Psychiatric Association, 85
Ontario Medical Association (OMA): position on effective referral policy, 156, 158; Psychiatry Section survey, 74, 76–7, 79, 81; Section of Palliative Medicine, 173
Ontario Psychiatric Association, 85
Ontario Superior Court, 27
opportunity cost, 419
Oregon, 21, 23, 340
oversight, 17, 40, 360n7, 403, 439

Pageau, Félix, 463–4
pain, psychological, 343–4, 352
palliative care: access to, 32–3, 39–40, 172–80, 298, 480; approach to addressing suffering, 168–9; for children, 480; conflation with MAiD, 169–72, 180; cost savings of MAiD versus, 199; definition of, 166–7; duty to inform of options, 35, 39–40; foundations of, 166; impact of effective referral policy on practice of, 161, 179; impact of MAiD on practice of, 177–8, 179–80; impact of MAiD on resources for, 172–3, 179–80; lack of input on Expert Panel on End-of-Life Decision-Making Report, 20; and MAiD terminology, 15; need to improve access to, 17, 25, 32–3, 173–7; not deemed essential health care service, 173; stigmatization of, 167–8. *See also* dignity: therapy
palliative sedation, 129–30

pandemic. *See* COVID-19
paramountcy, 399
parents. *See* children
Parkinson's disease, 171
parliamentary committees on MAiD. *See* Special Joint Committee on Physician-Assisted Dying (2015); Special Joint Committee on Medical Assistance in Dying (AMAD) (2021)
paternalism, 304, 309
patient-centred care, 171
Paulette, Francois, 288
Pearson, Karl, 224
Philpott, Jane, 26, 61, 63. *See also* minister of health
physicians. *See* doctors
poison, 100–1, 468
poverty: and choice, 78, 232–3, 312–13; cognitive load of, 233; Government of Canada definition of, 232; and Indigenous peoples, 283; as motivator for MAiD, 44, 105, 122–3, 192, 316; and people with disabilities, 78, 189, 228, 240, 243
power differential (between doctors and patients), 119
power of attorney, 461
practice standards, abandonment of, 79
prejudice and MAiD providers, 196, 287
premature death: of adolescents, 477, 483; and Bill C-7, 12; and Bill C-14, 37; and cost savings, 199; of Indigenous peoples, 287; lack of focus on protection against, 41; and MAiD by advance request, 452; of people with disabilities, 29, 114–15, 221, 403, 433; of people with mental illness, 67, 72, 89, 442, 444; and reflection period, 178; by suicide, 309, 442
pressure to choose MAiD: due to doctor, 42, 179, 189, 194–5; and eligibility, 124, 434; from family members, 178; due to lack of services and supports, 433; social, 214, 434
prime minister, 28, 63, 83, 111, 284. *See also* Trudeau, Justin
principles of fundamental justice, 308, 311. *See also* *Charter of Rights and Freedoms*
prison: and Indigenous peoples, 315, 479; and MAiD, 315; and people with disabilities, 231, 238, 241, 315
privilege and MAiD, 78, 90, 316, 493, 495
proportionality, 19, 311
prosecution, 18, 309, 495
provinces. *See* jurisdiction
Provincial-Territorial Expert Advisory Group on Physician-Assisted Dying, 23, 25, 60, 388
psychiatric care, 190, 425, 435–6. *See also* mental health care
psychiatric condition. *See* mental illness
psychiatrists: ability to separate suicidality from MAiD requests, 86, 430; and effective referrals, 160; lack of consultation with, 65; position on MAiD for mental illness, 38, 67, 73–4, 76–7, 86–7. *See also* Canadian Psychiatric Association; psychiatric care

Qualtrough, Carla, 32, 174. *See also* minister of employment, workforce development, and disability inclusion

Quebec: and 2014 MAiD law, 17–18; and advance requests for MAiD, 133; and effective referrals, 25; number of MAiD deaths in; 3, 18, 43, 489; and palliative care, 25, 174–5, 176; and racism in health care, 285; support for MAiD expansion, 28. *See also* Quebec EOL law

Quebec College of Physicians and Surgeons, 17

Quebec EOL law, 349, 350, 382, 387, 394–5. *See also Act Respecting End-of-Life Care*; Bill 11

Quebec Superior Court: decisions not binding on other provinces or Quebec appellate court, 32, 341; distinguishing between requirements of *Carter* and of the *Charter*, 342, 347; finding that suicidality and MAiD are separable, 106; ruling regarding MAiD during suspension of declaration of invalidity in *Truchon*, 33; ruling that RFND criterion unconstitutional in *Truchon*, 28, 63, 349. See also *Truchon v. Canada (Attorney General)*

racism, 78, 89, 238, 493; anti-Black, 155, 219–20, 231; in health care, 154–5, 284–7, 480; against Indigenous peoples, 280–1, 284–7, 300, 480; scientific, 221, 226

randomized controlled trials (RTC), 418–19

reasonably foreseeable natural death (RFND): and dementia, 133; interpretation of, 27, 42, 135, 192–3, 475; and minors, 476; and persons with disabilities, 193; purpose of criterion, 363n18, 376–7n142; removal of criterion, 296, 349, 488; and track 1, 188

reconciliation, 277, 282, 286

Reference re Genetic Non-Discrimination Act, 384

reflection period, 31, 35, 177–8, 488

regulation of MAiD, 383–4, 386, 388, 399, 403

regulatory college, 37, 41, 135. *See also* College of Family Physicians of Canada; College of Physicians and Surgeons of Ontario; Quebec College of Physicians and Surgeons

religion, freedom of, 122, 151, 158, 160–1. *See also* conscience, freedom of; *Charter of Rights and Freedoms*

reluctant welfareism, 229

remote communities, 284, 480

reserves, 278, 280, 281, 283, 479–80

residential schools, 281–3, 285, 479

resources: access to, 189, 219, 238, 310; doctors as gatekeepers to, 300; and interpretation of medically necessary service, 390; lack of, 32, 189, 191, 286–7; palliative care, 172–3, 179–80

Richardson, Lisa, 287

rights: to equality under the *Charter*, 15, 303–8, 312, 333,

349–50; to health care, 398; to life, liberty, and security of person under the *Charter*, 15, 308–12, 333, 339, 349–50; to MAiD, 102, 333–4, 398, 400–1; positive, 382, 396–8, 400; to refuse treatment, 119, 121, 126, 128–30, 315. See also *Charter of Rights and Freedoms*; human rights
risk/benefit analysis, 118, 120, 439, 457–8. See also cost/benefit analysis; harm/benefit analysis
RJR-MacDonald Inc. v. Canada (Attorney General), 385
Rodriguez, Sue, 15–16, 18
Rodriguez v. British Columbia (Attorney General), 16–17, 19, 21, 295, 385
Royal Society of Canada Expert Panel on End-of-Life Decision-Making, 13, 20
Russell, Marta, 229
R v. Bedford, 308

safeguards: 10-day reflection period, 31, 112, 177–8; 90-day assessment period, 35–6, 42, 113–14, 132; under Bill C-7, 35; under Bill C-14, 26–7, 490–1; compliance with, 344–5; consent requirements, 35–6; expertise of assessor, 36; final consent, 112, 133–5, 452; interpretation of, 27, 42, 128, 135, 344–5; and involuntary detention, 315; irremediability, 75; for MAiD for mental illness, 41, 62, 65, 83, 86; mental illness exclusion, 12, 67–9, 352, 488; non-ambivalence, 64, 65; palliative care access, 174; and public opinion of doctors, 300; removal of, 12, 25, 31, 112, 488; RFND criterion, 27, 132, 135, 192–3, 475–6; serious consideration, 35, 126; treatment futility, 65, 81, 83; under track 1, 35, 112; under track 2, 35–6, 113–14; voluntary request, 123–5, 131, 434; witnessed written request, 27, 112
Saskatchewan Court of Appeal, 16, 397
Saunders, Cicely, 166, 168
Schafer, Arthur, 24
schizophrenia, 113, 298
scientific evidence: and intolerable suffering, 425; and irremediability, 38, 425, 436; and MAiD for mental illness, 76, 82, 417, 443; and randomized controlled trials, 418. See also empirical evidence
segregation, 222, 230, 232
self-determination, 118, 128, 261–2n18, 314, 394
self-governance (by Indigenous peoples), 277
Seguin, Marilynne, 253
Sequenced Treatment Alternatives to Relieve Depression Study (STAR*D), 423–6
shame and desires to die, 195, 214, 245, 478
Singer, Peter, 256
slippery slope, 335–6, 343–4, 494
Smith, Lynn, 18–22, 337–8, 340
social acceptability of MAiD, 214, 221, 305
social determinants of health, 78, 138, 283, 286
social murder, 243, 495

social supports, availability of, 36, 78, 79, 296, 312
social utility, 463
Society of Canadian Psychiatry (SocPsych), 85, 86
Socrates, 100–1, 105
Sopinka, John, 16, 385
South Africa, 155
Soviet Union, 155
Special Committee on the Question of Dying with Dignity (Quebec), 17
Special Joint Committee on Medical Assistance in Dying (AMAD) (2021): recommendations on MAiD by advance directive, 44, 415n96, 452; recommendations on MAiD for mature minors, 44, 415n96, 473; recommendations on MAiD for mental illness, 11, 87–8, 356n2; testimony before, 37, 86–8, 192, 479, 494
Special Joint Committee on Physician-Assisted Dying (2015), 14, 24, 25, 27
special rapporteur on extreme poverty and human rights (United Nations), 190, 308
special rapporteur on the rights of persons with disabilities (United Nations), 115, 190, 299, 308
Special Senate Committee on Euthanasia and Assisted Suicide, 16
spinal cord injury, 194, 198, 237, 294
standard of care, 117–18; for defining when psychiatric condition irremediable, 61; impact of MAiD on, 115–17, 119–32, 135–8; and informed consent, 123–31, 132, 136; treatments, 277
Standing Committee on Justice and Human Rights, 32, 225
state-assisted suicide, 64
state interference, 310
sterilization: and eugenics, 222–3; of Indigenous peoples, 281, 285, 287, 300, 479; of people with disabilities, 226, 300
stigma: and dementia, 451, 467; and disability, 230, 299, 301, 310, 462; and exclusion of MAiD for mental illness, 70; and MAiD terminology, 14; and mental illness, 332; and palliative care, 167–8, 174; and suicide, 214
stress (financial), 196
stroke, 196, 198–9
structural oppression, 207, 213, 237
subjectivity (in MAiD assessments), 75, 104, 113, 126, 420
substance use disorders, 331. *See also* addiction
suffering: assessments of in patients with dementia, 453; distinction between disability-related and other suffering, 302, 305, 333–4, 403; enduring, 335, 420, 423–4; government's ability to reduce, 296, 307, 313; identifying cause of, 195–7; intolerable, 123, 306, 420–3, 424; medical condition as cause of, 122–3; medicalization of, 296, 301, 315; no requirement to access means to alleviate, 83, 122, 188, 488; prolonging of, 32; psychological, 60, 352; psychosocial, 44, 66,

192, 337; social, 62, 72, 489, 493, 494–5; social creation of, 244; subjectivity in assessments of, 104, 126, 420; understanding of, 236; and wait times, 190, 192, 306

suicidal ideation: as distinct from MAiD requests, 79, 86–7, 394, 430; and doctors bringing up MAiD, 159, 194; and hope, 106–7, 286; and onset of chronic condition, 197–8

suicide: contagion, 78, 217, 430–1, 478–81; impact of MAiD on rates of, 305, 431–2, 481, 491; legality of, 441; rates, 278, 280–1, 285, 479; right to, 102; stigma against, 214. *See also* aiding or abetting suicide; suicidal ideation; suicide prevention

suicide prevention: application to people with disabilities, 114, 305, 334; and autonomy, 106; court's rejection of characterization as legislative objective, 29; and duty to bring up MAiD, 135; as important social goal, 307; as an objective in Bill C-14, 26; undermining of, 286, 394, 431

sunset clause, 34, 67–9, 75–7, 89, 492

Supreme Court of Canada: and *A.C. v. Manitoba*, 475; and concurrent jurisdiction, 383; declaration of unconstitutionality in *Carter*, 12, 22, 335, 474; description of relationship between courts and legislature, 347–8, 353; and discrimination against people with disabilities, 304; discussion of concurrent jurisdiction over health, 382–3; discussion of informed consent in *Carter*, 127–30; discussion of irremediability in *Carter*, 338–9; and *E.F.*, 341, 348; evidence from Belgium in *Carter*, 343–6; hearing of new evidence in *Carter*, 22, 335; and MAiD terminology in *Carter*, 13; and *Murray-Hall v. Quebec (Attorney General)*, 382, 384, 391, 396–400, 403; new proportionality test, 19; and *Norberg v. Wynrib*, 119; no ruling on MAiD for mental illness in *Carter*, 341; no ruling on MAiD for minors, 402; no ruling that restricting access to MAiD discriminatory, 29; and personal constitutional exemptions permitted by *Carter*, 342; and *P.H.S.*, 385; presentation of palliative care as a safeguard in *Carter*, 174; rationale for legalizing MAiD in *Carter*, 247, 442; recognition of doctors' freedom of conscience and religion in *Carter*, 151; recognition of right to suicide in *Carter*, 102; and *R.J.R. MacDonald*, 385; and *Rodriguez*, 15; and *R. v. Latimer*, 16; and section 7 of the *Charter*, 121, 308–10; and section 15 of the *Charter*, 303, 307; suspension of declaration of invalidity in *Carter*, 23, 60, 341; and *Truchon*, 341, 353, 402, 490; and *United States v. Burns*, 311–12

Switzerland, 18, 23, 100, 101, 254

Sylvester v. Crits et al., 117

systemic inequalities, 313, 332

Taylor, Gloria, 18, 21, 128–30, 335–7, 339–41. See also *Carter v. Canada*
Taylor, Maureen, 23–4
teenagers, 280, 478, 480–1, 483. See also adolescents; children; mature minors
teleology, 418
terminal illness. *See* reasonably foreseeable natural death
Titchkofsky, Tanya, 208, 228, 236
total pain, 166
Toujours Vivant – Not Dead Yet, 478
track 1 (of MAiD): data on, 297–8; and dementia, 133; eligibility under, 126, 188, 199; safeguards under, 35, 112; transferring patients from track 2 to track 1, 132, 192–3; and waiver of consent, 35, 44, 112, 133, 452. *See also* MAiD; reasonably foreseeable natural death
track 2 (of MAiD): 90-day assessment period, 35–6, 42, 113–14, 132; additional consent requirements, 35; data on, 297–8; and discrimination, 34, 114, 303–6, 308, 464; eligibility under, 113–14; expert consultation, 36; safeguards, 35–6, 113–14; serious consideration to other options, 35, 126; transferring patients from track 2 to track 1, 132, 192–3
trauma: childhood, 478; and Indigenous peoples, 282, 284; intergenerational, 285–6, 286, 478–9; and psychiatric MAiD, 298

treatment: availability of, 69, 81, 188; contraindicated, 440–1; evidence-based, 339; first-line, 120; futility, 65, 435–6; indicated, 118, 120, 440–1, 444; MAiD as, 106, 115, 120, 124, 131; right to refuse, 122, 126, 128–30, 481; standard, 69, 188, 194, 488
trolley problem, 417–18, 440
Truchon, Jean, 28, 190, 349. See also *Truchon v. Canada (Attorney General)*
Truchon c. procureur général du Canada. See *Truchon v. Canada (Attorney General)*
Truchon v. Canada (Attorney General): and capacity assessments, 351; and *Charter* analysis, 309, 349–52; decision not to appeal, 28, 63, 74, 111; factual circumstances, 28, 190, 349; feasibility of separating suicidality from MAiD requests, 106–7; framing of legislative objectives, 350, 395; no ruling on MAiD for mental illness, 350–2; no ruling on MAiD for minors or by advance request, 402; not binding on other provinces, 401–2, 488; recognition of dignity and autonomy, 350, 395; RFND criterion unconstitutional, 63. *See also* Gladu, Nicole; Quebec EOL law; Truchon, Jean
Trudeau, Justin: and boil water advisories, 284; and decision not to appeal *Truchon*, 28, 63, 74, 111; and disability support

program, 295; and MAiD expansion, 67–8, 83; and mandate of Expert Panel on Options for a Legislative Response to *Carter v. Canada*, 23; and SNC-Lavalin affair, 63. *See also* prime minister
true positives, 427–8
trust: and the doctor-patient relationship, 119, 131; and doctors bringing up MAiD, 179, 197, 306; of public in doctors, 154, 171, 311
Truth and Reconciliation Commission. *See* Canadian Truth and Reconciliation Commission

Ugly Laws, 228
unconsciousness, 452–3, 456, 457
unconstitutionality. See *Carter v. Canada (Attorney General)*; *Charter of Rights and Freedoms*; invalidity, declaration of; *Truchon v. Canada (Attorney General)*
understaffing, 249, 250, 462
undue influence, 125, 136, 189
unintended participants, 208, 228
Union of British Columbia Indian Chiefs, 282
United Kingdom (UK), 108, 237
United Nations: Committee Against Torture, 281; concerns of, 39; experts, 12, 115, 190, 333; human rights rapporteurs, 115; Office of the Commissioner for Human Rights, 433
United Nations Declaration on the Rights of Indigenous Peoples (UNDRIP), 277, 288

United States (US), 211–12, 223, 237, 242. *See also* California; Oregon
United States v. Burns, 311–12
Universal Declaration of Human Rights (United Nations), 333
universal health care system, 204, 249
utilitarianism, 20, 160, 418, 444

vagrancy, 228, 230
values: and advance care planning, 457–8; of assessors, 75, 195; and the *Charter*, 308, 311–12; and choice, 217; cultural, 158, 278, 281; human, 106; Indigenous, 282, 285, 286, 289, 479; of patients, 42, 125, 152, 157, 195; societal, 354
values-based decision, 104
veterans, 105, 310
violence: by care providers, 252; and children, 285, 474; against people with disabilities, 251–2, 257; against women, 251
Virani, Arif, 68, 278. *See also* minister of justice
Vivre dans la dignité, 17
voluntary request, 123–5, 131, 176–7, 434, 474
vulnerability: assessment of, 351; and autonomy, 464, 491; as a burden, 468; cognitive, 460; and doctor-patient relationship, 119, 125, 131, 198, 306; human experience of, 227, 464–5; and Indigenous peoples, 278, 281; and legislative objective of prohibiting assisted suicide, 334, 377n142, 403; and mental

illness, 351–2, 394; and minors, 106, 346, 475; and safeguards, 495; structural, 332

wait times: and 90-day assessment period, 36, 190; and intolerable suffering, 306; and irremediability, 36, 192
waiver of consent, 35, 44, 112, 133–5, 452
Warner, Ellen, 161
water, access to, 283–4
welfare, 300
Wiebe, Ellen, 192
Wilson-Raybould, Jody: and Bill C-7, 32; and Bill C-14, 25–6, 61; comments on jurisdiction over MAiD, 386–7; and SNC-Lavalin affair, 63. *See also* minister of justice
withdrawal of life support, 13, 19, 129, 474, 481
women: and ableism, 221, 231, 239; and abuse, 257; and MAiD for mental illness, 298–9, 305; sterilization of, 281, 300; and track 2 of MAiD, 297, 305, 489; violence against, 251. *See also* missing and murdered Indigenous women (MMIW)
World Health Organization, 166
World Medical Association, 104, 168
wrongful death: and Bill C-7, 12, 31; and Bill C-14, 26, 37; and fallibility of systems, 311–12; and MAiD for mental illness, 89; and people with disabilities, 189; and public perception, 37–8

Yellowknife Stanton Territorial Health Authority Elders' Advisory Council, 288
Young, Margot, 314
youth. *See* adolescents; mature minors; teenagers

zealotry, 59